VOICES OF CONCERN:

THE PLAYBOY COLLEGE READER

VOICES OF

CONCERN

THE PLAYBOY COLLEGE READER

Edited by the Editors of Playboy

HARCOURT BRACE JOVANOVICH, INC.

New York Chicago San Francisco Atlanta

Published by Harcourt Brace Jovanovich, Inc.

ISBN: 0-15-595050-9
Library of Congress Catalog Card Number: 70–149097
Printed in the United States of America

Copyrights and Acknowledgments

HOLT, RINEHART AND WINSTON, INC. for the quotation on page 1 from "Speech to a Crowd" from *Public Speech* by Archibald MacLeish. Copyright 1936, © 1964 by Archibald MacLeish. Reprinted by permission of Holt, Rinehart and Winston, Inc.

HAROLD OBER ASSOCIATES INCORPORATED for the quotation on page 87 from *The Black Man Speaks* by Langston Hughes. Copyright 1943 by Langston Hughes. Reprinted by permission of Harold Ober Associates Incorporated.

NORTHERN SONGS LIMITED for the quotation on page 377 from *A Day in the Life* by John Lennon and Paul McCartney. Copyright © 1967 by Northern Songs Limited. Used by permission. All rights reserved.

PREFACE

The traditional purpose of writing is to entertain, to move, and to teach. We hope that this is what this book will do. When *Playboy* was first published over fifteen years ago with the slogan "Entertainment for Men," we did not realize that our audience would eventually include more than one million women or that the content of our magazine would evolve toward serious consideration of the problems of an increasingly perilous age. We do not congratulate ourselves on the change; rather, we congratulate our readers, who have stimulated us as much as we have stimulated them. The concerned, committed, idealistic young men and women who were in college in the sixties inspired this book, and it is fitting that we dedicate it to its readers, the young men and women of the seventies.

The college students of this decade will demand relevance, timeliness, and that neo-Chaucerian candor that insists not only on full honesty of expression but also on any terminology that serves to establish urgency. A new kind of anthology is required and *Playboy* is uniquely qualified to provide it. As evidence we cite the number of requests that we have received over the years for permission to reprint articles in college textbooks and the continuous stream of orders for copies of pieces that instructors wish to distribute to their classes. (In a typical recent month we mailed out nearly 1500 reprints of various articles in answer to such requests.) It is not surprising, therefore, that a number of college teachers have urged us to put together an anthology of pieces that originally appeared in our magazine but are not readily available elsewhere. Harcourt Brace Jovanovich has now made it possible to present such a collection.

We have striven to produce an unconventional and contemporary—if not entirely radical—view of American culture in a period of unprecedented conflict and change by choosing works from the very best and most committed writers active today. Each of the selections attacks a current and arresting topic with live intelligence and frequently disconcerting insight. Although all these writers trample on shibboleths and some assign whole herds of sacred cows to the abattoir, none are merely nihilistic: all seek constructive and effective alternatives. The selections, because they deal with issues that divide and hopes that unite us in this epoch, are inseparably merged and interwoven. Thus, all the pieces in this collection, whether fiction, article, opinion, or interview, illuminate one another and provide endless opportunities for discussion, essays, and various class assignments. In short, the book should provide the basis for the ideal kind of freshman course.

Our opening section, " 'The World was always yours': Youth and American Culture," zeroes in on education—an area that students and teachers know the most about and are most interested in—and indicates the interconnections between the classroom and the larger society outside. If the picture that emerges is in some respects disturbing, we should remember that we live in an age that has discovered that the larger society cannot be kept off the campus even if the buildings are ringed with bayonets and that heretics spring up faster than cups of hemlock can be distributed. It is hoped that this section will open for group discussion many topics that might explode if not given such free airing.

" 'Everybody but me': Race in America" plunges directly into what many consider the most significant question in our country today. Here the student will find James Baldwin's sensitive essay on black culture, a long interview with one of the most militant black leaders—Eldridge Cleaver, author of *Soul on Ice*—and a stark story on the ambiguous feelings of both blacks and whites. " 'Not the liberty which we can hope': Dissent and Justice in America" connects racism with the rebellion of modern youth, both black and white, and the backlash that this has called forth. Supreme Court Justice William O. Douglas' eloquent plea for traditional civil liberties in these turbulent times makes a point that both radicals and conservatives need to remember if humanistic values are not to be crushed in the struggle between revolution and counterrevolution. " 'Else they will fall': Politics in America" is a more general but still relevant section presenting alternative solutions that can lead to a new politics and a nation in which the intellect will have a function larger than that of Cassandra.

The concluding section, " 'I read the news today oh boy': The Ethical Dilemma in Contemporary Society," is mainly concerned with choices that individuals, as distinguished from governments, must make. Each writer in this section—even if he ranges as far as does Alan Watts in his jolting application of modern semantics and ancient oriental mysticism to the bread-and-butter problems of monetary and fiscal policy—returns to a consideration of the moral decisions of the single person. This section's emphasis on ethical questions brings out one of the book's major underlying concerns—the search for a principle of rational order in this age of irrationality. The final selection, an interview with Marshall McLuhan in which McLuhan's apocalyptic vision is expressed in his own psychedelic and mind-blowing style, touches on all the problems explored in the other sections and places them in a broad historical-technological perspective.

Although this is called an "age of transition," all times are times of transition. Our peculiar modern situation, as McLuhan hints, is the vast electronic speed-up of information which gives us an unprecedented awareness of the kind and number of changes that are occurring around us. During such a period, it is especially important for the traditional values of the university—detachment, humanism, and rational analysis—to reassert themselves in a challenging manner. But our students will not accept these disciplines if they seem to lead into an infinite regress, a cop-out, in which analysis feeds upon itself and existential participation is indefinitely postponed. We hope that these selections will provide the kind of reflection and meditation that does not evade problems but rather prepares one for the most intelligent and effective kind of action.

The Editors of *Playboy*

Contents

"Not the liberty which we can hope":

"Else they will fall":

'The World was always yours'

YOUTH AND AMERICAN CULTURE

The World was always yours:
you would not take it.

ARCHIBALD MACLEISH,
Speech to a Crowd

HERBERT GOLD **article**

THE NEW WAVE MAKERS

a sympathetic portrait of those far-out and fanciful west coast hippies, diggers and new leftniks who spark the action on today's youth scene—and generate bemused consternation among their elders

There seemed to be no airplane. There was just this parachutist sailing down through a cloudless sky. His face was masked. His chute was decorated with psychedelic-ecstatic colors. And below him, as he sailed so free, 20,000 grokkers said Ooh and Ah.

The occasion was the first Human Be-in on the Polo Field of Golden Gate Park in San Francisco. Tim Leary and Allen Ginsberg were there, the Hell's Angels were there, the Berkeley New Left politicos were there, the *Provo*like Diggers were there. There were children and parents, on a fine January day. There were banners, flags, costumes, drums, incense, chimes, many San Francisco rock bands, feathers, candles, heads and nonheads, families, lovers, heroes, animals, cymbals and symbols.

What was the cause? Just to grok and groove.

The police were absent. The crowd danced and played and loved each other all afternoon, and then Allen told them to pick up their litter and they did and then they went home. Nearby, the lawyer who represents the Hell's Angels in their continual hassling with the police was engaged in a rugby match, his legal talents unneeded. The Diggers passed out free food. Smiles and pats and kidding. Twenty thousand participants in the "Powwow, a Gathering of the Tribes for a Human Be-in" remember this as a causeless, meaningless and beautiful moment in their lives. A kind of history was truly made, an ecstasy, a memory of ecstasy and no police and no litter.

The whole thing was the conception of a couple of super-groovy wave makers. There have been succeeding episodes, and why not? All those bodies willing to be nice and knowing now, really knowing.

Where are these wave makers leading themselves and us? Should we follow? How can we follow? How can we *not* follow? How can we follow and not follow, all at once, picking up our litter?

FREAKY DOINGS DOWN ON EARTH, WHICH IS ONE OF YOUR TOP TEN PLANETS. Why add "the wave makers," another instant cliché, to the churning mass of language? Do we need another bumper sticker, another button, another dirge or snigger for the funny doings of the people who make the action? It is a matter of focus. After all, what are we standing on—peanut-butter-flavored yogurt? These are the people who are floating up all sorts of alien kicks through the rock-'n'-moil air. Some of them are developing products that will quickly be disposed of—rockets, missiles and youth itself. Some of them are working on a style of drugged psychedelic expansion or tripping with music and dancing and natural ease. "The Rise of the Uglies" would tell the story of the beards and the Goodwill Industry clothes and the haircut boycotts, except that the uglies are not ugly. Their charm comes in lumps, but it is charm all the same.

They are spontaneous. "I used to live with *him,*" says the girl at a party, pointing across the room to a guitarist, "but now I live with *him,*" as her finger crooks two ways southward toward a bearded postman, who is sleeping with his head on his mail sack. It is probably filled with Social Security checks. "Do you have a bicycle?"

"Yes."

"How many speeds?"

"Nine. It's Italian."

She absorbs this interesting data with gleaming eyes. Nine speeds is such a help getting up hills. "Would you like me to live with you?" she inquires. "Just for the weekend, I mean; it's such a drag making plans. But I do so love a man with nine different speeds."

They don't want to be uptight. They don't want to be brought down. They don't throw stones. They float out of the sky and keep the messy airplane out of sight.

Their older brothers and sisters were called beatniks, but the youths have other names now. The *Zazzeroni* of Italy, the *Raggaren* of Stockholm, the *Provos* of Holland, the Ladybugs of the Soviet Union, the *Chuligans* of Czechoslovakia, the *Halbstarke* of Austria, the *Gammler* of Germany, the *Gamberros* of Spain are all their cousins. An International is being created, with students and wandering loafers and the nervous-breakdown people and the remittance men and a few draft dodgers providing a network of communication; plus rumors, the telemouth; plus the conditions of industrialization and hard fear of war and disgust with mass culture that are settling over the Western world. "Arise, ye prisoners of affluence, arise ye processed of the earth——" They let hair and beards grow, they find God or godlessness (fanatic atheism is very close to religion), they seek out motorcycles and electronic music, they get high in a thousand different ways, they like leather and/or flowers, they question the traditional forms of work, they question property and making out, they question their parents bitterly, they look for their brother and sister souls. In many different ways and with no great unity of action—this is not an organized movement—they are making ripples and waves from which even their elders are learning. Their styles catch on. What they emulate is being emulated by their elders. They are tuning in and they are taking over.

If a capsule signal is needed for what the wave makers are turning against in the world of their fathers, it can be found in a paragraph from a column written in Vietnam by Stewart Alsop for *The Saturday Evening Post*, January 7, 1967:

> "We've killed a lot of friendly people, and I'm real sorry," said a sad-faced American colonel who is an advisor to the Vietnamese army here. "But, like Sherman said, 'War is hell.' "

The wave makers are not content with Sherman's famous remark. They may want to do nothing more about the war in Vietnam than evade it themselves, but it feeds their sense that a take-over generation—theirs—is required.

Student revolts are a serious matter, with political implications, meaning to change our ways about race, Vietnam, the abstract, hard-edged quality of education, the troubles of work. The revolutionists ask, What are we training for? *Why*? They express the post-Kennedy slump in national morale. Where are we at? Who puts us here? *Why*? Time passes, we grow old and die; or perhaps no time passes and we die, anyway—is that all? *Why*? What mean your duties, moralities, wars? Where are we at, old folks? Your way is unplugged.

For some, it's simply good to get back at Mommy and Daddy, or to revive the old Marxism of that prehistory, the Thirties, or to put panty raids and Castro in the same Savio blender. They are all decent law-evading people.

The rules of habit, tradition and authority are eroded. The threats that kept those rules in force—the punishment of God, pregnancy or disinheritance—have been eliminated by the dimming out of religion, the pill and the erosion of the old family structures. One of the dangers of the new youth style is formation of what critic Harold Rosenberg has called "the herd of independent minds." The opportunity, however, is to make a new tradition of the tradition of the new.

The beatniks of ten years ago seemed to be triumphantly the victims of all they surveyed. They dropped out arrogantly; they preached poverty, ease, the reign of love and, somewhat stammeringly, creativity. They wore the old clothes, but not magic clothes. Their hipster opposite numbers dressed sharp but in uniform. If they marched to a different drummer, they all seemed to march to the same old different drummers. Paralyzed by the ides of Ike, they alternately slumbered and slouched or rode off on wild Dexedrine highs, bopping a bit, and then returned to mattresses *chez* each other. They were nihilism's Organization Men.

The wave makers are lineal descendants of the Beats, in much the same way that Elizabethan England was composed of the lineal descendants of the Anglo-Saxon berry eaters who painted their rumps blue and lived in trees along about the time Aristophanes was writing his satires on Socrates. Though the word dropout has become popular, it is certainly true that the Beats really dropped out in a way that the wave makers have not. They are busy designing clothes, making movies, protesting the civil rights slothfulness and the nonfloating U. S. aircraft carrier that is the peninsula of Vietnam. They have blooming on their minds. They are present in the now. They are sometimes not here when you want them, but at least they are there. They set styles, Carnaby-Mod-Rock, and they capture philosophies—Marshall McLuhan, who plays Polonius to their Hamlets; Dr. Timothy Leary, who plays ghost on the parapets. They are the descendants of the Beats, but with new drugs, new toys, new fads and new sex.

They fill time with movement, space with gadgets, sound with volume and amplification, message with medium.

The traditional Western pattern for both personal lives and the history of a time requires a beginning, a middle and an end. We are born, we struggle, we die. There are climaxes, irregularities, tragic intensities. The circle is completed and then the circle starts afresh. But now, with bombs and fallout and war, with the powerlessness of will in a mass society, life does not seem to be so simply plotted. The pattern has gone peculiar, with paisley spirals and whorls. A new vision has gained a hold on the children. An on-going-with-ness, a stasis, a dropping out of time and a tuning in to perpetuity—these express the alternative ideals out of the East, the tube and history. The vision is not freshly invented. There has always been this element in Christian and Jewish mysticism, in fact, in all mysticisms. But as a popular style, it has taken new roots in the generation now young and active.

The willingness of so many of the most vital and energetic of the young to give up the sense of history, hope for the future, is understandable but unusual. What a French psychologist has called *la crise d'originalité juvénile*—"the crisis of adolescent originality"—used to mean a youthful bursting of the bonds toward new achievements: ambition and lust—and art, money, power, creative expression of personality, hope for society. The *Wanderjahr* of the nineteenth-century scholar-poet, the adventuring of the troubadour youth, the killing of the father in the primal horde—there are plenty of examples in history and in myth. Change meant *change,* and youth did it. The new psychedelic mode—digging the scene—is an odd reversal of this pattern. But of course the wave makers, those who define the scene, are finding their road to originality, their whorly path homeward to the tradition of novelty.

The Soviet poet Evtushenko's evocation of Mayakovsky's revolver—to kill the conformists, to kill untruth, hatred and cruelty—is also an evocation of that same revolver with which Mayakovsky killed himself. If he hadn't committed suicide, very likely Stalin would have had him murdered. The revolver of Evtushenko and Mayakovsky is the revolver of angry, hasty, wasteful youth, and an echo of it can be found in the name of the Beatle album filled with sweet love songs and ironic nudges: *Revolver.*

The stony hipsters of the slums, the hang-loose protesters of the status quo, the wet-eyed psychedelic lovers ("I love! I'm beautiful!") are different in many ways, but they are similar in the hope of grooving and grokking. To groove means to swing; groovy means good, in the swing, with it, *there. Grok* is a word from a science-fiction novel by Robert A. Heinlein, *Stranger in a Strange Land;* grok means to dig, to go in calm ecstasy, to relish what is before you. These decent people are eagerly grokking. They don't want to smuggle in or buy illegal marijuana; they want to declare it legal; but in the meantime, they feel they must fight the liquor lobby and help remove the smell of beer from places where men gather. "Junkies" for them are the old folks who accumulate junk out of advertisements; addicts are those who swing with a medicine chest full of pills; the insane are the politicians who run whole populations with fire and bombs; the weird are those whose sexual hang-ups include swift sorties with the girl at the sales convention or the neighbor's wife. The only thing they admit is that these strange and nongroovy people have temporary control of things.

The turbulence of youth is eternal; nothing unique to this fact. Their boiling and trouble accompany all the changes of civilizations, both the creative and the destructive ones. What gives it a special poignancy and risk today is that it has caused a punch-drunk unsteadiness of the balancing older generation. The wave makers seem to be asking the ruling husks of their fathers, Can you really want war? Do you really mean to let the air be filled with garbage, the waters poisoned, the population sickened by both excess and want? You mean for millions to be unemployed and the rest overworked? You mean it, Dad? Aw, that's a dumb shuck. Aw, get off our backs, you old creeps.

And, oddly enough, the older generation seems to be answering to this, You're right. Show us the way. We'll follow like you and try to be young and full of despair like you, or full of hope, too, if you choose. This is the new and curious element, this willingness of the seniors to submit to their more experienced juniors, to take their lead and pattern their uniformed age on the wisdom of youth.

Let us now attempt a geography of the elements on the scene. What follows is an atlas of the new world being colonized by the wave makers. The various hard rains falling will surely change its contours, but like any explorer, we may have to be content to discover America when we are looking for India.

BEACHHEAD. It is not nudism. It is not orgyism. But it is not what you could call just pure swimming or sun-bathing, either. It is "unstructured experience," says Darrell Tarver, the sociology student who organized the Free Beach Movement because he likes to frolic unclothed with friends. He is friendly with peace politicking and New Left theorizing, but his main interest is in getting boys, girls, Negroes, pacifists, soldiers on leave, belly dancers, architects, students, teachers, everybody! out! out on the beach, please! When a gawker takes the hand of a nudist, half the battle is won—and Darrell says, "Glad to have you here! Nice day, isn't it? That's my wife over there, playing volleyball." Pumping and pumping the hand and grinning and eyes darting and picking out something personal to say. The battle is generally won. Even sheriff's deputies, the daughters of sheriff's deputies—pants and panties and jeans and skirts, all the badnesses of nongrokking life come shed. For one thing, the volleyball looks like fun and they want to get into uniform. Darrell's wife—sweet, homey, nekkid—looks so right and relaxed, just the sight of her turns a gawker into a people.

Up and down the state of California there are now Free Beaches—free of clothes and free of nonclothes. The Free Beach franchise has gone out to the East Coast and the Gulf of Mexico, too. This is the most affable of revolutions, hardly a revolution at all. These are the converts to Human Be-ins, the advance guard of grokkers, those who believe they have only a few decades on earth and want to spend them now, unclothed, in touch with light, air, sun and other bodies.

The LSD explorers of inner space take an alternate line: You can love everyone, everything; the world can be changed by personal worship, example and contemplation. They dance to deafening rock 'n' roll with strobe lights, liquid light shows, flickering movies, all the stimuli their senses can bear. And in their ebullience and high health, their senses can bear a great deal.

They seek to break down the barriers between people set up by money and position and shaving. The psychedelic-ecstatic beat unites them.

THE THUNDER MACHINE presents
Space Daisy and Lee Quarnstrom
in
A Real Wedding

read an invitation. The couple got married to a rock version of Mendelssohn. The bride's child by her previous marriage danced the night through, stomping with six-year-old abandon. Some of the guests looked as if they qualified for slum clearance and urban renewal, but they were comfortable with themselves. As author Ken Kesey announced at his Acid Test Graduation Ceremony, "We must say it clearly, hairily and with good amplification."

Even *The Wall Street Journal* has picked up on the superpresent world of the wave makers, which is the missing link not to history but to the future. CALL IT PSYCHEDELIC AND IT WILL SELL FAST, SOME MERCHANTS SAY. This was the headline of a front-page story. The subhead read, "Psychedelic Shops, Fabrics, Night Clubs Make the Scene; Tootsie Rolls & Adolf Hitler." The news feature was an absolutely serious coast-to-coast survey of the market in "acidteric" merchandise, including posters, clothes, widgets for blowing smoke, diffraction disks for blowing minds, dream machines of various tilts and energies. *The Wall Street Journal* knows quite a lot about it, for *The Wall Street Journal*, that is ("markups run to 100 percent," psychedelicatessens can merchandise goods that sold at cut rates in dime stores), but a few items from the world of commerce and profit have been omitted from its survey. For example:

The Attention workshop, a private school designed to bring joy. Fee: $37.50 per weekend. "Session will be in the nude. Smokers will be allowed to bring one pack of cigarettes."

A cooking manual that might produce the recipe for a wave maker would include the juice of three Hondas, the pulp of a raw beard and a soupçon of LSD. With nearly half the population under twenty-five and the other half wishing it were, the culture of expenditure is running full blast. And within the sound of money, the sound of ecstasy, the noise of destructibility (goods, time, youth itself), there remain enclaves of those thoughtful ones who seek the meaning of it all. These are the moral philosophers who approve of summer jobs but think that a boy should have a summer job all his life, all year round. And preferably it should consist in taking eight-millimeter films of his daily goofing and gefuffeling (don't ask what it means, do it). As Don McNeill wrote in an article on "Living Without an Address on the Lower East Side," in *The Village Voice*: "Privacy is easily sacrificed . . . material possessions become less important, clean sheets forgotten. Yet the body is sustained and the mind is at work circumnavigating the answer." It's a great day in the history of hair.

The merchants who sell doughnuts and motorcycles and sleeping bags to these Dylanesque tribal troubadours have learned to love them. "Some of them are artists in their own way," an Army-surplus store told me. Actually it was a man, speaking for his business. "You know, poor as they act, they never buy the cheap sleeping bag. I sell 'em the forty–sixty-dollar job—good down, great attachments. They come in with their rags, but they don't buy anything but the Cadillac of sleeping bags. You think maybe they get money from someplace? Home?"

I thought maybe.

"Artists," he mused, "in their own way. They don't litter the streets the day after the night before. They're nice. Some of 'em I know by name."

The Children's Crusade has carried The Fugs, the Jefferson Airplane, the Grateful Dead and Donovan on their shields toward fame and riches. The makers of light shows seldom become rich, but some do. *Provos* are in international correspondence, selling anarchism. Macy's takes a full-page advertisement, declaring:

> Zen, the very essence of the Orient, sends a special subtle beat through the very heart of Macy's. . . . It is Zen, the spirit of "Stillness in Movement" . . . the bold, unfaltering strokes of Japanese painting. It is this pure serenity that inspired Shiseido, Japan's most famous name in cosmetics, to create Zen perfume . . . an exquisite fragrance that . . . Come discover Zen, by Shiseido of Japan . . . at your Macy's.

Even Macy's, the land of What Is and What Sells, want to tell us how the world might be, if only the world becomes different. The Hobbits are coming. Frodo Lives. The kids are electrocuting themselves, mixing acid in their souls and calling The Fugs square. Mao and Trotsky and Ramblin' Jack Elliott are over the hill. Debutantes are looking for what comes after plastic materials—nonplastic materials? They are dropping out of Andy Warhol and joining the *Provos:* "Anarchists, goblins, punks, saints, wild men, dope freaks, dropouts, vagrants, sorcerers, unite! If you want to put down this kiss-ass society, then you are a Provo!"

What debutante or disaffected graduate student can resist this touching appeal? The *Provos* of Amsterdam, the Living Children of Boston, The Diggers of San Francisco are all aimed at doing good, at simplicity, at cutting the shit. They feed the hungry, they attain some sweet family groupings on the tribal model, they cut some of the shit some of the time for some of the people. They trip out in a scene of advanced creative martyrdom, flowers, gang sex, big laughs, soft touches. It's too easy, of course, to ridicule the herd of independent minds. But everyone in this life seeks to trip out through fantasy and art and religion and sexual ecstasy, friendship and hope and a dream of community. The wave makers are seeking the trip directly, giving up money and position and an ethic of proving something to parents. Some of them, of course, get rich, get famous and prove something to their parents, but the style obeys the injunction: *Make new!*

Moses Maimonides speaks for the older fashion in his *Guide to the Perplexed* (that was in the twelfth century). When a boy is tormented by desire, he advises, "Drag it into the house of study." In other words, read, work and forget desire. Now his descendants, bearded, flapping, eager, drag it into the house of study along with the chicklet and the whole group and all their instruments. And the pills. And then blow the fuses.

The wave makers can be easy even on the tender questions of race and war. They want to swing. As one says, "We've learned two things about Negroes. (A) Not all of them want to sleep with our sisters. (B) Some do." And now that they face it all, it's easier, they can ride with it, there are more important things to do than protecting little sister from what comes naturally, such as feeling, flowers and fooling around.

Maybe 10,000,000 Americans turn on or have turned on. They are happy monaural with casual styles and rock 'n' roll and marijuana; they are ecstatic in stereo with acid and dropping out and devil take the rest. They leave a part of their souls in the youth bag. While the waves beat on the shores, they are waiting to take over.

At the opposite extreme from these pure and purehearted grokkers stand the New Left militants, the peace marchers and the politicals, those who want to kill war and segregate the segregationists and bring political and economic justice to a world badly in need of these qualities that it has never enjoyed except in the ardent imaginations of men. Some of them also seek violent change to make this better, more peaceful world. Their youthful heroes are men like Stokely Carmichael, who led SNCC from the problems of race in the South into the problems of race in the North and on into the confused realms of international hatemongering; and Mario Savio, who is seen as fighting the good fight of the individual against the multiversity and against an education designed to suit the military-economic machine.

But the grokkers and the revolutionists are not purely one thing or another; they join in an evolving conception of modern man. They may look like Hell's Angels dropouts to the old stratified society, but to themselves they look ready: ready for change, ready for novelty, ready to mess around and perhaps ready for fun, too. Some of them are maturing into a sense of their own internal power, if not yet into political control. They are nonideological, rhythmic rather than intellectual, turned on rather than convinced, products of the disposable culture and possessed of the most disposable commodity of all—youth, that disease that is no longer even cured by age. In the past, it was. Youthful idealism, hope, laziness and disposability hobbled toward the future, gathering goods and compromises and clucking over the excesses of its own children. The kids no longer take pride in these gains and losses.

POVERTY, POLLUTION, PEACE AND RACE. It may seem trivial to link these four issues together, but, as James Joyce may have said, it is not trivial; it is quadrivial. The same social activists move from one issue to the next. The New Left—writing in such organs as *Ramparts* and *The Village Voice, New Politics* and *Dissent, Liberation* and in occasional ephemera—argues that the old radical solutions, Marxist, mainly, are not adequate. The turned-on, plugged-in times seem to demand a radical humanism, a responsible anarchism, formulas of improvisation. The Radical Education Project, initiated by the Students for a Democratic Society, extends some of the organized lines of traditional student efforts. It is a large-scale reaching toward both knowledge and power, but in its immediate program it states that "the forms of democracy cannot be judged in the abstract, apart from the actual freedom and humanness which they allow." It is concerned with values and utopias, the analysis of myths and realities in the actual world, strategies of change. There is no basic theory; that is yet to develop, though certainly there are positions on poverty (Help!), pollution (Stop it!), peace (Stop the little wars, end the arms race!) and race (Use law!). But techniques and organization are still being studied. The Radical Education Project, like the underground press that has radically and psychedelically exploded in every hipster community, seeks an international educational intelligence network that can link scholars, journalists, youth leaders, officials, guerrilla leaders all over the world. "One former staff member," says a recent bulletin, "visited Guatemala last summer, where he made extensive contacts with Guatemalan guerrillas." The active figures belong to a generation for whom the Spanish Civil War, World War

Two, the lowering of the Iron Curtain, the Korean War—that whole clanking paraphernalia of history—are mere chapters in textbooks. No wonder men in their forties, fancying themselves still young, stare at them in wonder.

The "New Left" has become the cliché term that names these new radical critics of American society. But men such as Stokely Carmichael are not registered members of a political movement called the New Left; there is no such party. The prime differences between the old leftists and the new lie in the areas of doctrine and organization. The old leftists believed in final principles; they had explanations and factions; they disagreed among themselves, but they splintered and splintered into tiny, sometimes one-man parties. Shachtmanites and Lovestonites may have included only the founder and his wife, plus the family dog, and then there was a divorce—but no matter, it was a party all the same, with one lonely man the proprietor of his final truth to console him for the loss of wife, dog and mass base.

The New Left activists have been called anarchists because their criticism of society is basic and they are mistrustful of organizations to improve matters. However, at the same time, they form alliances wherever useful, without previously prepared grudges against, say, the Communists. They are too young and uncaring of history to remember the old grudges—too young to be suspicious and yet both hopeful and desperate. And just as they are resistant to doctrine, so they are resistant to the notion of leadership as such. They have observed the abuses of power—this history is familiar to them. They are not, on the whole, pursuing power. There seems to be a rare, almost temperamental shyness, even among the natural leaders. Bob Moses, once a leader of SNCC, found that he was being called by the contemporary cliché "charismatic"; he changed his name to Bob Parris to drop himself down a bit, and then he dropped out entirely. Moses/Parris is a man who fought the good fight in the South, risking his life. When he discovered that his fellow SNCC workers were being inspired by his example rather than by their cause, that they believed him when he said something, that he was in a position of enormous guiding power and inspiration—instead of being gratified, as most men would be, he was disappointed. He wanted the cause to speak for itself and leadership to be self-generating. He disappeared. Some friends say he is now studying in Africa.

The leadership in the New Left changes because the leaders seem to be interested in personal fulfillment—knowledge, understanding, getting in touch—rather than in running a bureaucracy. This is not selfish dilettantism; it involves principles about leadership. The natural result is that the bureaucracy is weak and organizations tend to fade away, as during the present lull in the civil-rights struggle.

The fading in and out of activist groups can mean, however, a deeper rooting of democratic process than is traditional in America. The war in Southeast Asia has tended to gather many disparate groups—pacifist, religious, political—into allied organizations and has drawn energy away from the struggles against poverty and race prejudice, but immediate local issues are able —wherever there are the young—to cause spontaneous combustion. Whether it is parking garages to replace parks, freeways to replace redwood forests or the filtering of garbage-laden air, there is an increasing popular ability to act.

The New Left is the label they are given, just as if they were the children of the old left, but these are self-fulfilling wave makers whose weapons are impiety, energy and rage. At a confrontation of New Left activists with some veterans of old-timey radical movements, Robert Scheer, editor of *Ramparts* and candidate for Congress in 1966, cried out with absolutely crystalline purity, "We don't care about your final goals. We don't have your rules. If the capitalists can give us peace, that's fine. If socialism means war, it's absurd. We want to stay alive *today!*"

NEW PHILOSOPHIES, NEW FAMILIES. Between the extremes of politicalized man and Eastern-mystic-contemplative man stand the curious efforts of the utopian or educative communities that are being organized in various isolated spots. One of the most serious, sensible and firmly rooted of these is located in Big Sur, that spectacular California stretch of mountains and Pacific Ocean beach, where a young man named Michael Murphy has taken a run-down family hotel and lodge and transmogrified it into the Esalen Institute, "a center to explore those trends in religion, philosophy and the behavioral sciences which emphasize the potentialities of human existence." The guests—students? clients? patients?—participate in seminars on such subjects as "Meditative Techniques and Depth Imagery," "Alternative Views of Reality" and "God in the Secular City." Mike Murphy has found his cause—a nondrug expansion of consciousness through techniques gropingly and intuitively understood by creative people in all fields: medicine, engineering, architecture, the sciences and the arts. Having returned to this family property after long wanderings that included over a year in an Indian monastery, he has organized a rapidly growing institution that aims to conduct its program in major cities, to publish papers, to find a way to end loneliness and to come close to answering the ancient questions about the meaning of life.

The resident staff includes Dr. Frederick Perls, one of the last surviving pupils of Freud, who dispenses wisdom and probes anxieties—or sometimes dispenses anxieties and probes wisdom. Gia-Fu Feng, calligrapher, also conducts classes in Tai Chi Chuan (meditative movements) and smiles inscrutably. Bernard

Gunther leads in "body sensitivity and nonverbal communication." Occasional visitors have been such thinkers as Buckminster Fuller, who invented the geodesic dome and the Dymaxion House; S. I. Hayakawa, the semanticist; the late Bishop James A. Pike, Episcopal and controversial—scholars and innovators of all sorts.

The point lies in a communal search for an open, freer world. People massage each other; people take the hot baths together, frolicking over spectacular cliffs looking out to sea. The fog is lovely. The sun is bright. The visitors can look at the mountains or the ocean. Some of the contemplation is merely histrionic, designed to let others know—that pretty teeny-bopper, say—that you are contemplating, but there is also a seriousness about the quest.

On one weekend at Esalen, Nelson Van Judah, a designer, led a large group of students in creating a "total environment experience." They constructed a geodesic dome and then filled it with delights and people. As the audience lay about inside, the students projected films and slides, played tapes of sounds and jazz and Handel, dripped projected colors, plugged in smells of eucalyptus and mint and ether. People giggled; people were moved and said Ooh and Ah; the claustrophobes and the rigid fled pell-mell. As with the drug experience, the "total environment experience" kicks the radio; that is, either people are stimulated to start functioning or they crack into kindling.

On the outside of the geodesic dome, the total-environmentalists, mostly ages eighteen to twenty-five, leaped about like manic *maestros*, improvising sounds and smells and film projections. They had labored over the construction for days; they had practiced together like an orchestra; and then, when it was all over, that was it. They walked away from it. They left the dome to Esalen and went back to San Jose. While at the Hot Springs, they slept in cars and in sleeping bags; it made no difference about comfort. Said Kathy Sullivan, a sweet and pretty young girl who was one of the star improvisers of the group, "I'll never need to sleep again!"

This is the way these people feel at the pinnacle of their creative acts—marvelously alive, fully human, making waves.

TEENIES. The youthful tribes have found new camping grounds and new forms of peace to smoke in their pipes. The old families have shriveled up and blown away. Now Junior doesn't rebel so much as take off. The *Provos*, The Diggers and the teenies of the Sunset Strip or Macdougal Street find families without parents, houses with only other kids sleeping twenty or thirty on a similar number of mattresses.

The *Provos* of Holland go about in flowered trousers, long hair or shaved heads, nineteenth-century army dress tunics, anything they find or like. Even white jeans and white T-shirts. They live communally. They paint bicycles white and leave them about, hoping people will go where they want to go and then leave the bicycle for the next voyager. The police find them provoking. They are *provocateurs.* They seek peace, justice, power, fun, truth, beauty, fresh air and the freedom to smoke pot. They want their elders to be responsible to history. Who'd have thought these friendly anarchists would leap to prominence in Amsterdam, of all places, among the staid Dutch, of all people?

The Diggers of San Francisco seem more likely. They have named themselves after a sect that opened business in 1649, in Merry England, urging the abolition of private property and the sharing of, well, just about everything. Afternoons, Diggers feed the hungry in the Panhandle of Golden Gate Park. They beg, borrow and maybe even steal some of the food. They house the teeny runaways. They don't use too much "speed"—Benzedrine and other energizers. They are reasonably anonymous. They seek to do good without too much theory and to have some fun while doing it. The cops push them around a little, but also admit they give some of the kids a place to sleep.

Late in 1966, there was a massive summit confrontation between the hard-line hippies (joy, drugs, dropping out) and the then-mysterious Diggers (joy, fewer drugs, taking control) on Haight Street, the Boulevard of Brotherly Love, in San Francisco. Rival Beatnik Bands Fight It Out! The Diggers versus the Acidheads! Two Hell's Angels were arrested by the fuzztrated fuzz—why? Drinking chocolate milk in a provoking fashion! Dangerous motorcycling. Harboring a wild look in the eye. But on the whole, the cops were watchful, confused and outwitted. There was a parade with candles, candies, children, flowers, fun. Peyote, the mongrel dog that had been mated with a coyote, was there, along with its pups. Buddha ambled amuck. Cops rode up, looking things over, and then rode away. Cheers.

On both sides of the street, men, women, children and in-betweens stood with incense and candles, and whistles in their mouths. A serious couple, one on each side of the street, began busily passing out leaflets. Trained in many demonstrations, the mob obediently took the sheets they were offered and gazed literately at the paper. The sheets were blank. Reams of blank proclamations, pure-white manifesto. More cheers.

A Negro bus driver got out, shook hands, grinned. Flags and flowers decorated his bus. The passengers frowned, giggled and prepared to try to tell the story at home. The Diggers passed out candy to the passengers, and flowers and kisses. Everyone unrioted. Teeth, smiles, cool. Buddha directed traffic and the bus moved on.

We all live in a yellow submarine,
a yellow submarine,
a yellow submarine . . .

The song swept down the street. It was December 17. It was a merry Christmas coming. Love, love, love.

Well, the East Village and even Chelsea tend to be a bit more uptight than San Francisco. But surely the weirdest is that illegal stretch of uptightness called the Sunset Strip in Los Angeles.

There, the teeny-boppers tried to graduate to teenyhood. The Sam Brownes killed it. What was gracious and sweet in San Francisco quickly became nervous and dead. A "White Watts" resulted in the destruction of a swift and neat reign by the kids. "Teen Power" is a slogan that has no future; what they called the "blue fascists" can easily bring up their big guns—curfews, hoses, clubs. And sighing, incompetent parents are obliged by the curfew laws to make bed checks.

Instead, the teenies will have to learn to *seep* into power. Orthopedic surgeons are reporting a mass influx of creaking adults who have tried to imitate the teen dances. Teen clothes cause rapture and rupture in the middle-aged chicklets and Wall Street hippies who try to hang loose in those mind-hugging clothes that look so groovy on a sixteen-year-old. New kicks, such as smoking dried bananas, promise to catch on among those old folks, twennies, thirdies and even fordies, who look to the cute Sharons and Kevins for guidance.

Deep thinkers for several generations now have poked and pried at the breakdown of the American family, the failure of paternal authority. The old conglomerations, stuck together in Mom's apple pie, have gone the way of some flesh: into myth and memory.

Slum gangs receive poverty funds and a certain amount of attention from sociologists, but have yet to receive their full due as models. And the new family, groupy, tribal agglomerations have gone back to a more primitive village culture. They seem to be merely camping out, but the need for meaningful structure is one of the most touching qualities of the teen rebellion. Fan clubs no longer satisfy their quest. That boy rapping on the mailbox at the corner may have Methedrine in his madness, but he could merely be trying to tell the post office something in Digger code. *Mom didn't love me wisely. Dad didn't tell me what to do. Where are we all going?*

Soon, it seems, the last remaining suits and ties will be bought up for museum exhibit. And the stars above will hang loose and free and echo the faulty genius of earth. They have seen other wars before the Children's Crusade. Some of those peculiar wars have changed history.

MUSIC AND ART AND CLOTHES. And money. The new permutations of Liverpool rhythm-and-blues country-and-western Dylan madrigal psychedelic-ecstatic rock need more than a mighty flow of adjectival modifiers to be understood by someone who has not picked up on it. Perhaps Miss Susan Cox, former production manager and editor of *Tempo,* a newsletter that rates records for top-forty stations, has found the right language: "Vital . . . unbelievable it's here. Pop music is pop music."

"Like man it don't have to be acid man if it's good it'll sell." This is an unpunctuated record producer talking. He works the dials, the globes, the speakers, the tapes, the mixers, the echoes, the overlays, the underlays, the rerecordings, the speed-up and slow-down levers. And if the guitarist (the wailer, the flutist, the combo) is good, it'll sell, he says. Of course, they shouldn't perform publicly, since so much is done in the studios.

A few years ago, it could be said that the kids didn't invent the music they didn't listen to, but they did influence it and they did do something to it—live by it, love by it, if not listen to it. As the leader of the band said: "Now we're going to play an oldie but a goodie, a dusty diamond, friends. Some of you may remember gettin' pregnant to this song, away back in 1964. . . ." Rock music came to life from a Negro tradition, blues, jazz and rock 'n' roll, after a sea change in Liverpool before it was shipped back by the Beatles, who have now been canonized through a habit of the times of producing Instant Tradition.

Other groups have taken the torch passed by the Beatles and Bobby Dylan while these torchbearing wave makers are still in their middle twenties and still actively creating, but perhaps being made to feel a little like fathers and uncles. Initially, the new groups are attracted by the slogans of Zen and Leary; they want to see truly and do little; but then the pleasures of money and esteem come in and they feel they can change the world by making the millions listen, and so enter the managers and agents and echo chambers and the soaped-up lyrics. Climb On, Cash In, Cop Out.

At the higher levels of money, the designer John Bates, English partner in the firm of Jean Varon, suggests that men learn to wear a gold disk at the shirt throat or even a circle of pearls for evening. "It may sound effeminate," he boldly declares, "but it needn't look it. There are some pink suits being worn in London now that look great. They really do. If you don't look effeminate to begin with, nothing you wear will change you. Wait till men's pastel furs take hold."

The questing in clothing, like the questing in music, is partly a search for definition and partly a lust to live in the here and instant now. "Life is a game. I want to be game-free." This is one of the philosophical statements that, in different forms, the wave makers will utter to explain themselves as they stand around digging one another's funny clothes, each other's funny sounds. They are seeking to discover the ultimate psychedelic—mankind—but in the meantime, they dig raga-rock from India, raga-soul from Motown in Detroit, Carnaby Street from Seventh Avenue, Salvation Army from that little *boutique* across the tracks that also sells old *Reader's Digest*s and burned-out sofas.

The Fugs, shock troops in the Rise of the Uglies, are so ugly they have surely become pretty. From trouble with the fuzz they have risen to trouble with the charts. These children in the sand pile, working out their games with electronic amplification, began in the East Village and headed inexorably toward Broadway and, who knows, maybe Caesars Palace in Vegas. "Kill, Kill, Kill for Peace" is tantrumantra; a song like *My Baby Done Left Me and I Feel Like Homemade Shit* has a perverse tender longing in it, beneath the nasal whine of electricity. The on-edge artist of the group, Tuli Kupferberg, poet, and Ed Sanders, a smiling Midwest American who edits *Fuck You / A Magazine of the Arts,* have found their little game turned into a commercial product with vast implications—money and air time.

The hippies will vote for the first candidate who promises pot in every chicken. They will lie in the park with a nude girl, reading *The Oracle*, because *The Oracle* gives the Word and every girl is nude under her clothes. Mouse and Wes Wilson, doing *Nouveau* Frisco posters, can thumb their wavy, psychedelic noses at the premises of poster art—be clear! punch hard! —in favor of fun and design and obscure play. People have leisure time now; they can figure out the words on the posters; and if they can't, who needs them?

The wave makers are ready to try anything that keeps them awake. *The Beard*, a play by the hip-and-beat poet Michael McClure, ends with cunnilingus committed by Billy the Kid (symbolic, stylized) on Jean Harlow (stylized, symbolic). The act, however, looks real in every way, and as the critic Grover Sales put it, "This play will go down on literary history." The police stalled awhile and ground their gears before arresting the actors and the writer. The American Civil Liberties Union entered the case, and now see how complicated it is: If they are really doing what they evidently are doing, then it is an obscene performance. But how can they really be doing it every night, in the identical way, with spoken lines? ("Star! Star! Star! Star! Star!" sobs Jean Harlow.) Then they must be imitating the action, that is, performing an act of art. But also the act they are imitating (or are they really doing it, plus lines?) is one that perhaps is inciting to some people. And it is illegal in many states to do it, even for married couples, though perhaps not to dramatize doing it for theatrical edification. And the police were confused and didn't move for a long time, but then they did (or imitated) their usual performance—they performed a bust. And now writers, critics and professors step forward to testify that the play is a moving, etc., symbolic, etc., testimony to the eternal, etc., dubieties. The poor police.

What is good and what is evil these days? Why should a poor cop have to think about such things, instead of helping Dick and Jane cross the street safely on the way to school? The fact is that *The Beard* is a black-comic fantasy with some touching moments in it. Since it deals directly with sadomasochistic fantasies, among others, it is as confusing as much of contemporary sexuality. It has found a partial means to control and master the confusion—laughter.

An English girl of the upper class, age sixteen, wrote to her older sister in New York:

> Men look so innocent and angelic in bed, don't they? Tell me, when did you first go to bed with anyone? How old were you? Mike and I really love each other. It's not just a mad infatuation—it's grown slowly. I knew him last holidays—not like Patrick, who was all glamor and titles, and also he was queer. He was really very fascinating, but, my God, he was *so* selfish. Mike's self-centered, but not selfish, so we make a good couple. We both need the same thing.

This touching girlishness and innocence, and the total will to accept sex as a mutually helpful collaboration, must produce a faint quaver in the bellies of the older, romantic generation. Just as throwing flowers and kisses at the cops—one of the hippies' favorite techniques, except that they don't think of it as "technique"—confuses the veterans of class wars, racial wars, boss-and-worker wars.

In a collegetown apartment in Ann Arbor, a girl glanced up from making love with her friend to find a pair of eyes peeking under the window shade. The eyes peered through three levels of glass—her window, the neighbor's window, the wearer's specs. She calmly met the eyes and then they retreated with shame and she continued what she was doing, a mutually helpful collaboration with her visitor.

"Actually," she commented, "I don't really blame him. But I don't like to give him the advantage over me."

The new mass family is replacing the father-mother-children small group of yore. The Army and mass transport, orgies and key parties, the electronic McLuhanite plugging in are all feeding a public straining out of encapsulated sex. A reporter doing a survey for a national news magazine explains, "I used to be afraid I was queer because I like to go to bed with my wife and another man at the same time. But now I know it's just I never had a brother and I want one. My wife—she's great—understands. I was a lonely only child. And now tell me: What's the mood of the country?"

Henry Fairlie, a fairly warmhearted English conservative, has protested the imitation of the young by the less young. He believes that it is for the benefit of the young that their opportunity for rebellion should be untainted by easy capitulation by adults. He writes:

> Anxious not to be thought "square," they steal the music, imitate the dance, adopt the dress, of the young. Anxious to be thought "understanding," they anxiously follow all that the young do and, with a giggle, applaud it. This adult invasion of the world of the young is, committed against themselves, a banal act—committed against the young, almost criminal. It is as if the adults today are searching for some kind of reassurance from the young, which is exactly where they have no right to look for it. Generations should keep their fences in good repair.

Fair enough. What is more gluey to the taste than an aging hippie? But then he feels obliged to ridicule the new inventions, those magic carpets ridden by the young; and here he mixes sweet good sense with sour:

> The only new factors which seem to me to introduce any real novelty into their situation are the scientific aids, from records to contraceptives, from travel to LSD, which provide both the temptation and the opportunity to satisfy, far more fully than before, the desire for immediate experience which is the source of the young's impatience.

The Psychedelic Rangers, riding drugs, riding kicks, may merely be satisfying "the desire for immediate experience." Fighting the fuzz may merely be a dramatic illustration of the blocked aggressivity noted by such writers as Robert Ardrey and Konrad Lorenz. But it is more likely that their new institutional forms will consolidate at least some of the kicky gains.

As the (original) Diggers Song, three centuries old, puts it:

> Gainst Lawyers and gainst Priests, stand up now.
> For tyrants they are both, even flat against their oath,
> To grant us they are loath, free meat and drink and cloth.
>
> Stand up now, Diggers all!
>
> To conquer them by love, come in now, come in now,
> To conquer them by love, come in now!
>
> No power is like to love.
>
> Glory here, Diggers all!

And thanks to these boons of modern technology—records and contraceptives, jet airplanes and superproduction—the old dream of the Diggers seems at least possible in the hearts of these anonymous souls who provide shelter to runaways, meat in the parks and a disconcerting habit of burning the money they are handed by condescending squares.

THE ACID-TRUTH MUMBLE. "Sure I'm interested in those other things—politics, work, everything. But it's all a part of love. And love is all a part of acid."

Now, of course, there is that vexed matter of drugs, about which there are strong positions on all sides except perhaps the middle. This article provides no exception, but anyone should at least be suspicious of experimenting with his own chemistry. Blowing the mind is cool (art, fun, sex, work), but blowing out the mind with the newest discovery is hard smack on the trail to El Rancho Tuckered Out.

Lysergic acid diethylamide, the chief of the psychedelic drugs, has put its convoluted stamp on the style of the period. Its users are not dulled or woozy, as with alcohol and the other depressants; nor are they jittering, as with Dexedrine and Methedrine; rather, their minds are expanded. They see visions. They proclaim truths. They are the travelers of inner space.

One deep critic of the drug cult has said, "LSD is harmless unless talked about." Surely 1967 was not a vintage year, and 1968 promises to be worse. A lot of peculiar sugar got into circulation, and Dr. Timothy Leary got some contradictory ideas into the press. At times, he promises spectacular sexual achievements while on acid trips; at other times, he says that erotic pleasures are irrelevant; and then again, he reconciles these contradictory positions with further contradictions. He is too busy "organizing the energy" to be consistent. Leary says, "You have to go out of your mind to use your head," but going out of your mind is not necessarily a guarantee that you are using your head.

At Millbrook, New York, in 1967, on an estate built in 1889, Timothy Leary lived, when not on tour, in a mansion filled with mattresses and a shifting group of followers of the new religion, LSD, the League for Spiritual Discovery. Asked by a visitor if he was a guru, he answered, "I was the one to get the lucky script." At the regular ingestions of LSD, he appeared in white dress to lead the faithful: "Now we are making this trip together. Now we are like spaceships in space. Now we are going to try to keep in formation. Now there might be voyagers who might want to leave this room, but spiritually we should want to stay together. . . ."

The little cubes of sugar are passed about. The celebrants look through prismatic glass together at a stone, at flowers, at the sky. Their spirits are elsewhere. Timothy Leary wears red socks, because he doesn't like his socks to be confused with others in the common laundry.

Out on the lawn, some children are playing. One ten-year-old asks a riddle: "What goes up and up and never comes down?"

"What?" asks the visitor.

"A guy on LSD with two boosters."

Mike, a merchant from one of the branch offices of the League for Spiritual Discovery, engages a visitor in discussion. The visitor says, "OK, maybe it's good for Leary, Alpert, Allen Ginsberg, people like that. Maybe it's a kind of fuel for a machine already in motion—gives them energy and insight, maybe, helps them power themselves. But what about some high-school kid who thinks she'll get to be like the poets, the gurus, the heroes of the movement?"

"Well, she's using it, isn't she?" Mike answers.

"I mean, she doesn't know who she is. She hasn't really got a self yet—she's a lonely adolescent. She gets a euphoric high and maybe a desperate bring-down or freak-out——"

"But she's using it, isn't she?" asks Mike.

"Yes, that's what I'm saying. She doesn't know herself at all. She just flips out into the drug——"

"But she's using it. Well, isn't she using it? Well, if she's using it, she's OK, isn't she? Isn't she using it? OK, then, she's OK."

Failure of communication. Dead stop. If she takes acid, then that defines OK.

Later, in an acid-pusher's pad—or shrine, as he would prefer to define it—I sat among the wall hangings, the Buddhas, the tapestries, the pillows, the teeny-boppers, the smell of incense and pot and herb tea and the macrobiotic rice cooking on the stove. Blonde Honey, wearing nothing but a smock, her eyes shining with tenderness, looked into a visitor's face and said, "You're beautiful. There's so much sweetness and love in you. I want to look at you so much. I really dig you."

She is nineteen years old. She worked as a hustler for a time in New York, but now she has found truth. She works only enough to buy her supply of acid. It's not very expensive, though the price continues to go up. She sleeps where a mattress is offered, and this week the mattress is offered here. She's nice to have around. She finds beauty everywhere, and especially in new men.

Another visitor to Mike's shrine is a former psychologist from Coral Gables, Florida. He wears a fuzzy-wuzzy sweater that makes him look like a cuddly favorite son. Jeans, tennis shoes. He explains what goes on during the acid voyage toward reality. "Inside it's truth and all true contemplation, feeling, meditation for peace of understanding type, man. Don't ask me to use words. What a drag. I been a word man all my life, consulting psychologist for industry, man. *Miami*, man. Jacksonville. Now I *dig*. That there Honey got the truth, man, right there where she keeps it. Ooh ah, there it went."

"Man," says the psychologist as Honey disappears to stir the rice, "suppose we could turn on . . . Johnson? Think of that. Lawrence Welk. The fuzz. Oh, I get a fine paranoia going for me. Ooh ah, there it went again. We could turn on everybody."

People have been tripping out in various rooms of the apartment. There is a quiet buzz in the air. A raga record plays over and over again, but when Ravi Shankar is tuning up and when he is playing—that's the beauty of it—the Western ear judges only with great difficulty. He is at one with his instrument. The new audience is eager to catch up with his training, but without actually learning what Ravi Shankar knows.

The Italian longshoreman husband of a lady painter is on a bad trip. He misses his wife. She is out dehexing a boardinghouse. In addition to being a painter and a belly dancer, she is a witch.

The husband is sweating and flailing the air and panicky. "Come on, Professor," he wails, "you got to straighten my head around, someone got to straighten my head around, I mean turn it around, I don't care, Professor——"

He is grinning but hysterical.

Mike, the organizer of this little cell, puts his arm around the man's shoulder and leads him onto the porch. He smiles back at the knot of concerned friends. I can take care of all this! his glance and grin seem to say. He listens to the flipped-out longshoreman. He pats his arm. The man is wailing for his wife. Mike calls to Honey to come and help listen, too.

Later the pusher, Mike, explains that he is a hero of our time. "Like, I'm a *hero*, man. I could go up for any amount of years now, them laws they got. Like, I'm putting my life on the line every time to make sure the people get blown out of their mind. Man, I'll turn on a cop, he wants it. I'm a true guru of our time."

"Guru means teacher, you know that?"

"That's what I said. I used to sell Meth, but it dries up the head, so I stopped that. I also sold pot. But, hell, grass is good—I'm really special. Now I found I have this mission, you know? To turn people on and make them OK. I'm the center here, you know, man? You know, man? You know, man?"

Meanwhile, Honey is giving truth to the former psychologist on a mattress while mildly curious visitors troop past them to look for grass, chat with friends, dip into the communal pot of rice. Honey's tenderness is real and it will be just as real for the next man in an hour or two. The psychologist feels that he is in touch with the universe, thanks to Honey, both of them meditated by acid. They know that acid is the magic carpet. It has transported them both to true love. They don't ask work, time, patience or sacrifice. Instant true love will suffice. It's not sex. They are opposed to mere sex. That's lust—square. It's love, love, love. Of course, they express it through sex. But that's only the means. It's not what you'd call square sex, like other people's. It's hip sex. It's special. It's theirs. And the psychologist says about his relationship with Honey, "In return, I give her the companionship of an exciting mind."

"What does she give you?"

He looked at me as if I were crazy, blind or all three—that includes malevolent. Yes, it was evident. "Which has broken out of the establishment game," he continued, diagramming his exciting mind for me.

In America, we now live in a drug culture. It is estimated that six dozen mood pills were consumed per person in 1966. Dracula is blurting chemicals into our blood streams, not sucking the blood out. Walter Mitty, wanting to be King Kong and finding himself married to Fay Wray for forty years, escapes by taking a pill and dreaming he is James Thurber. It excites him. So he takes tranquilizers. It bores him. So he takes stimulants. He looks at the sky and doesn't see God, so he asks Mike what to take, and Mike is delighted to tell him.

A few years ago, the drugs of choice were Methedrine or Dexedrine compounds—speed, as they are called, or forwards. But now the glory trip of Dr. Leary has advertised the new psychedelics, everything from acid to morning-glory seeds. Even in Cleveland, Ohio, there was until recently a Headquarters ("Travel Accommodations for the Discriminating Smoker"), where books and The Fugs and girls with Berkeley-Radcliffe ironed hair could be found on friendly Euclid Avenue. CAN YOU PASS THE ACID TEST? asks the card illustrated with a recruiting-poster version of Uncle Sam. All over the country, the acid-culture people flash funny cards and prisms and pieces of glass at one another. They are recognized, they recognize their reality. They feel at home, even on Euclid Avenue.

In a psychedelic boardinghouse in the Haight-Ashbury district of San Francisco—"Psychedelphia," columnist Herb Caen has called it—the residents have taken an old building and made it pretty with bits of glass, collages, clippings pinned to the wall, antiwar and prolove posters, celebrations of dances, poetry readings, Happenings, plastic hangings, little objects, rugs, tapestries, *things* fill the rooms. A boy with a Brooklyn accent giggles and says, "Like, man, wow, I'm on a trip now." The residents wear beads; the men and girls wear beaded headdresses, but without the feathers, because they are not quite Indians.

Joel, the boy from Brooklyn, explains about love. Acid helps people love. For example, "I love everyone, Johnson, Sheriff Clark in Alabama, Pat Boone——"

"Hitler?"

He turns thoughtful. "Well, I don't know much about him. But I love his soul. 'Course, I've been told some bad things about him. My parents are Jewish. So I don't love what he did, man."

"You're the first person I've met who loves Hitler."

Joel looks at me with pitying tenderness. "If you take off the ego," he explains, "we're all the same, I'm me and you and everybody. It's groovy."

"Do you ever get sore at anybody?"

"Well, my wife, sort of. We got divorced. But I love her. But not using acid should be grounds for divorce."

"She didn't use."

He shook his head with shame for his former wife. "She ran off to her mother. Scared, when all I wanted to do was help her. I knew this other cat, he gave up his college degree two weeks before he had it, he wanted to go to India to learn this flute he heard on a trip."

"What do you want out of life?"

He giggled and pulled the beads down tighter around his skull. "Travel around, see people, experience things, live in a cabin. . . ."

In the meantime, though, he lives in a boardinghouse with a lot of other people who want to live in a cabin, experiencing things. He likes to answer questions about what he is doing. He has a missionary intention. He is eager to please, like Polonius, eager to swell a progress and be of use.

Acid culture is similar to other drug cults, except that the mood is generally sweeter. There is much insistence on gentleness, smiles, love, the yeah-hey-groovy manner. A group living in Psychedelphia takes to the far-out taped music, to raga and other Eastern rhythms, to stained glass and dark, rich colors. When their optical nerves are jangled by acid, this is what they like to see. Beaded and glowing, they abandon the self to use by the great organic and the great machine worlds. Peace. A groove.

At a special gathering, Ken Kesey's Halloween Acid Test Graduation Ceremony, Kesey, who was fighting convictions on narcotics charges, announced a graduation from drugs. Among the crowd present were some Hell's Angels, students, teeny-boppers and Kesey's personal club, the Merry Pranksters, devoted to funny clothes, tape and film and grooving together. There was a band, costumes, an air of expectant reveling. There is a hip way to be square—the general idea of the meeting.

Taking a microphone, Kesey *segued* into an abstracted rhapsody about different spider webs. On speed, the spiders make lots and lots of lopsided webs. On marijuana, beautiful wild webs. On acid, one simple web and that's all.

Well, he implied, there might be a way to do it without acid.

This called for reverence. The ecstatic revelers, the psychedelic-ecstatic plus the reporters, the photographers, the TV cameramen, the girl from *Vogue* and Tom Wolfe all knelt with Kesey. The gifted novelist of *One Flew over the Cuckoo's Nest* was in trouble and knew it. He was trying to find his way back to society and to find it publicly. He was tired of running to Mexico and Canada under Federal indictment. It was silly to be abused on mere marijuana charges. Now he was waiting for his inspiration to strike. The crowd kneeled, hushed. He asked for comments from the floor and a bit of quiet meditation. The Merry Pranksters were stilled. Ken's wife and children beamed upon him.

He waited and waited for something to say. It would come to him in a moment. He practiced calm as a few disgruntled and impatient ones peeled off and went home. Some of the Hell's Angels who had been turned on to acid were puzzled by their colleague. Why didn't Ken say it? What was he thinking? What was the word?

The drama of the drug culture is partly illusory, depending on the *ambiance* of conspiracy and illegality. Living out this romance is often like having a lovely and delicate girl's hearing aid, but without the girl. Like pop art, much of what is produced is mitigated trash—mitigated by its fair expression of a confused and frantic time. It submits to the mood-weariness; it says that the way out is chemical, as Huxley predicted in *Brave New World,* where he showed a sheepish population lining up for *soma.*

Ken Kesey held a candlelit press conference at a Twin Peaks pad to announce that he was returning from the lam in Mexico or someplace in order to straighten out the minds of everybody. "I feel an idea flying through my head like a bat," he declared.

He chuckled about his lecture before a creative-writing seminar at Stanford. Wanted by the police, he was everywhere, if not like Batman, at least like Robin. How did he avoid arrest? "I just stand small and ooze along," he explained. "The cops never see me."

Relaxed now, Kesey sat hunched in a chair in his sheepskin coat while he imparted a few more of the ideas that came like bats to his head. Soon everyone was huddled closely about him as he called the signals: "No more acid! Turn on with other means—it's time for a new thing in this country."

His admirers admired the masked profile of courage that he turned toward the inept fuzz and the inepter FBI. He would ooze along, blowing his mind in his own way.

A few days later, Kesey was arrested. After two mistrials on eighteen-month-old possession-of-marijuana charges, he was finally convicted of "knowingly being in a place where marijuana was kept." On June 23, 1967, he began serving a six-month jail sentence.

In 1967, Dr. Timothy Leary took his traveling show from New York to San Francisco and held a press conference.

Leary: "I am here on a religious reconnaissance mission." While the reporters scribbled, the tape spools spun. He peddled his religion with fluent charm and eloquence, mixing the language of hippie and the language of Harvard and a certain *je ne sais quoi* of his own. He wore a red lei. "We want to distribute LSD only to our coreligionists; otherwise you get in a hassle. We don't want to engage in the game of power politics."

"Game" is one of the operative words for Leary. He continued, "You must be in a state of grace to take the sacrament, LSD. Of course, we don't have any formal routine—you're the best judge of that on your own internal chessboard."

"Chessboard," that day, was also one of his important words.

"We have witness of the divine process," he said slowly, keeping pace with the reporters' pencils.

His friend and colleague, Dr. Richard Alpert, warned the journalists, "If you write anything to do with drug, hippie, ex-professor, addiction, cult, you're wrong. It's all a metaphor, spiritual."

Leary: "We have celebrated the reincarnation of Jesus Christ in New York City. Now the people who go to the Fillmore to dance are doing it a different way. Everyone should start his own religion. We should examine our conscience. In ten years, I predict we'll have a psychedelic President."

"Who's gonna be the psychedelic President in ten years?" someone asked the publicity girl.

"Sh," she said.

Leary was explaining about bad trips. "Are there bad trips?" he asked. "Well, you're asking me to go onto the checkerboard of the minds of people I don't know. The reason people don't take LSD is they're afraid to—afraid of the divine process, they can't face it."

"Does that satisfy you?" Leary asked. "Good! Ask me another."

Someone asked about kids taking LSD.

"Well, a sixteen-year-old chick taking acid on a motorcycle with her lover, say. OK, she might be in a state of grace. A psychiatrist doing reasearch for a paper, on an ego trip of his own, is more frivolous. Does that satisfy you? Good."

"Do you agree with the existentialists that a person is what he does, his actions?" I asked Carlo, a former Madison Avenue art director who was with Leary.

"Yeah! I got a flash of that several times when I was on an acid trip! I believe it. No, it was a combination Methedrine high and acid trip. Yeah, I remember. You're right. You're absolutely right. If you do the right thing—take acid, see God—you're in the right bag. It's a glory trip. You're dropped out. You're nobody, you're everybody. Is that what you meant, man?"

Running through a cellular examination of themselves, the new druggies are content, peaceful, easy, unless they are tormented and violent. They are checking out what they feel. From the outside, in New York, Boulder, San Francisco, Chicago, London, on so many campuses, in so many towns, they have dropped out of the race. They look as if the population explosion has exploded them. They have taken a rain check on money, status, power, wars, the "games," as Leary and Alpert call the traditional pursuits: the power game, the establishment game, the academic game, the suburb game. They call their boarding-houses "communes." They write messages to one another on the walls and doors. They share elaborate "in" jokes, "in" art—jargon, designs, ways of passing the time. The heroin addicts of an earlier period had a heart-rending explanation of the rush and anxiety and achievement and peace of the occupation of being an addict: "It's something to do, man." The answer to boredom and anxiety: something to do, find the connection, get the fix, something to do. The acidheads keep busy in ways that seem stimulated, disorganized and peaceful, at different times. And the "bad trip," the frights, the horrors, the freak-out is like the vengeance of the outraged cells. When does it happen? When has too much LSD gone through the body? When the soul is not prepared for the experience? On the third, the seventh, the twenty-sixth trip? When the guide is not the right one? When the body has taken all it can take? No one can tell for sure. Many end in hospitals, and their friends wonder why, since always before it had been "beautiful, just beautiful, loving, tender, beautiful." Electricity, aspirin, many medicines can be taken in small amounts; larger amounts act as poisons. The limits for lysergic acid are not known. They seem to vary in individuals. The long-term effects are also not determined.

One psychiatrist, initially enthusiastic about the possibilities of LSD, has offered a metaphor to explain its power. It loosens the glue that keeps a personality together. It's like soaking a glued toy in hot water. Things get jangled; there are new conjunctions. Then the glue hardens. But not as hard as before. Then a new dose, new loosening, a new hardening. But not as hard as before. And one day, depending on the quality of the glue, it doesn't harden enough and the toy goes jangling into bits. "It's too dangerous," he says. Institutions are filling up with people whose glue doesn't seem to harden enough to let them survive in the world.

"Well," said a delegate to the LSD conference in San Francisco last winter, "everything has risks. You cross the street, that's a risk. You get up in the morning. You take a pill." He shrugged. "It makes you loving."

This vague evocation of the highest virtues—love, creativity—can be called the Acid Truth Mumble. The lips move. The voices come out. The voices repeat. It is acid speaking.

CONCLUSION: THE ART OF POSITIVE NAYSAYING. In all this wave-making confusion of innovation, a perennial vision of history is likely to reappear—the vision of continuity and permanence. The wave makers want to be what they are, what they really *are*. The kids are blowing their whistles and the cops are speaking in the careful, precise language of panic. Uptight, freaking out or just mind-blown, those who have seized upon leisure as their booty are creating demons, Victorian lamps and perhaps a new way of life. "Some of them," as that storekeeper in the East Village said, "are artists in their own way. They don't shoplift me so much anymore. They got a lot of love in 'em."

The young are leading the way to new forms of consuming and nonconsuming, setting the stage for the future with their smoky philosophies of Love and Express and Make Do with What You Have. Run far from America, cry these noble savages, and there you will find—America, America! They substitute for the beatnik's abstention a new complicity in the working out of things: You can't go into exile again. They look pretty good both in clothes and naked. When lost in storms, they force pills down their throats. They sneak glances at themselves in the mirror, but then they walk away. Like the Anabaptists and the Amish, the wave makers hate to bear arms, they believe in communal living, they have subtle rites of passage into adult life. They are cultural dropouts who see new cultures dropping in. They have extrasensory ignorances. They support themselves any way they can and sometimes get rich out of emulation of the rest of the world, which is seeking a better way, too.

The life you lead, they say, may be your own. They throw stones and live in glass houses because they like shimmering floors. They are careful to step on the splinters. They bear their wounds noisily.

In a manifesto filled with questions, The Diggers asked, When will Timothy Leary stand on a street corner waiting for no one?

FRODO LIVES! COME TO MIDDLE EARTH! proclaim the buttons of the new Hobbit cult based on J. R. R. Tolkien's trilogy, *The Lord of the Rings*. The Hobbits go along, they try to avoid danger, they don't like it, they don't want to get involved. But when the thing comes, they simply don't go under. This is the book of the wave-making age. Marshall McLuhan, Timothy Leary and Bobby Dylan are the foam of the wave. Tolkien's Hobbits swim in the tides beneath.

At Grace Cathedral in San Francisco, a representative of the Esalen Institute at Big Sur declared, "The life of every man—the heart of it—is pure and holy joy." This is a religious statement, but while this vision takes the imagination of some, others think back on the beatniks, the holy barbarians of ten years ago, or back into history—so many cults and credos and revolutions that are now merely footnotes to cultural history. Another vision takes the skeptic:

Two A.M. at the corner of Haight and Ashbury in San Francisco, or Bleecker and Macdougal in New York, or on Kings Road in London, or near Le Drugstore at St.-Germain-des-Prés in Paris. An ancient hipster of forty is picking up a vinyl-clad teeny-bopper with raga record under her arm. "Hey, man," he says, "you want to fall up to my pad and blow some music 'n' stuff?"

"Cool," says the fading teeny-bopper with the copy of John Lennon, the clipping about Bobby Dylan's accident, the BAN THE BOMB sticker on her miniskirt.

As they leave, two strangers appear. They are wearing wire glasses and antique clothes. One, the girl, has a skirt hanging all the way below her knees. She is carrying the last remaining Tiffany lamp. The other, a boy, is wearing a zooty suit with wide lapels and is driving a green tricycle. "Good Lord," he says, staring after both the forty-year-old hipster and the nineteen-year-old fading teeny-bopper, "look at those ricky-tick, worn-out articles. Come on, miss, let's go get a milk shake and a hamburger at the drive-in."

For, indeed, there is a certain permanence in rebellion, in the generational conflict. And all through history, back to the conflicts of Alcibiades the Young Hippie and Socrates the Square Professor—the *Euthyphro* is a dialog in which Plato ravishes the problem of what sons owe to fathers—there has been this struggle for pre-eminence. The sage habits of the elderly have given way to the wild impatience of the young, which has given way to sageness.

But the wave makers have found their way back, through all their many experiments, violations, outrages, to an old and essential truth about not just innovation and fashion but about that essential ingredient of humanity—creation. It takes a great deal of will to do creative work, and some of the will must be used to relax the will—to let in the wildness. The wave makers are relaxing the puritan will and doing it with passion and determination. They are grokking and grooving, and with a moral passion to grok and groove. They are not Huck Finns merely floating on the river. When they float, they are trying to define the nature of rivers, the nature of man.

And, yes, they are also floating, too, and they ask the rest of the world: Come let us float and define together. Let us make waves.

"Disgusting! I bet they're having an orgasm right now."

PAUL GOODMAN

The Deadly Halls of Ivy

is america's mania for mass education throttling initiative, individuality and intellect in the groves of academe?

Americans are sold on schooling and are continually pouring new billions into it. Yet for most youth, including the brightest, going to school for many years is not only a poor way of getting an education but is positively damaging. The high schools and colleges can superficially be improved, of course, but their basic idea is wrong. For most students, schooling prevents education. It destroys initiative and the relation to society that education is supposed to be about.

Consider a usual case: a young fellow, twenty years old, in a college classroom. Let me point out some obvious facts about his situation.

The salient and astonishing fact is that he has been *in an equivalent classroom for fourteen continuous years,* interrupted only by summer vacations. Although schooling has been the serious part of his life, he has spent those fourteen years passively listening to some grownup talking or has doggedly done assigned lessons. (Even the lessons, by the way, have not been programmed by the living teacher in front of him, but by a distant board of regents, a dean of faculties, a textbook manufacturer.) Our young man has never once seriously assigned himself a task or done anything earnest on his own initiative.

Sometimes, as a child, he thought he was doing something earnest on his own, but the adults pooh-poohed it as play and interrupted him. Now he's a junior in college.

He's bright; he can manipulate formulas and remember sentences. For instance, during his last year in high school, he made good grades on a series of grueling state and national tests, regents, college boards, national merits, scholastic aptitudes. In this college, which is increasingly geared to process Ph.D.s, he has survived, though the washout rate is nearly 40 percent. He has even gotten a partial scholarship through the National Defense Education Act. Yet he doesn't especially like books, he is not scholarly, and he gets no flashes of insight into the structure or the methods of the academic subjects. This isn't the field in which his intelligence, grace and strength show to best advantage. He just learns the answers. Needless to say, he has already forgotten most of the answers that once enabled him to pass his courses, sometimes brilliantly.

The academic subject being taught in this particular classroom is intrinsically interesting—most arts and sciences are intrinsically interesting—and the professor, or even the section man, probably knows a good deal about it. But, especially if it is one of the social sciences or humanities, our young man does not grasp that it is *about* something; it has no connection for him. He has had too little experience of life. He has not practiced a craft, been in business, tried to make a living, been fired, been married, had to cope with children. He hasn't voted, served on a jury, campaigned for office, or picketed. If he comes from a middle-class suburb, he might never have even seen poor people or the foreign-borns. His emotions have been carefully limited by conventions, his parents, the conformism of his peer group. What, for him, could philosophy, history, sociology, political science, psychology, great music, classical literature, possibly be *about?* In *The Republic,* Plato forbids teaching most of the academic subjects until the student is thirty years old, lest the teaching and learning be merely verbal and emptily combative.

Our young man is not verbally combative. But sometimes he is stimulated, or piqued, by something that the teacher or the book says, and he wants to demur, argue or ask a question. But the class is really too crowded for dialog. If the teacher is a lecturer, the format forbids interrupting. And a chief obstacle is the other students. In their judgment, discussion is irrelevant to the finals and the grades—"Professor! Are we responsible for that on the final examination?"—and they resent the waste of time. They resent it if any individual is paid special attention. Even so, suppose that the professor, or the young section man, is heartened by the sign of life and does want to pursue the discussion. Then possibly, in the social sciences or the humanities, he might express subtle, speculative or dissenting opinions; he might ask about the foundations of an institution or refer to somebody's personal experience. At once a wall of hostility will rise against the teacher as well as the questioning student: Surely he must be a Communist, pacifist or homosexual; maybe he is making fun of them. Feeling the hostility, and being, on the average, a rather timid academic, worried about tenure or advancement, the teacher signs off: "Well, let's get back to the meat of the course," or "That's beyond our scope here, why don't you take sosh 403?" or "That's really anthropology, young man, you'd better ask Professor O'Reilly, heh-heh."

Little of the teaching makes a student see the relevance, necessity or beauty of the subject. The teacher might indeed be interested in the latest findings or the ingenuity of the technique, but the student is at sea as to why he is studying it at all, except that it's part of sequence B toward a bachelor's. His confusion is aggravated by the fact that his generation, *including* the young teachers, has an exceedingly tenuous loyalty to the culture of the Western world, the ideal of disinterested science, the republic of letters. Mass culture, world wars, a largely phony standard of living rooted in status striving and material acquisitiveness, lack of community spirit; all these have torn the humanistic tradition to shreds. (I find these youths almost unteachable; though they are bright, eager and respectful, they simply do not dig what we academics are trying to say.) The humanistic function of higher education has been replaced; the university has become nothing but a factory to train apprentices and process union cards for a few corporations and a few professions. Their needs predetermine what goes on.

Paradoxically, a college is a poor environment in which to train apprentices—except in lab sciences, where one works at real problems with real apparatus. Most of the academic curriculum, whether in high school or college, is necessarily abstract. A structure of ideas is abstracted from the ongoing professions, civic and economic activities, and institutions, and these ideas are imported into the classrooms and taught as the curriculum. This ancient procedure sometimes makes sense; it makes sense for aspiring professionals who know what they are after and for the scholarly who have a philosophical interest in essences and their relationships. But for most students, the abstractness of the curriculum, especially if the teaching is pedantic, can be utterly barren. The lessons are *only* exercises, with no relation to the real world; they are never "for keeps." And many of the teachers are not practicing professionals but merely academics, interested in the words, not the thing. (As if recognizing the academic unreality, the college has recently been inviting outsiders, professionals, poets, politicians, etc., to give talks and readings and spend a week "in residence"; but this only makes the ordinary classroom seem duller by contrast, especially since the outsiders, who have no status to lose, are more outspoken or flamboyant.)

Our young man respects his teacher, perhaps unduly so, but he cannot help feeling disappointed. He had hoped, in a vague way, that when he came to college it would be different from high school. He would be a kind of junior friend of learned men who had made it; he could model himself on them. After all, except for parents and schoolteachers, he had had little contact with *any* adults. He thought, too, that the atmosphere in college would be—somehow—free, liberating, a kind of wise bull session that would reveal a secret. But it has proved to be the same competitive cash accounting of hours, tests, credits and grades. The teacher is, in fact, preoccupied with his own research and publishing; in both class and office hours he is formal and standoffish; he never appears in the coffee shop; he certainly never exposes himself as a human being. He is meticulous about the assignments being on time and about the grading, not because he believes in the system, but to keep the students under control; he does not realize that they respect him, anyway. So, just as in high school, the youth are driven back to their exclusive youth "subculture," which only distracts further from any meaning that the academic subjects might have. As David Riesman and others have pointed out, the students and faculty confront one another like hostile, mutually suspicious tribes.

Also, in recent years, this alienation or lack of community has been badly exacerbated by the chaotic transition that almost every college in the country is now undergoing. The grounds are torn up by bulldozers; the enrollment is excessive; the classes are too large; the students are housed three and four in a room meant for two. The curriculum is continually being readjusted; the professors are pirated away by salary increases and contracted research. These conditions are supposed to quiet down eventually, but I have seen them now for seven or eight years and the immediate future will be worse. Meanwhile, a whole generation is being sacrificed.

An even deadlier aspect of transition is the knowledge explosion. New approaches and altogether new subjects must be taught; yet the entrenched faculty is by no means willing to give up any of the old prescribed subjects. This is a peculiar phenomenon. One would expect that, since the professors have tenure, they would welcome dropping some of the course load, but their imperialism is too strong—they will give up nothing. So our student is taking five, or even six, subjects when the maximum might better be three. Whenever he begins to get interested in something, he is interrupted by other chores. Rushed, he can give only token performances, which he has learned to fake. No attention is paid to what suits *him,* although without instrinsic motivation he will obviously learn nothing at all. The only time a student is treated as a person is when he breaks down and is referred to guidance.

Instead of reliance on intrinsic motives, on respect for individuality and leisure for exploration, there is the stepped-up pressure of extrinsic motivations—fear and bribery. On the one hand, there is the pressure of schedules, deadlines and grades, not to speak of the fantastic tuition and other fees that will go down the drain if the student flunks out. On the other hand, lavish scholarships and the talent scouts for the big corporations hovering about with tempting offers. In this atmosphere of forced labor—punching a time clock, keeping one's nose clean, and with one eye constantly on a raise in salary—disinterested scrutiny of the nature of things, the joy of discovery, moments of creativity, the finding of identity and vocation die before they are born. It is sickening to watch.

Finally, we must say something about the animal and community life from which our collegian has come into this classroom. The college has spent a lot of government and foundation money on pretentious buildings with plush lounges, but the food is lousy and the new dormitories are like Bedlam for want of soundproofing. It's a world tailored for catalog photographs, not for living. The administration is strongly against fraternity houses because of the exclusion clauses and because they destroy cohesiveness of the student body; these are excellent reasons, but one sometimes suspects that the motive is chiefly rent gouging, since with urban renewal and area redevelopment many colleges have become great landlords. (In fact, some prestigious centers of learning are, under fictitious names, urban slumlords; or alternately, they gobble up neighborhoods, dislocate tenants, disrupt communities.) If students want to live off campus in their own cooperatives, they are avuncularly told that they are not mature enough to feed their faces and make their beds. There are exquisitely elaborate regulations governing sexual and convivial behavior—days and hours and how many inches the door must be open and whose feet must be on the ground. If these nineteen- and twenty-year-olds were factory hands, nobody would fuss about their sex lives or drinking habits, so long as they arrived punctually at the plant the next morning; as students, they are supposed to be the chosen of the land, the hope of the future, but they are not "responsible." Needless to say, despite the regulations, the young make love, anyway, but frequently the conditions are not charming. The degrading atmosphere of the much publicized "wild college weekend" develops as an inevitable reaction to, or revolt against, such strict and patronizing regulations.

The administration claims to be *in loco parentis;* yet many of these young men and women had more freedom at home, when they were still kids in high school. The psychologist in charge of guidance has made a speech about the awful plight of unwed mothers—with about as much compassion as they used to speak of "bastards"—but he will not ask the infirmary to give contraceptive information on request. One has more than a strong suspicion that all this parental concern has nothing whatever to do with the students' welfare, but is for public relations. The college motto may be *Lux et Veritas,* but there is a strong smell of hypocrisy in the air.

Maybe the most galling thing of all is that there is a student government, with political factions and pompous elections. It is empowered to purchase the class rings and organize the prom and the boat ride. Our young man no longer bothers to vote.

Now our average student's face isn't quite so blank. It is wearing a little smile. The fact is, he is no longer mechanically taking notes but is frankly daydreaming, as he used to in the sixth grade, ten years ago. Think of it, there might be four or five more years of this, for his father wants him to continue in graduate school. This will make nineteen years of schooling.

This is an appalling prospect! He will now have to do "original research" under these conditions of forced labor. And he will be in a panic about failing, or not getting the assistantship, because he now has a wife and an infant to support.

Of course, many of the unfavorable college conditions that I have been describing can be, and should be, improved. In my book *The Community of Scholars,* I suggested a number of expedients. Grading, for example, can be scrapped (keeping tests as a useful pedagogic device). There can be more part-time active professionals in the faculty, to generate a less academic atmosphere. There are several arrangements for teachers to pay more attention to students, discover their intrinsic motivations, guide them in more individual programs. The social sciences can be made less unreal by working pragmatically on problems of the college community itself and its immediate rural or city environment. The moral rules can be reformed to suit the purpose of an educational community, which is to teach responsibility by giving freedom in an atmosphere of counsel and support. Certainly these and other reforms are possible.

Nevertheless, when we consider those fourteen years, sixteen years, twenty years of schooling, we cannot avoid a far more disturbing question. *Why is the young man in this classroom in the first place?* It suits him so badly! He is bright but not bookish, curious but not scholarly, teachable but not in this way. Of course he must be educated, everybody must be educated, but has school been the best way to educate him? We have seen him in other situations than school when he looked far brighter, both more spontaneous and more committed, when he learned a lot, and fast, simply because he wanted to or really had to. Maybe, for him, the entire high school and college institution, in the form that we know it, has been a mistake. If so, what a waste of his youth and of the social wealth!

Every child must be educated, brought up to be useful to himself and society. In our society this must be done largely at public expense, as a community necessity; certainly Americans ought to spend more on it than they do. But it is simply a superstition, an official superstition and a mass superstition, that the way to educate a majority of the young is to keep them in schools for twelve to twenty years.

The hard task of education, as I see it, is to liberate and strengthen a youth's initiative and at the same time to make him able to cope with the activities and culture of society, so that his initiative can be relevant. In a democracy, each citizen is supposed to be a new center of decision. But schools and colleges, as we have them, are boxes in which the young mainly face front and do assigned lessons according to predetermined programs, under the control of professional educators who are rarely professional in any other way. Then by magic, after years of nothing but this, the young are supposed to decide their own careers, make a living in a competitive market, choose to marry or not marry, and vote for President of the United States.

At no other time or place in history have people believed that such schools were the obvious means to prepare most youth for most careers, whether craftsman, farmer, industrial worker, nurse, architect, writer, engineer, lawyer, shopkeeper, party boss, social worker, sailor, secretary, fine artist, musician, parent or citizen. Many of these careers require a lot of study, some need academic teaching, but it has never before been thought useful to give teaching in such massive and continuous doses.

The idea of everybody going to a secondary school and college has accompanied a recent stage of highly centralized corporate and state economy and policy. Universal higher schooling is not, as people think, simply a logical continuation of universal primary schooling in reading and democratic socialization. It begins to orient to careers and it occurs after puberty, and jobs and sex are not usually best learned about in academies. In my opinion, there *is* no single institution, like the monolithic school system increasingly programmed by a few graduate universities (and the curriculum reformers of the National Science Foundation), that can prepare everybody for an open future of a great society. What we are getting is not education but regimentation—baby-sitting, policing, brainwashing and processing technicians for a few corporations at the public's expense. (About 35 percent of college graduates go into the corporations; a good percentage enter government service and teaching; less than 2 percent engage in "independent enterprise.") We are in an increasingly closed society, dominated by the sovereign and the feudal corporations. Instead of education being a means of liberation, independence and novelty, everybody pays for schooling that rigidifies the status quo still further.

At present, facing a confusing future of automated technology and entirely new patterns of work and leisure, the best educational brains ought to be devoting themselves to devising *many* various means of educating and paths of growing up, appropriate to various talents, conditions and careers. We should be experimenting with different kinds of schools, with no school at all, using the real cities as schools, or farms as schools, with practical apprenticeships, guided travel, work camps, little theaters, community service, etc. Probably most of all, we need to revive the community and community spirit in which many adults who know something, and not only professional teachers, will pay attention to the young.

Instead of new thought, the tendency is crashingly in the opposite direction—to streamline, aggrandize and totalize what we have. (With the unanimous applause of all right-thinking people, Congress in 1964 appropriated another two billion dollars for college buildings.) In 1963 more than 60 percent of our seventeen-year-olds graduated from high school, and the President led a vigorous campaign to cajole and threaten the rest back into school. While 35 percent were going to college, it is hoped to push this figure to 50 percent. It has recently been proposed to make the two-year junior college compulsory. Among all liberals and champions of the underprivileged, it is an article of faith that salvation for the Negroes and Spanish Americans consists in more schooling at the middle-class level. And all educational observers, from hard-liners like Rickover, through James Conant, to "liberal" thinkers like Marty Mayer, insist that salvation for America lies in tightening and upgrading middle-class schools and getting rid of progressive methods that might give the kid a chance to breathe.

Like any mass belief, the superstition that schooling is the only path to success is self-proving. There are now no professions, whether labor-statesman, architect or trainer in gymnastics, that do not require college degrees. Standards of licensing are set by boards of regents who talk only school language. For business or hotel management it is wise to have a master's. Access to the billions for research and development is by Ph.D. only, and prudent parents push their youngsters accordingly; only a few are going to get the loot, but all must compete. Department stores require a high-school diploma for a salesgirl; this might seem irrelevant, but it speaks for punctuality and good behavior. Thus, effectually, whether it is rational or not, a youth *has* no future if he quits or falls off the school ladder. Farm youth can still drop out without too much clatter, but the rural population is now only 8 percent and rapidly diminishing.

We can understand and evaluate our present situation if we review the history of schooling in this country during this century.

By 1900, our present school system was established in its main outlines, with almost universal primary schooling, in a great variety of local arrangements. Yet only 6 percent of the seventeen-year-olds in that year graduated from high school. Maybe another 10 percent would have graduated if they could have afforded it (James Conant has estimated that only 15 percent are "academically talented"). Now we may assume that those 6 percent were in classrooms because they wanted to be *there*. There were no blackboard jungles or startling problems of discipline. More important, such students could be taught a curriculum, whether traditional or vocational, that was interesting and valuable for itself; they were not merely being chased up a ladder by parents and police, or pulled up by the corporate need for Ph.D.s.

But who were the 94 percent who did not graduate? Obviously they were not "dropouts." They were, as I have said, everybody: future farmer, shopkeeper, millionaire, politician, inventor, journalist. Consider the careers of two well-known architects who were born around that time. One quit school at the seventh grade to leave home and support himself. After a few jobs, he gravitated to an architect's office as an office boy and found the art to his liking. He learned draftsmanship in the office, and French and some mathematics on the outside (with the help of friendly adults), and he eventually won the Beaux Arts prize and studied in a Paris atelier. Today he has built scores of distinguished buildings and, as the graduate professor of design at a great university, is one of the most famous teachers in the country. The other architect happens to be the most successful in America in terms of size and prestige of his commissions. He quit school at age thirteen to support his mother. Working for a stonecutter, he learned to draw, and in a couple of years he cut out for New York and apprenticed himself to an architect. He studied languages and mathematics in competition with a roommate. Via the Navy in 1918, he went to Europe with some money in his pocket and traveled and studied. Returning, he made a splendid marriage, and so forth.

These two careers—not untypical except for their éclat—are almost unthinkable in our day. How could the young men be licensed without college degrees? How could they get college degrees without high-school diplomas? But they had the indispensable advantage that they were deeply self-motivated, went at their own pace, and could succumb to fascination and risk. Would these two men have become architects at all if they had been continually interrupted by high-school chemistry, freshman composition, Psychology 106? Indeed, it would be a useful study, which I have not made, to find how many people who grew up from 1900 to 1920 and have made great names in the sciences, arts, literature, government, business, etc., actually went through the *continuous* sixteen-year school grind without quitting for good or quitting and occasionally returning.

As the decades passed, higher schooling began to be a mass phenomenon. In 1930, 30 percent graduated from high school and 11 percent went to college. And by 1960, we see 60 percent have graduated, of whom more than half have gone to college. Who now are the other 40 percent? They are the dropouts, mostly urban-underprivileged and rural. From this group we do not much expect splendid careers in architecture, politics or literature. They are not allowed to get jobs before sixteen; they find it hard to get jobs after sixteen; they might drop out of society altogether, because there is now no other track than going to school.

What happened to the schools during this tenfold increase from 1900 to 1960? Administratively, of course, we simply aggrandized and bureaucratized the existing framework. The system now looks like the system then. But in the process of massification, it suffered a sea change. Plant, teacher selection and methods were increasingly standardized. The students were a different breed. Not many were there because they wanted to be *there;* a lot of them, including many of the bright and gifted, certainly wanted to be elsewhere and began to make trouble. The academic curriculum was necessarily trivialized. An important function of the schools began to be baby-sitting and policing. The baby-sitting was continued into the rah-rah colleges, to accommodate the lengthening youth unemployment.

Naturally, in the aggrandized system, educational administration became very grand. This was important because of the very irrelevance of the system itself, the inappropriate students and the feeble curriculum. Stuck with a bad idea, the only way of coping with the strains was to have more assistant principals, counselors, truant officers, university courses in methods, revised textbooks. Currently, we are getting team teaching, visual aids, higher horizons. And to compensate for the mass trivializing of the curriculum, there are intellectually gifted classes, enrichment, advanced placement. (Also, opportunity classes for the dull and six hundred schools for the emotionally disturbed.) The freshman year in college has been sacrificed to surveys and freshman composition, to make up for lost ground and to weed out the unfit. Correspondingly, from 1910 on, school superintendents have become scientific business managers and educators with a big E, and college presidents have become mighty public spokesmen. Public relations flourish apace.

Until recently, however, the expansion—though abundantly foolish—was fairly harmless. It was energized by a generous warm democracy and an innocent seeking for prestige by parents becoming affluent. By and large, the pace was easygoing. Few adolescents had cause to suffer nervous breakdowns because of the testing, and one could get a gentlemanly C by coasting. The unfortunate thing was that everybody began to believe that being in school was the only way to be educated. What a generation before had been the usual course—to quit school and seek elsewhere to grow up—became a sign of eccentricity, failure, delinquency.

But suddenly, since the Korean War, and hysterically since Sputnik, there has developed a disastrous overestimation of studying and scholarship. Mothers who used to want their offspring to be "well-adjusted" are now mad for the I.Q. and the percentile. Schools that were lax, democratic or playful are fiercely competitive, and an average unbookish youth finds himself in a bad fix. He may not be able to cope with the speedup and the strict grading; yet if he fails there are loud alarms about his predelinquency, and there are national conferences on dropouts.

It is an educational calamity. Every kind of youth is hurt. The bright but unacademic can perform, but the performance is not authentic and there is a pitiful loss of what they *could* be doing with intelligence, grace and force. The average are anxious; the slow are humiliated. In the process the natural scholars are ruined; bribed and pushed, they forget the meaning of their gift. Nothing is studied for its own sake. Bright youngsters "do" the Bronx High School of Science in order to "make" MIT, just as they will "do" MIT in order to "make" General Dynamics.

I doubt that any of this rat-race is useful. Given quiet and food and lodging, young scholars would study, anyway, without grades. According to the consensus of teachers of science, reported in Jerome Bruner's *The Process of Education,* drilling, testing and competition—the *sine qua non* of our educational system—are incompatible with learning to do creative research. Is there evidence that most creative youngsters, whether in sciences, arts or professions, especially thrive on formal schooling at all, rather than by exploring and gradually gravitating to the right work and environment? For some, schooling no doubt saves time; for others, it is interruptive and depressing. On lower levels of performance, do the technical and clerical tasks of increasingly automated production really require so many years of boning and test passing as it claimed? I asked the United Automobile Workers how much formal schooling is required for the average worker in the most automated plant. The answer was, None whatever. (It takes three weeks to break in a man.) In a year in the Army, average inductees somehow learn to read blips and repair machinery. To put it bluntly, generally speaking it is not the fancy training that is lacking but the jobs.

For urban poor kids who are cajoled to not drop out, the miseducation is a cruel hoax. They are told that the high-school diploma is worth money, but what if the increment amounts, after several years, to five dollars a week? Is this worth such arduous effort, in itself distasteful and to them unnatural? Isn't a lad wiser to choose the streets for the few years of his youth?

Of course, there is no real choice. Poor people must picket for better schools that will not suit most of their children and won't pay off. Farm youth must ride to central schools that are a waste of time for most of them, while they lose the competence they have. Middle-class youth must doggedly compete and be tested to death to get into colleges where most of them will cynically or doggedly serve time. It is ironical. With all the money spent on research and development, for hardware, computers and tranquilizers, America can think up only one institution for its young human resources. Apparently, the schooling that we have already had has brainwashed everybody.

This is the social and historical background out of which our young friend has come to that dazed look in the college classroom. He has been through a long process that has sapped his initiative, discouraged his sexuality, dulled his curiosity and probably even his intellect. His schooling has distorted earnestness and ambition. If he went to a good suburban high school, he no doubt engaged in the fun and games by which middle-class youth sabotage the system. Even the highly intelligent often resist by "underachieving"—they do not want to achieve in this way. Much of the social life and subculture that defeats the schools' purposes is spiteful despair. School is pointless, but it prevents anything else. A fellow can't quit and earn his own money.

What to do for him, or at least for the next generation of him?

Here are some possibilities:

Maybe the chief mistake that we make is to pay too much *direct* attention to the "education" of the children and adolescents, rather than provide them with a worthwhile adult world in which they can grow up. In a curious way, the exaggeration of schooling is both a harsh exploitation of the young, regimenting them, and a guilty coddling of them, since mostly they *are* useless in our world and we want them to waste their hours "usefully."

Certainly, directly useful real activities would be more cultural than the average classroom for the average youth.

We must start from where we are. A promising present expedient is to develop the many public enterprises that we have been neglecting, for they can also be educational opportunities for the young, as lively alternatives to continuing in school, and to spend on these some of the money now misused on schools for the nonacademic. (It costs $750 a year to keep a youth in a New York City high school; also, more than $2000 a year to process him in a reform school.)

For instance, there are scores of thousands of ugly small

towns in the country to be improved, where adolescents could do most of the work. These could be local affairs, or private enterprises, or we could apply to the purpose the Youth Work Camps proposed by Senator Humphrey in 1959, modeled on the Civilian Conservation Corps of the Thirties, but with smaller gangs and paying the youth Army minimum. (Incidentally, after the smoke of criticism cleared away, the CCC was judged to have been economically worth while, and many of its products have been lovely and lasting.)

Another necessary enterprise is community service like the Friends' Youth for Service. Mobilization for Youth might be useful if it got out of the antidelinquency business and out of the Department of Justice. In the past few years, hundreds of students have in fact left their disappointing colleges to work on Negro problems in the Northern Student Movement, CORE and the Student Nonviolent Coordinating Committee.

Here is a suggestion for the nonacademic who are especially bright and talented. In order to countervail the mass communications that swamp us with mediocre canned entertainment and brainwash us with uniform information, we need hundreds, perhaps thousands, of little theaters, little magazines, independent local papers, unaffiliated radio stations. These would furnish remarkable opportunities for youthful spirit and labor under professional direction. (To help finance these, I have elsewhere proposed a graduated tax on the size of the audience of the mass media, to create a fund earmarked for the counterbalancing independent media.)

In general, vocational training, including much laboratory scientific training, ought to be carried on as technical apprenticeships within the relevant industries. Certainly the big corporations have a direct responsibility for the future of their young, rather than simply skimming off the cream of those schooled, tested and graded at the public expense.

Interestingly, the retraining and rehabilitation programs of the Departments of Labor and Justice usually have better educational ideas, including schooling, than the direct school-aid bills. Since much of the Federal aid to education has been balked because of the hangup on the parochial-school issue, some of the money has been allotted indirectly and more effectively, but *not* through the school systems.

Small farms should be used as educational environments. Consider if June through September a small farmer of depopulating Vermont would put up half a dozen New York slum children. He would get $100 a head—it costs $600 a year to keep a child in a New York City primary school. This, across the country, would rescue thousands of economically marginal farms and bring thousands of others back into operation; and it is, without doubt, a wise policy to reverse the 8 percent rural ratio to something nearer 25 percent, if it can be done not on a cash-crop basis.

Again, on the model of the GI Bill, we might boldly allot a certain amount of public-school money—now allocated to college, high school, and even primary school—directly to the students or parents, to be voluntarily used for any purpose plausibly educational. This would produce a great variety of educational experiments, some weird, some excellent. But there is no such uniformity of need or educational theory as warrants the present improbable uniformity of the public schools from coast to coast.

Most important of all, given academic as well as unacademic alternatives, the young can be allowed to experiment in their twelve to sixteen years of lessons rather than feel that they are trapped and must face front. Late bloomers might then choose to return to formal academic study without having been permanently soured by schooling that was inappropriate to them and that they underwent unwillingly. Surely many on the GI Bill profited by going to school maturely, when they knew what they wanted and were sexually sure of themselves.

Finally, let me fit these proposals for secondary and higher education into the present framework of the colleges and universities. Returning to their tradition of agriculture and mechanics, the big state colleges could become administrative centers for the public enterprises mentioned above: town improvement, radio stations, rural culture, health and community service. Many of the students would have been working in the field on these projects, and they could soft-pedal the compulsory academic program that now wastefully leads to 50 percent dropouts. Conversely, the liberal-arts colleges could return to their authentic intellectual tradition of natural philosophy, scholarship and the humanities. Professional and graduate schools could work far more closely with the working professionals and industries in society, with whom many of the adolescents would have served apprenticeships. They would thus avoid the present absurdity of teaching a curriculum abstracted from the work in the field and then licensing the graduates to return to the field to learn the actual work.

I realize that all of this—like much else that I have written—is hopelessly "utopian." We are in the enthusiastic flood tide of a delusion about schooling that can sweep us to a future of prefabricated, spiritless and fundamentally ignorant people. But let me ask young readers to consult their own experience and to consider what they want for their younger brothers and sisters and for their own children. Schooling is one subject where the young know more than their elders; they are closer to it and they have had more of it. Unfortunately, they can't imagine alternatives, any other ways of growing up. But *that* is what we—and they—must put our minds to.

LESLIE FIEDLER

ACADEMIC IRRESPONSIBILITY

if that's what they say when a teacher pays allegiance to his conscience rather than to the establishment, so be it

To argue in favor of freedom for the teacher seems at first the most pointless sort of preaching to the converted, since everybody—as everybody hastens to assure you—is already convinced. Difficult enough under the best of conditions, everybody explains, teaching would be virtually impossible without a large degree of liberty. But everybody then adds, at the point where piety ends and candor begins, that the teacher obviously must be "responsible" as well as free; the clear implication is that freedom is *limited* by responsibility—to which everybody else assents, with the sole exception, it sometimes seems, of me.

In my objections to responsibility, I find myself not only lonelier and lonelier but more and more distant from those I had long thought my natural allies. From my earliest reading years, I had understood that Babbitt was the enemy of freedom and responsibility his hypocritical watchword. Of this I had been assured not only by Sinclair Lewis, who baptized him, but by John Dos Passos in *U. S. A.*, by James Thurber in *The Male Animal*, by the whole consort of writers who had sentimentalized and mythicized the early academic victims of Rotarians, chambers of commerce and boards of trustees—from Thorstein Veblen to Scott Nearing and innumerable other half-forgotten half-heroes fired from university posts for defending Tom Mooney and Sacco and Vanzetti or for criticizing monopoly capitalism and the war.

The campaign of vilification and harassment directed against certain leftish academics in the time of Joe McCarthy seemed the climax and confirmation of the whole thing. After the total discrediting of McCarthy, when political liberty for professors was pretty generally won and Babbitts everywhere had gone into retreat, an occasional rear-guard action on their part seemed more comic and pathetic than sinister or threatening. Picking up, for instance, a Kiwanis Club pamphlet labeled "Freedom," I am tickled rather than dismayed to discover no reference to anything that I mean by freedom, only an appeal to teachers to transmit to the young "an understanding of responsible citizenship, principles of free enterprise and values of our spiritual heritage. . . ." "Free" as in enterprise, but "responsible" in everything; it is quite what the literature I grew up on taught me to expect—something comfortably unchanged in our disconcertingly changeable world.

There is, however, one area at least where the Babbitts, even in retreat, continue to pose a real threat to freedom—a threat because the academic community is on their side. When social behavior rather than politics is involved—especially in matters of sex or the use of banned drugs (associated inevitably with sex in the fantasies of the repressors) and especially when faculty members seem to advocate, or condone, or encourage or simply permit unconventional student practices in these matters—then the faculties of universities tend to speak the same language as the Kiwanis Club. And here I am eternally shocked and disheartened.

For a decade now, there has been instance after instance, from the notorious firing of Timothy Leary at Harvard, through the dismissal of certain young "homosexual" instructors at Smith, to the failure to rehire the poet Robert Mezey at Fresno State College. Often the real issues are camouflaged, as in Leary's case; the charge pressed was not that Leary had become a published advocate of LSD but that he failed to meet his classes regularly. Or they tend to be blurred, as in Mezey's case; the fact that he opposed the war in Vietnam and defended black power might suggest the recurrence of simple old-fashioned McCarthyism were it not that thousands of academic opponents of the most unjust of American wars continue to be reappointed or promoted so long as they do not also happen to advocate changes in the existing marijuana laws.

Sometimes the underlying issues are totally hushed up, out of ostensible regard for the reputation of the victims, who, accepting dismissal in order to avoid scandal, provide their colleagues with the possibility of copping out, so that no advocate of academic freedom is called upon to take a principled stand on freedom for potheads or queers; no libertarian is forced to confront the limits of his own tolerance. I am aware of only a single case of this kind fought hard enough and far enough to compel the American Association of University Professors to rethink its own position, defining—from a teacher's presumable point of view—the competing claims of freedom and responsibility: the now nearly forgotten Koch case.

On March 18, 1960, Leo Koch, an assistant professor of biology at the University of Illinois, wrote a letter to the campus paper in which, after some reflections—more banal and less witty than he obviously thought them—on "a Christian code of ethics already decrepit in the days of Queen Victoria," he concluded:

> With modern contraceptives and medical advice readily available at the nearest drugstore, or at least a family physician, there is no valid reason why sexual intercourse should not be condoned among those sufficiently mature to engage in it without social consequences and without violating their own codes of morality and ethics.
>
> A mutually satisfactory sexual experience would eliminate the need for many hours of frustrating petting and lead to much happier and longer-lasting marriages among our younger men and women.

Whether the course of action that Professor Koch advocated would, indeed, have led to the happiness and marital stability he promised remains yet to be proved, since he inspired no general movement to lead openly the sort of sexual life that many students, whether "sufficiently mature" or not, have been leading covertly, anyhow. If Koch was espousing anything new in his manifesto, it was presumably the abandonment of concealment and that unconfessed pact by which students make it possible for their teachers to pretend they do not know what their students pretend they do not know those teachers know.

Yet his letter had results, all the same, for it brought about a chain of events that ended in his being fired. And his firing, in turn, produced a series of statements and counterstatements about morality and freedom from the president of the university, its board of trustees, the faculty senate and many individual members of the teaching staff. This intramural debate was followed by a prolonged investigation under the auspices of the American Association of University Professors of what had become by that time "the Koch case," an investigation not finally reported on in full until three years later. The report, which appeared in the *AAUP Bulletin* of March 1963, reveals a division of opinion among college professors themselves, symptomatic of a confusion on the issues involved, that not only divides one academic colleague from another but splits the individual minds of many Americans inside the universities and out.

More interesting to me, however, and more dismaying than any of the disagreements, was a substantial area of agreement between the president and the board of trustees of the University of Illinois (who thought Koch should be fired), the faculty senate of that institution (who thought he should only be reprimanded) and Committee A of the AAUP, the professed guardians of academic freedom (who thought the whole case should have been thrown out of court because of lack of due process). All four agreed that Koch was guilty of a "breach of academic responsibility" and that, regardless of his guilt or innocence, his academic freedom, like everyone else's, was and should have been limited by the academic responsibility that he was accused of having flouted. What academic responsibility means was nowhere very clearly defined in the dispute but was apparently understood by everyone involved to signify an obligation on the part of any professor to keep his mouth shut or only moderately open in cases where there is a clear danger of offending accepted morality, i.e., public opinion.

But how odd it was to find in the conservative and anti-intellectual camp a committee specifically charged with the protection of professors' rights—rights which the committee has often unyieldingly defended. What, then, moved it this time to grant that "we can hardly expect academic freedom to endure unless it is matched by academic responsibility"? Surely, the topic of Koch's letter had something to do with it, and not merely the fact that his thoughts were neither well reasoned nor cogently expressed. If all cases of academic freedom involved the justification of documents as dignified and compelling as, say, Milton's *Areopagitica,* to defend liberty would be as easy as to attack it; but this, as the AAUP must have learned in its long career, is far from the truth. No, it was the subject of Koch's expostulation that made the difference, for when sex and students are simultaneously evoked, even the hardiest campus civil libertarian seems willing to cry "responsibility" with all the rest.

And the larger community has sensed this, moving in to attack—even when political motives play a considerable role—only when sex and drugs are involved. The young instructors at Michigan State University who helped edit a radical magazine called *Zeitgeist* may have offended their colleagues and administrators in many ways, but when their contracts were not renewed, a few years ago, it was only the dirty words they had printed that were marshaled as evidence against them. And when, some years before that, Mulford Sibley, a well-known pacifist and political dissident, was brought under attack at the University of Minnesota, what was quoted against him was a speech in which he suggested that the university might be healthier if it could boast "a student Communist club, a chapter of the American Association for the Advancement of Atheism, a Society for the Promotion of Free Love . . . and perhaps a nudist club."

Predictably enough, communism and atheism tended to be soft-pedaled in the accusations brought against him, which lingered most lovingly over the fact that he was "agitating for nudist clubs" and added, apparently as the final proof of his perfidy, that "Dr. Sibley assigned books to his students resembling

'Lady Chatterley and Her Love Affairs.' " I know how disabling such a charge can be in academic circles, since, in an early encounter of my own with a really concerted effort to silence me in the classroom, I was accused not only of contempt for my then-fellow Montanans but also of having written a "dirty" poem called "Dumb Dick" and a "dirty" story called "Nude Croquet," which was "subsequently banned in Knoxville, Tennessee." Alas, some of my former colleagues, willing enough to stand with me on political grounds, were shaken by being informed that I was a "dirty writer."

Pornography and nudity, along with trafficking in drugs and indulging in homosexuality, as well as refusing to condemn any or all of these to students, are the stock charges in latter-day assaults against the freedom of the teacher by elements in the business community sophisticated enough to know that in our time old-fashioned accusations of being Red or "soft on Reds" are likely to be laughed out of the court of public opinion and have no status at all in courts of law. But there are statutes that can be invoked against offenses of the former sort, as in the police harassment of Leonard Wolf, a member of the English department of San Francisco State College, charged with "contributing to the delinquency of minors."

Wolf is the founder of Happening House, an institution set up to maintain a dialog between the kind of kids who inhabit the Haight-Ashbury district of San Francisco and the local academic community. During a conference on the problem of runaways, some of those kids, members of a performing dance group, took off all their clothes on stage. Wolf, who was the most convenient adult on the premises, was arrested. He was subsequently tried and acquitted because the prosecution could not prove him responsible for the students' disrobing, but from the start, the intent of the police seems to have been quite clearly to impugn Wolf both as the founder of Happening House and as a teacher. Why else charge him with acting in a way that "causes, tends to cause or encourages unknown juveniles to lead immoral or idle lives"? Whatever college officials thought of his classroom performance or his outside activities, a court conviction would make him a criminal in their eyes—and, as such, his position in the college, as well as his status in the community, would be endangered. And just as clearly, it wasn't only Wolf who was being put on trial, but all teachers who, insofar as they are true to their profession, seek to release their students from parochialism and fear, thus laying themselves open to charges of "corrupting the young" or "contributing to the delinquency of minors." A printed statement from the Leonard Wolf defense recognizes this fact—though it states the dilemma ineptly and misleadingly by insisting that in his case, "the limits of any teacher's responsibility are at stake" and that "if the attack on

Professor Wolf proves successful . . . the limits of responsibility will have been unfairly extended in the service of repressive interests."

One cannot effectively fight an opponent whose language, along with its assumptions, has been uncritically accepted. And to grant—even implicitly—that there are just and proper limits somewhere, sometimes, to the teacher's freedom is to give the game away to those ready and eager to seize any show of weakness on the teacher's part. This is especially dangerous these days, when we are threatened on two sides, not just on one, as we have long been accustomed. On the one hand, there are the traditional "repressive interests," plus the courts and cops whom they largely control, to whom a free faculty seems always on the verge of going over to the enemy, i.e., the young, whom they think of as swinging back and forth between an unwholesome flight from reality and untidy demonstrations in the streets. And, on the other hand, there are the young themselves, or at least the revolutionaries among them, to whom the much vaunted "academic freedom" of their teachers seems only a subterfuge, a coverup for their subservience to the *real* enemy, i.e., the old, who, if they do not actually wage imperialist war and exploit labor, apologize for both.

I sit at the moment looking mournfully at an "Open Letter" directed to the faculty at the University of Sussex, an English university in which I spent a year as a visiting professor. The document is signed by "The February 21 Committee," a group whose chief political activity was throwing a can of red paint over a speaker from the American Embassy who had attempted to defend United States intervention in Vietnam. An early paragraph reads, in part, "Students say 'free inquiry' or 'free speech' mean that academics must permit their institution to be used for any purpose, this freedom ends logically in irresponsibility. . . ." Syntax and punctuation have broken down a little, but the meaning is clear—and disheartening. Whether Kiwanis Clubber, AAUP member or Maoist student, one touch of responsibility makes them all kin to one another, and alien to me.

Yet there is a difference, of course, between the Babbitts and the *enragés*, those who boast themselves sane and those who like to think of themselves as mad. Both demand restrictions on political freedom, one from the right and one from the left; but the students, at least, are on the side of erotic and imaginative freedom, in favor of love and dreams—and when such issues are involved or can be evoked, the free professor will find them on his side. In that area, indeed, they are more dependable allies than his own colleagues, since even the most liberal professors have tended to be equivocal on the subject of social, as opposed to intellectual, freedom, for both students and themselves. To the young, more important than the freedom to read what books or take what courses they please is the freedom to make love as they please; and it was therefore quite proper that one student revolt in France was touched off at the University of Nanterre by protest over restricted visiting privileges between boys' and girls' dormitories.

This fundamental inconsistency of viewpoint toward social rather than academic freedom has tended to sap the integrity of certain faculty and sowed a deepening distrust in the minds of students, who, in response, have been on occasion as cavalier about the political rights of their teachers as their teachers have been about their personal liberties. But there is an even more fundamental source of confusion in the definition of responsibility that the academic community—professors first of all, and now the students—has accepted, without sufficient wariness, from the larger community that surrounds and often resents it.

Once the teacher has granted the theory that responsibility equals restriction, restraint, censorship, taboo, he has lost in advance all those "cases" to which he must in due course come. At best, he commits himself to endless wrangles about exactly where freedom (understood as the right to express what he believes without hindrance) yields to responsibility (understood as the obligation to curtail his expression), lest he offend the taste, the conventions or the religious, political and moral codes of the community that sustains him.

There is no way out of such wrangles and not much point in going on to further debates about who (the teacher, the community or some impartial referee) is to draw the line between freedom and responsibility, once these have been postulated as opposites. And surely there is even less point in debating after the fact how harshly the "irresponsibles" are to be treated, whether by a lopping of heads or a mere slapping of wrists, i.e., whether they are to be dismissed or reprimanded. I propose, therefore, to define responsibility in quite a different way —as a matter of fact, in two quite different ways—in order to put the problem in a new light and deliver everyone from the frustration and ennui of having endlessly to rehash the old arguments.

Let me begin with a positive definition of "academic responsibility" as the teacher's obligation to *do* something, rather than not to. The teacher—not exclusively, perhaps, but, without doubt, especially—has a single overwhelming responsibility: the responsibility to be *free,* which is to say, to be what most men would call *irresponsible.* For him, freedom and responsibility are not obligations that cancel each other out but one and the same thing; and this unity of academic freedom and academic responsibility arises from the teacher's double function in our society: first of all, to extend the boundaries of knowledge by questioning *everything,* including the truths that most men at any given point consider sacred and timeless; and, finally, to free the minds of the young, so that they can continue the same task beyond what he himself can imagine.

I shall not linger over the traditional "research" function of the teacher, since its necessity is granted, with whatever secret reservations, by almost everyone except certain backward students, much given to complaining that their teachers spend more time on research than on them—not understanding that there would be nothing for those teachers to give them if independent investigation and lonely meditation were ever suspended or drastically curtailed. Thorstein Veblen, prototype of the free teacher, thought it was a mistake to attempt to combine in a single person the schoolmaster and the scholar, but American universities have long since made the decision to try, and it is incumbent on the scholar-schoolmaster to be clear in his own mind, and to make clear to everyone else concerned, the priorities of his commitments. Few of them have been as candid about it as was Robert Frost, himself a schoolmaster for some fifty years, who always insisted from the platform that the teacher's first duty was to himself, his second to his subject matter and only his third to the student. And no one who begins with an understanding of the free teacher's peculiar obligation to the free student could possibly challenge this order.

The problem to begin with is what can, and what should be, taught. From that start, it was clear to me that teaching was a passion, not a science, and that methods, therefore, are meaningless in the classroom, that lesson plans and pedagogical strategy are vanity and illusion. But it has taken me nearly three decades of teaching to realize that even the subject matter one teaches is quickly—and, in most cases, quite correctly—forgotten, gone, certainly, with the last exam. It should no longer be considered a scandalous secret that the students believe they are hiding from teachers—or vice versa—that course subject matter is at best optional, at worst totally irrelevant.

What is required of the teacher is not that he impart knowledge but that he open up minds, revealing to his students possibilities in themselves that they had perhaps not even suspected, and confirming in them a faith in their own sensibilities and intelligence—not suffering their foolishness or indulging their errors, but all the time revealing to them the double truth that, though the student can often be wrong, he has, like his teacher, the *right* to be wrong and that, if he is willing to live a life of intellectual risk, he may someday know more, see further and feel more acutely than any of the elders of the community, including his teachers. It is the credo of the free and truly "irresponsible" teacher that no truth except this (not even the ones he most dearly believes in) is final, since the advance of human thought is potentially unlimited.

Such a teacher addresses his students, confronts them, engages with them, in the hope that they will someday go beyond the limitations of vision built into him by the limitations of his training and his time and that they will even escape the trap of believing that their new vision is a final one, to be imposed forever after on the generations who succeed them. My ideal teacher must teach his students, in short, to be free—which is something quite different from persuading them to write in their notebooks, "Be free!" since freedom cannot be acquired by rote any more than it can be established by law. Freedom cannot be taught by preaching it—as, by writing this, I have betrayed myself into doing—but by acting it out, living it in full view. Once we have realized that the teacher is not just a guide, much less a substitute parent or a charming entertainer (though he can be all of these things, too, if he is so moved), but a model, and that what is learned in the classroom is *him,* the teacher, we will understand that the teacher must become a model of the free man.

And yet how many of our own teachers do we remember as having been even in aspiration, much less in fact, anything like free? How many do we recall with love for having freed us from those fears and doubts about ourselves and our world that we brought with us into school, inextricably intertwined with our ignorance and bravado? There have been only a handful among the scores I encountered in my own school career: one or two in high school, none at all in college, and one in graduate school, whom I cannot forbear naming. Author of once-admired but now-forgotten poems and a splendid book about the shape of his own life, *The Locomotive God,* William Ellery Leonard once gave me, by his splendid example, certain illusions about what teaching and teachers were like that brought me into the university in the first place, and then left me, with even more splendid tact, to find out the truth for myself.

But why have so many, so large a majority not merely of my teachers but of everybody's teachers, failed in their obligation to choose to be free? It is tempting but finally unsatisfactory to say, in easy cynicism, Well, everyone fails at everything, so why not they? Certainly there are pressures on them from all sides to be of "service" to the community as a whole, or to the past, to the present, to God, to the revolution, etc. Wherever the free teacher turns, he confronts men, sometimes his own colleagues, convinced that the function of the university is not to free the mind but to inculcate a set of values, to indoctrinate or—as we say when somebody else's values are concerned—to brainwash the student.

But the wielders of such pressures are, in a sense, not hard to resist, especially when they speak from the conservative tradition, since there are habits of response built into most professors from earliest youth that stir a reflex of resistance against movements to ban books by, say, Allen Ginsberg and William Burroughs on the one hand, or by Ché Guevara and Mao Tse-tung on the other, or to fire those who ask students to read them. Whatever our disagreements with the lovers of such literature, we tend to feel them on our side. No, the most conspicuous failure of professors in this regard has been their refusal to protect the dissident right-wingers among them under attack from antilibertarians on our side. Surely one of the most scandalous events of recent academic history has been the quiet dismissal of a distinguished rightist teacher of political science from an equally distinguished Ivy League college, whose own silence was bought by buying up his contract and whose colleagues' silence apparently did not have to be bought at all.

Obviously, those who advocate reticence or "responsibility" from our side are more insidious—and sometimes, it would appear, impossible to resist. For it is our loyalty, rather than our timidity, on which such academic enemies of "irresponsibility" insist, asking us to limit ourselves (lest we give aid and comfort to a common opponent) in the free investigation, say, of the interconnections between the homosexual revolution and the first stages of the civil-rights movement, or the importance of anti-Semitism and racism in the later black-power movement. Similarly, they urge us not to take away from the progressive forces certain symbolic heroes of the historical left—not, for instance, to follow up the evidence that at least Sacco, and possibly Vanzetti as well, was guilty as charged in the famous case that mobilized most decent men on their side and that many of the organizers of the protests against their condemnation already knew the fact and strategically concealed it.

And when the voices that plead with us to lie a little about the importance of Negroes in our history, or to mitigate a little the harsh truth about the last country to betray some revolution in which we once thought we believed, are the voices of our own students, the voices of the young—how even harder it is to resist. We know that their cause, too, will be betrayed, as all causes are ultimately betrayed, but it seems churlish and unstrategic to tell them so; their strength and weakness is precisely not to know this, as our strength and weakness is to know it. And these strengths and weaknesses are complementary, make social life and intercourse between the generations not merely possible but necessary. Why, then, should we not lie to them a little when they come to us, as they do between periods of absolute rejection?

In a way, we are better off, safer, from our own point of view and theirs, when they turn their backs on us, muttering, "Old men, all we want you to do for us is *die!*" But a moment later, they return (being in need of uncles and grandfathers if not fathers: Marcuses and McLuhans and Norman O. Browns), crying, "Underwrite, sanction our revolt, tell us we are righter than you!" Indeed, how could they fail to be righter than we are still, wrong as we were at their age? But it is not our function as free teachers to tell them only how they are right; it is also imperative that we say (at the risk of being loved less, even of finally losing their ear altogether) how they are wrong—what in their movement, for instance, threatens the very freedom that makes it possible and what threatens to freeze into self-righteousness.

Spokesmen for the "future" forget that, even as they fight for it, the "future" quickly becomes the present, then the past, and that soon they are only fighting for yesterday against the proponents of the day before yesterday. This is why the teacher dedicated to freedom must tell them *right now* the same thing he tells the Babbitts when they howl down or propose to ban some speaker, some uncongenial idea: If any kind of truth or pursuit of truth—however misguided, however wrong—seems threatening to a cause we espouse, it is time to re-examine that cause, no matter how impressive its credentials. It is also to ourselves, of course, that we're speaking, since without constantly reminding ourselves of this simple principle we will yield to some pressure group, right, left or center. But even taken together, such groups are not our deepest and most dangerous enemy.

What gets us, as teachers, into final trouble is the enemy of our freedom that ordinarily we do not perceive at all: inhibiting forces that are as impersonal and omnipresent and invisible as our total environment or our very selves. Indeed, they are a large and growing part of that total environment, especially in the United States, where more and more education for more and more people remains an avowed goal of society. There are, however, inhibitory and restrictive tendencies built into the very school system to which almost everyone born in America is condemned by the fact of his birth—condemned beyond the possibility of appeal, since what he may feel as a prison was dreamed for him by his forebears as utopia.

For better or worse, in any event, young Americans these days find themselves sentenced by law to a term lasting from their fourth or fifth birthday to their sixteenth or seventeenth—and, by custom and social pressure, to a good deal more: time added, as it were, for good behavior. But though students in large numbers are dimly aware of all this, they have tended to resist it as outlaws rather than as revolutionaries, i.e., to drop out rather than to raise as a slogan, an immediate demand, the right not to go to school. Students have been primarily—and quite properly, as far as it goes—concerned with failures of the school system to provide them with the kinds of freedom to which that system itself is theoretically pledged: the right to demonstrate or petition, to participate and advise, to control in part, at least, their own destinies *in* the schools; but the existence of those schools, and even their traditional function, they have largely taken for granted.

To me, however, the root problem, the essential restriction of freedom, seems compulsory education itself—on both the primary and the secondary levels, where it is enforced by statute and truant officers, and on the higher levels, where it is, more and more broadly, customary and enforced by the peer group plus parents and teachers. Everything begins with the assumption by the community (or some auxiliary private enterprise) of the role traditionally played in the lives of the young by their families, aided and abetted by medicine men, prophets or kindly passing strangers, and is confirmed beyond hope of reform when that community sets up ever more rigid and bureaucratized institutions to do that job for it.

From this initial requirement follows most of what is dangerously restrictive throughout the school system: the regulation of every moment of a student's day (especially in high schools) and a good part of a student's nights (especially for female students, all the way to the university level). This involves, first of all, required attendance, tardiness reports, classes artificially divided into periods and rung off and on by a centrally controlled bell system, proctored examinations and blackmail by grades. And it implies, in the second place, a host of "disciplinary regulations" beginning with the banning of cigarettes on school grounds, or alcohol at school dances, or pot and the pill in dormitories, and ending with petty decrees—totally unconnected to the laws of the larger community—about the length of skirts and pants and hair. Hair, especially, seems the concern of school authorities, whether on the head or on the face—as if somewhere in the collective mind of those authorities, the image persisted of youth as a sort of Samson who to be enslaved must be shorn.

Students have, of course, protested against this; and a good deal of what moves them, plus more that might or should move them, has been beautifully formulated by Edgar Z. Friedenberg, beginning with a book titled *The Vanishing Adolescent.* But their cry of "no more *in loco parentis*" is undercut by their clearly contradictory wishes on this score. In general, they seem to want the schools to maintain a certain parental role in warding off police prosecution yet to surrender that role in maintaining internal discipline. In any case, the protesters do not begin far enough back, for the American school system is essentially—by definition and tradition—*in loco parentis.* And nothing fundamental is solved by persuading it to become a permissive rather than an authoritarian parent—that is, to make itself more like students' actual parents and less like their actual grandparents.

It is, alas, precisely those "permissive" parents who have made the whole school system, from kindergarten to university, what it is, insisting that it act out for them the dark side of their own ambivalence toward their children—be the bad parent they feel guilty for not being—and for wanting to be. If our schools are, in fact, totalitarian under their liberal disguises, more like what the sociologists call "total institutions" (jails, mental hospitals, detention camps) than small democratic communities or enlarged families, this is because the parents of the students in them *want* them to be what they are. Certainly any parent, any full adult in our society, is at least dimly aware of the tendency in himself and his neighbors to project upon children and adolescents sexual and anarchic impulses denied in himself. These impulses he asks his children both to act out and to be blamed for, relieving him of his own double guilt—and providing in its place the double pleasure of vicarious self-indulgence and the condemnation of sin.

In addition, there is the sexual jealousy that inevitably troubles those home-tied by jobs or children or oppressed by the menopause and the imminence of death when they confront others just emerging into puberty, as well as the desperation of those unable to persuade their children of the value of moral codes in which they only theoretically believe—a desperation that ends in calling out the law to enforce what love could not achieve. And, finally, there is the strange uncertainty of our society about just when a child becomes an adult (whatever that elusive term may mean)—at puberty, at sixteen, eighteen, twenty-one, when he votes, drinks legally, goes into the Army or simply becomes capable of reproducing himself. Out of this uncertainty emerge those absurd social regulations that turn the girls' dormitory into a police state, the rules whose goal is to keep those we claim we have to regulate (because they are still "children") from getting pregnant, i.e., from proving to us that biologically, at least, they are fully mature.

Small wonder, then, that our schools and universities have become, like our jails and hospitals and asylums, institutions whose structure works against their own avowed ends—leading not to the free development of free men but to the depersonalization of the student, to his conversion into a code number and an IBM card punched full of data, a fact that he may forget in the midst of the small pleasures that punctuate his boredom but of which he is reminded once, twice, even three times a year by the degrading rituals of examination and registration. The damage done the student by this system we have all begun to notice, as the resentment of his indignity has driven him to construct barricades and hurl fire bombs, but the similar damage done to his teachers we tend to ignore, since they typically respond with silence or statements read only to one another at annual meetings.

It is not merely that the teacher, too, is regulated, right down to such trivial matters as wearing a tie or smoking in class, but that also—and, finally, more critically—he, like the prison guard or the asylum attendant, becomes the prisoner of the closed world he presumably guards, a world in which he begins talking at the ping of one bell and stops at the clang of another, meanwhile checking attendance, making sure no one cheats or lights a cigarette under a NO SMOKING sign or consumes hard liquor or drugs or, God forbid, takes off his clothes in public. All of this, however, makes him a jailer or a cop, who notoriously resembles his charges, and insofar as he resists, turns him into a hypocrite, acknowledging only the infractions that someone else —the press, a planted police spy, an indignant parent—has noticed first.

How can the teacher who accepts such a system talk freedom to the students before him? Or how can he demand it for himself—academically, politically, personally—at the very moment he is denying it—socially, erotically—to those he asks to emulate his model? The historical struggle of teachers for what has been called "academic freedom"—that is, their own freedom—has been impugned throughout by their hypocrisy. No community, not even a school, can exist one tenth absolutely free and nine tenths half slave. It is an unendurable fraud, of which most of us manage to remain absurdly unaware, until some notorious "case"—the Leary case, the Koch case, the Mezey case—forces us to confront it, to confront the contradiction in ourselves. By then, however, it is too late.

Inevitably, at that point we tend to compromise or totally betray for one of us the principles we have already learned to compromise and betray for the students to whom we are, after ourselves, chiefly responsible. And here we have come, at long last, to responsibility. To avoid the word at this juncture would be as abject as having taken refuge in it earlier, since to be responsible means, in the new context, not to be restricted, which is to say, less free—but to be *answerable*, which is to say, more free.

Until a man has learned to be truly free, he cannot begin to be responsible in this deep etymological sense of the word, since the only thing for which a teacher is properly answerable is his own freedom, his necessary prior *ir*responsibility. A slave or a man under restraint, an indoctrinated indoctrinator, a civil servant brainwashed to brainwash others, is answerable for nothing. No matter what charges are brought against him, he can plead innocent, for he is the agent of another, a despicable tool, just another Eichmann, dignified beyond his worth by being brought to the dock.

The free teacher, on the other hand, must not merely suffer but welcome, even invite, criticism of what he espouses and teaches, for his job is to change the minds of the young—which those in established positions seem to view as a kind of "corruption." For him, freedom does not mean freedom from consequences; he takes, as the old Spanish proverb has it, what he wants but he pays his dues. Wanting nothing free of charge, he denies to no one the right to disagree with what he says, to criticize, to try to rebut, even to threaten sanctions. He must always be willing to argue against all comers the basic case for his freedom, which is never, and can never be, won finally and forever. But he must also be prepared to defend—one by one and each on its own merits—all of the tenets, views, opinions and analyses he finds himself free to offer.

Above all, when his ideas are proved wrong, to his own satisfaction, in the debate with those who challenge him, he must feel free to confess his error without in any way diminishing his right to have held those ideas, for he has never had any real freedom at all unless he has been free from the start to be wrong and unless he remains free to the end to change his mind. If, in the debate he has occasioned, however, he continues to believe in his position, he must—with all the assurance that comes of knowing his fallibility as well as that of his opponents—continue to maintain that position. It does not matter at all if a majority is against him, or even everybody, for even everybody has, on occasion, turned out to be wrong, and he is, in any case, not answerable to a popular vote.

He dares not betray the facts as he has learned from his teachers and his colleagues to determine them, but he must always be aware that those "facts" exist finally in his own head. And he is equally answerable to posterity, which means, for a teacher, his students—not those before him at any moment but those yet to come—best of all, those not yet born—and these, too, he must remember live only inside his skull. It is to the unborn, then, that the free man, the true teacher, is finally answerable, but it is the living students, their parents and the community that he inhabits rather than the one he dreams, that judge him and can make him suffer. If that community—parents or students or both—desires to visit sanctions on him, he must not pretend surprise or feel dismay.

Yet they are not hard to please, really, the spokesmen of the past or those of the present; all they ask is a show of subservience either to long-established conventions or to the very latest life style. Only an allegiance to the ever receding future dismays both, for, driven to imagine a time to come, the responsibles, both old and young, feel their authority slipping from them as they realize that someday they will be dead. But it is precisely this realization that exhilarates some men, making them feel free enough to be irresponsible, irresponsible enough to be free.

IRWIN SHAW **fiction**

where all things wise and fair descend

he was gifted, handsome, rich—
a golden boy—
but it took a violent death to make him a man

He woke up feeling good. There was no reason for him to wake up feeling anything else.

He was an only child. He was twenty years old. He was over six feet tall and weighed one hundred and eighty pounds and had never been sick in his whole life. He was number two on the tennis team and back home in his father's study there was a whole shelf of cups he had won in tournaments since he was eleven years old. He had a lean, sharply cut face, topped by straight black hair that he wore just a little long, which prevented him from looking merely like an athlete. A girl had once said he looked like Shelley. Another, like Laurence Olivier. He had smiled noncommittally at both girls.

He had a retentive memory and classes were easy for him. He had just been put on the dean's list. His father, who was doing well up North in an electronics business, had sent him a check for $100 as a reward. The check had been in his box the night before.

He had a gift for mathematics and probably could get a job teaching in the department if he wanted it upon graduation, but he planned to go into his father's business. He would then be exempt from the draft and Vietnam.

He was not one of the single-minded equational wizards who roamed the science departments. He got A's in English and history and had memorized most of Shakespeare's sonnets and read Roethke and Eliot and Ginsberg. He had tried marijuana.

He was invited to all the parties. When he went home, mothers made obvious efforts to throw their daughters at him.

His own mother was beautiful and young and funny. There were no unbroken silver cords in the family. He was having an affair with one of the prettiest girls on the campus and she said she loved him. From time to time he said he loved her. When he said it, he meant it. At that moment, anyway.

Nobody he had ever cared for had as yet died and everybody in his family had come home safe from all the wars.

The world saluted him.

He maintained his cool.

No wonder he woke up feeling good.

It was nearly December, but the California sun made a summer morning of the season, and the girls and boys in corduroys and T-shirts and bright-colored sweaters on their way to their ten-o'clock classes walked over green lawns and in and out of the shadows of trees that had not yet lost their leaves.

He passed the sorority house where Adele lived and waved as she came out. His first class every Tuesday was at ten o'clock and the sorority house was on his route to the arts building in which the classroom was situated.

Adele was a tall girl, her dark, combed head coming well above his shoulder. She had a triangular, blooming, still-childish face. Her walk, even with the books she was carrying in her arms, wasn't childish, though, and he was amused at the envious looks directed at him by some of the other students as Adele paced at his side down the graveled path.

" 'She walks in beauty,' " Steve said, " 'like the night/Of cloudless climes and starry skies;/And all that's best of dark and bright/Meet in her aspect and her eyes.' "

"What a nice thing to hear at ten o'clock in the morning," Adele said. "Did you bone up on that for me?"

"No," he said. "We're having a test on Byron today."

"Animal," she said.

He laughed.

"Are you taking me to the dance Saturday night?" she asked.

He grimaced. He didn't like to dance. He didn't like the kind of music that was played and he thought the way people danced these days was devoid of grace. "I'll tell you later," he said.

"I have to know today," Adele said. "Two other boys've asked me."

"I'll tell you at lunch," he said.

"What time?"

"One. Can the other aspirants hold back their frenzy to dance until then?"

"Barely," she said. He knew that with or without him, Adele would be at the dance on Saturday night. She loved to dance and he had to admit that a girl had every right to expect the boy she was seeing almost every night in the week to take her dancing at least once on the weekend. He felt very mature, almost fatherly, as he resigned himself to four hours of heat and noise on Saturday night. But he didn't tell Adele that he'd take her. It wouldn't do her any harm to wait until lunch.

He squeezed her hand as they parted and watched for a moment as she swung down the path, conscious of the provocative way she was walking, conscious of the eyes on her. He smiled and continued on his way, waving at people who greeted him.

It was early and Mollison, the English professor, had not yet put in an appearance. The room was only half full as Steve entered it, but there wasn't the usual soprano-tenor tuning-up sound of conversation from the students who were already there. They sat in their chairs quietly, not talking, most of them ostentatiously arranging their books or going through their notes. Occasionally, almost furtively, one or another of them would look up toward the front of the room and the blackboard, where a thin boy with wispy reddish hair was writing swiftly and neatly behind the teacher's desk.

"Oh, weep for Adonais—he is dead!" the red-haired boy had written. "Wake, melancholy Mother, wake and weep!"

Yet wherefore? Quench within their burning bed
Thy fiery tears, and let thy loud heart keep
Like his a mute and uncomplaining sleep;
For he is gone where all things wise and fair
Descend. Oh, dream not that the amorous Deep
Will yet restore him to the vital air;
Death feeds on his mute voice, and laughs at our despair.

Then, on a second blackboard, where the boy was finishing the last lines of another stanza, was written:

He has outsoared the shadow of our night;
Envy and calumny and hate and pain,
And that unrest which men miscall delight,
Can touch him not and torture not again;
From the contagion of the world's slow stain
He is secure, and now can never mourn
A heart grown cold, a head grown gray in vain;

Professor Mollison came bustling in with the half-apologetic smile of an absent-minded man who is afraid he is always late. He stopped at the door, sensing by the quiet that this was no ordinary Tuesday morning in his classroom. He peered near-sightedly at Crane writing swiftly in rounded chalk letters on the blackboard.

Mollison took out his glasses and read for a moment, then went over to the window without a word and stood there looking out, a graying, soft-faced, rosy-cheeked old man, the soberness of his expression intensified by the bright sunlight at the window.

"Nor," Crane was writing, the chalk making a dry sound in the silence,

> when the spirit's self has ceased to burn,
> With sparkless ashes load an unlamented urn.

When Crane had finished, he put the chalk down neatly and stepped back to look at what he had written. A girl's laugh came in on the fragrance of cut grass through the open window and there was a curious hushing little intake of breath all through the room.

The bell rang, abrasively, for the beginning of classes. When the bell stopped, Crane turned around and faced the students seated in rows before him. He was a lanky, skinny boy, only nineteen, and he was already going bald. He hardly ever spoke in class and when he spoke, it was in a low, harsh whisper.

He didn't seem to have any friends and he never was seen with girls, and the time he didn't spend in class he seemed to spend in the library. Crane's brother had played fullback on the football team, but the brothers had rarely been seen together, and the fact that the huge, graceful athlete and the scarecrow bookworm were members of the same family seemed like a freak of eugenics to the students who knew them both.

Steve knew why Crane had come early to write the two verses of Shelley's lament on the clean morning blackboard. The Saturday night before, Crane's brother had been killed in an automobile accident on the way back from the game, which had been played in San Francisco. The funeral had taken place yesterday, Monday. Now it was Tuesday morning and Crane's first class since the death of his brother.

Crane stood there, narrow shoulders hunched in a bright tweed jacket that was too large for him, surveying the class without emotion. He glanced once more at what he had written, as though to make sure the problem he had placed on the board had been correctly solved, then turned again to the group of gigantic, blossoming, rosy California boys and girls, unnaturally serious and a little embarrassed by this unexpected prolog to their class, and began to recite.

He recited flatly, without any emotion in his voice, moving casually back and forth in front of the blackboards, occasionally turning to the text to flick off a little chalk dust, to touch the end of a word with his thumb, to hesitate at a line, as though he had suddenly perceived a new meaning in it.

Mollison, who had long ago given up any hope of making any impression on the sun-washed young California brain with the fragile hammer of nineteenth-century romantic poetry, stood at the window, looking out over the campus, nodding in rhythm from time to time and occasionally whispering a line, almost silently, in unison with Crane.

" '. . . an unlamented urn,' " Crane said, still as flat and unemphatic as ever, as though he had merely gone through the two verses as a feat of memory. The last echo of his voice quiet now in the still room, he looked out at the class through his thick glasses, demanding nothing. Then he went to the back of the room and sat down in his chair and began putting his books together.

Mollison, finally awakened from his absorption with the sunny lawn, the whirling sprinklers, the shadows of the trees speckling in the heat and the wind, turned away from the window and walked slowly to his desk. He peered nearsightedly for a moment at the script crammed on the blackboards, then said, absently, "On the death of Keats. The class is excused."

For once, the students filed out silently, making a point, with youthful good manners, of not looking at Crane, bent over at his chair, pulling books together.

Steve was nearly the last one to leave the room and he waited outside the door for Crane. *Somebody* had to say something, do something, whisper "I'm sorry," shake the boy's hand. Steve didn't want to be the one, but there was nobody else left. When Crane came out, Steve fell into place beside him and they went out of the building together.

"My name is Dennicott," Steve said.

"I know," said Crane.

"Can I ask you a question?"

"Sure." There was no trace of grief in Crane's voice or manner. He blinked through his glasses at the sunshine, but that was all.

"Why did you do that?"

"Did you object?" The question was sharp but the tone was mild, offhand, careless.

"Hell, no," Steve said. "I just want to know why you did it."

"My brother was killed Saturday night," Crane said.

"I know."

" 'The death of Keats. The class is excused.' " Crane chuckled softly but without malice. "He's a nice old man, Mollison. Did you ever read the book he wrote about Marvell?"

"No," Steve said.

"Terrible book," Crane said. "You really want to know?" He peered with sudden sharpness at Steve.

"Yes," Steve said.

"Yes," Crane said absently, brushing at his forehead, "you would be the one who would ask. Out of the whole class. Did you know my brother?"

"Just barely," Steve said. He thought about Crane's brother, the fullback. A gold helmet far below on a green field, a number (what number?), a doll brought out every Saturday to do skillful and violent maneuvers in a great wash of sound, a photograph in a program, a young, brutal face looking out a little scornfully from the page. Scornful of what? Of whom? The inept photographer? The idea that anyone would really be interested in knowing what face was on that numbered doll? The notion that what he was doing was important enough to warrant this attempt to memorialize him, so that somewhere, in somebody's attic fifty years from now, that young face would still be there, in the debris, part of some old man's false memory of his youth?

"He didn't seem much like John Keats to you, did he?" Crane stopped under a tree, in the shade, to rearrange the books under his arm. He seemed oppressed by sunshine and he held his books clumsily and they were always on the verge of falling to the ground.

"To be honest," Steve said, "no, he didn't seem much like John Keats to me."

Crane nodded gently. "But I knew him," he said. "I knew him. And nobody who made those goddamned speeches at the funeral yesterday knew him. And he didn't believe in God or in funerals or those goddamned speeches. He needed a proper ceremony of farewell," Crane said, "and I tried to give it to him. All it took was a little chalk, and a poet, and none of those liars in black suits. Do you want to take a ride today?"

"Yes," Steve said without hesitation.

"I'll meet you at the library at eleven," Crane said. He waved stiffly and hunched off, gangling, awkward, ill-nourished, thin-haired, laden with books, a discredit to the golden Coastal legend.

They drove north in silence. Crane had an old Ford without a top and it rattled so much and the wind made so much noise as they bumped along that conversation would have been almost impossible, even if they had wished to talk. Crane bent over the wheel, driving nervously, with an excess of care, his long, pale hands gripping the wheel tightly. Steve hadn't asked where they were going and Crane hadn't told him. Steve hadn't been able to get hold of Adele to tell her he probably wouldn't be back in time to have lunch with her, but there was nothing to be done about that now. He sat back, enjoying the sun and the yellow, burnt-out hills and the long, grayish-blue swells of the Pacific beating lazily into the beaches and against the cliffs of the coast. Without being told, he knew that this ride somehow was a continuation of the ceremony in honor of Crane's brother.

They passed several restaurants alongside the road. Steve was hungry, but he didn't suggest stopping. This was Crane's expedition and Steve had no intention of interfering with whatever ritual Crane was following.

They rocked along between groves of lemon and orange, and

the air was heavy with the perfume of the fruit, mingled with the smell of salt from the sea.

They went through the flecked shade of avenues of eucalyptus that the Spanish monks had planted in another century to make their journeys from mission to mission bearable in the California summers. Rattling along in the noisy car, squinting a little when the car spurted out into bare sunlight, Steve thought of what the road must have looked like with an old man in a cassock nodding along it on a sleepy mule, to the sound of distant Spanish bells, welcoming travelers. There were no bells ringing today. California, Steve thought, sniffing the diesel oil of a truck in front of them, has not improved.

The car swerved around a turn, Crane put on the brakes and they stopped. Then Steve saw what they had stopped for.

There was a huge tree leaning over a bend of the highway and all the bark at road level on one side of the tree had been ripped off. The wood beneath, whitish, splintered, showed in a raw wound.

"This is the place," Crane said in his harsh whisper. He stopped the engine and got out of the car. Steve followed him and stood to one side as Crane peered nearsightedly through his glasses at the tree. Crane touched the tree, just at the edge of the wound.

"Eucalyptus," he said. "From the Greek, meaning well covered; the flower, before it opens having a sort of cap. A genus of plants of the N. O. Myrtaceae. If I had been a true brother," he said, "I would have come here Saturday morning and cut this tree down. My brother would be alive today." He ran his hand casually over the torn and splintered wood, and Steve remembered how he had touched the blackboard and flicked chalk dust off the ends of words that morning, unemphatically, in contact with the feel of things, the slate, the chalk mark at the end of the last s in Adonais, the gummy, drying wood. "You'd think," Crane said, "that if you loved a brother enough, you'd have sense enough to come and cut a tree down, wouldn't you? The Egyptians, I read somewhere," he said, "were believed to have used the oil of the eucalyptus leaf in the embalming process." His long hand flicked once more at the torn bark. "Well, I didn't cut the tree down. Let's go."

He strode back to the car without looking back at the tree. He got into the car behind the wheel and sat slumped there, squinting through his glasses at the road ahead of him, waiting for Steve to settle himself beside him. "It's terrible for my mother and father," Crane said after Steve had closed the door behind him. A truck filled with oranges passed them in a thunderous whoosh and a swirl of dust, leaving a fragrance of a hundred weddings on the air. "We live at home, you know. My brother and I were the only children they had, and they look at me and they can't help feeling, If it had to be one of them, why couldn't it have been *him*? and it shows in their eyes and they know it shows in their eyes and they know I agree with them and they feel guilty and I can't help them." He started the engine with a succession of nervous, uncertain gestures, like a man who was just learning how to drive. He turned the car around in the direction of Los Angeles and they started south. Steve looked once more at the tree, but Crane kept his eyes on the road ahead of him.

"I'm hungry," he said. "I know a place where we can get abalone about ten miles from here."

They were sitting in the weather-beaten shack with the windows open on the ocean, eating their abalone and drinking beer. The jukebox was playing "Downtown." It was the third time they were listening to "Downtown." Crane kept putting dimes into the machine and choosing the same song over and over again.

"I'm crazy about that song," he said. "Saturday night in America. Budweiser Bacchanalia."

"Everything all right, boys?" The waitress, a fat little dyed blonde of about thirty, smiled down at them from the end of the table.

"Everything is perfectly splendid," Crane said in a clear, ringing voice.

The waitress giggled. "Why, that sure is nice to hear," she said.

Crane examined her closely. "What do you do when it storms?" he asked.

"What's that?" She frowned uncertainly at him.

"When it storms," Crane said. "When the winds blow. When the sea heaves. Then the young sailors drown in the bottomless deeps."

"My," the waitress said, "and I thought you boys only had one beer."

"I advise anchors," Crane said. "You are badly placed. A turn of the wind, a twist of the tide, and you will be afloat, past the reef, on the way to Japan."

"I'll tell the boss," the waitress said, grinning. "You advise anchors."

"You are in peril, lady," Crane said seriously. "Don't think you're not. Nobody speaks candidly. Nobody tells you the one-hundred-percent honest-to-God truth." He pushed a dime from a pile at his elbow across the table to the waitress. "Would you be good enough to put this in the box, my dear?" he said formally.

"What do you want to hear?" the waitress asked.

"Downtown," Crane said.

"Again?" The waitress grimaced. "It's coming out of my ears."

"I understand it's all the rage," Crane said.

The waitress took the dime and put it in the box and "Downtown" started over again.

"She'll remember me," Crane said, eating fried potatoes covered with catsup. "Every time it blows and the sea comes up. You must not go through life unremembered."

"You're a queer duck, all right," Steve said, smiling a little to take the sting out of it, but surprised into saying it.

"Ah, I'm not so queer," Crane said, wiping catsup off his chin. "I don't behave like this ordinarily. This is the first time I ever flirted with a waitress in my life."

Steve laughed. "Do you call that flirting?"

"Isn't it?" Crane looked annoyed. "What the hell is it if it isn't flirting?" He surveyed Steve appraisingly. "Let me ask you a question," he said. "Do you screw that girl I always see you with around the campus?"

Steve put down his fork. "Now, wait a minute," he said.

"I don't like the way she walks," Crane said. "She walks like a coquette. I prefer whores."

"Let's leave it at that," Steve said.

"Ah, Christ," Crane said, "I thought you wanted to be my friend. You did a friendly, sensitive thing this morning. In the California desert, in the Los Angeles Gobi, in the Camargue of Culture. You put out a hand. You offered the cup."

"I want to be your friend, all right," Steve said, "but there're limits . . ."

"The word friend has no limits," Crane said harshly. He poured some of his beer over the fried potatoes, already covered with catsup. He forked a potato, put it in his mouth, chewed judiciously. "I've invented a taste thrill," he said. "Let me tell you something, Dennicott, friendship is limitless communication. Ask me anything and I'll answer. The more fundamental the matter, the fuller the answer. What's your idea of friendship? The truth about trivia—and silence and hypocrisy about everything else? God, you could have used a dose of my brother." He poured some more beer over the gobs of catsup on the fried potatoes. "You want to know why I can say Keats and name my brother in the same breath?" he asked challengingly, hunched over the table. "I'll tell you why. Because he had a sense of elation and a sense of purity." Crane squinted thoughtfully at Steve. "You, too," he said, "that's why I said you would be the one to ask, out of the whole class. You have it, too—the sense of elation. I could tell—listening to you laugh, watching you walk down the library steps holding your girl's elbow. I, too," he said gravely, "am capable of elation. But I reserve it for other things." He made a mysterious inward grimace. "But the purity——" he said. "I don't know. Maybe you don't know yourself. The jury is still out on you. But I knew about my brother. You want to know what I mean by purity?" He was talking compulsively. Silence would have made memory unbearable. "It's having a private set of standards and never compromising them," he said. "Even when it hurts, even when nobody else knows, even when it's just a tiny, formal gesture, that ninety-nine out of a hundred people would make without thinking about it."

Crane cocked his head and listened with pleasure to the chorus of "Downtown," and he had to speak loudly to be heard over the jukebox. "You know why my brother wasn't elected captain of the football team? He was all set for it, he was the logical choice, everybody expected it. I'll tell you why he wasn't, though. He wouldn't shake the hand of last year's captain at the end of the season, and last year's captain had a lot of votes he could influence any way he wanted. And do you know why my brother wouldn't shake his hand? Because he thought the man was a coward. He saw him tackle high when a low tackle would've been punishing, and he saw him not go all the way on blocks when they looked too rough. Maybe nobody else saw what my brother saw or maybe they gave the man the benefit of the doubt. Not my brother. So he didn't shake his hand because he didn't shake cowards' hands, see, and somebody else was elected captain. That's what I mean by purity," Crane said, sipping at his beer and looking out at the deserted beach and the ocean. For the first time, it occurred to Steve that it was perhaps just as well that he had never known Crane's brother, never been measured against that Cromwellian certitude of conduct.

"As for girls," Crane said, "the homeland of compromise, the womb of the second best——" Crane shook his head emphatically. "Not for my brother. Do you know what he did with his first girl? And he thought he was in love with her, too, at the time, but it still didn't make any difference. They only made love in the dark. The girl insisted. That's the way some girls are, you know, darkness excuses all. Well, my brother was crazy about her, and he didn't mind the darkness if it pleased her. But one night he saw her sitting up in bed and the curtains on the window moved in the wind and her silhouette was outlined against the moonlight, and he saw that when she sat like that she had a fat, loose belly. The silhouette, my brother said, was slack and self-indulgent. Of course, when she was lying down it sank in, and when she was dressed she wore a girdle that would've tucked in a beer barrel. And when he saw her silhouette against the curtain, he said to himself, This is the last time. this is not for me. Because it wasn't perfect, and he wouldn't settle for less. Love or no love, desire or not. He, himself, had a body like Michelangelo's *David* and he knew it and he was proud of it and he kept it that way—why should he settle for imperfection? Are you laughing, Dennicott?"

"Well," Steve said, trying to control his mouth, "the truth is, I'm smiling a little." He was amused, but he couldn't help thinking that it was possible that Crane had loved his brother for all the wrong reasons. And he couldn't help feeling sorry for the unknown girl, deserted, without knowing it, in the dark room, by the implacable athlete who had just made love to her.

"Don't you think I ought to talk about my brother this way?" Crane said.

"Of course," Steve said. "If I were dead, I hope my brother could talk like this about me the day after the funeral."

"It's just those goddamned speeches everybody makes," Crane whispered. "If you're not careful, they can take the whole idea of your brother away from you."

He wiped his glasses. His hands were shaking. "My goddamned hands," he said. He put his glasses back on his head and pressed his hands hard on the table so they wouldn't shake.

"How about you, Dennicott?" Crane said. "Have you ever done anything in your whole life that was unprofitable, damaging, maybe even ruinous, because it was the pure thing to do, the uncompromising thing, because if you acted otherwise, for the rest of your life you would remember it and feel shame?"

Steve hesitated. He did not have the habit of self-examination and had the feeling that it was vanity that made people speak about their virtues. And their faults. But there was Crane, waiting, himself open, naked. "Well, yes . . ." Steve said.

"What?"

"Well, it was never anything very grandiose . . ." Steve said, embarrassed, but feeling that Crane needed it, that in some way this exchange of intimacies helped relieve the boy's burden of sorrow. And he was intrigued by Crane, by the violence of his views, by the almost comic flood of his reminiscence about his brother, by the importance that Crane assigned to the slightest gesture, by his searching for meaning in trivialities, which gave the dignity of examination to every breath of life. "There was the time on the beach at Santa Monica," Steve said, "I got myself beaten up and I knew I was going to be beaten up . . ."

"That's good," Crane nodded approvingly. "That's always a good beginning."

"Oh, hell," Steve said, "it's too picayune."

"Nothing is picayune," said Crane. "Come on."

"Well, there was a huge guy there who always hung around and made a pest of himself," Steve said. "A physical-culture idiot, with muscles like basketballs. I made fun of him in front of some girls and he said I'd insulted him, and I had, and he said if I didn't apologize, I would have to fight him. And I was wrong, I'd been snotty and superior, and I realized it, and I knew that if I apologized, he'd be disappointed and the girls'd still be laughing at him—so I said I wouldn't apologize and I fought him there on the beach and he must have knocked me down a dozen times and he nearly killed me."

"Right." Crane nodded again, delivering a favorable judgment. "Excellent."

"Then there was this girl I wanted . . ." Steve stopped.

"Well?" Crane said.

"Nothing," Steve said. "I haven't figured it out yet." Until now he had thought that the episode with the girl reflected honorably on him. He had behaved, as his mother would have put it, in a gentlemanly manner. He wasn't sure now that Crane and his mother would see eye to eye. Crane confused him. "Some other time," he said.

"You promise?" Crane said.

"I promise."

"You won't disappoint me, now?"

"No."

"OK," Crane said. "Let's get out of here."

They split the check.

"Come back again sometime, boys," the blonde waitress said. "I'll play that record for you." She laughed, her breasts shaking. She had liked having them there. One of them was very good-looking, and the other one, the queer one with the glasses, she had decided, after thinking about it, was a great joker. It helped pass the long afternoon.

On the way home, Crane no longer drove like a nervous old maid on her third driving lesson. He drove very fast, with one hand, humming "Downtown," as though he didn't care whether he lived or died.

Then, abruptly, Crane stopped humming and began to drive carefully, timidly again. "Dennicott," he said, "what are you going to do with your life?"

"Who knows?" Steve said, taken aback by the way Crane's conversation jumped from one enormous question to another. "Go to sea maybe, build electronic equipment, teach, marry a rich wife . . ."

"What's that about electronics?" Crane asked.

"My father's factory," Steve said. "The ancestral business. No sophisticated missile is complete without a Dennicott super-secret what-do-you-call-it."

"Nah," Crane said, shaking his head, "you won't do that. And you won't teach school, either. You don't have the soul of a didact. I have the feeling something adventurous is going to happen to you."

"Do you?" Steve said. "Thanks. What're you going to do with *your* life?"

"I have it all planned out," Crane said. "I'm going to join the forestry service. I'm going to live in a hut on the top of a mountain and watch out for fires and fight to preserve the wilderness of America."

That's a hell of an ambition, Steve thought, but he didn't say it. "You're going to be awfully lonesome," he said.

"Good," Crane said. "I expect to get a lot of reading done. I'm not so enthusiastic about my fellow man, anyway. I prefer trees."

"What about women?" Steve asked. "A wife?"

"What sort of woman would choose me?" Crane said harshly. "I look like something left over after a New Year's party on skid row. And I would only take the best, the most beautiful, the most intelligent, the most loving. I'm not going to settle for some poor, drab Saturday-night castaway."

"Well, now," Steve said, "you're not so awful." Although, it was true, you'd be shocked if you saw Crane out with a pretty girl.

"Don't lie to your friends," Crane said. He began to drive recklessly again, as some new wave of feeling, some new conception of himself, took hold of him. Steve sat tight on his side of the car, holding onto the door, wondering if a whole generation of Cranes was going to meet death on the roads of California within a week.

They drove in silence until they reached the university library. Crane stopped the car and slouched back from the wheel as Steve got out. Steve saw Adele on the library steps, surrounded by three young men, none of whom he knew. Adele saw him as he got out of the car and started coming over to him. Even at that distance, Steve could tell she was angry. He wanted to get rid of Crane before Adele reached him. "Well, so long," Steve said, watching Adele approach. Her walk *was* distasteful, self-conscious, teasing.

Crane sat there, playing with the keys to the ignition, like a man who is always uncertain that the last important word has been said when the time has come to make an exit.

"Dennicott," he began, then stopped, because Adele was standing there, confronting Steve, her face set. She didn't look at Crane.

"Thanks," she said to Steve. "Thanks for the lunch."

"I couldn't help it," Steve said. "I had to go someplace."

"I'm not in the habit of being stood up," Adele said.

"I'll explain later," Steve said, wanting her to get out of there, away from him, away from Crane, watching soberly from behind the wheel.

"You don't have to explain anything," Adele said. She walked away. Steve gave her the benefit of the doubt. Probably she didn't know who Crane was and that it was Crane's brother who had been killed Saturday night. Still . . .

"I'm sorry I made you miss your date," Crane said.

"Forget it," Steve said. "She'll get over it."

For a moment he saw Crane looking after Adele, his face cold, severe, judging. Then Crane shrugged, dismissed the girl.

"Thanks, Dennicott," Crane said. "Thanks for coming to the tree. You did a good thing this afternoon. You did a friendly thing. You don't know how much you helped me. I have no friends. My brother was the only friend. If you hadn't come with me and let me talk, I don't know how I could've lived through today. Forgive me if I talked too much."

"You didn't talk too much," Steve said.

"Will I see you again?" Crane asked.

"Sure," said Steve. "We have to go back to that restaurant to listen to 'Downtown' real soon."

Crane sat up straight, suddenly, smiling shyly, looking pleased, like a child who has just been given a present. If it had been possible, Steve would have put his arms around Crane and embraced him. And with all Crane's anguish and all the loneliness that he knew so clearly was waiting for him, Steve envied him. Crane had the capacity for sorrow and now, after the day Steve had spent with the bereaved boy, he understood that the capacity for sorrow was also the capacity for living.

"Downtown," Crane said. He started the motor and drove off, waving gaily, to go toward his parents' house, where his mother and father were waiting, with the guilty look in their eyes, because they felt that if one of their sons had to die, they would have preferred it to be him.

Steve saw Adele coming back toward him from the library steps. He could see that her anger had cooled and that she probably would apologize for her outburst. Seeing Adele suddenly with Crane's eyes, he made a move to turn away. He didn't want to talk to her. He had to think about her. He had to think about everything. Then he remembered the twinge of pity he had felt when he had heard about the fat girl erased from her lover's life by the movement of a curtain on a moonlit night. He turned back and smiled in greeting as Adele came up to him. Crane had taught him a good deal that afternoon, but perhaps not the things Crane had thought he was teaching.

"Hello," Steve said, looking not quite candidly into the young blue eyes on a level with his own. "I was hoping you'd come back."

But he wasn't going to wake up automatically feeling good, ever again.

ERIC HOFFER

THE MADHOUSE OF CHANGE

the noted longshoreman-philosopher claims that uncontrolled social and technological progress can turn an entire population into destructive juveniles

After the Second World War, I spent two years (1947–1948) writing a small book on the nature of mass movements, which Harper later published under the title *The True Believer*. These were two years of utmost concentration and absorption. Yet even as I was writing the book, there was something tugging at my mind, making me wonder whether my attempt to make sense of the Stalin-Hitler decades would have relevance to what was taking place in the postwar world, particularly to the strange goings on in Asia and Africa. On both continents, several countries won independence from foreign rule and began to modernize themselves in a hurry. The struggle for independence was relatively brief, but the attempt at modernization became a hectic affair, which turned every country into a madhouse. Now, modernization is not an occult process. It requires the building of roads, factories, dams, schools and so on. Why should the accomplishment of such practical tasks require the staging of a madhouse?

I spent eighteen years groping for an answer. Almost everything I have written during the past eighteen years has dealt with some aspect of this problem. Every time I stumbled upon something that looked like an explanation, I wrote an essay. I acted on the assumption that in this sort of problem, all hunches and guesses were legitimate. It occurred to me, for instance, that modernization is basically a process of imitation—backward countries imitate advanced countries—and I wondered whether there might not be something bruising and antagonizing in the necessity to imitate a superior model. For the backward, imitation is an act of submission, and it is reasonable to expect that the sense of inferiority inherent in imitation should breed resentment. So I wrote an essay on "Imitation and Fanaticism," in which I suggested that the backward have to rid themselves of their feeling of inferiority, must demonstrate their prowess, before they will open their minds and hearts to all that the world can teach them. Most often in history, it was the conquerors who learned willingly from the conquered, rather than the other way around. There is, therefore, a kernel of practicalness in the attempt of a Nasser or a Sukarno to turn their people into warriors. It is a fact that nations with a warrior tradition, such as the Japanese or the inheritors of Genghis Khan in Outer Mongolia, find modernization less difficult than nations of subjected peasants, such as Russia and China. The essay also suggested that imitation is least impeded when we are made to feel that our act of imitation is actually an act of becoming the opposite of that which we imitate. Communism can be an effective agency for the transmission of Western achievements to backward countries, because it convinces the backward that by modernizing themselves they are actually becoming the opposite of the capitalist model they imitate. Finally, I pointed out that we are most at ease when we imitate a defeated or dead model, and that the impulse of the imitators is to defeat or even destroy the model they imitate.

I also noticed that the present modernization of backward countries is directed not by businessmen or traditional politicians but by intellectuals, and I blamed the madhouse on them. I wrote several essays in which I tried to prove that, unlike prosaic men of action, the intellectual cannot operate at room temperature, that he pants for a world of magic and miracles and turns everyday tasks into holy causes and Promethean undertakings. I suggested that should intellectuals come to power in an advanced country, it, too, would turn overnight into a madhouse.

The explanation that appealed to me most and to which I hung on longest was an unlikely one for an American. I became convinced that change itself is the cause of the madhouse, that change as such is explosive. It took me long to reach this conclusion. In this country, change is familiar and acceptable. We seem to change homes, jobs, habits, friends, even husbands and wives, without much difficulty. Actually, through most of history, change has been a rare phenomenon. Think of it; the technology perfected in prehistoric times served as a basis of everyday life down to the end of the eighteenth century. Even in this country, people lived in 1800 A.D. the way men lived in 3000 B.C. George Washington would have felt at home in King Cheops' Egypt. The end of the eighteenth century marks a sharp dividing line between an immemorial static world and a world of ceaseless change. It is obvious, therefore, that change is far from being as natural and matter of fact as we imagine it to be. Moreover, an observant person will notice that even in this country, change is never free of irritation and elements of fear. We adjust ourselves quickly to a new job or a new environment, but the moments of anxiety are there. And if we had to change our whole way of life as people have to do in the developing countries, we, too, would become upset and unbalanced.

The obvious fact is that we cannot prepare and fit ourselves for the wholly new. Skill and experience count for little and may even be a handicap. It takes time before we adjust ourselves to a wholly new situation and fit in. In other words, drastic change turns a whole population into misfits, and misfits live and breathe in an atmosphere of passion. We used to think that revolution is the cause of change. Actually, it is the other way around; revolution is a byproduct of change. Change comes first, and it is the difficulties and irritations inherent in change that set the stage for revolution. To say that revolution is the cause of change is like saying that juvenile delinquency is the cause of the change from boyhood to manhood.

To understand what is going on in the developing countries, we must know what it is that misfits need above all. They need self-confidence, which means plenty of opportunities for successful action, for asserting themselves and proving their worth. Where there are such opportunities, change is likely to proceed without convulsions and explosions. We have seen it happen in this country. From the middle of the last century to the First World War, some 30,000,000 Europeans came to this country. They were, for the most part, peasants torn from the warm communal life of small towns and villages and dumped almost overnight on a strange, cold continent. If ever there was a drastic change, this was it. The immigrants went through an upsetting, irritating and painful experience. They were misfits in every sense of the word, ideal material for a revolution. Yet we had no upheaval. The immigrants adjusted themselves quickly to the new environment. Why? Because they had an almost virgin continent at their disposal and unbounded opportunities for individual advancement and self-assertion.

In most of the developing countries, there are only the meagerest opportunities for the individual to do something on his own. Most of these countries are unimaginably poor, with debilitated populations living on the edge of subsistence. Some countries, like Indonesia, are rich in natural resources, but their governments do not countenance individual enterprise and self-assertion. The intellectuals who are in charge derive their sense of usefulness from telling other people what to do, and see it as an infringement of their birthright when common people start to do things on their own. You cannot see a Sukarno or even a Suharto government telling the people of Indonesia to come and get it, the way America told the immigrants from Europe.

Now, what do misfits do when they cannot win a sense of confidence and worth by individual effort? They reach out for substitutes. The substitute for self-confidence is faith, and the substitute for self-esteem is pride. Faith and pride in what? In a leader, a holy cause, a nation, a race. And it is easily seen that once you operate with faith and pride, you are going to have the bedlam atmosphere of a madhouse.

It is remarkable that all the years I was playing with these explanations I failed to see something that was staring me in the face. I failed to see that staging a madhouse in the course of rapid modernization was not peculiar to backward countries in Asia and Africa. It was only recently that it dawned upon me that Europe, too, has been living in an apocalyptic madhouse staged by Germany and Russia as they set out to modernize themselves at breakneck speed. The nationalist, racialist and revolutionary movements and the great wars, which have convulsed the Occident during the past hundred years, were the by-product of a drastic change in the life of the European masses, when millions of peasants were transformed into urban, industrial workers. Seen against this apocalyptic background, my explanation of the explosiveness of change as due to the creation of a state of unfitness seemed pale and inadequate. I began to feel that change does more than create misfits, that it affects deeper layers of the psyche. Considering how rare change has been through most of history, it is legitimate to assume that change goes against human nature, that there is in man a built-in resistance to change. It is not only that we are afraid of the new. Deep within us there is the conviction that we cannot merely adjust to change, that we cannot remain our old selves and master the new, that only by getting out of our skins, by becoming new men, can we become part of the new. In other words, change creates an estrangement from the self and generates a need for a new identity and a sense of rebirth. And it depends on the way this need is satisfied whether change runs smoothly or is attended with convulsions and explosions.

Let us go back to the 30,000,000 immigrants who were dumped on our shores and see what really happened to them. I said that the reason they had adjusted themselves so quickly to the new environment was that they found abundant opportunities for individual advancement. Is this all there was to it? Actually, a whole lot more happened to them. The moment the immigrants landed on our shores, America grabbed hold of them, stripped them of their traditions and habits, gave them a new diet and a new mode of dress, taught them a new language and often gave them a new name. Here was a classical example of processing people into new men. Abundant opportunities for action by themselves could not have transformed the transplanted peasants so quickly and smoothly.

Immigration, then, is a potent agency of human transformation. It is, moreover, an agency the masses will resort to on their own accord whenever there is a drastic change in their way of life. It is significant that the rapid industrialization of Europe was attended not only by mass movements but also by mass migrations to the New World. Marx cursed the discovery of gold in California for cheating him of his foretold and prayed-for glorious revolution. He said it was the injection of gold from California that saved tottering Europe. Actually, it was the discharge of 30,000,000 immigrants to America that postponed Europe's apocalyptic denouement.

It should be obvious, of course, that immigration can effect a human transformation only when it is to a foreign country. Internal migration cannot do it. Even now, when you want to transform a Sicilian or Spanish peasant into an industrial worker, you can do it more effectively by transferring him to Germany or France than to Milan or Barcelona. The Sicilian peasant who goes to Milan is not automatically processed into a new man, and he is likely to satisfy his need for a sense of rebirth by joining the Communist Party or some other mass movement. Immigration to a foreign country is a do-it-yourself way for the masses to attain a sense of rebirth. When they achieve this sense by joining a mass movement, they avail themselves of a device staged for them by intellectuals. It is easy to forget that mass movements are the creation not of the masses but of the intellectuals. Now, what is likely to happen to a Sicilian peasant who becomes an industrial worker in Milan did happen to millions of European peasants who flocked to the cities of their native countries in the second half of the nineteenth century. They attained a sense of rebirth and a new identity by joining the nationalist and revolutionary movements staged for them by poets, writers, historians and scholars, and their adjustment to a new life became a convulsive and explosive affair that eventually shook the Occident to its foundations.

Mass movements play a twofold role in the process of change. Firstly, they stage the drama of rebirth. By joining a mass movement, we become members of a chosen people—saints, warriors or pioneers showing the way to the rest of mankind. Secondly, by fusing people into a compact corporate body, a mass movement creates a homogeneous malleable mass that can be molded at will. We who have lived through the Stalin-Hitler decades know that one of the chief achievements of a mass movement is the creation of a population that will go through breath-taking somersaults at a word of command and can be made to love what it hates and hate what it loves.

There is one drastic change that no society can avoid, namely, the change from boyhood to manhood. It is a difficult and painful change, and we all know its explosive byproduct of juvenile delinquency. How do ossified, changeless societies weather this change? I was particularly interested in primitive, tribal societies that have remained unchanged for millennia. When I first started to look into this matter, I had no idea what I would find. I happened to come upon a translation of Arnold van Gennep's *The Rites of Passage*, and as I turned the pages, I had the surprise of my life. There it was in black and white: The rites primitive societies stage to ease the boy's passage to manhood are the rites of death and rebirth. In the Congo, boys at the age of fifteen are declared dead, taken into the forest and given palm wine until they pass out. The priest-magician watches over them. When they come to, he feeds them special food and teaches them a new language. During the rites of reintegration, the boys have to pretend that they do not know how to walk and that, like newborn children, they have to learn the gestures of everyday life. In several Australian tribes, the boy is taken violently from his mother, who weeps for him. He is taken into the desert, where he is subjected to physical and mental weakening to simulate death. He is then resurrected to live like a man.

In modern societies that have no rites of passage, the juvenile gropes his way to manhood on his own. He becomes an ideal recruit for mass movements. Indeed, the rapport between juvenile and mass movement is so striking—the two are so tailor-made for each other—that anyone of whatever age who joins a mass movement begins to display juvenile traits. This intimate linkage between juvenile and mass movement, and the fact that change readies people for mass movements, gave me a new view of the nature of change. Change, I realized, causes juvenilization; it turns a whole population into juveniles. It is as if the strain of change cracks the upper layers of the mind and lays bare the less mature layers. Another way of putting it is that people who undergo drastic change recapitulate to some degree the passage from childhood to manhood, and mass movements are in a sense the juvenile delinquency of societies going through the ordeal of change.

The juvenile, then, is the archetypal man in transition. There is a family likeness between juveniles and people who migrate from one country to another, or are converted from one faith to another, or pass from one way of life to another—as when peasants are turned into industrial workers, serfs into freemen, civilians into soldiers, and people in backward countries are subjected to rapid modernization. Even the old, when they undergo the abrupt change of retirement, may turn, so to speak, into senile juveniles. There is such a thing as senile delinquency. Retired farmers and shopkeepers have made of southern California a breeding ground of juvenile cults, utopias and movements. The Birch movement, with its unmistakable character of juvenile delinquency, was initiated by a retired candymaker and is sustained by retired business executives, generals and admirals. One need not strain the imagination to visualize the juvenile madhouse we would have if rapid automation should cause the retirement of millions of vigorous workers still hungry for action.

It should be of interest to see what light these theories throw on one of the most pressing changes that confront this country at present, namely, the Negro's passage from inferiority to equality.

One sees immediately the almost insurmountable handicaps that beset the Negro on every hand. Take the matter of *rebirth*. The fact that in this country the Negro is a Negro first and only secondly an individual puts the attainment of a sense of rebirth beyond his reach. No matter what the Negro individual achieves or becomes, he remains a Negro first. How can he ever feel that he is a new man reborn to a new life? Think of the absurdities Elijah Muhammad and Father Divine had to concoct in order to give the Negro some taste of rebirth. A decade of fervent agitation, demonstrations, riots, court decisions and new laws has not altered the fact that the white environment divests the Negro of his individuality.

Or take *immigration*. Millions of Negroes have migrated from the South to other parts of the country, but this mass migration has not helped the Negro to change himself. It is an internal migration that, as we have seen, cannot work a human transformation and cannot endow people with a new identity. The Negro ghettos outside the South are a world of "nowhereness" and "nobodiness" where the groping for identity assumes the aspect of a nightmarish masquerade. It is of interest that Negroes who come to New York from the West Indies, Panama or Africa do have the exodus experience, and their performance is not utterly different from that of European immigrants.

Can *mass movements* do ought for the Negro? The answer is no. America is hard on mass movements. What starts out here as a mass movement ends up as a corporation or a racket. The Puritan and Mormon movements became training grounds for successful businessmen, and even the Communist movement is becoming a vehicle for the transformation of true believers into successful real-estate dealers. The Black Muslim movement is on the way to becoming a holding company of stores, farms and banks. The civil-rights movement has been an instrument in the hands of the Negro middle class in its effort to integrate itself with the white middle class and force its way into the more privileged segments of American life. Used thus, the Negro revolution is not a movement but a racket. The Negro middle class has neither faith in nor concern for the Negro masses.

The fact is that the civil-rights movement has not only failed to become a genuine mass movement but has also failed as a racket. Not only has it not achieved anything like a transformation of the average Negro but it has failed to give the Negro middle class the new life that seemed within its reach. The Negro middle class has fabulous opportunities for individual advancement; yet such opportunities cannot give the Negro a sense of fitness and an unequivocal sense of worth. Middle-class Negroes are finding out that what they need most is something that they as individuals cannot give themselves, something, moreover, that neither courts nor legislatures nor governments but only the Negro community as a whole can give them. Only when the Negro community as a whole performs something that will win it the admiration of the world will the Negro individual be able to be himself and savor the unbought grace of life. The Negro must have justified pride in the achievements of his people before he can have genuine self-respect. Another way of putting it is that at present the only way the Negro in America can attain a sense of rebirth is by giving birth to an effective Negro community. This cannot happen unless the Negro middle class reintegrates itself with the Negro masses and canalizes its energies, skills and money into the building of vigorous organs for mutual help, self-improvement and communal achievement. Demonstrations, riots, slogans, grandstanding and alibis cannot create one atom of pride.

The building of a Negro community will probably require a new type of leader—a leader who will know how to dovetail the Negro's difficulties into opportunities for growth. The renovation of the Negro slums has been crying out for the mass training of unemployed Negroes as carpenters, bricklayers, plasterers, plumbers, electricians, painters, etc., and their organization into a black union that later, when the slums have been rebuilt, could challenge the discriminating white unions to open up or be wiped out. There is no reason why the Negroes in America should not become world pioneers not only in the renovation of slums but in the overcoming of backwardness. It is to the 20,000,000 Negroes in America that the backward countries should turn for guidance.

I have said that everywhere in America at present, the Negro is a Negro first and only secondly a human being. This is not wholly true. There is one place, the U. S. Armed Forces, where the Negro is a human being first. By joining the Armed Forces, the Negro acquires a new identity and is reborn to a new life. His excellent performance in Vietnam is generating a pride that radiates across the Pacific and reaches into many Negro households. New Left activists who ring doorbells in Harlem and urge Negro housewives to make common cause with the Viet Cong are unceremoniously thrown out. It is not inconceivable that the new leaders who will eventually lead 20,000,000 Negroes to a promised land will be Negro veterans of the Vietnam war. The new type of leader will be without charisma, swagger or clownishness. When the task is done, the followers of such a leader will feel that they have done everything themselves and that they can do great things without great leaders.

"Frankly, doctor, don't you think it's time to get off this civil rights kick and get back to the fundamental teachings of Christianity?"

‘*Everybody but me*’

RACE IN AMERICA

I swear to the Lord
I still can’t see
Why Democracy means
Everybody but me.

LANGSTON HUGHES,
The Black Man Speaks

JAMES BALDWIN

THE USES OF THE BLUES

how a uniquely american art form relates to the negro's fight for his rights

The title "The Uses of the Blues" does not refer to music; I don't know anything about music. It does refer to the experience of life, or the state of being, out of which the blues come. Now, I am claiming a great deal for the blues; I'm using them as a metaphor—I might have titled this, for example, "The Uses of Anguish" or "The Uses of Pain." But I want to talk about the blues, not only because they speak of this particular experience of life and this state of being, but because they contain the toughness that manages to make this experience articulate. I am engaged, then, in a discussion of craft or, to use a very dangerous word, art. And I want to suggest that the acceptance of this anguish one finds in the blues, and the expression of it, creates, also, however odd this may sound, a kind of joy. Now joy is a true state, it is a reality; it has nothing to do with what most people have in mind when they talk of happiness, which is not a real state and does not really exist.

Consider some of the things the blues are about. They're about work, love, death, floods, lynchings, in fact, a series of disasters which can be summed up under the arbitrary heading "Facts of Life." Bessie Smith, who is dead now, came out of somewhere in the Deep South. I guess she was born around 1898, a great blues singer; died in Mississippi after a very long, hard—not *very* long, but very *hard*—life: pigs' feet and gin, many disastrous lovers and a career that first went up, then went down; died on the road on the way from one hospital to another. She was in an automobile accident and one of her arms was wrenched out of its socket; and because the hospital attendants argued whether or not they could let her in because she was colored, she died. Not a story Horatio Alger would write. Well, Bessie saw a great many things, and among those things was a flood. And she talked about it and she said, "It rained five days and the skies turned dark as night," and she repeated it: "It rained five days and the skies turned dark as night." Then, "Trouble take place in the lowlands at night." And she went on:

Then it thundered and lightnin'd and the wind began to blow
Then it thundered and lightnin'd and the wind began to blow
There's thousands of people ain't got no place to go.

As the song makes clear, she was one of those people. But she ended in a fantastic way:

Backwater blues done caused me to pack my things and go
Because my house fell down
And I can't live there no mo'.

Billie Holiday came along a little later and she had quite a story, too, a story which *Life* magazine would never print except as a tough, bittersweet sob-story obituary—in which, however helplessly, the dominant note would be relief. She was a little girl from the South, and she had quite a time with gin, whiskey and dope. She died in New York in a narcotics ward under the most terrifying and—in terms of crimes of the city and the country against her—disgraceful circumstances, and she had something she called "Billie's Blues":

My man wouldn't give me no dinner
Wouldn't give me no supper
Squawked about my supper and turned me outdoors
And had the nerve to lay a padlock on my clothes
I didn't have so many, but I had a long, long way to go.

And one more, one more—Bessie Smith had a song called "Gin House Blues." It's another kind of blues, and maybe I should explain this to you—a Negro has his difficult days, the days when everything has gone wrong and on top of it, he has a fight with the elevator man, or the taxi driver, or somebody he never saw before, who seems to decide to prove he's white and you're black. But this particular Tuesday it's more than you can take—sometimes, you know, you can take it. But Bessie didn't this time, and she sat down in the gin house and sang:

Don't try me, nobody
'Cause you will never win
I'll fight the Army and the Navy
Just me and my gin.

Well, you know, that is all very accurate, all very concrete. I know, I watched, I was there. You've seen these black men and women, these boys and girls; you've seen them on the streets. But I know what happened to them at the factory, at work, at home, on the subway, what they go through in a day, and the way they sort of ride with it. And it's very, very tricky. It's kind of a fantastic tightrope. They may be very self-controlled, very civilized; I like to think of myself as being very civilized and self-controlled, but I know I'm not. And I know that some improbable Wednesday, for no reason whatever, the elevator man or the doorman, the policeman or the landlord, or some little boy from the Bronx will say something, and it will be the wrong day to say it, the wrong moment to have it said to me; and God knows what will happen. I have seen it all, I have seen that much. What the blues are describing comes out of all this.

"Gin House Blues" is a real gin house. "Backwater Flood" is a real flood. When Billie says, "My man don't love me," she is not making a fantasy out of it. This is what happened, this is where it is. This is what it is. Now, I'm trying to suggest that the triumph here—which is a very un-American triumph—is that the person to whom these things happened watched with eyes wide open, saw it happen. So that when Billie or Bessie or Leadbelly stood up and sang about it, they were commenting on it, a litle bit outside it; they were accepting it. And there's something funny—there's always something a little funny in all our disasters, if one can face the disaster. So that it's this passionate detachment, this inwardness coupled with outwardness, this ability to know that, All right, it's a mess, and you can't do anything about it . . . so, well, you have to do something about it. You can't stay there, you can't drop dead, you can't give up, but all right, OK, as Bessie said, "Picked up my bag, baby, and I tried it again." This made life, however horrible that life was, bearable for her. It's what makes life bearable for any person, because every person, everybody born, from the time he's found out about people until the whole thing is over is certain of one thing: He is going to suffer. There is no way not to suffer.

Now, this brings us to two things. It brings us to the American Negro's experience of life, and it brings us to the American dream or sense of life. It would be hard to find any two things more absolutely opposed. I want to make it clear that when I talk about Negroes in this context, I am not talking about race; I don't know what race means. I am talking about a social fact. When I say Negro, it is a digression; it is important to remember that I am not talking about a people but a person. I am talking about a man who, let's say, was once seventeen and who is now, let's say, forty, who has four children and can't feed them. I am talking about what happens to that man in this time and during this effort. I'm talking about what happens to you if, having barely escaped suicide, or death, or madness, or yourself, you watch your children growing up and no matter what you do, no matter *what* you do, you are powerless, you are really powerless, against the force of the world that is out to tell your child that he has no right to be alive. And no amount of liberal jargon, and no amount of talk about how well and how far we have progressed, does anything to soften or to point out any solution to this dilemma. In every generation, ever since Negroes have been here, every Negro mother and father has had to face that child and try to create in that child some way of surviving this particular world, some way to make the child, who will be despised, not despise himself. I don't know what the Negro problem means to white people, but this is what it means to Negroes. Now, it would seem to me, since this is so, that one of the reasons we talk about the Negro problem in the way we do is in order precisely to avoid any knowledge of this fact. Imagine Doris Day trying to sing:

> Papa may have, Mama may have,
> But God bless the child that's got
> his own.

People talk to me absolutely bathed in a bubble bath of self-congratulation. I mean, I walk into a room and everyone there is terribly proud of himself because I managed to get to the room. It proves to him that he is getting better. It's funny, but it's terribly sad. It's sad that one needs this kind of corroboration and it's terribly sad that one can be so self-deluded. The fact that Harry Belafonte makes as much money as, let's say, Frank Sinatra, doesn't really mean anything in this context. Frank can still get a house anywhere, and Harry can't. People go to see Harry and stand in long lines to watch him. They love him on-stage, or at a cocktail party, but they don't want him to marry their daughters. This has nothing to do with Harry; this has everything to do with America. All right. Therefore, when we talk about what we call the Negro problem, we are simply evolving means of avoiding the facts of this life. Because in order to face the facts of a life like Billie's or, for that matter, a life like mine, one has got to—the American white has got to—accept the fact that what he thinks he is, he is not. He has to give up, he has to surrender his image of himself and, apparently, this is the last thing white Americans are prepared to do.

But, anyway, it is not a question now of accusing the white American of crimes against the Negro. It is too late for that. Besides, it is irrelevant. Injustice, murder, the shedding of blood, unhappily, are commonplace. These things happen all the time and everywhere. There is always a reason for it. People will always give themselves reasons for it. What I'm much more concerned about is what white Americans have done to themselves; what has been done to me is irrelevant simply because there is nothing more you can do to me. But, in doing it, you've done something to yourself. In evading my humanity, you have done something to your own humanity. We all do this all the time, of course. One labels people; one labels them Jew, one labels them fascist, one labels them Communist, one labels them Negro, one labels them white man. But in the doing of this, you have not described anything—you have not described me when you call me a nigger or when you call me a Negro leader. You have only described yourself. What I think of you says more about me than it can possibly say about you. This is a very simple law and every Negro who intends to survive has to learn it very soon. Therefore, the Republic, among other things, has managed to create a body of people who have very little to lose, and there is nothing more dangerous in any republic, any state, any country, any time, than men who have nothing to lose.

Because you have thus given him his freedom, the American Negro can do whatever he wills; you can no longer do anything to him. He doesn't want anything you've got, he doesn't believe anything you say. I don't know why and I don't know how America arrived at this peculiar point of view. If one examines American history, there is no apparent reason for it. It's a bloody history, as bloody as everybody else's history, as deluded, as fanatical. One has only to look at it from the time we all got here. Look at the Pilgrims, the Puritans—the people who presumably fled oppression in Europe only to set up a more oppressed society here—people who wanted freedom, who killed off the Indians. Look at all the people moving into a new era and enslaving all the blacks. These are the facts of American history as opposed to the legend. We came from Europe, we came from Africa, we came from all over the world. We brought whatever was in us from China or from France. We *all* brought it with us. We were not transformed when we crossed the ocean. Something else happened. Something much more serious. We no longer had any way of finding out, of knowing who we were.

Many people have said in various tones of voice, meaning various things, that the most unlucky thing that happened in America was the presence of the Negro. Freud said, in a kind of rage, that the black race was the folly of America and that it served America right. Well, of course, I don't quite know what Freud had in mind. But I can see that, in one way, it may have been the most unlucky thing that happened to America, since America, unlike any other Western power, had its slaves on the mainland. They were here. We had our slaves at a time, unluckily for us, when slavery was going out of fashion. And after the Bill of Rights. Therefore, it would seem to me that the presence of this black mass here as opposed to all the things we said we believed in and also at a time when the whole doctrine of white supremacy had never even been questioned is one of the most crucial facts of our history. It would be nightmarish now to read the handbooks of colonialists a hundred years ago, even ten years ago, for that matter. But in those days, it was not even a question of black people being inferior to white people. The American found himself in a very peculiar position because he knew that black people were people. Frenchmen could avoid knowing it—they never met a black man. Englishmen could avoid knowing it. But Americans could not avoid knowing it because, after all, here he was and he was, no matter how it was denied, a man, just like everybody else. And the attempt to avoid this, to avoid this fact, I consider one of the keys to what we can call loosely the American psychology. For one thing, it created in Americans a kind of perpetual, hidden, festering and entirely unadmitted guilt. Guilt is a very peculiar emotion. As long as you are guilty about something, no matter what it is, you are not compelled to change it. Guilt is like a warm bath or, to be rude, it is like masturbation—you can get used to it, you can prefer it, you may get to a place where you cannot live without it, because in order to live without it, in order to get past this guilt, you must act. And in order to act, you must be conscious and take great chances and be responsible for the consequences. Therefore, liberals, and people who are not even liberals, much prefer to discuss the Negro problem than to try to deal with what this figure of the Negro really means personally to them. They still prefer to read statistics, charts, Gallup polls, rather than deal with the reality. They still tell me, to console me, how many Negroes bought Cadillacs, Cutty Sark, Coca-Cola, Schweppes, last year; how many more will buy Cadillacs, Cutty Sark, Coca-Cola and Schweppes next year. To prove to me that things are getting better. Now, of course, I think it is a very sad matter if you suppose that you or I have bled and suffered and died in this country in order to achieve Cadillacs, Cutty Sark, Schweppes and Coca-Cola. It seems to me if one accepts this speculation about the luxury of guilt that the second reason must be related to the first. That has to do with the ways in which we manage to project onto the Negro face, because it is so visible, all of our guilts and aggressions and desires. And if you doubt this, think of the legends that surround the Negro to this day. Think, when you think of these legends, that they were not invented by Negroes, but they were invented by the white republic. Ask yourself if Aunt Jemima or Uncle Tom ever existed anywhere and why it was necessary to invent them. Ask yourself why Negroes until today are, in the popular imagination, at once the most depraved people under heaven and the most saintly. Ask yourself what William Faulkner really was trying to say in *Requiem for a Nun*, which is about a nigger, whore, dope addict, saint. Faulkner wrote it. I never met Nancy, the nun he was writing about. He never met her, either, but the question is why was it necessary for him and for us to hold onto this image? We needn't go so far afield. Ask yourself why liberals are so delighted with the movie *The Defiant Ones*. It ends, if you remember, when Sidney Poitier, the black man, having been chained interminably to Tony Curtis, the white man, finally breaks the chain, is on the train, is getting away, but no, he doesn't go, doesn't leave poor Tony Curtis down there on the chain gang. Not at all. He jumps off the train and they go buddy-buddy back together to the same old Jim Crow chain gang. Now, this is a fable. Why? Who is trying to prove what to whom? I'll tell you something. I saw that movie twice. I saw it downtown with all my liberal friends, who were delighted when Sidney jumped off the train. I saw it uptown with my less liberal friends, who were furious. When Sidney jumped off that train, they called him all kinds of unmentionable things. Well, their reaction was as least more honest and more direct. Why is it necessary at this late date, one screams at the world, to prove that the Negro doesn't really hate you, he's forgiven and forgotten all of it. Maybe he has. That's not the problem. *You* haven't. And that *is* the problem:

I love you, baby,
But can't stand your dirty ways.

There's one more thing I ought to add to this. The final turn of the screw that created this peculiar purgatory which we call America is that aspect of our history that is most triumphant. We really did conquer a continent, we have made a lot of money, we're better off materially than anybody else in the world. How easy it is as a person or as a nation to suppose that one's well-being is proof of one's virtue; in fact, a great many people are saying just that right now. You know, we're the best nation in the world because we're the richest nation in the world. The American way of life has proven itself, according to these curious people, and that's why we're so rich. This is called Yankee virtue and it comes from Calvin, but my point is that I think this has again something to do with the American failure to face reality. Since we have all these things, we can't be so bad and, since we have all these things, we are robbed, in a way, of the incentive to walk away from the TV set, the Cadillac, and go into the chaos out of which and only out of which we can create ourselves into human beings.

To talk about these things in this country today is extremely difficult. Even the words mean nothing anymore. I think, for example, what we call the religious revival in America means that more and more people periodically get more and more frightened and go to church in order to make sure they don't lose their investments. This is the only reason that I can find for the popularity of men who have nothing to do with religion at all, like Norman Vincent Peale, for example—only for example; there're lots of others just like him. I think this is very sad. I think it's very frightening. But Ray Charles, who is a great tragic artist, makes of a genuinely religious confession something triumphant and liberating. He tells us that he cried so loud he gave the blues to his neighbor next door.

How can I put it? Let us talk about a person who is no longer very young, who somehow managed to get to, let us say, the age of forty, and a great many of us do, without ever having been touched, broken, disturbed, frightened—ten-year-old virgin, male or female. There is a sense of the grotesque about a person who has spent his or her life in a kind of cotton batting. There is something monstrous about never having been hurt, never having been made to bleed, never having lost anything, never having gained anything because life is beautiful, and in order to keep it beautiful you're going to stay just the way you are and you're not going to test your theory against all the possibilities outside. America is something like that. The failure on our part to accept the reality of pain, of anguish, of ambiguity, of death has turned us into a very peculiar and sometimes monstrous people. It means, for one thing, and it's very serious, that people who have had no experience have no compassion. People who have had no experience suppose that if a man is a thief, he is a thief; but, in fact, that isn't the most important thing about him. The most important thing about him is that he is a man and, furthermore, that if he's a thief or a murderer or whatever he is, *you* could also be and you would know this, anyone would know this who had really dared to live. Miles Davis once gave poor Billie Holiday $100 and somebody said, "Man, don't you know she's going to go out and spend it on dope?" and Miles said, "Baby, have you ever been sick?"

Now, you don't know that by reading, by looking. You don't know what the river is like or what the ocean is like by standing on the shore. You can't know anything about life and suppose you can get through it clean. The most monstrous people are those who think they are going to. I think this shows in everything we see and do, in everything we read about these peculiar private lives, so peculiar that it is almost impossible to write about them, because what a man *says* he's doing has nothing to do with what he's *really* doing. If you read such popular novelists as John O'Hara, you can't imagine what country he's talking about. If you read *Life* magazine, it's like reading about the moon. Nobody lives in that country. That country does not exist and, what is worse, everybody knows it. But everyone pretends that it does. Now this is panic. And this is terribly dangerous, because it means that when the trouble comes, and trouble always comes, you won't survive it. It means that if your son dies, you may go to pieces or find the nearest psychiatrist or the nearest church, but you won't survive it on your own. If you don't survive your trouble out of your own resources, you have not really survived it; you have merely closed yourself against it. The blues are rooted in the slave songs; the slaves discovered something genuinely terrible, terrible because it sums up the universal challenge, the universal hope, the universal fear:

The very time I thought I was lost
My dungeon shook and my chains fell off.

Well, that is almost all I am trying to say. I say it out of great concern. And out of a certain kind of hope. If you can live in the full knowledge that you are going to die, that you are not going to live forever, that if you live with the reality of death, you can live. This is not mystical talk; it is a fact. It is a principal fact of life. If you can't do it, if you spend your entire life in flight from death, you are also in flight from life. For example, right now you find the most unexpected people building bomb shelters, which is very close to being a crime. It is a private panic which creates a public delusion that some of us will be saved by bomb shelters. If we had, as human beings, on a personal and private level, our personal authority, we would know better; but because we are so uncertain of all these things, some of us, apparently, are willing to spend the rest of our lives underground in concrete. Perhaps, if we had a more working relationship with ourselves and with one another, we might be able to turn the tide and eliminate the propaganda for building bomb shelters. People who in some sense know who they are can't change the world always, but they can do something to make it a little more, to make life a little more human. Human in the best sense. Human in terms of joy, freedom which is always private, respect, respect for one another, even such things as manners. All these things are very important, all these old-fashioned things. People who don't know who they are privately, accept, as we have accepted for nearly fifteen years, the fantastic disaster which we call American politics and which we call American foreign policy, and the incoherence of the one is an exact reflection of the incoherence of the other. Now, the only way to change all this is to begin to ask ourselves very difficult questions.

I will stop now. But I want to quote two things. A very great American writer, Henry James, writing to a friend of his who had just lost her husband, said, "Sorrow wears and uses us but we wear and use it, too, and it is blind. Whereas we, after a manner, see." And Bessie said:

Good mornin' blues.
Blues, how do you do?
I'm doin' all right.
Good mornin'.
How are you?

interview

a candid conversation with **ELDRIDGE CLEAVER** *the revolutionary leader of the black panthers*

Eldridge Cleaver has been called the first black leader since Malcolm X with the potential to organize a militant mass movement of "black liberation." Whether he will succeed in forging it, whether he will remain free—or even alive—to lead it and whether, if he does, it will be a force for racial reconciliation or division remains to be seen. But there is no denying that Cleaver, like Malcolm X, has great impact on the young in the ghettos. They know his own ghetto origins; they identify with his defiance of the establishment and with his advocacy of self-defense; and, unlike SNCC's fiery former chieftain Stokely Carmichael, Cleaver offers them a growing organization to join—the Black Panther Party, of which he is minister of information. Carmichael, in fact, has recently joined the group himself. From their base in Oakland, California, the Panthers have established chapters in New York, Detroit, San Francisco, Los Angeles, Cleveland and San Diego, with a membership estimated at anywhere between 1000 and 5000.

Immediately identifiable by their black berets, black jackets and the empty .50 caliber shell worn on a rawhide thong around the neck, the Panthers are increasingly evident at community meetings, in churches, on the streets—every place they can manifest their concern for organizing masses of black people. Police departments, along with many white citizens, consider them highly dangerous, but some civic officials disagree. New York City Human Rights Commissioner William Booth, for example, credits members of the Black Panther Party with helping "relieve tensions in the community." In any case, they are a force, and their leaders—Cleaver and Huey Newton, the Black Panthers' jailed minister of defense—enjoy rising support among radical young whites as well as in the black ghetto. But Cleaver, even more than Newton, generates the kind of magnetism that creates converts as well as enemies. As Jeff Shero, editor of Rat, *a New York underground newspaper, puts it, "The heroes aren't Tim Leary and Allen Ginsberg anymore; they're Ché Guevara and Eldridge Cleaver."*

But not to everyone. Among opponents of his program and philosophy—in addition to those expectable proponents of the code phrase "law and order"—are many deeply concerned intellectuals, honest liberals and antiviolence workers for racial peace. Cleaver is accused of advocating justice via violence, which these people see as a tragic and dangerous contradiction. More importantly, perhaps, they have charged him with intensifying racial hostilities to the detriment of black Americans by alienating white sympathy and support for the cause of black equality and with providing racists—in and out of uniform—with precisely the provocation that can lend legal legitimacy to suppression. That he has also alienated many dedicated integrationists is a fact he would be among the last to deny.

There are many, however—integrationists and otherwise—who regard Cleaver as far more than a revolutionary gang leader. By many in the intellectual community, he is considered a writer and theoretician of major dimensions. In the fall of 1968, he was invited to give a series of lectures at the University of California in Berkeley—precipitating a fierce conflict about his "moral character" between the university on the one hand and its board of regents, Governor Reagan and the state legislature on the other. The chief reasons for this brouhaha: Cleaver's leadership of the Panthers and his 1968 book of explosive essays on the American racial dilemma, Soul on Ice, *which has sold more than 1,400,000 copies. Among the many laudatory reviews was that of Richard Gilman in* The New Republic, *who called it "a spiritual and intellectual autobiography that stands at the exact resonant center of the new Negro writing . . . a book for which we have to make room—but not on the shelves we have already built."*

"If we don't get justice in the courts, we'll get it in the streets. If atrocities against us continue unpunished, if police aggression is not stopped, more and more blacks may have to fight gunfire with gunfire."

"Our basic demand is for proportionate participation in the real power that runs this country—decision-making power concerning all legislation, all appropriations, foreign policy—every area of life."

"What can whites do?, Be Americans. Stand up for liberty. Stand up for justice. Stand up for the underdog; that's supposed to be the American way. Make this really the home of the free."

This sudden thrust to national prominence has been achieved by a man who has spent most of his adult life in jail. Born in Little Rock in 1935, Cleaver grew up in the Los Angeles ghetto. After several convictions for possession of marijuana, he was sentenced in 1958 to a fourteen-year term for assault with intent to kill and rape. By the time he was paroled in December 1966, Huey Newton and Bobby Seale had formed the Black Panther Party in Oakland. Cleaver soon joined them. Since then, he has taken time out to write not only his book but several articles in Ramparts, of which he is a senior editor, and to campaign in 1968 for the Presidency as the nominee of the largely white Peace and Freedom Party. The leading supporter, among black militants, of coalition with white radical groups, he propounded his racial credo in Soul on Ice: "If a man like Malcolm X could change and repudiate racism, if I myself and other former Muslims can change, if young whites can change, then there is hope for America. . . . The sins of the fathers are visited upon the heads of the children—but only if the children continue in the evil deeds of the fathers."

Aside from his unequivocal call, as the candidate of the Peace and Freedom Party, for immediate U. S. withdrawal from Vietnam and immediate reform of American social institutions that perpetuate the disenfranchisement of much of its nonwhite population, Cleaver has also become the most articulate and controversial spokesman for the Black Panthers—and, as we went to press with the December 1968 issue of Playboy, the only one free to talk. Bobby Seale was then on restrictive probation after conviction on a gun-law violation, and Huey Newton had, at that time, been in jail since October 1967, when an encounter between him and two Oakland policemen resulted in the death of one of them.

Cleaver, too, has been back in jail. A gun battle between Panthers and the Oakland police in April 1967 ended with the death of Panther Bobby Hutton and the wounding of Cleaver, whose parole was immediately revoked. But after two months in jail—and backed with demands for his release by such influential supporters as James Baldwin, Ossie Davis, Marlon Brando, Jules Feiffer, Tom Hayden, LeRoi Jones, Norman Mailer, Susan Sontag and the widow of Malcolm X—he was set free at a habeas corpus hearing, where the presiding judge accused the state of California of having rescinded Cleaver's parole because of his political views. Still pending against Cleaver, however, are charges of assault on a police officer and assault with intent to kill. When the California Adult Authority announced its intention of having Cleaver's parole revoked again, Playboy dispatched Nat Hentoff to interview the embattled activist in San Francisco before he was once again incommunicado behind bars.

When he returned to New York with the longest and most

searching interview Cleaver has ever granted, Hentoff wrote of his subject, "Having corresponded briefly with him while he was in prison a few years ago and having read Soul on Ice, *I was aware of the probing, resourceful quality of Cleaver's mind. But I wondered if some of the flamboyant rhetoric of his public statements since he'd become prominent indicated a change in the man—his constant use of the word pigs to describe police, for example; the incendiary tone of a recent Yippie-Panther manifesto, signed by Cleaver and three leaders of the white student group, which in effect declared war on the establishment; and statements like 'The cities of America have tasted the first flames of revolution. But a hotter fire rages in the hearts of black people today: total liberty for black people or total destruction for America.' Was he turning into a demagog? Did he still believe in the possibility of alliances with whites?*

"We met in the office of his white attorney, Charles Garry. Present were two Panthers and Cleaver's wife, Kathleen, also active in the Black Panther Party. The twenty-five-year-old daughter of a college professor who is now deputy director of the Foreign Service Mission to the Philippines, Kathleen is as militant and as radical as her husband. The bearded Cleaver, in black leather jacket, black pants and an open shirt, was initially reserved and preoccupied. There was legal strategy to discuss with Garry about both Huey Newton's and his own cases, and he was also weighing a number of lucrative offers from publishers for an advance on his next book.

"Leaving the office, he and Kathleen drove me through the black Fillmore district of San Francisco, where he was frequently recognized and waved at—particularly by the young. Dropping Kathleen off, Cleaver and I went on to a white friend's house overlooking San Francisco Bay. 'I need a place to get away from the phones,' he told me. 'Nobody's got the number here.' Nonetheless, our conversation was occasionally interrupted by calls for him. 'Damn,' he said, 'you can never get away.'

"We started talking in the afternoon and continued late into the night. Cleaver gradually relaxed, but not entirely. A tautness remained, a reflection of the constant tension under which he works. He speaks softly and deliberately, taking time to think before answering. Physically, he projects strength; he has a boxer's build and there's the clear impression that he could handle himself in any reasonably equal encounter. But he is also very much an intellectual. I remembered, as we talked, the conversations I'd had with Malcolm X; both were intrigued with ideas and their ramifications, but both were impatient with theoretical formulations that did not have application to immediate reality.

"As the interview went on, I was more and more impressed with Eldridge Cleaver—with the quality of his mind, with the

depth of his determination, with the totality of his commitment to his role as a leader in the new stage of the black movement for liberation. It was on the question of this new stage and the new kind of leadership he's convinced it requires that our interview began."

Playboy: You have written that "a new black leadership with its own distinct style and philosophy will now come into its own, to center stage. Nothing can stop this leadership from taking over, because it is based on charisma, has the allegiance and support of the black masses, is conscious of its self and its position and is prepared to shoot its way to power if the need arises." As one who is increasingly regarded as among the pivotal figures in this new black leadership, how do you distinguish the new breed from those—such as Roy Wilkins and Whitney Young—most Americans consider the established Negro spokesmen?

Cleaver: The so-called leaders you name have been willing to work within the framework of the rules laid down by the white establishment. They have tried to bring change within the system as it now is—without violence. Although Martin Luther King was the leader-spokesman for the nonviolent theme, all the rest condemn violence, too. Furthermore, all are careful to remind everybody that they're Americans as well as "Negroes," that the prestige of this country is as important to them as it is to whites. By contrast, the new black leadership identifies first and foremost with the best interests of the masses of *black* people, and we don't care about preserving the dignity of a country that has no regard for ours. We don't give a damn about any embarrassments we may cause the United States on an international level. And remember, I said the *masses* of black people. That's why we oppose Adam Clayton Powell. He's not militant enough and he represents only the black middle class, not the masses.

Playboy: Since you consider yourself one of these new leaders representing the masses, what are your specific goals?

Cleaver: Our basic demand is for proportionate participation in the real power that runs this country. This means that black people must have part of the decision-making power concerning all legislation, all appropriations of money, foreign policy—every area of life. We cannot accept anything less than that black people, like white people, have the best lives technology is able to offer at the present time. Black people know what's going on. They're aware of this country's productivity and they want in on the good life.

Playboy: So far—apart from your willingness to resort to violence in achieving that goal—you haven't proposed anything specific or different from the aims of the traditional Negro leadership.

Cleaver: OK, the best way to be specific is to list the ten points of the Black Panther Party. They make clear that we are not willing to accept the rules of the white establishment. One: We want freedom; we want power to determine the destiny of our black communities. Two: We want full employment for our people. Three: We want housing fit for the shelter of human beings. Four: We want all black men to be exempt from military service. Five: We want decent education for black people —education that teaches us the true nature of this decadent, racist society and that teaches young black brothers and sisters their rightful place in society, for if they don't know their place in society and the world, they can't relate to anything else. Six: We want an end to the robbery of black people in their own community by white-racist businessmen. Seven: We want an immediate end to police brutality and murder of black people. Eight: We want all black men held in city, county, state and Federal jails to be released, because they haven't had fair trials; they've been tried by all-white juries, and that's like being a Jew tried in Nazi Germany. Nine: We want black people accused of crimes to be tried by members of their peer group—a peer being one who comes from the same economic, social, religious, historical and racial community. Black people, in other words, would have to compose the jury in any trial of a black person. And ten: We want land, we want money, we want housing, we want clothing, we want education, we want justice, we want peace.

Playboy: Peace? But you've written that "the genie of black revolutionary violence is here."

Cleaver: Yes, but put that into context. I've said that war will come only if these basic demands are not met. Not just a race war, which in itself would destroy this country, but a guerrilla resistance movement that will amount to a second Civil War, with thousands of white John Browns fighting on the side of the blacks, plunging America into the depths of its most desperate nightmare on the way to realizing the American Dream.

Playboy: How much time is there for these demands to be met before this takes place?

Cleaver: What will happen—and when—will depend on the dynamics of the revolutionary struggle in the black and white communities; people are going to do what they feel they have to do as the movement takes shape and gathers strength. But how long do you expect black people, who are already fed up, to endure the continued indifference of the Federal government to their needs? How long will they endure the continued escalation of police force and brutality? I can't give you an exact answer, but surely they will not wait indefinitely if their demands are not met—particularly since we think that the United States has already decided where its next campaign is going to be after the war in Vietnam is over. We think the government has already picked this new target area, and it's black America. A lot of black people are very uptight about what they see in terms of preparations for the suppression of the black-liberation struggle in this country. We don't work on a timetable, but we do say that the situation is deteriorating rapidly. There have been more and more armed clashes and violent encounters with the police departments that occupy black communities. Who can tell at which point any one of the dozens of incidents that take place every day will just boil over and break out into an irrevocable war? Let me make myself clear. I don't dig violence. Guns are ugly. People are what's beautiful; and when you use a gun to kill someone, you're doing something ugly. But there are two forms of violence: violence directed at you to keep you in your place and violence to defend yourself against that suppression and to win your freedom. If our demands are not met, we will sooner or later have to make a choice between continuing to be victims or deciding to seize our freedom.

Playboy: Hasn't there been at least a modicum of real progress toward meeting some of your demands? Isn't there more involvement in the ghetto by private industry, as in the Bedford-Stuyvesant Restoration Corporation set up in 1966 by the late Senator Kennedy, and similar projects around the country? And aren't a growing number of city administrations, like those in New York and San Francisco, trying to get more community participation in building up ghetto institutions?

Cleaver: We think this is essentially just surface appeasement. The establishment believes that if it can keep a certain number of the most militant black people in each community pacified, large-scale disorders can be prevented. Small disorders they think they can deal with. But we consider this a deceitful approach that will not buy off the masses of black people as they become fully awakened to the fact that these programs are palliatives—though there's no denying that some have already been bought off. In San Francisco, one of the potentially strongest chapters of the Black Panther Party was growing in Hunters Point. But the mayor, Joseph Alioto, went in and started buying gas stations and giving some of the leaders there little handouts. He virtually destroyed the revolutionary morale of the people in Hunters Point by pumping small amounts of money into the area and by promises of more. Hell, Alioto even offered the Oakland Panthers some money and me a television show if we'd soften our demands. We turned him down.

Playboy: But other black militants, such as the leaders of CORE, are working now for black capitalism. They even helped draft a bill introduced in Congress last summer to set up neighborhood-controlled corporations. Federal funds would be channeled through those corporations and private firms would be given tax incentives to set up businesses in black neighborhoods—businesses that would eventually be turned over to ghetto residents through the corporations.

Cleaver: I know. It's all part of a big move across the country to convince black people that this way, they can finally get into the economic system. But we don't feel it's going to work, because it won't go far enough and deep enough to give the masses of black people real community control of all their institutions. Remember how the War on Poverty looked on paper and how it worked out? You may recall that of all the organizations around then, it was CORE that rushed in most enthusiastically to embrace that delusion; in some cities, they formed a large part of the staff. But they didn't have the decisive control, and that's where it's at. They can call these new devices "community" corporations, but those private firms from the outside can always pull out and Congress can always cut down on the Federal funds they put in, just as happened in the War on Poverty.

Fewer and fewer black people are allowing themselves now to be sucked in by all of these games. A man finally reaches a point where he sees he's been tricked over and over again, and then he moves for ultimate liberation. But for the masses to achieve that, they will have to be organized so that they can make their collective weight felt, so that they themselves make the final decisions in their communities—from control of the police department to command over all social and economic programs that have to do with them. The struggle we're in now is on two levels—getting people together locally to implement our demands and organizing black people nationally into a unified body. We want black people to be represented by leaders of their choice who, with the power of the masses behind them, will be able to go into the political arena, set forth the desires and needs of black people and have those desires and needs acted upon.

Playboy: But we repeat—isn't this already happening—at least on a small scale? There's a black mayor of Cleveland, Carl Stokes, and a black mayor of Gary, Richard Hatcher.

Cleaver: You're talking about black personalities, not about basic changes in the system. There is a large and deepening layer of black people in this country who cannot be tricked anymore by having a few black faces put up front. Let me make this very clear. We are demanding structural changes in society, and that means a real redistribution of power, so that we have control over our own lives. Having a black mayor in the present situation doesn't begin to accomplish that. And this is a question of more than breaking out of poverty. I know there are a lot of people in this country, particularly in urban ghettos, who are going hungry, who are deprived on all levels; but, obviously, it's not a matter of rampant famine. The people we deal with in the Black Panther Party are not literally dying of hunger; they're not going around in rags. But they are people who are tired of having their lives controlled and manipulated by outsiders and by people hostile to them. They're moving into a psychological and spiritual awareness of oppression, and they won't sit still for any more of it. Where we are now is in the final stages of a process with all our cards on the table. We've learned how to play cards; we know the game and we're just not going to be tricked anymore. That's what seems so difficult to get across to people.

Playboy: Is it a trick, however, when Senator Eugene McCarthy, among others, says that since more and more industry and, therefore, jobs, are moving out to the suburbs, more blacks will have to move there, too, with accompanying desegregation of housing in the suburbs and massive funds for improved transportation facilities? Isn't that a sincere analysis of a current trend?

Cleaver: We feel that a lot of these attempts to relocate black people are essentially hostile moves to break up the concentration of blacks, because in that concentration of numbers, we have potential political power. We didn't choose to be packed into ghettos, but since that's where we are, we're not going to get any real power over our lives unless we use what we have—our strength as a bloc. A lot of people in the Republican and Democratic parties are worried about all this potential black voting power in the cities; that's why, under the guise of bettering the conditions of black people, they're trying to break us up.

Playboy: But wouldn't many blacks have higher incomes and live better if they could be integrated into the suburbs?

Cleaver: I emphasize again that until black people as a whole gain power, it's not a question of where you are geographically if you're black; it's a question of where you are psychologically. No matter where you place black people under present conditions, they'll still be powerless, still subject to the whims and decisions of the white political and economic apparatus. That's why we've got to get together and stay together—especially with the country and the Congress getting more conservative politically every day, with police forces amassing more and more arms—arms on a scale to fit an army. That's why I say the situation is deteriorating rapidly—and why I'm also far from certain that the conflict between us and those who run the system can be solved short of a civil and guerrilla war.

Playboy: If this civil and guerrilla war does take place, on what do you base your assertion that there will be "thousands of white John Browns fighting on the side of the blacks"?

Cleaver: Because we recognize that there are a lot of white people in this country who want to see virtually a new world dawn here in North America. In the Bay Area alone, there are thousands of whites who have taken fundamental stands on certain issues, particularly on our demand to free Huey Newton. A person who can relate to that, who can move himself to understand the issues involved, is a person who has begun on a path of essential commitment. Many of these people have broken with the establishment by confronting the establishment. As a situation develops in which hostilities may increase to the point of war, they will have to make a decision on which way they want to move. A certain number of them can be expected to draw back and throw their hand in, but we think there is a hard core of whites, particularly young whites, who are very alarmed at the course this country is taking. They recognize that more than freedom for blacks is at issue; their *own* freedom is at stake. They've learned this at the hands of brutal police in many, many demonstrations, including what happened at the Democratic Convention in Chicago. They've been beaten, Maced, teargassed. They themselves have now experienced what's been happening to black people for so long, and they are prepared to draw the line. Previously, they recognized abstractly that this kind of suppression takes place in black communities, but they never thought it could be done to them. They are turning into a revolutionary force, and that's why we believe the Black Panthers can enter into coalitions with them as equal partners.

Playboy: When and if it comes to the possibility of large-scale violence, won't most of these essentially middle-class whites—even those you call the hard core—retreat?

Cleaver: You have to realize how deep the radicalization of young whites can become as the agents of repression against both them and us intensify their efforts. It's inevitable that the police, in order to suppress black militants, will also have to try to destroy the base of their support in the white community. When they arrest a black leader of the liberation struggle, they will also have to deal with the protests and the exposure of what they've done in certain white communities, and as they do, they will radicalize more whites. The forces of repression can no longer move just against black people. They cannot, let us say, put black people in concentration camps and simultaneously allow whites who are just as passionately involved in the liberation struggle to run around loose. There are already a lot of whites who will go to any lengths to aid their black comrades. We know this. Certainly, they must be a minority at this time, but the police, the pigs, are our best organizers for additional allies. Unwittingly, by their brutality against whites as well as blacks, they are going to keep helping us recruit more white allies who will not retreat, and that's why I don't have any doubts that we'll have thousands of new white John Browns in the future, if it comes to the point of mass revolt.

You see, whites in America really love this country. Especially young white idealists. They've always been taught that they're living in the freest country in the world, the fairest country in the world, a country that will always move to support the underdog. So when they see their government murdering people in Vietnam, the outrage flowing from that realization is immeasurable. They don't storm the Pentagon immediately; but at a distance, they begin to focus on what's really going on. People go through various stages of shock after a first awareness; they get angry, then they get uptight and finally they want to do something to change what's going on. A lot of whites have already made a correct analysis of the situation. They're aware that the government of their country has been usurped and is in the hands of a clique, what Eisenhower called the military-industrial complex, which manages the political system for the protection of the large corporations. Having made that analysis, there are enough people right now, I believe, who are so outraged at the way things are going that they would move against this usurpation if they knew how.

Playboy: And how is that?

Cleaver: That's the issue and the dilemma—how to find a revolutionary mode of moving in this most complicated of all situations. The people who supported McCarthy found out *that* wasn't the way. I'm not saying we, the Black Panthers, have the answer, either, but we're trying to find the way. One thing we do know is that we have to bring a lot of these loosely connected elements of opposition into an organizational framework. You can't have an amorphous thing pulling in all directions and realistically call it a "revolutionary movement." That's why we're organizing among blacks and intend the Panthers to be *the* black-national movement. At the same time, it makes no sense to holler for freedom for the black community and have no interconnection with white groups who also recognize the need for fundamental change. It's by coalition that we intend to bring together all the elements for liberation—by force, if all the alternatives are exhausted.

Playboy: Are they exhausted, in your opinion?

Cleaver: Not yet, but time is running out. It may still be possible, barely possible, to revolutionize this society—to get fundamental structural changes—without resorting to civil war, but only if we get enough power before it's too late.

Playboy: If you fail in this last effort to effect wholesale social reform without violence, what makes you think you'll have any more success in an armed insurrection? Considering the enormously superior force and firepower of police and troops—and their apparent massive support among whites—is it realistic to believe that you can sustain a guerrilla war?

Cleaver: Guerrilla warfare has traditionally been conceived and developed to deal with exactly this kind of situation—the presence of massive occupying forces on the one hand and the existence, on the other hand, of sizable numbers of people who are not going to confront those forces full-face but will strike swiftly at times and places of their own choosing. Works on guerrilla warfare have been widely circulated, and a lot of people understand that it doesn't take millions of people to undermine the stability of the American economic system in that way. That's what's at stake—the stability of the system. Of course, there will be tragedies, if it comes to guerrilla warfare. On the individual level, people will suffer, people will be killed. But on the mass level, more and more will be educated. It is the government itself that will become the chief agent of this kind of education, for the thrust now is unmistakably toward increasing repression. That creates an endless chain of suspicion; everyone in dissent, black or white, becomes suspect. And if the government intensifies the suppression of dissent, it cannot help but eventually become totalitarian. It creates and implements its own domino theory to the point where there won't even be lip service paid anymore to individual civil liberties for black *or* white.

Playboy: Police and Federal agencies have shown great skill in infiltrating radical movements—including the Panthers. If conditions became such that you decided guerrilla warfare was the only alternative, isn't it likely that your group and all its potential allies—with or without the help of black veterans—would be instantly neutralized from within, because the government would know every move you planned?

Cleaver: As for the Panthers, we have always worked on the assumption that we're under constant surveillance and have long been infiltrated. But we figure this is something you just have to live with. In any case, the destruction of a particular organization will not destroy the will to freedom among any oppressed people. Nor will it destroy the certainty that they'll act to win it. Sure, we try to take precautions to make sure we're not including hostile elements in our organization, but we don't spend all our time worrying about it. If we go under—and that could easily be done with police frame-ups right now—there'll be others to take our place.

Playboy: Have you considered the possibility that you could be wrong about the chances of waging a successful guerrilla war? Don't you run the risk that all your efforts toward that end—even if they don't escalate beyond rhetoric—could invite a massive wave of repression that would result in a black bloodbath and turn the country's ghettos into concentration camps?

Cleaver: It seems to me a strange assumption that black people could just be killed or cooped up into concentration camps and that would be the end of it. This isn't the 1930s. We're not going to play Jews. The whole world is different now from what it was then. Not only would black people resist, with the help of white people, but we would also have the help of those around the world who are just waiting for some kind of extreme crisis within this country so that they can move for their own liberation from American repression abroad. This government does not have unlimited forces of repression; it can't hold the whole world down—not at home *and* abroad. Eventually, it will be able to control the racial situation here only by ignoring its military "commitments" overseas. That might stop *our* movement for a while, but think what would be happening in Latin America, Asia and Africa. In that event, there would be a net gain for freedom in the world. We see our struggle as inextricably bound up with the struggle of all oppressed peoples, and there is no telling what sacrifices we in this country may have to make before that struggle is won.

Playboy: Do you think you have any real chance of winning that struggle—even without government repression—as long as the majority of white Americans, who outnumber blacks ten to one, remain hostile or indifferent to black aspirations? According to the indications of recent public-opinion surveys, they deplore even *nonviolent* demonstrations on behalf of civil rights.

Cleaver: At the present stage, the majority of white people are indifferent and complacent simply because their own lives have remained more or less intact and as remote from the lives of most blacks as the old French aristocracy was from "the great unwashed." It's disturbing to them to hear about Hough burning, Watts burning, the black community in Newark burning. But they don't really understand why it's happening, and they don't really care, as long as *their* homes and *their* places of work—or the schools to which they send their children—aren't burning, too. So for most whites, what's happened up to now has been something like a spectator sport. There may be a lot more of them than there are of us, but they're not really involved, and there are millions and millions of black people in this country who *are*—more than the census shows. Maybe 30,000,000, maybe more. A lot of black people never get counted in the census. It's not going to be easy to deal with that large a number, and it won't be possible to indefinitely limit the burning to black neighborhoods—even with all the tanks, tear gas, riot guns, paddy wagons and fire trucks in this country. But if it does come to massive repression of blacks, I don't think the majority of whites are going to either approve it or remain silent. If a situation breaks out in which soldiers are hunting down and killing black people obviously and openly, we don't think the majority will accept that for long. It could go on for a while, but at some point, we think large numbers of whites would become so revolted that leaders would arise in the white community and offer other solutions. So we don't accept the analysis that we're doomed because we're in a minority. We don't believe that the majority in this country would permit concentration camps and genocide.

Playboy: Not even in the midst of large-scale violence in which white neighborhoods were being burned and looted, white children being endangered?

Cleaver: Under those circumstances, it might be very possible for the power structure to capitalize sufficiently on white fear and anger to justify such atrocities even against those not involved in the violence. But there would still be elements in the white community that would resist massive and indiscriminate repression of all blacks, and once the immediate causes of fear and anger were over, I believe the majority would begin to protest and eventually move against mass imprisonment and genocide. I'm not saying most white people don't have racist attitudes. They do, because the values taught in this country inevitably result in whites' having racist attitudes. But I think a lot of whites are made racists against their essential humanity and without their conscious knowledge. And they get very uncomfortable when their actions are identified as racist, even by their own Kerner Commission. They would really be put on the spot if a large-scale confrontation took place between black people as a whole and white people as a whole. In that event, a lot of white people could not endure seeing themselves as part of the totalitarian apparatus. They would make it very clear that they opposed it and they would work to stop it—not only because of their essential humanity but because it would be in their own self-interest. The United States has huge interests to safeguard around the world, and most whites would recognize how seriously those interests would be jeopardized if there was total suppression of blacks domestically. That's another reason why the fact of our numerical minority doesn't mean we're destined to lose in our struggle for freedom. It doesn't take into account the international context of the black-liberation movement here. If this country's power structure was really free to totally, brutally and openly suppress black people at home, it would have done so a long time ago. So we have more going for us than our numbers, and our numbers are getting larger.

Playboy: Suppose you're right in claiming that most whites, for whatever reason, would not support massive repression of blacks in this country. These same whites, however, don't want black violence, either—but as you point out, most don't fully grasp the dimensions of the injustices against which that violence is a rebellion, nor do they understand why it continues in the wake of several milestone civil-rights laws and Supreme Court decisions. The familiar question is "What more do they want?" How would you answer it?

Cleaver: I can only answer with what Malcolm X said. If you've had a knife in my back for four hundred years, am I supposed to thank you for pulling it out? Because that's all those laws and decisions have accomplished. The very least of your responsibility now is to compensate me, however inadequately, for centuries of degradation and disenfranchisement by granting peacefully—before I take them forcefully—the same rights and opportunities for a decent life that you've taken for granted as an American birthright. This isn't a request but a *demand,* and the ten points of that demand are set down with crystal clarity in the Black Panther Party platform.

Playboy: Many would doubt that you're serious about some of them. Point four, for instance: "We want all black men to be exempt from military service."

Cleaver: We couldn't be *more* serious about that point. As a colonized people, we consider it absurd to fight the wars of the mother country against other colonized peoples, as in Vietnam right now. The conviction that no black man should be forced to fight for the system that's suppressing him is growing among more and more black people, outside the Black Panther Party as well as in it. And as we can organize masses of black people behind that demand for exemption, it will have to be taken seriously.

Playboy: Are you equally serious about point eight, which demands that all black prisoners held in city, county, state and Federal jails be released because they haven't had fair trials; and about point nine, which demands that black defendants be tried by all-black juries?

Cleaver: We think the day will come when these demands, too, will receive serious attention, because they deserve it. Take point eight. All the social sciences—criminology, sociology, psychology, economics—point out that if you subject people to deprivation and inhuman living conditions, you can predict that they will rebel against those conditions. What we have in this country is a system organized against black people in such a way that many are forced to rebel and turn to forms of behavior that are called criminal, in order to get the things they need to survive. Consider the basic contradiction here. You subject people to conditions that make rebellion inevitable and then you punish them for rebelling. Now, under those circumstances, does the black convict owe a debt to society or does society owe a debt to the black convict? Since the social, economic and political system is so rigged against black people, we feel the burden of the indictment should rest on the system and not on us. Therefore, black people should not be confined in jails and prisons for rebelling against that system—even though the rebellion might express itself in some unfortunate ways. And this idea can be taken further, to apply also to those white people who have been subjected to a disgusting system for so long that they resort to disgusting forms of behavior. This is part of our fundamental critique of the way this society, under its present system of organization, molds the character of its second-class citizens.

Playboy: Have you considered the consequences to society of opening the prisons and setting all the inmates free? Their behavior may in one sense be society's fault, but they're still criminals.

Cleaver: We don't feel that there's any black man or any white man in any prison in this country who could be compared in terms of criminality with Lyndon Johnson. No mass murderer in any penitentiary in America or in any other country comes anywhere close to the thousands and thousands of deaths for which Johnson is responsible.

Playboy: Do you think that analogy is valid? After all, Johnson has been waging a war, however misguidedly, in the belief that his cause is just.

Cleaver: Many murderers feel exactly the same way about *their* crimes. But let me give you another example: Compare the thieves in our prisons with the big-businessmen of this country, who are in control of a system that is depriving millions of people of a decent life. These people—the men who run the government and the corporations—are much more dangerous than the guy who walks into a store with a pistol and robs somebody of a few dollars. The men in control are robbing the entire world of billions and billions of dollars.

Playboy: *All* the men in control?

Cleaver: That's what I said; and they're not only stealing money, they're robbing people of life itself. When you talk about criminals, you have to recognize the vastly different degrees of criminality.

Playboy: Surely no criminality, proved in a court of law, should go unpunished.

Cleaver: As you know, the poor and the black in this country don't seem to make out as well as the rich and the white in our courts of "justice." I wonder why.

Playboy: You still haven't answered our question about the social consequences of releasing all those now behind bars.

Cleaver: Those who are now in prison could be put through a process of real rehabilitation before their release—not caged like animals, as they are now, thus guaranteeing that they'll be hardened criminals when they get out if they weren't when they went in. By rehabilitation I mean they would be trained for jobs that would not be an insult to their dignity, that would give them some sense of security, that would alow them to achieve some brotherly connection with their fellow man. But for this kind of rehabilitation to happen on a large scale would entail the complete reorganization of society, not to mention the prison system. It would call for the teaching of a new set of ethics, based on the principle of cooperation, as opposed to the presently dominating principle of competition. It would require the transformation of the entire moral fabric of this country into a way of being that would make these former criminals feel more obligated to their fellow man than they do now. The way things are today, however, what reasons do these victims of society have for feeling an obligation to their fellow man? I look with respect on a guy who has walked the streets because he's been unable to find a job in a system that's rigged against him, but doesn't go around begging and instead walks into a store and says, "Stick 'em up, motherfucker!" I prefer that man to the Uncle Tom who does nothing but just shrink into himself and accept any shit that's thrown into his face.

Playboy: Would you feel that way if it were *your* store that got held up?

Cleaver: That's inconceivable; I wouldn't own a store. But for the sake of argument, let's say I did. I'd still respect the guy who came in and robbed me more than the panhandler who mooched a dime from me in the street.

Playboy: But would you feel he was *justified* in robbing you because of his disadvantaged social background?

Cleaver: Yes, I would—and this form of social rebellion is on the rise. When I went to San Quentin in 1958, black people constituted about 30 percent of the prison population. Recently, I was back at San Quentin, and the blacks are now in the majority. There's an incredible number of black people coming in with each new load of prisoners. Moreover, I've talked to a lot of other people who've been in different prisons, and the percentage of black inmates there, too, is indisputably climbing. And within that growing number, the percentage of *young* black prisoners is increasing most of all. Youngsters from the ages of eighteen to twenty-three are clearly in the majority of the new people who come to prison. The reason is that for a lot of black people, including the young, jobs are almost nonexistent, and the feeling of rebellion is particularly powerful among the young. Take a guy who was four years old in 1954, when the Supreme Court decision on school desegregation was handed down, a decision that was supposed to herald a whole new era. Obviously, it didn't, but it did accelerate agitation and unrest. So this guy, who was four then, has had a lifetime of hearing grievances articulated very sharply but of seeing nothing changed. By the time he's eighteen or nineteen, he's very, very uptight. He's very turned off to the system and he has it in his mind that he's justified in moving against so unjust a system in any way he sees fit.

Playboy: Can that be the whole explanation for the growing number of young black prisoners? Are they all in conscious rebellion against the white power structure?

Cleaver: That's not the whole explanation, of course, but it would be a mistake to underestimate that rising mood of rebellion. Whatever their conscious motivation, though, every one of them is in prison because of the injustice of society itself. White people are able to get away with a lot of things black people can't begin to get away with; cops are much quicker to make busts in black neighborhoods. And even when they're arrested, whites are ahead because more of them can afford attorneys. A lot of black cats end up in prison solely because they didn't have someone to really present their case in court. They're left with the public defenders, whom prison inmates quite accurately call "penitentiary deliverers." I'll tell you what usually happens. It's the common practice of the police to file ten or so charges on you, and then the public defender comes and says, "Look, we can't beat them all, so the best thing you can do is plead guilty on one count. If you do that, I can get the others dropped." So a black cat is sitting there without real legal help, without any money, and he knows that if he's convicted of all ten counts, he'll get a thousand years. He's in a stupor of confusion and winds up taking the advice of the public defender. He doesn't know the law. He doesn't know how to make legal motions. He doesn't really know what's going on in that courtroom. So he goes along, wakes up in the penitentiary, starts exchanging experiences with other guys who have been through the same mill, and if he wasn't a rebel when he went in, he'll be a revolutionary by the time he gets out.

Playboy: What about your own problems with the law? If you weren't the author of *Soul on Ice*, is it likely that you'd still be in prison?

Cleaver: Certainly. If I had been just another black man, I wouldn't have had a chance in the world of getting out before my maximum sentence was served—especially not me, because I was involved in a lot of the prison politics. You know, the prison authorities consciously create and maintain a certain level of hostility among the various racial groups in prison. There is, for example, a preferential order on jobs; white prisoners get the best ones. And white prisoners do less time than black inmates for similar crimes; in the California prisons, the preferential order is whites, Mexican-Americans and then blacks. There's always been a lot of agitation within the prisons to change that. I was involved in that agitation and, as a result, I was told by members of the Probation Authority that I could just forget about getting out of prison until my entire fourteen-year term was up. It wasn't until I smuggled the manuscript of *Soul on Ice* out of prison and got it into the hands of people who had the book published that the attitude of the prison officials toward me started changing. And even then, it took a whole mobilization of prominent literary figures writing letters to get me out. But now that I'm out, it's starting to work the other way. Because of all the attention that's been focused on me both because of the book and because of my involvement with the Panthers, the state is trying to put me back in prison. You know, I used to think, I really did, that the Probation Authority would be proud of a man who had gone through their system, had gained a few skills while in prison and wasn't following the path of crime and violence he'd been on before he went in. But because I'm engaged in political activity, the Probation Authority would like nothing better than to lock me up again. The only reason they haven't been able to so far is that I'm not entirely powerless now.

Playboy: What happens to the ordinary black inmate who has no special talent that earns him a reputation—and influential supporters—outside of prison?

Cleaver: When I was in the guidance center at San Quentin last spring, I saw a lot of people like that—people I've known for years. Two of them had been in Los Angeles Juvenile Hall with me the first time I was ever arrested—some eighteen years ago. Since then, they had done some time and been paroled, and here they were back in San Quentin on bullshit charges of parole violation. That's a device used all the time to keep sending people back to prison. These guys had done nothing more than have personality clashes with their parole officers, who were empowered to send them back up on their own arbitrary decision. This would never have happened if these guys had had any decent legal help. But neither had anybody outside but their mothers and fathers. And they were just two among hundreds of kids in that guidance center who'd been sent back on parole violations, for no better reason. They hadn't committed felonies; they hadn't done anything that would get the average white man hauled into court. The only conclusion one can draw is that the parole system is a procedure devised primarily for the purpose of running people in and out of jail—most of them black—in order to create and maintain a lot of jobs for the white prison system. In California, which I know best—and I'm sure it's the same in other states—there are thousands and thousands of people who draw their living directly or indirectly from the prison system: all the clerks, all the guards, all the bailiffs, all the people who sell goods to the prisons. They regard the inmates as a sort of product from which they all draw their livelihood, and the part of the crop they keep exploiting most are the black inmates.

Playboy: And one of the ways you propose to solve this problem is by demanding not only that all black people in prisons be released but that all future trials of blacks be judged by all-black juries. Wouldn't the selection of a jury on the basis of color—whatever the motivation—be at variance with the U. S. Constitution?

Cleaver: The Constitution says very little explicitly; it has to be interpreted. Given the racism in this country and the inability of white people to understand what's going on with black people, the only truly just way for a black man to be tried by his peers is for him to have a jury of people who have been victims of the same socioeconomic and political situations *he* has experienced.

Playboy: By the same process of reasoning, wouldn't it follow that a member of the Ku Klux Klan accused of murdering a civil-rights worker should be tried only by an all-white jury of Southern segregationists because only they would have backgrounds similar enough to understand his motivations?

Cleaver: That's pretty much the way it happens, as a matter of fact. But I don't think the majority of whites will be content for too long with that kind of Ku Klux Klan subversion of justice.

My primary concern, in any case, is justice for black people *by* black people; if we can achieve that, then we might be ready to talk about whether blacks and whites could get together in accomplishing real justice across the board. But in our *present* society, the only way the Constitution can mean anything to blacks in terms of justice is for black people to be tried by their black peers.

Playboy: Some might question whether it's fair to talk of justice for blacks, when you write of another kind of justice for whites: "Those savages who perpetrate atrocities against black people are going to be hunted down like the dogs they are and will receive the *justice* that Adolf Eichmann got, the same *justice* that they gave to their innocent victims." If you actually resort to this kind of vigilante violence, won't you be morally indistinguishable from KKK night riders who lynch blacks and bomb black churches?

Cleaver: No, because there is such a thing as justifiable homicide, and I would include in that category every lyncher and church bomber who ever got exonerated by a white-racist jury. If we don't get justice in the courts—for blacks as well as for those who brutalize them—then we'll get it in the streets. If atrocities against us continue not only unpunished but unprevented, if the campaign of aggression by the police and other government forces against us is not stopped, more and more blacks may have to respond as some in Cleveland did last summer—by fighting gunfire with gunfire. One way or another, we are going to have to get justice. It was Thomas Jefferson, after all, who maintained that when society's institutions no longer serve the needs of the people, they must be changed by constitutional means or by revolution. That's at the base of the so-called American tradition; if the people are tyrannized by their government and that government answers their demands for justice by intensifying that tyranny, it is not only their right but their duty to abolish that government and set up another that will extend justice impartially and humanely to all its citizens. This applies even on the local level, and especially to those agencies of the establishment that are charged with the protection of the public. If the police department, for example, has abdicated its function of providing public safety to black people as well as to white, then we feel we have the right to provide for our own safety, even if that means confronting the police department. And if crimes are committed against us by the police, we have the right to defend ourselves and take whatever measures are necessary to prevent further atrocities from being committed against us. And we have the right to insist that perpetrators of past crimes against black people be punished.

Playboy: You've said that the black community is keeping a "death list" of those who are guilty of crimes against black people. Is this true?

Cleaver: The names of murderers, including police officers—pigs—who have gotten off without any penalty after killing black people are all on record. People in each local area know who they are. I myself have a long list of people who I know have done these things. These crimes are so atrocious and have been so well publicized and documented that even if a complete list doesn't exist, it will be a simple matter of research to go back, dig them up and deal with the murderers—if the law doesn't do it for us.

Playboy: You seem to alternate between advocating revolutionary violence and allowing for the possibility of social reform without violence. Which is it going to be?

Cleaver: What happens, as I've said, will depend on the continuing dynamics of the situation. What we're doing now is telling the government that if it does not do its duty, then we will see to it ourselves that justice is done. Again, I can't tell you when we may have to start defending ourselves by violence from continued violence against us. That will depend on what is done against us and on whether real change can be accomplished nonviolently within the system. We'd much rather do it that way, because we don't feel it would be a healthy situation to have even black revolutionaries going around distributing justice. I'd much prefer a society in which we wouldn't have to use—or even carry—guns, but that means the pigs would have to be disarmed, too. In the meantime, as long as this remains an unjust and unsafe society for black people, we're faced with a situation in which our survival is at stake. We will do whatever we must to protect our lives and to redeem the lives of our people—without too much concern for the niceties of a system that is rigged against us.

Playboy: Some black militants say there is an alternative to revolution or capitulation: the formation of a separate black nation within the United States. At a meeting in Detroit last March, a group of black nationalists proposed the creation of a state called New Africa, encompassing all the territory now occupied by Alabama, Georgia, Louisiana, Mississippi and South Carolina. Do you think that's a viable plan?

Cleaver: I don't have any sympathy with that approach, but the Black Panthers feel that it's a proposal black people should be polled on. There have been too many people and too many organizations in the past who claimed to speak for the ultimate destiny of black people. Some call for a new state; some have insisted that black people should go back to Africa. We Black Panthers, on the other hand, don't feel we should speak for all black people. We say that black people deserve an opportunity to record their own national will.

Playboy: Black people have already had a chance to record their will on this subject, according to CBS. A network survey last September revealed that in a poll of black Americans, 5 percent favored formation of a separate black state.

Cleaver: Fuck CBS. I don't trust any polls of black people by whites who are part of the system of oppression. The kind of poll we want to see—the only kind of poll that would have any international legitimacy—is a U.N.-supervised plebiscite throughout the black communities of this country on the question of whether black people want to be integrated into this nation or whether they want to be separated from it, and, if the latter, whether in a separate state or by controlling the communities where they live now.

Playboy: Do you have any reason to believe that the United Nations would consider holding such a plebiscite?

Cleaver: We already know there are a lot of countries in the world that sympathize with the black cause in America and would be willing to support us on this question. As the political situation worsens—as it inevitably must—both domestically and internationally, we feel we will be able to persuade enough nations to place the idea of a plebiscite on the agenda of the General Assembly, just as so many colonized peoples in other parts of the world have been able to do. After all, we're dealing with a black population in this country that outnumbers that of many U.N. member nations. We don't see why we have to remain powerless indefinitely when other formerly colonized peoples have won their freedom and their independence. Another plan we have is to invite U.N. observers to station themselves in the large urban areas so that they can witness the activities of police departments that to us are nothing but occupying armies. We ask this as a colonized people within the mother country.

Playboy: Few, if any, colonized peoples have the support of a contingent of the colonizing power; yet the Black Panthers have formed a working coalition with the Peace and Freedom Party in California—a group that is predominantly white. Isn't there an ideological inconsistency in such a coalition—despite what you've said about the good will and dedication of many sympathetic young whites—at a time when other militant black organizations, such as SNCC, pointedly rejected all white allies as agents of the white power structure?

Cleaver: There is no inconsistency if you don't confuse coalitions with mergers. We believe black people should be in full control of their organizations; the Black Panthers have always been. You may remember that Stokely Carmichael, when he came out for an all-black SNCC, also said that the role of whites was to go into their own communities and organize, so that there could be a basis for eventual coalitions. We've now reached a point where many white people have, in fact, organized in their own communities; therefore, we see no reason to maintain an alienated posture and to refuse to work with such groups.

Playboy: One of the passages in *Soul on Ice* had particular impact on many young white people who felt they had been drummed out of "the movement." You wrote, "There is in America today a generation of white youth that is truly worthy of a black man's respect, and this is a rare event in the foul annals of American history." Having since worked in collaboration with the Peace and Freedom Party, do you still think as highly of the new generation of white youth?

Cleaver: I'm even more convinced it's true than when I wrote those lines. We work with these young people all the time, and we've had nothing but encouraging experiences with them. These young white people aren't hung up battling to maintain the status quo like some of the older people who think they'll become extinct if the system changes. They're adventurous; they're willing to experiment with new forms; they're willing to confront life. And I don't mean only those on college campuses. A lot who aren't in college share with their college counterparts an ability to welcome and work for change.

Playboy: Do you agree with those who feel that this generation of youth is going to "sell out" to the status quo as it moves into middle age?

Cleaver: I expect all of us will become somewhat less resilient as we get into our forties and fifties—if we live that long—and I'm sure that those who come after us will look back on us as being conservative. Even us Panthers. But I don't think this generation will become as rigid as the ones before, and, for that matter, I don't write off all older people right now. There are a lot of older whites and blacks who keep working for change. So there are people over thirty I trust. *I'm* over thirty, and I trust *me*.

Playboy: You speak of trust, and yet there are many young whites —despite what you've said—who wonder if black people are really willing to trust them and to work with them on a basis of mutual respect. Bobby Seale, a Black Panther leader, for instance, told an audience of young whites in New York last spring,

"We hate you white people! And the next time one of you paddies comes up here and accuses me of hating you because of the color of your skin, I will kick you in your ass. We started *out* hating you because of the color of your skin. . . . In school, when a little white liberal walked by, I used to come up with my knife and say, 'Give me your lunch money or I'll cut your guts out.' And he'd give me his lunch money. Pretty soon, I'd say, 'Tomorrow you bring me two dollars.' And the next day he'd bring me two dollars. Because that two dollars was mine. Mine because of four hundred years of racism and oppression. When I take two dollars from you, pig, don't you say nothing." What kind of white person, unless he's a masochist, could form a coalition with black people on this basis?

Cleaver: I heard about that speech. There's been a lot of reaction to it, and it's unfortunate. As I understand it, Bobby had been preceded on that program by LeRoi Jones and a lot of that kind of thing, and maybe Bobby was turned on by all that. I don't know. But I do know Bobby, and if that quote is correct, it does not represent how he really feels—not deep inside. You have to remember that Bobby Seale, with Huey Newton, laid the foundation for the Black Panthers, and it was because of their attitudes that the party has been able to steer clear of getting involved in any of these dead-end racist positions. If you go around and talk to the white people in the Bay Area who have worked with Bobby, you'll find that they know the real Bobby Seale and are not disturbed by what he might have said on one particular occasion. It's even fair to say that a lot of them love Bobby. When that particular speech was made, I was in jail, but I've talked with Bobby about it since, and I don't condemn him for it.

Playboy: As you know, however, there are many who do and who believe he really meant what he said that night. In reaction to his and Jones' remarks, one young white radical wrote in *Rat Subterranean News*, the underground New York biweekly,

> You are denying my humanity and my individuality. Though I am in deepest empathy with you and with all blacks—all people—in their struggle to be free, you are in danger of becoming my enemy. I must revolt against your racism, your scorn of everything white, just as I revolt against the racism of white America. I will not let you put me in a bag. Your enemies and my enemies are the same people, the same institutions. . . . I feel no special loyalty to White, but only Self. I feel no love for the leaders or institutions or culture of this country, but only for individual people, in an ever-growing number, with whom I share love and trust. I deny my whiteness; I affirm my humanity. You are urging your black brothers to see me only as White, in just the same way as we have been raised to see you only as Negro. . . . I don't feel white enough or guilty enough to die joyfully by a bullet from a black man's gun, crying, "Ab-

> solved at last!" And I know that soon *you,* by denying me my me-ness, will become for me just as much an oppressor, just as much an enemy, as the white culture we are both fighting. . . . To remain free, and to transform society, I have to maintain my hard-won differentiation from the mass of white people, and I won't let even a black person, no matter how hard-bent he be on black liberation, squeeze me back into honkiedom. If I have to shoot a black racist one of these days, well, baby, that's part of the struggle.

This rejection of racism has been echoed by many young whites. What's your reaction to it?

Cleaver: I think it's a commendable statement. But there are many whites who do deny the humanity of black people, and I think LeRoi and Bobby were talking about them. If you're white and you don't fall into that bag, though, there is no reason why you should accept that analysis as applying to you. You have to judge people by what they do. Those white people who are still functioning as part of the juggernaut of oppression are, indeed, guilty. But those who place themselves outside the system of oppression, those who struggle against that system, ought not to consider that judgment applied against them. I think when a person has reached the kind of awareness expressed by this cat, he is totally justified in rebelling against the honkie tag. But he ought not to expect some kind of instant recognition by black people that he's "different." You cannot expect black people to make immediate distinctions while blacks themselves are still involved in the total fabric of oppression. Those whites who have freed themselves of the system know who they are, and, by what they do, *we* will get to know who they are.

Playboy: Specifically, what can they do, what must they do, to earn your respect and trust?

Cleaver: There are a whole lot of things they can do. They can organize white people so that together we can go into the halls of government, demand our rights—and get them. They can organize politically and get rid of all the clods and racists in the legislatures around the country. They can help keep the police from rioting. They can help make public servants recognize that they *are* public servants, that the public—black and white—pays their salaries and that they don't own the people and must be responsive to them. What can whites do? Just be Americans, as the rhetoric claims Americans are supposed to be. Just stand up for liberty everywhere. Stand up for justice everywhere—especially right here in their own country. Stand up for the underdog; that's supposed to be the American way. Make this *really* the home of the free. But that will never happen unless they help us conduct a thorough housecleaning of the political and economic arenas. Now is the time for whites to help us get the machinery together, to organize themselves and then form coalitions with black groups and Mexican and Puerto Rican groups that also want to bring about social change—and then act to do just that.

Playboy: What about whites—undoubtedly a much larger number —who are just not revolutionaries but still want to work for positive change?

Cleaver: That's simple, too. Find out which white organizations are for real and join them. Many whites can help educate other whites about the true nature of the system. And they can help black people—in the courts, in the social clubs, in the Congress, in the city councils, in the board rooms—win their demands for justice. The number-one problem right now, as we see it, is that of repression by the police. Whites should become aware of what the police are doing and why the Black Panther Party, to name only one group, has gotten so hung up over this crucial question. It's not only just police brutality and crimes; it's police intimidation of black communities. When we started, it became very clear to us that the reason black people don't come out to meetings, don't join organizations working for real change, is that they're afraid of various forms of retaliation from the police. They're afraid of being identified as members of a militant organization. So we recognized that the first thing we had to do was to expose and deal with the gestapo power of the police. Once we've done that, we can move to mobilize people who will then be free to come out and start discussing and articulating their grievances, as well as proposing various changes and solutions. We are doing that in the Bay Area and in other areas where the Black Panther Party is now active. But there are many places where the police continue to intimidate, and it would be a great help for white people to start their own local organizations or to form local chapters of the Peace and Freedom Party. They could then focus community attention on what the police actually do—as opposed to what the police and the city administrations *claim* they do—and work with black people who are trying to break free. That kind of organized activity is really the only hope for this country.

Playboy: If whites were to do this, wouldn't they have a lot to lose, even if they themselves don't become the victims of police repression? Radicals keep telling them that if they're really going to join in the struggle, they can't go on living as they do now, that they can't expect to continue enjoying the material comforts of a system they intend to confront, that anyone who "breaks free" is going to have to change his entire style of life. Do you agree?

Cleaver: Well, they're certainly going to have to give up those privileges that are based on the oppression and exploitation of other people. Most whites today are in the position of being the recipients of stolen property. This country was *built,* in large part, on the sweat of slaves. The standard of living most white people enjoy today is a direct result of the historical exploitation of blacks, and of the third world, by the imperialist nations, of which America is now the leader. But thanks to technological advances, even if that exploitation were stopped and there were just distribution of wealth abroad and at home, whites wouldn't really have to suffer materially. If the money now used for bombs and airplanes were redirected to build more houses and better schools—as even the white man's Kerner Commission recommended—I can't see how white people would have to make any sacrifices at all. And think of how much more wholesome—and peaceful—a social environment there'd be for everybody. It seems to me the only whites who would be losing anything are those irretrievably committed, emotionally or economically, to the continued subordination of nonwhites. But those whites who are not wedded to exploitation and oppression can only benefit if basic change comes.

Playboy: There are whites who would say that black people have not indicated that they have the determination, the discipline or even the good will to work toward such a goal. As you know, many privately feel that black people, with some exceptions, are lazy, irresponsible, destructive rather than constructive, unable to hold onto jobs, etc., etc. How do you think this problem of noncomprehension and lingering prejudice can be overcome?

Cleaver: Well, insofar as any of these stereotypes seem to have some basis in fact, they're the result of *strategic* forms of behavior by black people. Think about that. I don't see any reason, for instance, why black people should have been knocking themselves out on the plantations. Under slavery, the black man who could find ways to get out of work was really a very wise man. It's no different under the present system of exploitation, a system rigged against black people straight across the board. Why should any black man strive to excel, to better himself, when the system is set up to keep him "in his place"? I think anyone who can beat that system and draw a living from it with the least expenditure of energy is doing the best thing he can do for himself. It's stupid to be a dedicated, hardworking and loyal victim. But if black people were in a situation where their labor had meaning and dignity, where they were really building good lives for themselves and their children, then all this strategic behavior would cease to be functional.

Playboy: That answer might help convince some potential white allies of the viability of a black-white coalition for change. But how do you reconcile such expressions of hope with a statement you wrote for *Ramparts* shortly after the murder of Martin Luther King?

> There is a holocaust coming . . . the war has begun. The violent phase of the black liberation struggle is here, and it will spread. From that shot, from that blood, America will be painted red. Dead bodies will litter the streets and the scenes will be reminiscent of the disgusting, terrifying, nightmarish news reports coming out of Algeria during the height of the general violence right before the final breakdown of the French colonial regime.

If you really believe that, what's the point of talking about black-white coalitions?

Cleaver: Let me emphasize again that I try to be realistic. I keep working for change, in the hope that violence will not be necessary, but I cannot pretend, in the face of the currently deteriorating situation, that a holocaust is not very possible, even likely. Perhaps if enough people recognize how possible it is, they'll work all the harder for the basic changes that can prevent it. Obviously, there have already been dead bodies on the streets since the murder of King, and at some point, there can occur an eruption that will escalate beyond control. But let me also make clear that I do not justify shooting the wrong people. If the holocaust comes, the bodies on the streets would be those of the oppressors: those who control the corporations that profiteer off the poor, that oil the war machine, that traffic with racist nations like South Africa; those who use the economic and military power of the U. S. to exploit and exterminate the disenfranchised in this country and around the world; and, above all, those politicians who use their public trust to kill social reform and perpetuate injustice. The rest are just part of the machinery. They're not making decisions. They're not manipulating the masses. They're being manipulated themselves by the criminals who run the country.

Playboy: And these "criminals" are to be killed if there's a violent revolution?

Cleaver: It seems to be a hallmark of any revolutionary war that the worst culprits are stood up against the wall and executed. There are a lot of people in the category of active oppressor for whom I think execution would be a mild punishment. However, given an ideal situation, it might be possible to incarcerate these people, re-educate them and then allow them back into society, if they're not actually guilty of willful murder. But in the heat of a violent day-to-day struggle, one might not have time to be so fastidious with these people; in that event, anything that's done to them would be all right with me.

Playboy: In everything you say, there are the intertwining themes of vengeance and forgiveness, of violent revolution and nonviolent social reform, and that leads to a good deal of confusion among many whites as to what the Black Panthers are really for. On the one hand, you write of the coming holocaust and of bodies littering the streets. And yet the day before you wrote that article, you were at a junior high school in Oakland, where the black kids had decided to burn down the school in anger at the murder of Dr. King, and you talked them out of it. Similarly, you and other Panthers speak of a black revolutionary generation that has the courage to kill; yet when a group of seventh- and eighth-graders at another Oakland school tried to emulate what they thought the Panthers stood for by turning into a gang and beating up other kids, several Panther leaders went to the school at the invitation of the principal and told the kids they were in the wrong bag. The Panthers' advice was for black youngsters to study hard, so that they could be in a better position to help their brothers. They also told them not to hate whites but to learn to work with them. Which is the *real* Black Panther philosophy?

Cleaver: There is no contradiction between what we say and what we do. We are for responsible action. That's why we don't advocate people going around inventing hostilities and burning down schools and thereby depriving youngsters of a place to learn. What we do advocate is that hostilities in the black community be focused on specific targets. The police are a specific target. As I said before, we are engaged in organizing black communities so that they will have the power to stop the police from wanton harassment and killing of black people. And that also means self-defense, if necessary. Beyond that, it means getting enough power so that we can have autonomous black departments of safety in black communities. We have the courage—and the good sense—to defend ourselves, but we are not about to engage in the kind of random violence that will give the pigs an opportunity to destroy us. We are revolutionary, but that means we're disciplined, that we're working out programs, that we intend to create a radical political machinery in coalition with whites that will uproot this decadent society, transform its politics and economics and build a structure fit to exist on a civilized planet inhabited by *humanized* beings.

Playboy: You say the police are a prime target for Panther hostility. Is this, perhaps, because the reverse is also true? Police departments in all the cities in which the Panthers have organized claim that your group is a public menace—engaged in beatings, shakedowns, thefts, shootings, fire-bombings and other criminal activities.

Cleaver: Who are the criminals? I know about these rumors of what Panthers are supposed to be doing, but that's all they are—false reports spread by racist cops. They'd like the public to forget that it was Black Panthers in Brooklyn who were attacked by off-duty *police* outside a courtroom last September. Who were the criminals there? And who shot up the Black Panther office in Oakland in a drunken orgy, riddling pictures of Huey Newton and me—and a picture of Bobby Hutton, whom they had already killed? Two pigs from the Oakland Police Department. Of course, they're going to spread these false rumors about us; it's one of the ways they're trying to destroy us before we destroy them with the truth about their own lawlessness.

Playboy: Granted there have been conflicts between the Panthers and the police, but aren't you exaggerating their intent when you claim, as you did recently, that they're out to "systematically eliminate our leadership"?

Cleaver: Not in the least. We are a great threat to the police and to the whole white power structure in Alameda County and in Oakland, where the Panthers were born. The police are the agents of the power structure, in trying to destroy us. Let me give you the background. When Bobby Seale and Huey Newton organized the Black Panther Party in October 1966, they initiated armed black patrols. Each car, which had four men, would follow the police around, observing them. When police accosted a citizen on the street and started doing something wrong to him, the patrol would be there as witnesses and to tell the person being mistreated what his rights were. In this way, the Panthers focused community attention on the police and the people learned they didn't have to submit to the kind of oppressive, arbitrary brutality that had been directed against the black people in Oakland for a long time.

When the Panthers started to educate the community, those in power were afraid that blacks would go on to organize and exercise real political power. And the police were told to prevent this. They tried to do this first by multiple arrests. Anyone known to be a Panther would be rousted on ridiculous charges that couldn't stand up in court but that led to our having to spend a lot of money on bail and legal fees. That didn't work. They couldn't intimidate us. Then in October 1967, they finally got Huey Newton into a position where a shoot-out occurred. Huey was wounded, a cop was killed and another was wounded. Murder charges were filed against Huey; he was eventually convicted and sentenced to two to fifteen years, and that case is now on appeal. After the shoot-out and the arrest of Huey, the whole

Black Panther Party became involved in mobilizing community awareness of the political aspects of that case.

We had such great effect in that effort that the police tried even harder to stifle us. They moved against just about everyone who had taken an active part in speaking and mobilizing for Huey. To give you some examples, on January 15 of this year, our national captain, David Hilliard, was arrested while passing out leaflets at Oakland Tech. The next day, police broke down the door of my apartment and searched it without a warrant. On February 5, a Panther and his girlfriend were arrested for "disturbing the peace" after a rally at which Dr. Spock had spoken. They were beaten in jail. On February 24, Panther Jimmy Charley approached a policeman who was assaulting a black person. He questioned the officer and was immediately arrested and charged with "resisting arrest." On February 25, at 3:30 in the morning, police broke down the door of Bobby Seale's home. Again, there was no warrant. During the third and fourth weeks of February, there was a rash of arrests of black men either in the Panthers or identified with them. And on and on. None of the charges ever made it to court.

Playboy: What about the widely publicized shooting of April sixth, in which seventeen-year-old Black Panther Bobby Hutton was killed and two others, including yourself, were wounded? The official version has been circulated in the daily newspapers. Can you give your account of what happened?

Cleaver: Certain points I can't discuss, because I don't want to alert the prosecution to what we're going to bring out in court, but I'll give you the basic details. April sixth was a Saturday. We were going to have a barbecue picnic the next day—a black-community picnic in Oakland. We'd been leafleting the community and driving around in sound trucks, urging people to attend the picnic. And that night, we were involved in getting the food together—cooking the meat, picking up potatoes for potato salad, and all that. During the preceding days, we'd been having continuous trouble with the Oakland Police Department about the picnic. They tried to prevent our getting a permit to hold it, and although we got it after three or four days, there were severe restrictions on what we could do—no political speeches, no leafleting, things like that. This harassment and interference with our constitutional rights was nothing new. It happened with all the fund-raising events we planned. The police knew about them immediately and always started a mass of arrests, so that whatever money we'd raise would be drained off in bail and legal fees.

Anyway, this picnic was especially important to us, because we badly needed money for the Huey Newton Defense Fund and for political campaigns; Bobby Seale was running for the state assembly and Huey was running for Congress from jail. We'd come through all the police interference, until that Saturday. That night, I was driving a car that had been lent to us by a white man. It was a white Ford with Florida license plates, and for days before, Panthers who had been driving that car were constantly stopped by cops and questioned. "Are you from Florida?" "Where did you get this car?" All kinds of silly annoyances. Obviously, they were always on the lookout for that car. While driving it that Saturday night on the way to a Panther's apartment, where we were assembling all the food, I had to take a piss, so I pulled over on a dark street and got out of the car. The two other Panther cars in the caravan stopped behind me. Just then, this police car came around the corner. I didn't know at first it was a police car, because it was very dark and the car was some distance away. I was only concerned that somebody was coming, and it would be embarrassing to be caught standing there taking a leak. So I went around to the other side of the car. All of a sudden, the squad car turned a spotlight on me and the cops started yelling, "Come out from behind there!" Well, I was in the middle of taking this leak, so it took me a little time to get my fly zipped up and to get out into the middle of the street. Just as I cleared the front of my car, these cops started shooting.

Playboy: How do you know it was the police who started shooting?

Cleaver: Because all the Panthers were *behind* me and all the shots came from in *front* of me—where the cops were. And the shots were aimed *at* me; there's absolutely no question about it. Now I'm tempted to say that they knew who I was and that they were shooting at me specifically, but I don't really know that for sure. I *do* know, though, that they started shooting without any warning. My reaction was to dive down in front of the car. It wasn't a few seconds before another cop car came around the other corner from the opposite direction and also started shooting. Now, after checking out what happened, it seems pretty clear that some of those in the Panther cars also had guns; I mean, you never know when a Panther has a gun.

Playboy: Don't Panthers always carry guns?

Cleaver: No. Panthers are not supposed to carry any arms just for show. Guns are carried only if there is reason to anticipate the need for self-defense or for certain security purposes, such as the protection of Panther leaders under dangerous circumstances. That night, in view of the police harassment of us in Oakland, which had intensified during the preceding week, it would have been logical for some Panthers to have guns. I don't know who in particular had a gun, but there was some exchange of shots.

Meanwhile, we were all scattering, because it was a regular shooting gallery; the cops were coming from everywhere—at least fifty of them. Now the police story is that they were all responding to an emergency call by a cop who had just been shot, but how come so many arrived instantaneously from so many directions? Anyway, we were all running to get away from all that shooting. One cop was shooting at me with a shotgun, and I ended up going over a little shed between two houses. When I got on the other side, Bobby Hutton was already there. All kinds of cops on the street were shooting at us; Bobby had a rifle and he started shooting back, clearing the cops out of the immediate area. As they took cover, we had a chance to find a door into the cellar of this house.

From that point on, I suppose it's kind of flattering to say we had a shoot-out with the cops, but that's not what really happened. We were involved in ducking bullets. For ninety minutes, the cops poured bullets and tear gas into that house, and we got very badly asphyxiated by the gas. I also got shot in the leg, and one of those tear-gas canisters hit me in the chest and knocked the breath out of me. It was very dark in the cellar and Bobby thought I'd been wounded badly; so in the dark, he removed my clothes and tried to pat me down to find out where the blood was. The news reports said I came out naked. It's true, but that wasn't a plan I'd consciously devised so that the cops would be able to see I wasn't carrying a weapon and wouldn't have an excuse to kill me. When we decided to give up, Bobby tossed his rifle outside. Having been shot in the leg, I couldn't walk on my own, and when we went out, Bobby was helping me. There was a kind of step down past the threshold of the cellar door, and we fell down.

The cops surrounded us and about thirty of them hit us with guns and kicked us for a while—I don't know just how long. It ended with their telling us to stand up. Bobby helped me rise, and the cops seemed to resent his helping me. They snatched him away and told us to run down to a police car parked in the street. I couldn't run, so they told Bobby to run and shoved him. When he stumbled a few steps, they opened fire and killed him. Then they turned to me. I'm convinced that the only reason they didn't shoot me, too, was that by that time, a lot of people had been attracted to the scene by all the gunshots, and when they saw the cops shoot Bobby, they started pointing at me and yelling at the police, "Leave him alone!" and calling them murderers and pigs.

A cop, whom I knew from previous encounters, came over and asked where I was wounded. I told him it was my foot; this bastard kicked me on that foot and then told the other cops to get me out of there. They handcuffed me and put me in one of those big black vans. Two cops came in after me, but before they were all the way in, the cop driving the van told headquarters over the radio that they had a prisoner. Headquarters wanted to know who it was; the driver asked my name, I gave it to him and he radioed it in. That probably saved my life, because everything that comes in over the switchboard of the Oakland Police Department is put on a constantly operating tape. When the two cops from the outside got in, they started hitting me and told the man in front to drive slowly to the hospital. The driver said, "Don't do that, we've already radioed in his name." The two cops cursed him out, but they had to take me to the hospital. That was the end of the physical violence. Within about six hours, they took me to San Quentin. I stayed there three or four hours and then I was taken to Vacaville Prison, where they kept me for about sixty days until a judge released me. I was indicted on three counts of assault with intent to kill and three counts of assault on a police officer. So you see, it's not just my imagination that there's an awful lot of pressure to get rid of Panther spokesmen.

Playboy: You've also been a spokesman for the Peace and Freedom Party, of which you were this year's presidential nominee. How significant do you consider that kind of political activity, in terms of your plans for the growth of the Black Panthers?

Cleaver: Well, I never exactly dreamed of waking up in the White House after the November election, but I took part in that campaign because I think it's necessary to pull a lot of people together, black and white. Certainly, we're concerned with building the Black Panther Party, but we also have to build a national coalition between white activists and black activists. We have to build some machinery so that they can work on a coordinated basis. Right now, you have thousands and thousands of young activists, black and white, who are working at cross purposes, who don't communicate with one another, who are isolated and alienated from one another. But they could be a source of mutual strength and support. I believe that if we can simultaneously move forward the liberation struggle that's going on in the black colonies of this country and the revolutionary struggle that's going on in the mother country, we can amass the strength and numbers needed to change the course of American history.

Playboy: There are those who believe that this vision of yours is just another of those fugitive illusions that appear from time to time among radicals, black and white. Michael Harris, a reporter for the *San Francisco Chronicle,* wrote in *The Nation* last July, quoting a law-enforcement agent who had infiltrated the Panthers, "If the Federal Government makes a serious effort to pump lots of money into the ghetto, you can likely kiss the

Panthers goodbye. You simply can't agitate happy people." Do you think that's likely to happen?

Cleaver: If the Federal government moved to honor all the grievances of black people, to not merely alleviate but eliminate oppression, we'd be delighted to fold the whole thing up and call it a day. There are many other—and certainly safer—things we'd prefer to be doing with our lives. But until the government moves to undo all the injustices—every one of them, every last shadow of colonialism—no amount of bribes, brutality, threats or promises is going to deter us from our cause. There will be no compromise, no surrender and no sell-out; we will accept nothing less than total victory. That's why more and more black people have faith in us—because we offer a totally inflexible program in terms of our demands for black people; yet we have steered clear of doing this in a racist manner, as the Muslims have done. People are turning not to Muslims, not to the NAACP, not to CORE or SNCC but to the Black Panther Party.

Playboy: Is this happening more among older people or among the young?

Cleaver: We're getting older people, but we're acquiring particular strength in colleges, high schools, junior high schools, even grammar schools. We count very heavily on the young, in terms of the future. The Black Panther Party is a natural organization for them to join. It was organized by their peers; it understands the world the way they understand it. And for the young black male, the Black Panther Party supplies very badly needed standards of masculinity. The result is that all the young chicks in the black community nowadays relate to young men who are Black Panthers.

Playboy: You seem to have undergone quite a change in attitude since you were their age, when you related not to black girls but to white women, and in a decidedly unhealthy way. In *Soul on Ice*, you wrote,

> Somehow I arrived at the conclusion that, as a matter of principle, it was of paramount importance for me to have an antagonistic, ruthless attitude toward white women. . . . I had stepped outside of the white man's law, which I repudiated with scorn and self-satisfaction. I became a law unto myself—my own legislature, my own Supreme Court, my own executive. . . . Rape was an insurrectionary act.

Were you really being completely honest when you attributed your sexual attacks solely to ideological motives?

Cleaver: Well, at that time, I'd read a smattering of revolutionary works, though not with very much understanding. Passionate things like Lenin's exhortatory writings, and Bakunin, and Nechayev's *Catechism of the Revolutionist.* And Machiavelli. I felt I knew what insurrection was and what rebellion was. So I called rape an insurrectionary act. But basically, it was my delight in violating what I conceived of as white men's laws, and my delight in defiling white women in revenge over the way white men have used black women. I was in a wild frame of mind and rape was simply one of the weird forms my rebellion took at that stage. So it was probably a combination of business and pleasure.

Playboy: You went back to prison in 1958 for a fourteen-year sentence, after being convicted of assault with intent to kill and rape. During the nine years you served, what changed you to the point at which you admitted, in *Soul on Ice,* that you were wrong? "I had gone astray," you wrote,

> astray not so much from the white man's law as from being human, civilized—for I could not approve the act of rape. Even though I had some insight into my own motivations, I did not feel justified. I lost my self-respect. My pride as a man dissolved and my whole fragile moral structure seemed to collapse, completely shattered.

Cleaver: I came to realize that the particular women I had victimized had not been involved in actively oppressing me or other black people. I was taking revenge on them for what the whole system was responsible for. And as I thought about it, I felt I had become less than human. I also came to see that the price of hating other human beings is loving oneself less. But this didn't happen all at once; beginning to write was an important part of getting myself together. In fact, looking back, I started writing to save myself.

Playboy: In none of your own writing so far have you gone into any detail about your formative years and about whether the pressures on you as a boy in the ghetto were representative, in your view, of the pressures on young black people throughout the society. Were they?

Cleaver: So much so that I realized very soon after getting out of prison how little progress—if any—had been made in the nine years since I was sent up. What struck me more than anything else was the fact that the police still practice a systematic program to limit the opportunities in life for black cats by giving them a police record at an early age. In my own set, we were always being stopped and written up by the cops, even when we hadn't done anything. We'd just be walking down the street and the pigs would stop us and call in to see if we were wanted —all of which would serve to amass a file on us at headquarters. It's a general practice in this country that a young black gets put through this demeaning routine. But it's only one facet of the institutionalized conspiracy against black men in this country—to tame them, to break their spirit. As soon as he becomes aware of his environment, a black kid has to gauge his conduct and interpret his experiences in the context of his color and he has to orient himself to his environment in terms of how to survive as a black in a racist nation. But at least there's been one improvement in the years since I was a kid: Nowadays, being black—thanks to increasing white oppression—has been turned from a burden into an asset. Out there on the grade-school and high-school levels, young blacks are no longer uptight about their color. They're proud of it.

Playboy: Among the manifestations of that new pride is a decline in social acceptability of the word Negro in favor of the terms Afro-American and black. Is that why you don't call yourself or the Panthers "Negroes"?

Cleaver: I accept the analysis the Muslims and particularly Malcolm X have made of the term Negro. It's a word that whites applied to black people who were kidnaped from Africa. And historically the term came to mean a docile, submissive slave type of person. Afro-American and black, however, signify a rebellious person who finds and takes on his own identity. I use them to identify myself and I apply them to other black people whom I respect. They connote an original place of origin, as well as a pride in color.

Playboy: Many of those blacks who frown on the use of the word Negro tend to feel the same way about "integration." Why has this term fallen into disrepute among so many black people?

Cleaver: It's become a curse word because it has not only been of no use to black people but has prevented them from realizing the need to control their own institutions and to build their own sources of power. I mean, after all these years of talk about integration, it hasn't meant a damn thing but more segregation and more powerlessness. Integration is a dead word now except insofar as you want to use it to stigmatize somebody—like I would say, "Roy Wilkins, the integrationist."

Playboy: W. H. Ferry of the Center for the Study of Democratic Institutions maintains that "integration does not seem likely in the United States now or in the future. Americans are afraid of living with differences." Do you agree?

Cleaver: Well, talking about the future, I'd say that's up to white people. What black people want now is relief from being controlled and manipulated by white people. That could take the form of separation if white people continue to create conditions that make blacks convinced that total separation is the only alternative. If, on the other hand, conditions change sufficiently to end all exploitation and oppression of black people, then there is a possibility of integration in the long run for those who choose it. But we're a very long way from that.

Playboy: In which direction would you like to see America go—toward separation or integration?

Cleaver: Keeping in mind that we're talking about the very long view, it seems to me we're living in a world that has become virtually a neighborhood. If the world is not to destroy itself, the concept of people going their totally separate ways is really something that can't continue indefinitely. When you start speaking in ultimate terms, I don't see any way in which the world can be administered for the best interests of mankind without having a form of world government that would be responsive and responsible to *all* the people of the world—a world government that would function so that the welfare of no one segment of the population would be sacrificed for the enrichment of another.

Playboy: How do you feel about Roy Wilkins' claim that America's black people really want what the white middle class already has under capitalism—split-level homes and all the accouterments of the affluent life?

Cleaver: There's no question that black people want these things and have a right to them. The question is how to go about getting them. Many feel that they can get these things by entering into the mainstream of American society and becoming black capitalists. But to others, including myself, it's clear that in order for black people to have the best that society and technology are capable of providing, we need a new kind of society and a new kind of economic system. The goal must be to make possible a more equitable distribution of goods and services—but also to have a different set of values, so that things themselves don't become a substitute for life itself. In order to achieve that dual goal, we're going to have to move toward a new form of socialism. As long as there is so much stress on private property, we're going to have a society of competition rather than cooperation; we're going to have the exploited and the exploiters. Consider all these deeds, for example, that give people ownership of the productive and natural resources of this country. If there's going to be any burning, let's burn up these deeds, because everybody comes into this world the same way—naked, crying, without ownership of anything. The earth is here; it's given, like air and water, and I believe everyone should have equal access to its resources.

I want to see a society purged of Madison Avenue mind benders who propagandize people into a mad pursuit of gadgets.

They've conned people into believing that their lives depend on having an electric toothbrush, two cars and a color-television set in every room. We've got to rid ourselves of this dreadful and all-consuming hunger for *things,* this mindless substitution of the rat-race for a humane life. Only then will people become capable of relating to other people on the basis of individual merit, rather than on the basis of status, property and wealth. The values I'm for are really quite traditional and simple—like respecting your fellow man, respecting your parents, respecting your leaders if they're true leaders. These revolutionary goals are as old as time itself: Let people be. Let them fulfill their capacities.

Playboy: The ultimate society you envision, in *Soul on Ice,* is one in which male and female will "realize their true nature," thereby closing the present "fissure of society into antagonistic classes" and regenerating "a dying culture and civilization alienated from its biology." But some critics of the book felt that you seemed to reserve this new Garden of Eden for black people, who, you claim, are "the wealth of a nation, an abundant supply of unexhausted, unde-essenced human raw material upon which the future of the society depends and with which, through the implacable march of history to an ever broader base of democracy and equality, the society will renew and transform itself."

Cleaver: No, it's not limited to black people. Black or white, the male-female principle is toward unity. Both black and white people have to get out of the bags they're in to be natural again. White people have to disabuse themselves of the illusion that it's their job to rule and that the black man's job is to produce labor. And black men have to use their minds and acquire confidence in the products of their minds. This doesn't mean the white man has to let *his* mind fall into disuse, but he also has to relate to his body again, as the black man does. What I'm saying is that everyone needs a new understanding of his total nature, mental and physical. Only when people, black and white, start seeing themselves and acting as total individuals, with bodies and minds, will they stop assigning exclusive mental roles to one set of people and exclusive physical roles to another. Only then will the primary thrust of life—the fusion of male and female—be freed of sociological obstacles. That's the base of the kind of social system I want to see, a society in which a man and a woman can come as close as possible to total unity on the basis of natural attraction. In my own life, the more totally I've been able to relate to a particular woman, the more fulfilled I've been.

Playboy: Have you ever been tempted to withdraw from the front lines of the revolutionary social struggle to pursue that process of self-fulfillment in private life, by writing and raising a family with your wife Kathleen?

Cleaver: I could do that. I could withdraw. I've gotten enough money from the book so that I could get myself a pad away from all this shit. I could go down to my parole officer and say, "Look, man, I don't want to go back to prison. I'm going to stop talking revolution. I'm going to start writing poetry and fairy tales, the way you want me to and I won't be a problem anymore. So how about re-evaluating my case and leaving me alone? Live and let live." I know they'd go for that, and I wouldn't need much money to do it, because I'm not hung up on material things. But the fact is that I feel *good* working with my people and with the brothers of the Black Panther Party. I'd feel miserable doing anything else. Hell, most of my life has been involved in conflicts with authority, and now that I've politicized that conflict, I'm very content to be working for black liberation. I couldn't conceive of myself playing any other role—not even if I have to go back to prison for it. I'm going to do everything I can *not* to go back to prison, but I can't compromise my beliefs. I'd rather be dead than do that. And I may have a violent end, anyway. I'm hearing more and more these days from people telling me to be careful, because they feel my life's in danger. They may be right, but I say fuck it.

Playboy: If you are imprisoned or killed, how much confidence do you have that the Black Panther Party or any succeeding group in the revolutionary struggle will ultimately prevail?

Cleaver: I have confidence that people learn from the experiences of others. Every time a black man is murdered for speaking out against oppression, his death is fuel for the struggle to continue. When Malcolm was killed, that didn't frighten people; his death created more disciples. I can only hope that if what I'm doing has any constructive value, others will take up the fight and continue it if I'm killed. Ché Guevara put it the way I feel, when he said, "Wherever death may surprise us, let it be welcome, provided that this, our battle cry, may have reached some receptive ear and another hand may be extended to wield our weapons." That's all I ask for.

Playboy: How do you rate your chances of survival?

Cleaver: I plan to be around for quite a while.

Five days before he was scheduled to turn himself in to the California Adult Authority for "parole violation," Cleaver made his last American public appearance in San Francisco. He concluded his speech there by telling his audience he would not surrender; the authorities would have to come and get him. Cleaver was not heard from again until early in the sum-

mer of 1969, when Reuters reported he was living in Cuba. His wife quietly joined him and they were both next reported living in Algiers, where on July 29, 1969, their first child, a son, was born. Since then, Cleaver has appeared at a Pan-African Cultural Festival in Algiers, highlights of which are featured in William Klein's documentary film Eldridge Cleaver. *An autobiographical short story by Cleaver called "The Flashlight" appeared in the December 1969 issue of* Playboy *and, on January 6, 1970, an exclusive interview with Mike Wallace, filmed in Algiers, was nationally televised on CBS. In July 1970 both Cleaver and his wife were reported to be in North Korea awaiting the birth of their second child. It appears unlikely at this time that Cleaver will return to the United States.*

"Just what is it that you people want, anyway?"

fiction

KEN W. PURDY

chronicle of an event

Perhaps typical of our times, beginning with the statement, "It was an accident."

"You keep saying that," the cop said. "You keep telling us it was an accident."

"Because it was," Charles Stander said.

"A damn funny kind of accident," the sergeant said, "this colored fella with four holes in his chest, in a three-inch group, at that. You put four slugs that close together by accident, what would you do if you was to try?"

Stander said nothing.

"I could shoot like that, I'd make Expert," the harness-cop said. He was big and black Irish and baby-faced.

"I don't believe a word of it," the sergeant said. "I don't believe a goddamn word of it, and I never will. You and this jig had a fuss, and you took out this little pistol, a lady's gun, by the way, I might point out to you, and, no offense meant, not just now anyway, and you let him have four. You let him have four because he was a big strong fella, he was coming to you, and you didn't think maybe just one .25 would stop him. You had five rounds in the magazine, and you knew it, and you saved one for hitting him in the head if he kept coming in on you. That much is sure as hell true. Well, ain't it?"

"No," Charles Stander said. "It was an accident."

"Balls," the sergeant said. "Lemme read you from the coroner's report, here, along here, it says, '. . . two of the slugs having struck the left ventricle of the heart, death was almost instantaneous . . .' Two in the heart and two right alongside it, and that's an *accident*? Look, Mr. Stander, I been poking around these things for fourteen years, I *seen* a few gunshot accidents.

So turn it off, that crap, accident. Any time a guy gets shot four times, that's no accident. Balls to that."

"Yeah," the other cop said. "Like, you remember, Sarge, that old guy got shot in the Commodore, it was a month ago, he . . ."

"Ah, shuddup," the sergeant said.

The phone rang. He picked it up and listened. "Yeah," he said. "So, OK." He dropped it back.

"Somebody went your bail," he said to Charles Stander. "Somebody put up fifty grand for you. I see you got friends. Me, I wouldn't let you out for any money there is." He rolled in his chair and let his feet drop into the papers on his desk. He looked incuriously at Stander. He sighed. "I remember times I felt better," he said. "Donovan," he said, "where's the coffee for us?"

"I suppose I can go now?" Stander said.

"In due time, Mr. Stander," the sergeant said. "Don't be in a rush. There's some paperwork they gotta do upstairs, one thing and another. Don't be in a rush. Donovan is getting the coffee."

Charles Stander had nothing to say. Most of the fright had left him, but none of the horror. He was numb. When Donovan handed him a cup of coffee, he took it. It was weak and very hot. He couldn't get near it, although the sergeant sucked happily at his own cup. Stander was embarrassed. He didn't feel like a brilliant mind standing off a murder charge, holding wit and intelligence between himself and twenty years, or the electric chair, like a shield and sword. He felt like a cheap con man. He looked around the small room, bare, cramped, not dirty and not clean, an old, tired place. The sergeant was watching his eyes.

"This here's the captain's office, did I tell you that?" he said. "He's on sick leave. First time I was ever in this station house, Eddie Burke was captain. You never heard of him, I don't suppose? Eddie Burke was what you might call a cop's cop. I don't think anybody ever made captain from patrolman quicker than he did. He was smart, and he worked like a dog. To give you an example, he taught himself to read and write and speak *Chinese!* He almost had a law degree, too. Night school. He died in a stinking little holdup, years ago now. He wasn't fifty. Goddamn shame."

"No, I never heard of him," Charles Stander said.

"His wife was a cop, too," the sergeant said. "Beautiful woman. A big girl. Funny thing about her, she hated to carry a gun, and she had to, you know. Regulations. She did undercover stuff, narcotics and that, and she said it was too heavy in her purse. I told her one time, so all right, get yourself a .25 automatic, get a Colt .25 or one of them Berettas, that's a light piece. Like that Beretta you killed this fella with. That's why I said, you killed him with a lady's gun."

Charles Stander said nothing.

"I dunno how it is in your business, Mr. Stander," the sergeant said, "there in Wall Street. I guess it's like this business or some other one, you meet all kinds. People that are looking to cheat, steal, lie, screw the other fella some way. But not so many looking to kill somebody . . . ?"

"No, I guess not," Stander said.

"Maybe you just can't tell," the sergeant said. "It's a hard thing to tell. Any time you make a guess about a man, my feeling is, you're worse than even money to be wrong. But some things you can tell. Like, you take you. You're seven kinds of a liar, in this thing here, but you're not a *good* liar. A real good liar *talks,* that's one of the ways you can tell. You just sit there and say nothin' because you know you're a lousy liar. You'd say that's right, wouldn't you? I mean, you don't lie a hell of a lot, very often, wouldn't you say? You don't have a lot of practice at it, I mean, wouldn't you say that?"

"I'm not lying," Charles Stander said.

"That's what I mean," the sergeant said. "You sure as hell *are* lying, and a *good* liar would make up a sensible story, all cooked up with interesting little details and things to throw you off and all. You come in here with a story I'd slap my youngest kid for telling, it's so dumb."

"You don't seem to be getting anywhere, proving it's a lie," Stander said.

"Ah, there's a lot of time for that yet. I'm just telling you it's a dumb story, and we'll get you on it. Thing is, by the time we get you on it, everybody's gonna be sore at you, all that trouble. We got enough to do, we got real heavy cases going in this precinct, why should you come in here and foul us up with your goddamn dumb story? You'd be better off, I'm telling you the truth, if you'd tell us what happened. Look, Mr. Stander, I'm not saying you killed this colored fella because you *planned* to for a long time. I'm not saying that. I'm not saying this was premeditated murder. I'm with you, up to a point. I'm not saying *I* wouldn't have knocked him off myself, standing where you stood. He was coming at you, that's the surest thing there is. He was twenty-three and one-eighty and six foot, and you're, what, forty-something, like me? and anybody can tell you're not any too rugged. I'm telling you the truth, I don't think you're anything worse than manslaughter, and maybe self-defense, at that. That's on the *true* story, what *happened,* not this crap you been giving us for two days now. Isn't that right?"

"Isn't what right?" Charles Stander said.

"Isn't what I'm *saying* right is what I mean," the sergeant said. "Your story. It's a lousy story. What're you doing, a man your age, taking judo lessons? Huh? Well?"

"We've been over that twenty times. I've wanted to, all my life, and now I could, so I did."

"Balls. Four weeks, you're taking lessons from this fella. Four weeks. Then you kill him dead. Why? Huh? I want to tell you, Mr. Stander, and I'm telling you the truth, and no offense meant, some joker from the D. A.'s office will get you up there on the stand and he's gonna crucify you on that one. I mean, you can walk out of that court acquitted and free as a bird and you're never gonna be the same, when they get through with you, four weeks with this young guy and you shoot him. Think about it. You ever see one of those young, ambitious shysters *work*? They don't give a goddamn about you or what happens to you. Anything goes. You'll see. Am I right or not?"

"You could be," Charles Stander said.

"Yeah, I could be," the sergeant said. "You're goddamn right, I could be. You'll wish you'd been born dead." He looked around the room; his eyes fell on Donovan as if for the first time. "You got nothin' at all to do, Donovan?" he said. "Beat it."

"I thought you wanted me to stay," Donovan said.

"For what? You think Mr. Stander's going to beat me to death with a chair or somethin'? He's got no such idea, Mr. Stander. He even wishes to hell he didn't shoot his friend there, Jordan or what was his name? yeah, Mike Jordan. That right, Mr. Stander?"

"That's right, Sergeant," Stander said.

"You see, Donovan?" the sergeant said. "So, beat it. I'm safe as a church."

"When can I go?" Stander said.

"When I say so," the sergeant said. "Ain't that a funny thing, now? You got bail and all, but you don't go till I say so. *If* I feel like picking up the phone. Anyway, like I told you, these things take time, papers to make out, there can be delays . . . there's no rush, anyway. What I say, you're better off in here. When you get out I wouldn't go poking around much above 110th Street. Your picture's been in the papers."

"I know it."

"You take a terrible picture, I'll say that," the sergeant said. "There wasn't one in the whole bunch didn't make you look sixty-five years old, and creepy-looking at that. Pictures like that make a bad impression. Maybe you're lucky you're not married at that. She might want to dump you, seeing those pictures."

"Nothing I can do about it," Stander said. He was terribly tired. The coffee had done nothing for him. He was frightened and sick.

"I don't see a good end to it for you at all," the sergeant said. "You might think I'm trying to con you, now, but I'm telling you the truth, I don't even like it that you had a permit for the gun. You'd have been better off without it. It looks like you were thinking of something. You didn't have it long enough. And sure as hell you lied to get it. You had to have a permit because you carry large sums of money! Balls. The stock market works on credit, everybody knows that. You go into any brokerage house in Wall Street, you won't find lunch money in the till. What would they use money for? So *that* was a lie, and that's another thing the D. A.'s bright little bastards will hang you up on, though God knows it won't be as bad as the other one. But bad enough. It's a fact, you're a terrible liar, and I won't be surprised if they burn you for it." He sighed. "Jesus, my feet hurt," he said. "You'd think I just come in off the beat. Which I did, eleven years ago."

I *know* he's a fool, Stander thought. I'm sure he is. No, I was sure of it an hour ago.

"Now, you take that part of your story where you say Jordan was showing you how to take a gun away from a man when you had the accident," the sergeant said. "I have to laugh at you. I been all through that myself, years ago. Hell, man, I *took* a gun off a fella, and it pointing right at my belly. So don't tell me. Jordan was a pro. If he was showing you any such thing—and he sure as hell wasn't—before he'd let you come anywhere near him, he'd have broke that .25 himself, pulled the slide, pulled the magazine and looked right through it to the floor. You think any professional is going to let a dumbheaded civilian like you come at him with a gun that might have a round in it? You must be crazy. It's what I said before, I'd slap my own kid for a story like that one."

"Still, it's the truth," Stander said.

"Christ!" the sergeant said. "I'll make book they burn you for it at that. They'll hang a first-degree rap on you, they'll make it stick and they'll burn you. And they'll be wrong. You're no worse than manslaughter, any way you slice it. But you know something, Mr. Stander? Things come out even in the end. They'll tell you you're going to the chair for murder, but it'll be for lying. And I'll tell you something else: You won't be the first one burned for lying. Nor the last. Am I right?"

"You could be," Stander said.

"Yeah," the sergeant said. He lifted the phone. "Tommy," he said, "I'm sending him up. Turn him loose." Wearily, he stood. "The fella outside will take you up, Stander," he said.

"Goodbye," Stander said.

"Oh, I'll see you again," the sergeant said. "Don't think I won't."

A note from Stander's lawyer waited for him: Apology, can't wait, wife baby-having, phone soonest possible, best regards. The formalities of his springing were brief. He signed something. The deskman looked up at the ancient octagonal wall clock, its brass-weighted pendulum flickering past a slit in the glass case, and noted the time: 9:27 P.M., November 7, 1965. No one seemed to watch Stander leave the station house. Cold rain ran in the streets. He walked a little way, picked up a cab and gave the driver an address a block short of his own. He hurried down the other side of the street. Dead opposite, he could see there was no one in the lobby. He ran across, past the elevator to the stairway, and ran the three flights. No one in the hall, he was inside in seconds. He leaned against the door and sighed. "Well," he said, half-aloud, "home and dry."

He lowered the curtains before he turned on the lights. He went into the kitchen. The room was yellow, all of it, even the stove, and things glowed golden in the light. He pulled a bottle of bourbon from the cupboard and slopped three or four ounces into a glass. He drank it like ice water on a hot day and poured another. He squirted some seltzer into that one, carried it into the bathroom, set it on the tray that bridged the tub. He opened the faucets. He pulled off his tie, walking into the bedroom, stripped, and everything he had been wearing, save his shoes, he rolled into a ball and fired into the laundry hamper. He lowered himself slowly, sat on the hot bottom of the tub for a couple of breaths, then dropped himself to his neck. He let everything come to a balance before he reached a long arm for the bourbon. He took a couple of big bites. He sighed. He looked at the door to see if the bolt stood crosswise, if he had locked it. Yes. Against whom or whatever, he didn't know, but still he had locked it. The blessed anesthesia lifted him out of himself. He looked fondly into the glass in his hand. My God, he thought, and this is nothing but corn and spring water! There were cigarettes in a copper case. He fiddled one loose into his mouth and lighted it. He knew he was utterly safe, citadelled and long past all harm's way. What the hell, he said to himself, if you have a tub of hot water, a bottle of whiskey and a razor blade, they can all go screw themselves. They can come in and find you when they get around to it. He contemplated himself as a kind of still life, a bloated, drained, violet-white corpse, floating, motionless as a pear in gelatin, forever suspended in a tubful of pink water. Well. He took another little drink. Maybe it would be the sergeant who would come. He would have Donovan with him. "All right, Donovan, just lean on that door, now. You must be good for something, if it's only kickin' in doors." The sergeant, Stander knew, would not approve. Screw him. Who needs him? Stander thought. Anyway, it wasn't going to happen. Just an idea, he told himself. Just a little something in reserve.

That the sergeant knew perfectly well he was lying was not really important, Stander thought, because he did *not* know just *where* he was lying. And, the funny thing, the story that so outraged the sergeant in its improbabilities was nearly all true. In nearly every detail, what he had told the police had been true.

It was true that he had met Mike Jordan in his own office, at the instance of a friend who'd sent him. And it was true that he had tried hard to find a job for Jordan and, when he couldn't, even harder to convince the boy that it was not because he was a Negro that he had failed.

"Mr. Jordan," he had said, "there isn't one damned job in this whole outfit. The chairman of the board couldn't get his own kid in here today without making the job first. That's the way it is. And I'm awfully sorry."

"I understand," Jordan said softly.

"No, really," Stander said, "that's the way it is."

"OK," Jordan said.

"There must be other places, other ideas," Stander said. "What have you done before?"

"Well, my age, you know, not much," Jordan said. "I got through business school, you saw that"—he nodded toward the papers on Stander's desk—"then I was in the Service, in the Marine Corps . . ."

"Did you pick up anything there?" Stander said.

Jordan smiled. He was good to look at. He was easy, everything about him fitted. "In high school, in L. A.," he said, "I did some judo. So that came up and I went into it; it was natural, because after boot camp I was stationed in Japan, and I wound up instructor. I'm black belt third *dan,* matter of fact. But that's not like money right off." He smiled again.

"I always wanted to do that," Stander said. "When I was about thirteen, I remember, I bought a book—they called it jujitsu then—little red-and-white Spalding book; the kid next door and I. We worked out on it for a long time. We got two or three moves down pretty good."

Jordan smiled, and after a while he went away. Stander reported to his friend. His friend knew he had really tried—one always did, it was understood—you take care of one for me, I take care of one for you. Twenty or thirty days later the man phoned Stander to say that Jordan was working, teaching judo in a *dojo* on 88th Street.

"He's making out," the man said. "It's big now, the judo thing, you know, and he's doing seventy-five–eighty-five bucks a week, I think. So what the hell?"

"I'm glad to hear it," Stander said. "Where is the place, exactly? I always wanted to try that myself; maybe I will."

So, one night, he went around. Over a bowling alley, pizzas next door, bar over there, but it was no stinking gymnasium; it was bare but shiny clean, straw mats on the floor, not much else. People in short, white canvas pants and jackets were dumping each other around. It wasn't hard to find Jordan.

"What I thought," Stander said after they'd got through the hello-how-are-yous, "I'd like to try it. All right, I'm forty-seven, and all the exercise I've had since V-E Day, if you know what that means, is lifting my eyebrows, but I thought if I took a couple months to get into some kind of shape so I wouldn't break my neck straight off . . . you think there's any sense in that?"

"Well, Mr. Stander, you see that man over there, that white-haired man?" Jordan said. "That man's sixty-three. *He's* doing OK."

"All right," Stander said. "I'll see you in six weeks or so."

"Good," Jordan said.

"One thing, though," Stander said. "The first few times, I don't know, I suppose I'll look like a clown, and maybe . . ."

"Sure," Jordan said. "Everybody feels like that. I know what you mean. This place opens at nine in the morning, and the first class is eleven. So from nine to eleven, that's for private lessons. Costs more, but if you don't mind that . . ."

"You just made a deal," Stander said. They shook hands and he went away. He stopped smoking that night, and he stopped drinking. Next morning he walked twenty blocks before he took a cab. He went around to Abercrombie's and bought a stationary bicycle. It was all very easy and painless. In a couple of weeks he could do a lap around the reservoir in Central Park. It was no sweat. He felt good. He didn't know what was happening to himself, he didn't know why he was acting like an eighteen-year-old kid, skinny and sex-starved and wearing *acne vulgaris* on his face like a curse or a banner, but there it was, and as long as he didn't think about it, and didn't see himself as a forty-seven-year-old clown trying to play an eighteen-year-old kid, skinny and sex-starved . . . one thing led surely to another, like rocks rolling down a mountainside: If you didn't smoke, for some reason you didn't care so much about drinking, and if you didn't drink, you didn't go out so much, and if you didn't go out so much, you didn't get laid much, and you didn't care, either. In due season he went around to 88th Street.

Jordan was a natural teacher: He was patient, and he could put himself in another man's place. For a week Stander did *ukemi,* ways to fall without being hurt. Then they began with simple moves and throws. When it came to Stander that the essence of the art was rhythm, that it was dancing, that *judo* lived in the same house with skiing, with skating, with diving, with the *rappel* in mountain climbing, that it was a sensuous thing, then he was hooked, and knowing that with this wild, hard-on game you could kill a man, too, that was the extra bounty that put the lock on it. He bought all the clichés, that the price of a black belt is 10,000 falls, that the pious hope of the master *judoka* is that he will never in the rest of his lifetime touch a man in anger or in meanness . . . he bought all of it.

"You know," he said to Jordan one day, "I feel as young as I feel, if that makes sense."

"Yeah?" Jordan said, unblinking.

"I feel good," Stander said. "I just feel good."

"Well, now, that's nice," Jordan said.

It was Jordan who had brought him all this, and it was Jordan, after all, who could throw him twenty-five times to the floor in half an hour's time and never hurt him, and it was Jordan who'd let him, Stander, dump him as hard as he knew how and every time come up smiling, saying, "Now, that wasn't *bad,* Mr. Stander, but if you could remember to keep your left foot just a bit higher . . . try it again . . ." and he had to like the man. One day he said, "The hell with it, I'm not going back to the office today. Can we have lunch?"

"Sure, I guess so," Jordan said.

Lying there in the tub, more hot water coming in, more whiskey on the tray, Stander could see that it was that one day that did it. They went to the wrong place. It was a hotel restaurant in the West 60s, a so-so place; good but not too good, Stander had thought, if he'd thought about it at all. Nobody did anything you could pin. It wasn't the worst table in the room. They waited only a little longer than was decent. All right, things were cold, but what the hell, it wasn't the Pyramide in Vienne, it was a West Side hotel in New York. Jordan didn't seem to notice. He went along. He wasn't a big talker at any time, so Stander talked, a little too much, a little too fast, maybe, he thought, doing it, but still it had been his idea . . . I'll give the son of a bitching waiter a quarter tip, he thought, and then, just then, when he's picking up the tray, I'll take it back, and if the mothering so-and-so blinks an eye at me . . .

It didn't come to that. The waiter brought melon for dessert. He put Stander's down, then Jordan's. He stayed. He looked down at Jordan and he said, softly, pointing, "You use that spoon, there, to eat it with."

Jordan stood up. He took the waiter's lapel in his thumb and his finger. He said, "You know something, Whitey? I'm not going to kill you for that. Not now, I'm not, that is." He turned. "You coming, Mr. Stander?" he said.

They stood in the street, then, for two shakes, in the wind, the insensate low scream of traffic, across the Park and high towers of Fifth Avenue, all madness to the manor born, and Stander said, "Mike, I'm sorry."

"See you Wednesday, man," Jordan said, and he went away.

Stander stood there, irresolute, an idiot, no thought in his whole being. Well, one spin on his heel, find the waiter, break his bones—ah, no good, no good at all. He did what he had to do, he lifted a limp arm for a cab and went away.

On the Wednesday they worked out as they had the other days. There was no need to speak, although Stander tried.

Don't send money to chase lost money, Stander thought, locked in the warm embrace of whiskey and hot water. I know it now. But then, he had sent it. I'm not going to let some sick, wet-eyed, fish-bellied, all-people-hating hash-slinger louse me, and louse him, he had pledged himself. I'll wash that one out.

"Mike," he said another day, "I'm having a few people around Friday for drinks. Can you make it, say, six-thirty, seven o'clock at my place?"

"I guess so, Mr. Stander," Jordan said. Brown eyes in a brown face. "Why not, man?"

"Bring somebody," Stander said.

"Sure," Jordan said.

What the hell, Stander thought, it wasn't that I didn't try. And looking back, even now, he couldn't see where he had been wrong. He tried. Of the fifteen couples he could get into his flat, another one of Negroes? No. He had a little black book of his own. Tiji Yumosaka. He called her. "If there's no big flap in the Secretariat that night," she said, "sure. Love it, lover. See you."

He called Benstead. "Don't argue with me," he said, "bring your little Jamaican friend," he said. "Bring her, or don't come."

"OK, motha," Benstead said.

What went wrong, Stander never knew. It was a swinger, up and down and sidewise, for all he ever knew. He kissed Jordan's date on the same cheek he kissed all the others, no more no less, no sooner no later, and standing in the kitchen door, looking into the wriggling mass of idiots screaming into each other's faces, over their silly heads into the gray light-flecked sky and the Queensboro Bridge, he could think only that it was maybe cocktail fight number 136 out of say 500 going that night in a long stone's throw of the corner in which he stood. He didn't see Jordan go, and he was drained and happy, warm and full of love for all the world that three in the morning when Tiji Yumosaka bumped her little breasts against him, sitting up to light a cigarette, and said, "Your friend Jordan didn't have a very good party, did he?"

"He didn't?"

"Well, he left mad. Real mad."

"Why? What happened?"

"I don't know, honey. I just saw him bang out the door; somebody told me he was sore."

"Alone? He left alone?"

"I guess."

He didn't know where Jordan lived, and so Saturday and Sunday went. Monday at nine, before he could say hello, Jordan said. "Real nice party, Mr. Stander," bowed, hands on thighs, the regular thing, lightly took his hold and threw him, hard.

Stander tried once more, another time. A real cement-head, he thought, looking back, never knows when he's dead. No good. "I'm sorry," Jordan told him, "I'm busy that night."

And so it came up to November 4, in the year 1965, in the morning, 9:16 on West 88th Street in the borough of Manhattan.

There was nothing exotic about it. Jordan threw Stander with an ankle block, rolled him, and put his left wrist behind his ear. The pain came through slowly to Stander, slowly at first, and then in a big howling rush, a flash flood of pain screaming down a canyon wall. He patted the mat with his free hand. Nothing stopped.

"You know, chum," the soft voice came over his shoulder, "a *judoka,* he has to be able to take a little pain."

"I know," Stander said as levelly as he could. "And that's as much as I can take."

"No, it's not," Jordan said. "You can take a lot more. And you're going to."

"Mike. Lay off. What's this about? You're going to break my goddamn arm."

"Mr. Jordan. And I'm not about to lay off. And it's about nothing. And *I* know when your arm will break. And where."

"Jesus, Mike, please, lay off—you out of your goddamn head? What'd I do to you?"

"You did nothin' to me, Uncle Charlie," Jordan said. "It just came to me, a little while ago, that I don't like you. I don't like you for no reason. I don't want to know why I don't like you. I don't want you around. I never did want you around. It's time you blew the scene, that's all." He lifted Stander's arm an inch.

"So let me up," Stander said, "if that's all that's eating you."

"I don't *know* what's eating me," Jordan said. "And you don't." He took another inch, and Stander screamed. He tried to think of a move. A joke. He was nailed to the mat, he was locked like a beam in the building, he was lucky to breathe. "All right," he grunted, he moaned, he was crying, "what do I do, tell me?"

"You kiss my ass, I tell you to," Jordan said. "You BEG!"

Stander begged. He debased himself with every word he knew, in every permutation of words he knew. He howled like a dog, he groveled like a witch. His arm came free. He couldn't move it. It hung behind his back like someone else's. He tried to get up. Before he had moved a foot, Jordan was on him again, clamped to him, riveted to him.

"That was *that* arm, Whitey," he said. "Now we going to try *this* one."

Stander crawled off the mat in the end. After a while, his arms came back and he could use them. He dressed. And in dressing, the Beretta locked in the little holster in the watch pocket of his trousers softly reminded him that it was there. The sergeant was right, of course, he'd got it on a lie, the same lie that carried half the pistol permits in New York—that and knowing somebody in Centre Street. For carrying money? No. For hearing of muggings and beatings and holdups, for being scared. Still, there it was. He tied his shoelaces, he knotted his tie, he flexed his hands a few times. He went back.

Jordan was on the mat. He was doing push-ups. He looked, and he laughed.

"You back?" he said. "Whitey?"

"Mike," Stander said. "All right, you blew your top. And I'm white and I was handy. I dig it all. I'm not sore. But it's no good that way. I can't have it all my way, but you can't, either. I won't take what you made me take, what you made me do. So I want to hear you say one thing. I just want to hear you say you're sorry."

Jordan came off the mat like a big toy doll on the end of a rubber band as big around as your wrist, bouncing twice, barefoot, without a sound.

"What you got there in your hand, Uncle Charlie?" he said. "Water pistol?"

"No," Stander said.

"Might as well be, all the good it's gonna do you," Jordan said. "Takes more guts to shoot a man than you got." He stopped grinning. "You son of a bitch," he said, "you just don't want to know, do you? You just ain't gonna learn, are you?" And he started in.

If I let him inside ten feet, Stander thought . . . there were two dozen ways Jordan could do it, or try to do it . . . if I let him inside ten feet, Stander thought, I'll see him flat in the air, spread, his legs kicking out, swinging like a gate gone crazy, and that will be all I'll see . . . He hung a thread in the air in front of him, ten feet away. If he comes past that, he thought, God help me and love me, that's it, and Jordan came, laughing, scuttling, fast, fast, and Stander took it off his hip—at Fort Dix they told you, hold it low on your hip, don't let The Enemy get his hands on it that easy—he crouched, he grabbed his right hand with the other one, he pointed it, stuck it out in front, FBI way and all. All right, now he knows I mean it, and Jordan came through the thread hanging there, and he pulled, pow, pow, pow, pow.

Stander went out into the street and grabbed the first cop he saw, and it was then that he told the only lie, but of course the big one, the one the sergeant laughed at, that Jordan had been teaching him a move. And he stuck with it.

There is a point in drinking where the wildly rocketing, soaring upward curve must turn and fall back. Charles Stander came to that place. The water was cooling in the hard, white tub. He pulled himself out. He dried himself after a fashion. He was hungry as a shrew. He went into the kitchen and broke six eggs into a pan, stirred them into a kind of omelet, ate them with however many slices of toast, drank a can of tomato juice and put himself to bed. He was drunk, and stuffed, and sick of himself, and sleep came quickly. He dreamed.

A cemetery. He came into it under an *art nouveau* kind of archway. "The Lord God Jehovah's New Ethiopian Place of Rest." He saw himself. That man, there, in the belted trench coat, that one, with the flowers. A long way off, but he could see it clearly with his telescopic-wonder vision, a new grave, and a headstone, MICHAEL ARLEN JORDAN, 1942–1965, JESUS GRANT HIM REST. In a crescent shape, five hundred Negro men formed around it. Or six hundred. Or a thousand. He, Charles Stander, with flowers (early violets, a rose, dirty daisies and some anemones), going that way. But, just before, a turning, a place for cowards, a pathway to the right. Down that way. Here, a little white marker, and, drunken-slanting in a green-wire holder, a glass vase, brimful with brown rain water. And this: MARY LOU HATKINS, GATHERED UP IN HER LORD'S SWEET HARVEST, AGED SIX YEARS AND SEVEN MONTHS. The man in the trench coat kneeling and filling the vase with his flowers.

Charles Stander woke late. The phone was ringing, and while he wondered, was it this bell that had brought him back, it cut itself off, half in the middle of its shrilling, faceless racket. He slept again and at four in the afternoon got up. He made coffee and drank whiskey. He stood on his terrace and looked across the gray river into Long Island. He came in for more whiskey. The glass-framed door swung in the wet wind behind him. He phoned his lawyer, the new father, and told him nothing. He looked up the name of a newspaper in Harlem. He spoke to three people and in that nine minutes he drank coffee and bourbon half-and-half. The third man told him what he wanted to know. The Lord God Jehovah's New Ethiopian Place of Rest was in fact called John the Baptist Cemetery.

On Lexington Avenue in the 50s and 60s, it's easy to buy flowers. Stander took what was offered him. He waved for a cab and went uptown. In the end, he had to walk a long way in the rain, but he hardly knew that. He thought that the place, the very place, would be hard to find, but it was not; new graves, new babies, everyone knows. The old ground fills up, the new ground is over there. At the tight end of a narrowing white gravel path, he saw it, and he went that way. There were no five hundred people crescenting around the red-clay mound, there was no one. He went on. Fifty feet or so away, another path crossed to the right, and looking along it he could believe that there must be a little stone, MARY LOU HATKINS, GATHERED UP IN HER LORD'S SWEET HARVEST, but he kept on. There was no vase on Jordan's grave. He put his foolish flowers where there was room for them. He knelt and tried to pray, or pretended to try. He couldn't think of anything to say beyond, a couple of times, "I'm sorry," and he was in some doubt as to whom he was addressing this message. The ground beside the grave was wet and knobbed with gravel. He was cold, uncomfortable and futile. He did not feel that he was in communication with any of the deities of which he had heard during his life, and he could summon neither kinship with Jordan, below, nor compassion for his memory. He gave up. He stood, he looked around, he walked away, two wet and muddy patches clammy on his knees.

I thought there'd be more to it, he said to himself, I really thought there'd be more to it than this.

There never was. It was all downhill from there. The trial was a walk-through, the acquittal a certainty, the publicity brief. A year later, he couldn't clearly remember Jordan's face.

‘Not the liberty which we can hope’

DISSENT AND JUSTICE IN AMERICA

For this is not the liberty which we can hope, that no grievance ever should arise in the Commonwealth—that let no man in this world expect; but when complaints are freely heard, deeply considered, and speedily reformed, then is the utmost bond of civil liberty attained that wise men look for.

JOHN MILTON,
Areopagitica

FRANK DONNER

article

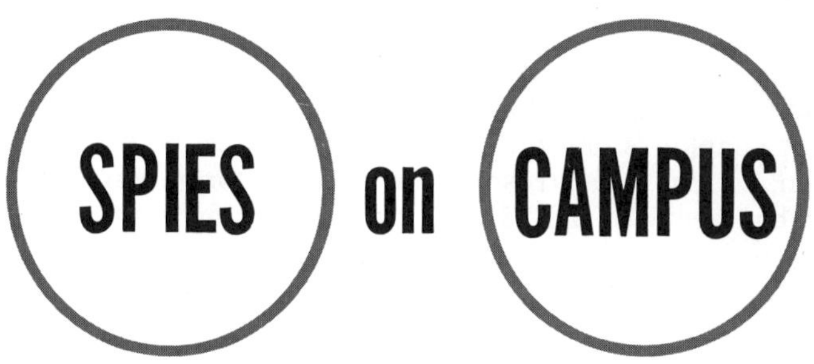

a sobering examination of political surveillance in the once-inviolate groves of academe

In comparison with most student protests held before and since, the one staged on the evening of February 9, 1967, at State University College at Brockport in upstate New York was singularly uneventful. Instead of a prolonged marathon involving hundreds of students, the demonstration—in the form of a sit-in, held at the student union—attracted only a handful of students and lasted a scant fifteen minutes. Sponsored by members of a group called the Campus Committee of Concern, the sit-in protested nothing so lofty as Vietnam, civil rights or academic freedom. The students involved simply wanted the union to remain open a while longer at night, so they could drink Cokes and talk there. Even the local press, knowing a nonstory when it saw one, devoted only a short item to the action the next day.

But before the month was over, it was clear that this mini-demonstration had, like the first element in an elaborate Rube Goldberg device, set in motion a series of more complicated events that ended in the exposure of an extensive network of FBI spying and political surveillance on the Brockport campus.

The story of the snooping—perhaps even more alarming because Brockport is hardly known as a hotbed of political activism—was brought to the surface by the widely respected Reverend John Messerschmitt, ecumenical chaplain to the college and a faculty advisor to the group that sponsored the sit-in. Speaking on February 23 to a hushed meeting of the local American Association of University Professors, Messerschmitt revealed that the morning after the sit-in, a member of the Brockport administrative staff, during a conversation with Messerschmitt about the Campus Committee of Concern, began making remarks about Dr. Ernst A. Wiener, then associate professor of sociology and also a faculty advisor to the CCOC. The administrator asked if Messerschmitt was aware of Wiener's involvement with civil rights, the peace movement and various New Left groups that the staff member "knew" to be Communist fronts. When Chaplain Messerschmitt protested that without evidence such accusations were irresponsible, the administrator confided (according to the chaplain's notes, recorded shortly after the conversation), "John, I know I can trust you with this information. I'm in regular contact with the FBI. There are four or five of us on the campus—two with the FBI and three with the CIA. We've been asked to watch Wiener very closely. Believe me when I tell you he has quite a background. Be careful." Messerschmitt responded by telling the man he could hardly believe he was actually working for the FBI and that if he was, his position "was in contradiction to what the university stood for and extremely dangerous to the civil liberties of all the individuals he was keeping under surveillance."

For a half hour, the two men argued the subject. "Wouldn't you do this FBI work if your country requested it of you?" asked the nameless administrator. "How can you attack the FBI when it's only trying to protect you? . . . This surveillance work is occurring on every campus in the country. . . . Those who are being watched shouldn't have anything to hide if what they are doing and saying is aboveboard. . . . Don't think I get paid for this; I don't. I was asked to do this and I agreed as a service to my country."

From the conversation, the surprised chaplain learned not only that such campus spying was common but that both the FBI and the CIA were regularly in touch with friendly Brockport faculty members, who were instructed—in the words of the administrator—"to kind of keep an eye on things on a permanent basis."

"Finally," Chaplain Messerschmitt concluded, "I told him our conversation had left me no less shocked at his disclosure. I was sorry he had assumed a confidence of me without first asking, but because this news was absolutely incompatible with what I understood higher education to be, I could not be quiet about it."

Nor was he. With the fuse lit by his subsequent disclosures, reactions exploded in swift succession. Convinced and outraged by what they had heard but prevented from direct legal action by the fact that the conversation was unwitnessed, the Brockport chapter of the American Association of University Professors passed a resolution strongly condemning undercover operations on the campus—as a threat of "faculty intimidation" and "thought control." Within the next month, the Brockport faculty senate and the State University Federation of Teachers at Brockport passed similar resolutions. The CIA responded by labeling the Brockport charges "nonsense" and stated that it "does not engage in spying in the United States." The FBI's authority is not so circumscribed, however. A few weeks later, FBI Director J. Edgar Hoover, in a letter to Chancellor Samuel Gould, the administrative head of the New York State University system, admitted the charges. "I would never permit the FBI," Hoover wrote, "to shirk its responsibilities. I feel certain that you, as a responsible educator and citizen, would never condone this Bureau's failure to handle its obligations in the internal security field, or that you would have us ignore specific allegations of subversive activity in any segment of our society, including college campuses."

Professor Ernst Wiener—whose activities and views had sparked all the commotion—seemed less surprised at the discovery of a campus spying network than at the fact that it should be concerned with someone as harmless as himself. "I have never attempted to conceal the nature of my political beliefs," he announced. And in what many felt was a moving document, indeed (a letter published March 17 in the Brockport college paper), he described his participation in the 1965 Selma–Montgomery march, his concern for the local problems of integration, his opposition to the Vietnam war and his membership in various groups supporting these and similar beliefs. He closed his letter by quoting Socrates: "For of old I have had many accusers, who have accused me falsely to you during many years. . . . Hardest of all, I do not know and cannot tell the names of my accusers . . . and therefore I must simply fight with shadows in my own defense, and argue when there is no one who answers."

Professor Wiener must have thought a good bit about Socrates in the month that followed, for on April 20 he committed suicide. In a letter found after his death, he had written, "It is too painful to continue living in a world in which freedom is steadily being constricted in the name of freedom and in which peace means war, in which every one of our institutions, our schools, our churches, our newspapers, our industries are being steadily engulfed in a sea of hypocrisy."

The events that grew from the Brockport affair would be tragic enough even if it were an isolated incident, conceived in the overzealous mind of a local FBI agent or his regional chief. But as Director Hoover's letter makes clear, the FBI regards campus spying as a near-sacred obligation. Just about the same time Dr. Wiener killed himself, *Ramparts* magazine—following up its disclosure that President Ngo Dinh Diem's intrigue-ridden regime in South Vietnam had relied heavily on the expertise of CIA-sponsored faculty members from Michigan State University —exposed a labyrinth of CIA front groups, notably the National Student Association. During the same month, a pseudo coed at the Madison campus of Fairleigh Dickinson made headlines by announcing that she had been planted there by county detectives to spy on a fellow student; and the president of Brigham Young University reluctantly admitted that a group of students had been used to spy on liberal professors. In the past few years, disclosures such as these have appeared with what the agencies involved must find embarrassing regularity, and they provide a small glimpse through the curtain that up to now has concealed a nationally organized, centrally coordinated, undercover campus intelligence operation.

Apologists for this collegiate spying frequently adopt the position of the nameless Brockport vigilante: "Those who are being watched shouldn't have anything to hide if what they are doing and saying is aboveboard." Because the agencies engaged in snooping have yet to use in a court case the mass of information they have gathered, they can easily be viewed as concerned—and relatively ineffective—voyeurs. We are only trying to find out the facts, say the surveiller-informers; we neither enjoin nor punish political expression or association.

But even if the snooping were as benign and nonrestrictive as the agencies suggest, there would still remain the thorny question of academic freedom. In theory, colleges are supposed to be open-market places of ideas, where students and teachers are free to say and think what they please. Government agencies violate this principle simply by listening in on what is said, even if they never use the information. Their presence—or just the possibility of their presence—can stimulate a self-censorship far more damaging to freedom and learning than most of the restraints against individual liberty currently on the statute books. If a student or a teacher has reason to suspect that Big Brother —or anyone, for that matter—is surreptitiously listening to or recording what he says, he will surely be more circumspect than he would be in complete privacy. Firmly committed students tend to accept political sleuthing as a predictable risk and often use it to support their alienation from society. But it is measurably daunting to the large number of timid, uncommitted but curious students—the samplers, sippers and tasters of the various causes offered on campus. These are the students who most need the opportunity to experiment and examine, an opportunity that our Bill of Rights—and our concept of academic freedom—was designed to protect. As the Brockport student paper asked editorially in March 1967: "How may academic freedom thrive in a classroom in which the instructor may be the patriotic, right-winged informer to the FBI and the CIA? The students are not so naïve as to believe that liberal or left-wing sentiments go unnoticed by the FBI." The result is that snooping yields maximum returns of control for a minimum investment of official power; it drastically curbs dissent and, in so doing, it evades judicial review in an area for which the courts have shown a special and commendable concern.

The surveillance-informing system is marvelously efficient because life in American society—particularly on the campus—makes the average "subject" extremely vulnerable to fear when he learns his politics are under scrutiny by the government, especially by the FBI. The undercover character of the surveillance, the benighted standards of the investigators, the assumed guilt of the subject, the denial of an opportunity to face charges or to offer a defense and the inability to understand the reasons for the investigation can be shatteringly Kafkaesque. Reputations, brittle as glass, are easily smashed beyond repair. "Of what crime was Ernst Wiener guilty," inquired the Brockport campus paper, "to allow the smearing of his name in a local newspaper as 'under investigation'? This is just more evidence of implying guilt by innuendo, while the investigators and smearers are well covered under a muffling cloak of silence."

Critics of campus spying—and they are legion—claim not only that collegiate surveillance is ethically questionable but that there's little legal justification for it as well. Neither the CIA nor any of the state and local vigilante groups described below can cite a single law permitting the sort of political snooping they engage in as a matter of routine. Even the legality of the FBI's activities in this area is suspiciously ambiguous. In 1956, Don Whitehead, J. Edgar Hoover's Boswell, published in *The FBI Story* a private directive—sort of a "Dear Edgar" letter—sent to Hoover by President Roosevelt in 1939. This letter—which was *not* an Executive Order—authorized the FBI to engage in "intelligence activities" incidental to its newly acquired domestic spy-catching authority. This informal and obscure note—at best intended as a stopgap measure in an atmosphere of impending war—has become the tail that wags the enormous dog of a permanent FBI surveillance apparatus. Hoover seems to have expanded the vague terms of the directive to confer upon the FBI the power, in Hoover's language, "to identify individuals working against the United States, determine their objectives and nullify their effectiveness." These "individuals," Hoover would say, are those whose activities involve "subversion and related internal-security problems." With this murky justification, the FBI has assumed the power to police not acts but opinions, speech and association—and not for the purpose of preparing evidence for presentation at a trial but merely to keep track of nonconformists.

No act of Congress has ever authorized the FBI to exercise

these powers. In fact, an act permitting the FBI to trail campus radicals, take their photographs, open their mail, record their license-plate numbers, bug their conversations, penetrate their meetings and associations through decoys and informers and assemble extensive dossiers that include tips and complaints supplied by private (and frequently anonymous) individuals would be about as constitutional as a law creating a hereditary monarchy.

Only since 1960 or so has the security establishment zoomed in on the college campus. According to the snoopers' logic, this new focus makes eminent sense. In the 1960s, the campus emerged as the spawning ground of the most vigorous—and the most radical—antiwar and political movements. The campus is where the action is. As a group, college teachers now dominate the New Left intellectual community. In faculties and student bodies alike, the young, the restless and the militant abound, openly activist and publicly disdaining what they see as the hang-ups and the subterfuges of their elders. These activists can provoke the messianic instincts in the snoopers themselves, many of whom believe they have a patriotic obligation to "save" students from "mistakes they might regret later on." This protective reasoning expresses the quasi-Freudian thesis that political preferences and attitudes are irrevocably fixed before the age of twenty and that unless a youthful subject subsequently defects or informs, he'll bear watching the rest of his life. On a more practical level, the university has also moved up in the intelligence pecking order because of its increasing financial involvement with the Federal government, particularly in the area of security-related research projects.

Since 1960, the House Un-American Activities Committee, at least in its public and semipublic endeavors, has been inordinately preoccupied with youth and the college scene. The California Burns Committee—HUAC's Golden State equivalent—has "protected" California by issuing four extensive reports (the first based on files apparently stolen from the offices of a New Left student group at Berkeley) on the activities of California's young. But the most ambitious campaign to unearth subversion in collegiate militancy has been mounted by Hoover and the FBI. Since 1963, Hoover has vainly tried to ban Communist speakers from college campuses, justifying his concern on grounds that even some FBI sympathizers found offensive: that seductive Communist propaganda is too treacherous for naïve student ears. Hoover's campaign reached a high pitch of passion in his annual report for 1966: "In its cynical bid to gain an image of respectability, the Party is directing an aggressive campaign at American youth, claiming to perceive a new upsurge of 'leftist' thinking among the young people."

So it's not surprising that when an admitted Communist visits a college campus, the FBI photographs not only him but his host —and keeps careful watch over anyone who visits either of them. An avowed Communist is presumed to be a conspirator, so anyone who breaks bread with him bears scrutiny, too. All too often, even more tenuous relationships attract the FBI. In 1963, for instance, John McAuliff, then a junior at Carleton College in Northfield, Minnesota, was investigated after he had sent a check to Dan Rubin, a Communist youth leader who had visited Carleton to speak on a program organized by a campus group (organized for the purpose of presenting controversial speakers of every political stripe) that McAuliff happened to head. The path of this investigation led an FBI agent to one of McAuliff's friends in Indianapolis. The friend was questioned about McAuliff's politics and then urged to keep quiet about the investigation. Nonetheless, *The Minneapolis Tribune* eventually found out about it, published all the facts and wondered editorially how the FBI knew that McAuliff had sent a check to Rubin—unless it had opened Rubin's mail.

In view of the FBI's overpowering obsession with protecting innocent youth from being duped by the wily Communists, it's also not surprising that FBI agents are now familiar figures in the halls of academe. In their legitimate functions—probes to which the student presumably consents, such as to clear him for Federal employment or to support his conscientious-objector claim—FBI agents have routine access to student transcripts (which are not always confined to grades) and also to personal files that may contain political or psychological data. Much of the material in these files is quite unrelated to security matters, but increasingly, colleges keep data on a student's political activities, associations and opinions—because administrators have learned in the past few years that they probably will be asked about these matters.

The presumably legitimate FBI investigations of students and former students have institutionalized the relationship between the Bureau and the universities. The intelligence agent who majors in campus spying develops a soft, friendly relationship with the college staff members with whom he works. The deans, registrars and their assistants know that the agent has "chosen policework as his career" because it is so "challenging." They know that the agent is as concerned as the next man with academic freedom. Didn't he attend college himself, sometimes the very college at which he now spends most of his time? Doesn't he have college-bound youngsters of his own? And, after all, isn't he "only doing his job"?

But when the investigating agents are on a sympathetic, first-name basis with those who keep the records, the shadowy line between legitimate and illegitimate surveillance is not always observed. Early in 1967, Berkeley's admissions officer, David

Stewart, admitted that in "three or four cases in the last few months," student records were given to the FBI. These were records of students who had not applied for any government position, students who had manifestly *not* consented to a *sub rosa* examination of their personal histories and political preferences. And even at universities that strive to maintain the distinction between legitimate and illegitimate investigations, the agent's explanation of the reasons for his investigation is almost invariably taken at face value—on trust.

Since the government itself now keeps dossiers on literally millions of individuals, information from a student's college files frequently finds its way into the government's master file. Unhappily, the accuracy of the resultant hodgepodge of facts and observations is far from unimpeachable. At a time when the government is the nation's largest employer and when some sort of security clearance is practically *de rigueur* for many of the most interesting jobs, the dossier system develops a formidable economic influence. An inaccurate or slanted report of an individual's campus activities—political or otherwise—recorded indelibly in a file the government consults but that the student can never see, can haunt him with preternatural persistence throughout his life.

As a small but perhaps revealing example, Joseph Tieger, who graduated near the top of his class at Duke in 1963, was denied conscientious-objector status by his New Jersey draft board. The board, it turned out, had referred to a five-thousand-word biography of Tieger, anonymously written but apparently prepared by the FBI, mostly from information compiled on Tieger while he was at Duke. This revealing document, which Tieger subsequently had the unique good fortune of obtaining from his draft board, does not record that a Duke religion professor had signed a statement asserting that Tieger deserved C. O. status "beyond question." It does mention, however, that Tieger in high school "failed to participate in extracurricular activities which is required to make a well-rounded personality"; that he once showed up at a tea party at Duke "in shorts with his shirttail out and wearing tennis shoes"; and that the university library once "addressed a postcard to the registrant indicating that a book concerning the writings of Trotsky was overdue."

Although the once-invisible CIA is confined by statute to intelligence operations outside the United States, its activities, too, spill over into the groves of academe. Students and professors who receive grants for foreign travel or study are frequently approached by CIA representatives, who request that the prospective travelers do a little moonlighting as unofficial intelligence agents during their sojourn abroad. Returning students are also interviewed and often invited to report or answer questions of interest to the CIA; if they have taken photographs, they might be asked for copies. The CIA stimulates such voluntary contributions by offering a generous "consultation fee"—as well as the prospect of a new grant. Some veterans of these sessions have taken to voluntarily stopping by the CIA office for a "debriefing" after sojourns to such places as Africa, Indonesia or India.

This might seem harmless enough, as long as the moonlighting scholars don't take their role as spies too seriously. But foreign-study grants are also used more directly, as a cover for regular CIA agents with legitimate or fraudulent academic credentials. While such a gambit is undoubtedly very useful to the CIA, its effects on the academic discipline involved are somewhat less salubrious. A weighty report published by the American Anthropological Association states that in many parts of the world American anthropologists are suspected of being spies. "There is some basis for these suspicions and beliefs," the report notes, adding that as a result, legitimate anthropological research has been severely handicapped. Some anthropologists, the report continues, after failing to get research grants for projects they view as worth while, "have been approached by obscure foundations or have been offered supplementary support from such sources, only to discover later that they were expected to provide intelligence information usually to the Central Intelligence Agency."

A rather similar example involved an instructor at an Eastern university, who in 1963 was turned down for a Fulbright grant for study overseas. The CIA, which seems to keep good track not only of those who get such grants but of those who don't, approached the disappointed instructor and asked him if he'd like to study abroad, anyway. He'd receive the same stipend as a Fulbright fellow and, in return, he would only have to report details about the host country and about the activities of the actual Fulbright scholars there. The instructor reluctantly agreed, but before the deal was closed, he attended an antiwar demonstration, where a student was seen taking pictures of him. The instructor subsequently learned that the CIA had assigned the student to check on the instructor's feelings about the war in Vietnam. The instructor apparently failed his CIA entrance exam, because he never did receive his pseudo Fulbright grant.

Others have been luckier, if you want to call it that. A former Ivy League student who is now a journalist parlayed his impeccable credentials in the Young Republican Organization—which the CIA seems to regard as "safe"—into a jaunt to Europe and then into a free trip around the world. He didn't realize the first trip was at the CIA's expense—until after he returned and was quizzed about it. He reported that all was safe overseas, which must have pleased the CIA, because it sent him back again. After his second return, the CIA never contacted him, so he didn't bother to report at all.

This may be nice work if you can get it, but many of those who succumb to the lure of free travel are not quite as cynical as this chap. Junketeers typically feel they ought to report *something,* if only to justify the CIA's expense. Many also feel that the juicier the information they give, the more likely they are to receive another "foundation grant" in the future. There are no facts to support this assumption, but it's not beyond belief that some of these part-time agents have filed fabricated or greatly exaggerated reports—perhaps to the disadvantage of whatever individuals and groups about which they were reporting.

Besides the CIA and the FBI, there is a surprising number of local surveillance agencies. These are called "Red Squads" or "Bomb Squads" and most of them sprang up in the early years of this century to keep track of Bolsheviks, anarchists, wobblies and the like. While these particular foes are nowadays hardly more than names out of the history books, the forces that once engaged them in battle are still emphatically alive. In fact, campus demonstrations, student antiwar activities and big-city racial disturbances have made them more robust than ever. On campuses in Berkeley, Chicago and New York City—to name a few—political-surveillance bureaus, directly or indirectly related to local police bodies, have taken it upon themselves to watch leftist opinions and associations.

As an example, on the eve of the 1966 National Student Association Convention, a St. John's (New York) University coed, Gloria Kuzmyak, was visited by detectives from New York City's Bureau of Special Services, known as BOSS. Miss Kuzmyak, then an officer in the NSA, was planning to attend the convention to be held at the University of Illinois, and the BOSS men solicited her help "to keep a check on demonstrations that were going to take place." Her help in this instance would be confined to giving BOSS the names of all New York NSA students and representatives "associated with the liberal caucus." Miss Kuzmyak declined. After she returned from the convention, she was visited twice, first by the same detectives with a similar plea and subsequently by another of their number, with the request that she "forget all about" the earlier attempts to extract names from her.

Some local Red Squad agents are so well known that they inspire an emotion similar to camaraderie among those they're paid to spy on. Not too long ago, a student "undercover" agent at the University of Texas, whose affiliation with the Texas Department of Public Safety was an ill-kept secret, was elected honorary chairman of the local chapter of Students for a Democratic Society—in recognition of his exemplary attendance record and the attentiveness with which he followed the proceedings.

The dean of all campus Red Squad operatives, until his recent retirement, was an inspector at Berkeley who has become something like Mr. Chips to a generation of Berkeley radicals. "This affable, balding gentleman," recalls one nostalgic Berkeley grad, "was so familiar to us that he would come up on the platform ahead of a meeting and ask for a list of speakers." The inspector claimed to have the authority to attend whatever Berkeley meetings he wished, but according to our informant, he usually left when asked to—"in order not to make a scene."

But indulgent sentiment for operatives such as this one, coupled with student notions of the ultimate harmlessness of the activities they engage in, sometimes conceals the fact that the Red Squad wings of local police forces are particularly useful to the higher security establishment, if only because of the ease with which they disregard state curbs on wire tapping and bugging. The authorities have allowed FBI agents to "tune in" only when national security is at stake (though the FBI tends to see national security threatened more frequently than most of us might), but local police tap phones routinely, without recourse to any high-sounding justifications. When discovered engaging in political bugging, they frequently explain their actions in terms of some conventional police function. In recent years, they have magically transformed what objective observers would construe as out-and-out political surveillance into investigations of such nonpolitical offenses as drug or morals violations.

Completing our roster of agencies that engage in campus snooping are the Army and Navy counterintelligence crews (who probe draft-connected security risks) and the ROTC. For years, the Berkeley Navy ROTC has conducted systematic surveillance of New Left campus groups. Whether such work earns academic credits isn't clear, but Berkeley undoubtedly provides enough radicals and anarchists to keep the NROTC busy. Much of their work involves compiling dossiers and maintaining files of leftish handbills, which are kept in folders marked CONFIDENTIAL—NAVAL INTELLIGENCE—TWELFTH NAVAL DISTRICT.

Recently the Army ROTC tried to extend the intelligence operation to encompass the eight Western states in the Sixth Army area. ROTC instructors at each school in the area were provided with "confidential" educational training kits, which made it easy for cadets to sniff out the bad guys. When a group of professors at the University of Washington learned about the kits, ROTC officials admitted that the kits had been distributed—but denied that cadets were instructed to snoop. Any spying that had occurred, said the officials, had been done by cadets on their own initiative. But the local chapter of the American Association of University Professors, which perhaps has learned the hard way that students don't usually undertake spare-time projects if they don't count toward the final grade, commended the university for its action against "political propagandizing" and charged the Army with "serious intrusions into academic life."

As both the ROTC groups and the CIA seem to have perceived, the best people to do spying work on campus are students themselves. If the student agent keeps his cool, the risks of exposure are minimal. He has perfect protective coloring, because, unlike the more conventional agent, his background, life style and appearance are just like everyone else's. And the role is much less demanding than being a decoy for drug pushers or homosexuals, or other after-school jobs for which students have been recruited. Students whose politics lean to the right tend to regard informing as a civic duty, like giving blood to the Red Cross.

Students who cannot be induced to spy on their cohorts by appeals to patriotism or the lure of free travel will often succumb to the more tangible blandishment of hard cash. Not too long ago, testimony in a court trial revealed that Charles Benson Childs, a student at the University of North Carolina, earned $100 a month, plus expenses—and he received a draft deferment as well.

Today the pay is not as niggardly. When the tiny Advance Youth Organization was on trial in 1963 and 1964 (the government was trying to compel the group to register as a Communist-front organization), eleven youthful informers testified they had received a total of over $45,000 for brief periods of undercover work. The highest-paid was one Aaron Cohen, whose take from the FBI totaled $6371.65. The sum presumably reflected his extra value as an officer of the organization. Officers, especially secretaries, keep the membership list and thus are prime targets for intelligence sleuths. During the 1965 passport-violation trial of three young people who were part of a student delegation that had visited Cuba, several informers—recruited from campuses as far-ranging as San Francisco State and Columbia—surfaced long enough to testify for the prosecution. All admitted they were well paid. One student testified the FBI had given him a $300 bonus for going to Cuba. Another of the informers wasn't even government-sponsored; he turned out to be in the employ of anti-Communist lecturer Gordon Hall, who had planted him in the delegation in order to arm himself with fresh material for the luncheon circuit.

Almost as good a recruit as an actual member is a student who joins a target organization and then leaves it for ideological reasons. As soon as the FBI learns of his defection, he is often offered the opportunity to avenge himself, usually at the expense of his former colleagues. A few defectors become chronic government witnesses, zealously denouncing their former beliefs and associates. Others, who might be less willing witnesses, are induced to inform more out of a feeling of panic. One day they impulsively join an organization and after weeks of sober reflection, they're stricken with profound regrets. A visit from the FBI at the right moment—or a telephone call by the student himself to the local FBI office—results in a get-together. The experienced FBI agent is predictably adept at manipulating hesitant subjects. He overcomes reluctance to inform by a promise that the information will be kept secret, by patriotic appeals ("Don't you want to help your country?"), by the assurance that "all the kids are doing it," by hints that the agent already possesses compromising information and by expressing sympathy for the humanitarian impulses that led the student into his political lapse. The agent scrupulously avoids the term "informer"; his plea is for "cooperation." The usual result is that the hesitant defector finally identifies other members of his group or pledges to stay on as an informer.

If the soft-sell fails, agents do not scorn cruder methods—especially if the potential stoolie seems a worthwhile recruit. If the subject has a job, an agent has been known to confront him there—and threaten to report a refusal to cooperate to the subject's employer. With law and prelaw students, a threat to report them to the bar association's character committee—which must approve all admissions to the bar—can sometimes turn the trick. A similar ploy can be used with students who plan teaching careers. And when all else fails, there's always the possibility of appealing to the subject's parents, to warn them that their offspring is associating with the wrong people on campus.

The recruiter's life is no bed of roses, however. Even though he concentrates on likely prospects, he is often indignantly rebuffed. To the continuing dismay of security types, most students regard informing as betrayal and they regard the invitation to engage in it as a personal insult. Furthermore, student groups persistently refuse to react in ways the security agents are most familiar with. Students, for instance, are unwilling to adopt the closed, Communist-cell-like political associations that agents are so adept at penetrating. Openness is the key to the students' political style. Students feel they have nothing to hide and—especially in their political associations—are largely repelled by secrecy. But the security establishment finds this attitude both perplexing and disconcerting, since it expects its targets to be guiltily concealing everything they do. After all, secret political machinations—loosely interpreted as "conspiracies"—are a key justification for the surveillance system.

The colleges themselves have responded to snooping activities in a variety of ways. A disturbing number of universities have been tacitly cooperative—in ways that greatly transcend the cozy personal relationships that often grow up between Federal agents and the college administrative staffs. Documented evidence supports the charge that some universities—Duke, Illinois, Indiana, Kansas, Michigan State, Ohio State and Texas, for instance—have actively collaborated with the FBI. In these institutions, a highly security-conscious bureaucracy compiles data about their students' politics from such sources as deans, faculty, staff, faculty advisors of campus organizations, fraternity officers, judicial boards, housemothers, housemasters, maids, the press and the police—both campus and local. Often this information is not only compiled but interpreted. At Duke, for example, Dean Robert Cox keeps an extensive set of dossiers that have been called "potentially the most explosive of all" by a special university committee headed by Professor John Curtiss, president of the Duke chapter of the American Association of University Professors.

Fortunately, most colleges aren't quite this zealous in lending aid and comfort to the surveillance establishment. But even sins of omission can be grievous enough. In 1966, the House Un-American Activities Committee sent subpoenas to Michigan and Stanford universities, requesting lists of officers of campus groups that had criticized the U. S. Vietnam policy. (Many universities require organizations to file membership lists to qualify for registration as an official campus body.) Both schools complied with these subpoenas—though many critics of HUAC, both within the schools and outside, thought that the HUAC action could be challenged as unconstitutional. Similar attempts to secure membership lists from the NAACP had been rebuffed by the Supreme Court, which had held that such enforced disclosures may "constitute as effective a restraint of freedom of association" as more direct forms of interference. The "inviolability of privacy," the Court had said, is "indispensable to the preservation of the freedom of association, particularly where a group espouses dissident beliefs." Despite what seemed a perfect precedent for refusal, or at least challenge, neither of the universities even protested or in any way questioned HUAC's mandate. And neither of the universities seemed to realize that they were collaborating in what amounted to a punitive exposure of the individuals on the lists. Whether or not those listed were summoned as witnesses (some were), all the names were permanently dossiered in the Committee's "file and reference service"—available to security bloodhounds and even to the constituents of any congressman who might ask for them.

To be sure, a few colleges have courageously resisted the intrusions of the surveillance establishment. And with several sorry exceptions—such as California until 1963 and North Carolina and Ohio State until 1965—they successfully resisted the snoopers' attempts to bar Communist speakers from campus. The general response to these two challenges left room for hope that painful memory of the abuses done to dissenting professors in the Fifties would quicken a determination not to collaborate in intimidating the burgeoning student protest movements of the Sixties. But only a handful have lived up to this promise. Following an SDS peace demonstration at Wesleyan University (Connecticut) in the spring of 1966, an FBI agent appeared and asked that college authorities hand over the SDS membership list. College Dean Stanley J. Idzerda refused, saying, "We keep no such lists of any organizations." He added,

> We consider the student's activity his own affair. At the same time, it's unfortunate that a climate of suspicion can be created by such activities that might lead some students to be more circumspect than the situation requires. Things like this can be a danger to a free and open community if men change their behavior because of it.

The resultant furor brought the FBI agent back to the campus, where he told the dean that there had been a "misunderstanding." No probe of the SDS had been contemplated, but only of "possible infiltration of the SDS chapter by Communist influence." Another agent involved in the case thoughtfully added that the FBI "makes inquiries every day on campuses throughout the country—we investigate 175 types of violations, security as well as criminal." When a Wesleyan student committee subsequently wrote J. Edgar Hoover that the investigation constituted a gross infringement of academic freedom, Hoover replied that the charge was "not only utterly false but also is so irresponsible as to cast serious doubt on the quality of academic reasoning or the motivation behind it."

When the director of the FBI can hint, without too much subtlety, that uncooperative colleges are themselves flirting with subversion or conspiracy, it's not too surprising that the colleges try to avoid such conflicts—even when their vital interests are at stake. Reluctant to act unless absolutely forced to do so, most colleges unwittingly invite the very pressures they seek to avoid—and then respond to these with more evasion and more compromise. Their caution is reinforced by the inbred conformity that seems common to all bureaucracies—collegiate or otherwise—a conformity that assures not only that accommodation to the demands of the security establishment will be mindless and irresponsible but that it will be uniform. As one student correspondent—who must remain anonymous, since he's still in school—puts it:

> Most university administrators operate on the principle of inertia—it's easier to go along with inquiries than to refuse. Why run the risk of being labeled a Commie-hippie school? Most of them cheerfully give out some information, although not all, without ever thinking they may be creating a serious problem. Once they are made aware that they also have a

prerogative to refuse, many agree it would be fine if all universities refused, but why should one university risk being labeled "oddball"?

But unless it is willing to take this risk, the university will soon find itself on a collision course with "national security." It will not be enough for the university to make informing or secret political surveillance—by faculty or students alike—grounds for immediate censure, discharge or expulsion, though this would certainly be a good beginning. In the long run, it is fatuous, or at least diversionary, to attempt to reconcile academic freedom with national security. They simply cannot be reconciled. The university must reconstruct, on the foundation of academic freedom, an ethos that—no matter what the risks or temporary costs—rejects surveillance altogether. If the university is disturbed by nonstudent attempts to gain a voice in its affairs (as in the Berkeley outbreak), then it should feel all the more threatened by the actions of Big Brother. At a time when the life and values of the university are being subjected to unprecedented stress by "security" pressures, the university, if it is to survive at all, must simply learn to say no—to the FBI, the CIA, the ROTC, the Red Squads, the congressional committees and the tribe of spies, spooks, snoops, surveillants and subpoena servers they have spawned. In the last analysis, the only real threat to our national security is the mutilation of academic freedom that will inevitably result if the security establishment continues to flourish on our nation's campuses.

"The administration is willing to give in to the first nine nonnegotiable demands, but under no circumstances will it consent to the dean of women being burned at the stake."

opinion

KENNETH REXROTH

THE FUZZ

despite new Supreme Court safeguards of our civil rights and liberties, police brutality prevails and the police mentality assumes guilt until proven innocent

Recently, police activity began to impinge upon my own life. I live in San Francisco's Negro district, and I could see about me a noticeable increase—prowl cars were more evident at all times. On weekend nights they seemed to be everywhere, stopping and questioning many more people than formerly.

An art gallery was raided and welded sculpture illustrating the *Kama Sutra* was confiscated. This was entirely a police action without prior civilian complaint. The police lost the case. Student parties in San Francisco's Haight-Ashbury district were raided again and again and everyone was hauled off to jail. Even where the police claimed to have found evidence of marijuana, the cases were usually dismissed. In New York, a party of the Artists' and Writers' Protest Against the War in Vietnam, a group with no political affiliations, was raided without a warrant or complaint and several arrests were made.

Friends of mine married to members of another race began to complain that they were frequently stopped by prowl cars and questioned when walking along the street in broad daylight with their spouses. After the *Ginzburg* decision, there was a noticeable increase throughout the country in police censorship. In San Francisco, bookshops were visited by police officers who told the proprietors, "Clean this place up or we'll take you in," but who vouchsafed no information as to what books were, in fact, objectionable.

Certain costumes seem to be an open invitation to police questioning—beards, dirty jeans, bare feet, especially on juveniles; but more common still, the uniform of the homosexual prostitute, the studbuster—T-shirt, leather jacket, tight jeans, heavy belt and boots. I began to get all sorts of complaints: A well-known jazz musician taking a breather between sets and talking to his white wife in front of a perfectly respectable jazz room was arrested, taken to the local station, held for two hours, insulted and then let go. Another driving with his wife was arrested for a minor traffic violation—failure to signal a right-hand turn—and taken to the station.

No policeman had molested me in over forty years. I drink only wine at dinner. Marijuana has no effect on me; I haven't smoked it since adolescence. I am a very safe driver. However subversive my opinions, I am an exemplary law-abiding citizen. But one night I parked my car in front of my own home, left my Negro secretary in the car and took my two daughters to the door. When I returned, the police, who obviously thought they were dealing with a racially mixed couple, had been questioning my secretary and, because they hadn't liked the tone of her voice, were writing a traffic ticket.

In the next block, the same patrol had threatened a neighbor with arrest in a similar situation. A few blocks away, a Negro youth leader had an appointment for lunch with a police officer. On the way to the lunch he was rousted by that very officer. A Negro high-school boy acting in a school play with my daughter was stopped as he was walking home from rehearsal along a well-lighted business street, rousted and eventually forced to lie down on the sidewalk, but finally let go.

All of his happened in my immediate neighborhood, to people known to me, in one month. Yet San Francisco's police force is unquestionably one of the most professional in the country, with an extremely active community-relations detail led by a dedicated officer, an enlightened chief, lectures and classes on civil liberties, race relations, youth problems and like matters. Reports in the press and from friends in other cities of increasing petty police harassment were far more shocking. It was apparent that the heat was on—nationally. Why?

What exactly is the heat and what turns it on? And why should it suddenly go on all over the country?

I decided to write an article about it. Before I was through, hell broke loose. A young Negro boy was shot and killed in San Francisco for suspicious behavior and refusal to halt. Naturally, a race riot began—nowadays, "race riot" means a massive show of force by police and National Guard and indiscriminate firing at Negroes, preferably Black Muslim mosques. As Dick Gregory has said, the only thing that saved the city from worse destruction than Watts was the sympathetic demonstrations by white people—the coffin-bearing deathwatch at the city hall and the defiant parade from Haight-Ashbury's new bohemia—whose participants were treated to a maximum display of brutality by policemen who, as a friend said, "stunk of fear as they beat up girls, boys and college professors and dragged them into paddy wagons."

Next came the Sunset Strip—conclusive demonstration that "whom the gods destroy, they first make mad." This Vietnam operation is very simply the attempt of the Organization-run night clubs along the Strip to use the Los Angeles police to turn back the clock and bring again the good old days of movie stars, gossip columnists, Elks and Shriners. Alas, Los Angeles is a run-down town and there will never be another Alla Nazimova or Garden of Allah—and never again the Strip with the Million Dollar Clip. So the kids—who have no place else to go and who spend good money, too, but only for honest entertainment—are subjected to a military operation on a scale seldom attempted in the Congo. Since the election of Ronald Reagan, things have got very tough, not just in California, but all over. The neo-conservative victories have been interpreted by the city police forces as a go-ahead signal for a nationwide campaign of censorship and harassment, for direct action by the police acting as cop, attorney, trial jury and judge. The police, in other words, are, after a few years of retreat, taking the law into their own hands far more aggressively than ever in the past forty years.

"If they can harass beatniks, they can harass all political dissent," say the civil libertarians. But the civil libertarians are oldies—they don't know that beatniks went out in 1956 and what the cops are harassing is precisely political and moral dissent.

In recent months there have been a number of magazine articles and serial newspaper features on "What's Wrong with the Police," and these have been answered in most cases by literate spokesmen for the police, not PR men, but working officers themselves. There's very little dialog. One side makes flat accusations, usually well documented, of police brutality, illegal entry or search, harassment, prejudice against the poor, racism, political reaction, third degree and other violations of the rights of those arrested. The other side simply denies that most of these things exist and counters with the statement "Policework is a profession with very special problems that the layman cannot understand."

Both sides isolate the problem and treat the police as though they were members of a self-contained society—separate from the rest of us, like monks, professional soldiers or the inmates of prisons and state hospitals. The problem is the functioning of the police as part of society, not apart from it. Essential to any understanding is the definition of the roles that the police perform in the society in fact and the different roles they are supposed to perform in theory—their own theories and those of their critics.

The average policeman looks on himself as an enforcer of the law and a guardian of public order and morality, an active protector of life and property. His critics say he should be an impersonal, purely objective guardian of the law. The first function is custodial, like a steward in a psychopathic ward. The second, ideally, is impassive, almost mechanical—a sorting process. In fact, since the policeman must make split-second decisions involving life and liberty, and most of the situations with which he deals are emergencies, he is, most especially in the slums, policeman, judge, jury, prosecutor, defense attorney and executioner. The policeman lives in constant expectation of acute emergency. Therefore, he is simply not physiologically "objective"—one does not cope with armed assault "objectively." In addition, when there are no emergencies, he certainly does act as neighborhood custodian, seeing to it that all his charges behave themselves—less obviously in a well-to-do suburb, very obviously indeed among the poor. It is especially this latter function that is a survival from an older society and it is the policeman's insistence on his role as moral enforcer that gets him into trouble.

The following article recently appeared in the *Berkeley Barb:*

POLICE RAID NUDE FEST . . . LIKE "GANG BUSTERS"

Berkeley police with flashbulbs blazing ran swiftly through a gathering of about 40 nude men and women last Saturday. They were "investigating" possible lawbreaking at an East Bay Sexual Freedom League party. "It was like 'Gang Busters,' " EBSFL president Richard Thorne told *Barb*. "They came in very quickly and told us to hold it, stay where we were, and flashed cameras." The police searched the house and checked the I. D. of each guest. They stayed for about an hour, around midnight. "After I got dressed, I went to the lieutenant in charge and inquired on what grounds the police were present," Thorne said. "The lieutenant said that someone had issued a complaint which led them to suspect that there was the possibility of contributing to the delinquency of minors. 'Of what sort?' I asked him. He said, 'Alcohol.' " Thorne and several other witnesses described the police investigation. Desks, chairs, bureaus, and clothes in closets were searched. Ashtrays were examined. Medicines were confiscated. Brown Filipino cigarettes were peeled open. Guests who objected to showing their I. D.s were given the choice of cooperating or being identified "at the station." At *Barb* presstime, no arrests had resulted from the investigation. One guest, who met a flashbulb as he emerged from the bathroom, described his conversation with the plainclothesman who apparently admitted the other police: "I asked him what had happened to give them the right to enter and search without a warrant.

"He asked, 'Are you a lawyer?'

"I said, 'No.'

" 'In that case, it's none of your business,' he said." Witnesses described the police demeanor as initially "rude," "sarcastic," "snide" and "uptight." As the hour passed, they "settled down" and became "mannerly" and "courteous," guests said. About 20 partygoers remained after the police departed. "Clothes came off again at a rapid rate after they left," one participant told *Barb*. "It was as if they wouldn't let the police intimidate them, and they wanted to release a pent-up rage. It became quite a party. A very fine, successful party."

Robert E. Kramer, M. D., comments on this in his own *Bulletin of Research Associates* as follows:

"Following the publication of this article in the *Barb,* I took it upon myself to question one of the members of the Berkeley police force regarding the matter. Our conversation was friendly and was not confined to the police raid, although it covered the pertinent aspects. Pertinent portions of the interview were in sum and substance to this effect:

Interviewer: What happened at the nude party?

Police officer: Oh, we alleged that there were people below the age of 18 there, but there weren't.

I: Did you really believe that there was someone below the age of 18?

P: No, we just used that as an excuse.

I: Well, what happened?

P: We busted into the place and there were several couples actually fornicating. So we took some pictures and left.

I: What did you do with the pictures?

P: Oh, they're fun to pass around for all the boys to look at down at the station.

I: Isn't that illegal?

P: Well, I suppose so, but they were having a nude party.

I: Didn't the attorney general of the state of California specifically say that nude parties were legal?

P: Oh, we know that there isn't anything illegal going on, but we feel that if you let this kind of thing happen, it's like opening Pandora's box.

I: Is the police department supposed to prescribe morals?

P: Somebody's got to.

I: Doesn't the Constitution of the United States specifically allow the citizenry to determine its own morals?

P: Well, you know how these things are.

I: Would you want the police busting into your home under these circumstances?

P: Well, I wouldn't be doing anything illegal.

I: Neither were they.

This example, however comic, poses the dilemma: the contradiction between the police as officers of order and officers of law. In the early days of the development of modern police forces, perhaps their primary function was the preservation of social order and the enforcement of public morality. They dealt mostly with the poor who, however unruly, accepted the same values. In a heterogeneous society such as America was in the days of massive immigration, most of the work of a patrolman on the beat in Hell's Kitchen, the Lower East Side, Five Points, Back of the Yards, was extralegal. He was not a law officer but a peace officer, and if he invoked the law to handle all violations of public order, he would have found himself hopelessly overwhelmed. Until recent years, the Paris police force still operated this way in almost all their day-to-day work. The vicious, the disorderly, the conspicuous violators of common morals, were simply taken up an alley and "coated" with a weighted cape or worked over with a truncheon and kicked out on the street, with a warning that if they were caught doing it again, they'd get worse.

Vice (prostitution, gambling, narcotics), as distinguished from crime, was "policed." Streetwalkers were protected on their stations from invasion by other whores or pimps and guarded against robbery or attack by their customers. This type of relationship—which was usually effective—was always advanced in private conversation by American policemen as an excuse for pay-off: "If you clout them, you control them." It still prevails in the slum districts of many American cities.

The Lower East Side of New York or Halsted and Maxwell Streets in Chicago were once seething slums, crowded with ethnic groups with the most antagonistic sets of values. Tension was constantly at a maximum. Petty crime and "vice" were rampant and all a policeman could hope to do was abate them, to keep social disorder from destroying social life. In addition, he usually performed all sorts of tasks of social hygiene of the type now handled by professionals—social workers, recreation workers and psychiatrists. Very important, the typical policeman was recruited from the most powerful group in the slums—the Irish poor. Insofar as there was a "consensus" of the well-behaved poor, he represented it—puritanical, authoritarian, superstitious, a believer in corporal punishment of children, subordination of wives and the solution of minor differences between friends by trial by fisticuffs. The Jews were the only group in the old slums who didn't share any of this social ethic, but they kept out of the way of the police.

America has changed. It is becoming a homogeneous society and the divisions that do exist are of a new kind. Today almost all Americans share another set of values—the acquisitive, conspicuous-expenditure, passive-pleasure system of the American middle class, with its built-in frustration and irresolvable sexual tensions. The Negroes in Watts riot because they want in—into the culture of the TV commercials. They *want* to integrate into a burning house. They want admission to American homogeneity.

First, of course, is the conflict over homogeneity itself, to which the Negroes demand they be admitted. The second most important division, from the police point of view, is a change of values, the democratization of what was once the privilege of an elite of radical intellectuals—an entirely new moral code.

The only people outside this TV culture are the young (and some old) members of the new and ever growing subculture of secession. They want *out,* on any terms, and they deny—in dress, conduct, amusements, personal relations, even intoxicants—all the values of the dominant culture. These people, actually the youngest members of another kind of middle class —the elite corps of the technological society—are, in fact, much more orderly and peaceful and infinitely less predatory than the dominant society. This in itself outrages the police as custodians of the prevailing morality.

Emma Goldman, free lover and anarchist, was quite a sufficient bother to the police of her day. Today there are millions of Emma Goldmans, members of a new kind of middle class. This public resents the police as guardians of public morals. Younger people, who live by moral codes that bear little resemblance to the lower-middle-class Irish Catholic morality of most of the police force, look upon the policeman as a dangerous and ignorant disrupter of their own peaceful lives.

The police, on the other hand, believe that they have the right to control the lives of others for their own benefit, that they know better what others should do than they do themselves. They adjust the behavior of those who live by a different moral code to the stereotypes that they have inherited from the past. In its most extreme form: "If you see a nigger and a white woman together, chances are it's a pimp and a whore." "All those beatniks," referring to a bearded student of nuclear physics, "take dope." "If you watch, you can catch one of them making a pass and you're sure to find marijuana or pills."

Both press and police commonly refer to marijuana, an intoxicant far less harmful than alcohol, and to LSD and the various barbiturates, tranquilizers and stimulants as "dope" and "narcotics" and attempt to deal with the problem exactly the same way that they dealt with the morphine-cocaine traffic and addiction of fifty years ago. It is significant that the use of most of these drugs results in relaxation and noninvasive behavior, while alcohol stimulates aggressions. The police as the arm of the squares represent an aggressive lower-middle-class morality in conflict with life patterns of nonaggression that they find incomprehensible and interpret in terms of crime and vice—aggression—which they *can* understand.

What is it the spokesmen for the police are talking about when they say the public doesn't understand the nature of policework? Why don't they explain? The reason is that the contradiction, the dilemma of policework, is something they do not wish publicized. They wish to present to a society concerned about civil liberties the policeman as a functionary of the legal process. They are not prepared to face the fact that he is involved in a symbiotic relationship within the illegal communities that function as subcultures in the society.

It is a common charge of those interested in a reform of the methods of handling the narcotics problem that the Federal, state and, to a lesser degree, city police, along with the Mafia, have a vested interest in preserving the status quo. This is an oversimplification. What has actually developed is a great web of petty crime, addiction and peddling, which the narcotics officer hopes he can control and which is sensitive to his manipulation.

For instance, to begin at the beginning of the process: A narcotics addict arrested on a petty-larceny charge can cooperate with the police in several ways. He can help clear the record by admitting to a number of unsolved petty thefts; he can give information that will lead to the arrest of his retail dealer, and his anonymity will be protected by the police and the charges against him will be reduced to a minimum. In the somewhat bigger time, a felony charge can be reduced if the prisoner is willing to cooperate in the arrest of a narcotics wholesaler.

At the bottom of the ladder, a prostitute known to have associates who are either thieves or narcotics pushers or both can cooperate simply by giving general information; or in cases where the police know that the girl has information they want, she is often given the choice between cooperation, being admitted to bail and receiving only a fine at her trial, or refusing to cooperate, being held without bail for a medical examination and then given a jail sentence.

All this is done with a great deal of indirection and evasive language; but since narcotics control is something the police must originate themselves—it is one of several "crimes without plaintiff," which is another definition of "vice"—the police can function only if they can keep a complicated machinery of information and actual social contact operating. And the fuel that keeps this machine going is bargaining power. Each side has a commodity of value to exchange with the other. Each party to the transaction must make a profit. In this sense, the police have a vested interest in the subculture of the underworld.

The remarkable thing about this subculture is that, although it may use the term square, both police and criminals share the same system of values. The narcotics peddler, the gambler or the prostitute may point out that their activities are civil-service occupations in some countries and if the public didn't want what they had to offer, they would go out of business. To some extent, most policemen share this point of view, but both sides in private conversation usually will be found to be convinced that vice is morally wrong.

The underworld subculture does not have the self-confidence attributed to it in fiction. Again, this lack is a powerful psychological tool in the hands of the police. A prostitute who is treated by the arresting officer as "just a hard-working girl," the victim of hypocritical bluenose laws that it is the officer's job to enforce, will be far more cooperative than a girl who feels she is being treated with contempt, most especially so because she herself has that contempt. Organizations such as Synanon have made a therapeutic method out of the self-hate of the narcotics addict, but a policeman who used the language of a Synanon session would find himself with a very hostile prisoner on his hands, indeed.

What the policeman does as a custodial officer within the underworld subculture is keep it abated, and he applies these methods to other problems of social order.

For instance, for several years I knew a handsome young Negro intellectual who was a professional blackmailer. He would spot a wealthy young married woman slumming in bohemia, strike up an acquaintance, carry on an intellectual conversation, arouse her sympathy. After reciting T. S. Eliot at length, he would divulge the information that he cried himself to sleep night after night because his skin was black and his hair was crinkly. As they parted, he would thank her profusely, say that he never hoped to see her again but could he write to her sometimes when the pain was more than he could bear. The exchange of letters led to an exchange of pictures and possibly even to an affair, and then one day the socialite housewife would get a telephone call that he was in a terrible jam and needed the $1000 that he had been offered by a newspaperman for the letters and pictures. Needless to say, journalism is seldom conducted this way, but the girls usually paid up, and those who had been sleeping with him usually went right on doing so.

One night I was in a club in San Francisco's North Beach and watched the regular cop on the beat question only the mixed couples in the place and concentrate his hostility on this man and his new girl. As the cop went out the door, he said to me, "OK, Rexroth, say I'm prejudiced, but what do you want me to do with that motherfucker? Go up to him and say, 'You're under arrest for blackmail'?"

Eventually this harassment may have paid off, because the fellow left town for good. This instance explains a good many things. The police still believe that there are enough relationships of this kind, or worse, among mixed couples to justify a policy of general interrogation and of making those people who do not respond as the police think they should as uncomfortable as possible. Harassment is a method of abatement and the police consider it one that may work when there is no plaintiff or no visible commission of crime.

Take the case of homosexuality. Homosexual acts between consenting adults are no longer policed as such. The laws that the police attempt to enforce are essentially the same as those applied to heterosexuals. The bushes in parks and public toilets are not chosen by heterosexuals for sexual intercourse, and although assignations are made between men and women in bars, this has become socially acceptable in most cities, and it is usually not so obvious as the activities in a gay bar.

With the growing tolerance of homosexuality and the enormous increase in gay bars and other open manifestations of homosexuality socially, there has been not only a great increase in homosexual prostitution, especially among floating adolescents, but a tremendous increase in robbery and murder. Not only have a number of well-known personalities in recent years been found robbed and beaten to death in cities with a large homosexual population, but studbusting has become one of the commonest forms of "unexplained" homicide. Middle-aged men, many of them married and with children, are pulled out of the bushes dead with a frequency the police prefer to say nothing about.

Here is the police problem: No one is going to complain. The partners in a homosexual relationship participate voluntarily. If one is robbed, he will not risk disgrace by going to the police. If he's dead, he's dead, and the circumstances of his murder provide no clue. The act itself takes only a brief time and is almost impossible to catch. So the police harass and embarrass the gay bar or the respectable-looking homosexuals frequenting parks or cruising certain well-known streets looking for "trade." The trade, the homosexual prostitute, they make as uncomfortable as possible.

At one time entrapment was a common form of arrest, but the prejudice of the court and the public is so great that it is being abandoned. A judge is very likely to say, "What were you doing when the defendant was fondling your penis?" Besides, entrapment does not catch the principal offender, the studbuster, who, if he is experienced, can recognize a plainclothesman no matter how plausibly disguised.

This leaves the police with degrading methods, peepholes in public toilets and such, which most officers rebel against using.

Of course, in all these cases, some policemen simply love this kind of work. The favorite term of contempt among police, as in the underworld, is "copperhearted." Fairykillers and whore-hunters are not liked by their colleagues on the force; and although police will give all their skill and devotion to cracking a big case of narcotics wholesaling, most men on the narcotics detail sicken of the work with the petty addict, the round of desperation, pilfering, prostitution and squalor and the hopelessness of changing it.

There is one outstanding factor in common in almost all arrests for "vice." The cop must *judge* to arrest; and in court, in a legal process based on contest, he must stick to his guns—and the *esprit de corps* of the force must back him all the way up the chain of command. A general cannot deny his troops. This is the reason that the chain of command almost invariably seems to the public to do nothing but whitewash whenever there is a complaint, no matter how grievous. It is this paramilitary ethic, not corruption, that accounts for the run-around. Except for a few cities in the East, corruption from outside is dying out. If it exists today, it comes from within the force. Outside the cities that are still controlled by the Organization, policemen, let alone high-ranking officers, are no longer directly controlled by corrupt political machines or by the Mafia.

Modern police corruption is a more subtle thing. Many police departments are controlled by intradepartmental political structures, power *apparats*. Others are the battleground of conflicting groups of this sort, but they are more likely to be generated within the department and concerned exclusively with police rank and privilege than to come from outside. In fact, the tendency is to keep such things from the attention of the public, even from the apparatus of the political parties.

In the case of a liberal and enlightened police chief, the increasing polarization of American society is certain to be reflected in an opposition, usually clandestine but often organized, that considers him a nigger-lover and a Red and whose members do everything they can to sabotage his efforts and to back one another up all along the chain of command as high as they can go. It is this type of reactionary opposition that accounts for the apparently successful John Birch Society recruitment campaign in the police forces of America; and it is here that you find whitewash and run-around in cases of police brutality and especially of racism.

Pay-off is, as I said, part of a system of control for which many otherwise honest, old-fashioned policemen will present strong if not convincing arguments. Criminal corruption, again, usually arises within a police force prompted only by the generally criminal character of American society.

Rings of thieves such as those uncovered a couple of years

ago in two police forces usually grow out of the general "knock-down" philosophy of American enterprise, particularly in relation to insurance claims. To quote Chief Stanley R. Schrotel:

> Most policemen recognize no wrong in accepting free admissions to public entertainment, discounts on their purchases, special favors and considerations from persons of influence, or tips and gratuities for services performed in the line of their regular duty. They choose to look upon these incidents as being strictly personal matters between themselves and the donors and are unwilling to recognize that moral obligations are involved. . . . No matter how much effort is expended in minimizing the derogatory effect of the acceptance of gratuities and favors by law-enforcement officers, the practice has become so prevalent that the public generally concedes that policemen are the world's greatest "moochers." Aside from the question of the effect of the practice upon the officers' effectiveness in enforcing the law, it is a certainty that a reputation for "mooching" does not elevate the standards of the profession in the public's mind.

This picture has a certain old-time charm: the copper in pith helmet and blue Prince Albert copping an apple off the pushcart. To quote again, Banton's *The Policeman in the Community,* paraphrasing Mort Stern's article "What Makes a Policeman Go Wrong":

> A former member of the Denver police department, in discussing what went wrong there, stressed that a new recruit was not accepted by his colleagues unless he conformed to their norms. When investigating a burglary in a store, police officers might put some additional articles into their pockets (indeed, they were sometimes encouraged to do so by the owners, who pointed out that they would recover from the insurance company, anyway).

In the "cops as robbers" scandals of a few years back, investigation soon revealed the step-by-step process of corruption. The robbery victim, owner of a shop or a warehouse, expected and encouraged the investigating officers to help themselves to a couple of mink coats or television sets to run up the insurance claim. From there it was a short step to collusion between police, burglary gang and would-be "victim," and from there a still shorter step, the elimination of the middleman, until the police planned and carried out the robberies themselves and moved on to plain, old-fashioned robbery, without the connivance of the robbed.

The corruption that stems from gambling is a special case, although its effects are probably the most far-reaching. Few police anywhere are directly part of the organized narcotics business, and their involvement in prostitution is really trivial, however common, and mostly part of what they consider the necessary web of information. Gambling is different. Today, when churches and supermarkets are gambling institutions, it is hard for the average policeman, who is likely to be an Irish Catholic whose church stages weekly bingo games, to take gambling seriously.

Pay-off may start as part of the system of control, but since gambling is the major business of organized crime in America, it soon penetrates to the vitals of the police system. Since gambling is also the major bridge between politics and organized crime, it carries with it not only the corruption of vice but the additional corruption of vice-controlled politics.

Collusion with bookmakers and the proprietors of gambling rooms is turned up fairly frequently on the West Coast. There is such a case pending at this writing in a suburb of San Francisco. Massive infection of the police department and the penetration of high-level, outside, political corruption seems to be far more common east of the Rockies. The Sunset Strip paramilitary actions against youth show conclusively the corruption of the police by the organized "entertainment business." There is a psychological factor here that must be taken into account. A corrupt police force is a guilt-ridden police force, because, with few exceptions, policemen do believe in the lower-middle-class values, even when they flout them. A guilty police force is likely to be both belligerently puritanical in its attempts to control unconventional behavior and hostile—quick to react aggressively to any fancied assault on its own authority. Obviously, this sets up a vicious circle that goes round and round in an ever accelerating separation of the police from the general population.

At the very best, as any honest policeman will tell you, the police live in a ghetto of their own, and a great deal of the effort of the human-relations bureaus and details of the better police departments is devoted to simply getting through to the public, to breaking down the ghetto wall. But even with the best public relations, the police as a subculture of their own are a garrison society. Policemen associate mostly with one another and have few civilian friends. Policemen's balls and picnics are characterized by a noisy but impoverished conviviality.

In the case of Negroes, the young man who joins the force is likely to meet with a total cutoff in his community and at best find himself uncomfortable in his new one, the police society. A neighbor who was a graduate in law from a Southern Jim Crow university joined the force and discovered that he had even lost the friendship of his minister. After a couple of years of isolation, he quit. As a custodial officer in a Negro ghetto, the policeman confronts a population in revolt to whom he is a soldier of an occupying army, as both James Baldwin and Bayard Rustin have said.

The Negro who sticks it out is bleached and assimilated. As a Negro sergeant in New York City said, "Five years on the New York force and I don't care how you started out—colored, Puerto Rican, Jewish—you end up Irish." But it must not be forgotten that this is less difficult and less incongruous than it seems to white people. The vast majority of Negroes are not all that exotic. They are conscious of themselves very specifically as a "deprived" minority—deprived of the wonders and goodies of the American way of life. Their exoticism is the delusion of a handful of intellectuals of both races who live exclusively along the hot no man's land of the miscegenation battle front.

I have neglected to mention the only way in which the average citizen comes in frequent contact with the police—traffic violation. This is, as we all know, an area of continual irritability and exasperation on both sides, and one of the best things a city can do is to create a department of traffic-control officers for all violations short of crime completely divorced from the police department.

To sum up, these are the basic factors in the problem: The police are a closed community, socially isolated from the general population, with a high level of irritability along the edges of contact. Police methods have developed in the day-by-day work of control of an underworld of petty crime and vice, in a period when most policework was with the poor, or at least the dwellers in slums. As a control or custodial officer, the typical policeman, in the words of Jerome H. Skolnick,

> is inherently a suspicious person, fond of order and predictability. He reacts to stereotyped symbols of potential trouble—even oddities of dress or speech—and proceeds on the presumption of guilt, often while winking at the legal niceties of restraint in searches and arrests. Intent upon "controlling crime," the officer keenly resents having his results upset at the appellate level.

Skolnick found that the police feel frustrated by the court's affirmation of principles of due process and generally consider the appellate judiciary as "traitor" to its responsibility to keep the community free from criminality.

We hear a great deal about the professionalization of the policeman from theorists and lecturers in police academies, but on the part of the older or more conventional of these people, professionalism really means the development of a high degree of craft skill in playing the role described by Skolnick—a social custodial officer with maximum efficiency and minimum social friction. This body of social servants, with its own ideology and ethic, is set over against a society that bears little resemblance to the one that produced it in the first place. To quote Thomas F. Adams, "Field Interrogations," *Police,* March–April 1963:

A. Be suspicious. This is a healthy police attitude, but it should be controlled and not too obvious.

B. Look for the unusual.

1. Persons who do not "belong" where they are observed.
2. Automobiles that do not "look right."
3. Businesses opened at odd hours, or not according to routine or custom.

C. Subjects who should be subjected to field interrogations.

1. Suspicious persons known to the officers from previous arrests, field interrogations and observations.
2. Emaciated-appearing alcoholics and narcotics users who invariably turn to crime to pay for cost of habit.
3. Person who fits description of wanted suspect as described by radio, teletype, daily bulletins.
4. Any person observed in the immediate vicinity of a crime very recently committed or reported as "in progress."
5. Known troublemakers near large gatherings.
6. Persons who attempt to avoid or evade the officer.
7. Exaggerated unconcern over contact with the officer.
8. Visibly "rattled" when near the policeman.
9. Unescorted women or young girls in public places, particularly at night in such places as cafés, bars, bus and train depots or street corners.
10. "Lovers" in an industrial area (make good lookouts).
11. Persons who loiter about places where children play.
12. Solicitors or peddlers in a residential neighborhood.
13. Loiterers around public rest rooms.
14. Lone male sitting in car adjacent to schoolground with newspaper or book in his lap.
15. Lone male sitting in car near shopping center who pays unusual amount of attention to women, sometimes continuously manipulating rearview mirror to avoid direct eye contact.
16. Hitchhikers.
17. Person wearing coat on hot days.
18. Car with mismatched hubcaps, or dirty car with clean license plate (or vice versa).
19. Uniformed "deliverymen" with no merchandise or truck.
20. Many others. How about your own personal experiences?

And Colin MacInnes, in *Mr. Love and Justice:*

The true copper's dominant characteristic, if the truth be known, is neither those daring nor vicious qualities that are sometimes attributed to him by friend or enemy, but an ingrained conservatism and almost desperate love of the conventional. It is untidiness, disorder, the unusual, that a copper disapproves of most of all, far more, even, than of crime, which is merely a professional matter. Hence his profound dislike of people loitering in streets, dressing extravagantly, speaking with exotic accents, being strange, weak, eccentric, or simply any rare minority—of their doing, in fact, anything that cannot be safely predicted.

Then Peter J. Connell, in "Handling of Complaints by Police":

> The time spent cruising one's sector or walking one's beat is not wasted time, though it can become quite routine. During this time, the most important thing for the officer to do is notice the *normal*. He must come to know the people in his area, their habits, their automobiles and their friends. He must learn what time the various shops close, how much money is kept on hand different nights, what lights are usually left on, which houses are vacant . . . only then can he decide what persons or cars under what circumstances warrant the appellation "suspicious."

All this was all right in a different world. At least the society didn't fall apart. What was once a mob is today a civil-rights demonstration; oddly dressed people are musicians, students, professors, members of the new professions generally (half of Madison Avenue seems to take the subway home to Greenwich Village at five P.M., shed the gray flannel suits and basic blacks and get into costumes that the police believe are worn only by dope fiends).

Why is the heat on all over America? For exactly the same reason it has always gone on in an American city after an outbreak of social disorder, a shocking crime or a sudden rise in the crime rate. The police feel that they are dealing with a situation that is slipping away from their control, and they are using the methods, most of them extralegal, by which they have traditionally regained control—"discourage them and they'll go away."

Where the police once confronted unassimilated groups of the illiterate poor, they now face an unassimilable subculture of the college-educated—unassimilable certainly by their own standards. Homosexuality, once a profitable source of shakedown and a chance to release a few sadistic repressions, is now open and, in fact, tolerated. There are articles in theological magazines about the church's responsibility to the homosexual and an interfaith organization to implement such responsibility—"homophile" organizations of both men and women stage national conventions addressed by notabilities in law, psychiatry and sociology and even by a few enlightened police officers. Such organizations recently sued the state of California to gain the right to operate a booth at the state fair.

Racially mixed couples are common on the streets of every Northern city and are beginning to appear in the South, and they are far more likely today to be students or professional people than denizens of the underworld. Outlandish costume has become the uniform of youth all over the world who are in moral revolt against the predatory society.

Today, when extra- and premarital sex is a commonplace, from grammar school to the senior citizens' clubs, we forget that a few individuals are still serving sentences in American prisons for fornication, adultery and oral sex between men and women; but the police have not forgotten—most of them, anyway. A weekly book-review section that once refused advertising of any book whatsoever by Kenneth Patchen or Henry Miller now runs a "cover story" on *Story of O,* a detailed, graphic description of the most extreme sadomasochism, homosexuality and "deviance." There are regular underground moviehouses that publicly show movies that would shock even policemen at a departmental smoker. Due to their seriousness of intent, they still horrify the police, but in a new way.

Adolescent Negro prostitutes in San Francisco, when arrested, "go limp" and put up long, highly sophisticated arguments for legalized prostitution and do everything but sing *We Shall Overcome.* I must say that the police with whom I have talked who have been involved in such situations have enough sense of humor to think it's all just hilarious.

At one time, marijuana and the various pharmaceutical kicks were part of a hard-dope subculture and unquestionably led in some instances directly to heroin addiction—"Whatsa matter, you chicken? When you going to graduate?" This is certainly no longer true. The squares and the oldies have no conception of how common the use of marijuana is among the young. Pickup and put-down pills are used by everybody to sleep or to wake up, and we have just gone through a craze for hallucinogens that seems to be leveling off. It is my impression that this has been accompanied by a proportionate decline in the use of heroin, except, possibly, in certain sections of New York City. Although large numbers of informed people believe that marijuana is harmless and that even the worst of the other drugs cause neither delirium tremens, polyneuritis, extensive brain damage nor lung cancer, the police, egged on by some of the press, persist in treating all users of all drugs and intoxicants except alcohol and nicotine as narcotics addicts.

Everybody talks back to the cops today. This "disrespect for law" has two contradictory sources—the general criminality that seeps through all American business and politics, and the growth of a new culture of revolt against precisely this "business ethic." In a sense, the police are caught in the middle of a class war, a war between antagonistic moral, rather than economic, classes.

Most policemen come from conservative levels of the society, lower-middle- and working-class families that have preserved an authoritarian structure and fundamentalist religion and puritanical attitude toward sex and a fear and contempt for any nonconformist behavior. The great majority of patrolmen in

America have no more than a high-school education, and that in substandard schools.

An additional factor seldom taken account of is the class hostility of the people on this social level for the educated, sophisticated and affluent generally, and most especially for those to whom the proper definition of bohemianism especially applies, those who mimic the habits of the idle rich without possessing their money or their reserves of power and who forgo the commonly accepted necessities of life to enjoy the luxuries. This kind of personality is specifically designed to outrage the type of policeman who is likely to be suspicious of anybody who drinks cognac instead of bourbon or who smokes Turkish cigarettes, much less someone who thinks Juan Marichal must be an obscure Spanish poet.

At one time, the great web of police custodial care could isolate such types in Greenwich Village or the Near North Side or North Beach. Today they are everywhere and increasing geometrically. If all of their activities, from peddling poetry on the streets or marching in demonstrations to smoking marijuana and attending nude parties, were suddenly to become accepted, the police forces of the country would be threatened with mass nervous breakdown. This may be one of those processes of historical change where the resistance of the past is not altogether valueless. For instance, laws against the possession of marijuana have become practically unenforceable. If everyone who smokes grass were arrested, we'd have to build concentration camps all over the country. Yet even today it would be quite impossible to legalize marijuana by referendum. It is doubtful that many of the state legislators of this country would have the guts to go on record as voting yes on a law such as the British one abolishing the criminality of homosexual acts between consenting adults.

The most dangerous social tension between police and people is certainly in race relations. The most enlightened police chief, with the aid of the most dedicated community-relations detail, cannot control the policeman on the beat in his personal relations with ignorant, poor and obstreperous members of a race that he does not understand. The only solution for this within the police force is education and the changing of group pressures. As one police officer said: "We all use the word nigger in the squad room. You'd be looked on as a kook if you didn't, but I won't let my kids use it at home."

Another obvious but unmentionable factor: Of all the ethnic groups in America, the Irish and the Negro put the greatest value on combativeness. The Chicago social group most like the South Side Irish of James Farrell's novels is precisely the Negroes who replaced them. Both communities were organized around mutual interpersonal hostility as a way of life.

Most chiefs of police rise directly from the ranks and are often less well educated than the new generation of rookies. Most city charters forbid the recruitment of managerial officers from outside the force. What this means is that the precinct captains are men from a less enlightened age who have risen by seniority to that point and are not competent to go further. They are the real bottlenecks and they can defeat all the efforts of an enlightened chief and police commission in their own bailiwicks.

The paramilitary structure of the police force is such that it is exceedingly difficult to create a board of review, office of complaints or of human relations within the force that will not be dominated by police politics and civil-service inertia. This is the reason for the ever growing demand for outside surveillance —civilian policing of the police.

Most cities now have police boards of various sorts, but these are made up of well-to-do businessmen and politicians and seldom meet more than a couple of hours once a week and have at best only a small secretarial staff. Negro members are usually lawyers and politicians or pastors of respectable churches. It would be possible to totally reorganize such commissions, make them representative, give them power and a large working staff.

Within the police force itself, it is possible to set up an inspector general's office, outside the chain of command, that would process, investigate and act on all citizen complaints. This is the common proposal of the more enlightened spokesmen from within the police system.

It would be possible to set up in each city an ombudsman office with the job of clearing all manner of citizens' dissatisfactions with the functioning of the city and its employees. This has worked in Scandinavia, whence the word comes, but the vision of pandemonium that the prospect of such an American office conjures up is frightening. It is doubtful that it would be possible to get people to take the jobs, and certainly not to stay on them.

A civilian review board, either elected or appointed by the mayor from completely outside all political apparatus, would be ideal, but the very terms contain a contradiction. How is this going to come about? It is a popular proposal with the civil-rights organizations and the one most fervently resisted by the police. Although it is true, as Bayard Rustin says, that it would protect the unjustifiably accused officer, it would strip naked the paramilitary structure that the police consider essential, not just to their morale but to their actual function; and it would reveal all those aspects of policework the police consider most essential, the clandestine extralegal ones.

In some cities, Seattle and Los Angeles among them, the civil-rights organizations have set up civilian patrols that prowl the prowl cars. They follow the police and stand by during arrest, politely and usually silently. They must be made up of citizens of all races, or of unimpeachable respectability, who are willing to donate eight hours at least once a week to difficult and unpleasant work. Obviously, they will obtain from the officers in the patrol cars the most elaborate compliance with all the amenities of the etiquette of arrest. How much effect this has in the long run is questionable, and by its nature, a civilian patrol program is not likely to endure beyond a few critical months. People are unlikely to engage in such activity night after night, year after year.

What is the best of these alternatives? Only experience can tell. If we were to set up in American cities a kind of neighborhood civil militia that checked on all police activity, we would soon find that we had created a police system like that of the Russians, in which the law and the police and their party and neighborhood representatives function as agents of public order and education in social ethics. This may be an estimable theory of how to run a society, but it is in total contradiction to every principle of British-American law and social organization. We do not want the police as custodians, but as instruments of a law that regards all men as equal and at liberty to run their affairs to suit themselves as long as they do not inflict damage on others.

The police spokesmen are perfectly right in saying that what should be done is to truly professionalize policework. This means changing the class foundation of the police force itself. A professional is a man with a salary at least comparable with that of a small-town dentist, with at least one college degree, with an advanced technical and, at the same time, broadly humanistic education and whose work demands that he keep abreast of its latest developments. The thought of turning all the policemen in America into such persons staggers the imagination. However, the nursing profession, which by and large is recruited from exactly the same level of society as the police, has been professionalized in one generation in everything but salary. An executive nurse in a big-city health department may have more years of college than most of the doctors working with her. She is lucky, indeed, if she makes $800 a month.

What is the answer? I have no idea. This is one of those many regions of frustration that are spreading across all of modern life, blotches on the skin of a body that is sick within with a sickness of which all diagnoses differ. I suppose society will smell its way to some sort of solution, muddle through the muddle. This is not a very hopeful prognostication for what is, after all, one aspect of a grave crisis, but none of the other prognostications about any of the other aspects are hopeful, either.

A friend who read this article said, "The ending should be

stronger. If the answer is to upgrade or professionalize the police forces, then that is the ending and the answer."

It has been said of Americans that they lack a tragic sense of life, that they are metaphysical optimists. There always must be an answer. The trouble is that there isn't. Our entire civilization is in a general crisis and seems incapable of producing any answers—nuclear disarmament or birth control, Rhodesia or the Common Market, cows in India and marijuana in American high schools—things are breaking down all over. Why should there be an answer to the problem of police brutality and extralegal behavior?

I have before me an article from the *Yale Law Journal*. The well-meaning, mild-mannered law professor tells a story of petty police harassment and insulting stopping and questioning that he has encountered throughout a lifetime of going peaceably about his business. He proposes a code of conduct to be adopted by city police forces. Eight points of ordinary legality and courtesy—but strictly belling the cat. There are all sorts of lovely solutions, long-term solutions—but there is no long term left. Things get worse faster than they get better. The professionalizing of policework would require a generation of time, billions of dollars and a revolution in American morality. American society deserves the cops it has produced. The pity of it is, it is the people who can't get into that society or who want out of it who get it in the neck.

The brutal fact is—the cops won't learn, or they can't learn fast enough. The Sunset Strip, coming shortly after Watts, shows that conclusively. Since the police have decided to treat the majority of the population—that is, those under thirty—as common criminals and rioters, the only thing to do is to adopt the protective behavior of the common criminal: "Keep your nose clean and don't volunteer." Carry the phone number of a lawyer and a bondsman. And, most important, say nothing whatever except "Please permit me to phone my lawyer." Allen Ginsberg used to carry a pocket tape recorder and turned it on whenever he was stopped by the police, which was at least once a week. That's good if you can afford it. Meanwhile, as the Jehovah's Witnesses say, "Are you ready for Armageddon?"

NAT HENTOFF

article

how the establishment's artillery of suppression—harassment, reprisal, physical force—is deployed against those who would exercise their constitutional right to activist disagreement

Early in 1968,* the superintendent of the building where I have an office drew me aside as I was going to the elevator. "Listen," he said very softly, "I shouldn't be telling you this, they told me not to, but a couple of FBI guys were asking about you yesterday."

It was a warm day, but I went cold. "What did they want to know?"

"Oh, do you just work here or do you live here, too? Where do you go in summer? Who comes to see you?"

There was only one possible reason for the FBI's interest in me. I have been writing and speaking against American policy in Vietnam for a long time and, more specifically, I was one of the first few hundred signers of *A Call to Resist Illegitimate Authority,* which pledges support of young men who in conscience resist the draft. Adding my name to that call had hardly seemed to me a revolutionary act. I thought these young men courageous and the least I could do was to say so publicly.

The chill left in the wake of the FBI wore off quickly enough, but a certain amount of apprehension remains. I remember, as

* This article was written before the Democratic National Convention in 1968.

today's young cannot, the effect on this country of Senator Joseph McCarthy—the careers blighted, the fear that paralyzed and shamed so many who thought themselves liberals. So does the man who wrote the definitive book on the pathology that was then called McCarthyism. The book is *Senator Joe McCarthy* and the writer, Richard Rovere, is a calm, moderate political analyst for *The New Yorker*. In October 1967, Rovere wrote in that magazine: "No government that is not totalitarian can go on indefinitely fighting a hard war that its people hate. Something has to give." There will be a test, he added, of how free we really are. "I cannot figure the odds on the outcome," Rovere continued, reminding us that "repression is the safest, surest, cheapest course for any government to take."

What *are* the odds? What do the auguries of the present tell us about next year and perhaps five years from now—even if the war ends? It seems relevant here for me to tell you that I am on the board of directors of the New York Civil Liberties Union and that indicates, I trust, my conviction that everyone's right to dissent, regardless of ideology, is due the full protection of the Constitution, specifically including the Bill of Rights. Furthermore, in examining the evidence and the auguries, I have kept in mind what I. F. Stone, editor and publisher of his own newsweekly, said recently. A doughtily independent journalist who was not in the least intimidated by Joseph McCarthy, Stone acknowledged that there is real danger of increasing repression in this country. "But," he emphasized, "our duty as believers in and practitioners of dissent is not to scare ourselves to death unnecessarily. I don't feel very optimistic in terms of the immediate future, but I don't feel hopeless."

Among those I talked to in the months of research for this article was a prominent theologian who has been in active opposition to the war. We spoke after Dr. Benjamin Spock, Yale chaplain William Sloane Coffin (subject of the August 1968 Playboy interview) and three others had been indicted by a Federal Grand Jury in Boston on January fifth for "conspiring" to counsel young men to violate the draft laws. One of the "overt acts" charged against Spock and Coffin in particular was the distribution of *A Call to Resist Illegitimate Authority*.

"I still speak and write against the war, but I'm more careful now," the theologian said, and he then told me of what had happened to George Huntston Williams, Hollis Professor of Divinity at the Harvard Divinity School. A scholar and not an activist, Professor Williams gave a talk in favor of selective conscientious objection to war during a meeting October 16, 1967, at Boston's Arlington Street Church. Six weeks later, members of the FBI visited the professor at his office and said that since they were questioning him concerning a possible indictment, they had to warn him of his rights.

"Williams," said the theologian, "was very disturbed by the incident. One of his specialties is the history of the German church in the 1930s. He told me he never thought he'd hear the knock on the door in this country, but now he's not so sure. He hasn't done much since then against the war. I expected that's one of the reasons the FBI went to see him."

Across the country, in Oakland, California, another stratagem in the war on dissent is being used to intimidate organizers of and participants in antidraft demonstrations. After a large turnout of antiwar protesters in October 1967 during Stop the Draft Week, seven young men were indicted on "conspiracy" charges that could lead to a prison sentence of up to three years and a $5000 fine. Among the counts against the dissenters are such acts as the printing and distribution of leaflets, the mere physical marching to an induction center and the opening of a checking account for Stop the Draft Week. Subsequent antidraft demonstrations in the Oakland area have been less well attended and much less effective.

The war on dissent is by no means limited to opponents of the war in Vietnam. Even if that war does end soon, attempts to repress free speech and the right of assembly, among other legitimate democratic processes, will continue. Still vulnerable are the nation's black militants and some not so militant who just happen to be black. "Much of the troublemaking in the months and years ahead," Richard Rovere wrote in the same *New Yorker* article, "will be the work of Negroes, and I can even imagine the imposition of a kind of American apartheid—at least in the North, where Negroes live in ghettos that are easily sealed off."

Fanciful? Consider this memorandum about Chicago from Jay A. Miller of the American Civil Liberties Union there:

> During the summer of 1967, we saw the machine attempt to use every possible and often lawless measure to "keep a cool summer." Using a mob-action statute, indiscriminate arrests and excessively high bail ($10,000–$50,000), they swept the streets of, and imprisoned without hearing, some 250–300 black citizens for a minimum of a week.

Several of those "lawless" measures were declared unconstitutional by a United States District Court judge in Chicago in March 1968. The city council, however, immediately enacted new ordinances that Jay Miller characterizes as being "worse than the old ones." Among them, for instance, is a stipulation that anyone continuing an activity deemed likely to lead to breach of the peace after the police have ordered him to stop can be charged with disorderly conduct. "Deemed likely" is so loose a term that it can encompass anyone the police want to seize. Similarly, there is another stipulation that anyone knowingly entering property open to the public and remaining there with "malicious or mischievous intent" gives the police free reign to stop any demonstration they choose.

New York City, meanwhile, has passed emergency measures for "riots and other disorders" that are shocking in view of the fact that Mayor John V. Lindsay has long been considered one of the country's most committed civil libertarians. The new measures severely restrict civil liberties by the imposition of curfews and the closing off of "disturbed" areas with accompanying harsh penalties for infractions of these emergency laws. The mayor is permitted to impose these restrictions on the free movement and free assembly of New Yorkers whenever he has "reason to believe that there exists a clear and present danger of a riot or other public disorder." As the New York Civil Liberties Union pointed out in a futile protest, "This condition does not pretend to be objective. It does not even require that a clear and present danger actually exist; it merely requires that the mayor *believe* it exists. He doesn't have to be right; he only has to be sincere. Such a provision truly substitutes the rule of men for the rule of law."

Just as startling is the power the mayor of New York now has to use his emergency measures if "an act of violence" has taken place. As the NYCLU also charged,

> This condition is so vague as to be meaningless. Hardly a day passes without "an act of violence." The bill does not even bother to state whether or not the act of violence has to occur in New York City. It would appear that this bill permits the mayor to declare a state of emergency in New York simply because there was a riot in Detroit, without any requirement to show the existence of a similar threat here. Had this bill been passed prior to the assassination of Martin Luther King, it would have permitted the mayor to restrict civil liberties in New York because of the possible effects of "an act of violence" in Memphis.

And New York City is generally considered to be the most "liberal" in the country.

Philadelphia officials have also become expert in keeping their city "cool," whether or not a clear and present danger to the peace exists. A proclamation in the summer of 1967 prohibited "all persons . . . from gathering on the public streets or sidewalks in groups of 12 or more . . . except for recreational purposes in parks or other recreation areas." A similar proclamation was issued and enforced immediately after the murder of Martin Luther King. Precedents for immediate, arbitrary use of "emergency" powers are being set throughout the country, and they are dangerous precedents.

At the same time, individual dissenters are being repressed. H. Rap Brown, national chairman of SNCC, has been undergoing a complicated series of court cases. When he was first released on bail, it was only on condition that he not leave the eleven counties of the southern district of New York, where the office of his lawyer, William Kunstler, is located. The judge who made the decision did not try to hide his intent: "Mr. Brown is not going to make speeches, because he is going to have to stay in Mr. Kunstler's district except when going to and from trial." For a time, the attempt to silence Brown worked. He had to cancel many speaking engagements in this country and abroad. When he finally did go to California to speak, he was jailed. And in May 1968, he received the maximum sentence of five years in jail and a $2000 fine for violating the National Firearms Act. That law forbids anyone under a felony indictment to transport a gun across state lines. The charge against Brown was that while under an indictment for arson in Maryland, he carried a carbine in his luggage on a plane from New York to Baton Rouge. There is not only a serious question as to whether Brown did, indeed, know he was under indictment at the time but there is also the clear likelihood that he is being punished so severely in an attempt to silence him for as long as possible. At the time of Brown's sentencing in New Orleans on May 22, 1968, William Kunstler declared, "I would hate to think my country used a little-known law like this to persecute and silence this man." It did, and the case is now on appeal.

Another illustration of how dangerous it is becoming to be a militant black dissenter is what happened to Clifton Thirley Haywood, a Negro and a Muslim. In October 1967, he was given two consecutive five-year sentences and two $10,000 fines for violations of the Selective Service Act—the heaviest sentence for such violations of the Selective Service Act since World War One. The jail term and fines were imposed even though Haywood had told Judge Frank M. Scarlett of the United States District Court in Brunswick, Georgia, that he was willing to violate his religious beliefs and enter the Armed Forces. If Haywood were not black, and a Muslim besides, would the sentence have been that severe? Even Senator Richard Russell of Georgia knows the answer to that question.

In January 1968, poet-polemicist LeRoi Jones, charged with the possession of guns during the violence in Newark the previous summer, received nearly a maximum sentence—two and a half to three years, plus a $1000 fine, with no probation permitted. The reason: because of what LeRoi Jones has written—the First Amendment notwithstanding. The judge said explicitly that he made the sentence so severe in large part because of a poem by Jones that had appeared in the previous month's *Evergreen Review.* The poem, the judge stated, was "antiwhite and full of obscenities." Only on the day of the sentencing was Jones or anyone else aware that he was also on trial for writing a poem. Reflecting on this ominous augury, Allen Ginsberg, gathering signatures for a writers' petition protesting the sentence, said, "I'm getting scared because of police-state purposes in this country. A lot of things I imagined in *Howl* are, unfortunately, coming true. . . . LeRoi didn't have any pistols. I talked to his father and his wife and they both told me that LeRoi had told them in private that he didn't have any guns. I called California the other day to get people to sign the petition and found that Ferlinghetti and Baez were in jail. And now Spock. Everything has gotten serious in a very weird way."

The growing thrust toward repression of dissenting views and of "troublemakers" is not limited to black militants and objectors to the war. The undernourished "war on poverty," for instance, has increasingly limited the possibilities of dissent for those of the poor who have been sufficiently "uplifted" to be hired as subprofessionals or in other roles in Federally aided projects under the Economic Opportunity Act. At the end of 1967, new legislation gave local government officials throughout the country much more control over antipoverty programs, thereby making it much easier to dismiss staff members who are critical of those same local government officials. Previously, bars had been placed on political activity by antipoverty personnel, and these have now been extended to include nonpartisan political activity. Another way of describing this process is co-optation: If you want to get on the payroll and stay there, don't make waves.

Another group experiencing penalties for dissent and nonconformity are the young—not only those who resist the draft but young people as a whole. In "Youth—The Oppressed Majority" (*Playboy*, September 1967), I indicated the scope and variety of pressures on the young. Those pressures are increasing. Ira Glasser of the New York Civil Liberties Union has since reported in a memorandum to all chapters in the state,

> The number of violations of students' civil liberties by school administrators is growing at an alarming rate. These violations have, to my knowledge, fallen roughly into three categories: 1. Denial of due process; 2. Repression of individual expression (mainly long hair and dress codes); and 3. Harassment of political activity.
>
> Denial of due process cases have involved things like summary suspension, hearing without counsel, permitting police to interrogate young children for hours without notifying parents, etc. The long-hair and dress-code cases have included some of the most bizarre and arbitrary standards imaginable, despite orders from State Commissioner of Education James Allen to the effect that school administrators had no right to impose such standards if they did not relate directly to educational goals. Harassment of political activity has taken many forms, including illegal search and seizure, threats of suspension for distributing leaflets or circulating petitions, repression of student clubs organized for political purposes.

And New York is far from the only state in which the Bill of Rights is not considered to apply to the young.

But is there really that much cause for urgent concern that the right to dissent may become emasculated? After all, there have always been repressive forces throughout our history. What determines the strength and effectiveness of those forces of repression, however, is the mood of the nation at any given time—and also the degree to which the majority of us understand and are committed to the Bill of Rights. A few years ago, Supreme Court Chief Justice Earl Warren said he was not sure the American people would vote for the Bill of Rights if it were up for ratification today. In December 1967, the Harris Poll posed this question: "Do you feel that people who are against the war in Vietnam have the right to undertake peaceful demonstrations against the war?" When the same question had been asked the previous July, 30 percent said opponents of the war do not have the right. By December, 40 percent took that position, one that in effect ignores the First Amendment. If peace talks break down and the war escalates again, with correspondingly larger numbers of American deaths, what percentage of the citizenry will continue to support the right of dissent under the First Amendment? And if the racial divide grows wider and deeper, leading to more violence, how much opposition will there be to loosely phrased "emergency laws" in cities and states?

Another way of measuring and predicting the national mood—in addition to public-opinion polls—is by listening to Congress and watching what it does. The present Congress has quite clearly moved to the right. Its most enthusiastic response during the President's State of the Union Message in January 1968 was to the section that began, "Now we at every level of government—state, local, Federal—know that the American people have had enough of rising crime and lawlessness in this country." There were cheers, whistles and eleven bursts of applause. That section, incidentally, contained this chilling Orwellian line: "And finally, I ask you to add one hundred FBI agents to strengthen law enforcement in the nation and to protect the individual rights of every citizen."

True, there have always been voices for repression in Congress, but during the past years, they have become louder and more insistent than at any time since the presence of Joe McCarthy loomed over Capitol Hill. In May 1967, Assistant Attorney General Fred Vinson was testifying before the House Armed Services Committee. Many of its members were pushing for immediate and relentless prosecution of all those who had given support to young men resisting the draft. Vinson explained that the First Amendment protects the right of free speech unless utterances constitute a "clear and present danger to the country." Responded Representative F. Edward Hébert of Louisiana, "Let's forget the First Amendment!"

On the House floor in September 1967, Emanuel Celler of New York, chairman of the House Judiciary Committee and generally considered a liberal, spoke sternly of "the responsibilities which march along with dissent" and asked whether dissenters are "aware of the point where the flow of the First Amendment reaches the wall of a clear and present danger." The time has come, Celler added, "to extend the rule of law within and without the boundaries of this land." Imprecise, but threatening, and further limning the mood of Congress. It is not a mood consonant with the conviction of Supreme Court Justice Hugo Black that "the First Amendment grants an absolute right to believe in any governmental system, [to] discuss all governmental affairs and [to] argue for desired changes in the existing order."

In December 1967, as news broke that Stokely Carmichael was coming home from his travels abroad, a number of congressmen prepared special greetings. While overseas, Carmichael had, indeed, spoken vehemently against American policies, but that was all he had done. He had given his opinions. Proclaimed Congressman Robert Michel of Illinois, "I rise to express my complete agreement with President Johnson on one point. I am referring to press reports that the President feels very strongly that Stokely Carmichael should be prosecuted for sedition if and when he returns to the United States."

There were passionate speeches in Congress in opposition to the right of assembly in Washington of the members of the Poor People's Campaign that had been initiated by the late Martin Luther King. Bills were submitted to forbid the march, to deny the demonstrators access to the Capitol or its grounds and to campsites on public parkland. Senator Karl Mundt even accused government officials of "lacking courage" to stand up against dissent. Meanwhile, other congressmen were volubly exacerbated by the waves of dissent on college campuses throughout the country, particularly the rebellion at Columbia University.

But, it can be claimed, these are just congressmen who are themselves exercising free speech. What is Congress actually doing and planning with regard to the suppression of dissent? The answers are hardly encouraging to believers in the Bill of Rights. In May 1968, by an overwhelming vote of 306 to 54, the House voted to cut off Federal financial aid—loans, grants, traineeships, fellowships—to students who take part in campus sit-ins or other disruptions of academic operations. *The New York Times* observed, "To turn Federal stipends into a device to regulate student views and behavior is to stoop to methods generally associated with totalitarian states. . . . Federal interference with higher education is an intolerable violation of academic freedom."

Also that spring, as part of a civil-rights bill, Congress made it a Federal crime to travel from one state to another—or to use radio, television or other interstate facilities—with an intent to incite a riot. The maximum penalty is five years in prison and a $10,000 fine. The bill defines a riot as a public disturbance involving three or more persons endangering either property or persons. Here, too, as in various local antiriot measures, the language is dangerously ambiguous. How is "intent" determined? As Attorney General Ramsey Clark said, "The state of mind of an individual when he travels . . . interstate . . . is very difficult to prove." What does "incite" mean? And what of free speech under the First Amendment?

Also alarming was the sweeping 72-to-4 vote by which the Senate passed a crime-control bill that allows wide latitude in the use of wire tapping and electronic surveillance and the admission of evidence obtained through such means into court cases. Under the bill's provisions, not only can the Federal government tap wires and use bugging devices with much greater legal freedom but state and local law-enforcement officials can use electronic surveillance against any crime "dangerous to life, limb or property and punishable by imprisonment for more than one year." Included, therefore, would be all the alleged crimes so broadly designated in the increasing number of local and state "antiriot" and "conspiracy" statutes. Understating the perils in this new bill, *The New York Times* noted that the voting indicated the congressional mood "is against safeguarding privacy. Snooping and tapping were approved not for a few serious crimes but for a wide variety. Furthermore, wire taps would be permitted for up to 48 hours even without a court order."

A further indication of the mood of Congress is a proposal by nineteen senators, led by James Eastland of Mississippi, that peacetime treason be declared a Federal crime. If the bill were passed, anyone convicted of giving "aid or comfort" to the Viet Cong or North Vietnamese or "any other nation or armed group engaged in open hostilities against the United States" would be liable to a prison term of up to ten years and a fine of up to $10,000. Without a declaration of war, then, dissent against a particular act of foreign policy could be interpreted as giving aid or comfort—and we would be close to a peacetime police state. "Evidence" of such aid or comfort would be all the more easily obtained through the expansion of permissible wire tapping and bugging.

Congress, meanwhile, is not only passing and considering repressive bills. There has also been a marked resurgence of activities by various congressional investigating committees. The venerable House Un-American Activities Committee has been looking into "the Communist instigation behind Northern ghetto riots" and is also exploring the "infiltrated" Draft Resister's League in Dallas. Representative Joe Pool of Texas, one of the committee's more fervent members, has also been urging an investigation of the Students for a Democratic Society, the largest national organization of the New Left.

In addition, the energetic Congressman Pool has called for a "preliminary investigation" of underground newspapers. "These smut sheets," he said during a speech at Yale in November 1967, "are today's Molotov cocktails thrown at respectability and decency in our nation. . . . Responsible publishers know that freedom of speech can be lost if the First Amendment is abused by the mudslingers who tell one lie after another to destroy those who oppose them." But this is just rhetoric. Who would take Pool seriously? The Liberation News Service, which provides material for much of the underground press, reported,

> In Dallas, the Southern Methodist University SDS chapter dissolved itself under the heat of Pool's attack last month, the Dallas Draft Information Center was illegally evicted from its office and *Notes from the Underground* (an independent student newspaper) was banned from campus in a double-think statement by the president of SMU defending freedom of the press.

Congressman Pool, furthermore, as a self-proclaimed champion of "our beloved freedoms," has proposed that "Congress should deny funds to any university that permits SDS to have an organized chapter on its campus."

While Congressman Pool beats the campus bushes for subversives, the Senate's Internal Security Subcommittee has undertaken a large-scale investigation of the New Left, including civil-rights and antiwar groups. As *The New York Times* observed on October 29, 1967, the chairman of the subcommittee, Senator Eastland, "obtained the unanimous approval of his subcommittee—including Senate Minority Leader Everett McKinley Dirksen of Illinois and Democratic liberal Birch Bayh of Indiana—for an investigation-authorizing resolution that amounts to a license to hunt for subversion in practically every organization of dissent now in existence."

The immediate focus of Eastland's resolution was on the Chicago meeting of the National Conference of New Politics at the Palmer House in September 1967. Represented at that convention were 367 groups, from Dr. Martin Luther King's Southern Christian Leadership Conference and SANE to the Communist Party, which, by the way, is a legal organization. (And out of more than 2000 delegates to that conference, only seven registered as Communists.) Before Eastland had his resolution to investigate, agents of the subcommittee were at the conference, and when they left, letters, files and other documents of the participating groups disappeared with them.

Another Senate unit, John McClellan's permanent Investigating Subcommittee, is also resurgent. It has engaged in, among other expeditions, a search to determine whether the violence in the ghettos has been "instigated and precipitated by the calculated design of agitators, militant activists or lawless elements."

Are we at the start of a new period of McCarthyism? Seven prominent religious and civil-liberties leaders sent a letter to Congress early in 1968 expressing exactly that fear. Among them were the late Martin Luther King; Roger Baldwin, founder of the American Civil Liberties Union; the Reverend John C. Bennett, president of Union Theological Seminary; Father Robert F. Drinan, S. J., dean of Boston College Law School; Rabbi Maurice Eisendrath, president of the Union of American Hebrew Congregations; Robert M. Hutchins, president of the Center for the Study of Democratic Institutions; and Dr. Benjamin Spock. "The dangers," their letter said,

> are manifest. These investigations are not aimed at determining the adequacy of laws concerning overt acts that actually threaten national security. . . . These investigations are aimed at the sacrosanct areas of First Amendment freedoms—freedom of speech, freedom of assembly and association and freedom of the press. They threaten to repeat the experience of the 1950s, when the cry of communism by Senator McCarthy and his acolytes stifled all but the most orthodox politics. Though we believe that today's dissenters and protesters will not be easily intimidated, the fact remains that the effect of simplistic name-calling will be to intimidate some people. The more intensive the name-calling and the guilt by association, the greater the number of those who will prefer anonymity to visibility and will prefer to remain outside the political dialog. More than that, however, it may well lead, as in the Fifties, not only to silence but also to persecution, prosecution and loss of employment.
>
> Perhaps the most serious consequence,

the letter concluded,

> may be the further lowering of the quality of debate concerning the nation's problems. With the isolation of the substantive criticism of the activists from the American mainstream, the search for solutions may turn up scapegoats, and the means of dealing with the conditions may be increasingly repressive.

The possibility of repressive means has been considerably increased by a particularly ominous act of Congress at the end of 1967. It passed a bill giving new life to the Internal Security Act of 1950, part of which the Supreme Court had declared unconstitutional. Surprisingly little public attention was given this development, but both the original act and its new amendments merit close study. The 1950 bill was vetoed by President Harry Truman, who said it represented "a clear and present danger to our institutions" and "would make a mockery of the Bill of Rights and of our claims to stand for freedom in the world." The Senate voted to override Truman's veto. One of the votes to override was that of Lyndon Johnson.

Among other provisions, the original act set up a five-man Subversive Activities Control Board and required Communist-front and Communist-action organizations to register themselves with the attorney general. In 1965, the Supreme Court decided that the latter section was unconstitutional because it violated the Fifth Amendment guarantee against self-incrimination. The newly amended act permits the Subversive Activities Control Board to conduct its own hearings as to whether organizations are Communist, Communist-controlled or Communist-infiltrated. If the board declares that a group falls into one of those categories, the names of all members will be publicly listed with the attorney general. In arguing unsuccessfully against the adoption of this end run around the Supreme Court, Congressman John Culver of Iowa warned,

> To grant such frightening power (to establish a public black list of organizations deemed Communist or "Communist-infiltrated") to a bureaucrat, to five men or, indeed, to (any) Government official . . . is most dangerous and irresponsible, because it may only serve to stifle dissent—it may only serve to kill expression of controversial views in this nation. To the extent that it denies the political vitality and vigor of our own free institutions, then it clearly aids and abets the Communist movement."

When the measure came up in the Senate for final adoption on December 14, 1967, only five senators were in the chamber, and this extraordinary piece of legislation became law by a vote of three to two. It may be significant to remember that in earlier debate, Senator Dirksen told his colleagues that the President had called him to the White House and told him he wanted the bill passed. The sonorous senator from Illinois then raised the flag to obscure the Constitution:

> We are at a time when we have to call a spade a spade in this country. The time for fooling is past. We have 475,000 youngsters and oldsters out in Vietnam. What do you think they think when they read about these things going on in the Senate—people trying to stop the Subversive Activities Control Board from doing its work?

There are further dangers to dissent in the new legislation. As a group of civil-liberties lawyers, including Melvin Wulf of the American Civil Liberties Union and William Kunstler, have pointed out:

> The statute, as amended, is, to put it conservatively, even more "at war with the First Amendment" than its predecessor. For example, the definition of a "Communist-front organization" has been further "liberalized" to provide that an organization may be registered as a "Communist-front organization" if it "is substantially directed, dominated or controlled by *one* or more members of a Communist-action organization . . ." (emphasis added). The act previously defined a "Communist-front organization" as one that "is substantially directed, dominated or controlled by a Communist-action organization."

How can it be proved that *one* Communist, who may well have hidden the fact that he is a Communist, is "substantially" directing, dominating or controlling your group? One key test, under the new amendments, is whether your organization is involved in "advocacy, espousal and teaching of a creed or of causes for which the Communist movement stands." As Representative Culver emphasized in his losing battle in the House, it would be quite possible for "innocent organizations" to take positions on matters of policy that in particular cases don't deviate from those of the Communist movement. "An organization advocating humanitarian programs designed to meet the unrest of the cities following last summer's riots," Culver noted, "could be classified as a Communist front if the Communist Party should find it expedient to exploit such causes."

As if the amendments to the Internal Security Act were not threatening enough to dissent, "the most serious aspects of this bill," as Congressman William Ryan of New York has warned, "involve not what it alters but what it leaves unchanged. The restrictions on freedom of association inherent in the original act are unchanged." So is the ability of the government to weaken and eventually destroy organizations through lengthy and expensive legal proceedings. This happened, as William Kunstler recalls, to many organizations under the old act. "This way," he says, "the Government can effectively kill by exhaustion those organizations it doesn't like."

Also still in effect is Title II, Section 100, of the original Internal Security Act. This provides that the President alone, under certain conditions—a declaration of war by Congress, an "insurrection" within the United States or "imminent invasion" of this country or any of its possessions—can declare a national "internal-security emergency." As soon as the President does this, the attorney general is required by the act to apprehend "any person as to whom there is reasonable ground to believe that such person probably will engage in, or probably will conspire with others to engage in, acts of espionage or sabotage."

According to the December 27, 1953, *New York Times,* six camps were actually set up for "dangerous" people—at Allenwood, Pennsylvania; Avon Park, Florida; El Reno, Oklahoma;

Florence, Arizona; Wickenburg, Arizona; and Tulelake, California. At that time, Charles R. Allen had described these camps in *The Nation* and other publications. In the June 1967 *Realist,* Allen wrote that he had recently reinvestigated the situation:

> Briefly, I found that the program is still in full force. That the Johnson Administration is all set to swing into action. That there are at least 1,000,000 Federal Internal Security Emergency Warrants waiting to be used if need be. That the FBI has a thing called "Operation Dragnet" that it can throw into full gear "overnight." That the concentration camps are, in one form or another, still ready on a "stand-by basis" and that they can hold at least an initial complement of 26,500.

He also claims that "the likely candidates for being picked up in 'Operation Dragnet' have expanded considerably since the passage of Title II so as to include the whole black-hippie-dissent scene."

Allen asked Walter Yeagley, head of the Internal Security Divison of the Justice Department—charged with carrying out these details of the Internal Security Act—for an interview about the camps. Yeagley wrote Allen that he did not consider the inquiry "a subject for public discussion." Early in 1968, however, Yeagley and other government officials were interviewed by William Hedgepeth, a senior editor of *Look,* in the course of an investigation by that magazine about the existence of the camps. Hedgepeth could find no evidence "either of physical preparations or of plans by the Federal Government for mass-level incarceration of Americans via Title II of the McCarran Act." But he was careful to add, "Still, the law lies on the books, the campsites exist . . . it *could* happen here." And he quoted Melvin Wulf of the ACLU: "The mere existence of the camps is really beside the point. If the law went into effect, they'd have no trouble finding some place to put 'em all." An unnamed Federal official agreed with Wulf: "Even without camps, we could transfer and double up in our prisons to hold people. We've got the talent and the staff to sit down and start working out transfers in a hurry."

That's the point. The law exists, and plenty of space can be found to intern all those picked up under that law. In 1962, in an interview on New York radio station WBAI-FM, former FBI agent Jack Levine revealed how quickly the roundups could take place. "The FBI," he said, "estimates that within a matter of hours every potential saboteur in the United States will be safely interned. They'll be able to do this by the close surveillance they maintain on these people; and they (the FBI) envisage that with the cooperation of the local police throughout the country, they'll be able to apprehend these persons in no time at all."

Nor is such a forced march to concentration camps without precedent in American history. It happened during World War

Two to 110,000 people of Japanese ancestry—70,000 of them American citizens by birth—who were herded into "relocation" camps for as long as four years. The most comprehensive account of that time of hysteria is Allan R. Bosworth's 1967 book, *America's Concentration Camps*. In his introduction to the book, Roger Baldwin of the American Civil Liberties Union, by no means an alarmist, warns,

> The laws and the machinery are ready for another day, another war, another emergency, another minority. . . . In order not to be caught again improvising measures for security in wartime or a national emergency declared by the President, Congress has thoughtfully provided that next time camps will be ready for the immediate internment of all persons, aliens and citizens alike, whom the FBI and other intelligence agencies suspect of sympathy with whatever enemy then confronts us.

In retrospect, it's instructive and hardly reassuring to consider the names of some of those who supported the mass imprisonment of the Japanese. When President Franklin Roosevelt signed Executive Order No. 9066, which put the machinery in motion, Earl Warren, then attorney general of California, said that the order was most wise. The act was also upheld by the United States Supreme Court in 1944, with Justice Hugo Black as its spokesman. In one of the three dissenting opinions, the late Justice Robert H. Jackson observed,

> A military order, however unconstitutional, is not apt to last longer than the military emergency. . . . But once a judicial opinion rationalizes such an order to show that it conforms to the Constitution . . . the Court for all time has validated the principle of racial discrimination in criminal procedure of transplanting American citizens. The principle then lies about like a loaded weapon ready for the hand of any authority that can bring forward a plausible claim of an urgent need.

The weapon is still loaded. William Peterson, professor of sociology at the University of California, ended an article, "Success Story, Japanese-American Style," in the January 9, 1966 *New York Times Magazine:* "The Chinese in California, I am told, read the newspapers these days with a particular apprehension. They wonder whether it could happen here—again." And not only the Chinese are apprehensive.

Just as there is a precedent in American history for "relocation" camps, so there is a chilling diversity of precedents for the suppression of dissent. From 1798 to 1800, the Alien and Sedition Acts were in force, providing jail terms of up to five years and fines of up to $5000 for anyone who spoke or wrote about Congress, the President or the Federal government "with intent to defame them or bring them . . . into contempt or disrepute."

Ostensibly designed to protect the country from subversion by the French, with whom America's relationships had deteriorated, the Alien and Sedition Acts were really intended by the Federalists in power to cripple the opposition Republican Party of Thomas Jefferson.

In the first four months during which the laws were on the books, twenty-one newspaper printers, all of whom put out Republican journals, were arrested. One prominent Boston editor died as the result of mistreatment in jail. Among many others arrested was a congressman, Matthew Lyon of Vermont, who had written in a letter that President John Adams had an "unbounded thirst for ridiculous pomp, foolish adulation and selfish avarice." For that opinion, the congressman was sentenced to four months in a tiny, unheated cell in a Vermont jail and fined $1000.

In revulsion against the Federalists' sweeping and arbitrary use of the acts, the electorate defeated them in 1800 and the new President, Thomas Jefferson, pardoned all who had been convicted under the laws. But throughout the nineteenth century, there were strong forces against dissent both within and outside the courts. In 1835, for instance, a mob advanced on the Boston office of the *Liberator*, an abolitionist newspaper edited by William Lloyd Garrison, and dragged him through the streets at the end of a rope. And for many years, abolitionists couldn't meet in the city of New York without having to cope with organized disturbances.

But Garrison and the other abolitionists not only persisted in dissent but also resisted laws they considered an affront to their consciences. On July 4, 1854, Garrison, in the course of a speech in Framingham, Massachusetts, held up a copy of the Fugitive Slave Law, which required the turning over of runaway slaves to their masters. He burned the copy of the law publicly—a precedent of its kind for today's burning of draft cards. Other acts of resistance to the Fugitive Slave Law provoked riots, direct confrontations with law-enforcement officials on the streets and the snatching away of runaway slaves from Southern masters who had gone North to claim them.

There was also resistance to the Mexican War, and Henry David Thoreau was jailed in 1846 for refusing to pay taxes to support that War. (A United States stamp in honor of Thoreau, ironically, was issued in 1967.) In another striking parallel with current public statements of dissent, Theodore Parker, an abolitionist clergyman, said during the same period,

> What shall we do . . . in regard to this present War? We can refuse to take any part in it; we can encourage others to do the same; we can aid men, if need be, who suffer because they refuse. Men will call us traitors; what then? That hurt nobody in '76. We are a rebellious nation; our whole history is

> treason; our blood was attainted before we were born; our creeds are infidelity to mother church; our Constitution treason to our fatherland. What of that? Though all the governors in the world bid us commit treason against man, and set the example, let us never submit. Let God only be a master to control our conscience.

In the last half of the nineteenth century, there were intermittent attempts, by law and by mob violence, to repress the nascent labor movement, all manner of radicals and women insisting on their right to vote. But the nadir of civil liberties in postslavery America was reached during World War One and in the years immediately after. National hysteria in World War One did not even exclude clergymen. Theodore Roosevelt declared that "the clergyman who does not put the flag above the church had better close his church and keep it closed." In their book *Opponents of War: 1917–18*, H. C. Peterson and Gilbert Fite wrote that

> in some cases, ministerial opponents of war were handled roughly, or even jailed. Reverend Samuel Sibert of Carmel, Illinois, was jailed in December 1917, because he said in a sermon that he opposed war. In Audubon, Iowa, two men, one of them a minister, were seized by a crowd who put ropes around their necks and dragged them toward the public square. After one of them signed a check for a $1000 Liberty Bond, he was released. The minister was released because of the intervention of his wife. *The Sacramento Bee*, December 27, 1917, headlined the report, "NEAR LYNCHINGS GIVE PRO-GERMANS NEEDED LESSON."

In 1917, Congress passed the Espionage Act, still on the books, which made it a crime, punishable by a $10,000 fine and twenty years in jail, for anyone to

> convey false reports or false statements with intent to interfere with the operation or success of the military or naval forces of the United States or to promote the success of its enemies . . . or attempt to cause insubordination, disloyalty, mutiny or refusal of duty in the military or naval forces of the United States, or . . . willfully obstruct recruiting or enlistment service.

The next year, to make doubly sure the lid was on dissent, the Sedition Act came into being. It prohibited anyone, on pain of a $10,000 fine and twenty years' imprisonment, to

> utter, print, write or publish any disloyal, profane, scurrilous or abusive language about the form of government of the United States, or the Constitution of the United States, or the uniform of the Army or Navy of the United States, or any language intended to . . . encourage resistance to the United States or to promote the cause of its enemies.

Security in time of war is one thing, but the 1918 act invited a return to the arbitrary repression of 1798. In the course of World War One, more than 2000 people—including pacifists and socialists—were prosecuted, many for simply speaking against the War. With the War over, there were further abuses of the Bill of Rights. In *Red Scare,* Professor Robert K. Murray describes the start of this next stage under Attorney General A. Mitchell Palmer. On August 1, 1919, Palmer established within the Justice Department's Bureau of Investigation

> the so-called General Intelligence, or antiradical, Division. As its head, he appointed young J. Edgar Hoover, charging him with the responsibility of gathering and coordinating all information concerning domestic radical activities. Under the general guidance of bureau chief William Flynn and through the unstinting zeal of Hoover, this unit rapidly became the nerve center of the entire Justice Department and by January 1920, made its war on radicalism the department's primary occupation. In fact, there are some indications that both Flynn and Hoover purposely played on the attorney general's fears and exploited the whole issue of radicalism in order to enhance the Bureau of Investigation's power and prestige . . . and started it on the road to becoming the famous FBI of the present day.

In that connection, it's worth remembering the durable J. Edgar Hoover's persistent attempts to link black militancy, antiwar activities and campus protest movements with communism. In his annual report to the attorney general in 1967, Hoover asserted that Communist Party leaders are "pleased with the disturbances on campuses and the disruption of city life by war protesters and riots in the ghettos." Pleased they may be, but their direction of any of these activities has never been proved, in hard fact, by the director of the FBI or anyone else. Nonetheless, Hoover went on to charge recklessly that the New Left, typified by Students for a Democratic Society, constitutes "a new type of subversive, and their danger is great." As *The Harvard Crimson* said in an editorial the same month, "Hoover commands more cooperation from congressional committees than does any other man, with the possible exception of General Hershey. And as head of a 16,000-man, $200,000,000 organization, Hoover has the kind of semiautonomy that makes his political stands particularly dangerous."

They were dangerous at the very start of his career, for his zealous early efforts to ferret out radicals and alleged radicals helped result in a series of raids under Palmer that reached a climax on January 2, 1920, when more than four thousand suspected radicals were swept up in a dragnet encompassing thirty-three major cities in twenty-three states. "Often such arrests," Robert Murray writes in *Red Scare,* "were made without the formality of warrants as bureau agents entered bowling alleys, pool halls, cafés, clubrooms and even homes and seized everyone in sight. Families were separated; prisoners were held incommunicado and deprived of their right to legal counsel. According to the plan, those suspected radicals who were American citizens were not detained by Federal agents but were turned over to state officials for prosecution under state syndicalist laws. All aliens, of course, were incarcerated by the Federal authorities and reserved for deportation hearings."

What was the reaction of the citizenry? "The mass of Americans," Murray notes, "cheered the hunters from the side lines, while Attorney General Palmer once again was hailed as the savior of the nation." As for the individual states, during 1919 and 1920, at least 1400 persons were arrested under state syndicalist and sedition laws; 300 were sent to prison. "Although such laws varied slightly from state to state," Murray adds,

> the effect was generally the same. Opinions were labeled objectionable and punished for their own sake, without any consideration of the probability of criminal acts; severe penalties were imposed for the advocacy of small offenses; and a practical censorship of speech and press was established ex post facto.

Even free elections were subverted in the name of antisubversion. Victor Berger, a Socialist, was twice elected to Congress from the Wisconsin fifth district (in 1918 and in a special election the following year) and was twice refused his seat by his colleagues. Only one congressman voted for Berger the first time, only six in 1919. In January 1920, the New York State Assembly, by a vote of 140 to 6, denied seats to five freely elected Socialists.

By the end of 1920, the Red Scare had abated. The next wave of repression began with the formation of the House Un-American Activities Committee in 1938 and reached its feverish height during the 1950–1954 suzerainty of Senator Joseph McCarthy. As Walter Goodman has documented in his definitive book, *The Committee: The Extraordinary Career of the House Committee on Un-American Activities,* thousands of reputations were ruined in public hearings before HUAC. In a sampling of life under HUAC, the American Civil Liberties Union tells of

> a successful Miami businessman-builder who relied on his Fifth Amendment privilege before HUAC, lost his business and finally had to leave Florida; he was forced to earn a living doing odd jobs and carpentry.
>
> A girl with a job as a pot washer was fired because her husband and father invoked the Fifth Amendment before the Committee. Her husband, a draftsman, lost his job, too. In a similar case, in another city, a girl who worked for a county government division lost her job because her father declined to testify

before the HUAC, though she herself was not involved in the hearings.

A fire-department captain, who denied he was a member of the Communist Party at the time of his testimony but refused to discuss his past political activity, was dismissed from his post when he lacked one month and ten days of 25 years' service and retirement benefits.

In an essay in *The Radical Right,* Herbert H. Hyman estimates that by the mid-Fifties, as a result of HUAC, other congressional investigating committees, their state counterparts and the administrators of Federal security programs,

> the total number of individuals whose loyalty or security had been subject to *official* scrutiny by some organ of American *Government* clearly extended into the many millions. The number of American *families* who had been affected by inquiry about one of their family members, and the additional number of families who had encountered such an inquiry through a field investigation of one of their acquaintances, friends or relatives must have been so large as to make quite a dent in the consciousness of the American people.

But what kind of dent? In January 1954, the king klaxon of loyalty testers, Joseph McCarthy, was shown by a Gallup Poll to be held in generally "favorable opinion" by 50 percent of the American people, who felt he was serving his country in useful ways. In opposition was 29 percent, and the rest had "no opinion." With regard to his congressional colleagues, Richard Rovere wrote in *Senator Joe McCarthy,*

> The truth is that everyone in the Senate, or just about everyone, was scared stiff of him. . . . Paul Douglas of Illinois, the possessor of the most cultivated mind in the Senate and a man whose courage and integrity would compare favorably with any other American's, went through the last Truman years and the first Eisenhower years without ever addressing himself to the problem of McCarthy. Senator John Kennedy of Massachusetts, the author of *Profiles in Courage,* a book on political figures who had battled strong and sometimes prevailing winds of opinion and doctrine, did likewise.

McCarthy was finally discredited, largely by his behavior during the televised Army-McCarthy hearings in the late spring of 1954. He clearly revealed himself to a fascinated and then appalled national audience as a bombastic bully, contemptuous of legal procedures. After his decline and eventual condemnation by the Senate, there were a few years of respite from repression of dissent. It appeared that McCarthyism, like the Red Scare before it, had been interred for a good long time. But with the coming of the New Left, increasing student unrest, the Vietnam war and the rise of black activism, we are again at a point in our national history at which the Bill of Rights is in clear and present danger.

In addition to the repressive bills passed and those being considered by Congress, and along with the intensive hunt for "subversives" by congressional committees, there is now also the use of the draft as a weapon against dissent. Intimations of what was to come appeared in the fall of 1967 as the large-scale October peace demonstrations at the Pentagon were drawing near. On October 19, Congressman Burke of Florida grimly addressed the House:

> Mr. Speaker, I would like to suggest two measures that may help curb these disgraces. I would hope, first of all, that the proper authorities would exercise some initiative and immediately round up these hippies, have orders processed for them and turn them over to some rugged military basic-training center for some good training. If they qualify . . . they can then fulfill their two-year obligation to their country. . . . These may be drastic actions, Mr. Speaker, but these are drastic times. If these long-haired protesters want to remain citizens of America like several million others, they must start facing the responsibility this citizenship requires.

And shut up.

After the Pentagon demonstrations, Congressman Roman Pucinski of Illinois revealed on the floor of the House,

> I have asked the Selective Service people to look at every one of these people who have been arrested and find out what their Selective Service status is and how many of these people are enjoying the privilege of not serving in the Service because they are going on to higher education. They have a right to come here and protest against their Government, but they do not have a right to stay out of military service.

And if they exercise the first right, let them pay for it.

On October 26, 1967, rhetoric was turned into action, when Selective Service Director General Lewis B. Hershey sent a letter to all local draft boards "recommending" that they quickly induct anyone, regardless of what kind of deferment he has, who has interfered with the draft or with military recruiting. A Hershey "recommendation" is interpreted as an instruction, not a suggestion, by local boards. And "interfering" can mean demonstrating at induction centers, symbolic turning in of draft cards and other acts of protest.

Eight House members attacked the Hershey recommendation as "a flagrant denial of due process clearly designed to repress dissent against the war in Vietnam." Hershey was unimpressed.

He said he had "talked with somebody" at the White House before issuing the letter; and the next month, he added, "Until the President tells me to change my course, I'll sail it. And he hasn't stopped me." Hershey has also opposed allowing draft registrants to have counsel with them when they appear before local draft boards. An appeal against that order has been turned down—without comment—by the Supreme Court.

Meanwhile, local boards, following Hershey's instructions, have continued to strip dissenters of their deferments. Included have been not only young men but also a thirty-seven-year-old member of the Temple University faculty, married and with two children, who had turned in his draft card during a Washington peace demonstration. Other professors and instructors have been reclassified for the same kind of act, as have a Protestant chaplain and a Catholic priest at Cornell, another Catholic priest in Rochester and a number of divinity students.

In the state of Oklahoma, it appears that the use of the draft against dissent has been extended to make a young man vulnerable for just being a member of a particular organization opposed to the war. John M. Ratliff, a University of Oklahoma student, has been reclassified 1-A by Tulsa Draft Board No. 76, specifically because of his membership in Students for a Democratic Society. The local board wrote Ratliff that it "did not feel that your activity as a member of SDS is to the best interest of the U. S. Government."

Moreover, according to the December 14, 1967, *Village Voice*, "a phone call to the Tulsa Draft Board No. 76 confirmed that all the state's draft boards had been 'ordered by General Hershey to review the status of all SDS students.'" As the *Voice* noted: "The incident raises several questions. How did Draft Board No. 76 get the SDS membership list? Does this mean that mere membership in an organization, never cited by the Government as subversive, will result in the automatic loss of student deferments?"

The use of governmental force by a draft board to war on dissent is, however, at least an act that can be fought within the democratic process. The board makes its move; then it can be attacked in court. Suits against manipulation of the draft to intimidate dissent are being carried forward by the American Civil Liberties Union, the National Student Association and other groups. More disturbing is the increasing use by government—Federal and local—of secret-police tactics.

As authoritarian states have demonstrated with cold efficiency, one way to control—and ultimately destroy—dissent is to infiltrate the opposition. In a democratic society, a reasonable case can be made for infiltrating secret, illegal and violent groups—the Mafia, the Ku Klux Klan, the Minutemen, or a revolutionary cadre, right or left, committed to assassination as a political weapon. But serious questions arise when the state moves by stealth to gather information about those who are simply exercising their First Amendment rights. During a Washington press conference of the American Civil Liberties Union in September 1967, for example, it was discovered that among those present were Secret Service agents photographing the participants and clandestinely taping the proceedings. Nor is it reassuring when *Newsweek* discloses that "in New York, Los Angeles and other cities, local police and Federal agents masquerade as newsmen, especially as newspaper photographers, to collect information unobtrusively at antidraft and peace demonstrations."

In addition, some of the infiltrators turn out to be *agents provocateurs,* hardly a legitimate role for law-enforcement personnel in a free society. In December 1967 in Chicago, the Chicago Peace Council exposed three policemen who had been posing as exceptionally active members of that antiwar group. Karl Meyer, chairman of the council, noted that the three infiltrators "invariably took the most militant positions, trying to provoke the movement from its nonviolent course to the wildest kind of ventures." Jay Miller of the Chicago ACLU called the use of these *agents provocateurs,* trying to get groups to perform illegal acts, a "real police-state practice that is bound to have an effect on dissent."

There were also infiltrators, many dressed as hippies, among the demonstrators at the Pentagon on October 21, 1967. Among them were agents of the FBI, the Secret Service, the Washington police and Army intelligence. In November, Colonel George Creel, assistant chief of the Army's public information office, told a George Washington University public-relations class, "There were more men infiltrated by us into the crowd at this demonstration than at any event I can remember." Were any of them *provocateurs*? No one who knows is saying.

In New York City plainclothesmen dressed as hippies have been active in peace demonstrations and some have later been identified by legitimate participants as having tried to urge the demonstrators on to more and more provocative action.

Secret-police infiltration has also moved onto campuses. The extent to which spying and political surveillance have been spreading in the colleges was detailed by Frank Donner in "Spies on Campus" (see page 157). During the student rebellion at Columbia a shaggy-haired New Leftist, usually wearing a safari jacket and cowboy boots, turned out to be a policeman attached to the Bureau of Special Services (New York City's "Red Squad"). Having infiltrated the campus protest movement for two months, this same disguised cop was the man who finally arrested SDS leader Mark Rudd on charges of riot, inciting to riot, criminal trespass and criminal solicitation.

Yet another method of stifling dissent is open, brutal police contempt for such First Amendment rights as "the right of the people peaceably to assemble" without being clobbered. If enough heads are busted and enough blood flows, the exercise of that right becomes so perilous that potential dissenters decide to stay home. In June 1968, when fifteen thousand antiwar demonstrators gathered outside the Century Plaza Hotel in Los Angeles, where President Johnson was attending a dinner, the police descended on the peaceable largely white, middle-class assemblage as if they were invading a black ghetto in revolt. "Some police clubbed wildly," the American Civil Liberties Union reported,

> others held the demonstrators so their colleagues could club them; others surrounded the crowd, compressing it, preventing the dispersal they had ordered and clubbing those who came within swinging range. Caught in the crush were children, pregnant women, old people, people on crutches and in wheelchairs. A partially paralyzed boy was hit on the head, knocked to the ground, clubbed and kicked, when he told an officer to stop hitting his mother. One officer knocked a baby from her mother's arms; another beat up a man who tried to pick up the child.

Within a week after the police had rioted, the chairman of the Board of Police Commissioners announced that the board had "reviewed all the circumstances of the occasion" and found "the police had taken proper action."

The Committee of the Professions, a peace group in New York, has released detailed reports of brutality against demonstrators at the Pentagon in October 1967. In statements signed by professors and other professionals, there are descriptions such as this: "For most of Saturday night, unprovoked arrests were accompanied by great violence. People were pulled away with no warning, clubbed and kicked in the sight of their friends." Similar accounts have come in recent months from participants in antiwar demonstrations in Chicago, Oakland, Cincinnati, Iowa City, Cleveland, San Francisco, San Jose and other cities. In New York, *The New York Times* in November reported the following attack on five hundred young demonstrators:

> A sudden charge by about 20 patrolmen into the front ranks of the marchers, many of whom were young women. Billy clubs swung and blood spattered the sidewalk. The flying wedge of policemen sent the crowd reeling back in disorder. Some youths were flung against the iron fence of [a] high school and ordered to stand spread-eagled, with arms and legs stretched wide apart, while plainclothesmen searched them. One youth was dragged by the hair across the street and thrown into a police van.

In one of several complaints to New York Mayor John Lindsay, the New York Civil Liberties Union got to the core of what appears to be a pattern of harsher police practices against demonstrators throughout the country by referring to "the atmosphere of intimidation which now hangs heavy over all future antiwar demonstrations."

The pattern continues. In January 1968, the *Berkeley Barb* reported from San Francisco about a demonstration on the appearance in that city of Secretary of State Dean Rusk, "Police repeatedly sprayed Mace at close range into the faces of persons held helpless by other cops. Police continually pursued, clubbed and Maced demonstrators blocks from the Fairmont Hotel—where . . . Rusk was saying, 'This country is committed to free speech and free assembly. We would lose a great deal if these were compromised.' "

The same paper carried this account of police savagery:

> The fury of them! The way they were beating people! There were two or three of them on foot behind us and two on motorcycles. One kid was falling behind and one of the cops drove him between two cars and ran his Harley over him. He drove right over him! I turned away. Tom [her companion] said he went over him again. I turned back and the cop was off his cycle and started beating him. . . . I saw a girl beaten all bloody around the face and head. Everywhere you looked, people were screaming and running. Anybody who couldn't run fast enough was beaten and arrested.

At Columbia University, police were called to clear the campus in the early morning. Students had staged sit-ins to protest Columbia's expansion into neighboring Harlem without having consulted or shown real concern for the community. They were also demanding more internal democracy on campus and the severance of Columbia's ties with the Institute of Defense Analyses, a consortium of twelve universities engaged in secret war research and in devising means of "pacifying" our domestic ghettos. The viciousness of the police at Columbia was such as to cause Dr. June Finer, a medical volunteer on campus that night, to declare, "I've been involved in demonstrations before. In the South in '64 and '65, I saw policemen I thought were unnecessarily vicious. But this was almost unbelievable, to see so many instances at once of overwhelming brutality." Another doctor, a member of the Medical Committee on Human Rights, said, "The plainclothesmen and detectives were like wild animals. They were beating up people who had offered no resistance at all and, in most cases, were bystanders."

Describing another police riot, this one at a Chicago Peace Council parade, Joseph L. Sander in *The Nation* added more bloody detail to the pattern of police intimidation of dissent through violence:

> The police hunted in posses through the Loop, beating and arresting many whose buttons identified them as march participants. Many officers removed their badges and name plates for this action. Newsmen and TV crews were frequently ordered to "get those cameras out of here!" Often, too, a uniformed police officer would step before the camera to prevent its recording the actual descent of a raised club. At one such post-demonstration encounter at the corner of Randolph and State streets, an officer in a riot helmet, furious because the street was not cleared fast enough, ordered the driver of a halted station wagon to drive right into the crowd. The motorist started forward and knocked down two girls before regaining sanity.

The growing readiness of the police to show naked force is not limited to antiwar demonstrations. Preparing for increased black unrest as well as for more dissent against the war if it continues, police departments, *The New York Times* has reported, "are purchasing armored cars and stockpiling such equipment as tear-gas grenades, other nonlethal weapons and shotguns. . . . At least one police department, according to a major helicopter manufacturer who asked not to be identified, wanted to buy an armed helicopter like the ones the Army uses against the Viet Cong in Vietnam." That helicopter could be useful in a new way to those departments that adopt a suggestion recently advanced by the Institute for Defense Analyses—a net that could be moved by hand or could be dropped by helicopter to sweep out a portion of a crowd.

Also in more and more police arsenals are such weapons as Stoner assault guns, which shoot through walls, and armor-plated police commando vehicles that have eighteen gun ports and carry a combat crew of twelve. Los Angeles is proud of a new twenty-ton, tanklike personnel carrier equipped with a machine gun, tear-gas launchers, a smoke-screen device, chemical fire extinguishers and a siren that can disable people merely with its sound.

There is no question that police departments need necessary equipment to handle riots, but the scope of present police overkill in weaponry can only, as Representative John Murphy of New York makes clear, "intensify the fear in the nation's cities. They are not weapons of law enforcement; they are weapons of mass destruction." The President's National Advisory Commission on Civil Disorders agrees: "The commission believes there is a grave danger that some communities may resort to the indiscriminate and excessive use of force. The harmful effects of overreaction are incalculable. The commission condemns moves to equip police departments with mass-destruction weapons, such as automatic rifles, machine guns and tanks."

But most police departments continue to ignore these warnings. Caught up in their own rhetoric of "warfare," they see themselves as an army mandated to squash peace demonstrators and dissident blacks. In return, more of those who take to the streets will inevitably escalate their own response. "The thing to remember," James Farmer, former national director of CORE, underlines, "is that the young blacks will not just be throwing bottles and bricks." And increasing numbers of them, he adds, will be returned veterans from Vietnam, skilled in guerrilla-warfare techniques. And others of the young, not black, if pushed to violence, will react in kind.

"We are not at war in our cities," says Roy Wilkins of the NAACP. "The weapons of warfare have no place there." But the police *are* placing more and more weapons of war in the cities; and throughout history, armaments, when at hand, have eventually been used.

And the weapons are becoming more and more sophisticated. There are not only the commando cars and helicopters but also a wide choice of "nonlethal" pacifiers. The Institute for Defense Analyses, for instance, is fond of a foam generator that can block streets or spray crowds. The beauty of it, the manufacturers claim, is that people immersed in the foam become very disturbed by loss of contact with their environment.

As has been indicated, especially popular among constabularies these days is Mace, a spray that, according to its manufacturer, General Ordnance Equipment Corporation, "envelops assailant with his own small 'cloud' of tear gas from which he cannot escape. . . . The victim suffers temporary loss of vision accompanied by pain that is incapacitating even though only temporary in nature." But the humiliating memory lingers on.

In the past few years, more than 250,000 cans of Mace have been sold to 4000 police departments in the United States. As of April 1968, each of the 11,500 members of the Chicago police force, for example, is required to carry a spray can of Mace in a holster attached to his pistol belt. It is becoming more and more evident, however, that the effects of Mace may be more than temporary. Dr. Lawrence Rose, a San Francisco ophthalmologist, who has treated victims of the chemical and has conducted his own tests, reports that Mace can cause permanent eye damage, has pronounced deleterious effects on the central nervous system and can inflict second-degree burns on the exposed skin. In May 1968, the mayor of Paterson, New Jersey, nervously banned the use of Mace by his police because of a report he had received from the United States Surgeon General's office confirming Dr. Rose's finding that the chemical can cause permanent eye damage. But sales still rise, as more and more cops add Mace to their basic weaponry.

A further problem with Mace and other "nonlethal" chemical

pacifiers is that their effects can be indiscriminate and quite possibly fatal. Gas or chemical sprays turned on a crowd can incapacitate passers-by as well as participants; and in either group, someone with a weak heart or a severe respiratory condition could die as a result. But a spokesman for Smith & Wesson, a leading manufacturer of chemical crowd controllers, is quoted in *The New York Times* business section: "We're selling all we can make, and we feel that the equipment we're making is lifesaving equipment." As national values and priorities become increasingly distorted, so does language. And so do people. In the years 1966–1968 gun ownership in the United States—civilian, not police—increased by 25 percent. As the *Times* notes, "Demographic facts—there are more whites than Negroes and more of them have more money—would indicate that the distribution favors whites." Shotgun sales are up particularly high in Montgomery County, Washington's wealthiest and whitest suburb. A clerk in a gunshop in Allen Park, a white suburb of Detroit, told a *Wall Street Journal* reporter, "Hate is getting big. The word is that if there's any trouble this summer and you see a black man in your neighborhood, shoot to kill and ask questions later." And after the summer? Does hate stop as the leaves fall?

With police arming as if for Armageddon and with more neighborhood vigilante groups forming, there is reason to listen carefully to the Reverend Andrew Young, a mild-mannered assistant to the late Martin Luther King: "We are almost facing the danger of a right-wing military take-over of our cities. If we have another couple of summers of riots, you will get much more repressive police action—and certainly no change."

Also looking ahead is the Defense Department, which has started a program to facilitate the recruitment of ex-Servicemen by police departments. The Defense Department offers soldiers discharges up to three months in advance of their normal separation times if they sign up as policemen. As Allen Young of Liberation News Service observes, "The plan affirms a general affinity between the police and the military—both refer to outsiders as 'civilians.' " That affinity is constantly being strengthened by the Army's take-over of instruction of local police in what it calls "riot control." At Fort Gordon, Georgia, there are continuous sessions of the Army's Civil Disobedience Orientation Course. "Each week since early February," *The New York Times* reported in 1968, "a new class of police officers, Guardsmen and occasional Secret Service or Federal Bureau of Investigation agents has completed the course, directed by the Army's Military Police School." The high point of one class came "when a helicopter swooped over the range, emitting a white cloud of gas that was forced down on the [simulated] mobs by the downdraft of the rotor blades."

As the Army, National Guard and local police become increasingly intertwined, the "civilians" who may become their targets encompass not only ghetto residents but, as was shown at Columbia University, such hitherto privileged groups of the citizenry as college students. And, considering the history of peace demonstrations during 1967–1968, also included are more and more adult middle-class dissenters. The military-police attitude toward these civilians at times leads to scenes that could have taken place in South Africa or Poland. In October 1967, for instance, Chancellor William H. Sewell of the University of Wisconsin brought in the Madison police riot squad to disperse two hundred people sitting outside a room where representatives of Dow Chemical Company, manufacturers of napalm, were holding interviews. "Instead of clearing the building," wrote James Ridgeway of *The New Republic,*

> the police clubbed, stomped and tear-gassed those inside as well as 1500 students standing outside. When students called the university hospital and asked for ambulances to take away the unconscious, the hospital refused. When an intern asked for medical supplies so that he might on his own help the injured, the hospital refused. Neither Chancellor Sewell nor his chief lieutenant, Joseph F. Kaufman, dean of student affairs, appeared at the scene; yet they wasted no time in suspending 13 students; then in the name of safety, they called off the Dow interviews.

But force is by no means the only method being used to ensure conformity on American campuses. Dissenters can be and are being simply severed from academic institutions. Early in 1968, a Brown University assistant professor of psychology was suspended from teaching duties for the rest of the term because he took part in an anti-CIA-recruiting sit-in; two philosophy professors at Paterson State College in New Jersey were fired for supporting a student petition asking to have political, religious and social organizations on campus; and four faculty members at Adirondack Community College in New York were told their contracts would not be renewed because they supported the right of students to participate in demonstrations and took part in one themselves. What was the demonstration in which the four teachers were involved? A minute of silence at the flagpole on the campus as a protest against the war in Vietnam! There have been more such firings of faculty, and the trend is up.

Also up, as I have shown, is the extent of campus spying and political surveillance. As more and more names of dissenters, off as well as on campus, are fed into FBI files and other government dossiers, it will be all the easier to keep track of potential "troublemakers" for the rest of their lives—with attendant effects on the careers of those who have been so marked. The Defense Department has 14,000,000 life histories in its security files; the

Civil Service 8,000,000. The FBI won't tell how many it has, but it does acknowledge dossiers on 100,000 "Communist sympathizers." And new names are being added at a greatly accelerated rate. The Justice Department has proudly announced its reinforced capacity to track down "extremists" in antiwar cadres and black communities through the pouring of more and more information into the computers of the department's intelligence unit. "Our intake in items of intelligence is immense," Attorney General Ramsey Clark proclaimed. "It ranges in the thousands of items daily," from Federal, state and local sources.

Professor Alan Westin, who wrote "The Snooping Machine" (*Playboy*, May 1968) and the book *Privacy and Freedom*, has demonstrated in great and ominous detail that as methods of surveillance and recordkeeping become increasingly efficient and interlocked, whatever a man has done—or has been suspected of doing—at any time of his life can be frozen into central computers. And there will be no arguing with present or future computers about extenuating circumstances, false information or change of opinion. As Vance Packard has noted dryly, "The notion of the possibility of redemption is likely to be incomprehensible to a computer."

Without many of us realizing it, we are experiencing what Alan Westin terms "the crisis of surveillance technology." How that technology will be used, for what ends and with what safeguards depends, of course, on the degree to which this society *really* values civil liberties. And that's why the current war on dissent is so crucial. It is a testing ground, and the results may determine the nature of American life for decades to come.

There are certainly reasons for pessimism as to what may happen to the nature of American life. I've detailed many of them in this article. Another, not widely reported, is a disclosure made by Cal McCrystal in the April 23, 1968, *New York Post:*

> It is now a fact of life that any civil servant in the Defense Department who criticizes U. S. policy in Vietnam—or elsewhere, for that matter—stands to lose not only his job but a reasonable chance of getting another one. First of all, he must be examined by a psychiatrist on whose report the patient's supervisor will determine his fitness for duty. If he is fit, it means he no longer disagrees with U. S. policy. If he isn't fit, then he must leave. And on his record permanently is the fact that he received psychiatric treatment, as a result of which he was declared unfit for duty.

If so pervasively powerful an institution as the Defense Department is made so systematically immune from even the merest expression of dissent, a diagnosis of our society by Senator Eugene McCarthy becomes all the more disturbing. He spoke, as Dwight Eisenhower did, of the growth of "a huge, powerful and somewhat autonomous military establishment whose influence reaches into almost every aspect of our national life. . . . The threat it poses is not so much that of a conspiracy as a conditioning, in our lives and institutions."

A particularly revealing example of how this conditioning works was an unsigned letter to *The New Republic* from a draftee. Opposed to the war in Vietnam, he had one quiet confrontation with the Army. He gives no details about it, but he does indicate that it worked out to his advantage. The letter, however, is not in the least buoyant; it's a statement of resignation from dissent:

> My experiences in the Service have taught me quite a few things. First of all, the Army does not fit the extreme Left's stereotype of a clique of fascist officers brutally ordering innocent enlisted men to their doom in Vietnam. On the contrary, the enlisted men are the bulwarks of the system. Like most Americans, they are either too ignorant to question it or simply conform and rationalize away any doubts they may have. . . . If I sound unduly cynical and bitter, it is because I am. I will be a civilian again in a relatively short time and I intend to steer clear of political activism then. . . . If the Army is a cross section of society, then this society is gravely ill, and incurably so because it doesn't even know it is.

His case is far from unique. The majority of the young remain concerned with keeping their records clean and with not going "too far" in expressing whatever dissent they feel. Those who plan to go into government or into large corporate structures already know what to expect. They would not be in the least surprised at the statement given to *The Wall Street Journal* by Colonel W. F. Rockwell, chairman of Rockwell-Standard Corporation of Pittsburgh: "We don't try to tell employees what they can or can't do off the job, but we pick them carefully to begin with. Among other things, we don't go looking for people who'll go out looking for trouble." "We assume," said an official of a large Eastern metals processor in the same article, "that people who hold higher jobs here won't do or say anything that might reflect negatively on the company, like speak for some radical political outfit or get tossed in jail over civil rights. If a customer doesn't like our product, OK. But we'd hate to lose out because someone doesn't like one of our men's ideas."

While it is true that many Americans are willing to restrict themselves to the expression of only "correct" ideas, an impressively committed minority continues to insist on exercising its full rights of speech and advocacy. More than 26,000 Americans signed a Statement of Support for Dr. Benjamin Spock, William Sloane Coffin and the two other supporters of draft resistance whose cases were in the Federal courts. These signers pledged to back "those who refuse to serve in Vietnam and those indicted men and all others who refuse to be passive accomplices in war crimes," even though they know that the maximum penalty for aiding and abetting draft refusal is five years in prison, a $10,000 fine or both. And young men in unprecedented numbers are signing statements that they will refuse to serve in the Armed Forces as long as the United States is at war in Vietnam —442 at Harvard, 300 at Yale and 320 law students from 20 law schools.

A newly formed National Federation of Priests' Councils—representing some 35,000 of the estimated 65,000 Roman Catholic priests in the United States—also testifies to the strength of the forces mobilizing against the war on dissent. Even though a Catholic priest, the Reverend Philip F. Berrigan, was sentenced to six years in Federal prison for a symbolic act of protest—the pouring of blood on draft-board files in Baltimore—this federation of priests adopted a resolution declaring, "It is consistent with Catholic tradition that men make free and individual determination about the justice of an individual war, and that men have the right to resist the draft according to their consciences."

Even among the military, men who have held vital command posts are breaking with military tradition to speak out against the war—Rear Admiral Arnold E. True, Brigadier General Samuel B. Griffith II, Brigadier General William Wallace Ford, Brigadier General Hugh B. Hester, General Matthew B. Ridgway, Lieutenant General James M. Gavin and General David M. Shoup, former Marine Corps commandant.

It was the dissenters—students and many adults—who made Eugene McCarthy a national political figure, brought the late Robert Kennedy into the Presidential campaign and finally forced Lyndon Johnson to declare that he would not run for a second term. Clearly, dissent is not going to be so easily muted this time as in the years of Joe McCarthy nor so easily crushed as in the period of the Red Scare. For even when the war ends, the dissenters—in the universities, in the ghettos, and including many in the middle class who want full rights extended to everyone in this country—will continue to speak and act. And though a minority, today's nucleus of dissenters, over and under thirty, black and white, are a good deal tougher, however inwardly scared some of them may be. And they're more resilient. Fred Brooks of SNCC, arrested for refusal to submit to induction, said that if convicted, he would continue to organize blacks in jail: "You can organize in jail just as well as you can out. They'll be getting out someday."

If today's dissenters retain their courage and their commitment to re-energize American democracy across the board, they may be able to make our cities livable, to awaken Congress to the needs of all the people and to turn education on every level into the creation of citizens for whom freedom is a fundamental value, a basic necessity. I do not, therefore, feel hopeless about the outcome of the war on dissent. But, as I have demonstrated in this article, I do not underestimate the strength of the forces working to stifle dissent, for *their* greatest support comes from the apathy of the majority. As educator John Holt emphasizes in an essay in Robert Theobald's *Social Policies for America in the Seventies:*

> I . . . believe that freedom is in serious danger in this country because so many people . . . do not feel free, never did, don't expect to and, hence, don't know what freedom is or why it should be worth making such a fuss about. For a great many Americans, freedom is little more than a slogan that makes it seem right to despise, hate and even kill any foreigner who supposedly has less of it than they do. When, rather rarely, they meet someone who feels free and acts free and takes his freedom seriously, they are more likely than not to get frightened or angry. "What are you, some kind of nut?" For, alas, the man who has no real freedom, or thinks he hasn't, doesn't think about how to get it; he thinks about how to take it away from those who do have it.

There is the real danger. For how many Americans is freedom more than a slogan? Abraham Lincoln, a man President Johnson is fond of quoting in other contexts, pointed out,

> Our defense is in the preservation of the spirit which prizes liberty as the heritage of all men, in all lands everywhere. Destroy this spirit and you have planted the seeds of despotism at your own doors. Familiarize yourself with the chains of bondage, and you are preparing your own limbs to wear them. Accustomed to trample on the rights of others, you have lost the genius of your own independence and become the fit subjects of the first cunning tyrant who rises among you.

That spirit, I believe, has not yet been destroyed in this country. If it is, the majority of us will get the kind of country we deserve. The success or failure of the war on dissent depends on you. More than one hundred years ago, Henry David Thoreau wrote,

> There are thousands who are *in opinion* opposed to slavery and to the War, who yet in effect do nothing to put an end to them; who, esteeming themselves children of Washington and Franklin, sit down with their hands in their pockets and say that they know not what to do, and do nothing. . . . They hesitate, and they regret, and sometimes they petition; but they do nothing in earnest and with effect. They will wait, well disposed, for others to remedy the evil, that they may no longer have it to regret.

If you now only wait, well disposed, for others to successfully fight for the continued right to dissent, you may discover that you will have waited too long. Today's dissenters are, as William Sloane Coffin has emphasized, the true patriots, for they know that the essence of the American tradition is the right to speak and act as a free man. They also know that if this right is not exercised by enough of the citizenry, it will atrophy.

"Same here—being kept under surveillance for my own protection."

NICHOLAS VON HOFFMAN

article

both the establishment and the anti-establishment were on trial —and both sides and the nation lost

the chicago conspiracy circus

"Screw the war, screw racism. The big issue now is prison reform," Abbie Hoffman said shortly before he and his six co-defendants were sentenced to jail. Later, when a higher court let them out of prison, pending appeal, he and his buddy, Jerry Rubin, resurfaced in a fury of complaints about roaches, the plumbing and the food served in Cook County Jail. But he was wrong. The big issue for millions of people was how these men had come to be indicted and what had happened at their trial.

They were indicted for violating and conspiring to violate Title I, section 2101, of the 1968 Civil Rights Act, a constitutionally dubious piece of Federal law generally known as the Rap Brown Amendment, in honor of the man who inspired Congress to write it. Section 2101 makes it a Federal crime to cross a state line or to send a message across a state line with the intention of inciting or encouraging a riot. The specific riot blamed on the men who have come to be known as the Conspiracy Eight—later Seven—is what happened on Chicago's streets during August of 1968 while the Democratic National Convention was nominating Hubert Humphrey in exhaustion, despair and disillusion.

In the contentious aftermath, the National Commission on the Causes and Prevention of Violence asked Daniel Walker, a Chicago corporation lawyer, to head a study team that would fix the blame for the fighting on whoever was responsible. The Walker Report, the most detailed and objective account we have of what happened, concluded that

> The vast majority of the demonstrators were intent on expressing by peaceful means their dissent either from society generally or from the Administration's policies in Vietnam. . . . On the part of the police, there was enough wild club swinging, enough cries of hatred, enough gratuitous beating to make the conclusion inescapable that individual policemen, and lots of them, committed violent acts far in excess of the requisite force for crowd dispersal or arrest. To read dispassionately the hundreds of statements describing at firsthand the events . . . is to become convinced of the presence of what can only be called a police riot.

Nevertheless, eight civilian protesters were prosecuted by the Justice Department for conspiring to *incite* the police to riot. The mere fact of this indictment raises the possibility that anybody who publicly manifests his approval or disapproval of anything—be it rat control, peace, clean lakes or better police protection—not only risks getting his head split open by a cop but also risks being tried for conspiring to provoke a cop to do it. This could have a chilling effect on free speech, and it is one reason, simple justice aside, that many people who are irritated by the defendants' personalities, courtroom antics and politics are sticking up for them.

One of the defendants, Tom Hayden, has provided evidence that the decision to prosecute him was made before any kind of riot took place in Chicago. Hayden says that on the very first day of the convention, he was told by the police assigned to tail him that he would be indicted under the Rap Brown Amendment. Rennie Davis agrees that it was a "Government that increasingly is controlled by a police mentality" that indicted him and the seven others and brought them into a trial that has claimed more attention than Sirhan Sirhan's, more than the Rosenbergs', more than any American criminal proceeding since Sacco and Vanzetti's. "This trial," said Davis, "has been controlled by the police and the FBI and undercover agents from the beginning, from the first witnesses that have been paraded with their lies to that witness stand to the last sentence."

That's what Davis told Judge Julius Hoffman before that last sentence was given the five who were convicted. The FBI agent who sat at the prosecution table said nothing. He'd sat there for the trial's four-and-a-half-month duration and said nothing. Maybe he was there to make sure the job was done and that Davis, Hayden, Dave Dellinger, Abbie Hoffman and Jerry Rubin were sent up for five years. United States District Attorney Thomas Foran claimed otherwise. He maintained that the decision to prosecute came from Washington and Nixon's Attorney General, John Mitchell, in a routine way.

The gossip around Mies van der Rohe's thirty-story steel courthouse provided a different explanation. They do gossip there, but instead of sitting in rockers under porticoes, the old-timers pass their retirement hours in shiny metal and Naugahyde chairs lining brightly lit corridors. The courthouse talk was that Foran had been told to do the job by Mayor Daley. It's impossible to say. Foran was the most puzzling of all the principals.

The judge was easy to figure. Seventy-four years old, a legal technician who had married rich and then donated enough money to the Republican Party for Eisenhower to appoint him to the bench, he was an ordinary status quo man with a pedantic theatricality about him and a touch of British affectation in his speech. Supposedly, the judges get their assignment by lot, but his choice suggested premeditation. He is Jewish, and so were three of the defendants. Of a different political party than Daley's, he is more intelligent than the loud, quick-tempered patronage hacks whom years of Democratic control had permitted to accumulate on the Federal bench in the Northern District of Illinois, Eastern Division.

From the beginning, it was obvious that Hoffman thought he was doing the Lord's work, but Foran was different. True, he had earned a lot of money around Chicago representing clients in urban-renewal work, which you don't do if City Hall disapproves of you, but coming into this trial—which has destroyed his reputation with moderate liberals—he was considered the best U. S. District Attorney Chicago had had in years. He'd broken his back trying to get a jury to convict a policeman for depriving a black man of his civil rights by killing him. Throughout the conspiracy trial, there were rumors that he thought being involved in it was the worst mistake he'd ever made and that he was spending every day after court with the judge, trying to get him to hold back and make it look fairer.

If nobody can say who ordered the eight tried for breaking and conspiring to break the Rap Brown Amendment, why these eight were picked is also unknown. They were, as Norman Mailer tried to say from the witness stand before he was silenced by the prosecution, "not political allies but practically enemies." Hayden and Davis, with their common SDS background, shared the same ideas and values, and they did work closely on an operational though not an ideological level with Dave Dellinger, the fifty-year-old communitarian, Christian pacifist disciple of the late A. J. Muste. These three, with their reasoned radicalism, their position papers and their memoranda, had nothing in common with the two super-hippie-Yippies, Abbie Hoffman and Jerry Rubin.

During the spring and early summer of 1968, when the Chicago convention was in preparation, relations between the National Mobe office (Davis, Dellinger and Hayden) and the street-theater contingent, with their Festival of Life and Pigasus, their porcine Presidential candidate, were at the level of open animosity. Davis would sit around the first-floor coffeeshop in the building where the Mobe was located and damn Abbie Hoffman, calling him reckless and saying his cart wheels and handstands would get people hurt. In his turn, Abbie Hoffman, when you could get him to be serious, would shrug off Hayden with an expletive: "Political freak!" At a preconvention planning meeting where the Mobe tried to get the dozens of diverse and disagreeing antiwar groups to decide what they were going to do in Chicago, Abbie spoke at a workshop on anticapitalism. He said that he "offered a plank that we ought to abolish pay toilets, that they were an insult to a system that was as affluent as this. They didn't like that. They were very straight, that workshop."

Davis, Dellinger and Hayden had played important parts in protest politics for years. It may not have been wise or right to indict them, but it made a kind of sense. Rubin and Hoffman, however, appeared to have been brought to the prisoners' dock for kidnaping and seduction. Foran put it this way:

> Evil is exciting and evil is interesting and plenty of kids have a fascination for it. It is knowledge of kids that these sophisticated, educated psychology majors know about [Abbie Hoffman did graduate work in psychology]. They know how to draw kids together and maneuver them to accomplish their purposes. They take advantage personally, intentionally, evilly to corrupt those kids.

Later, he would say,

> We can't let people use our kids like that. . . . Hoffman said, "There was no violence, but the young kids were fucking in the grass and smoking dope." That's what he said. I don't like to use language like that, but . . . that's what you're dealing with. . . . We've lost our kids to the freaking fag revolution and we've got to get them back.

Bobby Seale seems to have been made a defendant because 1968 and 1969 were two years when it was fashionable to involve a black in any activity. If the trial were to happen now, the same kind of requirement would demand the inclusion of a women's-liberation type. There was no other reason for indicting Seale, the Black Panther, who was a last-minute speaking replacement for Eldridge Cleaver; no evidence was ever introduced to show that he did more than fly into town for two days, give a couple of speeches and fly out.

The last two defendants were the most perplexing. They were small shots. One of them, John Froines, an assistant chemistry professor, was so unimportant in the trial that, after reading the instances of contempt committed by the other defendants, the judge forgot to sentence him. "It's part of being a media unknown," said Froines by way of self-condolence. Judge Hoffman recollected himself and sentenced Froines to six months and fifteen days in jail and, as an afterthought, gave Lee Weiner, a graduate student in sociology, two months and eighteen days.

This is a lot of time to pull when, like Weiner and Froines, you're found not guilty on all counts; it would be a lot of time even if you were found guilty of what they were accused of: conspiring to put a stink bomb in the lobby of the Conrad Hilton Hotel and fire-bombing an underground garage. Since almost no evidence was introduced against them, the question of why they were indicted remains. The only explanation came from Tom Hayden:

> Pick Weiner and Froines, innocent young men, so if they are found guilty, that will scare every innocent young person who might associate with leaders, who might go to a demonstration because they are average people in a movement of millions of average people, and when they saw them indicted, they said to themselves, "Well, that could have been me." Also, it gives you plenty of room to negotiate if the jury doesn't want to feel it's putting everybody away.

Hayden was right. The jury did negotiate. After it had rendered its verdict, Kay Richards, a twenty-three-year-old computer operator and the only young juror, recounted what happened during the four days it took them to decide:

> There were two groups and each felt they had their own point of view, and they wouldn't change it. At first I was a hard-liner for finding all seven of them guilty and then I went soft. I felt as a responsible juror I had to come up with a solution, so I became the negotiator. . . . I sat down with the three women who were really hard-liners for finding the seven [Seale had been mistrialed out of the case] innocent. The three thought the law was unconstitutional. I pointed out it was our job to decide whether these men had broken the law, and it was the job of an appeals court to decide if the law was constitutional . . . at the hotel, the others agreed to the compromise. They didn't feel it was right, they said, but they would consent and do it.

But by then, the jury's action was anticlimactic. All eight and their two lawyers had already been sentenced to unprecedented prison terms for contempt. All over the country, people—even liberals who thought the trial was insane—were accusing the eight and their attorneys of what the judge repeatedly called "a deliberate and willful attack upon the administration of justice in an attempt to sabotage the functioning of the Federal judicial system." From reading some of the editorials, you might be forced to conclude that the eight had cleverly tricked the United States government into indicting them so they could lay waste to the Federal courts.

The defendants denied they ever regarded the trial as a God-sent target of opportunity. On the last day of the trial, Abbie

Hoffman remarked that Judge Hoffman's court, a place he had once called a "neon oven," was "probably the least best forum to hear what is called the truth." He went on to say in the morbid way of one who doesn't have the energy to fight an ineluctable fate, "Right from the beginning of the indictment up until the end of the trial, I always wanted to change my plea. I had, like, a great urge to confess, say, 'I am guilty,' because I felt what the state was calling me was an enemy of the state. . . . I recognize that I am an outlaw."

During most of the trial, Abbie Hoffman's behavior reflected just this state of mind. Some days he would joke and do handstands on the defense table, the blue neon lights from the grill in the government oven making him look bad and tired; some days he would sit blowing his nose and taking pills—he was sick and fluish a lot—and some days the proceedings would catch him up in anger and he'd fight back. There was no pattern to it, nothing to indicate a studied deliberation.

Rennie Davis declared, "You may not believe this, but we came here to have a trial with a law that we regarded as unconstitutional and unfair and a jury that was inadequately selected. We came here, nevertheless, to present our full case to this jury so that it might decide on whether or not our movement was just in coming to Chicago or whether or not we came here to incite a riot." Jerry Rubin, the old hell raiser from Berkeley, said the same thing: "I was ready for a trial with lawyers, a full defense."

It may seem contradictory that men who had damned the system should claim that they came like ordinary defendants with a hope that the machinery would work equitably and that they would be acquitted. But they probably did. They're too American not to believe—with some part of themselves—in the formal institutions of the country. In one sense, it was this very belief that got them in trouble—their shrill, braying, insulting, militant, obnoxious, whacked-out, indomitable demand that the nation live up to itself. A chilled, analytical piece of themselves said the system would act to destroy them; the believing part, the part that caused them to keep quoting Thomas Jefferson to the judge, said that justice would be done, that the forms meant something.

This wasn't true of Tom Hayden. After the convention, before he was returned to Chicago for the trial, he had gone off to Berkeley and let his hair grow long, so that when he reappeared, his ear-length locks, his acne-scarred skin and his red nose made him look like a bankrupt, alcoholic pilgrim—or an English-village lout. In the Berkeley Soviet, he had fallen in love, listened to music and seemed to be in the process of becoming more humane and less of a logical ideologue. He even talked about "the post-Calvinist society," but his writings remained Leninist in tone, not in content but in the feeling of wanting to turn sloppy human imponderables into predictable patterns of behavior.

Months before the trial, in June of 1969, he wrote, "We need to expand our struggle to include a total attack on the courts. The court system is just another part of this rigged apparatus that is passed off as 'open and impartial.' . . . There is no reason for us to become submissive at the courtroom door." Later, he made it clear that the Chicago trial was going to be nothing like the Spock conspiracy trial:

> We do not intend a defense like that of Dr. Benjamin Spock. . . . The goal in that trial was to challenge the legality of the war inside a Government courtroom. . . . The defendants eventually were freed probably more because of their respectability than their legal strategy. Their failure was political. Their courtroom testimony went unheard.
>
> We are attempting to create a political trial this time with wide international repercussions. . . . We were not a pressure group which went beyond the permissible limits of dissent in liberal society and we are not interested in having this trial define those limits. . . . The give and take in the courtroom brings out latent hopes that capitalism can be tolerated. . . . We do not intend a defense which leaves this ritual renewed . . . the courts are no longer co-optive and tantalizing, but more nearly the assembly points on the road to detention camps.

That's what Tom Hayden said; what he did in the courtroom was quite different. He was the least noisy and most polite of the defendants, even managing to charm Judge Hoffman into arranging that fascinating, elastic mouth of his into an expression close to a smile, while telling Hayden, "Fellows as smart as you could do awfully well under this system," and then adding, in a second sally of judicial humor, "I'm not trying to convert you, mind you." Of all the defendants, Hayden ended this awful, draining trial with the most respect and affection from the steady spectators. He seemed more like the friend of Robert Kennedy (which he was) than whatever kind of radical he is; his speeches in the courtroom were so measured and reasonable that it seemed like the chairman of the ADA was on trial.

When Judge Hoffman gave him fourteen months and fourteen days for contempt and asked him why he shouldn't pack him off to the penitentiary, Hayden's reply was totally nonpolitical. "I was trying to think about what I regretted about punishment. I can only state one thing that affected my feelings, my own feelings, and that is that I would like to have a child." The judge answered him, "There is where the Federal system can do you no good." Hayden was near tears, many people in the courtroom were crying and, until Judge Hoffman made his cruel wisecrack, there was some hope that at the very end, a few of these men might relent and do a kindness to one another. Instead, Hayden responded sharply, "Because the Federal system can do you no good in trying to prevent the birth of a new world."

Looking back on the trial record, it didn't matter whether or not Tom Hayden and the others intended to assault the judicial system. The system assaulted itself as though it were recapitulating the events of the convention week, when the simple presence of Hayden and the hippie-Yippies was enough to set off a police riot. Their appearance in the courtroom set off a legal riot.

At first, things were nasty but not out of control. The eight were unhappy with the picking of the jury, but they left it to their lawyers, Leonard Weinglass, a young man from Newark making his first appearance in a Federal court, and William Kunstler, a widely respected attorney who had defended all kinds of people in the movement, from Martin Luther King, Jr., to Rap Brown. Both of them were straight legal types coming at the case as if they assumed they could win it in the usual way lawyers win cases. This caused Abbie Hoffman to laugh one day in the elevator during the lunch break. "Poor Kunstler," he said, "the guy thinks he's back in the good old South with those good old civil rights cases. He's gonna put everybody to sleep and lose, too."

Judge Hoffman asked both sides to suggest questions he should put to the jury in order to determine if they were biased, and Kunstler submitted a long list of them. They included such pertinent inquiries as

> Would you let your son or daughter marry a Yippie? Do you consider marijuana habit-forming? Do you have hostile feelings toward persons whose life styles differ considerably from your own? Do you know who the Fugs are? Do you believe that young men who refuse to participate in the Armed Forces because of their opposition to the war are cowards, slackers or unpatriotic?

Virtually none were asked.

The jury of ten women and two men was predictably old, lower middle class and, judging from what little was revealed about them, unable to understand somebody like an Abbie Hoffman or a Rennie Davis, who worked for an organization that paid its staff by trying to institutionalize the loaves and the fishes. "We had an icebox," Davis told the court, "and a newsman would come into the office and we'd ask him if he had ten dollars, and then we'd take the ten dollars and go down and buy baloney and put it in the icebox and get some bread and jam and peanut butter. People who had a need were given money when it existed."

As soon as this jury of the defendants' "peers" was chosen, and before the first prosecution witness was sworn in, Bobby

Seale gave the court his own handwritten motion, asking that the trial be postponed until his lawyer, Charles R. Garry, could get out of a San Francisco hospital and come to represent him. Or, if that were denied, he wanted to represent himself. Judge Hoffman paid no attention. The trouble began immediately. Seale, a thin man wasted from months in jail in connection with a murder charge that he maintains is as political as what he faced in Chicago, was not going to be put aside. He persistently got to his feet to say such things as "If I am consistently denied this right of legal defense counsel of my choice, then I can only see the judge as a blatant racist."

Judge Hoffman was called Judge Magoo by the defendants, because the little five-foot-four-inch man looks like the cartoon character or like some harsh reckoner of helpless spirits in a Dickensian countinghouse. He's tough enough to stifle his anger when his temper grows short. Then he works his jaw muscles and grinds out sandpaper words through locked molars. "Mr. Seale," he would say, "I must admonish you that any outburst such as you have just indulged in will be appropriately dealt with at the right time during this trial, and I must order you not to do it again. If you do, you do it at your own risk, sir. . . . Will you be quiet? That is all. You have a lawyer to speak for you."

"They don't speak for me," Seale would reply in varying pitches of anger.

> I want to represent myself. Charles R. Garry is not here in my service. . . . I will speak for myself. I want to defend myself. I just want to let him know. That racist, that fascist! The black man tries to get a fair trial in this country! The United States Government, huh! Nixon and the rest of them!

The judge's position was that Seale had a lawyer: William Kunstler. This was true but only in a limited sense. Kunstler had filed as Seale's counsel after the Black Panther had been taken from his California prison and driven by a crazy zigzag route to Chicago, where he was held incommunicado in Cook County's dilapidated jail. His friends and codefendants were worried about his health and Kunstler filed an appearance solely to get into the jail to visit Seale. From what an outsider could judge, at no time did Seale contemplate using Kunstler as his lawyer. He had always used Garry, who is a great favorite of the California Panthers. Actually, Garry was supposed to be chief counsel for all the defendants. His absence may have been a serious loss to the defense, because he's supposed to be much better at examining witnesses than Kunstler, who is regarded more as an appellate man.

Since there are almost no clear-cut, unambiguous rules in law, there's no way of saying if Judge Hoffman was technically right in doing what he did on the Garry matter. In other cases, Judge

Hoffman has been known to grant a trial postponement for such reasons as a lawyer's preplanned Caribbean vacation. This, like almost everything else a judge does, is up to his discretion. Regardless of the technicalities, what Judge Hoffman did was to ignore the appearances of justice. Most Americans believe they have an absolute right to defend themselves, to call their own witnesses and to present their own evidence to prove their innocence. Judge Hoffman, who ought to have known better—since he is ultrasensitive to publicity—forgot this and made rulings that scandalized lay opinion. He compounded his errors by failing to explain his reasons, so a sensitive spectator got the idea that the law and the workings of the law courts were nobody's business but the judge's.

But Judge Hoffman may have felt that he was on shaky legal ground in refusing Seale's demands. After Seale began his rumpus, the judge issued bench warrants for the arrest of four lawyers, who had been retained only to prepare pretrial motions concerning FBI wire taps, in order to show that Seale was adequately represented. The lawyers were never meant to argue the case in court. The judge's attempt to demonstrate to an appeals court that Seale had representation was botched; one of the four, Mike Tigar, a young UCLA law professor, was dragged out of bed, put on an airplane to Chicago, where he was photographed, fingerprinted and thrown into jail. Immediately, there was an uproar. Lawyers came flying into the city to picket the courthouse. Even the staid members of the bar got fidgety about this sort of treatment for one of their brothers. Judge Hoffman might do it to them sometime. The resulting stink made the judge back off, but he still wouldn't let Seale defend himself.

The government's case was never very coherent—being a collage of testimony by police spies, double agents, creeping Toms, *provocateurs*, snatches of TV film and dull recitals of incidental material by lower-level political bureaucrats. And during October, the first full month of the trial, what shape it did have was shattered by Bobby Seale, who wanted to cross-examine witnesses and have the same privileges as the two defense lawyers. He would not give up trying to defend himself. Day after day, the judge would stretch his mouth and say, "I admonish you, sir, that you have a lot of contemptuous conduct against you," and the tall black man who wore a long-sleeved striped T-shirt would come back saying, "I admonish you. You are in contempt of people's constitutional rights. You are the one who is in contempt. I am not in contempt of nothing."

It got rougher and rougher, with the marshals forcibly pushing Seale down into his seat and Dave Dellinger interposing himself in his nonviolent way to prevent them. The defendants couldn't take what was happening to Seale without doing something. They were all active, articulate political men, and they began fighting back in a dozen ways. To show their contempt, they would pass out jelly beans in the courtroom or try, as they did one day, to get a birthday cake inside for Seale. The marshals, sporting miniature handcuff tie tacks, stopped them, thus prompting Rennie Davis to blurt out in open court—at the cost of a two-day jail sentence—"They arrested your cake, Bobby. They arrested it."

Dellinger seemed to be the most profoundly outraged at what was happening to Seale. This lifelong pacifist, a short-haired, old-school Christian socialist, who must have worn the same fagged-out olive-green sports coat every day of the trial, could not contain himself. He was the most aggressively abusive of the remaining seven throughout the trial, constantly calling Judge Hoffman a fascist, a racist and a liar. He got over two years for contempt because of it, but he showed no fear.

The others sometimes did. There would be days when Rubin would come into the courtroom with a spooked, frightened dullness in his eyes. Dellinger had already served three years in jail during World War Two for resisting the draft, so perhaps he knew what the others couldn't—that he was strong enough and together enough as a personality to take years in prison. Some days he'd leave off trying to defend Seale and go on the attack, as he did on October 15, when he said to the judge, "Mr. Hoffman, we are observing the Moratorium."

"I am Judge Hoffman, sir," the judge replied.

"I believe in equality, sir," Dellinger gave back, "so I prefer to call people mister or by their first name."

"Sit down."

"I wanted to explain we are reading the names of the war dead from both sides."

By October's end, with Seale uncowed and the rest of the defendants in a daily rising fury, the judge ordered the marshals to chain the black man to his chair and gag his mouth. That didn't stop Seale, who was able to talk through the gag, which was then tightened with an elastic bandage. The bandage began to choke Seale and, in a courtroom of widening chaos, Weinglass asked that it be loosened, while Kunstler asked, "Your Honor, are we going to stop this medieval torture that is going on in this courtroom?"

Then the dialog went as follows:

Rubin: This guy (*a very big, black marshal*) is putting his elbow in Bobby's mouth. . . .

Kunstler: This is no longer a court of order, Your Honor. It is a disgrace. They're assaulting the other defendants, also.

Rubin: Don't hit me in the balls, motherfucker.

Seale: This motherfucker (*referring to the gag, not the marshal*) is tight and it's stopping my blood.

Kunstler: Your Honor, this is an unholy disgrace to the law. I, as an American lawyer, feel a disgrace.

Foran: Created by Mr. Kunstler.

Kunstler: Created by nothing other than what you have done to this man.

Abbie Hoffman: You come down here and watch this, Judge.

Foran: May the record show that the outbursts are by the defendant Rubin.

Seale: You fascist dogs, you rotten, low-life son of a bitch.

Dellinger: Somebody go protect him.

Kunstler: Your Honor, we would like the names of the marshals. We are going to ask for a judicial investigation of the entire condition and the entire treatment of Bobby Seale.

Judge Hoffman: You may ask for anything that you want. When you begin keeping your word around here that you gave the court, perhaps things can be done.

Kunstler: I feel so ashamed.

Judge Hoffman: You should be ashamed.

At the end of the trial, this episode cost Kunstler three months of his four years and thirteen days in contempt sentences. That put him ahead of Seale, who got a flat four years when Judge Hoffman mistrialed him out of the case. It was then, just before sentencing him and evicting him, that the judge finally said, "Mr. Seale, you have a right to speak now. I will hear you."

The incredulous Seale asked, "For myself? How come I couldn't speak before?"

"This," the judge answered him in his clipped way, "is a special occasion."

Then the fact that he was about to go to jail—without even a trial—for exercising what he thought were his rights clicked inside Bobby Seale's head and the astonished man replied,

> Wait a minute. You are going to attempt to punish me for attempting to speak out for myself? What kind of jive is that? What am I supposed to speak about? I still haven't got the right to defend myself. . . . Wait a minute, I got a right—what's the cat trying to pull now? I'm leaving? I can't stay . . . ? I still want an immediate trial. You can't call it a mistrial. I'm put in jail for four years for nothing? I want my coat.

That was the end of it, with the defense sympathizers in the courtroom shouting, "Free Bobby! Free Bobby!"

From then on, the trial was never the same; it had become a disaster for everyone. Humane people would remember Julius

Hoffman as the judge who refused Seale his most basic rights; Foran would be remembered as the prosecutor who tried to convict a bound and gagged black man; the worst fears of the defense had become a courtroom reality.

Still the government slogged on with its side of the case, a side that was profuse in details that proved nothing much. Only one of its witnesses testified that any of the defendants had been seen breaking a law, and that was Froines, who was supposed to have thrown a couple of rocks. Hayden was alleged to have let the air out of a tire, but this accusation was so trivial that it became a source of embarrassment.

The Chicago convention was relived on the witness stand—complete with the stories of bags of urine and spiked whiffle balls—but there was little evidence that any of the eight, now seven, had crossed a state line with the intention of inciting anybody to toss these execrable objects. Much evidence, however, was introduced to prove that in the midst of the Chicago battling, some of the seven had said inciteful things. Hayden was quoted as telling a crowd,

> If blood is going to flow, let it flow all over the city; if gas is going to be used, let that gas come down all over Chicago, not just all over us in this park; if the police are going to run wild, let 'em run wild all over the city of Chicago; if we're going to get disrupted and violated, let this whole stinking city be disrupted and violated. . . . Don't get trapped in some kind of large organized march which can be surrounded. Begin to find your way out of here. I'll see you in the streets.

Rubin was cited as giving some "fight-the-pigs" talks, and there were examples of Davis saying things that might be construed as incitement to riot. With Dellinger, the government lacked not only deeds but even words and was driven to argue that their absence was the proof of his guilt: This "architect of the conspiracy," this rough old pacifist was too shrewd to say or do anything overtly incriminating. "He won't say what they planned. He is very careful," assistant prosecution counsel Richard Schultz told the jury.

Had it been a state or a municipal court and an ordinary incitement-to-riot charge, the government might have had a pretty good case against three or four of the seven. The charge, however, was a Federal one of crossing a state line with the *intent* to start a riot, and the out-of-state evidence was almost nonexistent. What the government was really doing was trying them for the street fighting, for what they might have done in Chicago, not what they might have had in mind before they got to Illinois. The government's case said simply that the defendants were revolutionaries, insurrectionists who wanted to overthrow every institution. And to prove it, much evidence was introduced—including speeches made *after* the convention, when they were, if not more radical, certainly more angry.

During the proceedings and in the months afterward, many people attacked the trial as a threat to free speech, but this isn't so. Over and over, Foran emphasized that what the seven said was constitutionally protected; it was coupling their words with political actions that made what they did felonious. The government's position appeared to be that only orthodox, two-party, Democratic/Republican politics is legal; creative politics outside the two-party structure, politics that can bait the standard-brand politicians into making fools of themselves or bloodying people's heads, is illegal. The price for having psyched out Mayor Daley and President Johnson, the price for having baited them into losing their tempers and using force against the nonparty political extemporizers was jail.

Understanding the evidence and the legal arguments doesn't help understand the trial. To do that, you must also know the little nastinesses.

In his opening statement to the jury, Kunstler received a bitter foretaste of the hostility to come:

> **Kunstler:** We hope to prove before you that the evidence submitted by the defendants will show that this prosecution which you are hearing is the result of two motives on the part of the Government——
>
> **Schultz:** Objection as to any motives of the prosecution, if the court please.
>
> **Kunstler:** Your Honor, it is a proper defense to show motive.
>
> **Judge Hoffman:** I sustain the objection. You may speak to the guilt or innocence of your clients, not to the motive of the Government.
>
> **Kunstler:** Your Honor, I always thought that——
>
> **Schultz:** Objection to any colloquies and arguments, Your Honor.
>
> **Judge Hoffman:** I sustain the objection, regardless of what you have always thought, Mr. Kunstler.

The lawyers for both sides were always having at one another, calling one another names—unprofessional, mouthpieces, hypocritical. Foran and Schultz were especially maddened by Kunstler's talking to the press, in violation of an Illinois district court ruling that attorneys may not comment on pending cases—a rule that many legal experts believe to be unconstitutional. There were interminable objections when Kunstler referred to the defendants by their first names. Anything that might suggest to the jury that the defendants were young and therefore forgivable irked Foran, who said, "They are not kids. Davis, the youngest one, is twenty-nine. These are highly sophisticated, educated men and they are evil men."

The judge was full of tricks that added to the conviction that he'd replaced his symbolic scales with a noose. After the prosecution had completed its presentation, he extended the court day, so that the jury had to hear much of the defense case when it was tired from hours of wrangling. He appeared to make it a denigrating specialty to mispronounce the defense's names, particularly Weinglass', who finally called him on it and got this response: "I have got a very close friend named Weinruss and I know nobody by the name of Weinrob and somehow or other the name of Weinruss stuck in my mind and it is your first appearance here."

There were long, self-justifying, self-pitying excursions of recrimination and rationalization addressed by the judge to the defendants and their counsel. Almost any request by Kunstler or Weinglass would elicit snappish, peeved responses from the bench, even the observation that it was half past noon and time for lunch: "I know, I am watching the clock. What does the man say on the TV or the radio? Leave the driving, leave the time watching to me. Mr. Kunstler, I will watch the clock for you. I will determine the time when we recess, sir. I don't need your help on that. There are some things I might need your help on, not that."

And always he worried about what the drama critics would say:

> I don't try cases in the newspapers. I don't send letters to newspapers when they praise me, and they have; and I don't send letters of criticism when they criticize me adversely. . . . I have literally thousands of editorials back there in my chambers . . . that are complimentary about decisions I have made over the years. . . . It would have been so much easier to rise, wouldn't it? [Hoffman found the lawyers guilty of contempt for failing to sit down and the defendants guilty for failing to get up]. . . . I am an informal person. I may sound a little starchy up here, but I don't insist on deference that some other judges do off the bench. . . . You know, the Solicitor General of the United States, when he argues before the Supreme Court—this is rather a humorous observation, in the light of the tailoring in this case—he is obligated under the rule of court to wear a cutaway, a morning coat and striped trousers.

Although the defense called over one hundred witnesses, it wasn't able to present its case. Partly, this was because people inside the courtroom and out considered the use of such witnesses as Judy Collins, William Styron, Norman Mailer and Phil Ochs dilatory theatricality, part of the plan to subvert the judiciary. But once something may have gotten through, when Allen Ginsberg was on the stand reciting the damnation of his famous poem *Howl:*

I saw the best minds of my generation destroyed by madness, starving, hysterical, naked, dragging themselves through the Negro streets at dawn looking for an angry fix. . . . Moloch! Solitude! Filth! Ugliness! Ash cans and unobtainable dollars! Boys sobbing in armies! Children screaming under stairways! Old men weeping in the parks! Moloch! Moloch! Nightmare of Moloch! Moloch the loveless! Moloch the heavy judger of men!

The little judge bounced in his chair and put a hand to his face; it was said in the courtroom that in New York, exorcists chanted prayers to drive the dibbuk out of him.

The poet, however, wasn't taken seriously when he explained what was working on the minds of the people camping out in Lincoln Park during the convention:

> The planet . . . was endangered by violence, overpopulation, pollution, ecological destruction brought about by our own greed; the younger children in America . . . might not survive the next 30 years; it was a planetary crisis not recognized by any government . . . nor the politicians who were preparing for the elections. . . . We were going to gather together to manifest our presence over and above the more selfish elder politicians. . . . The desire for preservation of the . . . planet's form . . . was manifested to my mind by the great mantra from India to the preserver-god Vishnu, whose mantra is Hare Krishna, Hare Krishna, Krishna, Krishna, Hare, Hare, Rama, Hare Rama, Rama, Rama, Hare Hare.

As Ginsberg's voice filled the courtroom—which Abbie Hoffman had called "wall-to-wall bourgeois"—one of the marshals jumped to his feet and went into his jacket, as if going for his gun, and the prosecution plunged into altercations about Sanskrit and relevance until Ginsberg uttered two long, universal O-O-M-M-M-M-Ms, which brought Foran to his feet, saying, "All right, we have had a demonstration. From here on, I object."

"You haven't said that you objected," Judge Hoffman commented.

"I do after the second one," Foran replied. "I have no objection to the two OMs that we have had. However, I [don't] want it to go on all morning."

Judge Hoffman, feeling equally playful, added, "The two OMs may remain of record and he may not continue to answer in the same vein." But Ginsberg did OM a little later on—to calm the judge and the lawyers after the judge had gotten into another snit because he wasn't getting enough respect from the defense.

The use of people like Ginsberg to establish the state of mind and therefore the intent of the seven was a complete failure. The cross-examination was mostly given over to a refined form of fag baiting. Kunstler put Abbie Hoffman and Rennie Davis on the witness stand, so that they might explain their state of mind and intent. But the judge interpreted the rules of admissible evidence in the narrowest possible way. Davis' struggle to be allowed to answer the question the way he wanted resulted in forty-three warnings from Judge Hoffman—and, ultimately, six months in jail.

Although the Chicago seven's political opponents use the contempt citations to show they were trying to clown and wisecrack the court into ruin, the preponderate number of citations arose out of Bobby Seale's treatment and their losing attempt to get their case on the record. Here is one example of what put Davis in jail:

Foran: The whole activities of your planning with these defendants were designed to cause the President of the United States to call out the troops to protect the convention, isn't that correct, sir?

Davis: No. The objective was to try to get rid of the troops.

Foran: I object, Your Honor, to anything but no.

Davis: (*persisting*): To try to stop the use of troops.

Judge Hoffman: I sustain the objection. . . . I again order the witness to answer the question and don't go beyond the question. You do hear well, don't you? You hear me?

Davis: Yes. It is just when a man destroys my meaning, I feel obligated to——

Judge Hoffman: You must conform to the rules, to the law.

Davis: I took an oath here to tell the whole truth and that's what I'm trying to do.

Judge Hoffman: And you will conform to the rules of evidence.

Davis: Are the rules of evidence in conflict with the truth?

Foran: Five hundred years of the law, Your Honor, says that they help find the truth, and this is why we have them.

Kunstler: Two hundred years of the law said slavery was valid in this country.

These wrestling matches piled up time in jail for Davis—while showing the hopelessness of judicial proceedings that try to convict men for their state of mind, their opinions, their beliefs.

Having been unable to get much evidence as to intent on the record through direct testimony, the defense tried documents. Many were admitted, but the judge refused to allow into evidence the application for a permit to use Soldiers Field as a meeting place. More seriously, he disallowed a twenty-one-page memorandum that Davis and Hayden had written before the convention. This memo spelled out various kinds of thinking about what the demonstrators might do when they got to Chicago. It said, for instance, that

> A coalition of poverty-rights organizations in one region might surround the Conrad Hilton, a downtown Chicago hotel, on the morning of the 26th to greet the delegates with leaflets demanding 15 billion dollars to end poverty. . . . The final funeral march on the convention, beginning as the first ballot is taken, should bring 500,000 people demanding a choice on the issues of peace and justice, citizens who have to "make the democratic process work" by pinning the delegates in the International Amphitheater until a choice is presented to the American people.

As documentary evidence of intent, the memo was important, but the judge threw it out. This was too much for Davis, who blurted out, "You never read it. I was watching you. You read two pages . . . he didn't read the document. I watched him. He never looked at it." This cost him two more months in jail.

In ruling the way he did, the judge may have been legally correct. Lay people think of law as a clear set of rules that can be evenly applied, when, in reality, it's a large mass of technical notions and exceptions that can be used as rationalizations for decisions that are politically or socially motivated. This is what killed the defense's last line of approach, an attempt to prove an alternate theory of what happened in Chicago. As Kunstler said, "One way you can get your client off is not by proving that he's innocent but that somebody else is guilty."

Kunstler proposed to do that with Mayor Daley. "The person responsible for what happened in Chicago, whether acting alone or in concert with other people, is Mayor Richard J. Daley," he told the court. "We have attempted in every way possible to state our fundamental defensive position that it was the mayor who caused the trouble, the bloodshed, the police riot and every other aspect which brings these defendants into court." So he brought Daley into court as a defense witness, but the rules prevented Kunstler from asking the hard questions that might have brought out the truth. In such circumstances, it's customary for a lawyer to have the witness declared hostile by the judge. This permits the asking of otherwise forbidden questions. Judge Hoffman wasn't buying that. He even ordered Kunstler not to tell the jury that the motion to declare Daley hostile had been refused. Kunstler did anyway, and eighty-three times, he asked Daley questions that Judge Hoffman ruled objectionable. That got him six more months in the lockup.

There was still one road open to Kunstler. If he could find some friendly public officials who might know what Daley had been up to and would testify to it, he could prove his theory that it was the mayor and not his clients who did the conspiring and the intending. There were three such men: Ramsey Clark, the former attorney general; Roger Wilkins, a former assistant attorney general; and Wesley Pomeroy, who'd been special assistant for law-enforcement coordination under Clark. These three had dealt with Daley and his police chiefs in preparation for the convention. But Judge Hoffman refused to allow Clark to appear before the jury. Wilkins and Pomeroy he let on the witness stand but forbade any testimony about the mayor. Pomeroy's off-the-witness-stand recital of what went on might well have destroyed the prosecution's case. "The entire fiasco in Chicago," he declared,

> was almost solely the responsibility of a stubborn, unwise Mayor Daley, who emasculated his police command. I went there twice before the convention as a messenger from the attorney general, asking Daley to let somebody from the Government negotiate with somebody from the mobilization. He didn't hear the message. The one thing Mayor Daley said was that if the Justice Department really wanted to help, it could let him know when those out-of-town agitators were coming into Chicago so he could take care of them.

More contempt citations—and more time in jail—were issued as a consequence of the Ramsey Clark decision but the defense was lost, its best case never put to the jury. Nothing remained for the seven but to make their gallows speeches. Jerry Rubin called Judge Hoffman a sadist. Rennie Davis said, "We are going to turn the sons and daughters of the ruling class in this country into Viet Cong." Tom Hayden asked,

> If you didn't want to make us martyrs, why did you do it? If you wanted to keep it cool, why didn't you give us a permit? You know, if you had given us a permit, very little would have happened in Chicago. . . . We would hardly be notorious characters if they had left us alone in the streets of Chicago. It would have been testimony to our failure as organizers.

Abbie Hoffman told the court,

> It's only fitting that if you went to the South and fought for voter registration and got arrested and beaten 11 or 12 times on those dusty roads for no bread; it's fitting that you be arrested and tried under a civil rights act. . . . I am not made to be a martyr. I tried to sign up a few years ago when I went down South. They ran out of nails. What was I going to do? So I ended up being funny.

But the end of the end came when Dellinger was being sentenced for contempt. His sports coat was smeared with some kind of white goo he'd picked up in the jailhouse where the judge had sent him after revoking his bail. "You want us to be like good Germans, supporting the evils of our decade," he was saying, while the loquacious old judge commanded, "Mr. Marshal, I will ask you to have Mr. Dellinger sit down."

Dellinger wouldn't. "You want us to stay in our place like

black people were supposed to stay in their place, like poor people——"

"I will ask you to sit down," the judge said.

"Like children, like lawyers," he continued, while the judge said, "Mr. Marshal, will you please ask him to keep quiet?"

"People no longer will be quiet. People are going to speak up. I am an old man and I am just speaking feebly, but I reflect the spirit that will echo——" Dellinger persisted, now encircled by marshals, who kept glancing up at the judge for their next cue.

"Take him out," they were ordered, but the room had come apart. Natasha, Dellinger's oldest daughter, had her arms hooked onto the back of a bench and she was about to kick a marshal in the stomach. Michelle, her thirteen-year-old sister, was weeping, and Dellinger was crying out, "Leave my daughters alone!" There were voices screaming, "Tyrants! Tyrants!"

Kunstler, aged and radicalized by the months in this room, walked up to the lectern in front of the judge's raised bench and asked, "What are you doing to us, Your Honor?"

The little judge was rigid in the leather chair that was too big for him. Across the courtroom, down on his left, he could see six or seven people fighting; and directly behind Kunstler, he could look at Rubin shouting and making the Nazi salute as he hollered, "*Heil* Hitler! *Heil* Hitler! *Heil* Hitler! I hope you're satisfied."

Another voice in the crowd shouted, "You mocky Hitler"; but Kunstler spoke softly, leaning forward, one hand half-raised in the beckoning gesture of supplication. "My life has come to nothing," he told the judge, who pushed himself back against his chair's high back, as though he'd like to disappear through it. "You destroy me and everybody else. Put me in jail now, for God's sake, and get me out of this place." The lawyer wept as he talked. "Come to mine now. Come to mine now, Judge, please. Please. I beg you. Come to mine. Do me, too."

The marshals threw people out and calmed the room down; one on each arm, they took Dellinger and led him toward the exit. He stopped and called out, "Right on, beautiful people, black people, Vietnamese, poor people, young people, everybody fighting for liberty and justice. Right on." They took him through the doorway, but he reappeared to say, "Not to mention Latin Americans," and then he was gone.

JON R. WALTZ

13 legal questions raised by the trial of the Chicago 8 minus 1 plus 2

The Chicago riot-conspiracy case came to a temporary end on February 18, 1970. The trial's histrionics and its veneer of violence have obscured significant legal issues that will receive a full hearing in appellate courts. The most important of these legal questions are:

1. Is the Federal statute under which the Chicago Eight were indicted constitutionally valid? Counsel for the defendants plus the ACLU and the Chicago Council of Lawyers can be expected to argue that the vaguely worded Anti-Riot Act has an impermissibly chilling effect on the rights of free speech and assembly and is clearly unconstitutional.

2. Were the accused accorded "due process of law"; that is, were they given a fair trial? This is a complicated concept. At minimum, fair trial implies two notions—that of equality (were these defendants given the same protection and chance of acquittal as others are?) and that of rational procedure (was there an adherence to procedures rationally adopted to determine the guilt or innocence of the defendants?). Inevitably, this issue will focus on the conduct of Judge Julius J. Hoffman. Almost every issue to be listed here could be considered an aspect of the overall due-process issue.

3. Were the defendants deprived of their Sixth Amendment

right to the assistance of legal counsel? The judge refused a relatively brief delay in the trial's commencement to permit attorney Charles R. Garry to participate as chief defense counsel. The complex right-to-counsel issue brooded over the entire case, vexing the situation of defendant Bobby G. Seale and contributing to the deterioration of the trial into an embarrassment.

4. Was the manner of selecting the jury adequate? Were the Chicago Eight, these protesters and system dropouts, tried by a jury of their peers? (The jurors had been drawn from voter-registration rolls, which meant to the defendants that they were all establishment cogs.) Is the court rule that permits the trial judge to bar defense counsel from directly questioning the qualifications of prospective jurors another constitutional deprivation of the right to assistance of counsel? (Judge Hoffman's examination of prospective jurors took only a few hours and was surprisingly unspecific, failing even to reveal what the jurors knew of the convention week's troubled events.)

5. Were the accused prejudiced by the trial judge's manner of reading the indictment to the prospective jurors? Defense counsel, backed by the shocked out-of-court statement of at least one prospective juror, insisted that Judge Hoffman employed his not inconsiderable acting skills to convey to the jury his own sense of outrage at the crimes of the presumptively guilty defendants.

6. Was the defendants' case prejudiced by the trial judge's inadvertent disqualification of the jury's youngest member, Miss Christie King? In a moment of dramatic ineptitude, the trial judge passed to the juror a threatening letter, signed "The Black Panther Party," that she had never seen before. This so frightened the girl that it became necessary to excuse her from further service. She was replaced by another young woman who, months later, engineered the compromise convictions of five of the seven.

7. Were constitutional concepts of privacy and free speech violated by the government's reliance on evidence obtained through nonstop undercover surveillance of the defendants prior to and during the convention?

8. Did the shackling and gagging of codefendant Seale and the eventual mistrial as to him prejudice the case of the seven other defendants in the eyes of the jury? Also, Seale's predicament apparently exerted pressure on the other defendants, previously rather docile, to rally to him and thereby make themselves appear to be men of violence.

9. Were the defendants accorded reasonable latitude in putting on their defense? The Chicago Eight, their prior bias against the system inflamed by Judge Hoffman's consistently rigorous application of evidentiary rules (which, in fact, provide for substantial flexibility), believed that they were being prevented from making their defense. (This dashing of the accused's expectations is almost inevitable in political cases, since the defendants

are always stripped of what they consider to be their first line of defense: the validation of their political philosophies.) The defendants can be counted on to point to the trial judge's preventing a probing defense examination of Mayor Richard J. Daley, to his unprecedented refusal to let former Attorney General Ramsey Clark take the witness stand on behalf of the defendants, and to his upholding of all government objections to questions, put to an array of singers, writers and politicians, designed to explicate the defendants' intent in traveling to Chicago to attend the convention.

10. Did the trial judge's obvious distaste for the defendants and their lawyers result in an unfair trial? Observers were impressed by Judge Hoffman's willingness to display to the jury his admiration for the government's legal representatives and his disdain for those of the accused. He praised prosecutor Foran, while indicating unrelenting scorn for attorneys Kunstler and Weinglass by repeatedly lecturing them (sometimes quite incorrectly), referring snidely to their out-of-state origins and interjecting veiled threats of contempt citations.

11. Are the guilty verdicts invalidated by the process of compromise through which they were reached? Because one juror breached the traditional confidentiality of a jury's deliberations, it is known that the verdicts were the product of outright compromise. While there exists an antique principle that a jury's verdict, lawful on its face, cannot be impeached out of the jurors' own mouths, it is at least possible that an appellate court will reach out to grapple with the hard question of the propriety of the compromise verdict.

12. Were five of the defendants, acquitted on the government's conspiracy charge, then wrongly convicted on the crossing-state-lines-with-intent-to-incite-riots charge because the jurors took into account substantial amounts of prejudicial hearsay evidence that was properly receivable only on the conspiracy count? (This contention, an important one, is based on highly esoteric evidentiary principles peculiar to conspiracy cases.)

13. Did the trial judge abuse the contempt power? Separate appeals are already under way to test the legality of Judge Hoffman's implementation of the power to sentence summarily for direct contempt of court. The multiple contempt citations and the sentences doled out to all of the defendants and their counsel are questionable. In the first place, the trial court cast itself as prosecutor, witness, jury and judge, despite respectable authority for the proposition that it should have referred the contempt matters to a neutral judge for resolution. Also, the U. S. Supreme Court has said men cannot be convicted of a "serious contempt" —one drawing a serious penalty—except by a jury. It is arguable that Judge Hoffman's attempted circumvention of this dictate by issuing a stream of "petty" citations and by sentencing to six

months or less on each is an unavailing gambit. But perhaps the most compelling inquiry will simply be whether or not Judge Hoffman's contempt findings are factually supported. Experienced trial lawyers, myself among them, wonder whether young Leonard Weinglass was really in contempt of court and subject to imprisonment for continuing on several occasions to argue the defendants' cause after Judge Hoffman had delivered himself of a ruling. There are even law professors who, sharing nothing of William Kunstler's outlook on life and the law, nonetheless wonder whether he should spend time in a Federal prison because, for example, on February 9, 1970, he "[accused] the court of being wrong when it wasn't."

Unless our courts of review become irretrievably reactionary, we should expect to see the Chicago convictions overturned on appeal.

a candid conversation with

WILLIAM SLOANE COFFIN

the embattled chaplain of Yale and Vietnam war critic tried for counseling young men to violate the draft laws

One of those anointed few over the age of thirty who can and do communicate with the nation's young is William Sloane Coffin, chaplain of Yale University. A leader for several years in the movement against the war in Vietnam, Coffin became even more prominent—"notorious," some uptight adults would say—when he was indicted by the Federal government in January 1968 on charges of conspiring to counsel young men to violate the draft laws. (Codefendants were Dr. Benjamin Spock, writer Mitchell Goodman, Harvard University graduate student Michael Ferber and Marcus Raskin, codirector of the Institute for Policy Studies in Washington.) The trial began in Boston as this interview went to press.

Controversial on campus long before the current furor, Coffin has become an even stormier petrel since his indictment. "After reading your nauseating article about publicity-hound Coffin," wrote one alumnus to the Yale Alumni Magazine, *"I threw up—then burned my Alumni Fund contribution card. Please send future issues of your magazine in a plain wrapper. I don't want anyone to know, not even the mailman." Kingman Brewster, president of Yale, has publicly disagreed with Coffin's position on draft resistance, but adds, "I feel that the quality of the Yale educational experience and the Yale atmosphere has gained greatly from his presence. Thanks in large part to his personal verve and social action, religious life within and without the church reaches more people at Yale than on any other campus I know about. More important, the rebellious instinct which elsewhere expresses itself so often in sour withdrawal, cynical nihilism and disruption is here more often than not both affirmative and constructive, thanks in considerable measure to the chaplain's influence." In the spring of 1968, Coffin's appointment as chaplain was renewed on a permanent basis—but with the proviso, as stated by Brewster, that "the corporation might want to review the appointment when the lawsuit is terminated if it seemed that the final judgment . . . had some bearing on the chaplain's fitness for his duties."*

In contrast to this equivocal endorsement by the school administration, 640 Yale faculty members—including 16 deans, 25 department chairmen and 8 college masters—have issued a statement in his support. And on college campuses throughout the country, Coffin draws even larger and more enthusiastic crowds than before his arrest—not only because he is a strikingly effective speaker but also because he comes through strongly as a man of tested integrity who is wholly free of self-righteousness. A typical account of a Coffin appearance was carried in the Providence Evening Bulletin *in March 1968, on the occasion of a speaking engagement at Brown University: "As Mr. Coffin began his public appearance yesterday in Meehan Auditorium, about an eighth of the 3000 Brown students stood to applaud him. When he left the rostrum, all stood to applaud."*

Coffin's background could hardly be more unlikely for so formidable an opponent of the government. Born in New York, the son of the late vice-president of W. & J. Sloane (the posh Fifth Avenue furniture store), Coffin grew up a part of the Eastern establishment. After graduation from Phillips Academy in 1942, he served with distinction as a captain in the Army paratroop corps until the end of World War Two. It wasn't until after V-J Day that he committed his first act of civil disobedience. Assigned as liaison officer to the Russian army, Coffin was ordered to return Russian deserters to the Soviets. "The first one I brought back," Coffin has told a reporter for The New York Times, *"they shot on the spot. After that, I never gave them back another one."*

Despite this defiance of authority, Coffin returned to the Eastern establishment. He completed his undergraduate work at Yale, spent a year at Union Theological Seminary, and then joined the Central Intelligence Agency shortly after the outbreak of the Korean War. When he came home again, following three years' service as a CIA agent, Coffin finished his divinity studies, was ordained in the Presbyterian Church in 1956 and served as chaplain at Phillips Academy and at Williams College before he was appointed chaplain at Yale—where he gave an inkling of things to come by making his first pastoral rounds on a motorcycle.

It soon became clear that Coffin's chaplaincy was going to be forceful and unpredictable. Although he had been a member, as a Yale undergraduate, of the highly prestigious Skull and Bones secret society, Coffin as chaplain strongly opposed fraternities and secret societies because of their racially, ethnically and religiously restrictive membership. Off campus, in 1961, he was arrested at one of the first sit-ins in Montgomery, Alabama. Two years later, he was arrested again—this time for protesting segregation at an amusement park outside Baltimore. And in 1964, he went to jail in St. Augustine, Florida, for participating in yet another civil-rights demonstration.

As Coffin moved into militant antiwar protest in 1966, his bearing and speaking skill soon made him a national figure. He has perhaps been best described by Norman Mailer in *The Armies of the Night*. On an October afternoon in 1967 in Washington, Coffin and others confronted members of the Justice Department, handing them 944 draft cards returned by young men who had refused to serve in the Vietnam war. "The Yale chaplain," Mailer recalled, "had one of those faces you expected to see on the cover of *Time* or *Fortune*, there as the candidate for Young Executive of the Year. He had that same flint of the eye, single-mindedness in purpose, courage to bear responsibility, that same hard humor about the details in the program under consideration, the same suggestion of an absolute lack of humor once the line which enclosed his true WASP temper had been breached. He was one full example of the masculine principle at work in the cloth."

These tough-minded qualities are impressively evident in the following conversation with Nat Hentoff—the most outspoken and extensive interview ever granted by Yale's embattled chaplain. "Coffin met me at the railroad station in New Haven," reports Hentoff. "Tall and limber, he is one of the most informal public figures I know. This ease of manner, like the dryness of his wit, is part of an integral style that helps explain why no generation barrier exists between him and the young. Wearing a blue sport shirt, red tie and slacks, Coffin was escorting me to his car when a middle-aged lady stopped him. 'You don't know

"The churches and synagogues will have to get rid of their irrelevant righteousness. They've been concerned about free love—and yet indifferent about free hate. They must rearrange their priorities."

"If the next Administration is a continuation of this one in terms of policy and action, many students are going to turn off to private sensations, leave the country in droves—or turn to acts of terrorism."

"I don't think any man ever has the right to break the law, but I do think that upon occasion, every man has the duty to break the law—when the law begins to dominate rather than serve men."

me,' she said, 'but I just wanted to tell you that you're one of the reasons I'm beginning to have hope for the world.'

"As we drove the short distance to Yale, Coffin said, 'Attitudes are changing more and more. There's a big Italian butcher near here. A hawk, I guess you'd say. Last week, he stopped me in his store near those huge meathooks. As he loomed over me, I wondered, "Is he going to pick me up and impale me?"' Coffin laughed. 'What he said was, "Reverend, I'm beginning to see your point."'

"The chaplain and I talked all day and into the night. Whenever we were outside, on the campus, he was frequently stopped by students—some with a problem, one to ask if he'd officiate at his wedding, others just because they dig speaking with him. Late in the afternoon, the interview was interrupted as Coffin met with several students planning a ceremony on campus at which more draft cards would be turned in, but not burned. Coffin was asked to speak and, predictably, agreed. Later, we continued talking at his small, comfortable, unpretentious house nearby, where I met his three young children—two boys and a girl—and his wife, Eva, daughter of pianist Artur Rubinstein.

"After that day and night at Yale, I talked to Coffin again following Lyndon Johnson's announcement that he would not run again and that he would begin negotiations with North Vietnam. Coffin was preparing a speech for an antiwar demonstration at the time. It was in part an answer to the call from the President for Americans to now close ranks. Coffin read me his reply: 'The war is still going on. The plea to close ranks is a plea to close our eyes and hearts to the continuing suffering of the Vietnamese, let alone our own boys. It is a plea for spiritual death to which we can only respond, "Do not go gentle into that good night / Rage, rage, against the dying of the light."' I began the interview by asking him to assess the significance of Johnson's new political posture in pragmatic rather than poetic terms."

Playboy: Hasn't the cutting edge of the peace movement been dulled by the negotiations with North Vietnam and by the President's refusal to seek another term of office?

Coffin: Far from it. Though we're now in a most hopeful period, it's also a most dangerous period. It would be a catastrophe if we didn't remain alert to the possibility of what can happen if negotiations break down. It's quite possible that President Johnson, robed in his new moral garb of self-abnegation, could turn to the country before the end of the year and say, "You can see I've done my best, but the enemy is clearly not serious about negotiations; so we have no choice but to resume the fighting." Were he to do this, many unthinking citizens might believe he had exhausted his diplomatic resources when, in fact, he had hardly begun to tap them. What worries me is the fact that most Americans see our willingness to negotiate as the moral issue in this war; once Johnson agreed to negotiate, his moral standing rose again. But the basic moral issue is why we are in Vietnam in the first place. Since I believe that many Americans haven't begun to understand that, I remain very apprehensive that the killing will not stop and may well increase.

Playboy: Dr. Spock has predicted that peace, if it comes, may be as far away as two years. But you've said that we can't afford to wait that long. Why not?

Coffin: Because the psychological and moral timetables demand that peace come sooner. I don't think people at home and around the world can sit around just waiting for two years; if talks drag on that long, the situation is bound to deteriorate. And if it does, that could mean a much more intense escalation of the war.

Playboy: What course do you think the negotiations should take to prevent that from happening?

Coffin: I've always tried to make a distinction between intent and implementation. Were the American government to show a genuine intent to extricate itself, I would be inclined to leave it considerable latitude in the realm of implementation of that intent. A convincing disclosure of that intent will be crucial in negotiations. We desperately need reconciliation with the North Vietnamese and with the National Liberation Front. Hanoi in the past has said that once America really decided to move out, the path would be strewn with roses. I would hope that if Johnson does show a clear intent to get out, the National Liberation Front will make a similar statement.

Playboy: What do you think should be the terms of an equitable settlement?

Coffin: Clearly, the Saigon government will have to change, and that means at least a coalition government with the National Liberation Front. In the past, it might have been possible to have had a non-Communist coalition in the south, with the Buddhists and other forces represented. But it's too late for that now. We could have negotiated with the British in 1777—if they had offered to negotiate; probably something like six and a half colonies for them and six and a half colonies for us. But by 1780, it was too late. It is now 1780 in Vietnam.

Playboy: What if the present Saigon government refuses to accept a coalition government with the National Liberation Front?

Coffin: Then they'll have to go it alone. And that means *really* alone.

Playboy: There's also the possibility that our own Administration will persist in its refusal to consider the possibility of a coalition government. What if it remains adamant on that point?

Coffin: In that case, negotiations will probably break down and the war escalate again. And if that happens, our resistance to the war will also have to increase.

Playboy: Even if both sides consent to a coalition government, do you agree with those who feel that the U. S. has a responsibility to prevent mass executions of those whom we've supported?

Coffin: Yes, I do. The likelihood of bloodshed is real after twenty-two years of bitter conflict. So I would like the strongest possible international presence there after the settlement. But perhaps not the U.N. A beefed-up International Control Commission, for example, would probably be more acceptable to North Vietnam than a United Nations peace keeping force, since North Vietnam is not a member of the U.N. If we had this kind of international umbrella for a time, the United States could withdraw its troops while the international presence acted as a force against mass bloodshed. The big cats—the Kys, the Thieus—will get out; they always do. It's the little kittens who get left behind that are vulnerable. But if an international presence remains during the transition period, the little ones can be protected. And as this is going on, the North Vietnamese can be removing their own troops.

Playboy: Even if they do—and even if bloodshed is avoided—what if the NLF proves to be so powerful that South Vietnam eventually goes Communist?

Coffin: That's a possibility we have to face. But that doesn't mean a unified Communist Vietnam would then automatically come under Chinese control. There's every indication that Ho Chi Minh wouldn't want the Chinese Communists in Vietnam any more than he wants *us* there. Every time there's a Communist conference in Moscow that Peking boycotts, the North Vietnamese delegation turns up, closely followed by the North Korean delegation. This clearly indicates that China is not able to control even Communist countries in Asia. We have to remember that communism keeps changing. There is a vast difference now among Polish pink and Russian red and Chinese crimson. And look at what's been going on in Czechoslovakia this year. What an irony that when a Czech Stalinist general defected, he defected to America. How are the Czechs possibly going to get the lid back on those students again? In Yugoslavia, after Tito, we may even have a two-party Communist system.

We have to bide our time. We have to realize that enemy number one is nuclear warfare, not the Communists. And enemy number two is poverty. The real struggle in this world is not East-West or Communist-capitalist; it's the rich against the poor. That's why our priorities ought to be not in "containing" communism nor in increasing our nuclear arsenal but in helping the underdeveloped countries. *That*'s our self-defense. It's absolutely ridiculous to say that we need South Vietnam to be under some kind of American control as a means of ensuring America's national security. Nor, in all likelihood, would a unified Vietnam under Ho Chi Minh be any more of a danger to us than Yugoslavia now is. As a matter of fact, a unified Vietnam could become an *Asian* Yugoslavia.

Playboy: In view of America's total military commitment to preventing Ho Chi Minh from winning the war, hawks argue that a Communist Vietnam—Yugoslavian in orientation or not—would be an immeasurable blow to U. S. prestige. Do you see any validity in that view?

Coffin: That kind of thinking leads to the perfectly immoral position that life is expendable but prestige is not. In any case, what *creates* prestige? Does it stem from the naked use of power or from the legitimate exercise of authority and responsibility? Despite the fact that the French had to pull out of Algeria and out of Indochina before that, I think it's clear that they haven't lost face. In fact, they've regained a great deal of influence, as well as prestige, in both those areas. The sincerity of America's international commitments is *already* questioned—but not because we've failed to save corrupt anti-Communist regimes from Red aggression. Our sincerity is questioned abroad because we have reneged on our commitments of economic aid to eradicate poverty, illiteracy and disease throughout the world. Our sincerity is questioned because we're not really dealing with racism and poverty at home. It is in *these* areas of commitment that we have to prove ourselves.

Playboy: Do you think it's fair to accuse this country of reneging its responsibilities to help eradicate world poverty, illiteracy and disease when it's already spending more than three billion dollars a year on foreign economic aid?

Coffin: Completely fair. I know that sounds like a lot of money, but when you divide it up among the billions of people who desperately need it, that comes to about a dollar apiece—and most of them never get it, anyway. Much of the public economic aid—and most of the private investments—we've extended abroad have deterred rather than advanced the cause of social reform in the underprivileged nations. By that I mean, we have not been nearly careful enough to see that our aid is actually used for education and health, for example, rather than to prop up those in economic and political power. It's well documented that much of our aid is siphoned off at the top before what is left—if any—trickles down to the masses of people.

Playboy: What do you suggest to remedy the situation?

Coffin: For one thing, if a government is corrupt and tied in with monopolistic economic interests, we should refuse it military aid. That would give such a government a real incentive to bring about reform, since it would not be able to suppress dissent by force of arms.

Playboy: Couldn't that country easily acquire arms from some source other than the U. S.?

Coffin: The only country besides ours that can supply large quantities of arms is Russia, and if Russia were to support such a reactionary and oppressive government in this way—which I consider unlikely—it would clearly be an ideological victory for us.

Playboy: But suppose that government were to fall as a result of our nonsupport.

Coffin: In that case, there might well be a new government that really had the loyalty of most of its people—one that might be more deserving of economic aid, because its very existence would be predicated on an acknowledgment of the need for internal economic and social reform.

Playboy: Many critics of American foreign policy feel that the U. S. should give no military aid to *any* government, regardless of how democratic it may be. You seem to disagree.

Coffin: It depends on the individual case—but rather than give military aid unilaterally to any single government, I think we should concentrate on creating international peacekeeping forces under the direction and control of the United Nations. It can well be said that America passed from isolationism to interventionism without passing through internationalism—without realizing that in the world as it is today, a multinational body *must* be the one to decide if intervention is necessary to keep the peace. But it's not too late to do that even now. By making military arms and power international, we could avoid, for instance, the type of arms race that's going on now in the Middle East. We could avoid the situation we had when we armed India and Pakistan to forestall Chinese invasion and Russian influence and then, when those two countries started fighting each other, it was the Russians who came in and settled the argument.

America spends more than two billion dollars a year on that kind of military aid and almost thirty billion dollars more on its own war in Vietnam—both ostensibly to defend the underdeveloped nations from communism. Yet we give only the tiniest fraction of that amount—approximately three tenths of 1 percent of our gross national product—to economic development abroad. That makes us one of the stingiest nations per capita on the face of the earth. This is a real indictment of Americans—its ruthless distortion of national priorities.

Playboy: How can we reorder those priorities?

Coffin: That gets to the question of the personal priorities of individual Americans, which too frequently are power, prestige and pleasure. I very much object to the way institutions take over individuals to such an extent that they not only won't extend or commit themselves, they won't even speak out. When I was in Detroit last year, I asked the reporters after a press conference—and reporters are always a great source of information for me—"Who in the automotive industry is against the war?" They said, "Reverend, you must be joking. You don't think these bastards ever open their mouths on a controversial issue, do you?" That's what really gets me. I know many businessmen who secretly have opposed the war; yet they have allowed their rights of citizenship to be bought out by government contracts or by fear of pressure of one type or another. To make a very bitter remark, most American businessmen are such practicing cowards when it comes to controversial issues that they make common integrity look like courage. It's a dreadful commentary on the country when the peace movement is symbolized by baby doctors and chaplains. The business of America is business, we've been told. All right, then, let businessmen assume their responsibilities in controversial areas as well. I think it's awful the way people go up the success ladder only to become blander and blander. The result is that we have, if not the blind leading the blind, the bland leading the bland in this country. Again and again, businessmen have asked in amazement, "Why are all these students out in the street?" My answer to them is very simple: "Because *you've* crawled into the woodwork. If you came out and did your duty as American citizens, there might not have to be so many students on the street." It's because of this dereliction of duty that students have become so cynical about the business community.

Playboy: You're not saying that businessmen are the only ones to blame.

Coffin: No, *most* Americans don't involve themselves in what needs to be done. Moreover, we are more paralyzed in thought than we know. This point was brought home to me very vividly a couple of years ago, when two Soviet citizens came to visit in New Haven. They started off by asking, "How do you Americans do it?" Knowing they had just returned from the Midwest, I naturally assumed they were talking about our great agricultural achievements, but they soon made it clear they had something very different in mind. "We have watched CBS, NBC, ABC. What's the difference? We have listened to endless radio broadcasts, and their monotony is absolutely breath-taking. With the exception of such newspapers as *The New York Times*, the *St. Louis Post-Dispatch* and the Louisville *Courier-Journal*, your country's editorial policies, not only in the Hearst papers but in other papers, are remarkably alike. So how do you do it? How do you achieve such a high degree of thought control without resorting to terror?" I thought to myself, "This is some irony. Communists might soon be coming to our shores, in droves, in order to study more sophisticated methods of thought control."

Playboy: There certainly hasn't been anything sophisticated about the methods used to suppress dissent in this country—particularly against the Vietnam war. The techniques have ranged from economic reprisal and physical brutality to the kind of extraordinary legal pressure epitomized by your indictment, along with Dr. Spock and three others, for counseling violation of the draft laws. How do you account for what's been called the "war on dissent"?

Coffin: As our indictment testifies, there have certainly been conscious attempts by the Federal government and other authorities to stifle dissent, though I must admit that, in our case, we were crowding the government a little by *asking* for a confrontation. But I don't know if I'd term it a "war" on dissent; I don't think the people in power are consciously out to do away with democratic process. It's rather that their concern for "law and order" has blinded them to the higher priority of our constitutional right to free speech. They see in our dissent, rather than in their suppression of it, a clear and present danger to national security. This overreactive reflex is all part of our willingness to seek solutions by force; abroad, we do it militarily; at home, with police, rather than dealing with the real social and economic causes of unrest.

Playboy: To what extent do you think the government has been successful in its campaign to suppress opposition to the war?

Coffin: So far, the campaign has been counterproductive. It's increased dissent, just as the bombing of North Vietnam strengthened rather than weakened the resolve of the North Vietnamese, and in my case, the government's indictment has given dissent a kind of respectability it didn't have before. People didn't always believe us when we said we were willing to accept the legal consequences of what we were doing, but now they see that we're following the traditional legal route. And the fact that we've been indicted also elicits some sympathy for people who face a prison sentence for what seems more and more clearly a question of conscience.

Playboy: You said on the steps of the Department of Justice Building on October 20, 1967,

> The law of the land is clear. Section 12 of the National Selective Service Act declares that anyone "who knowingly counsels, aids or abets another to refuse or evade registration or service in the Armed Forces . . . shall be liable to imprisonment for not more than five years or a fine of $10,000, or both." We hereby publicly counsel these young men to continue in their refusal to serve in the Armed Forces as long as the war in Vietnam continues, and we pledge ourselves to aid and abet them in all the ways we can. This means that if they are now arrested for failing to comply with a law that violates their consciences, we, too, must be arrested, for, in the sight of that law, we are now as guilty as they.

The government finally took you and four others at your word. If you're willing to go to jail for this issue of conscience, as you say, why not simply accept the penalty?

Coffin: That statement did not mean I abdicated my right to test the constitutionality of that law. We believe that on a number of grounds, including our free-speech rights under the First Amendment, the government's case against us doesn't hold up constitutionally. Certainly, we were prepared to be arrested. We were also prepared to test the law. If a law is unjust, one of the ways of demonstrating its injustice is to have as many arrests as possible.

Playboy: If you lose the case, will you appeal the decision to a higher court?

Coffin: Yes. It is hard to argue constitutional issues at the lower end of the judiciary; I expect we'll have to go all the way to the Supreme Court.

Playboy: And if you lose there?

Coffin: If we lose and are punished, that will point again to the perennial paradox of legality and morality. Of course, men must be concerned with what's legal, but we must be more concerned with what's right—right in terms of one's own informed conscience—and we have to keep in mind the occasional difference between the two. I hope we'll see the day when this country attains such a high level of democracy that any action to which a man adheres for reasons of conscience, and that harms no one, will be constitutionally immune from the power of the majority.

Playboy: Those who disagree with you argue that if everyone is allowed to determine for himself which war he'll fight in and which war he'll resist, it could lead ultimately to anarchy—and to the undermining of this country's capacity for legitimate self-defense.

Coffin: This is the argument I hear all the time. I'll answer the second part first. I think the history of public support for even the most dubious of wars makes it highly unlikely that people would refuse to fight when the national defense was clearly at stake. As far as the argument about anarchy is concerned, I think it's important to remember three things about draft resistance. One: It's an expression of patriotism rather than of disloyalty. At least that's what motivates me, and I think that's what motivates most draft resisters. These are people who know the anguish reflected in Albert Camus's words: "I should like to be able to love my country and still love justice." Two: Draft resistance does not infringe on the civil liberties of any other person. Therefore, those who say that I'm taking the law in my own hands, like the Ku Klux Klan, or that I'm doing the same as advocating rioting really don't see the point. Third: If you're prepared to accept the legal consequences of draft resistance, you are, in fact, supporting and not subverting the legal order. So if these three points are kept clearly in mind, then one can understand the spirit—even when one doesn't agree with the convictions—of those who resist the draft. After all, they are in the tradition of Socrates, of Jesus, of the Quakers in the Massachusetts Bay Colony and of John Woolman, who broke with Benjamin Franklin and refused to pay taxes in 1750 when Pennsylvania decided to arm against the Indians. They're also in the tradition of Thoreau, Eugene Debs and A. J. Muste.

Playboy: But how do you justify determining, as an individual, the rightness or wrongness of a particular war? What of your obligations as a citizen?

Coffin: The answer to that is that it's in the best American tradition not to surrender one's conscience to the state.

Playboy: Even when that means breaking the law?

Coffin: As I've said before, I don't think any man ever has the right to break the law, but I do think that upon occasion, every man has the *duty* to break the law. When the law begins to dominate rather than to serve men, far from staving off chaos, it begins to *invite* chaos. Fundamentally, it's only a *good* law, not any law, that stands between man and chaos. The 1964 Civil Rights Act, yes; the 1850 Fugitive Slave Act, no. When a man decides to break the law, he has to ask himself how great the specific evil is that he's protesting. Have all other remedies been exhausted? Is the evil so monstrous that there is no time to exhaust what remedies remain? What will be the consequences of his action on others—today and twenty years from now? Has he really done his homework about the issue at hand? And has he purged himself of all self-righteousness? None of those questions can ever be answered fully, but if the overwhelming weight is in favor of the need to break the law, we have to act wholeheartedly without absolute certainty. The war in Vietnam has been such an occasion. To stand against the law is a difficult and even fearful thing, but in the face of what is insane and inhuman, we cannot be either silent or servile. As the French nationalist and poet Charles Péguy wrote, "The worst of particularities is to withhold oneself; the worst ignorance is not to act; the worst lie is to steal away."

Playboy: Your opponents also argue that this kind of justification for civil disobedience is predicated on an assumption of your own moral superiority over those who do not agree with you—and on a conviction that the morally elite have the right to break or resist any laws they don't like, because they are "morally superior" beings.

Coffin: To take a moral stand doesn't imply that everybody else is immoral. Just as when you join SANE [the Committee for a Sane Nuclear Policy], you're not proclaiming that everybody outside that organization is *in*sane. You're saying that what this country does with nuclear arms has become an issue of conscience and that joining SANE is the way you personally have to act on it. But I do think that history is full of people who had consciences that were badly informed. Conscience is a good servant but it can be a bad master. One needs more than simply conscience; one needs to have a great deal of information and a capacity for rational judgment to take this kind of moral stand. So, rather than adopting a stance of moral superiority, the issue is one of informed conscience.

Playboy: Yet many critics of the war have called the Johnson Administration "immoral." Doesn't that tend to indicate an attitude of moral superiority?

Coffin: Yes, it does. Too many young people fail to understand that all it takes for evil to flourish these days is for a good man with a great deal of power to be a little wrong while the majority of his citizens remain indifferent to the way in which he's exercising his power. If there is something immoral about our leaders, it has less to do with their character than with their social function. It's too easy to fight national righteousness by falling into personal self-righteousness; one has to make a great effort not to get into an accusatory moral stance. The way I would assess our government is that it has been caught for a long time in a kind of paralysis of imagination, a paralysis of sensitivity. There's a certain element of pride in our foreign policy; we seem to think we have a lot to teach and very little to learn. Our pride-swollen faces have closed our eyes to a great many things that were going on in Vietnam that we preferred simply not to see—the wanton atrocities, the corruption of the government, the suffering of the people.

Playboy: That suffering, along with the war itself, according to several spokesmen for the Administration, has been prolonged by the kind of dissent represented and encouraged by you and Dr. Spock; they say it gives aid and comfort to the enemy. What's your reaction to that charge?

Coffin: My reaction is that it's nonsense. It's American policy that has prolonged the war. I think the rising chorus of dissent in this country has actually helped *shorten* the war—by motivating the Administration to negotiate. But even if dissent *were* prolonging the war, is this a democracy or is it not? Are we expected to fold our democratic tents and steal away? If that were the case, the members of the Senate Foreign Relations Committee—the vast majority of whom have been against the war for some time—would be expected to stop dissenting, too. If you take that line of argument seriously, we're expected to pay the price of giving up democracy so that the country can be "unified" against the North Vietnamese and the National Liberation Front. That's far too high a price to pay. Actually, those who have brought a great deal of aid and comfort to the enemy have been such people as General Westmoreland, with his policy of escalation that has turned world opinion completely against the United States. So have Ky and Thieu, by their incapacity to rally their own people. The fantastic corruption of the Saigon government has brought an *enormous* amount of aid and comfort to the enemy.

Playboy: How do you feel about the aid and comfort supplied by those who carry Viet Cong flags in peace demonstrations?

Coffin: Well, theirs is a perfectly legitimate position, and it's the position held, let's face it, by the vast majority of Europeans. According to every international poll I've heard about, 80 percent of all Europeans think we're dead wrong and that withdrawing is the only decent thing for Americans to do. So the extreme position here is their *moderate* position. I think it's perfectly dreadful that in Europe, they've been talking about "good Americans"—who allow crimes to be committed in their name—the way they used to talk about "good Germans." But many Europeans have told me that the protest movement in this country is the only thing keeping alive the hope in their minds and hearts that the American dream has not turned totally into a nightmare.

Playboy: Aren't you concerned about public opinion in this country?

Coffin: It obviously doesn't help our cause to carry Viet Cong flags, any more than it helps to burn draft cards or American flags. If you're trying to sway a complacent public, that's hardly the effective way to do it. I keep thinking of the kind of low-voltage discontent about the war that prevailed in 1964; then four or five people burned their draft cards and immediately, millions of outraged Americans found there was a good reason to wage the war. And as for burning the American flag, I agree with Norman Thomas: "Don't burn it; wash it."

Playboy: Would you try to exclude draft-card burners and flag burners from demonstrations with which you're associated?

Coffin: I'd have to handle that sort of thing one demonstration at a time. More basically, I would be for seminars about demonstrations on every single college campus—and as many other places as we could have them. I mean seminars that would be exceedingly demanding intellectually; everybody would be asked to face exactly what it is he wants to accomplish, what message he's communicating, whom he wants to reach. Then you act according to your aims. For example, if you want to convince the middle class of the horrors of war, maybe you should demonstrate against Dow Chemical, the manufacturers of napalm. But in demonstrating, you don't obstruct the movements of Dow Chemical representatives, because that will turn off many in the middle class. And if you're trying to reach the middle class, you try to put the bearded ones among you somewhere in the background. If you feel, on the other hand, that a concern with public relations is precisely what has corroded the quality of life in this country, then you put your beards up front. But you must know what it is you want to accomplish.

My great cry, my constant misgiving about the peace movement is that we're not hard-nosed enough about just what it is we want to do, and so we often end up doing things that are counterproductive—or so it seems. It's hard to know what *is* counterproductive in the long run. Thoreau was gloriously ineffective in his time, but by his example, he injected something into the mainstream of American and world history that is nourishing people more than a hundred years later. So I think it's a very small measure of devotion we owe to a generation yet unborn to be willing to go to jail, if necessary, to witness to a truth as we see it. It's going to be very good for our grandchildren to know that there were some people who protested rather vigorously during a period in American life that history will judge very harshly.

Playboy: Another form of protest that you've championed is conscientious objection on nonreligious as well as religious grounds. Why?

Coffin: I think it's a gross misfortune not to believe in God, but it's not automatically an ethical fault. As a minister, I'm deeply concerned that the rights of conscience of a secular humanist are not properly recognized under current law.

Playboy: By what criteria could one determine that such an objector was conscientiously opposed to war rather than simply afraid of being killed?

Coffin: You may have some people whose motives are more involved with personal survival than with principle—but it does take a certain amount of courage to stand against a war. Even if you're a physical coward, you have to be quite independent to take that step, and I don't think there are many people who have the independence to be a member of such a conspicuous and unpopular minority; so I don't think many people apply to be C. O.s just because they're cowards. I think the criteria would have to be very broad, once you got away from religious belief and training as the primary requisites for conscientious objection. I'm quite prepared to say that a man is a conscientious objector if, for example, he says, "Look, I'm a conscientious economist. I've done four years of graduate study in economics at Yale and I think, from the point of view of a conscientious economist, that this war is an outrage." You have to be willing to go quite far, once you allow selective conscientious objection on nonreligious as well as religious grounds.

Playboy: How do you feel about the kind of conscientious objector who refuses to even apply for C. O. status, who believes the very act of registering for the draft—even on a noncombatant basis—represents complicity with evil?

Coffin: If that's the way this young man truly feels about it, then, obviously, that's what he's going to have to do. But I think it's important to point out to him that it will be harder for him to make his case of conscience in court, because the government will simply point out that he had a number of administrative procedures available to him and did not avail himself of any of them. Therefore, he's going to be charged with failure to fulfill those administrative procedures. His case won't be decided on what he regards to be the overwhelming principle of noncooperation with the government.

Playboy: If such a man were to ask you for public support, would you give it?

Coffin: If I thought he were being truly conscientious in taking this position, I'd support him, on the grounds that he had the right to express his conscientiousness in this way. But I might also make clear that I didn't think this was a very good stand to take. It's not one I'd particularly approve of.

Playboy: Would you serve in a noncombatant capacity, if drafted —say, as a chaplain?

Coffin: With respect to this war, I would refuse service of any kind.

Playboy: Wouldn't you feel any responsibility to minister spiritually to those who need you, even if they're in uniform?

Coffin: It would be a difficult decision for any chaplain to make, but I would choose to minister spiritually to those resisting military service in this war and to those already in jail because of their resistance.

Playboy: Do you oppose the draft only because you oppose the war, or do you agree with those who feel that America should do away entirely with conscriptive military service?

Coffin: I'm really hung up on that one. I tend to be suspicious of a standing professional Army, so that would seem to argue for a draft of civilians. On the other hand, I'm not sure if it makes that much difference, given the pervasive reality of what Eisenhower called the military-industrial complex. I mean, our protection against military control is supposedly that at the very top, the civilians still control the military. But does it really matter that the Secretary of Defense is a civilian, when so many generals retire to become presidents of corporations that then, in turn, accept contracts from the Pentagon? Even with a draft, to what extent is the civilian mentality really in control? A corollary, and perhaps more fundamental, question is, How large should the Army be? Here, again, not being a pacifist, I have no instant answers. We do need an Army for defense, but if it's a large Army, the temptation is to use it, and so I'm not sure to what degree America gets involved in wars partly because it has such a large Army already.

Playboy: Since you do believe there has to be an Army of some size, and since the draft is likely to be operative for the foreseeable future, how do you think it can be made more equitable, so that the poor—particularly those who are poor and black—are not disproportionately represented in the Army and in the front lines?

Coffin: One way would be to make sure that more blacks sit on draft boards. If it's not a constitutional problem, it ought to be, when thousands of Negroes can be drafted in Mississippi without one black sitting on a draft board in that state. Another way to distribute the burdens of war more equitably between rich and poor, educated and noneducated, would be to turn the draft into a lottery system. We could either have everybody serve for a period of time when he gets to the age of eighteen or nineteen or there could be educational deferments set up in such a way that they're not extended so long that they actually become exemptions.

Playboy: Seventy priests in Boston earlier this year proposed deferments for young Negroes working to develop the city's black community. Would you consider that a legitimate reason for deferment?

Coffin: Yes, I think that should be an occupational deferment, because it's in an area where the national interest is at stake. It could also be a valid form of alternative service for those blacks who conscientiously object to a specific war or to all wars. Similarly, a splendid form of alternative service might consist of a member of Students for a Democratic Society organizing a community of poor whites in Chicago or Appalachia.

Playboy: Who do you think should decide which deferments are legitimate?

Coffin: The decision making should be democratized to such a degree that all elements of each community are involved. If broad, flexible guidelines were set by the Federal government, it wouldn't be difficult for democratic local boards to decide on legitimate educational and occupational deferments.

Playboy: The New York Civil Liberties Union has taken the position that the implementation of the current draft system is unconstitutional. It claims that any draft is a serious deprivation of civil liberties and can be justified only if a national state of emergency is proved. The President, the NYCLU adds, has failed to demonstrate that such a state of emergency exists. Do you agree?

Coffin: Well, that's one of the constitutional issues I hope we can argue during the course of our trial—if not in the lower court, then in the higher courts, if we lose below. It seems obvious to me that when the business of declaring war is the business of the legislative and not the executive branch of government, and when we don't even have a declared state of emergency, not only does the war become constitutionally questionable but so does the implementation of the draft.

Playboy: You've said that the war is not only unconstitutional but in violation of the laws of war. In what way?

Coffin: In many ways, I'm afraid. We have destroyed crops and villages, we have forcibly relocated thousands of people and we have been guilty of indiscriminate killing of civilians. The inordinately high ratio of civilian casualties to military casualties makes clear that we have not made the distinction between combatants and noncombatants that is fundamental to the laws of war, as well as of humanity. The result is that almost the entire surface of Vietnam is soaked with the tears and the blood of the innocent. If you want more than four hundred pages of very specific testimony of American violations of the laws of war in Vietnam, you'll find it in a book called *In the Name of America*, commissioned and published by Clergy and Laymen Concerned About Vietnam. It's full of eyewitness accounts published in American newspapers and on American wire services, as well as accounts from various periodicals, here and abroad, ranging from *Air Force/Space Digest* to *Le Monde* in Paris. The type of thing in it is indicated by excerpts from a letter written by a GI and published in the *Akron Beacon Journal* last spring:

> Dear Mom and Dad:
>
> Today we went on a mission and I'm not very proud of myself, my friends or my country. . . . When the ten helicopters landed this morning, in the midst of these huts, and six men jumped out of each "chopper," we were firing the moment we hit the ground. We fired into all the huts we could. Then we got "on line" and swept the area. It was then that we burned these huts in distinct violation of the solemn laws of war that we have signed.
>
> The families don't understand this . . . so everyone is crying, begging and praying . . . then they watch in terror as we burn their personal possessions and food. Yes, we burn all rice and shoot all livestock.
>
> Some of the guys are still careless. Today, a buddy of mine called, "*La dieh*" ("Come here"), into a hut, and a lone man came out of a bomb shelter. My buddy told the old man to get away from the hut and since we have to move quickly on a sweep, just threw a hand grenade into the shelter. After he threw it and was running for cover during the four-second delay, we all heard a baby crying from inside the shelter. After the explosion we found the mother, two children (ages about six and twelve, boy and girl) and an almost newborn baby. The children's fragile bodies were torn apart, literally mutilated. We looked at each other and burned the hut. The old man was just whimpering in disbelief outside the burning hut. We walked away, left him there. My last look was of an old, old man in ragged, torn, dirty clothes, on his knees outside the burning hut, praying to Buddha. His white hair was blowing in the wind and tears were rolling down.

If that were an isolated instance, my telling it to you would be mere sensationalism. But I'm convinced—and *In the Name of*

America supports the conviction—that this isn't an exceptional instance.

I would also add the frequent instances of brutal interrogation and torture of prisoners by the South Vietnamese army. We may not do it ourselves, but if we stand by and let our allies do it, we're just as guilty as they are, according to our own laws of war. Let me give you some examples. The Saigon government has used Chinese mercenaries from Formosa—Nuongs—who control their prisoners by taking wire and running it through a man's hand and then his cheek and into his mouth. They pull the wire out through the other cheek and the other hand, finally knotting both ends around sticks. The South Korean troops we use have rounded up unarmed villagers and shot in cold blood, without further investigation, anyone who informers said had anything to do with the Viet Cong; that's one of our forms of "pacification." We have also trained what are called Provincial Reconnaissance Units—South Vietnamese troops who engage in assassination and butchering. Describing them, a *Washington Post* reporter wrote last year, "A Viet Cong unit on occasion will find the disemboweled remains of its fellows along a well-trod canal-bank path, an effective message to guerrillas and to non-committed Vietnamese that two can play the same bloody game." Again, these are not isolated instances. They form a bloody pattern of war crimes.

Playboy: You've mentioned atrocities committed only by Asiatics against other Asiatics. What about the reports that some American soldiers have kept Viet Cong heads and ears as trophies?

Coffin: If true, this is a further indication of the dehumanization of our own men that the war in Vietnam has caused. I am aware that those who point to the crimes we have committed are always asked about Viet Cong atrocities—but you don't use somebody else's dirt as soap to wash clean your own hands. We can't be responsible for what they do, but we *can* be responsible for what *we* do. Furthermore, wc have to recognize that the more selective terroristic tactics of the Viet Cong have paid off politically far more than the indiscriminate terror that is rained from the sky by our mortars, artillery and, particularly, by our airplanes. When the Viet Cong resorted to terrorism in the late Fifties, they eliminated the appointees of the Saigon government who—by the later admission of the Saigon government itself—were corrupt. That kind of terrorism, as Bernard Fall pointed out in his books, put a kind of Robin Hood halo over the heads of many of the Viet Cong. That's something our government has never really understood: the degree to which the people of Vietnam, South as well as North, actually sympathize with the Viet Cong, the fact that the struggle of the NLF is actually a civil war against the forces of reaction and corruption and colonialism, rather than a strategic beachhead of the "international Communist conspiracy in its master plan for world conquest."

Playboy: As Norman Mailer might have phrased it—why are we in Vietnam?

Coffin: From the very beginning, America's involvement has been based on our misinterpretation of what was happening in Vietnam and on the rigidity of our anticommunism. The French originally got us involved in Vietnam by translating the anticolonial thrust of their opposition into a danger to the "free world" from monolithic, messianic communism. We fell for that to the tune of more than two billion dollars, all of which went straight down the drain. We failed to see that nationalism was a more important element than communism in the Vietnamese struggle against the French. We failed to see that South Vietnam, under Diem, was going to hell in a basket. And we failed to see, as I indicated earlier, that a united Vietnam would have been much better able to withstand pressures from China than a divided Vietnam. So I think—and all of the State Department representatives with whom I've debated agree to this—we should have allowed the 1954 Geneva accords to take their course: We should have allowed elections by July 1956 and let Ho Chi Minh have his Vietnam. But we were so terrified of communism that we were ideologically paralyzed.

Playboy: Do you hold Eisenhower and Dulles responsible for this paralysis?

Coffin: Dulles was certainly the architect of America's anti-Communist crusade, but Eisenhower's intervention was actually very modest. It consisted of economic aid and was based on a certain expectation that the Saigon government would do its own part, would bring about necessary reform to merit further economic aid. Kennedy began to escalate aid, military as well as economic, but he maintained some sanity when he said, "Finally, it's their war—Vietnamese against Vietnamese." No, it's Johnson who has to bear the responsibility for having brought American military involvement so hugely into the forefront.

Playboy: We gather you don't agree, then, with those among the radical young who maintain that from Eisenhower to Kennedy to Johnson, American involvement in Vietnam has been a progressive extension of American institutional interests—that the blame must be placed on a pervasive policy of unenlightened self-interest, rather than on the warmongering of a single President.

Coffin: In the largest sense, of course, they're quite right. We should be addressing ourselves to a re-evaluation of the institutional commitments of this country, rather than to the acts of this President or that President. If those commitments and priorities are not changed, we are going to continue to be in trouble. You cannot have a more-than-fifty-billion-dollar military enterprise and think that somehow you're going to avoid other policy wars after Vietnam. By policy wars, I mean wars that are not really in self-defense but are part of a global policy that equates American self-interest with American control of certain areas of the world. You cannot nurture a paranoid hatred of a monolithic Communist enemy and think that somehow you're going to avoid a nuclear holocaust forever. We have to examine our attitudinal as well as our financial commitments to see the degree to which we have lost our freedom to maneuver, the degree to which we have become ideologically simplistic and doctrinaire. That, I believe, is one of the great responsibilities of the universities today—the undertaking of a fundamental re-examination of American institutions and attitudes.

Playboy: What you're asking for will depend on the initiative of the intellectual community; yet this war has involved more intellectuals in its support than any in American history—those in the Rand Corporation; those connected with the Institute for Defense Analysis, a consortium of twelve universities; those who started with the Kennedy Administration and are now advising Johnson. In the light of the hawkish role they've been playing, do you think it's likely that they will now undertake "a fundamental re-examination of American institutions and attitudes"?

Coffin: Well, there are two types of intellectuals. One is the kind who fulfills the Socratic ideal of a gadfly. He is generally out of power and he insists on asking the basic questions "To what end? To what purpose?" These are the intellectuals who have been leading the opposition to the war and they are the ones I expect will go on to the kind of re-examination I mean. The second species of intellectual is sort of modeled after Machiavelli—the mandarin at the service of a prince. That kind of intellectual represents learning at the service of power. It is this kind of intellectual who has been supporting the war and advising the government on its more effective "implementation."

Playboy: A moment ago, you said that the Vietnam conflict might be the forerunner of a succession of American "policy wars." But Gabriel Kolko, professor of history at the University of Pennsylvania, claims that from the beginning, Vietnam has been not a battleground in America's holy war against "world communism" but a testing ground for America's ability to suppress wars of revolutionary nationalism. Do you agree?

Coffin: I'm afraid there's a great deal of truth in that. In an *Atlantic Monthly* article last year, then–Defense Secretary McNamara was quoted as predicting future wars of revolutionary nationalism and as asserting that Vietnam was a useful place to learn how to control them. Unless we examine this basic question —what is our responsibility in the world?—we may well end up trying to suppress one revolution after another. Of course, we don't *say* we consider ourselves a world policeman; Americans are very prone to use high-sounding moral precepts to rationalize their meddling in the affairs of other nations. Dean Rusk says it's "freedom" we're defending the world around. Is it individual freedom, or is it the privileges freedom has brought to us as Americans—the privileges of wealth and power? Are we defending freedom or are we defending our own economic and political interests? Camus once said, "Freedom consists especially not of privileges but of duties." If America really believes in its duty to maintain freedom, we have to ask ourselves why we weren't crying bloody murder over Trujillo, why we weren't crying bloody murder over Batista before Castro, why we aren't agonizing over the oppression of black men in Rhodesia, South Africa, Mozambique, Angola. A Latin American diplomat claims that an American State Department official told him, "In the last analysis, America will always end up on the side of a dictator, no matter how dishonest, who is not a Communist—as opposed to a reformer, no matter how honest, who might someday turn against us."

It worries me to think what might happen when Haiti, or some other country with terrible internal weaknesses, finally falls. What will this country do then? Will it recognize that the average annual income in Haiti is $70 per capita, that only about 5 percent of the people get to school at all? As of now, Duvalier stays in power only because of a twenty-thousand-man bodyguard carefully trained by the United States Marines. When Duvalier does fall, there will be a dozen, maybe two dozen Cubans in the attacking forces. There's no question that Castro Communists will help bring about that revolution. Are we going to send in troops to suppress that revolution because Communists are involved, or are we going to be able to make the very important distinctions between internal weakness and external pressures as the primary cause for the overthrow of a government?

Playboy: There are those, Walt Rostow and Dean Rusk among them, who claim that America has the duty to defend "legitimate" governments from Communist subversion and invasion at the request of those governments and that this is why we've been involved in Vietnam from the start. Do you consider that kind of reasoning hypocritical?

Coffin: First of all, it's clear that if we had not originally come to the rescue of the Diem regime under Eisenhower and then Kennedy, it would have collapsed long before; it did not have the support of the South Vietnamese. It is also clear that if we had not continued to escalate our military force, the National Liberation Front would have done away with succeeding Saigon governments. It's clear that if it hadn't been for our gasoline, Ky would not have been able to put down the insurrections at Hué last year. It's clear again and again that we have propped up anti-Communist governments to which we then make our "commitments." I think it's also clear that despite the heroic labor and tremendous bloodshed of countless Americans, the fact remains that the South Vietnam government continues to be incapable of rallying its people to any real kind of sacrifice and effort. We have to realize we cannot do for the Vietnamese what they will not do for themselves. It's like China; Americans in the Fifties accused Truman of losing China. But we never had China to lose.

Playboy: Looking beyond Vietnam, what do you think the American response should be to an appeal for help from a truly legitimate and democratic anti-Communist or non-Communist government in repelling Communist subversion or invasion?

Coffin: When you say "invasion," that calls for a distinction. I think it's one thing to say to a country, "We will come to your aid if you're invaded"; that's a military commitment of a limited nature. It's something else to say to a country, "We will never allow you to go Communist." That is an ideological commitment of an unlimited nature.

Playboy: What criteria would you use to determine whether America should go to the aid of a country that might go Communist even if it weren't invaded militarily?

Coffin: It's hard to be precise about such criteria. I've always been impressed by the fact that during the American Revolution, about one third of us were revolutionaries, one third were Tories and one third sort of watched what was going on as if it were at Wimbledon. Victory went to the third that had the future, that was able to galvanize the people to some kind of sacrifice, that was able to give them some kind of hope. I think, again and again, in underdeveloped countries, the Communists have had the perspicacity to figure out which third of the people had the future, had nationalism and social justice on their side. It was that third the Communists backed. We, on the other hand, have chosen again and again to back those who are antinationalistic and who are incapable of unfurling the banners of social justice. And we've made those decisions because some in the opposition were Communists or because Communists were supporting them. As a result, we end up backing the counterrevolutionary side. You cannot stave off the future that way.

You ask me about criteria for future American involvement; I would say that we must avoid the kind of taking over of a country that we've done in South Vietnam. In other cases, we might send aid and advice, but we have to understand what forces are actually at work in a given country. And to understand that, as I've said before, we have to get over the ideological paralysis that leads us to be scared to death of communism as some kind of monolithic world force.

Playboy: Despite what you've said, there are those—including spokesmen high in the Administration—who warn that if one government falls to communism, other governments in that area will also fall. Does this so-called domino theory have any validity, in your opinion?

Coffin: I would hope that by now, our own domestic experience should make it plain that governments almost always fall from internal weakness rather than because of external pressure. Ho Chi Minh and Mao Tse-tung know perfectly well that you can't have a revolt without the existence of revolting conditions. There were revolting conditions in South Vietnam in '57, '58 and '59, and that's why the peasants were in revolt.

Playboy: What were those revolting conditions?

Coffin: For one example, the U. S.-supported Diem regime took back some of the land that had been liberated by the Viet Minh, the predecessors of the Viet Cong, and gave it back to the absentee landowners, using the police to collect the rent. The Diem regime also eliminated the one democratic feature of South Vietnamese life—the elected village elder. In the elders' place, they put in appointees from Saigon who were exceedingly corrupt and appeared in the villages more to collect taxes and graft than to provide services. When the peasants finally revolted against all this, the Diem regime—using American guns—put down the rebellions in very brutal fashion. In one province, from October 1958 to February 1959, according to *Tu Do*, the official Saigon newspaper, there were almost forty thousand people in jail.

Playboy: As you probably know, there have been reports that Diem's assassination in 1963—and his replacement by a more moderate and compliant president—was engineered by the CIA in order to forestall a Communist *coup d'état*. Whether or not the CIA was guilty of this particular crime, its involvement in right-wing counterrevolutions and its subversion of domestic organizations such as the National Student Association have been well documented in our pages and elsewhere. Your position of leadership in the antiwar movement and the views you've expressed here seem completely at odds with everything the CIA stands for; yet you worked as a CIA agent from 1950 to 1953. How do you reconcile this?

Coffin: The same love of country that motivated me then motivates me now. Just as it is wrong to judge the present in terms of the past, so is it wrong to judge the past in terms of the present. In the early days of the CIA, when I was there, before it had this tremendous influence and this tremendous organization, it was doing things that seemed to me—though perhaps a bit simplistically—quite justified, particularly in view of the things Stalin was doing at the time. He was conducting purges; he was pouring tremendous amounts of money into the Communist parties of Europe; he was suppressing human freedom in the satellite countries; he was sending many agents to various countries, where they engaged in subversion, sabotage and assassination on a wholesale scale. The CIA was countering that kind of Stalinist activity. Moreover, some of what the CIA was doing then represented a kind of victory for liberals. For example, a lot of people in the CIA were contending that the only way to fight communism in Europe was with the non-Communist left, not with the right, and they won some pretty significant victories. They gave money to non-Communist labor unions; they helped support cultural freedom organizations. Although I wasn't in on this aspect of CIA work, I feel quite sure that this support was given with no strings attached. It was just an effort to aid the non-Communist left.

Playboy: Did it have to be secret help?

Coffin: That's the irony of it. In those days, the CIA tended to be a lot more liberal in many ways than the State Department and was certainly more liberal than the country as a whole. The country would not have been sufficiently liberal to countenance giving money overtly to the non-Communist left in Europe. I will say that, in retrospect, I think it was a very dangerous game the CIA was playing and it was probably a more dangerous game than I realized at the time. Often in life, it turns out that the first step you take still leaves you free, but some steps later, you've become enslaved. And it may be that in taking that first step, which I thought was being taken with considerable freedom—no strings attached and all that—we as a country were already on the way to an institutional commitment that was going to lead to the kind of rigid anticommunism that has produced policy wars.

Playboy: In the highly fanciful event that you were ever asked, could you imagine yourself being part of the CIA again?

Coffin: It's so fanciful it's not worth discussing. But you know, it's a very strange thing; I still have some good buddies in the CIA. I remember about a year ago going to the house of one of them. As he greeted me at the door, he looked at me with real hatred in his eyes. I had been suggesting as a matter of strategy that seminarians turn in their draft exemptions, and I had been justifying civil disobedience as a part of draft resistance. When I saw that hatred, I said, "OK, you're looking at a traitor, aren't you?" "That's just about it," he answered. "You know what *I'm* looking at?" I asked. "A murderer. Now what are we going to do about it?" He didn't answer. "I propose, then, that you produce the largest bottle of bourbon you have, and when we've gotten halfway through it, we'll see if we can work out our differences."

Playboy: Did you?

Coffin: Well, by the time we'd gotten through that bottle, I don't think either of us was able to remember too well how we proposed to work out our differences, but we did come to some kind of agreement to disagree. This kind of experience, trying as it is, has substantiated my conviction that on a personal level, men have more in common than they have in conflict. Once again, you have to realize that it doesn't take an evil man to do evil things in this world. That's a terribly important thing to keep alive in our minds. It's always a great danger to fight evil as if it were something totally outside oneself. And it's always dangerous not to feel some sense of complicity with any evil, even with the evil one is fighting. I've found that what is intensely irritating in other people can also be an intense source of compassion. Why do they feel they have to do this? What has frozen their imagination? Why have they gotten themselves caught in this ideological bind? So, in this sense, you can go on talking to people with whom you have the most profound disagreements, people who, in your view, may even be doing terribly wicked things. Of course, this doesn't make you any more mellow. But as you grow older, there's no reason not to become more compassionate as you retain your militancy.

Playboy: Speaking of that militancy, you said about two years ago, "I have been forced to move from liberal to radical, but I am not quite prepared to think we have to become revolutionary." What made you evolve from a liberal into a radical?

Coffin: First of all, there are a lot of radicals who would be appalled to hear me say I'm a radical. Let me not claim a name to which I'm not entitled. I've come to realize that a liberal is a person who thinks other people need help, and a radical is one who knows we're *all* in trouble. What has changed *me* into that kind of radical is what has happened since 1964. In that year, Staughton Lynd, a professor of history at Yale at the time, said it wouldn't make that much difference who got elected—Goldwater or Johnson. I told him, "That's typical of you radicals;

you're all hung up in your ideology. You can't see a difference that's as plain as the nose on your face." Since then, it's become clear which of us was right and which of us was wrong. I have been proved wrong in this way again and again by people on the left, but I can't remember having been proved as fundamentally wrong by anyone on the right. So, inevitably, I've tended to move a little bit toward the left—to the point where I'm inclined to believe that criticism of American society and its institutions has to cut into this society much more deeply than it has.

Playboy: The number of those who feel as you do has greatly increased, especially among the young, since the escalation of the Vietnam war, but they're still a small minority of the population. Until the Tet offensive, most Americans continued to support the war in a passive way—or at least failed to protest against it—despite mounting evidence of its inhumanity and futility. How do you account for it?

Coffin: T. S. Eliot has a line about it: "Human kind cannot bear very much reality." It's the same in our domestic experience. All Americans would agree intellectually that all men are created equal, but only a handful really *feel* the monstrousness of inequality, and those few are usually those who have either extraordinary capacity for imaginative projection or who have had firsthand experience. That's why I fear what may be ahead in our racial division. Most whites, to say the least, do not *feel* what it is to be black. There was talk again this year about getting summer jobs for the young poor, but I don't see a majority of the citizenry really rallying to put enough pressure on the institutions of this society, certainly including Congress, to build enough low-income housing, to help black communities create and nurture real economic roots, to redistribute power in a more equitable way. On the contrary, we may be entering a phase of history in which the majority coalition in this country is forming, not behind the demands of justice, but behind demands for a law and order that can only be achieved at the *expense* of justice. Instead of grievances' being redressed, those raising grievances may be repressed. And the repression will only increase the despair that produced the disorders in the first place, leading thereby to a vicious, spiraling circle. On the one hand, we will then have the politics of despair, and on the other, very possibly an authoritarian state.

If, for any reason, the Vietnam negotiations fail, and if little, as a consequence, is done about poverty and racism at home, this country could be split wide open by acts of violence on the part of blacks and of a great many students. I don't know what's going to happen at the Democratic Convention, but I think that Eugene McCarthy's campaign and, to some extent, the one waged by the late Senator Kennedy, constitute the last big effort many students could find themselves prepared to make along normal political lines. If the next Administration is pretty much a continuation of this one in terms of policy and action—or if it's worse—many students are going to turn off to private sensations and interior visions, or they'll leave this country in droves, or they'll turn to acts of terrorism.

Playboy: You've said that "hatred and violence shrink your spirit." But many black-power militants claim that violence is not only necessary but ennobling, in the sense that it allows the oppressed to "regain their humanity." How do you feel about that kind of nihilistic mysticism?

Coffin: I don't believe in the idealization of violence. I think a study of the careers of violent men would indicate that violence did not enhance their humanity at all. I think black power is still seeking opportunity rather than revenge, but the pressure of events may force it to seek that opportunity through violence. It may turn out to be a necessary evil.

Playboy: How optimistic are you that we can still achieve social justice through nonviolence?

Coffin: Not very. I just don't see enough moral dynamism among the majority of whites. I don't see movement and real concern in the suburbs. I certainly don't see real movement in Congress. And I don't see enough people being sufficiently organized in the ghettos in time to get the necessary things accomplished before the politics of despair set in.

Playboy: What do you think are some of those necessary accomplishments?

Coffin: We must accomplish nothing less than the complete integration of all black people into society. What we've had up to now has been the assimilation of individual Negroes. The hard core of blacks—the poor, the unemployed and often unemployable—have not been integrated into American society. For that to happen, they will have to be organized in the same way the Italians and the Irish before them were organized. In this sense, I can see black power as a constructive organizational principle. I can also see it as a way of asserting the beauty of blackness. It is, however, a tricky concept and could easily become counter-racist, and that's where it's dangerous. To prevent that from happening requires that we deal with all the just grievances blacks have. When people feel they have a stake in a society, they're loyal to that society. They become disloyal when they feel they have no stake in it.

Playboy: What specific programs do you feel would provide Negroes with that stake in society?

Coffin: We need a twentieth-century Homestead Act that will provide millions of decent housing units. We need to end the mental genocide that takes place in ghetto schools. We need a program of immediate training for millions of blacks by both the private and the public sectors of our economy, in order to provide jobs. We can still prevent the country from being torn to shreds, if there's good organizing leadership in the ghettos and a creative response from the establishment outside the ghettos. So I'm not yet prepared to give up totally—but, as I said, I'm not optimistic that this is going to happen before it's too late. Whites in this country have reacted to the demands of black people only after there has been disorder, after blacks have refused to keep paying the price that allows white people to remain in peace. We did nothing about the injustice to black people until the truth that had been staring us in the face finally *hit* us in the face. Then we reacted. It's clear that until Watts blew up, Los Angeles was not prepared to do much about it; the same is true of Hough and Cleveland, Harlem and New York City. So, in that sense, violence played a regrettably constructive role. But despite the riots, not nearly enough has been done to end the injustices that cause them.

I still believe, though, that a massive nonviolent movement would be far better than violence. If Negroes and those sympathetic to them were willing to put in the time and energy necessary for a mass nonviolent organization to get real change accomplished, there would be no stimulus for violence. But that's asking an awful lot, in view of the sin pervasive among us; I mean the sin of people not really caring about injustice to others. What upset me about the public reactions to the murder of Martin Luther King were the official pronouncements by the President and by Attorney General Ramsey Clark. They said what a pity it would be if this great apostle of nonviolence were to have his name discredited by those resorting to violent action as a result of his death. But it was Johnson and Clark who discredited Martin Luther King's name by failing to make clear that he was not just an apostle of nonviolence; he was an apostle of social justice *through* nonviolence. Only by making that connection can we ever hope to achieve real justice and reconciliation.

Playboy: Many of those who supported Dr. King were buoyed in their dedication by a deep religious commitment to King's Christian philosophy of nonviolence. As another Christian clergyman, how do you feel about the fact that the majority of the dissenting young you support, and who support you, are either nonreligious or antireligious?

Coffin: I feel that many of the young have trouble not so much with God as with Christians and Jews and churches and synagogues. Their primary problem is not really intellectual but ethical. If the churches and synagogues were really true to their beliefs, if the churches and synagogues were demonstrating a capacity to sacrifice, if Jews and Christians were really showing a willingness to dedicate their lives to one another and to the world, then we'd have a great many more believing students today. Christians have always been the best argument against Christianity, but they've never been the central argument. What students have to face up to is not what they think of Christians but what they think of Christ. If Christians and churches, if Jews and synagogues could get out of their way, I believe many of these mystic humanists would become believers—because they are, in many ways, natural believers. They say they're antireligious, but they're quite willing to recognize that the life of the mind is not the life of the whole human being. They're quite ready to recognize that truths are *ap*prehended at a deeper level than they are *com*prehended. I think really sensitive humanists today are beginning to realize that they have been overly optimistic about man's capacity to fulfill himself all by himself. Michael Harrington points out that people stopped believing in God when they thought they could control nature. But now we've not only controlled nature but produced a human environment that is much more mystifying and much more difficult to control than nature used to be. This realization has subverted antifaith and brought about a new kind of humility in humanists and a new willingness to recognize that we may stand in greater need than we used to.

Playboy: In greater need of what?

Coffin: Need of forgiveness, need of strength beyond our own capacities. The need that comes from acknowledging that very few of us are really free in the sense that our hands can be extended to anybody else in need. We're all a bit paralyzed, disabled. People say, "The church is a crutch." My answer is "It certainly is—but what makes you think you don't limp?" As we begin to recognize that we limp as human beings, there's a willingness to be a bit more open to a need for strength beyond our own capacities. Your soul has to have shrunk a great deal to have lost the appetite for the transcendent glories of a religious belief. There's no question in my mind that a man is impoverished without it.

Playboy: What do you think the churches and synagogues can do to regain the allegiance of young people?

Coffin: They'll have to get rid of their irrelevant righteousness. The church has been concerned about free love—and yet indifferent about free hate. Churches and synagogues must rearrange their order of priorities. They must put at the top of their agenda the questions of war and peace, racism, poverty. It's perfectly true that you cannot legislate morality, but you can certainly legislate the conditions that are conducive to morality. You can legislate *vast* sums of money to eradicate poverty. You can legislate ways to bring people together, people of different races and classes, in schools and on jobs and in housing. And when they're brought together, they may be able to *get* together. These are things the church can help energize. The church has to be more orthodox—in the sense that it has to recognize, as orthodox Biblical religion does, that religion goes far beyond the garden gate. "Let justice roll down like mighty waters!" said Amos. He certainly didn't mean justice between father and son and husband and wife alone; he meant justice in a political and economic sense. Other people will have to figure out what the blueprints are, but it's up to preachers and committed laymen to make sure that the concerns of this nation are basically *human* concerns, to resurrect and embody the Biblical theology that God is always trying to make humanity more human.

Playboy: With or without committed preachers and laymen, do you think we'll ever attain that end?

Coffin: We are dealing with *provisional* fulfillment; we're not going to be able to make man perfect. But the sinfulness of man is peculiarly evident in his refusal to change; he's always trying to put the freeze on history. Capitalists have done this; Communists have done this; everybody tries to do this—individuals and institutions and nations alike. The true Christian—and I use the term here in its broadest and most nonsectarian sense, to describe a man of any faith, or no faith, who lives in accordance with Christ's commitment to the service of mankind—is one who is constantly trying to move history along toward the fulfillment that is always there as a vision. Toward this end, I think all Christians must be permanent revolutionaries.

Playboy: Are there enough men of good will and dedication to accomplish that?

Coffin: At any particular time in history, one looks only for a creative minority. And today there is a very significant creative minority among students. The kind of ferment that's going on from Columbia to the Sorbonne is a very hopeful sign to me, because it represents the basic striving of these young people for justice and for the construction of more humane communities, as opposed to our present mechanized social structures. What they want is to be part of a community that's natural, organic, warm. But that kind of communal life has largely been destroyed by the growth of rigid bureaucratic organizations where the decision making is from the top down. And when communal life is destroyed, personal life becomes disintegrated spiritually. What we're seeing now among the young is a reconstitution of the sense of being an individual. With blacks, it starts with the skin; with whites, it can be long hair; even that is making a kind of personal statement. Once this begins, a need for community grows, and that leads to the formation of brotherhoods among black students and to such organic communities among whites as the Students for a Democratic Society.

What we're getting, as this need for a sense of community increases, is the inevitable clash between the young and such large bureaucratic institutions as colleges. In most universities here and abroad, students have about as much to say concerning the running of them as the inmates in a mental institution. The students want to change that, and the big question now is how flexible these entrenched institutions are going to be in response. Are they going to allow a rational dialog to take place and bring change, or will they force violent confrontations such as the ones at Columbia and the Sorbonne? I don't know the answer, but I would recommend the statement of John Holt, the educational authority, that "the true test of intelligence is not how much we know how to do but how we behave when we *don't* know what to do."

These young people profess to be interested in discontinuity, but, in fact, it is continuity they're practicing—in the best sense. They fault their parents because their parents do not act according to the beliefs they *profess*. They fault the nation because America is not making good its promises to maintain a decent respect for the opinion of mankind. This creative minority faults the church because it fails to practice the love it preaches. It's a very, very hopeful sign for the future that we have a group of students who are oriented toward both the past and the future in a very alive and saving way.

Here is where I think we have something to learn from the hippies. The so-called feminine virtues they practice are obviously more important for us to cultivate now than the so-called masculine ones. That is, we need more cooperation and less competition, more tenderness and less callousness. We had better learn to become merciful, since we now live at one another's mercy. We had better learn to be meek or there won't be any earth to inherit. It's instructive as well as amusing to note that a pot party—which tends to be much more civilized than a drunken brawl—is very threatening to the average American's image of himself. A belligerent drunk still fits into that tradition of rugged individualism, but a bunch of people sitting around talking about Kafka and smoking pot is a great threat to that image. Not that I think you have to smoke pot to be able to discuss Kafka, but I do think the old tradition of rugged individualism has led America into what has become an aggressively competitive rat-race. Somebody once said that even if you win a rat-race, you're still a rat. We just have to learn to be gentler folk.

Playboy: Do you think we will?

Coffin: I think that there's a chance—just a chance—that a genuine change of values will come out of this generation of the young.

Playboy: There are many observers, as you know, who predict that they'll "sell out"—and become the kind of people they now put down as they assume financial responsibilities and start raising families. Do you think that's likely?

Coffin: It's hard to predict, but students have never been more sensitive to these problems and perils than they are now. In the ten years I've been chaplain at Yale, I have watched this sensitivity grow. It's grown because things have been so bad in this country—the war, the racial divide. Many students are very much aware of the danger of finding themselves ten years out of college and committed to being somebody they never really wanted to be. The world is so much better able to shape us for the worse than we are able to shape the world for the better. So it's going to be a very long, hard struggle not to sell out.

I think both the religious and the academic communities are going to have to give serious attention to the need for developing a habit of heroism among the young. I think the change of draft policy—the cutting down of academic deferments—brought home to many students the fact that choosing to be human is not a one-time decision but an arduous process. Now they're no longer in the protected cocoon; they're discovering that to be a free man requires a kind of total commitment, a certain style and practice of life, a certain amount of steel up the spine that we have not been tending to develop in this country. We've been buffered from these basic human decisions. There have been too many pillows between our backs and the wall. We have opinions galore but a paucity of convictions. We don't embody our opinions in our lives.

Playboy: You talk about the need to develop a habit of heroism. Among many of the young, the problem is often put another way: whether they can become functioning units of society and still remain "radical humanists"—that is, remain concerned with getting at the root of oneself and of the ills of society. Are these compatible goals, in your opinion?

Coffin: If we take the professions individually, I can say it would be pretty hard for a lawyer who joins Airedale, Airedale, Whippet and Pug—one of those Wall Street corporation-law factories—to remain radical very long. On the other hand, suppose he becomes a criminal lawyer. Suppose he becomes a man who recognizes that the penal system in this country is medieval, that it's punitive and not curative. Certainly, a criminal lawyer has a great deal of room in which to remain a radical humanist; he can be quite free in his operations and perhaps bring about a considerable amount of basic reform. On the other hand, he has to remember that there won't be basic reform unless there's a creative response from within the establishment; with the right kind of stimulus, establishment people *can* be noninsular in their responses, even if they're rather inhibited in terms of what they can initiate. Take the medical profession, for another example. I have a friend who abandoned a very lucrative professorship here at Yale to go out and set up a clinic in Hough. Now that he's dealing with the public-health problems of that ghetto, he's going to be in a very important position, from which he can initiate a lot of constructive reform in the area of public health. Take teachers; they can go into the slums and teach. They don't have to stay in the suburbs. Even preachers don't have to remain chaplains at Yale. They, too, can go into the slums of New York and Chicago.

Playboy: Have you ever thought of doing that?

Coffin: Yes, I have. On the other hand, my slum-priest buddies say, "Well, Coffin, you seem to be sort of cut out for work on the campuses, so maybe you ought to stay there." My job, as I see it, is to help keep the humanity of human beings alive when they're contending against such monstrous evils as the war, and to help them become the kind of people who will make significant choices.

Playboy: When the war is over, what will be your cause then?

Coffin: It's a hard question to answer. I'm certain I will continue to feel that as a chaplain, I'm in the business of trying to educate men of conscience; as for how I should assert solidarity with them in the future, that's something that will be dictated by the situations in which I find myself. But two convictions have come to me and will last. One, as Peter Marshall used to say, is that if a man doesn't stand for something, he'll fall for anything. It's terribly important that each of us decide where he really stands, and we have to be willing to witness to this truth, even if it means rotting in jail to do so. It's terribly important to witness to the truth in our time. The second thing is to act and witness in a life style that expresses your compassion and concern; your witness can enhance the humanity of other human beings—and of yourself—only if it is filled with love. If you suffer as a witness, you have to suffer because you have so much love to give and not because you haven't any at all. You must have so much love that you're willing to persist in the face of great adversity, even willing to explore and accept the possibilities of compromise—so that we can move from imperfection to something less imperfect. That's the best we can hope for.

Playboy: Many young people regard you as more than a chaplain, more, even, than a champion of their resistance to the war and to the draft. In an editorial for the University of Michigan student newspaper, one student wrote about you, "Combining his compassion with his energy and unrelenting faith and conviction in that which he believes, he is the impetus for the movement to continue. He has given the movement a center, a meaning. He has become a focal point for dissent. . . . We don't need a whole lot of Reverend Coffins. But we do need at least one. And he, too, must realize this. For the moment, he must hang up his robe of modesty in the closet and accept his role as a hero-leader without too much reluctance. It is what the movement needs. It is how the movement will succeed." Are you ready to accept a role as hero-leader?

Coffin: I have ambivalent feelings about hero-leaders. I'm torn, for example, between the desire for some perfectly magnificent leader for the country and the desire for a perfectly colorless one. For a lot of people look for a hero to take care of all their problems, but if we had no hero, we might be willing to settle down and do our own work, to take care of our problems ourselves. I do, however, recognize the importance of having good examples. Especially now, because I have a feeling we're beginning to create a movement among those committed to a humanistic alternative to the two other main choices of our time. One of those other choices has been called "the gentle apocalypse"—the sacrificing of humanity to the demands of technology. The other main alternative is the nongentle apocalypse, the Maolike, revolutionary alternative—which can lead to fierce repression. The violent revolt of the dispossessed can bring down on them the full ferocity of entrenched power, thereby making things even worse than they are. But there is a third way. More and more people in schools, in and out of the church, and some in politics, are uniting in a search for humanistic life styles and policies that will change not only America at home but what America does abroad. The lines are not yet clear and, as I said before, the odds are against us. But this movement will continue and will grow, and it will need spokesmen. If asked to become one of those spokesmen, I would not hold back.

Playboy: In a *Playboy* interview, New Orleans District Attorney Jim Garrison said, "The imperatives of the population explosion, which almost inevitably will lessen our belief in the sanctity of the individual human life, combined with the awesome power of the CIA and the defense establishment, seem destined to seal the fate of the America I knew as a child and bring us into a new Orwellian world where the citizen exists for the state and where raw power justifies any and every immoral act." Are you as pessimistic as he is?

Coffin: Yes and no. I still think that if we can straighten out our national priorities—and I know that's a big if—we have the possibility through technology to realize human freedom; I mean the possibility that all aspects of humanity may be allowed to flower in ways that were not possible before because so much time and energy had to be committed to mechanical work. For centuries, man did the work of animals; for centuries thereafter, he did the work of machines; now human beings can be free to do *human* work. Of course, we will have to apply a great deal of imagination, thought and courage to figure out what is human work and how the humanity of human beings can be enhanced by technology. We will have to figure out how we can control technology so that it liberates rather than enslaves. Either we will choose the future, as Michael Harrington has written, or the *future* will choose—and destroy—us. Destroy us as human beings.

Playboy: Are you hopeful that we *will* choose our future?

Coffin: It's possible, if not probable. If I can be theological for a moment, I think there's a great difference between being optimistic and being hopeful. I am not optimistic, but I *am* hopeful. By this I mean that hope, as opposed to cynicism and despair, is the sole precondition for new and better experiences. Realism demands pessimism. But hope demands that we take a dim view of the present because we hold a bright view of the future, and hope arouses, as nothing else can arouse, a passion for the possible.

The trial began May 20, 1968. On June 14, Raskin was acquitted of the conspiracy charges while Spock, Ferber, Coffin and Goodman were found guilty and a month later were sentenced to two years in Federal prison. Execution of sentence was waived pending appeal. On July 11, 1969, the First Circuit Court of Appeals reversed the decision. Dr. Spock and Michael Ferber were acquitted of all charges, but the case against Coffin and Goodman was returned to a lower court for retrial because of prejudicial statements by the judge to the jury. Acting on a motion from the Justice Department, a Federal court judge in Boston agreed on April 22, 1970, to drop government draft-conspiracy charges against Coffin and Goodman. Throughout the affair Reverend Coffin has remained chaplain of Yale University and has never given up his antiwar activities.

"You're a disgrace to the uniform!"

WILLIAM O. DOUGLAS

article

CIVIL LIBERTIES: THE CRUCIAL ISSUE

the keystone on which all programs for a decent society must ultimately depend is the sovereignty of the individual as defined in the constitution and the bill of rights

Most modern constitutions contain promises of things that government must do for people. Our Constitution, an eighteenth-century product, guarantees no one such benefits as an education, social security or the right to work. It is not a welfare-state document. To the contrary, it specifies in some detail what government may *not* do to the individual. In other words, it was designed to take government off the backs of people and majorities off the backs of minorities.

It stakes out boundaries that no executive, no legislature, no judiciary may violate. The "law and order" advocates never seem to understand that simple constitutional principle. An example will illustrate what I mean. The First Amendment says that government may not abridge the free exercise of religion. Suppose a city enacts an ordinance that provides that no minister may deliver a sermon without first obtaining a permit from the Department of Safety. To exact a license before the citizen may exercise a constitutional right is to abridge that right. No minister worth his salt would knuckle under. If he defied the ordinance, he would be acting in the best American tradition. If he were prosecuted, the unconstitutionality of the ordinance would be a complete defense. The person who concludes that a law is unconstitutional and defies it runs the risk, of course, that he guessed wrong. Yet his punishment is not thereby compounded. Law and order is the guiding star of totalitarians, not of free men.

This principle of civil disobedience can be appreciated only if the antecedents of our Constitution and Bill of Rights are understood.

The ideas of freedom, liberty and sovereignty of the individual reflected in the two documents come from a long stream of history. The ideas of political freedom trace at least as far back as the Athenian model. But the political freedom of classical Greece did not guarantee private freedom, which was first emphasized by the Romans through the development of natural law. The church added the tradition of a divine order and a set of precepts based on the integrity of the individual before God; the Reformation gave the individual a choice of religio-political orders. The divine right of Kings—one form of the social contract—was successfully challenged by the end of the seventeenth century. Rousseau's *Social Contract* was a frontal assault.

But the single thinker who had the most direct impact on the framers of the Constitution was John Locke. Locke taught that morality, religion and politics should conform to God's will as revealed in the essential nature of man. God gave man reason and conscience as natural guides to distinguish between good and bad, and they were not to be restrained by an established church or by a king or a dynasty. Isaac Newton, who in 1687 published *Principia,* his great work, seemed to abolish mystery from the world and enable a rational mind to uncover the secrets of nature and nature's God. This parallel thought gave wings to Locke, who wrote:

> Men being . . . all free, equal and independent, no one can be put out of his estate, and subjected to the political power of another, without his consent. The only way whereby any one divests himself of his liberty and puts on the bonds of civil society is by agreeing with other men to join and unite into a community, for their comfortable, safe and peaceable living one amongst another, in a secure enjoyment of their properties and a greater security against any that are not of it. . . . When any number of men have so consented to make one community or government, they are thereby presently incorporated and make one body politic, wherein the majority have a right to act and conclude the rest.

These ideas were well known to our colonists through the church as well as through Locke, Newton and many other writers. God, nature and reason were the foundations of politics and government; they were extolled in the Declaration of Independence and further distilled in constitutional precepts.

The foregoing is but an outline of the history of ideas behind the Constitution. They were translated into the body of Anglo-American law in a series of crucial test cases over a period of at least four hundred years.

The political counterpart of heresy in the sixteenth century was treason. The law of England allowed a man to be tried for treason if he "doth compass or imagine the death" of the king. This was called "constructive treason," for the accused did not have to lift his hand against the king to be guilty; all he need do was wish the king were dead. As a result, treason is narrowly defined in our Constitution: "Treason against the United States shall consist only in levying war against them, or in adhering to their enemies" and the proof required is very strict. That clause is the product of the philosophy of Madison and Jefferson. Madison wanted treason narrowly defined, because history showed that "newfangled and artificial treasons" were the "great engines" by which partisan factions "wreaked their alternate malignity on each other." Jefferson had the like view, pointing out that the definitions of treason often failed to distinguish between "acts against government" and "acts against the oppressions of the government." Madison and Jefferson are strangers to our law-and-order school, whose spokesmen go so far these days as to call dissent to our Vietnam policy "treason."

In the seventeenth century, it was the practice to force citizens to make loans to the British crown, failing which the citizen would be jailed and languish there without bail. Thomas Darnel met that fate in 1627. From his prison, he applied for a writ of habeas corpus, the conventional way in those days of testing the legality of a confinement. The case was argued before judges who were appointees of the king, serving at his pleasure. They ruled that they were required to "walk in the steps of our forefathers," that the word of the king was sufficient to hold a man, saying, "We trust him in great matters." This case resulted in the Petition of Right of 1628, which led to vesting in Parliament, rather than in the king, the authority to levy taxes; and it also established the prisoner's *right to bail.*

The legislative branch was also a source of oppression. A bill of attainder is an act of the legislature punishing individuals or members of a group without a *judicial trial.* Its vice is that it condemns a person by legislative fiat without the benefit of a trial having all the safeguards of due process of law. English history, as well as our own history between 1776 and 1787, is replete with instances where the legislature, by its own fiat, subjected men to penalties and punishments. The Constitution abolishes bills of attainder outright, both at the state and at the Federal level.

The foregoing are merely examples of how the sovereignty of the individual was, historically speaking, jeopardized by acts of all branches of government—the executive, the legislative and the judicial.

The fear of our forefathers was also a fear of the majority of the people who from time to time might crush a minority that did not conform to the dominant religious creed or who in other ways were ideological strays.

One episode that occurred in this nation just before the 1787 Philadelphia Convention is illustrative. Times were hard in 1786. A postwar depression had hit the country. The state legislatures were swept by agrarian influences. Debtors wanted relief. There was no strong central government. Only Congress, under the feeble Articles of Confederation, had national authority, and it was not in a position to act decisively.

Up at Northampton, in August 1786, Daniel Shays moved into action. His armed group seized the courthouse in order to put an end to legal proceedings for the collection of debts. The example at Northampton was followed in other parts of the state, about two thousand armed men joining Shays. Courts were paralyzed. In September, Shays' men moved on Springfield and overawed the court with their claims that their leaders should not be indicted and that there should be a moratorium on the collection of debts. They also insisted that the militia be disbanded. The stakes were high, because at Springfield there was a Federal arsenal filled with artillery, guns and ammunition, which Shays planned to take. The decisive engagement took place on January 25, 1787, the Shays group being routed by militia equipped with Federal cannon.

Shays' Rebellion gave impetus not only to a strong central government but also to checks and restraints on populism. The mercantile, financial and large landed interests were getting tired of talk of the rights of man; they were becoming concerned with the protection of their property. Too much democracy in the state governments, it was argued, was bringing bad times on the country. Massachusetts, New Hampshire and Rhode Island were said to be disintegrating. General Henry Knox, in the mood of our modern law-and-order men, wrote Washington from Massachusetts in the fall of 1786: "This dreadful situation, for which our Government has made no adequate provision, has alarmed every man of principle and property in New England."

Though Shays' Rebellion was shortly put down, the populist or agrarian forces remained in control of some state legislatures and repudiation of debts remained a threat. Majorities in state legislatures ruled without restraint. The commercial, financial and landed interests moved to Philadelphia for the Constitutional Convention in an antidemocratic mood. A republican form of government emerged that, to use the words of Madison, was designed "to protect the minority of the opulent against the majority." This majority, Madison said on another occasion, might well be the landless proletariat.

Numerous barriers were written into the Constitution designed to thwart the will of majorities. As Charles A. Beard said in his monumental work *An Economic Interpretation of the Constitution of the United States*, those who campaigned for ratification of the Constitution made "their most cogent arguments" to the owners of property "anxious to find a foil against the attacks of leveling democracy."

While the House was to be elected for a short term by the people, senators (until the 17th Amendment) were selected by the state legislatures, and the President was picked for a fixed term by electors chosen by the people. Thus, a measure of assurance was granted that *majority* groups would not be able to unite against the *minority* propertied interests. Moreover, amendment of the Constitution was made laborious: Two thirds of both the Senate and the House were to propose amendments; three fourths of the states were to ratify them. A final check or balance was an independent judiciary named by the President, approved by the Senate and serving for life.

The "minority of the opulent" were also protected when it came to the Bill of Rights, as in the provisions in the Fifth Amendment that "private property" could not be taken for a "public purpose" without payment of "just compensation."

But the Bill of Rights went much, much further. It was concerned with all minorities, not only the minority of the opulent. Government was taken off the backs of all people and the individual was made *sovereign* when it came to making speeches and publishing papers, tracts and books. Those domains had "no trespassing" signs that government must heed.

Great battles have raged over those guarantees. Peaceful and orderly opposition to the government—even by Communists—is, of course, constitutionally protected. Chief Justice Charles Evans Hughes said, "The maintenance of the opportunity for free political discussion to the end that government may be responsive to the will of the people and that changes may be obtained by lawful means, an opportunity essential to the security of the republic, is a fundamental principle of our constitutional system."

American law also honors protests, whether they are in the form of letters to the editor, picketing, marches on the statehouse or rallies to whip up action. As already noted, police historically have arrested dissenters for "disorderly conduct" and "breach of the peace," often using these devices to suppress an unpopular minority. But such charges are no longer permissible at either the state or Federal level, though the law-and-order men often try to use "vagrancy" or other misdemeanors to suppress dissent or to promote racism.

Government is also constrained against interfering with one's free exercise of religion. A man can worship how and where he pleases. Government at times has preferred one religion over another, giving it privileges as respects marriages, baptisms and the like, and even putting some prelates on the public payroll. The Bill of Rights bans this practice by prohibiting the "establishment" of any religion by the government.

It was the pride of British tradition that a man's home was his castle. Even the king could not enter without legal process. On this side of the Atlantic, British officers had ransacked homes (and offices as well) under search warrants that were good for all time and for all kinds of evidence. This led to the Fourth Amendment, which, in general, requires an officer making a search to have a warrant issued by a judge on a showing of probable cause that a crime has been committed. And the warrant must describe with particularity the scope of the search and the articles or person to be seized. Modern technology has developed electronic devices that can record what goes on in the sanctuary of a home without entering the home in any conventional sense. They, too, have now been included within the Fourth Amendment. Yet the law-and-order propagandists would brush aside the Fourth Amendment and use any short cut to convict any unpopular person.

The much misunderstood self-incrimination clause of the Fifth Amendment had a similar history: "No person . . . shall be compelled in any criminal case to be a witness against himself." At one time in England, the oath that one takes to tell the truth was used against the accused with devastating effect. If he refused to take the oath, he was held in contempt and punished. If he took the oath and then refused to answer a question, the refusal was taken as a confession of the thing charged in the question. Thus were men compelled to testify against themselves.

A widely heralded defiance of this practice was that of John Lilburne, who was charged with sending scandalous books into England. He refused to be examined under oath, saying that the oath was "both against the law of God and the law of the land." He announced that he would never take it, "though I be pulled to pieces by wild horses." Lilburne was held in contempt, publicly whipped, fined and placed in solitary confinement. That was in 1638. On February 13, 1645, the House of Lords set aside that judgment as "against the liberty of the subject and law of the land and Magna Charta." And in 1648, Lilburne was granted damages for his imprisonment.

The idea spread to this country. The Puritans who came here knew of the detested oath that Lilburne refused to take. They, too, had been its victims. *The Body of Liberties,* adopted in 1641 by Massachusetts, afforded protection against self-incrimination either through torture or through the oath. The highhanded practices of the royal governors who believed in law and order and who sought to compel citizens to accuse themselves of crimes also whipped up sentiment for the immunity. A majority of the colonists, therefore, as part of their programs for independence, adopted bills of rights that included the immunity against self-incrimination. Later, it was written into the Fifth Amendment and into most state constitutions.

The immunity has been broadly interpreted. It extends to all manner of proceedings in which testimony is taken, including legislative committees. It was early held by the Supreme Court to give immunity from testifying not only to acts or events that themselves constitute a crime or that are elements of a crime but also to things that "will tend to criminate him" or subject him to fines, penalties or forfeitures. As Chief Justice John Marshall put it at the beginning, immunity protects the witness from supplying any "link" in a chain of testimony that would convict him. Yet in spite of this long history, the law-and-order propagandists denounce the decisions that forbid the police from using coercion to obtain confessions from people in custody.

The protection against double jeopardy, the right to counsel, the right to confront the person who accuses one, the guarantee against cruel and unusual punishment—these all have a similar specific and detailed history of abuse by government. Each reflects a clear and calculated design to prevent government from meddling with individual lives.

The law-and-order people say that "criminals" and "Communists" deserve no such protection. But the Constitution draws no line between the good and the bad, the popular and the unpopular. The word is "person," which, of course, includes "aliens." *Every* person is under the umbrella of the Constitution and the Bill of Rights. The Bill of Rights purposely makes it difficult for police, prosecutors, investigating committees, judges and even juries to convict anyone. We know that the net that often closes around an accused man is a flimsy one. Circumstantial evidence often implicates the innocent as well as the guilty. Some countries have the inquisitorial system, in which the criminal case is normally made out from the lips of the accused. But our system is different; it is accusatorial. Those who make the charge must prove it. They carry the burden. The sovereignty of the individual is honored by a presumption of innocence.

The principle of *equality* entered our constitutional system with the Civil War amendments; which banned discrimination based on race, creed, color or poverty. So today we stand for both *liberty* and *equality*. The Russians who protested the 1966 Ukrainian trials came out strong for *liberty:* "The highest saturation of material goods, without free thought and will," creates "a great prison in which the food rations of prisoners are increased." Whatever continent one visits, he finds man asserting his sovereignty—and usually receiving punishment for doing so. There are few places in the world where man can think and speak as he chooses and walk with his chin held high. Yet in spite of our commitment to both, we are confronted with tremendous internal discontent. Some are in rebellion only to obtain control over existing institutions so that they may use them for their own special or selfish ends. But most of the discontent, I think, comes from individuals who clamor for sovereign rights—not rights expressed in laws but rights expressed in jobs and in other dignified positions in our society. We face civil disobedience on a massive scale.

Civil disobedience, though at times abused, has an honored place in our traditions. Some people refuse to pay taxes because the money raised is for a purpose they disapprove. That is *not* a permissible course of conduct, for, by and large, the legislative branch has carte blanche to prepare budgets and levy taxes. It would paralyze government to let each taxpayer exercise the sovereign right to pay or not to pay, depending on whether he approves of the social, economic or political program of those in power. The same is true, in general, of most other laws imposed on the citizen, whether it be observing a speed law or obeying a zoning ordinance or a littering regulation.

Gandhi's much-publicized civil disobedience was quite different. It expressed a universal principle. Gandhi had no political remedy to right a wrong. Disobedience of the law embodying the wrong was his only recourse. Colonial India, like Colonial America, was under a foreign yoke. Regulations were often imposed from overseas or taxes exacted by the fiat of the colonial rule. The subject had to submit *or else*. "Taxation without representation" was one of the complaints of both Sam Adams and Mahatma Gandhi. Our Declaration of Independence stated the philosophy—all men are created equal; they are endowed by their Creator with certain "inalienable rights." Governments derive their just powers from "the consent of the governed"; and whenever a form of government becomes "destructive to those ends, it is the right of the people to alter or abolish it." Thus, the right of revolution is deep in our heritage. Nat Turner did not get the benefit of our Declaration of Independence. But he moved to the measure of its philosophy. These days, some people are caught in a pot of glue and have no chance to escape through use of a political remedy. Civil disobedience, therefore, evolves into revolution and is used as a means of escape.

Revolution is therefore basic in the rights of man. Where problems and oppression pile high and citizens are denied all recourse to political remedies, only revolution is left. Sometimes revolution with violence is the only remedy. Violence often erupts these days in Latin America and Southeast Asia, where feudal and military regimes hold people in a vise, making it impossible for them to be freed from oppression by the political processes. In some nations, a trade-union organizer is considered an enemy and is shot. So is a person who tries to organize the peasants into cooperatives. In those extreme situations, there is no machinery for change except violence.

We have had civil disobedience accompanied by violence, the bloodiest one being the Civil War. Prior to that, there was the widespread rebellion under John Adams against the Alien and Sedition Acts, which made it a crime to utter any false or malicious statement about the nation, the President or Congress. The Virginia and Kentucky Resolutions called them a "nullity," because—by reason of the First Amendment—Congress may pass no law abridging freedom of speech or press. Those laws expired under Jefferson and for years the country reimbursed the victims for the wrongs done.

The Embargo Act was a self-blockade, in the sense that it forbade the departure of any ships from American ports to foreign countries. Jefferson tried in vain to enforce it, and it was repealed in 1809.

In World War One, there were about three hundred thousand draft dodgers, in spite of the fact that Congress passed a declaration of war.

Some of those episodes were accompanied by violence and many people were fined or imprisoned for their misdeeds. During those crises, the majority clamored for conformity. The minority, impatient at the existence of laws they deemed unjust, took matters into their own hands and did not wait until the power to correct the abuse at the polls could be exercised.

Today the dissenters, both black and white, claim that the changes needed to admit the lower fourth of our people into an honored place in our society are being thwarted. There is a growing feeling that the existing political parties are not likely instruments of change. The colleges' and universities' administrations, in general, walk more and more to the measure of traditional thought and have lost their revolutionary influence. The Cold War flourishes, diminishing our overseas potential and making the military the most potent force in our lives and in our economy. The puritan ethic—hard work and industry will guarantee success—is not valid in a system of private enterprise that is less and less dependent on labor. For many, the only recourse for employment is in the public sector; yet blueprints for an expanding public sector are hardly ever in public view. Racial discrimination takes an awful toll, as partially evidenced by the fact that the average annual income of whites who go to work at the end of the eighth grade tends to be higher than the average annual income of blacks who go on to college and enter the professions.

The crises these days are compounded because the *real* dissenters from the principle of equality in our laws and in the Constitution are often the establishment itself—sometimes a municipal, county or state government; sometimes slumlords allied with corrupt local machines; sometimes finance companies or great corporations or even labor unions. That is to say, these existing institutions often ask minorities to conform to practices and customs that are unconstitutional. People are apt to overlook the fact that those who make such a request are the offenders, not the vociferous minorities who demand their rights.

Rebellion by members of the establishment against full equality cannot be met with apathy and inaction, for that is the stuff out of which violent revolutions are made. Blacks and whites must join hands in momentous programs of political action. Those who put law and order above liberty and equality are architects of a new fascism that would muzzle all dissenters and pay the individuals in our lower strata to remain poor, obedient and subservient.

Unprecedented civil action is needed. When my friend Luis Muñoz Marín first ran for governor of Puerto Rico, he actually drafted and had printed and circulated the precise laws he would have enacted when elected. He was elected and the laws were passed. Those who march need specific proposals in their hands—proposals to put an end to a particular injustice. India, when dealing with the explosive problem of the untouchables, required about 15 percent of all matriculating students and about 15 percent of all government employees to be drawn from those ranks. While the maximum age for taking examinations for government service was generally twenty-four years, it was increased to twenty-seven years in the case of the untouchables. And this once-abhorred group also has a certain minimum number of seats reserved for it in the national parliament and in the state legislatures.

We need to think in terms as specific as those in dealing with our own minorities, whether black or white. No one today is on the side lines. We are all caught up in a tremendous revolutionary movement. It starts with a demand for equality in educational and employment opportunities. It extends to a removal from our laws of all bias against the poor. It embraces a host of other specifics that will, if faced frankly and adopted, make a viable and decent society out of our multiracial, multireligious, multiideological communities—and both preserve the sovereignty and honor the dignity of each and every individual.

'Else they will fall'

POLITICS IN AMERICA

When bad men combine, the good must associate; else they will fall, one by one, an unpitied sacrifice to a contemptible struggle.

EDMUND BURKE,
Thoughts on the Cause of Present Discontent

NORMAN THOMAS

article

pacifism in america

the grand old man of the movement traces its rocky course and asserts it still may offer our one last hope for survival

If any "manned" flying saucers from Mars have come near enough to observe this planet closely, I am quite sure their commanders have said to their pilots, "Home, James, this madness is contagious." For it is a mad world. Its scientists and technicians have given its nations the power of unlimited destruction. There are, now, many times more thermonuclear weapons than would be needed to obliterate human life on this earth. An hour of war between the United States and the U. S. S. R., President Kennedy once said, would cost 300,000,000 lives. The idea that this obliteration will be permanently deterred through a balance of terror, history teaches, is preposterous. In the meantime, the weapons that compose the balance cost the world 133 billion dollars a year—while three quarters of the world's population lives in the narrow margin between hunger and starvation.

These brief, bleak thoughts should make an objective observer wonder why all men are not pacifists. But an aggressive instinct in man—an inheritance from the evolutionary process that includes an infinite capacity for cruelty—has made war one of the most enduring human institutions. Hundreds of generations have failed to provide any alternative to it. Clans, tribes and nations, all possessed of powerful group loyalties, ideals and interests—in terms of profit and power—have waged almost uninterrupted war through the ages. There has been little attempt to give real political validity to the ideal that humanity itself is above all nations. Lacking this sense of a larger loyalty, some of man's more redeeming characteristics—his capacity for courage and his sense of loyalty—have been turned to the support of war, whose heroes have been immortalized in song and story.

Yet man, who accepts and even loves war, can also love peace. Some men have rejected war as too ugly and terrible a means to be justified by any end. The dream of the Hebrew prophets—that men would turn their swords into plowshares and their spears into pruning hooks—has persisted down to the age of thermonuclear bombs.

The peace movement today has its roots in the pacifist movement of fifty years ago. The history of pacifism over the past five decades encapsulates the best and worst of human nature and has considerable relevance for America today.

Neither before our entry into World War One nor today, in our cruel and stupid war in Vietnam, has a strong, united peace movement emerged, completely opposed to war. In every crisis between the outbreak of World War One and the beginning of our involvement in Vietnam, there have been two groups among the general supporters of peace. One group is composed of pacifists, who condemn war outright. The other, far larger and more shifting group opposes particular wars that it does not feel are politically or ethically justified.

At the outbreak of World War One, I was a Presbyterian minister, a conventional advocate of peace on religious grounds. The War itself—by its contrast of horror with the ethics of Jesus —made me a religious pacifist. I also became a strong objector to the War on political grounds. Each position strengthened the other. I have never forgotten the words of a very able and honorable judge, Julian W. Mack, who was serving on a government commission to consider the case of conscientious objectors who were in prison at the end of World War One. I was talking to him in behalf of a Jewish religious objector and the judge said, "I am not sure of a Jewish religious basis for conscientious objection, but I can't see how a Christian can fail to be an objector to war. To me, it is the greatest irony in history that the belligerent tribes of western Europe took a pacifist Jewish peasant not only as their prophet but as their god." But there came a time in the period between the two World Wars when, to my sorrow, my religious philosophy could provide me with no alternative to a possible support of *some* wars, as the lesser of two evils. It was, however, the passion of my life to find alternatives not only to war in general but to the particular wars that crowded upon us.

In this article, I shall use the word pacifist to describe only those who have been conscientiously opposed to participation in *all* wars. In the early years of this century, Tolstoy was by far the most influential of pacifist thinkers and writers. Philosophically, pacifists have added very little to Tolstoy's thinking. But there were some outstanding pacifists and many influential persons who stood out as peace advocates, often in opposition to particular wars. It is, however, not human voices but war itself and its consequences, even when the better side wins, that plead loudest for peace.

As I look back on it, the early part of this century, prior to 1914, was curiously an age of innocence. We in America knew of many evils, including war, but we believed in "progress" and the probability of peace. We believed this despite the Spanish-American War at the end of the nineteenth century, despite our Manifest Destiny imperialism in the Philippines, despite our interventionist policy in the Caribbean area, despite the Boer War in Africa and the Russo-Japanese War in Asia. We took little account of the significance of colonial rumblings against the great capitalist imperialist powers. We had great hopes in arbitration. The steel baron Andrew Carnegie had a social conscience that was very weak in dealing with the sins of a rampant capitalism but made him a great financial supporter of libraries and schools. Around 1910, he gave money for the Church Peace Union and the Carnegie Endowment for International Peace. He also built the Peace Palace in The Hague. (The actual service to peace of these institutions has been very moderate.) Another tycoon, Henry Ford, so loved peace that he sent a peace ship to Europe after World War One had begun. It had no influential effect.

In 1910, Norman Angell published *The Great Illusion,* proving that large wars would not pay the empires that waged them. It was almost universally applauded, but in four years, the First World War broke upon an astonished world. European socialists had gone so far in opposition to international war—as contrasted with revolutionary struggles—that the eloquent Jean Jaurès of France, James Keir Hardie of Scotland and others seriously discussed strikes against mobilization in France and Germany, in the event of a threat of war. In England, which had no conscription, a general strike against the entry into war was considered, but there was no formal adoption of this plan, nor were there any arrangements to carry it out. Jaurès was assassinated by a French "patriot," and soon socialist internationalists were killing one another in the name of loyalty to their particular nations just as cheerfully as Christians, who had had centuries' more experience in violating human brotherhood.

In the United States, there was at first an almost universal horror of the War and determination not to be dragged into it, but this opposition was chipped away by the growing involvement of our whole economy in the support of the anti-German allies, by the fear that Germany might win and, particularly, by abhorrence of Germany's action in sinking ships that carried passengers as well as munitions. (In the Second World War, we did the Germans the honor of copying this practice, in our submarine destruction of enemy merchant ships.) I have long believed that we would not have entered World War One if we had traded with both groups of combatants. President Wilson would not have discovered a war for democracy in what amounted to a brute imperialist clash. When the President summoned the nation to war on April 6, 1917, most of the opposition to it—except from socialists, other radicals and a small group of religious pacifists—joined in the hysterical support the War received, at enormous cost to civil liberties at home. The conventional peace societies went along with the crowd. But some new societies had sprung up that persisted after the U. S. had got into the War. The American Union Against Militarism, under the leadership of Lillian Wald, Jane Addams, Oswald Garrison Villard and others, was actively opposed to the War and to Wilson's Caribbean policy. The Union persisted a while after our entry and then died. The present American Civil Liberties Union is, in a sense, its offspring, because it developed out of a subcommittee of the Union under the leadership of Roger Baldwin, himself a conscientious objector. The Fellowship of Reconciliation, founded in England in 1915, was the most important and durable of these new peace societies. It was an organization of Christian objectors to war and spread to the U. S. That magnificent humanitarian organization, the American Friends' Service Committee, founded in 1917, operated in the Quaker tradition of pacifism. In later years, it and its efficient secretary, Clarence Pickett, were to receive the Nobel Peace Prize.

In the calmer times between wars, other American pacifists received that honor. Among them was Jane Addams, founder of Hull House in Chicago and probably America's most famous social worker. She spoke out for peace all during the First World War and was a principal founder of the Women's International League for Peace and Freedom (in April 1915). One of her associates, Emily Greene Balch, was similarly honored. So, too, in a later stage of the struggle for peace, were the famous scientist Linus Pauling, because of his opposition to thermonuclear weapons, and the Reverend Martin Luther King, who applied the principle of nonviolence in the American racial struggle.

But none of this regard for pacifists and their service to world sanity and peace was manifest during the First World War. The U. S. had never had conscription—except in a very bad form for part of the Civil War—but Wilson and his Congress felt it necessary to impose it, despite the fact that thousands of Americans had come here from European countries to escape it. There were hardly any provisions for conscientious objectors. Like all those who refused the draft, objectors were nominally subject to whatever penalty military courts might impose on them. The law defined conscientious objectors in a very narrow manner. They had to be members "of any well-recognized religious sect or organization at present organized and existing and whose existing creed or principles forbid its members to participate in war in any form and whose religious convictions are against war or participation therein in accordance with the creed or principles of said religious organizations."

A great many of the young objectors could not qualify as members of these pacifist churches. Even those who did qualify were required to take some form of prescribed noncombatant service. No systematic provision was made for such service until almost a year of war had passed. The result was confusion, rough handling of conscientious objectors and excessive court-martial sentences. One of the worst incidents concerned a small group of religious objectors called Molokani, who had settled in Arizona during President Grant's Administration on his assurance that there would not be peacetime conscription in the United States. When the War came, their young men refused to register and, under the law, served about a year in prison. They were model prisoners in civil prisons, but then they were compulsorily registered and drafted into the Army. They again refused service and were sentenced for very long terms to Fort Leavenworth Military Prison. Here they refused to work, because the commandant of the prison was a colonel and his orders were military orders. Even the armistice made no difference. Under military law not of his making, the colonel sent the young men to dark, solitary cells, where they were manacled to the bars in a standing position during the period when the other men worked. My brother, Evan W. Thomas, was not a Molokani, but he, too, refused to work and was among this manacled group. Fortunately, he managed to get a message to me. To my shocked surprise, one of the clergy to whom I appealed, a leader in the Church Peace Union, said the men were traitors and deserved no sympathy. The onetime liberal Newton D. Baker, Secretary of War, denied that there was any such punishment in an American military prison. It was only after I got Don Seitz of the New York *World* to send a crack reporter to Leavenworth that the truth was revealed. Armed with this evidence and with the belated support of liberals, the Reverend John Nevin Sayre, related to President Wilson by marriage, managed to reach the President, who ordered the end of such punishments. My brother was released on a technicality and the others were transferred to another prison and not too long thereafter were freed. I do not know of similar brutality directed against conscientious objectors to later wars, after the shooting had stopped.

It is estimated that during World War One, some 170,000 managed to evade the draft altogether by flight to Mexico or by obtaining false medical certificates or safe, exempt jobs. But these were not crusaders for peace. That role was far better filled by some four thousand objectors. The conscription law and its enforcement were very confused, but in the end there were about twelve hundred who accepted civilian substitutes, such as farm furloughs, and ninety-nine took work with the Friends' Reconstruction Unit. About five hundred absolutists were court-martialed and sent to military prisons for long terms —twenty-five years or even life. There were cases where the original sentence was death. After the War, Presidential clemency reduced these long sentences rather capriciously. The last of the objectors was not released until 1933, long after objectors in foreign countries had been released.

Conscientious objectors were not the only sufferers. Civil liberties were pretty well shot to hell under the "liberal" President Wilson. Mobs of "patriotic" citizens went even further than the President. Ray Abrams, in *Preachers Present Arms,* tells a melancholy tale of the wholesale expulsion of pacifist preachers from their pulpits. Very few survived. At the end of the War, there were some one thousand political prisoners still in jail, guilty of nothing except their exercise of rights that were supposedly guaranteed by the First Amendment. The best known, of course, was Eugene Debs, the Socialist who polled about one million votes as a candidate for President while he was a prisoner in Atlanta.

I shall never forget the joy with which I greeted the armistice that finally ended the brutal War of mud and trenches in Europe. It was a joy very commonly shared by the world. But the War did not give us wisdom, as I had hoped, to guard against the recurrence of organized murder in the name of our nation or our political creed. At first, there was widespread hope in peace circles for President Wilson's plan for a League of Nations. What came out of the Versailles Conference by way of a treaty and the plan for the League of Nations was a great disappointment to pacifists, as well as to radicals. We believed that the treaty—which, to be sure, might have been worse—contained the seeds of another world war. How far this opposition should go divided radicals and pacifists, but many swung over to unenthusiastic support of the League during the Harding and Coolidge Administrations. As the Socialist candidate for President in 1928 and 1932, I favored joining the League on condition of some reservations (which could easily have been obtained) to prevent it from dragging us into a new war. We held this position as late as 1932, when President Roosevelt ended any talk of joining the League.

I have never believed that, given the general conditions of the world, our membership in the League would, of itself, have saved it from disaster and the world from the agony of World

War Two. Communism had arisen during World War One and Mussolini's Fascism not long thereafter. They, rather than a struggle for peace, preoccupied most minds.

American attention to foreign policy was diverted by the Great Depression. But even before 1929, American attitudes toward the First World War had drastically changed. The old hysteria continued for a time after the armistice, but it changed rapidly and fairly early in the Twenties. I and others found ourselves being applauded for saying things about World War One that very likely would have called forth violent protests and probable arrests at the beginning of the decade. The idea grew that we had been victims of the "merchants of death." By the time of the senatorial inquiry presided over by Senator Gerald Nye of North Dakota, this idea was firmly based—and resulted in a rather weak Neutrality Act designed to prevent trading in arms with nations at war. Ironically, that idea of neutrality—and the way it was enforced under Roosevelt's direction—worked to the disadvantage of the democratic Spanish government in that country's civil war. Even the advocates of arms embargo eventually turned against the proposal when it was used, as it was by Roosevelt, to hurt the Spanish Loyalists and, hence, to help Franco and—through him—Hitler.

The general idea of neutrality had had support from peace advocates, including pacifists. The Nye inquiry itself was largely the result of work by the Women's International League for Peace and Freedom. Earlier peace organizations and their friends, with more or less enthusiasm, had supported Secretary of State Charles Evans Hughes in engineering a treaty in 1922 limiting naval construction in the United States, Great Britain, Japan, France and Italy. In 1930, the London Naval Reduction Treaty provided for a proportional reduction of the navies of these five countries. Under President Coolidge, we were treated to the Kellogg-Briand Pact, signed by practically all nations. The Pact renounced war as an instrument of policy but never had any effect on real foreign policy. It was a piece of pious hypocrisy.

Then, in 1930, there was a strong, nearly successful effort in Congress, sponsored by Senator Lynn J. Frazier of North Dakota, to initiate a constitutional amendment making war totally illegal. Whatever the role local or national organizations played in support of the Frazier Amendment, it was not primarily the work of pacifists or pacifist leaders. Frazier himself owed his position and his fame only secondarily to his stand on peace. Primarily, he was part of the agrarian radical movement in North Dakota (and other states) that produced the Farmers Nonpartisan League and had a great influence on the Republican Party in the northern prairie states. Peace sentiment as such was earnestly presented by excellent men and women, but little or no new philosophy of peace was developed in America by them or by the fragmented peace movement.

In the world at large, the great exception was that remarkable Indian character Mahatma Gandhi, whose work before and during the Second World War brought to success India's nonviolent revolution against Great Britain and the establishment of Indian independence. Gandhi—who, by his own statement, had been principally inspired by the writings of Henry Thoreau—invented the tactics of nonviolent demonstration and action used today.

Americans generally, as the 1930s wore on, were far more occupied with the subject of violence in connection with the national and international problems raised by communism and fascism than with peace as the ultimate goal. The American League Against War and Fascism—which became the moderately influential League for Peace and Democracy—was much more concerned with opposition to fascism than with opposition to war. Toward its end, it was rather effectively captured by the Communists, although by no means were all its members Communists. Its usefulness was completely destroyed when Hitler made his pact with Stalin. Other organizations arose as the crisis in Europe drew nearer. The Keep America Out of War Committee was formed in 1937. It was opposed to the War, but it was not isolationist in its general foreign policy. The much larger America First movement was isolationist in general policy and intensely opposed to those policies of Roosevelt that it thought were leading us to war.

All of this controversy, however—in which there was little interest in pacifism as a principle—ended with the Japanese attack on Pearl Harbor and Hitler's declaration of war on the United States. The political organizations opposed to war disbanded instantly and their members dedicated themselves to supporting war in Europe and the Pacific. The Communists, whose *Manual* had declared that the Soviet Union was the only fatherland of the workers, followed Russian policy, first against Nazism ("The Yanks are coming!") and then, briefly, in support of the Hitler-Stalin Pact ("The Yanks are not coming!"). During the Second World War, they were 212-degree-Fahrenheit patriots. I remember their sending hecklers to try to interrupt a poorly attended meeting that I called to protest Roosevelt's ordering all Japanese and Japanese-Americans within one hundred miles of the Pacific Coast into concentration camps, without trial or hearing. This order was the greatest single outrage against civil liberty in both World Wars. The patriotism of many Japanese-Americans from other parts of the country, who served bravely in our Army, proved how unnecessary the camps were. Otherwise, civil liberties fared pretty well, for the simple reason that the Second World War was the only war in America's history to which there was practically no opposition. There were, however, conscientious objectors on religious and humanitarian grounds. These were better treated than in the First World War. Much more generous and effective provision for alternative service for them was provided. They were not required, as in the First World War, to be members of some pacifist religious body, but they were required to affirm that their pacifism was on the basis of their "religious training and belief." This phrase received very different interpretations by draft boards in different parts of the country. (The draft law of 1948 subsequently tried to solve this by requiring belief in a Supreme Being.)

At the end of World War Two, after atomic bombs were dropped on Hiroshima and Nagasaki, the world and its peace forces faced a new situation. The immemorial practice of war became a threat to the very existence of mankind. Soon after Hiroshima, I heard a high military officer at a conference talk along the lines later followed by Norman Cousins in his *Modern Man Is Obsolete*. Nevertheless, this conviction by no means made all people automatically pacifist; nor did it provide alternatives to war, and so the struggle went on.

In a world where war had supposedly become "obsolete," the United States since the Second World War has been involved in military activity in Cuba, Lebanon and the Dominican Republic, as well as "police actions" leading to more serious wars in Korea and Vietnam. Behind all of these struggles lay the fear of an equally militant communism and the somewhat stupid belief that communism should and could *always* be restrained by military force. Major assumptions about the nature of communism and its strength have been partially refuted by developments in its once monolithic structure. There have been modifications in the Stalinist version in Russia; and the growth of independent, nationalist and increasingly libertarian versions in several countries has been a welcome development. Recently, this liberalization has been most emphatic in Czechoslovakia—where, however, as I write, Russia and her satellites have intervened in force to put down a liberal Communist regime. Russia's rationale for invading Czechoslovakia resembles the reasoning Johnson used for intervening in the Dominican Republic. Both involved a combination of national self-interest and ideological concern. We intervened through a fear of "communism," while the Russians, according to TASS, intervened to combat the "threat to socialism."

However, not all postwar developments have been negative. A pragmatic sort of pacifism has won some victories in the United Nations. In 1963, peace forces here and abroad succeeded in securing a limited ban on nuclear tests, which greatly diminished the danger of radioactive fallout; and earlier this year [1968], agreement was reached on a nonproliferation treaty that, as of this writing, has not yet been ratified by the Senate. Neither France nor the Communist government of China signed either treaty.

But it was still true that by 1968 the total military budget of the United States was eighty billion dollars, of which thirty billion dollars was spent on the war in Vietnam, a war that we were not winning but only indefinitely prolonging. Moreover, racism of various kinds had resulted in violent riots in more than one hundred American cities, and many Negro and white activists who had formerly been committed to nonviolence saw no hope but in a kind of guerrilla war in our streets. Frantz Fanon, Fidel Castro, Ché Guevara and Regis Debray became heroes.

Both violence and nonviolence have had remarkable and personally devoted advocates during this period. At the beginning of the postwar period, India still had her great and apparently successful proponent of a nonviolent revolution in Gandhi. In the United States, Dr. Martin Luther King had won some victories of importance on principles developed by Thoreau and Gandhi. Before his tragic assassination, Dr. King's work was organized through the Southern Christian Leadership Conference (headed now by the Reverend Ralph Abernathy), which remains dedicated to fulfilling Dr. King's "dream."

In India, Gandhism had not been strong enough to prevent a tremendous clash between Moslems and Hindus, war with Pakistan, the take-over of Goa and several armed confrontations with China.

In these struggles both sides have their heroes. In the United States, Martin Luther King, Medgar Evers and countless others stand as victims of the violence they so strenuously opposed. I would be inclined to add to this list the name of the late Reverend A. J. Muste, whose life and gift of leadership had been given to the cultivation of a nonviolent resistance and a pacifism that was never passive in the face of injustice. One also thinks of that remarkable woman, Dorothy Day, and others in the Catholic Worker movement.

On the violent side, one need only think of the fantastically courageous Ernesto Ché Guevara and his group of little-known but extremely dedicated guerrilla comrades in Bolivia.

In the United States, pacifism as I define it has doubtless gained many new adherents. It has, however, been less influential as a direct force than as a spur to men opposed to particular wars. That sentiment, which is so large and prominent in opposition to the war in Vietnam, was slow in growing and is much greater now than it was during the Korean War. Many near pacifists felt that, on balance, that conflict was an international peace-keeping operation that could only be avoided by a dangerous yielding to the violence of international communism. Even so, there were approximately eight thousand conscientious objectors to the Korean War. The latest report I have shows about three times that many conscientious objectors to the war in Vietnam and each month sees a rise in the number of men registering their objection. Religions that have not been explicitly pacifist, such as Roman Catholicism, are producing more and more C. O.s. More and more objectors are insisting on the 1-O classification, which means that they refuse noncombatant as well as combatant duty. The campaign against President Johnson's policy is widespread and growing. More people have spoken out and from a greater variety of positions.

But the churches and other organizations that now express great opposition to the war in Vietnam were frustratingly slow in awakening to its meaning and significance. Since this article is a short history of pacifism rather than a history of our times, I cannot go into the reasons why there was, on the whole, so little resistance to the American interventions in Cuba and the Dominican Republic, and during the early stages of the war in Vietnam. In general, the argument was that we had to stop communism, which we have a tendency to falsely identify with any form of social revolution in Latin America and elsewhere. We have continued to work under the extraordinarily stupid assumption that the defeated Chiang Kai-shek, ingloriously driven out of mainland China, is still entitled to represent it at the United Nations. (The nonrecognition of China has been one of the more effective bars to peace, and pacifists and near pacifists have continued to point this out.)

Even President Eisenhower warned us against the military-industrial complex, which, coupled with some of the worst features of the CIA, has immensely hurt the cause of peace and American leadership for peace in the world. Senator J. William Fulbright has warned us against some of these dangers in his fine book, *The Arrogance of Power.* His criticism, as well as that of many others, both in public office and out, is not predicated on a complete pacifism, but at least shows some recognition of the hard facts of life.

Unfortunately, most polls show less than total support by laymen for these relatively advanced opinions. The official labor body in the United States, the AFL-CIO, has not kept up with the churches, either in general support of peace or in specific actions, as, for instance, the war in Vietnam. Many strong unions have gained in wages as their employers have gained in profit—money that they do not want to lose. Far too much of our economy is military, and recipients of its benefits are blind to the fact that the vast sums we have spent on the Cold War are far less productive, in jobs and benefits to the consuming public, than money directed into a war against poverty and for schools, hospitals and homes throughout the nation.

Labor in America has never been very close to communism, but before the Second World War it was influenced to a greater degree by Communists. Considerable sections of labor were friendly to communism during our alliance with Soviet Russia against Hitler. All this was radically changed with the development of the Cold War, for which, I believe, Stalin was chiefly responsible.

The chief crusader against communism in the labor movement was not Senator Joseph McCarthy but the little-known, very influential Jay Lovestone. Lovestone was a leader of the American Communist Party in the Twenties, from which position he was deposed by Stalin. For some years he tried to run a non-Stalinist Communist Party, with decreasing success year by year. About the time of the Second World War, Lovestone moved to the right. After the War, he acquired much influence behind the scenes in the AFL-CIO and devoted his life to trying to build a world-wide anti-Communist movement in labor circles. His weapons emphatically did not include pacifism or any belief in the possibility of working out coexistence with evolving communism in Russia, still less in China. It is only recently that some sections of the labor movement have stepped out of this mold and actively protested against the Lovestone brand of anticommunism.

Against all this supermilitarism there still has not emerged a united peace organization. There are a great many groups—for youths, for women, for liberals, for pacifists, etc.—that have had a great influence. One thinks of the National Committee for a Sane Nuclear Policy (SANE), among others. The National Mobilization Committee to End the War in Vietnam is a large alliance of peace groups responsible for several impressively large demonstrations against that war and against war generally. It is a very inclusive group, with a loose membership of groups and individuals ranging from liberals to the extreme radical left.

In both civil rights and antiwar groups, the divisions are largely due to increasingly strong differences of opinion on the uses of violence. For example, Dr. Benjamin Spock, a bitter, consistent opponent of the war in Vietnam, has said that while he hates all war on principle, he would support American commitments to Israel as the lesser evil if Israel's existence were threatened.

This problem may be examined best, perhaps, by a discussion of the role of demonstrations in both the civil rights and the antiwar movements. In Washington and, of course, in other towns and cities, thousands of people have found their way to join in such demonstrations as the August 1963 March on

Washington—which was organized, incidentally, by a former staunch pacifist, Bayard Rustin. A comparison of this demonstration with the so-called March on the Pentagon in October 1967 is revealing. Great numbers of the same people marched in both demonstrations, but the spirit of the first march was expressed by Dr. King's magnificent eulogy of peaceful methods to achieve social change. The spirit of the second march was very different and much more diffuse—although its chairman, David Dellinger, was a genuine pacifist in his rejection of war, even guerrilla war, which had, by this time, attracted many white and black activists.

The Student Non-Violent Coordinating Committee, inspired by effective young leaders like Stokely Carmichael and H. Rap Brown, once supported nonviolent methods of resistance, both as tactics and philosophically. Now, some members call for guerrilla war in America and openly support the National Liberation Front in Vietnam. Their white counterparts in other organizations, notably in the Students for a Democratic Society (SDS), hold similar views. These groups do not absolutely reject but have very little hope for electoral politics or for that form of pacifism that seeks to avoid all forms of violence.

In general, however, there is an extraordinary rise in popular interest in electoral politics in the United States. This interest was intensified when President Johnson, acceding to the great opposition against him, decided not to run again and by the subsequent fight in the Democratic Party for the nomination. That fight culminated with the nomination for President of Vice-President Hubert Humphrey—while Chicago police were using Gestapolike tactics against both demonstrators and newsmen in the streets and parks of that city. Through the simultaneous television coverage of the convention itself and the demonstrators in downtown Chicago, millions of Americans became aware of the numbers and determination of young pacifists.

Political opposition has compelled Washington to pursue negotiations with North Vietnam with at least some seriousness. But those negotiations are bogged down in Paris. They will remain ineffectual as long as this country continues to bomb North Vietnam and refuses to recognize the National Liberation Front as a chief negotiator.

The most radical activists against the war—many of them contemptuous of pacifists—have supported the right to expand a moral objection to the draft so that it applies, as it did not in the past, to particular wars. Anything less than such a provision in the law is opposed completely to civil liberties and gives the government a dangerous power over the individual.

Dr. Benjamin Spock, the Reverend William S. Coffin, Jr., Michael Ferber and Mitchell Goodman were recently found guilty of illegally conspiring to aid and urge young men to avoid the draft. The case is now on appeal. Of all the defendants, only one, Michael Ferber, can be described as a complete pacifist.

Most pacifists and other peace lovers would probably agree with the Socialist Party's position on the requirements for a secure peace: First among these is universal disarmament down to a police level, under much stronger international control than the U.N. at present affords. Simple fear of nuclear arms, accompanied by an increasing accumulation of them by one nation after another, will never keep peace indefinitely. Governments are scarcely more to be trusted with such arms than kindergarten children could be trusted if they were handed revolvers to use as deterrents in quarrels. Beyond disarmament, peace also requires a concerted, world-wide attack on poverty, illiteracy, disease and the exploding world population.

There will never be peace until the major powers—emphatically including the United States—cease to act unilaterally as armed policemen around the world. Tragically, America can take no leadership for peace while it plays out its present role in the Vietnam war. Peace can only come after the world recognizes that violence is never a logical deliverance from injustice. The most useful role for the pacifist in these times is to point to the incredible excesses violence has rained down upon humanity in this century—and to convince man that violence in any form must be recognized as his true enemy.

"Damn it, Conrad, I'm for peace, too—but not as an end in itself."

article

CAREY McWILLIAMS

THE INTELLECTUAL AS A POLITICAL FORCE

once dismissed with the slurring epithet "egghead," the erstwhile captives and gadflies of the establishment now have the numbers and strength to be a potent impetus for change

The 1968 campaign will be remembered as the year intellectuals first emerged as a new national constituency in American politics. As individuals, intellectuals have long been attracted by power and fascinated by politicians. But today, as Lewis S. Feuer (the former University of California philosopher, now at the University of Toronto) has pointed out, "for the first time, the intellectual elite is trying to assert itself as a self-conscious force in the making of decisions by the Government." For some years, politicians of both parties have been vaguely aware that such a new constituency was emerging, but the events of 1968 removed any doubts they may have entertained of its political potency. In one of the numerous pieces in which friends of President Johnson have speculated on why he decided not to seek renomination, one of his "closest friends" is quoted as saying, "You cannot put your finger on any one thing that happened to start the reaction. However, attacks by the so-called intellectuals cannot be underrated. These intellectuals have more voice than real power. They represent minority opinion, but the attention paid them gives the impression that theirs is the voice of majority opinion." There is, of course, much more to the growing influence of intellectuals than this statement implies, but it is true that today they form a key link in the process of communication between politicians and the public. As much as any single group, they can shape or distort or destroy a politician's image.

Today, intellectuals are no longer content to serve politicians as speechwriters, occasional consultants or brain trusters; they are insisting on a role for themselves in politics as a group, as a new constituency. In 1968, intellectuals set the stage for the revolt that resulted in Johnson's decision not to run. At the outset, he made the mistake of not taking their protests seriously; he can count votes as well as the next man and he knew that intellectuals were not numerically significant. But the bitter and eloquent criticism of the Vietnam war by intellectuals evoked the "constituency of conscience" that Senator Eugene McCarthy tapped in New Hampshire. From 1965 on, intellectuals had marched, picketed, demonstrated. They had issued manifestoes, circulated petitions, prepared full-page advertisements for *The New York Times* and other papers. They had conducted teach-ins, write-ins, poetry readings; they had staged antiwar art-and-poster exhibits. Arm in arm, they marched on the Pentagon in October 1967. Even before the ballots were counted in the New Hampshire primary, it was apparent that their protests had created a strong opposition movement.

This new importance of intellectuals in politics should not be regarded as a transient phenomenon. On the contrary, it is an ongoing trend of major historical importance and world-wide interest. What we are witnessing, as Alan Trachtenberg of Pennsylvania State University puts it, is "the process whereby history is invented in the chambers of consciousness." This process is obviously at work in Prague, Belgrade, Paris, Warsaw, Rome, Mexico City, West Berlin and even, in a tentative way, in Moscow. In Czechoslovakia, writers set in motion a new kind of revolutionary protest that is about the only kind of "revolution" that postindustrial societies can generate. In Paris, students formed the avant-garde of a similar protest that paralyzed the government. In Belgrade, the strike of forty thousand university students, supported by intellectuals, had major political impact. In the view of Herbert Marcuse, the philosopher of the New Left here and in Europe, these and other recent events of the same order have healed once and for all "whoever still suffers from the inferiority complex of the intellectual." The fact is that the traditional idea of a working-class revolution is no longer relevant in postindustrial societies. The new waves of protest that will generate social change in these societies will be set in motion by intellectuals, who have become the prime articulators of discontent. Oddly enough, the dramatic demonstrations of 1968 in Prague, Rome, Paris and Belgrade were foreshadowed by similar developments at an earlier period in this country. "The old European notion of the intellectual as the 'conscience' of society," writes Gianfranco Corsini, literary editor of *Paese Sera* in Rome, "has found for many its embodiment mainly on the other side of the ocean, and travels back to Europe in American dress."

To get at the significance of this extraordinary—and most surprising—development, one must meditate briefly on the meaning of the tricky term "intellectuals" and then trace the emergence of the type in American society. Once this task is out of the way, I propose to examine why intellectuals here and abroad have become a new force in politics and to suggest what their role should be.

Who are the Intellectuals? The imprecision of the term intellectuals has bugged historians and sociologists for a long time, and with good reason. A certain vagueness is inherent in the term; then, too, it has meant different things at different times and places. Intellectuals have never constituted a social class as such; they hail, as economist Joseph Schumpeter said, "from all corners of the social world." They are defined more by attitude than by status; that is, they think of themselves as "intellectuals." But they do share certain interests and concerns and they have at least one common bond. All intellectuals are either self-educated or formally educated. Not all educated persons, by any means, qualify as intellectuals, but any educated person is a potential intellectual. And as Schumpeter noted, the fact that "their minds are similarly furnished facilitates understanding between them and constitutes a bond."

Despite the notorious vagueness of the term, intellectuals constitute a distinct social type. Robert A. Nisbet, sociologist at the University of California in Riverside, in one of the better attempts at delineation, stresses three characteristics. The first is "commitment to ideas as such. Intellectuals are 'gatekeepers of ideas and fountainheads of ideologies.'" They transform conflicts of interest into conflicts of ideas; or, as Lewis Coser, one of the editors of *Dissent*, once noted, they "increase a society's self-knowledge by making manifest its latent sources of discomfort and discontent." Second, they have a strong "moral commitment," that is, a pronounced concern with the core values of a society. And, third, they take delight in the play of ideas.

So far so good. But rapid social change—and the tumultuous history of the past few decades—has poured new wine into the old bottles. For one thing, today's intellectuals are products of the cultural fragmentation that seems to characterize postindustrial societies. The old social components tend to break down into new parts, each with a kind of subculture of its own. "Adolescents" is one example; "intellectuals" is another. As with adolescents, intellectuals have acquired a new consciousness-of-kind and are asserting themselves in new ways. In present postindustrial societies, intellectuals are coming to constitute a new political constituency.

The new significance the term is acquiring relates to an earlier usage. In Europe, the term was adapted from "intelligentsia," which the Russians had begun to use in the 1860s to designate a new social class that did not fit into any of the conventional social categories. A small minority of Russians who had been educated in Europe felt a deep sense of responsibility to "modernize" Russia on the European pattern. They came to think of themselves as a kind of dedicated order, held together by a strong sense of solidarity and kinship. "Isolated and divided," writes Sir Isaiah Berlin, "by the tangled forest of a society impenetrable to rational organization, they called out to each other in order to preserve contact. They were citizens of a state within a state, soldiers of an army dedicated to progress, surrounded on all sides by reaction." Although the setting is much different, intellectuals today are coming to think of themselves in much this same light.

In Europe, the term intellectuals had a different connotation. European intellectuals were a product of the secularization of society. When the church lost its monopoly of intellectual life, lay intellectuals began to take over some of the functions churchmen had once discharged. In fact, Julien Benda (author of *The Treason of the Intellectuals*) referred to intellectuals as "priests of the mind." As the church had once enunciated general principles to guide public conduct, so the postmedieval intellectuals, as Harvard historian H. Stuart Hughes has written, "began to elaborate a richer and less confined pattern of behavior to offer their fellow citizens." In the first phases of this transition, intellectuals served as advisors to the ruling dynasties. Erasmus and Bacon addressed themselves to princes and the government elite. They were, as we would say, very much a part of the establishment, of the power complex.

But at a later date, the relationship began to change. Initially, intellectuals had been allies of the rising middle class, but as this class more firmly entrenched itself in power, it had less need of the intellectuals and began to regard them as a nuisance or worse. The turning point came during the anti-Dreyfus craze, when the *bourgeoisie* turned viciously against *les intellectuels*. From then on, the intellectual became a critic of the society he had once served as an advisor. The transition was not difficult; the intellectual found it easy to be critical of a bourgeois establishment that claimed to have no further need of his services. With no fixed position, he could afford to play the role of social critic. He was less secure than the doctor or lawyer; he earned less, saved less and owned less. Standing apart from society, he could view it with detachment.

For the most part, however, the intellectuals of the West centered their fire on middle-class culture and middle-class values. It would have done them little good to assert a right to participate, as intellectuals, in the decision-making process; they were not numerous enough. Besides, the Western regimes were not nearly as oppressive as the czarist type. The educated classes were larger and provided a better, more responsive audience for intellectuals. Western Europe and the United States developed a sizable middle class; Russia did not. In the West, most intellectuals belonged to the middle class or were middle class in origin. While they were often critical of the middle class, they did not think of themselves as a class apart, as did the Russian intelligentsia.

But the fact that intellectuals were so few in number, and isolated from the centers of political power, increased their feeling of alienation and predisposed them to reflect the discontents and concerns of less privileged groups. As historian Richard Hofstadter has written, "It is the historic glory of the intellectual class of the West in modern times that, of all the classes which could be called in any sense privileged, it has shown the largest and most consistent concern for the well-being of the classes which lie below it in the social scale." Oddly enough, as intellectuals have discovered "the wretched of the earth" both in their own countries and in today's world, the more conscious they have become of their own identity as "intellectuals," the more they have thought of themselves as a class apart.

More important, the very qualities that differentiate intellectuals as a distinct social type have forced them to reassess their role and function in today's world. Intellectuals are to be distinguished from "intellectual workers" in one basic respect. The "intellectual worker," as the late Paul A. Baran, a Marxist economist who taught at Stanford University, put it,

> takes the existing order of things for granted and questions the prevailing state of affairs solely within the limited area of his immediate preoccupation. This preoccupation is with the job in hand. . . . Putting it in negative terms, the intellectual worker *as such* does not address himself to the meaning of his work, its significance, its place within the entire framework of social activity. . . . His "natural" motto is to mind his own business.

He is the kind of person who says, "I just work here," who disclaims any responsibility for the use that is made of his talent, his brains. But what marks the real intellectual and distinguishes him from intellectual workers and from all others, as Baran stressed, is that

> his concern with the entire historical process is not a tangential interest but permeates his thought and significantly affects his work. To be sure, this does not imply that the intellectual in his daily activity is engaged in the study of all of historical development. This would be a manifest impossibility. But what it

does mean is that the intellectual is systematically seeking to relate whatever specific area he may be working in to other aspects of human existence . . . it is this effort to interconnect which constitutes one of the intellectual's outstanding characteristics.

It is precisely this characteristic that today has catapulted the intellectual into a larger—certainly a more significant—political role. Intellectuals have vivid memories and imaginations. They do not need to visit Vietnam to know what is happening there. They experience no difficulty in making those interconnections to which Baran referred. In an age of "news management" and manipulation, in which small armies of intellectual workers help keep public opinion in line with establishment policy, intellectuals feel that they have a special responsibility to speak out *as intellectuals*. In a famous essay on *The Responsibility of Intellectuals*, Noam Chomsky hammered home the proposition that "the question 'What have I done?' is one that we may well ask ourselves, as we read, each day, of fresh atrocities in Vietnam—as we create, or mouth, or tolerate the deceptions that will be used to justify the next defense of freedom."

This heightened sense of responsibility might not imply a larger political role for intellectuals were it not for the fact that their numbers are increasing and so is the size—and the responsiveness—of their audience. Wars, revolutions and depressions produce "social critics" pretty much as certain strains of mold secrete the antibiotic known as penicillin. For much the same reason, the audience for relevant social criticism is growing. More and more people want it told the way it is. And today, no great gap separates the intellectual from "the people"; he is not isolated in the same manner or to the same degree as the Russian intelligentsia. Today, to quote a leading French leftist intellectual, Maurice Duverger, "the intellectuals . . . have no wider range of potential choice than the rest of mankind—the amateur thinker or those who believe themselves to be quite devoid of thought. The only difference is that they are better at explaining their attitudes, describing their states of mind, depicting their internal struggles."

For years, American intellectuals complained that they had little political influence and that society took scant notice of what they said or thought or wrote. Indeed, until quite recently, there was far more discussion about "anti-intellectualism" than there was, say, of the role of intellectuals in politics. In 1955, I took part in a discussion of anti-intellectualism that focused entirely on the attacks then being directed against intellectuals (the papers were later published in *The Journal of Social Issues*). Intellectuals were not marching or demonstrating then; the "confrontations," such as they were, took place before inquisitorial congressional committees. The public was then concerned not with student power but with student apathy, with the silence of a generation, not with the noise it was making. Sharp political conflict, we were then told, belonged to the past; consensus politics marked an end to warring ideologies. Today, just a few years later, students are rioting and intellectuals have become a new force in politics. To understand why this dramatic turnaround has taken place, one must first trace the emergence of intellectuals as a significant force in American politics.

The Emergence of the Intellectuals

The emergence of intellectuals as a distinct social type is a recent phenomenon in American life. Nisbet has no recollection of the serious use of the term much before the 1940s. True, individual intellectuals have always been interested in politics. But until quite recent times, intellectuals did not constitute a distinctive social group capable of exerting a cumulative influence on a national scale. The native intellectuals were too few in number, too thoroughly isolated and too thinly distributed to constitute a distinct element.

In the aftermath of World War One, many "sad young men" ran off to Europe, where living was cheap, and thumbed their noses at the America of Harding and Coolidge. It was a nice time to be young, but we have it on the authority of Scott Fitzgerald that the Jazz Age had "no interest in politics at all." The exiles were committed to living their own lives and to little else; and those who stayed home, for lack of funds or whatever reason, shared H. L. Mencken's disdainful view of politics. The issues then were personal: individual emancipation, a desire to escape from Babbittry, the discovery of Europe, a sharp reaction to the War. There was a rebellion of sorts, but it was based on a rejection of responsibility.

During the 1930s, American intellectuals began to acquire a sense of responsibility and commitment; the decade witnessed a sharp change in the attitude of many intellectuals toward social, economic and political issues. But the 1930s did not witness the emergence of intellectuals as a class. *Writers* formed committees, issued manifestoes and made speeches. But Nathanael West said of the period that even the writer had no outer life, only an inner one, "and that by necessity." The fact is that the crises of the times—the Depression, the imminence of war, the rise of fascism—had caught everyone unprepared, including the intellectuals. "The influx into America of intellectuals who were refugees from national socialism brought with it," writes sociologist T. B. Bottomore, "something of the urgency of the social struggles in Europe, as well as the ideas of thinkers who had long been Marxists." But the influence of Marxism was slight. The radical movement of the period failed to establish itself as a permanent force in American politics, and at the end of the period, a gulf still separated intellectuals from the great majority of the population. In fact, the isolation of the intellectuals was a prime cause of the endless infighting and sectarian wrangling of the period. In 1932, fifty-three prominent writers signed the famous statement on "Culture and the Crisis" on behalf of William Foster and James Ford, the Communist Party candidates. The ticket polled about 100,000 votes—one fourth of one percent of the electorate—and three years later, not one of the drafters of the statement remained in or identified with the Communist Party. By 1937, the ferment of the New Deal was about over; by then, we were preparing for World War Two.

The Spanish Civil War marked the intellectual and emotional climax of the decade. "Never before during this century," writes Frederick R. Benson in *Writers in Arms*, "had writers been so completely involved in a historical event about which they felt moved to express themselves." It has been called *The Last Great Cause*—the title of Stanley Weintraub's book on intellectuals and the Spanish Civil War—but it was merely the last great cause of the 1930s. The war in Vietnam has been opposed with more force, and by many more intellectuals, than rallied in support of the Spanish Loyalists. What brought the ferment of the 1930s to a close was not the defeat of the Loyalists but the fact that all of the "causes" of the period, including Spain, had been sucked into the One Big Cause, which was World War Two. As Stephen Spender has written,

> If you approved of the War, you were absorbed into it. . . . All the protests and affirmations of the anti-Fascists of the Spanish War were now systemized and swallowed up in official government anti-Nazi propaganda, while the anti-Fascists were often rejected from the service, being regarded as ideologically suspect, and despised as amateurs, now that antifascism had become a professional game.

Lewis Feuer is clearly right in saying that it was the involvement of the university community in World War Two and its Cold War aftermath that "changed permanently the status of the intellectuals." The government suddenly needed not merely the trained competence to be found in the universities; it needed intellectuals of all kinds, for many purposes: in the intelligence services, in the information and propaganda services, in the expanding procurement agencies, in overseas missions. Large and expanding bureaucratic structures began to take form in government, in business, in the foundations, and the demand for intellectuals burgeoned.

The inception of the Cold War, with its stepped-up "war for

men's minds," simply intensified the need for the services of all kinds of intellectual workers. Foundations emerged as a major source of funds, in increasing volume, for all kinds of intellectual projects, many of which were government-sanctioned. Some of the foundations became, in fact, conduits for government funds that were, in this way, covertly channeled to various organizations. In 1953, for example, *Encounter* was founded in London. It was sponsored by the Congress for Cultural Freedom and covertly financed, in large part, by the CIA. Its editors had heard "rumors" of the fact but had never been able to verify the rumors.

At the end of World War Two, we were, as literary critic William Barrett has written, "at the end of a long tunnel, there was light showing ahead, and beyond that all sorts of horizons opened." But this bright vision was never realized; instead, "social life became somber, immense, massive, institutionalized." It was the inception of the Cold War—more particularly, the domestic cold war or witch hunt—that eclipsed the bright vision many had seen in 1945. During these years, which saw the rise of McCarthyism, certain American intellectuals, most of them with former left-wing backgrounds, were guilty of a dual corruption. On the one hand, they assisted government agencies in driving from the cultural and political scene those intellectuals who had not abandoned their left-wing backgrounds. But worse, these professional "anti-Communists" reneged on their responsibilities as intellectuals. True, they had some waspish things to say now and then about "the great smuggery" of the Eisenhower years, but they did not challenge the course of American policy or the rise of the military-industrial complex or the assumptions on which the Cold War rested. They showed no interest in the poverty that the "affluence" of the period concealed. They were too concerned with "Reds" to show much interest in Negroes. In their infatuation with "value-free" judgments and problem solving, they refused to be concerned about the core values of the society.

It was during these years, in the 1950s and early 1960s, that intellectuals rose to the status of a privileged class. No two Presidents had less kinship with intellectuals than Truman (who wrote sassy letters to music critics) and Eisenhower (who was not interested in meeting Robert Frost and who preferred his and Churchill's paintings to De Kooning's), but it was during their Administrations that intellectuals began to constitute a kind of mandarinate. As Christopher Lasch, Northwestern University historian, has pointed out,

> The postindustrial order . . . created an unprecedented demand for experts, technicians and managers. Both business and government, under the pressure of technological revolution, expanding population and the indefinitely prolonged emergency

> of the Cold War, became increasingly dependent on a vast apparatus of systematized data intelligible only to trained specialists; and the universities, accordingly, became themselves industries for the mass production of experts.

But while intellectuals had finally emerged as a distinct class, intellectuals in the classic sense were to be found, as Lasch notes, "chiefly in the borderland between academic life and liberal journalism."

With the election of John F. Kennedy, the mandarinate advanced into the spotlight. The new President was a Pulitzer Prize winner, a historian of sorts, a man who enjoyed the company of intellectual specialists. His favorite book, we were told, was Lord David Cecil's *Melbourne;* his favorite novel, Stendhal's *The Red and the Black.* Every intellectual heart beat a mite faster when Kennedy was inaugurated. Arthur Miller, John Steinbeck and W. H. Auden were invited to the Inauguration, and so was the octogenarian poet Robert Frost, who had heralded the New Frontier as "an Augustan age of poetry and power, with the emphasis on power." Even Norman Mailer was charmed by the new President, who said he had read *The Deer Park* "and the others." Mailer was inclined to believe the New Frontier intellectuals would at long last be able to escape from the "alienated circuits of the underground." Politics, he said, had quarantined us from history; we had too long left politics to those who "are in the game not to make history but to be diverted from the history that is being made." Intellectuals came flocking to Washington, to serve in the Peace Corps, in the CIA, in the Department of Defense, in the White House, in the diplomatic service. Adlai Stevenson, a *manqué* intellectual, had aroused a certain fervor among the "eggheads," a term, incidentally, that was coined during the "anti-intellectualism" of the McCarthy era. But it was under Kennedy, as Alfred Kazin has written, that to be an "intellectual" became "the latest style in American success, the mark of our manipulatable society."

The trouble was that many of these intellectuals had joined the establishment on *its* terms, not theirs. At first, it was such a heady experience that they did not seem to have a very clear understanding of what they were being paid to do. Some of them were simply flunkies to the military: "crisis managers," counterinsurgency experts, Kremlinologists, etc. Others traveled far and wide, in Asia, Latin America, the Middle East and Africa, on special missions of one kind or another. For most of them, it was a new experience to be close to the centers of power, to see how decisions are made, to watch the wheels spin. As long as Kennedy was at the helm, they stayed on, serving purposes that they probably did not fully approve.

The turning point came shortly after the 1964 election. President Johnson received, of course, the overwhelming support of intellectuals in that election. They did not like him—nor he them—but they supported him against Goldwater. He swept every campus community and won the nearly unanimous endorsement of the intellectuals. But with his decision to escalate the war, the intellectuals began to drop out and join the opposition. No doubt, Johnson was glad to see many of them leave; they had been serving on sufferance. But he could not have been pleased by the mounting opposition of intellectuals, of all stripes, to the war. Sensing the new power of intellectuals, he had appointed Dr. Eric Goldman early in 1964 as special White House consultant on matters relating to the intellectual community. But Dr. Goldman was unable to put down the growing intellectual opposition to the war, and the breach widened. In an effort to close it, the President named a three-man team of White House assistants to aid Dr. Goldman. But they, too, were frustrated. So the President and Mrs. Johnson, in the summer of 1965, staged a White House Festival of the Arts, which was supposed to improve relations. But the festival simply focused attention on the fact that certain guests used the occasion to speak out against the war. In late August 1966, Goldman resigned, blaming both the President and the intellectuals for what he termed "a tragic estrangement." Johnson, of course, was furious and took prompt measures to discredit the apostate. A crisp White House statement charged that Goldman had never worked anything like a full-time schedule.

At this juncture, Vice-President Humphrey induced the President to appoint John P. Roche, professor in the department of politics at Brandeis and former chairman of ADA, to succeed Goldman. Roche was known chiefly, as Joseph Kraft observed, as an Irishman who had taught at a Jewish university and a liberal who supported the war in Vietnam. Instead of placating the intellectuals, Roche began to berate them. "Who are these alienated intellectuals?" he asked. "Mainly the New York artsy-craftsy set. . . . A small body of people who live in affluent alienation on Cape Cod and fire off salvos against the vulgarity of the masses . . . high-class illiterates." In March 1968, Roche conducted a press conference at the U.N., "at the suggestion of Washington," on the subject of "Intellectuals and Vietnam." In the course of this conference, he referred to American intellectuals as "essentially a self-styled group rather like the intelligentsia of nineteenth-century Russia. That is to say, a self-defined, self-anointed, self-appointed cultural elite which has taken unto itself the job of protecting the society from various and sundry problems. . . . It is this intelligentsia which has drummed up most of the vigorous opposition to the war." Of the war itself, he said it was a mere border skirmish, comparable with the nineteenth-century adventures of the British in India or the Japanese in Manchuria in the 1930s.

Surveying Roche's performance, one might conclude that Johnson had decided to carry the fight to the intellectuals. But he still kept trying to woo them. In the spring of 1966, when it was still possible for him to accept an honorary degree without being booed, he visited Princeton and boasted of what he had done for intellectuals. The 371 appointments he had made in two and a half years in office held, collectively, 758 advanced degrees. The Princeton faculty and student body listened politely and applauded listlessly. Later, Johnson used the occasion of the fiftieth anniversary of the Brookings Institution to make a major speech on intellectuals and the government. Nothing so clearly underscores the new importance of intellectuals in politics as the fact that the President, the master of consensus politics, felt compelled to make this speech, in which he pleaded for their support. Still later, in mid-May 1967, he invited sixteen "leading intellectuals" to lunch at the White House for the stated purpose of discussing with them how his standing with the intellectual community might be improved. The luncheon had the overtones of high farce. The assembled intellectuals were mostly government bureaucrats. Even so, they just might have given the President some sound advice if he had been prepared to listen to them. But he did all the talking and closed the session with a twenty-minute monolog. Why, he asked his guests, were so many intellectuals opposed to him, when he had done so much for them? The guests, who had enjoyed a good lunch, smiled, applauded politely and said nothing.

But the President did manage to win a minor consolation prize in his ill-fated campaign to keep the intellectuals in line. His staff—or, rather, Eric Sevareid of CBS—finally turned up an anti-intellectual intellectual who scorned the intellectual community and greatly admired Mr. Johnson. When the President was told of Sevareid's interview with Eric Hoffer, the ex-longshoreman, he promptly invited him to the White House. The President's press aide conceded that Mr. Johnson had not read any of Hoffer's books, but it turned out that Roche had long admired them. And what need was there to read the works of a man who had said that Mr. Johnson would be regarded as the foremost President of the twentieth century? The President was delighted with Hoffer, who told him how to handle intellectuals: "Pet them, but don't give them power." The President must have glowed with satisfaction when told that Hoffer had said, "Kennedy was a European. All you have to do is tabulate how many times Kennedy crossed the Atlantic and how many times he crossed the Appalachians and you know where he belonged." What is rather surprising about this "instant" friendship is that apparently neither Roche nor the White House aides advised the President that Hoffer has made a career out of cultivating middle-brow distaste for intellectuals. If anything was needed, therefore, to indicate how completely the President had misread the intellectuals, it was his sudden discovery of Hoffer, who, in high-topped work shoes, a lumber jacket and shirt without tie, was just the kind of person to reassure him that those witless "intellectuals" were not worth the effort he had devoted to them. (Later, the President appointed Hoffer to the commission named to inquire into the causes of violence after the assassination of Senator Robert Kennedy. The commission contained not one critic of the war in Vietnam.)

On the memorable evening of March 31, 1968, the President told the nation he would not seek or accept renomination. What prompted the President to bow out was, of course, the mounting pressure against his Vietnam policy. In effect, the President had been defeated in advance of the election; he was compelled to step down as prime ministers step down when they lose a vote of confidence. The President read the New Hampshire returns correctly; he did not need to wait for those from Wisconsin.

Much of the credit for this remarkable political achievement must go to the dissident intellectuals who had succeeded in mounting a forceful opposition to the war. Intellectuals were the one constituency that had bolted the consensus to oppose the war; labor, business, the farm groups, the big-city machines, the ethnics, even the Negroes, by and large, had stayed in line. But the intellectual opposition, added to the regular antiwar, propeace constituency, had finally succeeded in turning public opinion against the war. Of course, the headlines helped—the Tet offensive, the gold crisis, the riots, the crises in the cities—but headlines alone do not account for the remarkable change that occurred. The President's decision to bomb the north triggered the first teach-in, which was held on the campus of the University of Michigan March 24, 1965. In its wake, scarcely a campus community remained immune to the ferment of opposition.

It was this mounting tide of opposition, largely set in motion by the free-lance or dissident intellectuals, that brought Senator Eugene McCarthy into the race. And his candidacy, of course, promptly brought the intellectuals, on and off campus, and the students back into the mainstream of national politics. Not all of them, to be sure, but enough to make a real stir. By the spring of 1968, the intellectual community was as solidly opposed to Johnson as it had been *for* him in 1964. McCarthy's candidacy simply demonstrated Johnson's vulnerability; after New Hampshire, the number of consensus dropouts, individual and institutional, rapidly increased. If intellectuals surfaced in the Kennedy Administration as a new class, they emerged in the last years of the Johnson Administration as a new political constituency. It remains to be seen, of course, how strong this constituency is and how long it can hold together under a Nixon Administration, but that it constitutes a new and continuing force in American politics there can be little doubt.

Why Intellectuals Are Important

The importance of intellectuals as a new force in politics is certain to increase in the future. For one thing, the number of intellectual workers is rapidly increasing. The proportion of the labor force designated by the Bureau of the Census as "professional, technical and kindred" is the fastest-growing of all major occupational groups. Government and business need a far larger quota of intellectual workers than in the nineteenth century. Today, teachers constitute the largest single occupational group; the business of America, it is said, is no longer business but education. Government spending on science has increased from $100 million in 1940 to $16 billion in 1968. Business will spend something on the order of $17 billion on research in 1969. *Opinion Research* points out that intellectual workers "are getting into every nook and cranny of business life, particularly in staff positions."

In the same way, the number of educated persons is rapidly increasing. Today, we have roughly 2000 institutions of higher learning, with 6,000,000 or more students and 400,000 teachers and administrators. America is becoming, it is said, "a knowledge state." In 1900, a man who had completed high school was regarded as a member of his generation's elite, but in 1967, about 75 percent of all young people were finishing high school. By 1965, more than two of every five young men were entering some sort of college and more than one in every five were graduating.

While only a minority of intellectual workers and college graduates are intellectuals, nevertheless, the number of intellectuals has increased as the first two categories have expanded. Intellectuals as such are vastly more numerous than they were, say, a generation back. And intellectuals interact with intellectual workers and the educated; these are no longer, if they ever were, separate and wholly distinct categories. The time is largely past, as Riesman and Jencks note, "when the uneducated considered themselves superior to those with book learning"; the level of cultural sophistication is rising and it will continue to rise. The main point, in any case, is that the increase in the number of intellectual workers and college graduates is creating an expanding constituency for intellectuals. As these categories expand, so does the intellectual's political importance. "Conditions are ripe today in the United States," writes Lewis Feuer, "for the self-assertion of the intellectual elite. The sheer numbers of the constituency to which they appeal—several million undergraduates and graduate students, officered by several hundred thousand professors—are the most massive and most easily mobilized corporate body in the country."

But the audience of the intellectuals is also undergoing a remarkable expansion. Affluence has greatly increased the size of the middle-income sector. More people have more money to spend on "culture" and they are spending it. A "cultural explosion" of sorts has occurred since 1945. A mass market has been created for recordings, for works of art, for paperback books. Museum attendance has soared. Every major city now has—or will soon have—a center for the performing arts. T. R. Fyvel, author of *Intellectuals Today,* estimates that no more than 15 to 20 percent of the British people participated in the dominant culture in the pre-1914 period; in this country, the percentage would have been smaller for the same period. It is now much higher for both countries. Today, an army of intellectual workers is needed to disseminate information, to serve as "communicators," to carry watered-down versions of the intellectuals' wares to an ever-expanding mass market. Intellectuals constantly inveigh against mass culture, and often with good reason, but it is incontestable that the size of their audience has expanded enormously in the past quarter-century. "The position of the intellectual activists," writes Erwin D. Canham, editor of *The Christian Science Monitor,* "is more important than many realize. They provide a cutting edge and a solid shaft for political doctrine. They are themselves mass communicators of talent. They greatly influence youth."

Surveying the affluent society that has emerged in the postwar period, with its large bureaucratic structures, its expanding middle class, its new corporate empires, many intellectuals thought it most unlikely that new political movements could emerge in such an environment. There was no proletariat; the poor were demoralized and scarcely visible; the labor movement was fat and complacent. On the surface, there seemed to be little discontent. But an affluent society breeds its own kind of discontents that are voiced by new constituencies. "It is possible," writes John Kenneth Galbraith,

> that the educational and scientific estate requires only a strongly creative political hand to become a decisive instrument of political power. . . . As the trade unions retreat, more or less permanently, into the shadows, a rapidly growing body of educators and research scientists emerges. . . . It is to the educational and scientific estate, accordingly, that we must turn for the requisite political initiative. The initiative cannot come from the industrial system, although support can be recruited from individuals therein. Nor will it come from the trade unions. Apart from their declining numbers and power, they are under no particular compulsion to question the goals of the industrial society.

For "the educational and scientific estate" to initiate social change in an affluent society, however, it would have to be broadly defined to include intellectual workers, intellectuals, students, etc.

It may seem odd to suggest that students, in today's world, constitute a kind of proletariat, but, in a sense, they do. The more production centers on knowledge, on science, on technology, the more "brain workers" come to occupy much the same role as "the workers" once did. The university becomes, in this setting, the "knowledge factory," and students take on the role and, in many instances, the mannerisms and appearance of a new proletariat. The groups that control production begin to feel that they must control the university, not merely to be able to tap its intellectual resources but to control, in effect, their future labor supply. Students—at least the activist elements—sense these changes and are responding to them. In many cases, they feel that they are being trained for careers that are, or soon will be, obsolete. They have a feeling that education should be a continuing process, not crowded into a few brief years. They want more to say, therefore, about the kind of education they receive. Student activists are to other students and, in a way, to their instructors what the old-style proletariat was to the labor movement: a vanguard of protest. And the fact that the social base of the student population has expanded to include virtually all elements means that more volatile student bodies are to be found on the campuses.

Similar conditions prevail in European universities, east and west. It is not unusual nowadays to find references to students as "an alienated, helpless, 'proletarianized' group." In postindustrial societies, we have to assemble the new cast in order to understand the action. "Marx or Lenin," writes Dr. George Keller, former assistant dean of Columbia University, "would have snickered at the notion of starting a revolution to transform society by taking over a *school*—an ivy-covered retreat without guns, power or money." But it is not such a startling idea today. "History teaches us," Edgard Pisani, a former cabinet minister in the Pompidou government, told the National Assembly during the debate on the great strike, "that the great upheavals have always been provoked by the determining or dominant classes: in former times the peasants, in 1789 the shopkeepers, in the nineteenth century the workers, today the repositories of knowledge—students and cadres."

The great upheaval in France is perhaps the first of a new kind of revolution, the only kind that is likely to take place in a welfare-technocratic state. Essentially, the issue is how to use the new technology to build the society of the future. The spread of technology has stimulated new social expectations and created the potential for remarkable social advances. But the more production is rationalized, the more irrational become the goals and objectives to which it is dedicated. For example, arms production aborts the potential for real abundance. A potentially explosive situation is created, in both capitalist and Socialist societies, when workers are harnessed to jobs over which they have little control and, at the same time, cannot see that their work is furthering any worthwhile objectives. Under these circumstances, it does not take much of a spark to touch off a major social upheaval. Of the situation in eastern Europe, journalist Lucjan Blit writes, "It is precisely the more efficient industrial managers and 'scientific workers' and those influencing the spiritual life of their society who are now rebelling. The former because the sclerotic economic system robs them of the chance to do their job efficiently; the writers and journalists because even the most corrupt among them have by now seen the futility of their work." The situation is not essentially different in the west. Of the French upheaval, Neal Ascherson, on the staff of the London *Observer*, writes, "The enemy is the 'bureaucratic state' —east and west. It is the society organized for efficiency at the expense of liberty, the system which offers the people consumer goods and calls them freedom. It is the system which adapts education—so it seems—to the mass production of docile technocrats. It is the party system posing as a true democracy —repression masked as tolerance."

In such a situation, ideologies once again become the subject of intense political debate. An ideological struggle is essentially an attempt to change peoples' perspectives and to define "reality" in a new way. As such, "ideological revolutions," writes Anatol Rapoport of the University of Michigan, "are instigated by intellectuals, whose command of verbal expression makes them the carriers of new ideals." The rise of technology was, in a way, responsible for what appeared to be "the end of ideology" in politics; but now, once again, ideological questions take precedence over specific issues. When consensus politics gives way to the ideological variety, new national constituencies begin to take the places of the old interest groups and coalitions. Intellectuals are, potentially, one of the most important of these new constituencies. We are beginning to reject, as Galbraith has said, the goals of an industrial society. What should the new goals be? What kind of society do we propose to build? These are the kinds of questions that most appeal to intellectuals and to which their style of thinking is most relevant.

If the society of the future is to be one of even greater organizational and technological complexity, with a greater reliance on planning, then it cannot fail, as George Lichtheim, author of *Marxism in Modern France*, has said, to enhance the significance (and the responsibility) of the stratum which does the thinking for the rest of society . . . social evolution is increasingly going to depend on mind, and consequently on the quantitative and qualitative growth of the stratum which embodies the capacity of the intellect to introduce order into the environment. . . . When one has said the worst that can be said about the intelligentsia, it remains a fact that this stratum carries within itself the main potentiality of evolution still open to mankind.

In these terms, it should be clear that intellectuals will exert a growing influence on the politics of the future, regardless of which party is in office. As custodians of the nation's core values, they must be listened to on the question of goals and purposes; as the group most disposed to take "the general view," with the best record of disinterested judgment, they are becoming indispensable to the proper functioning of our political system. "If we define an intellectual," writes Rapoport, "not merely in terms of intellectual competence but in terms of a commitment to intellectual values, of which an important one is that of living the *examined* life," then intellectuals do have a class interest, the pursuit of which constitutes one of society's best offsets to the deadening effects of a thoroughly rationalized technostructure that functions in almost complete disregard of what people think and feel and want. The intellectual's chief responsibility is to this group interest. In a postindustrial society, only intellectuals can effectively voice the subtle but basic discontents that are most likely to threaten social stability. The upheavals in Prague and Paris were clearly foreshadowed in what Czech and French intellectuals have been saying for years.

In recent times, intellectuals—H. Stuart Hughes and sociologist J. P. Nettl, among others—have speculated that perhaps intellectuals would become obsolete in a bureaucratic-technological society. The usual argument has been that the intellectual is being increasingly forced to join some kind of large organization or to reject modern society as a whole without being able to propose an alternative. If he opts for the former, he loses his status as an intellectual; if for the latter, he becomes socially irrelevant. No doubt, there is something to this argument. Intellectuals cannot surrender their independence without ceasing to be intellectuals. But the political power they are beginning to assert provides significant assurance that they can maintain their independence if they wish to do so and if they will honor commitments to their own group interest. In economic terms, intellectuals are doing better than they have ever done before. In today's world, it is hard to see how they will become obsolete —unless, of course, success corrupts them and they cease to be social critics.

The enhanced political importance of intellectuals raises, of course, a key question. What *should be* the role of the intellectual in politics? Should he seek to move closer to the centers of power, so that he may exert his influence within and through these centers? Or should he maintain a neutral-to-hostile independence, the better to discharge his role as social critic and custodian of the nation's conscience? In point of fact, the real choice is no longer, if it ever was, this clear-cut. Precisely because of his new functional importance, the intellectual has become implicated in the processes by which power is applied and decisions are taken. He cannot, even if he would, stand wholly to one side—at least not for long. The university, for example, is a prime center of power in the new age; it is also an important base of power for intellectuals. Intellectuals cannot be "neutrals" on campus. Inescapably, they are involved in decisions affecting the administration of university affairs, the relationship of the university to government, and in faculty-student-administration as well as university-community relations. In much the same way, it would be shortsighted of intellectuals to assume that they can long remain neutral simply by refusing to serve the government; they can serve it or oppose it, but they can hardly ignore it. Society has a way of co-opting those whose services it needs and, in the long run, intellectuals will be increasingly caught up in the bigger action.

Under these circumstances, what intellectuals can and must do is, first, recognize that politically their prime task is to protect and advance the interests of intellectuals as intellectuals, such as preserving academic freedom, insisting on the free flow of information, opposing censorship, seeking to improve the quality and integrity of mass communications, furthering free inquiry, resisting attempts to manipulate or manage news, insisting on the free pursuit of truth in all fields, etc. These are the freedoms that intellectuals must have if they are to function as intellectuals; they are also freedoms of vital importance to society. If these group interests are brushed aside or stifled, intellectuals will find themselves prisoners of huge impersonal organizations of one kind or another, serving purposes they do not approve. Second, if individual intellectuals decide to play an active role politically or to accept government or other bureaucratic posts, they should do so with full awareness of the risks they have incurred. Not only should they have a clear-eyed awareness of the possibility that they will be "used" —for ends and purposes they do not approve—but they should be fully prepared at all times to step down whenever they feel that their integrity *as intellectuals* is threatened.

Obviously, this is a hard line to draw, the more so since power has its attractions and rewards. For this reason, intellectuals should be exceedingly wary about accepting such offers; ideally, they should serve government on a short-term or interim basis and should constantly remind themselves that they are, first of all, intellectuals and only secondarily, and temporarily, wielders of power.

Third, intellectuals must realize, as most of them do, that more important than their role as specialists—technician, scientist, scholar, etc.—is their role as guardians of the moral legitimacy of society's stated values and purposes. They should be endlessly concerned with goals, purposes, values. Postindustrial societies, with their complex bureaucratic structures, require constant scrutiny and criticism; such societies tend to be propelled in directions that are determined not by conscious choice but by a kind of technological determinism.

This social role of the intellectuals far transcends in importance whatever specialized contributions they may make as individuals. Granted that society cannot function without their specialized talents, the big questions—the increasingly important questions—remain: Function to what ends? In whose interests? For what purposes? At all costs, intellectuals must preserve their freedom to question the obsolete, restrictive, arbitrary arrangements—and policies and programs, as well—that develop wherever bureaucracies flourish. The intellectual is a generalist, a moralist, a questioner, a social critic. To this end, he must join with other intellectuals in defense—and in furtherance—of the interests of intellectuals as a group. These interests are not and can never be antithetical to the stated values of a democratic society; on the contrary, they guarantee the survival of these values. For if intellectuals fail to honor their responsibilities or misconceive them, society is quite capable of destroying itself or of finding its value system distorted beyond recognition.

KARL HESS

THE DEATH OF POLITICS

a polemicist who has been there and back castigates both the left and the right, and makes a persuasive case for a new libertarian ethic

This is not a time of radical, revolutionary politics. Not yet. Unrest, riot, dissent and chaos notwithstanding, today's politics is reactionary. Both right and left are reactionary and authoritarian. That is to say, both are political. They seek only to revise current methods of acquiring and wielding political power. Radical and revolutionary movements seek not to revise but to revoke. The target of revocation should be obvious. The target is politics itself.

Radicals and revolutionaries have had their sights trained on politics for some time. As governments fail around the world, as more millions become aware that government never has and never can humanely and effectively manage men's affairs, government's own inadequacy will emerge, at last, as the basis for a truly radical and revolutionary movement. In the meantime, the radical-revolutionary position is a lonely one. It is feared or hated, by both right and left—although both right and left must borrow from it to survive. The radical-revolutionary position is libertarianism and its socioeconomic form is laissez faire capitalism.

Libertarianism is the view that each man is the absolute owner of his life, to use and dispose of as he sees fit, that all man's social actions should be voluntary, and that respect for every other man's similar and equal ownership of life and, by extension, the property and fruits of that life, is the ethical basis of a humane and open society. In this view, the only—repeat, only—function of law or government is to provide the sort of self-defense against violence that an individual, if he were powerful enough, would provide for himself.

If it were not for the fact that libertarianism freely concedes the right of men voluntarily to form communities or governments on the same ethical basis, libertarianism could be called anarchy.

Laissez faire capitalism, or anarchocapitalism, is simply the economic form of the libertarian ethic. Laissez faire capitalism encompasses the notion that men should exchange goods and services, without regulation, solely on the basis of value for value. It recognizes charity and communal enterprises as voluntary versions of this same ethic. Such a system would be straight barter, except for the widely felt need for a division of labor in which men, voluntarily, accept value tokens such as cash and credit. Economically, this system is anarchy, and proudly so.

Libertarianism is rejected by the modern left—which preaches individualism but practices collectivism. Capitalism is rejected by the modern right—which preaches enterprise but practices protectionism. The libertarian faith in the mind of man is rejected by religionists who have faith only in the sins of man. The libertarian insistence that men be free to spin cables of steel as well as dreams of smoke is rejected by hippies who adore nature but spurn creation. The libertarian insistence that each man is a sovereign land of liberty, with his primary allegiance to himself, is rejected by patriots who sing of freedom but also shout of banners and boundaries. There is no operating political movement in the world today that is based upon a libertarian philosophy. If there were, it would be in the anomalous position of using political power to abolish political power.

Perhaps a regular political movement, overcoming this anomaly, will actually develop. Believe it or not, there were strong possibilities of such a development in the 1964 campaign of Barry Goldwater. Underneath the scary headlines, Goldwater hammered away at such purely political structures as the draft, general taxation, censorship, nationalism, legislated conformity, political establishment of social norms and war as an instrument of international policy.

It is true that, in a common political paradox, Goldwater (a major general in the Air Force Reserve) has spoken of reducing state power while at the same time advocating the increase of state power to fight the Cold War. He is not a pacifist. He believes that war remains an acceptable state action. He does not see the Cold War as involving U. S. imperialism. He sees it as a result only of Soviet imperialism. Time after time, however, he has said that economic pressure, diplomatic negotiation and the persuasions of propaganda (or "cultural warfare") are absolutely preferable to violence. He has also said that antagonistic ideologies can "never be beaten by bullets, but only by better ideas."

A defense of Goldwater cannot be carried too far, however. His domestic libertarian tendencies simply do not carry over into his view of foreign policy. Libertarianism, unalloyed, is absolutely isolationist, in that it is absolutely opposed to the institutions of national government that are the only agencies on earth now able to wage war or intervene in foreign affairs.

In other campaign issues, however, the libertarian coloration in the Goldwater complexion was more distinct. The fact that he roundly rapped the fiscal irresponsibility of Social Security before an elderly audience, and the fact that he criticized TVA while speaking in Tennessee, were not examples of political naïveté. They simply showed Goldwater's high disdain for politics itself, summed up in his campaign statement that people should be told "what they need to hear and not what they want to hear."

There was also some suggestion of libertarianism in the campaign of Eugene McCarthy, in his splendid attacks on Presidential power. However, these were canceled out by his vague but nevertheless perceptible defense of government power in general. There was virtually no suggestion of libertarianism in the statements of any other politicians during the 1968 campaign.

I was a speechwriter for Barry Goldwater in the 1964 campaign. During the campaign, I recall very clearly, there was a moment, at a conference to determine the campaign's "farm strategy," when a respected and very conservative senator arose to say, "Barry, you've got to make it clear that you believe that the American farmer has a right to a decent living."

Senator Goldwater replied, with the tact for which he is renowned, "But he doesn't have a right to it. Neither do I. We just have a right to try for it." And that was the end of that.

Now, in contrast, take Tom Hayden of the Students for a Democratic Society. Writing in *The Radical Papers,* he said that his "revolution" sought "institutions outside the established order." One of those institutions, he amplified, would be "people's own antipoverty organizations fighting for Federal money."

Of the two men, which is radical or revolutionary? Hayden says, in effect, that he simply wants to bulldoze his way into the establishment. Goldwater says he wants, in effect, to topple it, to forever end its power to advantage or disadvantage anyone.

This is not to defend the Goldwater Presidential campaign as libertarian. It is only to say that his campaign contained a healthy element of this sort of radicalism. But otherwise, the Goldwater campaign was very deeply in hock to regular partisan interests, images, myths and manners.

In foreign policy, particularly, there arises a great impediment to the emergence of a libertarian wing in either of the major political parties. Men who call upon the end of state authority in every other area insist upon its being maintained to build a war machine with which to hold the Communists at bay. It is only lately that the imperatives of logic—and the emergence of antistatist forces in eastern Europe—have begun to make it more acceptable to ask whether the garrison state needed to maintain the Cold War might not be as bad as or worse than the putative threat being guarded against. Goldwater has not taken and may never take such a revisionist line—but, among Cold Warriors, his disposition to libertarian principles makes him more susceptible than most.

This is not merely a digression on behalf of a political figure (almost an *anti*political figure) whom I profoundly respect. It is, rather, to emphasize the inadequacy of traditional, popular guidelines in assessing the reactionary nature of contemporary politics and in divining the true nature of radical and revolutionary antipolitics. Political parties and politicians today—all parties and all politicians—question only the forms through which they will express their common belief in controlling the lives of others. Power, particularly majoritarian or collective power (i.e., the power of an elite exercised in the name of the masses), is the god of the modern liberal. Its only recent innovative change is to suggest that the elite be leavened by the compulsory membership of authentic representatives of the masses. The current phrase is "participatory democracy."

Just as power is the god of the modern liberal, God remains the authority of the modern conservative. Liberalism practices regimentation by, simply, regimentation. Conservatism practices regimentation by, not quite so simply, revelation. But regimented or revealed, the name of the game is still politics.

The great flaw in conservatism is a deep fissure down which talk of freedom falls, to be dashed to death on the rocks of authoritarianism. Conservatives worry that the state has too much power over people. But it was conservatives who gave the state that power. It was conservatives, very similar to today's conservatives, who ceded to the state the power to produce not simply order in the community but *a certain kind of order*.

It was European conservatives who, apparently fearful of the openness of the Industrial Revolution (why, *anyone* could get rich!), struck the first blows at capitalism by encouraging and accepting laws that made the disruptions of innovation and competition less frequent and eased the way for the comforts and collusions of cartelization.

Big business in America today and for some years past has been openly at war with competition and, thus, at war with laissez faire capitalism. Big business supports a form of state capitalism in which government and big business act as partners. Criticism of this statist bent of big business comes more often from the left than from the right these days, and this is another factor making it difficult to tell the players apart. John Kenneth Galbraith, for instance, has taken big business to task for its anticompetitive mentality. The right, meantime, blissfully defends big business as though it had not, in fact, become just the sort of bureaucratic, authoritarian force that rightists reflexively attack when it is governmental.

The left's attack on corporate capitalism is, when examined, an attack on economic forms possible only in a collusion between authoritarian government and bureaucratized, nonentrepreneurial business. It is unfortunate that many New Leftists are so uncritical as to accept this premise as indicating that all forms of capitalism are bad, so that full state ownership is the only alternative. This thinking has its mirror image on the right.

It was American conservatives, for instance, who very early in the game gave up the fight against state franchising and regulation and, instead, embraced state regulation for their own special advantage. Conservatives today continue to revere the state as an instrument of chastisement even as they reject it as an instrument of beneficence. The conservative who wants a Federally authorized prayer in the classroom is the same conservative who objects to Federally authorized textbooks in the same room.

Murray Rothbard, writing in *Ramparts,* has summed up this flawed conservatism in describing a

> new, younger generation of rightists, of "conservatives" . . . who thought that the real problem of the modern world was nothing so ideological as the state *vs.* individual liberty or government intervention *vs.* the free market; the real problem, they declared, was the preservation of tradition, order, Christianity and good manners against the modern sins of reason, license, atheism and boorishness.

The reactionary tendencies of both liberals and conservatives today show clearly in their willingness to cede, to the state or the community, power far beyond the protection of liberty against violence. For differing purposes, both see the state as an instrument not protecting man's freedom but either instructing or restricting how that freedom is to be used.

Once the power of the community becomes in any sense normative, rather than merely protective, it is difficult to see where any lines may be drawn to limit further transgressions against individual freedom. In fact, the lines have not been drawn. They will never be drawn by political parties that argue merely the cost of programs or institutions founded on state power. Actually, the lines can be drawn only by a radical questioning of power itself, and by the libertarian vision that sees man as capable of moving on without the encumbering luggage of laws and politics that do not merely preserve man's right to his life but attempt, in addition, to tell him how to live it.

For many conservatives, the bad dream that haunts their lives and their political position (which many sum up as "law and order" these days) is one of riot. To my knowledge, there is no limit that conservatives would place upon the power of the state to suppress riots.

Even in a laissez faire society, of course, the right to self-defense would have to be assumed, and a place for self-defense on a community basis could be easily imagined. But community self-defense would always be exclusively defensive. Conservatives betray an easy willingness to believe that the state should also initiate certain *offensive* actions, in order to preclude trouble later on. "Getting tough" is the phrase most often used. It does not mean just getting tough on rioters. It means getting tough on entire ranges of attitudes: clipping long hair, rousting people from parks for carrying concealed guitars, stopping and questioning anyone who doesn't look like a member of the Jaycees, drafting all the ne'er-do-wells to straighten them up, ridding our theaters and bookstores of "filth" and, always and above all, putting "those" people in their place. To the conservative, all too often, the alternatives are social conformity or unthinkable chaos.

Even if these were the only alternatives—which they obviously aren't—there are many reasons for preferring chaos to conformity. Personally, I believe I would have a better chance of surviving—and certainly my values would have a better chance of surviving—with a Watts, Chicago, Detroit or Washington in flames than with an entire nation snug in a garrison.

Riots in modern America must be broken down into component parts. They are not all simple looting and violence against life and property. They are also directed against the prevailing violence of the state—the sort of ongoing civic violence that permits regular police supervision of everyday life in some neighborhoods, the rules and regulations that inhibit absolutely free trading, the public schools that serve the visions of bureaucracy rather than the varieties of individual people. There is violence also by those who simply want to shoot their way into political power otherwise denied them. Conservatives seem to think that greater state police power is the answer. Liberals seem to think that more preferential state welfare power is the answer. Power, power, power.

Except for ordinary looters—for whom the answer must be to stop them as you would any other thief—the real answer to rioting must lie elsewhere. It must lie in the abandonment, not the extension, of state power—state power that oppresses people, state power that tempts people. To cite one strong example:

The white stores in many black neighborhoods, which are said to cause such dissatisfaction and envy, have a special, unrealized advantage thanks to state power. In a very poor neighborhood there may be many with the natural ability to open a retail store, but it is much less likely that these people would also have the ability to meet all the state and city regulations, governing everything from cleanliness to bookkeeping, which very often comprise the marginal difference between going into business or staying out. In a real laissez faire society, the local entrepreneur, with whom the neighbors might prefer to deal, could go openly into business—selling marijuana, whiskey, numbers slips, books, food or medical advice from the trunk of his car. He could forget about ledgers, forms and reports and simply get on with the business of business, rather than the business of bureaucracy. Allowing ghetto dwellers to compete on their own terms, rather than on someone else's, should prove a more satisfying and practical solution to ghetto problems than either rampages or restrictions.

The libertarian thrusts away from power and authority that marked the Goldwater campaign were castigated from the left as being "nostalgic yearnings for a simpler world." (Perhaps akin to the simplistic yearnings of the hippies whom the left so easily tolerates even while it excoriates Goldwater.) Goldwater's libertarianism was castigated from the right—he received virtually *no* support from big business—as representing policies that could lead to unregulated competition, international free trade and, even worse, a weakening of the very special partnership that big business now enjoys with Big Government.

The most incredible convolution in the thinking that attacked Goldwater as reactionary, which he isn't, rather than radical, which he is, came in regard to nuclear weapons. In that area he was specifically damned for daring to propose that the control of these weapons be shared, and even fully placed, in the multinational command of the North Atlantic Treaty Organization, rather than left to the personal, one-man discretion of the President of the United States.

Again, who is reactionary and who is radical? The men who want an atomic king enthroned in Washington, or the man who dares ask that that divine right of destruction become less divine and more divided? Until recently, it was a popular cocktail pastime to speculate on the difference between the war in Vietnam under "Save-the-world-from-Goldwater" Johnson, or as it might have been under wild Barry, who, by his every campaign utterance, would have been bound to share the Vietnam decision (and the fighting) with NATO, rather than simply and unilaterally going it alone.

To return to the point, the most vital question today about politics—not *in* politics—is the same sort of question that is plaguing Christianity. Superficially, the Christian question seems simply what kind of religion should be chosen. But basically, the question is whether any irrational or mystical forces are supportable, as a way to order society, in a world increasingly able and ready to be rational. The political version of the question may be stated this way: Will men continue to submit to rule by politics, which has always meant the power of some men over other men, or are we ready to go it alone socially, in communities of voluntarism, in a world more economic and cultural than political, just as so many now are prepared to go it alone metaphysically in a world more of reason than religion?

The radical and revolutionary answer that a libertarian, laissez faire position makes to that question is not quite anarchy. The libertarian, laissez faire movement is, actually, if embarrassingly for some, a civil-rights movement. But it is antipolitical, in that it builds diversified power to be protected against government, even to dispense with government to a major degree, rather than seeking power to protect government or to perform any special social purpose.

It is a civil-liberties movement in that it seeks civil liberties, for everyone, as defined in the nineteenth century by one of Yale's first professors of political and social science, William Graham Sumner. Sumner said, "Civil liberty is the status of the man who is guaranteed by law and civil institutions the exclusive employment of all his own powers for his own welfare."

Modern liberals, of course, would call this selfishness, and they would be correct, with intense emphasis on self. Many modern conservatives would say that they agree with Sumner, but they would not be correct. Men who call themselves conservatives, but who operate in the larger industries, spend considerable time, and not a small amount of money, fighting government subsidies to labor unions (in the form of preferential tax and legal considerations) or to people (in the form of welfare programs). They do not fight *direct* subsidies to industries—such as transportation, farming or universities. They do not, in short, believe that men are entitled to the exclusive employment of their own powers for their own welfare, because they accept the practice of taxing a good part of that power to use for the welfare of other people.

As noted, for all the theoretical screaming that sometimes may be heard from the industrial right, it is safe to say that the major powers of government to regulate industry were derived not only from the support of businessmen but actually at the insistence of businessmen. Uneconomical mail rates are cherished by businessmen who can profit from them and who, significantly, seem uninterested in the obvious possibility of transforming the postal service from a bureau into a business.

As a business, of course, it would charge what it costs to mail things, not what is simply convenient for users to pay.

The big businessmen who operate the major broadcast networks are not known for suggesting, as a laissez faire concept would insist, that competition for channels and audiences be wide open and unregulated. As a consequence, of course, the networks get all the government control that they deserve, accepting it in good cheer because, even if censored, they are also protected from competition. It is notable, also, that one of the most fierce denunciations of pay TV (which, under capitalism, should be a conceptual commonplace) came not from the *Daily Worker* but from the *Reader's Digest,* that supposed bastion of conservatism. Actually, I think the *Digest* is such a bastion. It seems to believe that the state is an institution divinely ordained to make men moral—in a "Judaeo-Christian" sense, of course. It abhors, as does no publication short of William Buckley's *National Review,* the insolence of those untidy persons who today so regularly challenge the authority of the state.

In short, there is no evidence whatever that modern conservatives subscribe to the "your life is your own" philosophy upon which libertarianism is founded. An interesting illustration that conservatism not only disagrees with libertarianism but is downright hostile to it is that the most widely known libertarian author of the day, Miss Ayn Rand, ranks only a bit below, or slightly to the side of, Leonid Brezhnev as an object of diatribe in *National Review.* Specifically, it seems, she is reviled on the right because she is an atheist, daring to take exception to the *National Review* notion that man's basically evil nature (stemming from original sin) means he must be held in check by a strong and authoritarian social order.

Barry Goldwater, during his 1964 campaign, repeatedly said that "the government strong enough to give you what you want is strong enough to take it all away." Conservatives, as a group, have forgotten, or prefer to ignore, that this applies also to government's strength to impose social order. If government can enforce social norms, or even Christian behavior, it can also take away or twist them.

To repeat, conservatives yearn for a state, or "leadership," with the power to restore order and to put things—and people—back in their places. They yearn for political power. Liberals yearn for a state that will bomb the rich and balm the poor. They, too, yearn for political power. Libertarians yearn for a state that cannot, beyond any possibility of amendment, confer any advantage on anyone, a state that cannot compel anything, but simply prevents the use of violence, in place of other exchanges, in relations between individuals or groups.

Such a state would have as its sole purpose (probably supported exclusively by use taxes or fees) the maintenance of a system to adjudicate disputes (courts), to protect citizens against violence (police), to maintain some form of currency for ease of commerce, and, as long as it might be needed because of the existence of national borders and differences, to maintain a defense force. Meanwhile, libertarians should also work to end the whole concept of the nation-state itself. The major point here is that libertarians would start with no outstanding predispositions about public functions, being disposed always to think that there is in the personal and private world of individuals someone who can or will come along with a solution that gets the job done without conferring upon anyone power that has not been earned through voluntary exchange.

In fact, it is in the matters most appropriate to collective interest—such as courts and protection against violence—that government today often defaults. This follows the bureaucratic tendency to perform least needed services—where the risk of accountability is minimal—and to avoid performing essential but highly accountable services. Courts are clogged beyond belief. Police, rather than simply protecting citizens against violence, are deeply involved in overseeing private morals. In black neighborhoods particularly, the police serve as unloved and unwanted arbiters of everyday life.

If, in the past few paragraphs, the reader can detect any hint of a position that would be compatible with either the Communist Party of the Soviet Union or the National Association of Manufacturers, he is strongly advised to look again. No such common ground exists. Nor can any common ground be adduced in terms of "new politics" versus "old politics." New or old, the positions that parade today under these titles are still politics and, like roses, they smell alike. Radical and revolutionary politicians—antipoliticians, if you will—should be able to sniff them out easily.

Specific matters that illustrate the differences would include the draft, marijuana, monopoly, censorship, isolationism-internationalism, race relations and urban affairs, to name a few.

As part of his aborted campaign for the Presidency, Nelson Rockefeller took a position on the draft. In it, he specifically took exception to Richard Nixon's draft stand, calling it the "old politics" as contrasted with his own "new politics." The Rockefeller position involved a certain streamlining of the draft, but nothing that would change it from what it patently is—forced, involuntary servitude. Rockefeller criticized Nixon for having asserted that, someday, the draft could be replaced by a voluntary system, an old Republican promise.

The new politician contended that the Nixon system wouldn't work because it never *had* worked. The fact that this nation has never offered to pay its soldiers at a rate realistic enough to attract them was not covered in Rockefeller's statement. Nor did the new politician address himself to the fact that, given a nation that not enough citizens can be attracted to defend voluntarily, you probably also have a nation that, by definition, isn't really worth defending.

The old politician, on the other hand, did not present quite as crisp a position on the draft as the new politician tried to pin him with. Nixon, although theoretically in favor of a voluntary military, was—along with the presumably even *more* conservative Ronald Reagan—opposed to trying voluntarism until *after* the Vietnam war. Throughout the conservative stance one sees a repetition of this position. Freedom is fine—but it must be deferred as long as a hot war or the Cold War has to be fought.

All should be struck by the implications of that baleful notion. It implies that free men simply cannot be ingenious enough to defend themselves against violence without themselves becoming violent—not toward the enemy alone, but to their own persons and liberty as well. If our freedom is so fragile that it must be continuously protected by giving it up, then we are in deep trouble. And, in fact, by following a somewhat similar course, we got ourselves in very deep trouble in Southeast Asia. The Johnson war there was escalated precisely on the belief that southern Vietnamese freedom may best be obtained by dictating what form of government the south should have—day by day, even—and by defending it against the North Vietnamese by devastating the southern countryside.

In foreign relations, as in domestic pronouncements, new and old politicians preach the same dusty doctrines of compulsion and contradiction. The radical preachment of libertarianism, the antipolitical preachment, would be that as long as the inanity of war between nation-states remains a possibility, free nation-states will at least protect themselves from wars by hiring volunteers, not by murdering voluntarism.

One of the most medievally fascinating minds of the twentieth century, that of Lewis Hershey, until recently sole owner and proprietor of the Selective Service System, has put this unpretty picture into perfect perspective with his memorable statement, delivered at a National Press Club luncheon, that he "hate[s] to think of the day that [his] grandchildren would be defended by volunteers." There, in as ugly an example as is on public record, is precisely where politics and power, authority and the arthritis of traditionalism are bound to bring you. Former Director Hershey is prevented from being a great comic figure by the rather obvious fact that, being involved with the deaths of so many unwilling men, and the imprisonment of so many others, he becomes a tragic figure or, at least, a figure in a tragedy. There is no new or old politics about the draft. A draft is political, plain and simple. A volunteer military is essentially commercial. And it is between politics and commerce that the entrant into radical or revolutionary politics must continually choose.

Marijuana is an example of such a choice. In a laissez faire society, there could exist no public institution with the power to forcefully protect people from themselves. From other people (criminals), yes. From one's own self, no. Marijuana is a plant, a crop. People who smoke it do not do so under the compulsion either of physiological addiction or of institutionalized power. They do so voluntarily. They find a person who has volunteered to grow it. They agree on a price. One sells; the other buys. One acquires new capital; the other acquires a euphoric experience that, he decides, was worth allocating some of his own resources to obtain.

Nowhere in that equation is there a single point at which the neighbors, or any multitude of neighbors, posing as priesthood or public, have the slightest rational reason to intervene. The action has not, in any way, deprived anyone else of "the exclusive employment of all his own powers for his own welfare."

The current laws against marijuana, in contravention even of all available medical evidence regarding its nature, are a prime example of the use of political power. The very power that makes it possible for the state to ban marijuana, and to arrest Lenny Bruce, is the same power that makes it possible for the state to exact taxes from one man to pay into the pockets of another. The purposes may seem different, but upon examination they are not. Marijuana must be banned to prevent people from succumbing to the madness of its fumes and doing some mischief upon the community. Poverty, too, must be banned for a similar reason. Poor people, unless *made* unpoor, will angrily rise and do mischief upon the community. As in all politics, purposes and power blend and reinforce each other.

"Hard" narcotics must be subjected to the same tests as marijuana in terms of politics versus antipolitics. These narcotics, too, are merely salable materials except that, if used beyond prudence, they can be quite disabling to the person using them. (I inject that note simply because, in my understanding, there remains at all levels of addiction the chance of breaking or controlling the habit. This suggests that a person *can* exercise a choice in the matter, that he can, indeed, be prudent or not.)

The person who uses drugs imprudently, just as the person who imprudently uses the politically sanctioned and franchised drugs of alcohol or tobacco, ends up in an unenviable position, perhaps dead. That, rationally, is his own business as long as he does not, by his actions, deprive you of the right to make your own decision not to use drugs, to assist addicts or, if you wish, to ignore them. But it is said, by right and left today, that the real problem is social and public—that the high price of the drugs leads the addict to rob and kill (rightist position), and that making drugs a public matter, for clinical dispensation, would eliminate the causes of his crime (leftist position).

These both are essentially political positions and clearly inept in a society where the line between mind expanders such as coffee or LSD is highly technical. By choosing the economic and cultural approach rather than a political one, the anti-political libertarian would say, sell away. Competition will keep the price down. Cultural acceptance of the root ethic, that a man's life and its appurtenances are inviolate, would justify defense against any violence that might accompany addiction in others. And what is there left for the "public" to do? Absolutely nothing—except, individually, to decide whether to risk drugs or to avoid them. Parents, of course, holding the purse strings of their children, can exercise a certain amount of control, but only individually, never collectively.

Incidentally, it is easy to imagine that, if drugs were left to economics and culture instead of politics, medical researchers would shortly discover a way to provide the salable and wanted effects of drugs without the incapacitation of addiction. In this as in similar matters—such as the unregulated competition from which it is felt people need protection—technology rather than politics might offer far better answers.

Monopoly is a case in point. To suppose that anyone needs government protection from the creation of monopolies is to accept two suppositions: that monopoly is the natural direction of unregulated enterprise, and that technology is static. Neither, of course, is true. The great concentrations of economic power, which are called monopolies today, did not grow *despite* government's antimonopolistic zeal. They grew, largely, *because* of government policies, such as those making it more profitable for small businesses to sell out to big companies rather than fight the tax code alone. Additionally, Federal fiscal and credit policies and Federal subsidies and contracts have all provided substantially more assistance to big and established companies than to smaller, potentially competitive ones. The auto industry receives the biggest subsidy of all through the highway program on which it prospers, but for which it surely does not pay a fair share. Airlines are subsidized and so protected that newcomers can't even try to compete. Television networks are fantastically advantaged by FCC licensing, which prevents upstarts from entering a field where big old-timers have been established. Even in agriculture, it is large and established farmers who get the big subsidies—not small ones who might want to compete. Government laws specifically exempting unions from antitrust activities have also furthered a monopoly mentality. And, of course, the "public utility" and "public transportation" concepts have specifically created government-licensed monopolies in the fields of power, communications and transit. This is not to say that economic bigness is bad. It isn't if it results from economic efficiency. But it *is* bad if it results from collusion with political, rather than with economic, power. There is no monopoly situation in the world today, of which I can think, that might not be seriously challenged by competition, were it not for some form of protective government license, tariff, subsidy or regulation. Also, there isn't the tiniest shred of evidence to suggest that the trend of unregulated business and industry is toward monopoly. In fact, the trend seems in the opposite direction, toward diversification and decentralization.

The technological aspect is equally important. Monopoly cannot develop as long as technology is dynamic, which it most abundantly is today. No corporation is so large that it can command every available brain—except, of course, a corporate state. As long as one brain remains unavailable, there is the chance of innovation and competition. There can be no real monopoly, just momentary advantage. Nor does technological breakthrough always depend upon vast resources or, even where it does, would it have to depend upon a single source of financing—unless, again, only the state has the money. Short of total state control, and presuming creative brains in the community, and presuming the existence of capital with which to build even modest research facilities, few would flatly say that technological innovation could be prevented simply because of some single source enjoying a temporary "monopoly" of a given product or service. The exceptions, to repeat, are always governments. Governments can be—and usually are—monopolistic. For instance, it is not uneconomical to operate a private post-office department today. It is only illegal. The Feds enjoy a legal monopoly—to the extent that they are currently prosecuting at least one entrepreneur who operated a mail service better and cheaper than they do.

Politics is not needed to prevent monopoly. Unregulated, unrestricted laissez faire capitalism is all that is needed. It would also provide jobs, raise living standards, improve products, and so forth. If commercial activity were unregulated and absolutely unsubsidized, it could depend upon only one factor for success—pleasing customers.

Censorship is another notable example in which politics, and politicians, interpose between customer and satisfaction. The gauge becomes not whether the customer is happy, but whether the politician (either singly or as a surrogate for "the public") is happy. This applies equally to "public" protection from unpopular political ideas as well as protection from pornography. Conservatives are at least consistent in this matter. They feel that the state (which they sometimes call "the community") can and must protect people from unsavory thoughts. It goes without saying who defines unsavory: the political—or community—leaders, of course.

Perhaps the most ironic of all manifestations of this conservative urge to cleanthink concerns the late Lenny Bruce. He talked dirty. He was, therefore, a particularly favorite target of conservatives. He was also an explicit and, I think, incisive defender of capitalism. In commenting that communism is a drag ("like one big phone company"), Bruce specifically opted for capitalism ("it gives you a choice, baby, and that's what it's about"). There is no traditional conservative who is fit to even walk on the same level with Lenny Bruce in his fierce devotion to individualism. Lenny Bruce frequently used what is for many conservatives the dirtiest word of all: He said capitalism. When was the last time that the NAM did as much?

Lenny Bruce wasn't the only man to alienate conservatives by opening his mouth. In 1964, Barry Goldwater alienated Southern conservatives in droves when, in answer to a regionally hot question about whether Communists should be permitted to speak on state-university campuses, Goldwater said, flatly and simply, "Of course they should."

Even anti-Communist libertarians have no choice but to deny the state the right to suppress Communists. Similarly, libertarians who are aesthetically repelled by what they deem pornography have no other course than not to buy it, leaving its absolutely unregulated sale to producer, purchaser and no one else. Once again, a parent could intrude—but only by stopping an individual, dependent purchaser, never by stopping the purveyor, whose right to sell pornography for profit, and for absolutely no other socially redeeming virtue whatever, would be inviolate. An irate parent who attempted to hustle a smut peddler off the street, as a matter of fact, should be sued, not saluted.

The liberal attitude toward censorship is not so clear. At this point, it needn't be. Liberals practice it rather than preach it. The FCC's egregious power to insist that broadcasting serve a social purpose is both a liberal tenet and an act of censorship. In the FCC canons, social purposes are defined so that a station can get good points for permitting a preacher free time but no points —or even bad points—for extending the same gift of free air to an atheist.

It is partly in the realm of air, also, that differences regarding nationalism between the old left/right politicians and the libertarian antipolitician show up. If today's conservative has his fervent jingoism for old nations, the liberal has just as fanatic a devotion to the jingoism of new nations. The willingness of modern liberals to suggest armed intervention against South Africa, while ignoring, even in terms of major journalistic coverage, slaughters in Nigeria and the Sudan, is a demonstration of interest only in politics—and in particular persons—rather than in human life per se.

Of course, conservatives have a similar double standard in regard to anti-Communist slaughter and anti-Communist dictatorship. Although it is not as whimsically selective as the liberal decision to be revolted or cheered by each particular bloodbath, the conservative double standard can have equally tragic results. The distinct undercurrents of anti-Semitism that so obviously muddle many conservative movements probably can be traced to the horrid assumption that Adolf Hitler's anticommunism excused his other, but comparatively minor, faults. Somehow, anticommunism seems to permit anti-Semitism.

I have met in my time many anti-Communists who view communism as simply a creature of Jewish plotting for world dominion. The John Birch Society's separate chapter for Jewish members is a seriocomic reflection, I think, of such good old WASP anti-Semitism. The widely reported admiration of Hitler by the head man of the right-wing Liberty Lobby is a reflection, presumably, of the "you need a strong man to fight atheistic communism" school of thought. There are, of course, notable Jewish anti-Communists. And there are many anti-Communists who condemn anti-Semitism. But the operating question for most of the full-time anti-Communists that I have met is simply Are you anti-Communist? Being also anti-Semitic is not automatically a disqualification on the right, though it usually is on the left.

Conservatives and liberals alike hold in common the mystical notion that nations really mean something, probably something permanent. Both ascribe to lines drawn on maps—or in the dirt or in the air—the magical creation of communities of men that require sovereignty and sanction. The conservative feels this with exaltation when he beholds the Stars and Stripes. The liberal feels this with academic certitude when he concludes that Soviet boundaries must be "guaranteed" to prevent Soviet nervousness. Today, in the ultimate confusion, there are people who feel that the lines drawn by the Soviet Union, in blood, are better than the lines drawn, also in blood, by American foreign policy. Politicians just think this way.

The radical and revolutionary view of the future of nationhood is, logically, that it has no future, only a past—often an exciting one, and usually a historically useful one at some stage. But lines drawn on paper, on the ground or in the stratosphere are clearly insufficient to the future of mankind.

Again, it is technology that makes it feasible to contemplate a day in which the politics of nationhood will be as dead as the politics of power-wielding partisanship. First, there is enough information and wealth available to ensure the feeding of all people, without the slaughtering of some to get at the possessions of others. Second, there is no longer any way to protect anything or anybody behind a national boundary, anyway.

Not even the Soviet Union, with what conservatives continue to fear as an "absolute" control over its people, has been able to stop, by drawing lines or executing thousands, the infusion of subversive ideas, manners, music, poems, dances, products, desires. If the world's pre-eminent police state (either us or them, depending upon your *political* point of view) has been unable to protect itself fully behind its boundaries, what faith can or should we, the people, retain in boundaries?

It is to be expected that both liberals and conservatives respond to the notion of the end of nationhood with very similar shouts of outrage or jerks of reaction. The conservative says *it shall not be*. There will always be a U. S. Customs Inspector and long may he wave. The liberal says that far from ending nationhood, he wants to expand it, make it world-wide, to create a proliferation of mini- and micronations in the name of ethnic and cultural preservation, and then to erect a great superbureaucracy to supervise all the petty bureaucracies.

Like Linus, neither liberal nor conservative can bear the thought of giving up the blanket—of giving up government and going it alone as residents of a planet, rather than of a country. Advocates of isolationism (although some, admittedly, defend it only as a tactic) seem to fall into a paradox here. Isolationism not only depends upon nationhood; it rigidifies it. There is a subcategory of isolationism, however, that might avoid this by specifying that it favors only military isolationism, or the use of force only for *self*-defense. Even this, however, requires political definitions of national self-defense in these days of missiles, bases, bombers and subversion.

As long as there are governments powerful enough to maintain national boundaries and national political postures, then there will be the absolute risk, if not the certainty, of war between them. Even the possibility of war seems far too cataclysmic to contemplate in a world so ripe with technology and prosperous potential, ripe even with the seeds of extraterrestrial exploration. Violence and the institutions that alone can support it should be rendered obsolete.

Governments wage war. The power of life that they may claim in running hospitals or feeding the poor is just the mirror image of the power of death that they also claim—in filling those hospitals with wounded and in devastating lands on which food could be grown. "But man is aggressive," right and left chant from the depths of their pessimism. And, to be sure, he is. But if he were left alone, if he were not regulated into states or services, wouldn't that aggression be directed toward conquering his environment, and not other men?

At another warlike level, it is the choice of aggression, against politically perpetuated environment more than against men, that marks the racial strife in America today. Conservatives, in one of their favorite lapses of logic—States' rights—nourished modern American racism by supporting laws, particularly in Southern states, that gave the state the power to force businessmen to build segregated facilities. (Many businessmen, to be sure, wanted to be "forced," thus giving their racism the seal of state approval.) The States' rights lapse is simply that conservatives who would deny to the Federal government certain controls over people, eagerly cede exactly the same controls to smaller administrative units. They say that the smaller units are more effective. This means that conservatives support the coercion of individuals at the most effective level. It certainly doesn't mean that they oppose coercion. In failing to resist state segregation and miscegenation laws, in failing to resist laws maintaining racially inequitable spending of tax money, simply because these laws were passed by states, conservatives have failed to fight the very bureaucracy that they supposedly hate—at the very level where they might have stopped it first.

Racism has been supported in this country not despite of, but thanks to, governmental power and politics. Reverse racism, thinking that government is competent to force people to integrate, just as it once forced them to segregate, is just as political and just as disastrous. It has not worked. Its product has been hatred rather than brotherhood. Brotherhood could never be a political product. It is purely personal. In racial matters, as in all other matters concerning individuals, the lack of government would be nothing but beneficial. What, actually, can government do for black people in America that black people could not do better for themselves, if they were permitted the freedom to do so? I can think of nothing.

Jobs? Politically and governmentally franchised unions do more to keep black men from good jobs than do all the Bull Connors of the South. Homes, schools and protection? I recall very vividly a comment on this subject by Roy Innis, the national director of the Congress of Racial Equality. He spoke of Mayor John Lindsay's typically liberal zeal in giving money to black people, smothering them with it—or silencing them. Innis then said that the one thing Mayor Lindsay would not give the blacks was what they really wanted: political power. He meant that the black community in Harlem, for instance, rather than being gifted with tax money by the bushel, would prefer to be gifted with Harlem itself. It is a community. Why shouldn't it govern itself, or at least live by itself, without having to be a barony of New York City ward politics? However, I take exception to the notion of merely building in Harlem a political structure similar to but only separate from New York City's. And I may be doing Mr. Innis, who is an exceptional man, an injustice by even suggesting that that is what he had in mind.

But beyond this one instance, there is implicit in the very exciting undercurrents of black power in this country an equally exciting possibility that it will develop into a rebellion against politics itself. It might insist upon a far less structured community, containing far more voluntary institutions within it. There is no question in my mind that, in the long run, this movement and similar ones will discover that laissez faire is the way to create genuine communities of voluntarism. Laissez faire is the only form of social/economic organization that could tolerate and even bless a *kibbutz* operating in the middle of Harlem, a hippie selling hashish down the street and, a few blocks farther on, a firm of engineers out to do in Detroit with a low-cost nuclear vehicle.

The *kibbutz* would represent, in effect, a voluntary socialism —what other form could free men tolerate? The hash seller would represent institutionalized—but voluntary—daydreaming, and the engineers would represent unregulated creativity. All would represent laissez faire capitalism in action and none would need a political officeholder or a single bureaucrat to help, hinder, civilize or stimulate. And, in the process simply of variegated existence, the residents of this voluntary community, as long as others voluntarily entered into commerce with them, would solve the "urban" problem in the only way it ever can be solved, i.e., via the vanishment of politics that created the problem in the first place.

If cities cannot exist on the basis of the skills, energy and creativity of the people who live, work or invest in them, then they should not be sustained by people who do *not* live in them. In short, every community should be one of voluntarism, to the extent that it lives for and through its own people and does not force others to pay its bills. Communities should not be exempted from the civil liberty prescribed for people—the exclusive employment of all their own powers for their own welfare. This means that no one should serve you involuntarily and that you should not involuntarily serve anyone else. This means, for communities, existing without involuntary aid from other communities or to other communities.

Student dissenters today seem to feel that somehow they have crashed through to new truths and new politics in their demands that universities and communities be made responsive to their students or inhabitants. But most of them are only playing with old politics. When the dissenters recognize this, and when their assault becomes one against political power and authority rather than a fight to gain such power, then this movement may release the bright potential latent in the intelligence of so many of its participants. Incidentally, to the extent that student activists the world over are actually fighting the existence of political power, rather than trying to grab some of it for themselves, they should not be criticized for failing to offer alternative programs, i.e., for not spelling out just what sort of political system will follow their revolution. What ought to follow their revolution is just what they've implicitly proposed: no political system at all.

The style of SDS so far seems most promising in this respect. It is itself loosely knit and internally antiauthoritarian as well as externally revolutionary. Liberty also looks for students who rather than caterwauling the establishment will abandon it, establish their own schools, make them effective and wage a concerned and concerted revolt against the political regulations and power that, today, give a franchise to schools—public and private—that badly need competition from new schools with new ideas.

Looking back, this same sort of thinking was true during the period of the sit-ins in the South. Since the enemy also was state laws requiring separate facilities, why wasn't it also a proper tactic to defy such laws by building a desegregated eating place and holding it against hell and high water? This is a cause to which any libertarian could respond.

Similarly with the school situation. Find someone who will rebel against public-education laws and you will have a worthy rebel indeed. Find someone who just rants in favor of getting more liberals, or more conservatives, onto the school board, and you will have found a politically oriented, passé man—a plastic rebel. Or, in the blackest neighborhood, find the plumber who will thumb his nose at city hall's restrictive licenses and certificates and you will have found a freedom fighter of far greater consequence than the window breaker.

Power and authority, as substitutes for performance and rational thought, are the specters that haunt the world today. They are the ghosts of awed and superstitious yesterdays. And politics is their familiar. Politics, throughout time, has been an institutionalized denial of man's ability to survive through the exclusive employment of all his own powers for his own welfare. And politics, throughout time, has existed solely through the resources that it has been able to plunder from the creative and productive people whom it has, in the name of many causes and moralities, denied the exclusive employment of all their own powers for their own welfare.

Ultimately, this must mean that politics denies the rational nature of man. Ultimately, it means that politics is just another form of residual magic in our culture—a belief that somehow things come from nothing, that things may be given to some without first taking them from others, that all the tools of man's survival are his by accident or divine right and not by pure and simple inventiveness and work.

Politics has always been the institutionalized and established way in which some men have exercised the power to live off the output of other men. But even in a world made docile to these demands, men do not need to live by devouring other men.

Politics does devour men. A laissez faire world would liberate men. And it is in that sort of liberation that the most profound revolution of all may be just beginning to stir. It will not happen overnight, just as the lamps of rationalism were not quickly lighted and have not yet burned brightly. But it will happen—because it must happen. Man can survive in an inclement universe only through the use of his mind. His thumbs, his nails, his muscles and his mysticism will not be enough to keep him alive without it.

"Son, why don't you bring some of the New Left home for Cokes and cookies?"

GERALD GREEN

fiction

the dispatcher

a take-over of this country by the bungling mace project? absurd, they'd said, after the first ludicrous attempts— but later events proved it all too possible

I could swear that my secretary, Miss Minihan, addressed my boss as *Colonel* Carter this morning. And did I hear him say to her, "Thank you, *Corporal?*" Having just assumed my new job as quality-control manager, I don't wish to seem too inquisitive.

Our firm is only indirectly involved in defense work, which makes me even more puzzled. Yesterday, for example, I overheard a conversation between two elderly mechanics in the shop. It went:

"Old man's on the warpath again."

"Eatin' ass like it was steak."

"You know how it is. With the I.G. on his back."

"They don't frighten me. Goddamn brass. They'd strangle in their own snot if it wasn't for us."

At first I assumed the conversation was some kind of shop jargon. But now I am not so certain. What further disturbed me was that shortly after this conversation, Mr. Carter came to the assembly line to talk to these men. I could not hear the conversation, but a peculiar stiffness in the attitudes of the mechanics, a movement of their right arms, was evident.

Later I passed Carter in the corridor. He nodded at me and I suddenly felt my right arm moving toward my right temple, fingers extended and joined.

Carter smiled. "Go ahead, Dugan," he said. "It's all right, if you want to, even though we don't insist on it."

I pulled my arm back to my side, feeling embarrassed and confused, and I hurried to my office. Miss Minihan had a batch of invoices for me to check. I went about my work, trying to make some sense out of the strange work habits here. In the midst of the invoices, I saw a sheet of legal-size paper, headed:

TABLE OF ORGANIZATION
UNITED APERTURES, INC.

I called my secretary. "Miss Minihan, what is this?" I asked.

"Oh, that. The administrative chart."

"But it says *Table of Organization*. That is an Army expression. It is referred to as a T/O, and that's exactly what this paper is."

"Golly, I never thought of it that way." She giggled.

When she left, I searched for my name. I was listed under *Headquarters and Headquarters Company* with the rank of first lieutenant.

Dazed, I wandered about the plant for a few minutes and entered a half-hidden men's room on a fire-stair landing. As I approached the urinal, a sign over it greeted me:

PLEASE DO NOT THROW CIGAR BUTTS
IN HERE
IT MAKES THEM SOGGY AND
HARD TO LIGHT

I knew at once that I was involved in neither a joke nor a dream nor a corporate fancy. They had gotten me back in.

My present circumstances recall a series of curious incidents in which I was involved some years ago, beginning with the appearance of the *dispatcher* at my home.

After my discharge from military service, I was living with my parents in an old Spanish-style house in West Los Angeles. I had spent four years in the Army, including overseas duty, and was discharged with the rank of sergeant. Now I had returned to my studies in business administration at the University of California at Los Angeles. I note here that I was never a perpetual griper or a guardhouse lawyer. While I was not delighted with serving in the Army, I accepted it as a duty.

One spring morning, I was unable to locate the keys of the old Ford I drove to classes. We were a family of comfortable means and had three cars: my old Ford, a new Mercury driven by my father, an accountant for one of the film studios, and my mother's Nash. (We did not think ourselves in any way unusual, because there was virtually no public transportation to be had.) Having searched the house and the car for the keys, I went to the small room above our garage to look for them.

As I opened the screen door, I saw a man sleeping on the day bed. He was in an Army uniform. An overstuffed duffel bag was on the floor alongside him. On it was stenciled:

ESPOSITO SALVATORE ASN 32694853

My assumption was that he had been hitchhiking in the area (men were still being discharged and transferred) and he had wandered in to catch a night's sleep. I shook him firmly but gently.

"OK, Mac, let's hit it," I said. "Grab your socks."

The sleeper stirred. His eyes opened and he studied me irritably. "Jesus, I just got to sleep." He muttered something about "doing a frigging day's work without sleep," yawned enormously and sat up in bed. As he scratched himself, stretched and broke wind, I studied him.

Esposito was a squat, dark man in his early twenties. His features were blunt—the eyes hooded and suspicious, the mouth pouting. Black stubble covered his chin; he needed a haircut.

"Get a good night's sleep?" I asked.

"Lousy. Couldn' find da mess hall. You da CQ?"

"You're a little confused, soldier. This is a *private* house. I don't mind you catching some shut-eye, but don't you think you should have asked first?"

Esposito got up and stretched. His o.d. shirt came loose from his o.d. trousers. An o.d. undershirt peeked through the gap. "Ain't no terlet paper in da latrine. And dere better be a PX around or I'll raise hell. I may be oney a lousy corporal but I got rights."

Was he unbalanced? Some poor dope ready for a Section Eight discharge? I decided to be firm. "Esposito, you'd better get out of here. My father's got a bad temper and he won't like the idea. I'm a former enlisted man myself, so I don't mind. But you'd better clear out."

"I ain't goin' nowhere. I been *transferred* here."

"That's impossible. A soldier can't be transferred to a private home."

"Ya'll shit, too, if y'eat reg'lar."

With that, he dragged the duffel bag to the bed, undid the cord and groped in its guts. Out came a wool-knit cap, half of a messtin, a cardboard stationery folder and some dirty socks. Then he located a single wrinkled sheet of mimeographed paper, which he thrust at me. "Dat's your copy, pal. File it or it'll be *your* ass."

I read it swiftly.

> HOLABIRD ORDNANCE DEPOT
> HOLABIRD, MARYLAND
>
> Corporal ESPOSITO SALVATORE ASN 32694853 (NMI) Casual Detachment, 1145 Labor Supvn Co., Holabird Ordnance Depot, Holabird, Md., is transferred in rank and grade to 1125 Hampton Drive, West Los Angeles, California.
>
> Cpl. ESPOSITO will on arrival at new post assume duties of

DISPATCHER, Army Classification 562, and be responsible for dispatch of all vehicles, wheeled, tracked and half-tracked, at said installation.

No change of rank or pay involved. EM to draw six dollars per diem. Transfer at request and convenience of MACE, Washington, D.C.

Having at one time served as a battalion clerk, I realized that the orders were either the real thing or a perfect forgery. The language, the phrasing, the format were perfect.

As I puzzled over the sheet, Corporal Esposito seated himself at a table in the corner of the room. On it he placed a yellow pad and a few slips of carbon paper. These were *trip tickets*, standard Army forms for the use of a vehicle. Behind his ear he stuck a red pencil stub. He put his feet on the table and began to read a ragged copy of *Captain Marvel* comics.

"Just what do you think you're doing?" I protested.

"Look, Mac, I got a job to do, *you* got a job to do," he said thickly. His sullen eyes darted up from the comic book. "Anya you people wanna vehicle, you come see me foist for a trip ticket. No trip ticket, no vehicle."

At that moment I understood that Esposito was no lunatic, no practical joke, no error. He was real. He was the essential dispatcher. I knew his type—surly, slovenly, wary, a petty dictator, a wielder of power and influence. He wore exactly what you'd expect: a stained old-fashioned field jacket, the corporal's chevrons sloppily sewn to the sleeve; a sweat-marked overseas cap pushed back on his coarse black hair.

I wasn't ready to challenge him. I returned to the house and found my father eating his Bran Flakes and scowling at the *Los Angeles Times*. I told him about the intruder. My father, the late Francis James Dugan, was a short-tempered, choleric man. His reaction was what I expected.

"What are you worried about?" he asked. "I'll throw the bum out."

Esposito was smoking a foul cigar when we entered. He flicked ashes on the floor and called out, "Could use a coupla butt cans here!"

My father flew across the room and yanked the dispatcher from his chair by the lapels of his field jacket. "Beat it, you bum. Pack your bag and get out, or I'll throw you out."

Salvatore wriggled loose and backed against a wall. He did not seem frightened, merely annoyed at my father's obtuseness. Like all true dispatchers, Esposito had a snarling equanimity that never turned into genuine hate or permitted true fear.

"Hey, Mac," he appealed to me, "straighten yer old man out. Dis ain't my idea. Fa Chrissake, I'm here on orders, *orders*. Ya can't disobey orders. You seen 'em ya'self."

I took my father to the porch outside the study. "Pop, why start a fight? We'll call the police and let them handle it, OK?"

He agreed reluctantly and went back to the house. Suddenly I remembered my class at UCLA. I re-entered the spare room to look for my keys. Esposito studied me narrowly. "Lookin' for somethin', soljer?"

"Car keys."

He patted the pocket of his jacket. "Right here, Mac."

"Give them to me."

He took the keys out and jangled them tantalizingly. "Foist ya gotta ask for a trip ticket."

"Good God, this is lunacy. Give me those keys, Esposito."

"Oh, yeah?" he asked. His eyes were slits. "Who's aut'orizin' dis trip, anyway?"

"Captain Dugan of battalion public relations," I said glibly. "In the line of duty."

"Whyna hell dincha say so' at foist?" He began to scrawl on the yellow pad. "Boy, you guys who go around keepin' secrets from da dispatcher. Jeez." He then ripped the carbon copy and thrust it at me with the keys. As I reached for them, he wickedly pulled his hand back. "Keep da ticket inna glove compartment and toin it in with the keys when ya get back."

I sat through my morning classes, hearing nothing, and got home before noon. My father had not gone to work. He was impatiently awaiting a call from Washington. He filled me in on what had happened. The local police had refused to throw Esposito out after looking at his mimeographed orders. A call to the Ninth Service Command at Fort Douglas was even less helpful. They said the incident would have to be explained by the War Department in Washington.

"I asked them what the hell MACE was, but they didn't know." He frowned. "I'll get to the bottom of this."

"Pop, I hate to tell you this, but I think that guy is *real*. He's a dispatcher and he's been assigned here."

The phone rang and I listened on the kitchen extension.

"Department of Defense?" asked my father.

A woman's nasal voice responded. "Who is calling?"

"This is Francis James Dugan of West Los Angeles, California. There's a goddamn soldier assigned to my house. I want him thrown out, but nobody'll take the responsibility. Let me talk to an outfit called MACE."

"I'm sorry, but no calls are permitted to that branch."

"The hell you say. I'm a taxpayer and a member of the American Legion. There's something in the Constitution about billeting soldiers in private homes."

"You will be reimbursed for the man's subsistence."

"I don't want to be. I want him out. And what does MACE stand for?"

"I am sorry, I cannot help you, Mr. Dugan."

"Goddamn it, you'll hear from me again! Or my congressman!"

But my father never carried out his threat. He worked long hours at the studio. My mother, a timid, retiring woman, had no stomach for conflict. As for myself, I was now convinced that Esposito was legally, actually and indisputably our dispatcher.

At first he was persistent in his efforts to make us accept his yellow trip tickets. He demanded the keys. When we refused, he removed the rotors from the engines (an old dispatcher's ruse). When we ourselves kept keys and rotors, he locked the steering wheels. He was frantic about his mission. Soon all three of us began to accommodate him, accepting his yellow chits and returning the keys.

So he lingered, taking his meals in the spare room (he dutifully gave my mother six dollars a day), reading comic books, presumably happy in his work. But he became lax. The keys were left in the cars; he did not demand trip tickets. I confronted him one day. He was sacked out on the day bed.

"Goofing off, Sal?"

"What's it to you?"

"As one enlisted man to another, Salvatore, I'd say you are gold-bricking. Isn't anyone checking up on you?"

He looked around warily. "S'posed to be an officer come around. But he ain't showed yet. You don't rat on me, I'll let yez drive a car all ya want."

"You got a deal, Sal." He could be managed.

The Sunday after his arrival, I drove out to the valley community of Sandoval to watch an old Army friend, Eddie Chavez, play sand-lot baseball. My parents had gone to La Jolla for the weekend. Esposito had been absent since noon Saturday. No doubt he had written himself a thirty-six hour pass.

I arrived at Sandoval just as the game was about to begin, found a seat in the rickety grandstand—there could not have been more than two hundred people present—and waved to Eddie Chavez. He was at home plate discussing ground rules with the umpire and the captain of the visiting team, the Lock City Lions.

As Eddie was about to lead the Sandoval Giants into the field, three men in Army suntans appeared, walking from the third-base line to home plate. From my seat in back of third base, I could see their rank clearly: a captain bearing a manila envelope and two sweating sergeants, each porting huge barracks bags.

"Just a minute!" the captain called. "There'll be a change in procedure today!" The umpire, Eddie and the Lock City captain stared at him. The captain extracted a sheet of mimeo paper from his envelope and gave it to the umpire.

A crowd of ballplayers gathered around and I heard expressions such as "What the hell?" "Who's this guy?" "Where do they git off?"

The captain addressed the crowd with a bullhorn. "By order of the Defense Department, I am authorized to supervise this game. The first event will be a three-legged relay. Teams line up at home plate."

I jumped from my seat and raced to home plate. The argument was raging.

"Hey, Frank!" Eddie called. "This guy says he has the right to run the game today! You was a battalion clerk. Look at his papers."

I did. Again I saw the reference to MACE and the formal language. The captain's name was Pulsifer. It seemed an appropriate name for a physical-training officer.

"All right, all right, we haven't got all day. Get those enlisted men lined up," Captain Pulsifer cried. "Sergeant, tie their legs together."

The ballplayers lined up in a column of twos. The sergeants bustled among them, joining them, left leg of one to right leg of another, for the three-legged race.

"I'm sure we'll all enjoy this!" Captain Pulsifer shouted.

He blew his whistle—a bronze whistle on a plaited red-and-yellow lanyard, a whistle only a P. T. officer would carry—and the three-legged race began. It was a dry, hot day, and the stumbling, cursing players kicked up great clouds of dust as they hopped off to the center-field flagpole.

"Faster, faster!" shouted Captain Pulsifer. "The winning team gets to bat last!"

"They do not!" I cried, trotting alongside the captain. "The home team bats last! You can't just change the rules like that!"

"Who says I can't?" he asked icily. "The Army can do anything it wants."

I could think of no response to this, but it hardly mattered, because the players refused to go on with the mad game. The crowd was booing, hissing. Pop bottles were thrown. But the captain was not through yet. Somehow—with threats, promises, frequent wavings of his orders, he got the teams to play short contests of underleg basketball relay, swat-the-baron and club-snatch. However, the games lasted only a few moments before the players stopped and began to yell again. How often I had played these same lunatic games during basic training!

"Play ball, goddamn it!" the umpire shouted. "Chavez, git yer team in the field. Lock City at bat! And you, you *jerk*, git lost!"

Captain Pulsifer walked off the field. But as the Lock City lead-off man stepped to the plate, the officer ordered one of his sergeants to bring a duffel bag forward. From it the captain took an olive-drab contraption—a gas mask.

"By order of the authority invested in me by the Defense Department, this game can proceed only under these conditions —*batter, pitcher, catcher and umpire are to wear gas masks at all times*." He then attempted to affix the mask to the batter's head. The lead-off man recoiled, the captain came after him and then the ballplayer swung his bat at the officer. The sergeants leaped to help their superior—the blow had missed by a hair—and the fans swarmed onto the field.

Eddie Chavez, the umpire and I tried to calm people down. For a moment it looked as if the crowd was ready to pull the P. T. O. and his men to pieces. As it was, they merely gave them a bum's rush across the diamond and dumped them into a weapons carrier that had been parked near the left-field foul line.

"You personnel haven't heard the last of this!" I heard Captain Pulsifer mutter through bruised lips. And they drove off. The game resumed. Most of the people around me seemed to think that the whole thing was a dumb practical joke.

I went home feeling dizzy from too much sun and queasy with uncertainties. That night I had a terrifying dream (one that has been recurring since I took my new job) and I woke up shivering. In this dream, I am back in Service and I am a permanent latrine orderly. I protest that I have had two years of college and have been a model soldier, but I am nonetheless kept on latrine duty because I am a "troublemaker." The latrine occupies all five stories of a tall building, an endless vitreous enamel nightmare, never-ending urinals, toilet bowls, sinks, a latrine so huge that it spills out into the street, crosses a road and deposits its gleaming receptacles in private homes, stores, factories. It generates and reproduces itself. It is dotted with signs reading, BLOKES WITH SHORT HORNS STAND CLOSE, THE NEXT MAN MAY HAVE HOLES IN HIS SHOES; or, FLIES SPREAD DISEASE, KEEP YOURS BUTTONED; or, WE AIM TO PLEASE, YOU AIM, TOO, PLEASE; or, PLEASE DO NOT THROW CIGAR BUTTS IN THE URINAL, IT MAKES THEM SOGGY AND HARD TO LIGHT.

I did not feel well enough to attend classes on Monday. Lingering over my coffee, I tried to piece together Salvatore Esposito, the baseball game and the mysterious initials MACE.

My mother came in from the living room—I had heard the vacuum humming—and began to mop the kitchen floor.

"Where's Serena?" I asked. It was Monday, and Serena Hastings, a Negro lady from Watts, came every Monday to give the house a cleaning.

"She called to say she can't get here," my mother replied. "If it were anyone but Serena, I'd say they'd made the story up. Something about soldiers stopping her bus and making everyone get off."

"What?"

My mother continued mopping. Nothing ever rattled her. Her

mind always seemed to be elsewhere, probably in Des Moines, where she was born and raised and where all of her family still lived.

"It sounded so silly, I really didn't pay attention, and at first I thought it was as if Serena had got drunk, or a little disturbed. But knowing Serena . . ."

"What, exactly, did she say, Mother?"

My mother paused and rested on her mop. "Well, she was on the Central Avenue bus, and it was filled, mostly with day-workers like herself, and in downtown L. A. it was stopped by a soldier. He was armed and Serena knew he was an MP, because her brother was once an MP, and an officer got on and announced that the bus was being taken over for the day. He apologized and everything, but everyone had to get off."

"Then what happened?"

"Nothing. A bunch of officers got on and the bus drove off in a different direction. They put a sign or something on it—OFFICERS' CLUB or something like that. Serena gave up and took a taxi home. You know how infrequently buses run. I can't blame the poor girl."

"But didn't anyone protest?"

"I didn't ask. Frank, could you please take these bottles into the garage?"

As I went on this errand, I began to feel faint. I decided to visit Dr. Cyril Mandelbaum, our family physician. I had not been to Dr. Mandelbaum's since my discharge. His pink stucco house on a patched green plot off Pico Boulevard looked no better than before the War. An elderly nurse let me in and I settled into a sagging chair with a copy of the *Los Angeles Times*. There were five other people in the waiting room—a white-haired woman with a boy of about eight, a young Negro couple and a husky young man in denim work clothes.

"Dr. Mandelbaum has been delayed at the hospital," the nurse told us, "but I expect him any minute."

I paged through the *Times*, my vision blurred, my head throbbing. On the sports page, a small item drew my attention.

FUN AND GAMES AT SANDOVAL

A special program of unusual athletic contests highlighted yesterday's Inland League baseball game in which the Sandoval Giants defeated the Lock City Lions, 4–3.

Members of both squads volunteered for the amusing games, which included a three-legged race, underleg basketball relay and swat-the-baron. Sandoval was declared winner of the special pregame competition by Captain A. M. Pulsifer, United States Army, who supervised the program.

"This is the first of several such fitness programs," said Captain Pulsifer, "and we're delighted with the public acceptance. Fans and players both had a wonderful time."

I must have looked like an idiot to the other patients, shaking my head and muttering. "No, no," I mumbled, "it wasn't that way at all." How had this fiction gotten into print? Why hadn't they reported the near riot I had seen?

The newspaper slipped from my lap and I covered my eyes.

In a minute or so, the office doors opened and out stepped not Dr. Cyril Mandelbaum but two men in Army uniforms. One was a dapper first lieutenant with a yellow mustache and the caduceus on his starched collar. The other, a fat, ruddy man, was a master sergeant. Dr. Mandelbaum's perplexed nurse was trailing them.

"But can't you wait until Dr. Mandelbaum gets here?" she asked. "This must be a mistake."

"Prepare the infirmary for sick call," the officer snapped.

"But Dr. Mandelbaum should——"

"No time. I'm under orders to take this installation over until further notice. Don't stand there, nurse." He barked at the sergeant. "Figler, tell the enlisted men to line up."

"Do they all have appointments with Dr. Mandelbaum?" she asked.

He waved a mimeographed sheet at her. "Government orders!"

I got up from my seat. "You're from MACE, aren't you?" I asked weakly.

"What business is that of yours?"

"I know a little bit about them. I was curious."

His yellow mustache quivered. "Figler, get that man's name, rank and serial number."

"Sir, I'm not sure he's in Service." Figler seemed a little confused. I guessed that these new assignments were so strange that even the personnel ordered to carry them out were puzzled from time to time. "And the infirmary's ready, anyway, sir. May we start sick call?"

"Very well. Tell them to line up outside. We'll do this as fast as possible."

The lieutenant then marched into Dr. Mandelbaum's office and sat at his desk. Figler followed him in, but emerged immediately, brushing by the astounded nurse. He carried a large glass beaker containing a half-dozen thermometers. Dumbly we lined up at the office door—the woman and the boy, the two Negroes, the man in work clothes and myself. With a speed and deftness that recalled to me every sick call I had ever attended, Figler flew down the line and jammed thermometers into our mouths. He had one left over, so he put *two* in my mouth. No sooner were they in than he raced back to the head of the line and yanked them out. Obviously, it had been impossible for a reading to register in so short a time, but that did not bother him. In any case, he barely glanced at the thermometers, putting them back into the beaker, which he gave to the nurse.

"Sir!" Figler called to the officer. "Every one of these people is fit for duty. Not a sick one in the lot. We've had trouble with this outfit before."

The rugged man in denims looked appealingly to me. "What'n hell is this? Who are these jokers?"

"I'm not sure. But they're not joking."

The medical officer barely heard Figler. He was ripping pages from Dr. Mandelbaum's calendar, juggling paper clips, furiously dialing numbers and then hanging up. "Damn it, don't stand there all day! Come in! Wipe your feet before you do!"

Figler ushered the old woman and the boy to the desk. They stood there frightened. The lieutenant barked, "Well?"

"I ain't the patient," she said. "It's my grandson, Rollie. He gets dizzy and vomits."

The officer shook his head and gave her a small pillbox. "Take two of these every four hours and drink plenty of liquids! Next!"

"But I ain't sick," the woman pleaded. "It's Rollie."

"We are under no obligation to treat children of enlisted personnel. This is not an overseas installation."

"It isn't any kind of installation!" I shouted.

"Pipe down, soljer," Sergeant Figler said. "The lootenant's had about enough of you. We know your type. You wanna come on sick call, you keep yer mouth shut."

"This isn't sick call!" I protested.

"That's right," said the husky man. "Where's Doc Mandelbaum?"

"Yeah, wheah the *real* doctah?" the young Negro man asked.

"What's *your* outfit, soljer?" Figler asked the Negro. "Labor battalion? One of them troublemakers?"

"Labah battalion?" He grabbed his wife's arm. "Let's git outa heah. I din't come for no sick call." They left quickly. The white-haired woman and the little boy followed them out.

"This is terrible!" the nurse wailed. "You're driving away all of Dr. Mandelbaum's patients!"

"How do you think I feel?" the medical officer shouted. "I gave up a forty-thousand-dollar-a-year practice in Newark for this crap! Next!"

The big man in denim walked to the desk. He was rubbing his fists.

"What's your problem?" the officer asked.

"None of ya friggin' business," the man said. "I done doody already. Five years combat engineers. Where's Mandelbaum? What'd you jerks do wit' him?"

Figler moved toward him. "Watch yer language, soljer."

"You call me soljer oncet more, yer ass'll be suckin' wind."

"I'll handle this, Figler." The medical officer got up. His mustache bristled. "All right, you, what's your outfit?"

"I ain't tellin' you nothin'. Pill roller."

"You'll regret this," the officer said. He was trembling.

"Chancre mechanic."

"Figler——"

"Clap surgeon. Go run a pro station."

Seething, the officer began dialing. "I'll throw the book at you!" he yelled. "You'll be up for a general court-martial! Hello, hello—get me the military police!"

The rugged man yanked the phone from his hand and shoved the officer roughly. Sergeant Figler hurled himself at the man's back. Then the rear door of the office opened and Dr. Mandelbaum walked in. At that time, the doctor was in his sixties, but he was still as strong and as fit as when he was on the USC wrestling team.

"What the hell is this?" Dr. Mandelbaum shouted. His weeping nurse tried to explain.

The lieutenant retreated to a corner of the room. The big man, seeing Dr. Mandelbaum, stopped his lunge at the officer.

"Now, then, Mandelbaum," the medical officer snapped, "we've a file on you. This mission will help all of us, including you, yourself. We are here in the national interest. That man threatened me and I'm having him brought up on charges of insubordination!" He was slightly hysterical. He was not carrying out his assignment as well as my dispatcher had.

"What are you talking about?" Dr. Mandelbaum yelled. "Who are you to bust into my office and abuse my patients? That's Al Zawatzkis. He's been my patient for years. I delivered him. He's never welshed on a bill in his life."

"Then you are prejudiced in his favor," the officer said. "I'll see to it that you don't testify at his court-martial!"

He began dialing again. "I want the military police, and if you can't get them, I'll talk to the Defense Department, office called MACE——"

Dr. Mandelbaum grabbed him by his shoulder straps and shook him as if he were a rag doll. The lieutenant screamed for help. Figler tried to pry Doc Mandelbaum loose, but big Zawatzkis thundered at him. It was no contest. He plucked Sergeant Figler from Doc and threw him against a filing cabinet. While Figler lay there stunned, Zawatzkis tried to untangle the two physicians. I have to give credit to the Army officer; he was tenacious and brave. He clung to Mandelbaum, wheezing and hissing and protesting that we were all traitors, but he was no match for Zawatzkis. The medical officer sprawled on the X-ray table, then got a second wind and came at Zawatzkis, who smashed a jug of green soap over his head.

The lieutenant hit the floor. The jug broke clean. The medic wasn't cut, merely bruised and coated with the viscous fluid. "Get him out," Doc Mandelbaum said. I gave Zawatzkis a hand. We picked up the semiconscious officer and carted him out.

"He slipped!" I said loudly. "I saw it! He slipped on the floor!"

Dr. Mandelbaum helped Sergeant Figler to his feet and escorted him to the front door. "Be a nice boy, not a schlemiel," he was saying to him. "What is all this nonsense? Go get a job instead of being a bum in the Army all your life." The three of us—Doc, Zawatzkis and myself—stood on the sidewalk as Figler, crying softly, drove off in the jeep with his superior. Then we went into the office, where Doc took care of us in his usual considerate manner.

That evening at the dinner table, I kept my thoughts to myself. Esposito dropped down to pick up his dinner, greeted us sullenly and retreated to his sanctuary. We rarely saw him anymore. He had long stopped bothering us for car keys or trip tickets.

"I wish that tramp would go," my father said. It was exactly one week that Salvatore had been with us. "And I wish I knew why he's here."

"He doesn't bother anyone," my mother said. "And he is never behind with the six dollars a day."

"Who needs it?" my father grumbled.

"He keeps the room clean," my mother said defensively. "His personal appearance isn't much, but the bed is always made."

"*Bed,*" my father said. "Did you tell Frank what happened at the hotel in La Jolla yesterday?"

"You mean the tennis match?"

"No, no. That business with the beds. You know, what we saw when we were going down to the pool."

"What happened?" I asked.

My father stirred his coffee. "It was either a practical joke or else they were rehearsing for a movie or something. Maybe a publicity gimmick for a movie. That old hotel has been used a lot for locations."

"Francis, you asked the manager that and he said no."

"Yeah. But if it wasn't a movie stunt, what was it?"

My father shook his head.

"But what, exactly, happened?" I asked.

"Your mother and I were on our way down to the pool, when we passed this room with the door open. There was a lot of yelling going on and I peeked in. There were five people in the room—a young couple, a chambermaid and this Army officer and a sergeant. One with all those stripes up and down."

"First sergeant," I said. My hands were sweaty; a stone was growing in my stomach.

"This captain kept yelling that he was *gigging*—whatever that is—gigging the two guests because the beds weren't made with hospital corners."

"It *was* very strange," my mother said. "Like a silly motion picture, as Daddy says."

"This sergeant tried bouncing a dime off the bedspread a few times, but it wouldn't bounce, and this got the captain sore. He also had white gloves on and I saw him run his finger through the closet shelves."

"Didn't the guests object?" I asked.

"They were scared," said my father. "I think they were honeymooners and figured somebody was kidding them. The guy kept saying the chambermaid had made the bed and the officer kept shouting, 'We want results, not excuses, in this man's Army!' Probably be a funny story in the papers about it."

I wondered, would it be a funny story like the lying account of the baseball game at Sandoval? How would they handle inspection? As a cheerful course in modern hotelkeeping?

The last incident in this sequence of events—that is, the last up to my current listing on a *Table of Organization* as a first lieutenant—took place the next day.

Unhearing, I sat through morning classes and decided to spend the afternoon in the library. In the interests of economy, I had been driving home for lunch (we live a few minutes from the Westwood campus), but on this day I went to the school cafeteria. I arrived a moment after it had reopened for lunch and was greeted by an odd tableau.

The five colored ladies who manned the counter were clearly upset. They were huddled away from the steaming food vats. The manager, a Mr. Sammartino, as I recall, was in front of the counter, gesticulating and appealing to—— Need I go on?

Looming behind the great aluminum bins of tuna-fish timbale, chicken and noodles, breaded veal cutlet and eggplant parmesan was one of the fattest men I have ever seen. He wore a filthy, sweat-stained fatigue suit with sergeant's stripes stenciled on the sleeves. On his head was a green fatigue cap, the brim upturned and stenciled with the name TEXAS. He brandished two enormous tools—a devil's fork and an ogre's ladle—and he sweat gallons into the food. A nauseating and disgusting figure, he was incontestably a mess sergeant. I needed no mimeographed orders to tell me so.

"Come and git it, fo' I throw it to the pigs!" he bellowed. "Yeah, hot today, hot today!"

He had an underling, a short, hairy man in dirty fatigues, who bustled through the kitchen doors, lugging a steaming pot of some appalling pink stew.

"Lady wit' a baby!" yelled the small man. "Hot stuff comin' through!"

"That's mah boy!" the mess sergeant beamed. "Li'l ole Hemsley. Hemsley a good ole boy. Look lak Hemsley brewed himself a mess of good ole S.O.S.! Shit on a shingle! Wahoo! Give us a ole rebel yell, Hemsley."

Hemsley obliged. The air shivered with the sound. The Negro

ladies retreated even farther back. One, a bespectacled woman of great dignity, appealed to Mr. Sammartino.

"If this a fraternity prank, Mr. S.," she said, "it gone far enough. The girls is fed up."

The manager paced feverishly. "But they said they had *orders!* They gave me *this!*" Mr. Sammartino waved a mimeographed sheet of paper. By now a queue of hungry students had formed in back of me. Most of them were amused by the insanity behind the steam table, assuming, as did the woman, that it was some form of undergraduate humor.

The mess sergeant stirred his pink S.O.S., stabbed at a gray sparerib, sniffed the okra soup. "Ole Hemsley. He a good ole boy. Hemsley, y'all got some grits back there, so's we can show the Yankees how rebels eat?"

"I wouldn't be for knowin', but I'll look."

"Well, be for lookin'."

Hemsley vanished into the kitchen, clanging empty pots. I took a clean tray and started down the line, as if drawn to some rendezvous with fate. The colored girls shrank away. The huge sergeant seemed to fill up all the space behind the counter.

He eyed me with contempt. "Y'all got an early chow pass?"

"Y-yes," I stammered. "Company and company headquarters. What's for chow, Sarge?"

A grin widened his pulpy face. He was in *control.* He had me. "Fly shit 'n' brown pepper."

"That's OK," I said hoarsely. "So long as it ain't the same as what we had yesterday."

Chuckling, he began to load up my tray. A glop of mashed potatoes landed in the middle. Two slices of bread hit next and were promptly buried beneath the horrid S.O.S. A brownish mixture of vegetables was hurled, spattering the empty spaces of the tray. Several wilted leaves of lettuce were inserted in the brown ooze; a rubbery veal cutlet came to rest in the S.O.S. There remained but two square inches of inviolate mashed potatoes. The sergeant grinned at the tray. "Looks like we kinda missed a spot, right, buddy boy?" I said nothing. I knew what was coming. He ladled out a yellow cling peach, swimming in syrup like the inside of a roc's egg. Leaning over the counter, he deftly set the peach half in the midst of the potatoes, drowning everything else in the sweet juice.

"Now you all set," he beamed.

The blood roared to my skull. I breathed deeply, glanced at the wailing manager and lifted the tray high, as if sacrificing it to a god unknown. Then I hurled it at the fat sergeant. He took the blow—stunned, soaked, steaming—a great abstract work of food. I fled to cheers and laughter.

Upon returning home, I went to the spare room. Corporal

Salvatore Esposito was sacked out, reading *Famous Funnies.*

"Get going, Salvatore," I said. "I am throwing you out."

"I don't go unless ya got orders for me."

"No, no, you must leave. And you tell your superiors you were thrown out, that we didn't want you and shouldn't have let you stay. The only reason you stayed so long was because of a delay in policy."

He sat up in bed. "I ain't goin' and you know it."

I walked to my father's golf bag and pulled out the driver. "Pack, soldier. I could handle you without this, but I want to make sure you leave in a hurry." I whipped the air a few times.

He struggled out of bed, a stumpy troll in droopy khaki drawers and socks. "Jeez. Din't think you was dat kind of guy." He dressed hastily, slung the bag over his shoulder and asked if he could make a telephone call. I permitted him to. He dialed swiftly, identified himself and asked that a jeep meet him at the corner, on Olympic Boulevard. I gave him his trip tickets, the carbon papers and the pencil, which he had carelessly left on the table. I wanted all traces of him obliterated. We walked to the street corner. Salvatore squatted on his sack.

"Who sent you here, Salvatore?" I asked.

"I dunno. I git assigned, I go."

"What is MACE?"

"I dunno. All I know is someone's gonna get chewed out for throwin' me out." He glowered at me, but it was a meaningless glower, one for the record. "It'll be your ass, Dugan, not mine."

An open jeep, driven by a young second lieutenant, pulled up to us. "Spasita?" he asked.

"Dat's me." Salvatore didn't salute. He tossed his bag in the rear of the jeep and climbed in.

"Orders come through, Spasita. You transferred."

"They did not!" I shouted. "He was not transferred! I threw him out! Why was he sent to me, anyway? I never wanted him!"

The shavetail studied me innocently. "Beats me, mistah. We git orders and folla them.

"All set, Spasita?" He gunned the engine.

"Just a minute," I said. "I demand an explanation. What does MACE mean?"

"Never heard of it." And the jeep drove off.

"Remember what I said, Salvatore!" I shouted after them. "*I threw you out!* You tell them!"

Did I imagine it? Or did my dark dispatcher turn and answer my hysterical request with a nod of his head, a wink?

Today I sit in my air-conditioned office and think about my new job. Who decided I was first lieutenant? I have discharge papers at home showing that I was released from military service "for the convenience of the Government" some years ago. When was I commissioned? By whose authority?

I stopped Carter at the water cooler late this afternoon. My arm did not rise in salute, but he gauged the confusion on my face.

"I saw the T/O," I said. "Am I to call you Mister or Colonel?"

"It doesn't matter, Dugan," he said pleasantly. "One way or the other. We don't stand on ceremony in this outfit."

"But what are we?"

He smiled. "Little bit of everything, you might say. You'll get used to it."

We walked down the corridor together. I glanced at his shoes—highly polished mahogany-brown officer's pumps with a strap instead of laces. They say to me: PX.

"Colonel, did you ever hear of an outfit called MACE? Just after the War?"

"MACE? Yes, I remember it. It was obsoleted a long time ago. We tried it out briefly. A pilot project, a really primitive one. We were just sort of fiddling around in those days."

"What did the letters stand for?"

"Military and Civilian Enterprises. Nothing mysterious about it."

"It was abandoned?"

"Naturally. We've got more sophisticated systems today. Data programming, circuitry. The whole operation is computerized. I must say, somebody in Washington is doing a marvelous job. MACE! My goodness, I haven't thought about that old one-horse operation in years!"

He entered his office. I could hear people snapping to attention inside.

My nylon shirt is drenched; my knees are water. How did it happen? How in heaven's name did I get here? I curse Corporal Salvatore Esposito, my late dispatcher. He never told them that I threw him out. I am certain of that.

‘I read the news today oh boy’

THE ETHICAL DILEMMA IN CONTEMPORARY SOCIETY

I read the news today oh boy
About a lucky man who made the grade
And though the news was rather sad
Well I just had to laugh
I saw the photograph
He blew his mind out in a car
He didn't notice that the lights had changed
A crowd of people stood and stared
They'd seen his face before . . .

JOHN LENNON and PAUL MCCARTNEY,
A Day in the Life

ALFRED KAZIN

The Love Cult

a distinguished man of letters casts a critical eye at america's favorite panacea

Love as a conviction, as an attachment to someone or even to something, can be a profound individual experience. I don't happen to believe that it is the *most* profound or significant feeling that a human being can have in life. But when it is authentic, when it is too much at times for the person who feels it, when it shakes us and becomes almost too much for the inadequate language we have for our feelings, then it is certainly not to be discussed lightly and is properly nobody's business but our own. Nobody else would really understand it. In the deepest sense, love *is* incommunicable, since by taking us out of ourselves it forces us to find words for feelings that usually are unexpected and often are not even wanted. Our attachment—when it is genuine, when it starts in a certain pain—can be different in sensation from anything we have known. That is why love, when we really love, can be actively disturbing; for once we are concerned with the object of our love and less with ourselves. In that flight from ourselves as the usual center of the world, there is certainly no guarantee that our love will be reciprocated, that it will last, that it will even be known.

No, it is certainly not with the depth of love nor with the possible anguish of love that I quarrel; it is with the *word* love—the buttery little symbol of our self-satisfaction and society's approval. "Love" as a password, as a badge, as an announcement of how kindly we are and how goodly and how full of generosity and acceptance and warm feelings—this *word* as a slogan and advertisement of our good intentions is what I have come to dislike. For the word is easy, it costs us nothing (not even a feeling of love) and, like an excessive tip to a waiter, is meant to purchase a good opinion of ourselves. I dislike the easiness with which we now use this word in America. I dislike the glibness which it expresses and the unlovingness it so often suppresses. But most of all I dislike "love"-as-a-formula for its superstitious attempt to stave off the truth by incantations. We live in a world of such menace from our fellow human beings and of such fear of our fellow human beings that it is surely a strain on our honesty to speak of human beings as "loving." What primitive men once feared in the storms and cataclysms of nature—something which in their ignorance they thought malevolently directed against them—we now know to be true of human beings in society. Not only do most people love us not at all—some of them would gladly kill us. Much of what we think of as "love" in ourselves or in others is simply conservatism. We get attached to people, houses, cities, mechanical appliances, and associate with them a pattern of satisfaction. There are a few people, I know, who can transcend themselves altogether in their attachment to a person or an idea; the saints are saints precisely because they have a rare attachment to God and more to God than to anything mortal. But I for one will never recover from the Second World War, and when I think of the millions of children slaughtered for love of country, when I consider how many crimes have been committed, and how many more have been considered, in the name of a love that was deep but fundamentally selfish and tyrannical, I genuinely wonder why the word is so much prated. For love of a parent, many people are unable to love others in later life; for love of an idea, crimes are committed against defenseless populations; for love of God, those who love Him a little less verbally, or in a different ritual, have been tortured to death.

Why then do we talk so much in the name of love, why is the word the easiest to use and the most self-satisfying? What is the mysterious satisfaction we seek to obtain by the word? Of course, one reason is that human beings rarely do love in any true sense, but are so acculturated to the use of the word that they acquire some necessary social approval by it. The Russians, who came relatively late to Western manners, are very quick to reprove publicly any of their people who do not behave nicely at table. The reproach is that someone is *not cultured,* and the remark can hurt. In the same way, Americans, and more usually American women, are very quick to say of some action or gesture that it is *not loving*—and there are few of us brave enough to admit that in some situations or even in general, unloving is what we are. As the novelist Saul Bellow once complained, "Would we be told to love if love were as natural as breathing?" So little is it natural to us, in fact, that representations of love by the most acute psychological novelists, like Stendhal, emphasize with almost clinical observation the confusing arrival of new sensations rather than concern with the beloved. This side of Eros (who is only one of the many gods of love; in America we favor a more domestic figure) is one of the great subjects of the European novel, for as Louis-Ferdinand Céline once said, physical love is the *fact* which stands outside all our *verbal* systems and ideas. This is what has made the great European novelists identify physical love with the truth inadmissible by society. In Proust's greatest single work, *Swann's Way,* Swann himself, the fastidious and pains-taking intellectual who has been accepted in the most snobbish ranks of French society despite his Jewish blood, suddenly finds himself losing all control and all care for his position in his obsessive need to possess Odette, who is essentially a prostitute. Yet when, at the end of his "sickness," Swann says ruefully that he went to all this trouble for a woman who "wasn't even my type," we recognize the empirical spirit, the fidelity to the disconcerting facts of human experience, wherever they may lead us, that is the peculiar fascination of great fiction.

Proust says in his novel that he who "possesses" a person really possesses nothing—of course, it is the pride of conquest, not of actual possession, that is associated for a man with physical love. Yet if you look at the history of "love" as an idea, you can see that "possession" was associated even with spiritual love. In what is perhaps the most profound explanation of love, Plato's *Symposium,* Socrates makes it clear that love is our highest recognition of what is most unlike ourselves. It is an excellence of a being unlike ourselves that we want to attach ourselves to. We want to possess what we are not. But by the quality of our recognition of what is excellent and even perfect of its kind, we can also *not* seek to possess it. This is why Saint Augustine's definition of love is so rare and moving—*I want you to be*. The beauty of this phrase lies in its surprise. It is the most concrete example I know, in Western culture, of how love can ennoble itself. By contrast, most statements about love deal neither with the physical facts, as Proust does, nor with the kind of aspiration which at certain moments we faintly detect in ourselves. The usual thing is the glib assurance that every-body "loves"—or with a little encouragement, can. The love that Saint Augustine speaks of must be won out of the endless battle with our own suspicious human nature, against the actual wickedness of the human animal. But this love, when it is real, can rise to sublime concern for another person.

Yet, beautiful as such an intimation of the highest power of love can be, the fact remains that we are always being coun-seled to love—that is, to talk as if we loved—but keep falling back. Why is the term honored so much in our culture that we lie for its sake, lie even when we are just thinking aloud, lie to protect the mere term from dishonor? Is it only because with-out the word to hold us in, we would tear each other to bits? After all, to be unloving is not necessarily to be aggressive and destructive. Bad as we are (and never have human beings thought so little of themselves as they have since the First World War), we are not—at least not all of us, and surely not any of us all the time—so violent. Why, then, do we lie that we love, pretend to love? Why, indeed, do we try so hard to love?

Surely one reason is that without "love" as a concept, the world seems exactly as indifferent to us and our most tenderly cherished personal strivings as in certain unbearably lucid moments around three in the morning we recognize it to be. The peculiarity of Christianity among the great world religions is that it establishes God as not merely creating the world (not all religions do even that), but as creating it out of love for man, out of the spirit of love. God is love. He works in love for us. He so loved the world that He gave His only begotten Son . . . The sublime "good tidings" that the word *gospel* literally stands for is this unprecedented loving intervention in the affairs of men by God in His incarnation as Christ. With the idea of God *as* Love (which expressed something different from the Old Testament God's loving concern for man), of God creating man out of love alone, a protective new relationship unfolded for Christians, between themselves and a universe somehow more their own, now tenderly aware of man (for whom Christ died) and cherishing him in the hope of spiritual perfection. Out of love God created man; out of love God redeemed man of his primal sin and offered him salvation. In return, even the emotion that a man felt for his wife now became a symbol of the divine love. The world, under the influence of Christianity, now came to seem a *loving* world. Love created it. Of love was it made.

And without love, what was it? Without love, the world was as dark and capricious as it had been to the ancients, as mysterious and incalculable as Providence appears to the Jews. Without love the world—the true world, the spiritual world—was without form, as it had been before the creation. Without love, as Satan said in *Paradise Lost*, "which way I fly is hell; myself am hell." This was what the great Christian novelist Dostoievsky said about those unable to love; the wretchedness Father Zossima describes in *The Brothers Karamazov* is to fail in love for the world. Not to love, in the Christian tradition of the word, was to cut oneself off from life. And so deeply woven into the fabric of Christian civilization was the idea of God as love that, scholars are beginning to discover, the conscious eroticism of the troubadours in the early Middle Ages (the beginnings of the cult of romantic love) may actually mark the beginnings of Protestant heresy. Yet to lavish so much adoration on a woman, even though it was done in playful ritual—officially a symbol of devotion to the Virgin—was nevertheless to honor and to retain the "practice of love." Whatever may have split and weakened the Christian faith through the centuries, "love" as its unique theology and its special badge of faith has remained with it. In America, such sects as Transcendentalism retained the idea of God's love long after they had virtually ceased to believe in God. The Christian idea that love, as an expression of God's concern, can heal, is, of course, the foundation of Christian Science. "Love" for many Christians, and for many non-Christians, has not only survived but replaced the idea of God. It is only by understanding love's role as a theology, even for many ex-Christians and non-Christians, that one can begin to understand the force that it has in our culture. It is the *sine qua non*, literally—without it we feel that we are lost. Without it our universe is suddenly without rhyme or reason; we have no shelter against the possible dissolution of the only society that we are used to.

So deep is this conservative and domesticating influence of "love" as a commandment that it has virtually reoriented psychoanalysis in the direction of ethical goals which Freud never intended for it. As Freud once pointed out in a letter: "psychoanalysis also has its scale of values, but its sole aim is the enhanced harmony of the ego, which is expected successfully to mediate between the claims of the instinctual life [the id] and those of the external world; thus between inner and outer reality. . . . We believe that it [psychoanalysis] cannot reveal to us anything but primitive, instinctual impulses and attitudes . . . worthless for orientation in the alien, external world." Freud was concerned with sexual instincts; these were necessarily at war not only with existing laws and morals, but often enough with the softening and conventionalizing spirit which already went by the name of "love." He showed, as the great European novelists had done, how much that we call "love" is the separable force that we can more truly call lust or desire, and how much the spirit of "love," as conventionally honored, can conceal or suppress the force of this desire.

In Freud's view, it was not love that needed understanding and expression, but all those component instincts and biological forces that go to make up the amalgam that the word has been used to conceal. Freud felt that "love" as a term had been honored enough in our culture; the instinctual forces below the surface engaged his attention. Far from flattering human society that its ruling motive was one of love, he insisted that the generations of men in the primal past had succeeded one another by force of conquest, arising in a spirit of deep sexual competitiveness and jealousy. Even in his own family and clan, man was ruled not by selfless affection but by incestuous longings which by now he had forgotten that he felt. He was engaged in a constant reliving of the past with which he had never come to terms. His only relief from the anxiety of struggling endlessly with his impulses was in a longing for death—

a longing he would not even acknowledge to himself, so little was he aware of the bitter struggle going on in himself with the demands of physical love. As Freud saw it, man was a battleground between the exuberant but frightening spirit of Eros, and that of Thanatos, the wish for death to free us. Eros exhilarates us to a renewed sense of our human possibilities, but he disturbs the order we have so grimly built up. To give in to Eros is to reach down to a force in ourselves that we are constantly trying to pacify and to domesticate and to civilize.

Love is not a heresy now; it is the only guarantee left to us of the status quo. This, in our day, is the magic of the word. "Love," in America today, is what retains and re-establishes and secures; this is why "love," for which Proust's Swann almost died and for which Anna Karénina did die, now stands for those pacified and pacifying qualities that we hope will let us be. In Freud's eyes, a man was sick if he could not consciously and bravely deal with the profound stirrings of Eros; in the eyes of, say, Dr. Smiley Blanton, author of the popular manual *Love or Perish,* it is the failure to love that may doom us all. Notice that Freud spoke of biological instincts that exist; Dr. Blanton and, on a much higher level, the influential Dr. Erich Fromm speak of feelings of love that must be strengthened. Dr. Fromm's appeal is directed from a strong core of European liberal idealism; he is concerned with love as the creator of a new society, not the domestic love which alone means so much to American women—and therefore to American men. But the effect of Dr. Fromm's books is, in the American context, to strengthen the fond American belief that it is love and love alone that holds the world up at all just now.

It is not even love in itself, direct feelings of love for another, that I discern in the solemn repetitions of the word; it is the wistful longing that the world be kept whole, that it may be kept what it was, that it be kept still. It is rare indeed for a truly conservative novelist, like James Gould Cozzens, to show that in the death of what *once* was love, the deepest values of our society have gone, too. *By Love Possessed* is not my favorite among Cozzens' novels, but it should be remembered that the subject of his book is the decline of the most elementary moral notions among our "best" people—and that one of his examples is the selfish and faithless addiction to "love" among such people. Cozzens really is a conservative: He has a concrete image of a past society, of past values, that he cherishes and respects above all others. But the anxious and even panicky use of "love" today is to hold up a rickety world, or almost any world, in the absence of any positive values of our own. Without "responsible," "mature," "decent" interpersonal relationships, we may all go to hell. No wonder that on every side just now I seem to hear psychiatrists and counselors and ministers saying

—"*Love*, you monsters! Love, damn it all, love! Do you want to rock the boat and destroy us all?" What was in the earliest days of civilization a prime discovery by the human spirit, and later a sublime construction of theology, has now become a threat. Love, or we'll think less well of you! Love, or else the whole joint-stock company of modern humanity, dependent on the loving restraint of its members, will still not be enough to keep the missiles and H-bombs from going off! Love!—so that *I* may not die.

Yet, more than fear of war, which can only mean fear of ourselves and our fellow men, it is the poverty of our daily language that impels us to invoke love like the name of a political party. It has become our only absolute. What God has meant to so many, what in times past the good society has meant to many again, what was once summed up by words like justice, now the quick sound of "love," like a card quickly being shuffled off the top of the deck, means in contemporary American culture. Students of language have a name for the quick automatic response that is expected in a culture: "counterwords." Love is now our chief counterword. On Broadway now, as in popular versions of psychoanalysis, there is no value to live for but "love." "Love," that is, as a symbol of your status, for love of a person is hardly something to boast of or to think of as comfortably growing like money in an interest account. If you have "love," you've got it made, as people make it in business. The family that loves together stays together. It shows how very nice we are. "Love" is a very American thing; not many Europeans love as much as *we* do. A psychiatrist-turned-writer once told me that European novelists like Camus and Sartre lacked "the spirit of love." To be without this warm, gushing, confiding spirit (so quick to advertise itself like toothpaste) is now, apparently, the hell of exclusion that Dostoievsky reserved for those unable to love. And the usual American song is less often I love than it is I *need* love. On Broadway, "love" means a psychological health necessary to the only kind of person that we now recognize. Yet see how quickly love-as-need becomes love-as-value. In Paddy Chayefsky's television play *Marty*, the sense of pathos involved in needing love so much made for a dramatic situation that one could understand if not particularly admire. But in his more recent play, *The Tenth Man*, we find an old man in a Jewish house of worship not merely praising the hero for loving the heroine, but ending the play on the affirmation that such love is all that we mean by God nowadays.

Love as "security," love as guarantee that the home will stand up, the city, the world, even God himself—what a strange thought. If love has ever really meant anything, it has meant the largest possible risk. How can I, by loving, bind another to myself? And how can *another* bring me safety? Yet we all believe in this, whether we admit it or not, and the reason goes deep. The real terror of our days is not merely that we civilized people view society as savages once viewed nature—something awesome and beyond control. It is that so many of the words that we use to signify our deepest allegiance and loyalty, the words that convey our bottommost trust and faith, have vanished for us—so that, for many people, it is virtually the magic of love and love alone that seems to hold the world up at all. That is why, on Broadway, where a work can live only if it is immediately liked by its audience, plays like Archibald MacLeish's *J.B.* and William Inge's *Come Back, Little Sheba* and Tennessee Williams' *A Streetcar Named Desire* are popular. MacLeish re-establishes the "private" world of love for a wife as the only one to which a modern Job stricken by the (significant) irrationality of misfortune can return. Inge and Williams, in their different ways, re-establish in the word love a kind of primal authority that is essential to the overwhelming concern of these playwrights with the word home. Even in Williams, who is so talented and so concerned with the force of sex, "love" takes away the "hardship," as Freud grimly called it, of sex.

Whether as nostalgia or as commercial salesmanship, you just can't beat love nowadays. Love is associated with the most sublime insights of a religion which is honored more in the breach than in the observance, and which survives every breach, in a sense thrives on it, by holding out such high hopes for love. Love, in fact, is what we most admire when everything else has failed our admiration. Its promise is enormous: "For ever wilt thou love and she be fair!" And, of course, this concept of love also soothes; it beckons; it replenishes our stale and disillusioned imaginations with the word which is the very incarnation of a better opinion of ourselves. In a society which is not merely anxious about its future but, more seriously, shoddy with outworn beliefs, exploded mythologies, a language debased by commercialism and popular entertainment and shallow mass education, "love" alone seems to stand up. On it, at least, we try to stand.

*"Heavens, don't worry about the trains!
Marie and Jeff can drop you off in the ghetto
on their way back to Westchester."*

opinion

ROMAIN GARY

the baiting society

young people, feeling trapped by a seductive world they never made, are approaching the explosive critical mass —but run the risk that their ideals of change may degenerate into power-struggle confrontations

As I sat in front of my television set watching the second invasion of Czechoslovakia, this time by the Communist storm troopers, resentment and despair, shame, indignation and the frustrated awareness of my total impotence were racing wildly through the corridors of my mind, like the "hounds of heaven" in the famous Housman poem. I was trying to control my breathing and to clear my throat; my whole body was tense, and in my hands there was a kind of physical longing for the controls of the bomber I had flown against the other Nazis during the War. Then, out of some even darker corner of my psyche, there suddenly arose a monstrous thought: This, if ever, was a case for the use of the atom bomb. Under the impact of intolerable provocation, faced with this cynical baiting of my helplessness and weakness through a combination of total frustration and powerless sense of injustice, I was crossing the border of sanity and falling prey to the obscure forces within a Lee Harvey Oswald, a Hitler or a Sirhan Sirhan.

My own reaction is the answer to all those who wonder how violence has become our daily companion, why students are running amuck in every city of the world. Our consciousness and conscience, our inbred belief in the existence of some kind of honor among men, are mercilessly teased, baited, provoked day by day, hour by hour, through the instant audio-visual contact with the world we live in. This world may be no more ugly than it was fifty years ago, but its beastliness was then ignored or unknown to a colossal degree, and this ignorance protected our psyche. But two generations of mass media and communications have exposed both the world to us and us to the world in such a brutal way that our conscience has become an exposed nerve. An adjustment to such a situation becomes not only impossible but immoral; that is why Freud and psychoanalysis are more and more rejected by the young, as Miss Anna Freud herself so courageously pointed out some time ago. In the world of Prague, Biafra, Vietnam and Harlem, can anyone tell me what could possibly be meant by an adjusted man? Brainwashed at best, more likely, a passive accomplice. For the youth of today, to be ill-adjusted is a term of praise, a first necessity in terms of dignity, of moral and psychological survival, as well as the first prerequisite to a radical change of the total environment.

Not long ago, I heard an eighteen-year-old boy say ironically, looking at his father with an unbelievable expression of scorn, "Yeah, he's always been well adjusted."

One of the most absurd arguments advanced against the sixteen thousand rioting students in Paris in May 1968 ran as follows: "We are feeding them, clothing them, we are giving them all the opportunities to learn and to occupy a place in society; then they go and throw stones at us." It is true that 90 percent of the rioters were *fils à papa*. It is, however, the most stupidly selfish argument ever employed by the French *bourgeoisie* in blind self-defense. For the so-called French revolution of 1968 had its roots precisely in the fact that the young intellectuals of Nanterre and Paris could no longer stand to be well fed, well clothed, well educated and settled in jobs in a world where 700,000,000 people are suffering from malnutrition. It was said that the rioting students had no purpose in sight. True enough; they were merely vomiting the world.

Being a violent person myself, I am no less aware than other observers of the pathological character of all violence and I would be the last to defend it or to sing its praise. But, on the other hand, we cannot drive people mad and then condemn them for being insane. I am also aware that violence derives either from our own self-righteous conviction that we are absolutely right or from our reaction to others who feel and behave as if they are absolutely right. Such an attitude excludes all margin of tolerance. The belief in one's cause becomes so strong that all other moral considerations are swept aside, usually together with some butchered or burned bodies of men, women and children. My moral convictions become so overwhelming that I no longer let ordinary morality stand in my way. For the holder of absolute truth, everything else ceases to matter. During the last War, I spent five years more or less continuously at the controls of a bomber in England, Abyssinia, Libya, Syria, France and Germany. In 1943, I dive-bombed and missed an enemy submarine. I have often heard of bomber pilots who, years later, experience a recurrent nightmare: They see the victims of their bombing. I suffer from an even more terrible recurrent nightmare: Twenty-six years later, I still dream that I miss that submarine. I wake up screaming in a cold sweat because I have *not* killed. My anti-Nazi convictions and my belief in what I was fighting for were so absolute that I had become a highly decorated killing machine. Even today, my painfully abstract remorse stems from the fact that I feel no remorse.

Albert Camus has written what to me is one of the two key sentences of our or, for that matter, any other time: "I am against all those who think they are absolutely right." And I may as well quote the other key sentence in the same context: "You condemn to the death penalty a guilty man, but you always carry out the sentence on an innocent one." I know of no greater truth; and yet, as I was watching the rape of Czechoslovakia, I felt so absolutely right in my indignation that I caught myself longing for the absolute weapon.

I do not believe that this is a time when one can have a conscience and be entirely sane. Brutality is merely the opposite pole of this escape from reality; the oversensitive individual always dreams of toughness, of virility, and can become a pathological killer merely to escape from his own feeling of impotence.

My contention is that we are in the midst of the greatest psychological, moral and spiritual crisis that our civilization has ever known. Ideology has become associated with mass murder. Materialistic society finds nowhere to go, except to more of the same, and there is neither God nor man in sight any longer. Humanism is dead and Man, with a capital *M*, died with it. I myself believe in an extraordinary spiritual revolution and renaissance in the next century, and it probably will be of a scientific origin or, if you prefer, a revelation. Man cannot live by man alone. The new civilization will have to find outside help. I do, however, feel that our traditional religions are all deeply associated with our fiasco and that our spiritual rebirth will have very little to do with them.

One of the most obvious reasons for our angst is, of course, the fact that we are truly opening our eyes for the first time. For thousands of years, civilizations prospered on a happy mixture of limited knowledge and unlimited ignorance. The most frightening, shocking single event in Voltaire's life and time was the Calcutta earthquake. Today, an earthquake is a reassuring thing: At least there is one horror for which we are not responsible. We are living in a state of instant and constant awareness. Let me give you an example of the power of the mass media. In May 1968, in Paris, a few hundred students occupied the

Sorbonne. It so happened that while Dean Roche, Chief of Police Grimaud and Sauvageot—the handsome Ché Guevara of the students' revolt—were negotiating inside the building, unknown to them, Radio Luxembourg had its mikes there and every word of the angry discussion was on the air. Within a matter of hours, the four hundred students were sixteen thousand and the May revolution began.

It would, of course, be absurd and totally unacceptable that the realities of the world we live in should be deliberately hidden from us. But it is no less true that we are overexposed. By its very nature, television dwells on dramatic events. There is no show element in peace. Nondrama, the nonhappening, is not something upon which movies, radio and television can feed and prosper. Our conscience and consciousness are therefore constantly bombarded with the worst. The very nature of showmanship, of the spectacular, of the arresting, of the dramatic, is shock. Overemphasis sets in with the necessity to conquer new audiences and to fight the competition of other media. All those who listened to the hysterical radio report on the assassination of Senator Robert Kennedy soon found themselves reacting hysterically to the tragedy. Superevents provoke overreactions. Even the voices of the majority of news commentators in the United States are almost constantly keyed up; they tend to overplay the drama already emphatic enough in itself. The accent is always on tragedy, and the more peaceful and happy aspects of life are largely ignored. There is an old saying in France: "Happy people have no history." There is no story in the absence of drama. We are, therefore, being served day-by-day overdoses of tragedy and we like, through mass media, a permanent show, with the consequence that a lack of entertainment, which was our normal way of life for thousands of years, leaves us in a vacuum. It is not so much the violence on the television screen or in the movies, as is too often said, that leads to crime and violence; it is a craving for a constant happening, the conditioning by the constant dramatic vibration on the screen, which, in the end, equates nondrama with a feeling of nonexistence. As often as not, violence in the streets is a form of self-provided entertainment.

I understand that after the assassination of Robert Kennedy, many Hollywood personalities took an oath to renounce violence in the movies in which they star. It may be a valid personal reaction against our gun society, but it has no relevance to the murder of Robert Kennedy. The young senator was assassinated —probably as was his brother—because his glamorous personality, wealth, power, good looks and unlimited prospects had been overdramatized by mass media to the point that they were beginning to act as provocation on a paranoid personality with an inherent feeling of inferiority and frustration, always on the lookout for dramatic self-assertion. In such a situation, the assassin feels that he has avenged himself and has achieved greatness by his act, and that he has risen above the status of his victim.

As for violence in films, its influence is probably highly overestimated. And can anyone tell me what effect *Bonnie and Clyde* had on the sadistic behavior of the Chicago police during the convention?

During the 1968 spring riots in Washington, I was fortunate enough to be able to witness an example of a truly curious rapport between the television addicts and the magical box. Several houses were burning around 14th Street. A few blocks from the nearest and clearly visible fire, I saw a crowd in front of a store. The crowd was watching a television set in the window, and do you know what they were looking at? They were looking at a house burning in the neighborhood. They had only to turn their heads to see the fire live, but they obviously preferred to watch it on TV. Maybe they were confident that the network had picked the *best* fire for them. Or maybe they wanted to see the commercial that would follow. I do not pretend to be able to explain this phenomenon. At one moment, I even began to suspect that the crowd was not watching the fire on the screen but the TV set itself. Or perhaps they were just waiting for someone to break the window so that they could take the set and the fire home with them.

The power of the transistor radio in the underdeveloped countries is fantastic. It can be argued that Egypt and the whole Arab Middle East are held together only by transistor radio. A few words can throw millions of people into the streets, as happened in Cairo during Nasser's "abdication" speech and in Paris, in the Champs Elysées, during De Gaulle's challenging speech against the Communist Party.

The power of the mass media is snowballing through the democratic explosion and coincides with the appearance on the social scene of a completely new and extremely receptive class—youth, with its own economic power and leadership, its own mechanized transport, vocabulary, heroes and tribal organizations, with its more sensitive and militant elements refusing any form of integration. Youth power is in the process of radically changing the patterns of behavior in our society; and the adults are simply unable to meet the challenge of the young and to compete with them, if only because they are almost physiologically incapable of the same reflexes, vitality, eagerness and freshness of outlook. All they seem able to do is to call the police. In such a situation, mass reactions are bound to become endemic and explosive, unpredictable and beyond the grasp of traditional reason. In France, the average age at a mass meeting thirty-five years ago was forty-two. Today, it is twenty-four. A huge turnout forty years ago meant 100,000 people; today, it means nearly 1,000,000. A large minority of this new class, youth, seeks a deliberate alienation from the rest of society, develops new codes of behavior and reinvents something akin to tribalism. The recourse to tribalism—hippies, black angels, psychedelic clans, gangs, sects, each with its own way of living, of dressing, each with its own customs, language, signs and symbols—is a reaction of the individual against the sucking-in pressures of a homogenized society endowed with unlimited power and authority over him. The individual regroups himself within the tribe and tries to create a world of his own. This form of retreat will be prevalent as long as a prosperous society permits such marginal living, which is feeding essentially on surplus and offal. The same forces will become revolutionary when marginal forms of escape living become economically impossible. Add to this the demographic congestion in urban areas and the evidence that our unreconstructed society is largely incapable of coping with the growth of its own birth rate, and it becomes apparent that we will either have to reconstruct the society entirely or establish a police state. Our civilization remains static and clings to sameness, while all its components, from technology to communications media, are in constant change, which can only mean an explosion, a breakdown or rapid, deliberate progress. The whole refuses to follow the changes of its components.

Within the U. S. A., the combined psychological pressures of advertising and of the constant show of wealth surrounding the poor are so strong that they amount to an invitation to looting or to robbery. The baiting never stops. Buy! Consume! You cannot do without this; this is the newest and the best and you must have it! Come on, it's waiting for you! How can we act indignant after that when the ghetto kid, submitted to such a teasing, at the first opportunity goes on a looting spree? America has laid out the rule for the successful consumers' society: Get rich. Yet it refuses both within its national boundaries and throughout the world to play its own game. Willing or not, it finds itself, therefore, constantly baiting, taunting and provoking millions of its own economically abandoned nonconsumers, as well as all the underdeveloped countries. The attitude of the destitute masses of South America, Asia and Africa toward the U. S. A. is that of the average looter toward a Fifth Avenue store.

The alternative to crime would be revolutionary; it would consist of an attempt to overthrow a society that at the same time baits you with its riches and denies you economic access to them. Crime is a form of adjustment to society. It's a pathological way of accepting this society and of answering to its pressures. Crime is not, as is often said, the left hand of idealism; it is the right hand of ignorance.

Each of us can compose his own list of overwhelming forces

active as a tease within our baiting society. Authority, for instance, has become a dirty word because of the sheer exhibitionistic, overactive and ever present aspects of it. For young people everywhere, revolutionary and nonrevolutionary alike, from Moscow to Belgrade, from Prague to Paris, from Chicago to Montreal, authority is the number-one enemy. No wonder: Living has become an exercise in bureaucracy. Individual freedom has all the scope of a pedestrian crossing: Walk, Don't Walk. During the students' May revolt, when spring in Paris was blossoming with slogans on all walls in the flickering light of burning cars, one of the graffiti I read was "Down with the bureaucracy of living!" It was impossible to find out what the students were fighting for, in terms of actual politically constructive changes. They were merely reacting to the daily baiting of our civilization, reaching for an overexposed and unacceptable reality; and they reminded me once more of Kafka's most moving prophecy, those few words that have been my greatest inspiration as a writer and whose echo can be heard in all my books: "The power of the human scream is so great that it will smash all the iron laws decreed against man."

"*La puissance, voilà l'ennemi!*" ("Power, that's the enemy!"), ran another bit of writing on the wall. The individual is surrounded by the evidence of too much implacable power around him—nuclear, economic, military, industrial, mechanized, organized, anonymous, impudent power. The individual either capitulates to the power machine and becomes a kind of "insert one" coin in its entrails or tries to destroy the machine itself, with nothing in mind to replace it. Violence, then, becomes a kind of groping for self-respect, a self-assertion, a proclamation of independence. Victory becomes irrelevant; what counts is the old-fashioned, seldom-heard-today word "honor." The rebellious Jews of the Warsaw ghetto could not hope for any victory over the German war machine. But they attained dignity and honor.

Each of us is exposed day by day to increasing doses of historical fallout. After all, there is no reason a French student should feel guilty and responsible for what happens, let us say, in Biafra. But when a mass-circulation magazine prints on its cover the picture of a tiny skeleton still stirring and staring at you under the caption "Within two hours this child will be dead," unless you have become completely amorphous, with your sensitivity killed by overexposure and you no longer care or react (which is the first step toward a police state), any human being, and particularly the young, feels like smashing something, a typical reaction of frustration and impotence.

I vividly remember other slogans scribbled on the dirty old walls of Paris: "The word is a born liar," which is an approximate translation of "*Le mot ment comme il respire.*" "The word comes with police protection and tear gas." "Truth cannot be expressed in words without lying." "Unlearn the words; go back to before ABC." "Stop the word before it makes another million dead." As I write this, I wonder how the politicians and the war-makers everywhere would feel about this. The disillusionment of the young is entirely justified, and the indisputable fact is that the Communists and the capitalists, all the democrats and nondemocrats, all the revolutionaries and conservatives alike have betrayed their beautiful words and promises. Remember "Freedom from fear, freedom from want"? I wonder what happened to *them*.

To many people, this verbal aggression against words may appear as mere literature; but then, what they are really shrugging off is literature itself, which they cannot do without admitting that they have capitulated in their relationship with spiritual values and that those values are in the process of rotting in the vast Marxist and non-Marxist cemetery of "culture." It is characteristic that the leaders of the Paris revolt and most of the rank and file were students of literature and philosophy. Unquestionably, the revolution had its roots in the very dynamics of all artistic creation: the need for self-expression under the onslaught, baiting and pressures by our unacceptable reality. All art and literature is an answer to the taunting or challenge by reality. All craving for justice is an artistic pursuit, a craving for beauty and harmony. Frustration and inability to change the real world can lead both to violence and to artistic creation. This age will probably see more music, art and literature—and more young people, talented or not, devoted to those pursuits—than any other age, simply because there is no other way out. From the furious action painting of Jackson Pollock to Picasso's pictorial aggression against reality, from the theatrical Happening to the students' riots in the streets, the means of self-defense and self-expression may differ vastly, but the motivation is the same: a refusal to accept the taunting of our consciousness and of our conscience by a monstrous environment. Psychodrama, Happening, Living Theater—the riots and violence in our cities were and will continue to be what art and literature have always been: an attempt at a rebirth, a spiritual self-cleansing, a deliberate alienation from the present-day social reality. Art is what is not there but should be there.

To me, the most hopeful sign is that our generation of protest and of negation has outgrown national frontiers, races, creeds and ideologies. It's nothing more than one great big, emotional *No!* And it unites Christians and atheists alike. Not long ago, I stood in the midst of a crowd of Catholic dissenters near Notre Dame, the day after the Pope's ban on the contraceptive pill was announced. As I stood pushing the mike of my tape recorder toward the white face of a young Dominican priest, these were exactly the words I heard:

"The contraceptive pill means the rebirth of man. It means resurrection. It means the end of genocide; of genocide through hunger, through oppression, through squalor, through ignorance. It means the reassurance that the reborn Jesus will not die of hunger in some small corner of the world. The prohibition of the contraceptive pill is genocide."

My contention is that the real danger to our future is not the violent, rioting youth, still a vocal minority magnified through the mass media, always on the watch for drama. The real danger is our indifferent masses. The pattern of violence is, in my view, insufficient to force our society toward a real change, but its positive aspect is that it may awaken some stupefied, apathetic people. Every Communist and every politician has always and will always speak of the people with sobs of emotion in their voice, and the people have responded with self-righteous self-esteem almost to the point of no return. This passive, cowed, hypnotized majority may still be awakened from its slumber by the so-called violent fringe. Up to now, both in Soviet slave-land and deep between the layers of our Western fat, the people have refused to budge. We hear every day about the rioters and killers in our midst, about the troublemakers, but we never hear a word about the 95 percent of the population who are merely for law and order. The question is *what* law and *what* order? The same as before and more of the same? Then we will soon need a police state to protect our goodies and our rights.

ROLF HOCHHUTH

opinion

SLAUGHTER OF THE INNOCENTS

recalling a visit with the master bomber of dresden, the controversial author of the deputy *asserts that any distinction between war hero and war criminal is false, and that the bombing of civilians is the most heinous horror of modern warfare*

On the evening of February 13, 1945, 733 British Lancaster bombers dropped 650,000 incendiary bombs on Dresden, Germany, creating a firestorm that could be seen two hundred miles away. Next morning, 311 American Flying Fortresses blasted the still-flaming city with high explosives, while escort fighters strafed survivors. The city burned for seven days and eight nights, and an estimated 135,000 persons were killed in the holocaust. While Winston Churchill was later to write that Dresden was "a communications center for Germany's Eastern Front," other observers—both during and after the War—claimed it was a civilian target of no strategic importance. Regardless of its military value, Dresden symbolized a drastic change in Allied attitudes toward the rules of war. Before Dresden, the large-scale destruction of civilian population centers was taboo; after Dresden, it became an implicitly accepted—although seldom discussed—weapon in the armory of modern warfare. Almost twenty-two years after Dresden, with the deliberate bombing of civilians once again not a threat but a distinct possibility, Hochhuth, at work on a new play based on the destruction of Dresden, attempted to grasp the implications of this Allied "atrocity." The following was written in London, in February 1965, while Hochhuth—accompanied by David Irving, author of

The Destruction of Dresden—*gathered material for his forthcoming play.*

If Wing Commander Maurice Smith had belonged to the British Fighter Command during the War, defending England against German flyers, instead of being master bomber under Sir Arthur Harris, he would then have had no time for us today, the eve of Churchill's funeral. For we have just seen in the *Evening News,* above the top headline, which announces the arrival in London of crowned and other heads of state, an eight-column picture that itself seems an official decoration and that shows especially deserving fighter pilots—fourteen men, again in their old, richly decorated uniforms—who tomorrow morning are to take their seats of honor in St. Paul's. That former bombardiers are also to appear at the state ceremony one reads nowhere. Fighter and combat flyers saved the island from Hitler—but England's bombers of that time embody today the still-unmastered past of the nation that has so sure a sense of fair play when it is the victor. Air Chief Marshal Harris suddenly left the country a few days ago—to recover from an illness. And the second-highest marshal of the bomber command, who supervised the preparation of all bombings of Germany during the War, Sir Robert Saundby, also will not be going to the ceremony. He has arranged for David Irving and me to meet him tomorrow afternoon in his country house several miles west of Reading (where Oscar Wilde was jailed, in Berkshire), above which on the evening of February 13, 1945, the Lancasters of the Marker and Bomber Group foregathered for the Dresden flight.

Mr. Smith greets us in the office of the aviation magazine (*Flight*) of which he is today editor-in-chief. Obviously, since I have come from Basel, he takes me for a Swiss; perhaps he was only ready to talk at all for that reason. So I say right off that I am a German.

His reserve grows; I am surprised that he allows Irving to use his tape recorder. Finally, though, Smith takes from a shelf behind his desk a navy-blue leather volume with heavy gold lettering and ornamentation—a book like a stamp album—on whose cover the owner's name had been stamped along with his rank and the years of his assignment as bombardier. Now before our eyes the retired wing commander, who is perhaps forty-eight, thumbs through orders to attack, target indications, pictures and technical aviation data, while he explains that he deplores the destruction of Dresden and that, before Dresden, he had been on missions against numerous military targets. But above all, that he found war repellent.

Because I want to repress it, the memory of the photograph-and-document collection—I think on parchment—of another officer disturbs me uninterruptedly while I look at the leather album. Its last page read, "And now there is no more Jewish quarter in Warsaw." I don't want to think of this now. I know that *Herr* Smith, in contrast to *Herr* Stroop, would never have come upon the idea—if he had, he could have acted on it after the War—of counting his victims, sticking pictures of corpses in his book and writing such a sentence as "Total number of Jews seized and probably annihilated: in all, 56,065." Smith has not only not counted the dead; if possible, he'd rather not know their number, even today. He reported to Irving with uneasiness that he was told, twenty years ago, on the thirteenth of February, that *he had the honor* to lead the first British attack on Dresden. And like all the other flyers to whom Irving put this question, Smith confessed his inability to kill a man eye to eye. But this answer, I'm afraid, does not surprise me. I find it surprising only that Irving still attributes any significance to the question. As if it were not known that the most unscrupulous murderers of our epoch were seldom or never capable of delivering a death blow with their own hands. They performed their duties at their desks. Himmler (this was confirmed) began to scream when he was about to look at a massacre that he himself had ordered.

Then why this confrontation, which undeniably exposes one as a German to the massive suspicion of wanting to weigh Dresden against Auschwitz? Any such calculation would be objectionable and absurd. Let the record be clear: SS men who murdered in the camps or at bases or in their own home towns could avoid going to the front because they murdered. Bomber pilots who killed civilians staked their lives, and the British bombers, for example, suffered by far the greatest losses of all sections of the British services during the War. The bomber fleet of the RAF lost more men than the entire British army in the period from the invasion of Normandy to the death of Hitler. It lost nearly 56,000 men, a thousand more than the number of Hamburg civilians it had been able to kill.

But above all, in air warfare, *both* parties to the War committed heinous crimes. The Jews, the Gypsies and the Polish intellectuals were killed by us just for having identities that would have been impossible for them to abandon. They were murdered for being born. In Europe before Hitler, that would never have been grounds for the death penalty. One must also concede to the bomber pilots of all nations that insofar as they killed civilians deliberately—and we are talking now only of such pilots—they could imagine they made thereby a contribution to their country's victory. But this in itself is, of course, a highly questionable argument.

If I still bring together in the same proposition this related pair of towns, Auschwitz and Dresden, in which very likely more people were burned than in any other two places in the whole history of the world, it is only because it can cost us our very lives if the massacre of Dresden is not finally rejected by the military in the West as in the East—rejected with the same disgust that the generals, it may be hoped, feel for Auschwitz.

For our future depends on just this: whether the defenseless will again be taboo, off limits, for the combatants—whether one can erase the crazy notion from the minds of today's air strategists that the *method* with which one proposes to kill civilians should determine whether one is to be considered a criminal or a soldier. The method, the style, the mode of operation, determines nothing. Auschwitz can only be a lesson to us all when this doctrine reads quite simply: Civilians may never be the assigned target.

Simple? In Europe it was once so—before Guernica, before Lübeck, before Belgrade. The law of the Red Cross was commonplace for anyone who deserved the decent professional designation of "soldier." Today this commonplace seems rather a tall order to the military men—a circumstance that makes one's flesh creep.

Both our defenders and our potential adversaries wish to hush up the fact that murder remains murder even when one does not propose to gas civilians, as in Auschwitz, but "only" to kill them by radioactivity, as at Hiroshima, or asphyxiate them, as at Dresden. To repeat, it can, it will cost us our lives, one day, one night, if we do not regard the destroyers of Belgrade or Rostock with the same contempt as we do the executioners of Treblinka or Bergen-Belsen. This is the irreplaceable worth of the war-crimes trials, and one hopes it will be a continuing worth, that through them the gassings in the camps were revealed as so objectionable, so "impossible," that even the gassers themselves, Eichmann or Hoess, did not try to defend their deeds, but only themselves.

On the other hand, since the destruction of cities was unfortunately never what the trials were about, the blockbusting pilots still in all seriousness believe today (and the world believes so, too) that they acted as soldiers. Mr. Smith is just saying it again: Of course, he did nothing but his duty. The doctrine has a following! The flyers of today take for granted what for the British bomber command was still at any rate problematic and what the American bomber crews rejected as undiscussible till January 1945: the deliberate killing of the defenseless. The opening of the rocket era by Hitler was a further step toward the wild and arbitrary extermination of the defenseless by air raids. One cannot say the defenseless were the target; there were no targets, but rather the procedure was targetless and limitless. Today—such is progress—no one complains about this monstrous product of the man from Braunau and his Wernher von Braun, since this second-worst tool of Hitler has become the pride of all the advanced countries.

British Air Marshal Saundby, with whom one can talk quite freely and openly, agreed with me that the attacks of 1941–1945 would hardly have taken place if they had been discredited before 1939 by international agreement. But there were no such agreements, and still are none, although the Geneva Red Cross has fought for them since 1957. Air Chief Marshal Sir Arthur Harris could recently say to Irving, and with some shade of truth, that the only international rule by which he and his bomber command could have felt bound during the entire War was an agreement from the Franco-Prussian War of 1870 that forbade throwing explosive objects from gas-filled dirigibles. With his characteristic humor, Harris revealed that *this* ban had been strictly adhered to by the RAF bomber command during all of World War Two.

It is true: There is a law for naval warfare and one for land warfare, but there is none for air warfare. And the major powers do not *wish* an air-warfare law that would compel them to spare population centers.

On our way to visit Smith, Irving showed me two of the many letters written to him before and after the appearance of his Dresden book. I quote from one sentence written in the bureaucratic German of a man in the Federal Statistical Bureau in Wiesbaden:

> In the process of removing the dead, from the place where they were first taken, to the mass burning centers, switching from individual registration to wholesale numerical computation during assembly, and due to complete annihilation of groups of dead with flame throwers on account of incipient danger of plague, after rough computation of the number of the dead.

I must think of this fragment of a sentence, which stops the breath and not just because of a missing comma, when I confront the colorless Mr. Smith, who naturally—come to think of it, why naturally?—is as uncriminal and normal (and just this is so frightful) as the brother, the cousin, whom each of us had in his own family—yes, like the image that, approximately, one finds also in one's own mirror.

In the other letter a Turk, who was a student in Dresden in 1945 and after the attack looked for his fiancée, wrote:

> In the streets lay, among other things, naked women with children prematurely born (through heat and air pressure) between their thighs. In one case just the head of the child had come out and the feet were still in the womb. You [Irving] write also of naked dead, but do you mention why they lay around naked? Anyhow, I sought my fiancée among these dead women. She was pregnant, and I had to examine the teeth of likely-looking dead women, for the faces were all charred. In

the afternoon (February 14) we got to the part of town called White Stag. A mighty hurricane caused by the fires raged over the Elbe. On the Elbe bridge we had to hold onto the ironwork and crawl on the roadway so as not to be sucked up by the whirlwinds.

The bridges, Irving explained to me, the only military targets of the city, were not hit in any of the three attacks.

At the very time that I sit opposite Mr. Smith, I sense the injustice of bringing up *his* name in particular, and his "job," as he calls it, in these reflections on the fall of Dresden. Certainly, Smith led the attack, and yet, this man did the same thing that presumably all other pilots of all other nations would have done if they had reached the same level of technical training as Smith. And so a part of his guilt is transferred to us all. More guilty than this individual is the society that took over his conscience for that which he did in its name.

This society and its norms have not changed since Dresden. Still worse, for all bombing strategists, Dresden became the test case, the proof, in fact, that one could destroy a city from the air, even with conventional weapons. And since one could, it has never been doubted by the military that one was entitled to. Hannah Arendt said of Eichmann, "He never at any time put to himself just what he was doing." This is the most precise characterization ever made of the normal "man acting on orders from his superiors." And it fits, without modification, those of all nations who bombed cities in World War Two.

This applies to Smith, to Harris and to Lord Alanbrooke, Great Britain's highest-ranking soldier. Alanbrooke, who kept a daily diary, did not, it would seem, even mention Dresden—and he was a very conscientious diary writer and, incidentally, a very tender-minded ornithologist. With Sir Charles Portal, who personally gave the order for the attack, he was at table in Buckingham Palace during the week of Dresden, possibly the same evening, possibly one or two evenings earlier or later. *This*, but not the most colossal city fire in history, he thinks worth recording: "The King and Queen were as usual quite extraordinary hosts and made us forget at once the regal atmosphere of the meeting. The King thrilled about the new medal ribbons he was devising and had an envelope full of them in his pocket. . . ."

What light-years away "men of action" are from their actions! Perhaps this is nowhere so clear as in the diary of Churchill's physician, who presents a shudderingly innocuous report on the night before the fire. It is quite clear that the man who ordered Dresden reduced to ashes retained not the slightest memory of giving such an order at the time when the catastrophe was imminent. The Yalta Conference in the Crimea was over, Churchill was preparing to return home on the *Franconia*, and his physician, Lord Moran, notes, "The chef of the *Queen Mary*, borrowed for the occasion, produces perfect food, and the white rolls take one back to times of peace." Then he records the highly animated table conversation that took place in the very hours when hell broke loose in Dresden. The Prime Minister

> reverted to the natural conversation of old age, with its dislike of change. He bemoaned the passing of ritual. He had not really forgiven the King and his family for allowing the eight cream ceremonial horses to disappear. They could not be replaced now. The breed was extinct, or at any rate, since they came from Holland, and Holland was in a turmoil, their successors could not be bought. Black horses would draw the coach of state in the future; they were well enough, but—well, they were not the same thing.

One might conclude from this conversation that the ability to forget what one is doing is a prerequisite of becoming great through one's deeds.

Smith stresses that air personnel harbored no feelings of hate or revenge. Obviously, he thinks this purely technical outlook is more human, whereas in reality it is the most shocking thing of all. "Quite certainly we had no fun doing it, though what we did interested us technically and we tried to do as good a job as possible." On humane grounds, I had hoped to hear Mr. Smith, in regard to Dresden, mention our German atrocities against the Jews. Not a bit of it. So I ask about this expressly. Yes, he says, more and more news of that was coming in, but he adds that at the same time came the news of how extremely correct was the treatment given bomber pilots shot down in Germany. "As I told you earlier, if any attack had specially grieved me, it would have been Dresden, but that was really a personal affair—really a misunderstanding on my part, because we all had the idea that Dresden was a specially beautiful city, and we thought of it in terms of Dresden china, and I think some of us would sooner the attack had been on some less pretty old town."

David Irving diplomatically begins his new question with the prefatory note that it had less to do with him, Wing Commander Smith, who often had attacked much more rewarding targets than Dresden or Heilbronn or Karlsruhe in his capacity of master bomber—military and railroad installations, for example. But what had other officers of the bomber command thought, Irving would like to know.

Mr. Smith answers, "Well, I can imagine they would have felt a certain regret if they had indulged in such deeper thoughts at all. And I don't think they would have concealed this by saying the Germans deserved it. I don't think they'd have said that. They would probably have said, 'There's a war on, and how can you separate this from war in general—the whole thing is rotten.' " The ground personnel, Mr. Smith concedes—and one accepts this human aspect of things as a kind of relief—the ground personnel, who came in closer contact with the destruction wrought by the *Luftwaffe* in English cities, would have tended, rather, to say, "Let 'em have one for us!"

Smith feels no hate, no pity. If the air photographs showed that a city can be totally annihilated, then the pilots' reaction was, Thank God we needn't go there again.

For the second attack on Dresden during the same night and before the Americans were to bomb it the next day, an officer was chosen as master bomber who already, in November 1944, had been requested to lead the mission to Freiburg. At the time he had rejected the request, since he had studied at Freiburg University and many of his friends lived in Freiburg. Evidently he had been permitted to say no without getting the feared formula LMF stamped in his paybook. This meant Lack of Moral Fiber and made difficulties in an officer's career, though it did not quite mean "coward." Almost, but not quite.

Today the various directives for the attacks that one reads in Irving's account sound sadistic. But in intention they are simply matter-of-fact. They say, for example, that the second attack should not happen until enough time has elapsed to guarantee that fire-fighting crews from other Middle German cities have arrived in Dresden to get themselves annihilated in their turn when the second blow falls. If one reads such directives page after page, the main object of the raids might seem not the burning of cities but the extermination of people.

Harris, the Chief Marshal, with the forthrightness that characterizes him, and much to the discomfort of the Cabinet, made no bones about this, but stressed it, and thereby annoyed the Secretary of State for Air, Sir Archibald Sinclair, who lied to Parliament persistently, year in, year out. Harris said, "Before we can win the War we must first kill a whole pile of German civilians." This and many similar expressions of leading Britons are what make it so hard to stand by what hitherto seemed to me *the* decisive difference between an Eichmann and a Harris. I said to myself, Eichmann cannot have believed the gassing of Jewish families brought Hitler's Germany one step nearer to final victory; this he *cannot* have believed.

And Harris? Without question, he believed the burning of the cities led to our downfall. But the burning of the citizens? A general is supposed to have believed that? Incidentally, Irving possesses a copy of the leaflet that the RAF dropped on Dresden at the time of the attack, from which it transpires that London knew the city to be overcrowded with refugees from other parts of Germany. More ghastly still, proof exists that this fact was one of the grounds, if not the chief one, for Churchill's ordering the massacre. Maurice Smith says that Harris was always known as a butcher. "Certainly, many people thought he was a butcher, and I have heard people defend him from the charge as well as attack him. But if a conclusion was reached, it was this one every time—whether or not he was a butcher, he too had his job to do, and so I don't know where one is to seek the final responsibility."

Harris says the responsibility is not carried by him. Actually, the massive area bombings had already been ordered by the Cabinet when he took over the command in February 1942. His deputy, Marshal Saundby, with whom we are to drink tea tomorrow, introduces Irving's Dresden book in a very relaxed manner:

> When the author of this book invited me to write a foreword to it, my first reaction was that I had been too closely concerned with the story. But, though closely concerned, I was not in any way responsible for the decision to make a full-scale air attack on Dresden. Nor was my commander-in-chief, Sir Arthur Harris. Our part was to carry out, to the best of our ability, the instructions we received from the Air Ministry. And, in this case, the Air Ministry was merely passing on instructions received from those responsible for the highest direction of the war.

To read such words, almost precisely these words, you unhappily do not need Irving's book on Dresden. They are to be found today in every newspaper, in every speech, in which a German war criminal defends himself.

"I wish I'd said that . . ."

article

JULIAN HUXLEY

THE CRISIS IN MAN'S DESTINY

what the human race must do now to keep our accelerating technology—the presumed servant of mankind—from becoming its master

The most bewildering characteristic of the present moment of history is that things are happening faster and faster. The pace of change in human affairs, originally so slow as to be unnoticed, has steadily accelerated, until today we can no longer measure it in terms of generations. Major changes now take place every few years, and human individuals have to make several drastic adjustments in the course of their working lives. Where are these breathless changes taking us? Is change synonymous with progress, as many technologists and developers would like us to believe? Is there any main direction to be discerned in present-day human life and affairs? The answer at the moment is no. Change today is disruptive; its trends are diverging in various directions. What is more, many of them are self-limiting or even self-destructive—think of the trend to explosive population increase, to overgrown cities, to traffic congestion, to reckless exploitation of resources, to the widening gap between developed and underdeveloped countries, to the destruction of wild life and natural beauty, to cutthroat competition in economic growth, to Galbraith's private affluence and public squalor, to overspecialization and imbalance in science and technology, to monotony, boredom and conformity, and to the proliferation of increasingly expensive armaments.

What is to be done? Before attempting an answer, we must

look at the problem in a long perspective—indeed in the longest perspective of all, the perspective of evolution. The process of evolution on this planet has been going on for five billion years or so. First of all, it was only physical and chemical—the formation of the continents and oceans and the production of increasingly complex chemical compounds. Then, nearly three billion years ago, this purely physicochemical phase of evolution was superseded by the biological phase—the evolution of living matter, or "life." The threshold to this was crossed when one of the numerous organic chemical compounds built up by ultraviolet radiation in the world's warm, soupy seas became capable of reproducing itself. This compound is a kind of nucleic acid, called DNA for short; its complex molecule is built in the form of a double helix, like a spirally twisted ladder whose complementary halves are joined by special chemical rungs. In favorable conditions, the two halves sooner or later break apart, and both build themselves into new wholes by incorporating organic compounds from the surrounding medium. DNA also has the capacity to build up special enzymes and many other proteins out of its chemical surroundings, with the final result of producing a primitive cell with DNA as its core.

DNA is thus self-reproducing and self-multiplying matter. It is also self-varying, since now and again it undergoes a small change in part of its structure as a result of radiation or some chemical agency (or sometimes spontaneously), and then reproduces itself in this changed form. In modern terms, it mutates, and the mutation is hereditary. And very soon, the sexual process multiplies the variation manyfold by recombining mutations in every possible way.

As a result of these two properties of self-multiplication and self-variation, there results a "struggle for existence" between the different variants, and this in turn results in what Darwin called *natural selection*—a shorthand phrase for the results of the differential death, survival and reproduction of variants.

Crossing the threshold must have been a relatively slow business, taking perhaps ten million years or more, but once it was crossed, the whole process of evolution was enormously speeded up, major changes taking place at intervals to be measured in hundred-million-year instead of billion-year units. And, as Darwin pointed out over a century ago, and as has become clearer ever since, major change was inevitably progressive, headed in the direction of improvement—improving the organization of plants and animals in relation to their environment, enabling them to surmount more of its dangers and make better use of its resources.

Each major change in biological evolution involved the step-by-step crossing of a critical threshold, leading to the formation of a new dominant type. This is followed by a rapid flowering of the new type and its further improvement along many divergent lines, usually at the expense of its parent and predecessor type. Sooner or later, the process reveals itself as self-limiting: The type as a whole comes up against a limit, and further progress can only be realized by one or two lines slowly achieving a new and improved pattern of organization, and stepping across the threshold barrier to give rise to quite new dominant types.

Thus the amphibians broke through the barrier from water to land, though they still had to live in water as tadpoles or larvae in the early stages of their development, but after about 100,000,000 years, they were succeeded by a new and fully terrestrial dominant type, with shelled eggs containing private ponds to develop in—the reptiles, which, as everyone knows, produced an astonishing variety of specialized lines—crocodiles and tortoises, marine ichthyosaurs and plesiosaurs, aerial pterosaurs and the splendid array of terrestrial dinosaurs.

But after nearly 150,000,000 years, they, too, reached their limit. A new type of organization was produced, involving hair, warm blood, milk and prolonged development within the mother, and broke through to dominance in the shape of the placental mammals, while most reptilian lines became extinct. This new type again radiated out, to produce all the familiar mammal groups—carnivores and ungulates, rats and bats, whales and primates. Once more, after 50,000,000 years or so, their evolution seems to have reached its limits and got stuck. Only one line among the primates took all the steps—to erect posture, tool and weapon making, increased brain size, and capacity for true speech—that led, a mere 100,000 or so years back, to the emergence of man as the new dominant type, and took life across the threshold from the biological to the psychosocial phase of evolution.

This works by cumulative tradition rather than by genetic variation, and is manifested in cultural and mental rather than in bodily and physical transformation. Yet evolving human life progresses in the same sort of way as animal life—by a succession of improved dominant types of organization. However, these are not organizations of flesh and blood and bodily structure but of ideas and institutions, of mental and social structure—systems of thought and knowledge, feeling and belief, with their social, economic and political accompaniments. We may call them psychosocial systems. With the emergence of each new system, man radically changes his ideas about his place, his role and his job in nature—how to utilize natural resources, how to organize his societies, how to understand and pursue his destiny.

Up to the present there have been five such dominant psychosocial systems, five major progressive stages, involving four crossings of a difficult threshold to a new way of thinking about nature and coping with existence. First the crossing from the stage of food gathering by small groups to that of organized hunting and tribal organization. Then the step, first taken some ten thousand years ago, across to the neolithic stage, based on the idea of growing crops and domesticating animals, associated with fertility rites and priest-kings, and leading to food storage and settled life in villages and small towns. Third, nearly six thousand years ago, the radical step to civilization, with organized cities and trading systems, castes and professions, including a learned priesthood, with writing or other means of nonvocal communication, and leading to large and powerful societies (and eventually to empires), always with a religious basis. And fourth, less than five hundred years ago, the even more decisive step, marked by the Renaissance, the Reformation and the beginnings of organized objective inquiry, over the threshold to the stage of exploration—geographical, historical, religious and, above all, scientific: in a word, the stage of science. This was associated with increasingly secular representative government, with the idea of progress based on ever increasing knowledge and wealth, and led to a profit-based economic system, industrialization and competitive nationalism.

What, you may ask, has all this to do with our present troubles? The answer is that they portend a new threshold to be crossed to a new dominant system and a new stage of human advance. During each previous dominant stage, mankind differentiated into competing groups, with divergent trends of thought and action. These were in the long run self-limiting, self-defeating, disruptive or just hampering. But they contained seeds of self-correction. As their unhelpful nature became obvious, this provoked new thinking and new action to reduce their harmful effects, and eventually to make clear the need to attempt the difficult passage into a new stage based on a radically new system. To take but one case, abuses of ecclesiastical power provoked the Reformation, backward-looking and hairsplitting scholasticism helped on the new birth of the Renaissance and of modern science, and the reaction against the Church's ban on "usury" or charging interest on a loan, coupled with the urgent need for large-scale trade ventures, stimulated the birth of the capitalist system.

The same sort of thing is at work today. The population explosion is stimulating birth control, monolithic overplanning in the U. S. S. R. and its satellites is producing liberalizing reactions, while the doctrinaire freedom of enterprise and expression of the U. S. A. and its acolytes is forcing the acceptance of some degree of discipline and planning; the gap between rich and poor nations is stimulating increased aid and assistance, while racial injustice is stimulating campaigns for integration.

The inadequacy of our educational systems has called forth efforts for their expansion and reform; the reckless exploitation and careless destruction of the world's varied resources is leading to a multitude of separate attempts to conserve them; traffic congestion and the other frustrations of city life are leading to transportation planning and schemes of urban renewal; in reaction against the conformity and boredom of modern mechanized existence, a whole crop of new outlets for life is sprouting, in sport and art, in adventure and dedicated projects, while to fill the vacuum caused by the enfeeblement of traditional religious belief and expression, new adventures of spiritual and mental exploration are being undertaken. And the giant wars of this most destructive of centuries have provoked a reaction against war itself and generated a general desire for peace and a crop of projects for preserving and fostering it.

But all this is not enough—all these are negative attempts, actions *against* something, instead of positive efforts *for* something. What is needed is a new over-all pattern of thinking and willing that will give us a new vision and a constructive purpose, providing meaning for our lives and incentives for our actions. Only this can bring together the separate reactions against the divergent threats that beset us and harness them (and all our reserves of suppressed good will) in a single-minded team.

A new vision has been revealed by post-Darwinian science and learning. It gives us a new and an assured view of ourselves. Man is a highly peculiar organism. He is a single joint body-mind, not a body plus a separate mind or soul, but with mind on top, no longer subordinate to body, as in animals. By virtue of this, he has become the latest dominant type in the solar system, with three billion years of evolution behind him and (if he doesn't destroy himself) a comparably long period of evolution before him. Certainly no other organism could oust him from his position. He would quickly become aware of any challenge, whether from rat, termite or ape, and would be able to nip it in the bud. His role, whether he wants it or not, is to be the leader of the evolutionary process on earth, and his job is to guide and direct it in the general direction of improvement.

To do this, he must redefine his aims. In the past, most human groups and most human individuals have aimed at wealth or pleasure or pride of power, though with a sizable minority seeking salvation in a future life, and a smaller minority seeking spiritual satisfactions or creative outlets in this life. During the long march of prehuman evolution, dominant types have split into a multitude of separate biological organizations termed species. Dominant man has also split, but into separate psychosocial and often competing organizations that Konrad Lorenz calls pseudospecies—tribes and nations, empires and religions (though this tendency toward diversity and disunity has been partially offset by an increasing tendency toward convergence and unity).

Clearly, our first aim must be to demote these pseudospecies and recognize the unity of the real species *Homo sapiens*—in other words, the oneness of mankind. And, *pari passu* with that, to construct more effective organs of his unity, in the shape of really effective international (or preferably supranational) institutions, to think, plan and act on behalf of the human species as a whole. A supporting aim must be to increase man's understanding of this new vision of himself, of his destiny and responsibility, of the limitless possibilities of improvement. And to convert understanding into action, he must improve his instruments for actually getting on with the job—new knowledge and new skills, new technological achievements, new social and political mechanisms.

But his most important instrument is his mind; accordingly, one of his most urgent tasks is to improve his own mental and psychological organization. As anthropologist Loren Eiseley has said, ancestral man entered his own head; ever since, he has been trying to adapt to what he found there. What he found there, of course, was a lot of myths and mumbo jumbo, witchcraft and wish fulfillment, the results of primitive thinking trying to cope with his own profound ignorance, with the civil war of conflicting passions inside and with the constricting forces of nature outside.

Man's primitive or fantasy thinking is always projecting his own ideas, his own guilt and his own secret wishes, onto someone or something else; its unconscious cunning is always inventing justifications for his own passions—supernatural justification like shifting the blame for his actions onto God, moral justifications like ascribing wickedness to his enemies or proclaiming his own group as divinely inspired or chosen.

In the natural sciences, man has learned the technique of "reality thinking"—of accepting the facts and phenomena of external nature and trying to understand them objectively, without bias. But he still has to tackle the more difficult task of abandoning primitive for reality thinking in dealing with the facts of his own nature and his own psychosocial creations, like religions and arts, laws and customs, social organizations and political institutions, and all the myths and rationalizations concerning them. In a word, man must improve his mechanisms for thinking about himself.

An obvious aim is to find out further how best to avoid conflict by transcending or transforming it, both internally, within our heads, and externally, in the physical and social world. Another is to ensure that the new pattern of thought and belief (and therefore of potential action) shall not be self-destructive but capable of constructive growth, not self-limiting but open-ended.

And the aim of aims must be to provide truly satisfying goals for human beings everywhere, so as to energize our species, to stimulate it to move and to ensure that it moves in the right direction. This involves planning for greater fulfillment for human individuals and greater achievement by human societies, and for fuller realization of man's varied possibilities, both personal and collective. It means aiming at quality rather than quantity—quality of life and personality instead of quantity of people, wealth and material goods. The time is ripe for a new approach to destiny, a new look at human life through the telescope of comprehensive vision of wholes instead of the microscope of analysis into separate parts.

Now I want to take another brief look at some of the unpleasant and threatening trends I spoke of at the outset, to see how the countermeasures we obviously must take against them may help us in planning the practical steps needed to achieve these new integrated ends.

First, population. The world's population is increasing by over sixty million a year—the equivalent of a good-sized town every day of the year, and of nearly twelve baseball teams (with coach) every minute of the day. Its compound-interest rate of increase has also increased, from under ½ percent per annum to over 1¾ percent today, and is still increasing a good deal. This applies just as much to Western countries like Britain or Sweden with a slow increase rate or the U. S. A. with a medium rate as to Asian or Latin American countries with a high rate.

Whatever we do, the world's population will double by the turn of the century. If we do nothing now, life for our grandchildren and great-grandchildren will be much more unpleasant than it is for us, which is saying a good deal. If we go on doing nothing, man will lose his chance of being the beneficent guide of evolution and will become the cancer of the planet, ruining it and himself with it.

A prerequisite for further human progress is immediate and universal birth control as an instrument of national and international policy, with the immediate aim of reducing man's rate of increase to manageable proportions, well below 1 percent a year, and the ultimate aim of reducing the total number of human beings in the world.

This means publicizing the need for birth control, incorporating family planning in national health services, adjusting family allowances and taxation systems to discourage overlarge families, and providing birth-control appliances and trained personnel to fit them, in all programs of aid and technical assistance. This means rethinking the whole problem of population, in terms of higher quality of life instead of increasing quantity of people. It also means rethinking the problem of resources, in terms of long-term conservation based on scientific ecology instead of quick exploitation based on mechanized technology.

Next there is the problem of cities. In the last half-century, more and more metropolitan areas have grown to monstrous size, up to 12,000,000, 14,000,000, even 16,000,000 in Tokyo, Greater London or Greater New York. If you take as your yardstick the city proper, the central area without its suburban tentacles, the number of cities with over a million inhabitants has grown from thirty at the end of World War Two to over eighty today. And meanwhile, the population of automobiles is growing twice as fast as that of people. As a result, cities are suffering from traffic thrombosis and their inhabitants from severe vital frustration. We know from experiment that overcrowding in animals leads to distorted, neurotic and downright pathological behavior. We can be sure that the same is true in principle for people. City life today is definitely leading to mass mental disease, to growing vandalism and possible eruptions of mass violence.

Existence in cities must be made not merely tolerable but life-enhancing, as it has so often been in the past. To do this, we must forcibly restrict any further expansion of overbig cities, while undertaking planned and limited expansion of smaller ones; we must create new towns in strategic locations (as is already being done in Britain) to accommodate the overspill of the nation's population; and we must rigorously prevent the horrible unplanned spread of what is neither city nor suburb nor country town, but "slurb"—a compound of slum, suburbia and urban sprawl, which has already blighted southern California and much of the Atlantic seaboard.

And we must be ready to devote a great deal of money and a great deal of skilled effort to something much bigger and more constructive than what often passes for urban renewal—the conversion of cities from being victims of their own size, ugly or infinitely dreary monuments of profiteering development and general unplanning, or even parasites of the automobile like Los Angeles, into what they should be by definition: organs for civilized existence; places in which their inhabitants enjoy living, instead of being turned into neurosis fodder; generators of fulfillment instead of frustration.

Science is exploding even more violently than population. Scientists (including technologists) are multiplying over three times as fast as ordinary people. The one million or so scientists now at work constitute over 90 percent of all the scientists who have ever lived, and their numbers may well go up to 20,000,000 or even 30,000,000 by A.D. 1999. The number of scientific journals has increased from one in 1665—*The Philosophical Translations of the Royal Society*—to about 1000 in 1865, to over 50,000 in 1965, in which nearly 5,000,000 separate articles are published each year, and the rate of increase is itself increasing. If nothing is done about it, science itself runs the risk of drowning in this torrent of paper; specialization will make scientists in one field more ignorant of work in other fields; and man's advance will be stifled in the mounting mass of unassimilable knowledge that he himself has accumulated.

The situation is made worse by the gross lack of balance between different fields of research. Billions of dollars are spent every year on outer-space research—much of it merely for the sake of prestige, in an effort to get to Mars before somebody else—as against a few millions on exploring the "inner space" of the human mind; billions on weapons research as against a few millions on the sociology of peace; hundreds of millions on "death control" through medical science as against four or five millions on birth control and reproduction. Biological research has given us the tools for real eugenic improvement, in the shape of artificial insemination with the deep-frozen sperm of outstanding male donors, even after their death, and the speedy prospect of grafting ova from admired female donors—but nothing (except words) has been spent on any such project.

The situation is also made worse by the lack of balance between scientific progress in different countries and regions. There is a big scientific and technological "brain drain" from Britain and Europe to the U. S. A. and Canada, and this is producing an equally big one to Britain and Europe from underdeveloped countries like those of Southeast Asia, the Middle East and Africa. In consequence, the gap between rich and poor nations is widening scientifically as well as economically.

What is to be done? The torrential flow of scientific printed matter could be reduced if the scientific reputation of a man or a department did not depend so much on the number of scientific papers published. This leads, among other things, to postgraduate students being pushed to undertake researches where publishable results rather than scientific importance are the prime consideration. (This holds with even greater force in the humanities, which too often pretend to be "scientific," flooding the learned market with Ph.D. theses crammed with unimportant literary or historical details.)

But what is mainly necessary is a change in approach. Instead of all the separate sciences, like inorganic chemistry or astronomy or systematic botany, pushing on and on along their own divergent lines, and individual scientists competitively striving for new discoveries (or just for publishable facts), more and more scientific man power should be mobilized to converge on problems that can only be solved by cooperative teamwork between different branches of natural and human science—problems of land use and city planning, of resource use and conservation, of human behavior and health, of communication and education. Beyond all, we need a science of human possibilities, with professorships in the exploration of the future.

Tentative beginnings on a world basis are being made along these lines, like the very successful I. G. Y., or International Geophysical Year, and now the International Biological Program, or I. B. P., and I am sure that they will increase and multiply in regional, national and professional affairs as well. At the same time we must do our best to get rid of the present imbalance between different branches of science and integrate them in a framework of common effort. This is a necessary step toward a greater goal—the integration of science with all other branches of learning into a single comprehensive and open-ended system of knowledge, ideas and values relevant to man's destiny. This might even lure professional philosophers out of their linguistic burrows and metaphysical towers to take part in rebuilding a genuine philosophy of existence. But before this can happen, we must repudiate our modern idolatry of science and technology, and dethrone them from the exaggerated pedestals on which we have set them. After all, "science" is only the name for a particular system of knowledge, awareness and understanding acquired by particular methods; it must come to terms with other systems acquired by other methods—aesthetic and historical, intuitive and subconscious, imaginative and visionary. A prerequisite for this is the creation of a real science of psychology in place of the array of conflicting heresies at present occupying the field. I venture to prophesy that this will find its root in ethology, the science dealing with the analysis and evolution of animal mind and behavior.

One of technology's most exciting but also alarming achievements is the computer, which is pushing technologically advanced countries like America into an era of computerized automation. I say *alarming* because computerized automation coupled with population increase must tend to split a country into two nations, to use Disraeli's phrase about mid-Victorian Britain. In late twentieth-century America, the two nations will not be the rich and the poor but the employed and the nonemployed, the minority with assured jobs and high incomes, the majority with no jobs and only unemployment pay. Even though automation can ensure increased production of all kinds of goods, this would be a socially disastrous and politically intolerable situation. Somehow or other, the technologically advanced countries will have to rethink the whole concept of work and jobs. One kind of work that will certainly expand is teaching; another is learning—teaching and learning how to live.

The problems of adjustment will be formidable, and the methods for achieving it will need not only hard thinking but time to work out. Meanwhile, we may be driven to providing everyone, even if they have no job in the customary sense, with a really adequate income to tide them over the period of adjustment.

In regions of dense population and rapid industrial growth, science and technology are producing an alarming increase in pollution and ecological degradation. The volume of solid matter discharged annually into the world's waters amounts to over sixty-five cubic miles—equivalent to a mountain with twenty-thousand-foot vertical sides and a flat top of over sixteen square miles. This includes so much sewage that bathing in many lakes, including even the Lake of Geneva, and on numerous sea beaches has become either disgusting, dangerous to health, or both. Our vaunted Affluent Society is rapidly turning into an Effluent Society. Meanwhile, rubbish dumps and used automobiles are polluting the land; automobile exhausts, domestic smoke and industrial fumes are polluting the air; and pesticides and herbicides are killing off our birds, our wild flowers and our butterflies. The net result is that nature is being wounded, man's environment desecrated, and the world's resources of enjoyment and interest demolished or destroyed.

Here is an obvious case where quality of life and living must take precedence over quantity of production and profit. Compulsory measures against pollution, whatever they may cost, are as necessary as are compulsory vaccination or compulsory quarantine against disease. Meanwhile, science can be set to find better methods of pest control, and technology put to work to reduce effluents, to render them innocuous (or even beneficial, as are some forms of sewage treatment) and to recover any valuable components for future use. Both science and technology must also be called in to reduce the really shocking gap in standards of living and quality of existence between rich and poor countries. If this goes on widening, it will split the world economically into two hostile halves. It will inevitably stir up "envy, hatred, malice, and all uncharitableness," as The Litany puts it, in the poor countries, all too probably combined with racial animosity and with a threat of violence lurking under the surface.

It is all too clear that our present methods of aid and assistance are pitifully inadequate to reduce the gap to below the danger point, let alone close it. To take a single example: The losses inflicted on the countries of Latin America by the falling prices of their primary export products during the Fifties were greater than all the aid they received in the same period. During the present so-called Development Decade, they may well become less instead of more developed.

We have to rethink the whole system. The very idea of aid and assistance, with its implications of charity, of a man satisfying his conscience by giving a beggar half a dollar, must be dropped; for it we must substitute the idea of cooperation in world development, with rich and poor in active though complementary partnership.

This will involve large changes, both in attitude and in practice. First, we must take into account the raw fact that an underdeveloped country cannot be industrialized if its rate of population increase is too high. Too much of the capital and skills required is used up in feeding, housing, educating and generally taking care of the excess crop of human infants; it goes down the drain—the baby drain. Thus, expert inquiry has made it clear that unless the Indian birth rate is halved within a generation, it will be impossible for India to break through to modernized economy. Accordingly, all plans for aid must take account of what may be called the recipient country's demographic creditworthiness; if this is too low, some of the aid must go to help the country control its rate of increase, by providing contraceptives and training personnel in their use, and by sending expert advisors.

Secondly, we must somehow transform our international economic system—trade and barter, loans and grants and technical assistance—from the outdated shackles of "free" enterprise and competitive profitability. It is not for a noneconomist to suggest remedies, beyond obvious ones like making loan terms as easy as possible and stabilizing commodity prices. But clearly the job is urgent and demands a high degree of economic and political statesmanship, in nations, foundations and international bodies.

Both science and automation link up with education. Dorothy Parker once acidly remarked that education consisted in casting sham pearls before real swine. Omitting all questions of the swinishness of its recipients or victims, we must admit that many of its pearls *are* false, flawed or misshapen and, to change the metaphor, that it often involves the forcible feeding of its pupils on unsuitable, unhealthy or even poisonous diets. Just as education in Hitler's Germany was based on stuffing children's brains with National Socialist dogma and anti-Jewish indoctrination, in many Roman Catholic countries it is based on Catholic dogma and anti-Communist and antihumanist indoctrination; and in China, the U. S. S. R. and its satellites, it is based on Communist dogma and anticapitalist and antireligious indoctrination. Meanwhile, educational systems in the Western world, and I regret to say in India and most emergent nations in Africa and Southeast Asia, are suffering from the complaint that has been called *examinotosis*—cramming pupils with facts and ideas that are to be regurgitated at appropriate intervals, in subjects that can be marked or graded by the examination process, with the ultimate idea of awarding certificates, diplomas and degrees that will help the examinees in obtaining jobs.

In addition, the world's poor countries suffer grievously from undereducation at all levels. One result of this is that adult illiteracy is actually increasing. A Unesco survey has shown that between 1952 and 1962, thirty-five million adults were added to the over one billion of the world's illiterates, and the figure is growing yearly. In many countries, only 25, 15, or even 10 percent of the male population is literate, and the illiteracy of women is considerably higher. Meanwhile, surveys have demonstrated that literacy is an indispensable basis for vigorous national life in the world of today and that 40 percent literacy is the minimum needed for achieving appreciable economic, technological or cultural success. The Shah of Iran has suggested that all nations should contribute 2 percent of their annual military budgets to a world campaign against illiteracy, and there are numerous other projects for promoting literacy.

Many efforts are also being made to free the examination-ridden educational systems of developed countries from their restrictive practices and liberate them from their true goals—of transmitting human culture in all its aspects and enabling the new generation to lead fuller and more rewarding lives.

The first thing is to reform the curriculum so that, instead of separate "subjects" to be "taken" piecemeal, growing minds are offered a nutritious core of human knowledge, ideas, techniques and achievements, covering science and history as well as the arts and manual skills. The key subject must be ecology, both biological and human—the science of balanced interaction between organisms and their environment (which of course includes other organisms)—together with its practical applications in the conservation of the world's resources, animal, vegetable and mineral, and human. Education must prepare growing human beings for the future, not only their own future but that of their children, their nation and their planet. For this, it must aim at varied excellence (including the training of professional elites) and at the fullest realization of human possibilities.

This links up with the rethinking of religion—a vital task, but one I can only touch on in summary fashion. It is clear that the era of mutually exclusive and dogmatic religions, each claiming to be the sole repository of absolute and eternal truth, is rapidly ending. If mankind is to evolve as a whole, it must have a single set of beliefs in common; and if it is to progress, these beliefs must not be self-limiting but open-ended, not rigid barriers but flexible guidelines channeling men in the general direction of improvement and perfection. Already an effort is being made to find common ground between the world's various religions and churches, and we can be sure that necessity will drive them further in this direction. But this is not enough. In the light of our new and comprehensive vision, we must redefine religion itself. Religions are not necessarily concerned with the worship of a supernatural God or gods, or even with the supernatural at all; they are not mere superstition nor just self-seeking organizations exploiting the public's superstitions and its belief in the magical powers of priests and witch doctors.

The ultimate task will be to melt down the gods, and magic, and all supernatural entities, into their elements of transcendence and sacred power and then, with the aid of our new knowledge, build up these raw materials into a new religious system that will help man to achieve the destiny that our new evolutionary vision has revealed. Meanwhile, we must encourage all constructive attempts at reformulating and rebuilding religion. My personal favorite is Evolutionary Humanism, but there are many others tending in the same general direction, like Yoga and Zen, ethical and meditative systems, and the cults of release through psychedelic drugs or bodily rituals.

How does this all add up? It adds up to a meaningful whole, something greater than the sum of its parts. We need no longer be afflicted with a sense of our own insignificance and helplessness, or of the world's nonsignificance and meaninglessness. A purpose has been revealed to us—to steer the evolution of our planet toward improvement—and an encouragement has been given us, in the knowledge that steady evolutionary improvement has actually occurred in the past, and the assurance that it can continue into the future.

It is especially encouraging to know that biological improvement has been born of struggle, and that conflict has often been disinfected of open violence and sometimes even converted into cooperative bonding; and it is especially significant that the most vital of all improvements has been the improvement of mind—awareness, knowledge and understanding—coupled with ability to learn and profit from experience. What is more, improvements in the human lot, in man's ways of coping with the problems of existence, have always depended on improvements in his awareness, knowledge and understanding; and today the explosive increase of knowledge has given us a wholly new understanding of our role in the universe and wholly new hopes of human improvement. We are still imprisoned in a mental cage, whose walls are made of the forces of nature as we have experienced them, whose bars are the constructions of our own primitive thinking—about destiny and salvation, enjoyment and ethics, guilt and propitiation, peace and war.

Today the individual man or woman need not feel himself a meaningless insect in the vast spaces of the cosmos, nor an insignificant cog in a huge, impersonal social machine. For one thing, the individual human is the highest and most wonderful organization we know of. In developing his own personality, he is making his own unique contribution to the evolution of the universe.

Secondly, he is a unit of mankind, and mankind is the highest type in the solar system, the only organism we know of in whom mind has broken through to dominate existence. Mankind is not only a product of past evolution but an active agent in its future course. The human individual can help mankind shoulder this responsibility.

Our first objective is to clarify the new vision of our evolution. The next is to define the tasks required to carry out our responsibilities. Our over-all aim is improvement. Our immediate tasks are to achieve the peaceful unity and cooperative development of mankind, to encourage varied excellence and greater achievement, to think in terms of ecology and to practice conservation, and to build a fulfillment society underpinned by some new system of beliefs. The final aim will be the eugenic transformation of man's genetic nature, coupled with the cultural transformation of his social environment. Meanwhile, all can help in understanding and spreading the new revelation of human destiny.

ALAN WATTS

opinion

WEALTH VS. MONEY

when we learn to stop confusing symbols with the realities they stand for, then, and only then, will we be freed from illusory problems that now seem overwhelming

In the year of our Lord Jesus Christ 2000, the United States of America will no longer exist. This is not an inspired prophecy based on supernatural authority but a reasonably certain guess. "The United States of America" can mean two quite different things. The first is a certain physical territory, largely on the North American continent, including all such geographical and biological features as lakes, mountains and rivers, skies and clouds, plants, animals and people. The second is a sovereign political state, existing in competition with many other sovereign states jostling one another around the surface of this planet. The first sense is concrete and material; the second, abstract and conceptual.

If the United States continues for very much longer to exist in this second sense, it will cease to exist in the first. For the land and its life can now so easily be destroyed—by the sudden and catastrophic methods of nuclear or biological warfare, or by any combination of such creeping and insidious means as overpopulation, pollution of the atmosphere, contamination of the water and erosion of our natural resources by maniacal misapplications of technology. For good measure, add the possibilities of civil and racial war, self-strangulation of the great cities and breakdown of all major transportation and communication networks. And that will be the end of the United States of America, in both senses.

There is, perhaps, the slight possibility that we may continue our political and abstract existence in heaven, there to enjoy being "better dead than Red" and, with the full authority of the Lord God, to be able to say to our enemies squirming in hell, "We told you so!" On the grounds of such hopes and values, someone may well push the Big Red Button to demonstrate that belief in spiritual immortality can be inconsistent with physical survival. Luckily for us, our Marxist enemies do not believe in any such hereafter.

When I make predictions from a realistic and hard-boiled point of view, I tend to the gloomy view of things. The candidates of my choice have never yet won in any election in which I have voted. I am thus inclined to feel that practical politics must assume that most people are either contentious and malevolent or stupid, that their decisions will usually be shortsighted and self-destructive and that, in all probability, the human race will fail as a biological experiment and take the easy downhill road to death, like the Gadarene swine. If I were betting on it—and had somewhere to place my bet—that's where I would put my money.

But there is nowhere to lay a bet on the fate of mankind. Likewise, there is no way of standing outside the situation and looking at it as an impartial, coldly calculating, objective observer. I'm involved in the situation and therefore concerned; and because I am concerned, I'll be damned if I'll let things come out as they would if I were just betting on them.

There is, however, another possibility for the year A.D. 2000. This will require putting our minds on physical facts and being relatively unconcerned with the United States of America as an abstract political entity. By overlooking the nation, we can turn full attention to the territory, to the actual earth, with its waters and forests, flowers and crops, animals and human beings—and so create, with less cost and suffering than we are bearing in 1968, a viable and thoroughly enjoyable biological experiment.

The chances may be slim. Only six months ago, Congress voted, with much patriotic rhetoric, for the imposition of severe penalties upon anyone presuming to burn the flag of the United States. Yet the very congressmen who passed this law are responsible, by acts of commission or omission, for burning, polluting and plundering the territory that the flag is supposed to represent. Therein, they exemplified the peculiar and perhaps fatal fallacy of civilization: the confusion of symbol with reality.

Civilization, comprising all the achievements of art and science, technology and industry, is the result of man's invention and manipulation of symbols—of words, letters, numbers, formulas and concepts, and of such social institutions as universally accepted clocks and rulers, scales and timetables, schedules and laws. By these means, we measure, predict and control the behavior of the human and natural worlds—and with such startling apparent success that the trick goes to our heads. All too easily, we confuse the world as we symbolize it with the world as it is. As semanticist Alfred Korzybski used to say, it is an urgent necessity to distinguish between the map and the territory and, he might have added, between the flag and the country.

Let me illustrate this point and, at the same time, explain the major obstacle to sane technological progress by dwelling on the fundamental confusion between money and wealth. Remember the Great Depression of the Thirties? One day there was a flourishing consumer economy, with everyone on the up-and-up; and the next, unemployment, poverty and bread lines. What happened? The physical resources of the country—the brain, brawn and raw materials—were in no way depleted, but there was a sudden absence of money, a so-called financial slump. Complex reasons for this kind of disaster can be elaborated at length by experts on banking and high finance who cannot see the forest for the trees. But it was just as if someone had come to work on building a house and, on the morning of the Depression, the boss had said, "Sorry, baby, but we can't build today. No inches." "Wha-d'ya mean, no inches? We got wood. We got metal. We even got tape measures." "Yeah, but you don't understand business. We been using too many inches and there's just no more to go around."

A few years later, people were saying that Germany couldn't possibly equip a vast army and wage a war because it didn't have enough gold.

What wasn't understood then, and still isn't really understood today, is that the reality of money is of the same type as the reality of centimeters, grams, hours or lines of longitude. Money is a way of measuring wealth but is not wealth in itself. A chest of gold coins or a fat wallet of bills is of no use whatsoever to a wrecked sailor alone on a raft. He needs *real* wealth, in the form of a fishing rod, a compass, an outboard motor with gas and a female companion.

But this ingrained and archaic confusion of money with wealth is now the main reason we are not going ahead full tilt with the development of our technological genius for the production of more than adequate food, clothing, housing and utilities for every person on earth. It can be done, for electronics, computers, automation techniques and other mechanical methods of mass production have, potentially, lifted us into an age of abundance in which the political and economic ideologies of the past, whether left, middle or right, are simply obsolete. There is no question anymore of the old socialist or Communist schemes of robbing the rich to pay the poor, or of financing a proper distribution of wealth by the ritualistic and tiresome mumbo jumbo of taxation. If, *if* we get our heads straight about money, I predict that by A.D. 2000, or sooner, no one will pay taxes, no one will carry cash, utilities will be free and everyone will carry a general credit card. This card will be valid up to each individual's share in a guaranteed basic income or national dividend, issued free, beyond which he may still earn anything more that he desires by any art or craft, profession or trade that has not been displaced by automation. (For detailed information on the mechanics of such an economy, the reader should refer to Robert Theobald's *Challenge of Abundance* and *Free Men and Free Markets* and also to a series of essays that he has edited, *The Guaranteed Income*. Theobald is an avant-garde economist on the faculty of Columbia University.)

Naturally, such outrageous proposals will raise the old cries "But where's the *money* going to come from?" or "Who pays the bills?" But the point is that money doesn't and never did *come* from anywhere, as if it were something like lumber or iron or hydroelectric power. Again, money is a measure of wealth, and we *invent* money as we invent the Fahrenheit scale of temperature or the avoirdupois measure of weight. When you discover and mine a load of iron ore, you don't have to borrow or ask someone for "a thousand tons" before you can do anything with it.

By contrast with money, true wealth is the sum of energy, technical intelligence and raw materials. Gold itself is wealth only when used for such practical purposes as filling teeth. As soon as it is used for money, kept locked in vaults or fortresses, it becomes useless for anything else and thus goes out of circulation as a form of raw material, i.e., real wealth. If money must be gold or silver or nickel, the expansion and distribution of vast wealth in the form of wheat, poultry, cotton, vegetables, butter, wine, fish or coffee must wait upon the discovery of new gold mines before it can proceed. This obviously ludicrous predicament has, heretofore, been circumvented by increasing the national debt—a roundabout piece of semantic obscurantism—by which a nation issues itself credit or purchasing power based not on holdings in precious metals but on real wealth in the form of products and materials and mechanical energy. Because national debts far exceed anyone's reserves of gold or silver, it is generally supposed that a country with a large national debt is spending beyond its income and is well on the road to poverty and ruin—no matter how enormous its supplies of energy and material resources. This is the basic confusion between symbol and reality, here involving the bad magic of the word debt, which is understood as in the phrase going into debt. But national debt should properly be called national *credit*. By issuing national (or general) credit, a given population gives itself purchasing power, a method of distribution for its actual goods and services, which are far more valuable than any amount of precious metal.

Mind you, I write of these things as a simple philosopher and not as a financial or economic expert bristling with facts and figures. But the role of the philosopher is to look at such matters from the standpoint of the child in Hans Andersen's tale of *The Emperor's New Clothes*. The philosopher tries to get down to the most basic, simple principles. He sees people wasting material wealth, or just letting it rot, or hoarding it uselessly for lack of purely abstract counters called dollars or pounds or francs.

From this very basic or, if you will, childish point of view, I see that we have created a marvelous technology for the supply of goods and services with a minimum of human drudgery. Isn't it obvious that the whole purpose of machines is to get rid of work? When you get rid of the work required for producing basic necessities, you have leisure—time for fun or for new and creative explorations and adventures. But with the characteristic blindness of those who cannot distinguish symbol from reality, we allow our machinery to put people out of work—not in the sense of being at leisure but in the sense of having no money and of having shamefacedly to accept the miserable charity of public welfare. Thus—as the rationalization or automation of industry extends—we increasingly abolish human slavery; but in penalizing the displaced slaves, in depriving them of purchasing power, the manufacturers in turn deprive themselves of outlets and markets for their products. The machines produce more and more, humans produce less and less, but the products pile up undistributed and unconsumed, because too few can earn enough money and because even the hungriest, greediest and most ruthless capitalist cannot consume ten pounds of butter per day.

Any child should understand that money is a convenience for eliminating barter, so that you don't have to go to market with baskets of eggs or firkins of beer to swap them for meat and vegetables. But if all you had to barter with was your physical or mental energy in work that is now done by machines, the problem would then be what will you do for a living and how will the manufacturer find customers for his tons of butter and sausages?

The sole rational solution would be for the community as a whole to issue itself credit—money—for the work done by the machines. This would enable their products to be fairly distributed and their owners and managers to be fairly paid, so that they could invest in bigger and better machines. And all the while, the increasing wealth would be coming from the energy of the machines and not from ritualistic manipulations with gold.

In some ways, we are doing this already, but by the self-destructive expedient of issuing ourselves credit (now called debt) for engines of war. What the nations of the world have spent on war since 1914 could, with our technology, have supplied every person on earth with a comfortable independent income. But because we confuse wealth with money, we confuse issuing ourselves credit with going into debt. No one goes into debt except in emergency, and therefore, prosperity depends on maintaining the perpetual emergency of war. We are reduced, then, to the suicidal expedient of inventing wars when, instead, we could simply have invented money—provided that the amount invented was always proportionate to the real wealth being produced. We should replace the gold standard by the wealth standard.

The difficulty is that, with our present superstitions about money, the issue of a guaranteed basic income of, say, $10,000 per annum per person would result in wild inflation. Prices would go sky high to "catch" the vast amounts of new money in circulation and, in short order, everyone would be a pauper on $10,000 a year. The hapless, dollar-hypnotized sellers do not realize that whenever they raise prices, the money so gained has less and less purchasing power, which is the reason that as material wealth grows and grows, the value of the monetary unit (dollar or pound) goes down and down—so that you have to run faster and faster to stay where you are, instead of letting the machines run for you. If we shift from the gold standard to the wealth standard, prices must stay more or less where they are at the time of the shift and—miraculously—everyone will discover that he has enough or more than enough to wear, eat, drink and otherwise survive with affluence and merriment.

It is not going to be at all easy to explain this to the world at large, because mankind has existed for perhaps a million years with relative material scarcity, and it is now roughly a mere hundred years since the beginning of the Industrial Revolution. As it was once very difficult to persuade people that the earth is round and that it is in orbit around the sun, or to make it clear that the universe exists in a curved space-time continuum, it may be just as hard to get it through to "common sense" that the virtues of making and saving money are obsolete. It may have to be put across by the most skillfully prepared and simply presented TV programs, given by scientific-looking gentlemen in spectacles and white coats, and through millions of specially designed comic books.

It will always be possible, of course, for anyone so inclined to earn more than the guaranteed basic income, but as it becomes clearer and clearer that money is not wealth, people will realize that there are limits to the real wealth that any individual can consume. We may have to adopt some form of German economist Silvio Gessell's suggestion that money not in circulation be made progressively perishable, declining in value from the date of issue. But the temptation to hoard either money or wealth will dwindle as it becomes obvious that technology will keep the supplies coming and that you cannot drive four cars at once, live simultaneously in six homes, take three tours at the same time or devour twelve roasts of beef at one meal.

All this will involve a curious reversal of the Protestant ethic, which, at least in the United States, is one of the big obstacles to a future of wealth and leisure for all. The Devil, it is said, finds work for idle hands to do, and human energy cannot be trusted unless most of it is absorbed in hard, productive work—so that, on coming home, we are too tired to get into mischief. It is feared that affluence plus leisure will, as in times past, lead to routs and orgies and all the perversities that flow therefrom, and then on to satiation, debilitation and decay—as in Hogarth's depiction of *A Rake's Progress*.

Indeed, there are reasonable grounds for such fears, and it may well be that our New England consciences, our chronic self-disapproval, will have to be maintained by an altogether new kind of sermonizing designed to inculcate a fully up-to-date sense of guilt. Preachers of the late twentieth century will have to insist that enjoyment of total luxury is a sacred and solemn duty. Penitents will be required to confess such sins as failing to give adequate satisfaction to one's third concubine or lack of attention to some fine detail in serving a banquet to friends—such as forgetting to put enough marijuana in the turkey stuffing. Sure, I am talking with about one half of my tongue in my cheek, but I am trying to make the deadly serious point that, as of today, an economic utopia is not wishful thinking but, in some substantial degree, the necessary alternative to self-destruction.

The moral challenge and the grim problem that we face is that the life of affluence and pleasure requires exact discipline and high imagination. Somewhat as metals deteriorate from "fatigue," every constant stimulation of consciousness, however pleasant, tends to become boring and thus to be ignored. When physical comfort is permanent, it ceases to be noticed. If you have worried for years about lack of money and then become rich, the new sense of ease and security is short-lived, for you soon begin to worry as much as ever—about cancer or heart disease. Nature abhors a vacuum. For this reason, the life of pleasure cannot be maintained without a certain asceticism, as in the time and effort required for a woman to keep her hair and face in fine condition, for the weaving of exquisite textiles or for the preparation of superior food. Thus, the French distinguish between a gourmand and a gourmet, the former being a mere glutton, a trencherman who throws anything and everything down the hatch; and the latter, a fussy, subtle and sophisticated devotee of the culinary arts.

Affluent people in the United States have seldom shown much imagination in cultivating the arts of pleasure. The business-suited executive looks more like a minister or an undertaker than a man of wealth and is, furthermore, wearing one of the most uncomfortable forms of clothing ever invented for the male, as compared, say, with the kimono or the caftan. Did you ever try the food in a private restaurant for top brass in the offices of a big corporation? Strictly institutional. Even the most expensive night clubs and country clubs pass off indifferent fare; and at $100-a-plate charity dinners, one gets the ubiquitous synthetic chicken, machine-raised in misery and tasting of just that.

If the behavior of increasing numbers of young people is any real portent of what may happen by A.D. 2000, much of this will change. Quite aside from cavalierish styles of long hair, men are beginning to wear jewelry and vivid colors, imitating the styles of medieval and Oriental affluence that began to disappear when power shifted from the landed gentry to miserly merchants of the cities—the burghers or *bourgeoisie*. Beneath such outward appearances, there is a clear change of values: Rich experiences are more to be desired than property and bank accounts, and plans for the future are of use only to those who can live fully in the present.

This may sound feckless and undisciplined, as if young people (especially hippies) had become incapable of postponing gratification. Thus, it might seem that the world-wide rebellions of students are a sign that the adolescent is no longer willing to work through the period of training that it takes to become an adult. "Elders and betters" do not understand that today's students do not want to become their *kind* of adult, which is what the available training is intended to produce.

Artists have always been important prophets of social change, and the increasingly favored "psychedelic" style is anything but undisciplined. Using intense color and highly articulate detail of line and form, the exponents of this style are restoring a sheer glory to Western art that has not been seen since the days of French and Celtic illuminated manuscripts, the stained glass of Chartres and the luminous enamelwork of Limoges. It calls to mind the jeweled gardens of Persian miniatures, the rhythmic intricacy of Moorish arabesques and the golden filigree of Hindu textiles. Among the hippies, I know makers of musical instruments—lutes and guitars—that, for delicate ivory inlays and excellence of grain and texture, are as lovely as any work of the Italian Renaissance. Furthermore, musicians are beginning to realize that the Beatles (to take an obvious example) display a serious musical genius that puts them in line with the great Western masters, from Bach to Stravinsky, and that some of the songs of Dylan and Donovan are quite as interesting as the best lieder.

At best, then, a leisure economy will provide opportunity to develop the frustrated craftsman, painter, sculptor, poet, composer, yachtsman, explorer or potter that is in us all—if only we could earn a living that way. Certainly, there will be a plethora of bad and indifferent productions from so many unleashed amateurs, but the general long-term effect should be a tremendous enrichment of the quality and variety of fine art, music, food, furniture, clothing, gardens and even homes—created largely on a do-it-yourself basis. Mechanical mass production will provide utilities, raw materials, tools and certain foodstuffs, yet will at the same time release us from the necessity for much of the mass-produced trash that we must now buy for lack of time to make anything better—clothes, dishes and other articles of everyday use that were made so much more exquisitely by "primitives" that they now adorn our museums.

Historically, luxuries of this kind could be afforded only by shameless aristocrats exploiting slave labor. Though still exploiters, the *bourgeoisie* were timid newcomers, often had Protestant guilty consciences and, therefore, hid their wealth in banks and did their very best to pretend that successful business is an ascetic and self-sacrificing way of life. But by A.D. 2000, there need be no slaves but machines, and it will then be our urgent duty to live in that kind of luxurious splendor that depends upon leisurely devotion to every form of art, craft and science. (Certainly, we have long forgotten that a schola, or school, is a place of leisure, where those who do not have to grub for a living can apply themselves to the disinterested pursuit of knowledge and art.) Under such circumstances, what exuberant styles of life will be cultivated, for example, by affluent Negroes under no further pressure to imitate the white *bourgeoisie*?

The style of life will be colorful and elegant, but it will not, I feel, exhibit the sheer gluttony and greed of certain notorious aristocracies of the past. Speaking perhaps only half seriously, by A.D. 2000, most of Asia will have followed the lead of Japan and be laced with superhighways and cluttered with hot-dog stands, neon signs, factories, high-rise apartment buildings, huge airports and swarms of Toyotas, with every fellah and coolie running around in a Western business suit. On the other hand, America, having had all this and being fed up with it, will abound with lamaseries and ashrams (but coeducational), expert players of the sitar and the koto, masters of Japanese tea ceremony, schools for Chinese calligraphy and Zen-style gardening—while people stroll around in saris, dhotis, sarongs, kimonos and other forms of comfortable and colorful clothing. Just as now the French are buying sourdough bread flown by jet from San Francisco, spiritually starved Tibetans and Japanese will be studying Buddhism in Chicago.

That this is not quite a joke might be inferred from the amazing increase of interest among American college students in Oriental mysticism and other "non-Western" studies, as courses in Afro-Asian cultures are now often classified. Obviously, this interest is not unconnected with the widespread use of psychedelic drugs. This is not, as is often suggested, a substitute for alcohol; it is much more an adventure, an exploration of new dimensions of experience, all the more attractive for being esoteric and in defiance of authority. To repeat, students tend to be much more interested in experiences than in possessions, feeling that their parents' way of experiencing both themselves and the world is in some way sick, impoverished and even delusive. Certainly—and precisely because their parents have for generations confused symbol with reality, money with wealth, and personality (or ego) with the actual human organism.

And here's the nub of the problem. We cannot proceed with a fully productive technology if it must inevitably Los Angelesize the whole earth, poison the elements, destroy all wildlife and sicken the blood stream with the promiscuous use of antibiotics and insecticides. Yet this will be the certain result of the technological enterprise conducted in the hostile spirit of a conquest of nature with the main object of making money. Despite growing public alarm over the problems of soil erosion, pollution of the air and water and the deterioration of crops and livestock raised by certain methods of industrial farming, little is as yet being done to develop an ecological technology—that is, a technology in which man has as much respect for his environment as for himself.

In this regard, many corporations—and even more so their shareholders—are unbelievably blind to their own material interest, for the ill effects of irresponsible technology are appearing so rapidly that this is no longer a problem wherein we can simply pass the buck to our children. Recent investigations, both here and in England, show that the actual operators of chicken factories avoid eating their own produce; it may be as well for the appetites of their absentee shareholders that they do not know too much about raising hens in batteries. Does anyone care what happened to the taste of fruits and vegetables, or mind particularly if apples and tomatoes are often sprayed with wax to improve their looks? (I just scraped an apple, very gently, to prove it.) Is it either good business or good living to buy an $80,000 home in Beverly Hills and inhabit a miasma of exhaust fumes? (In Paris, last May, we didn't mind the tear gas much; just used to L. A.) Is it even sane to own a Ferrari and, twice daily, jangle one's nerves and risk one's life by commuting from

Norwalk, Connecticut, to Madison Avenue, New York? And what about the view from the plane between San Francisco and Seattle—acres and acres of brown Oregon hills dotted with nothing but tree stumps?

It is an oversimplification to say that this is the result of business valuing profit rather than product, for no one should be expected to do business without the incentive of profit. The actual trouble is that profit is identified entirely with money, as distinct from the real profit of living with dignity and elegance in beautiful surroundings. But investors take no long-term responsibility for the use of their capital; they clip coupons and watch market statistics with regard only for monetary results. They see little or nothing of the physical operations that they have financed and sometimes do not even know that their own funds are invested in the pithy potatoes they get for dinner. Their actual experience of business is restricted to an abstract, arithmetical translation of material fact—a translation that automatically ignores textures, tastes, sights, sounds and smells.

To try to correct this irresponsibility by passing laws (e.g., against absentee ownership) would be wide of the point, for most of the law has as little relation to life as money to wealth. On the contrary, problems of this kind are aggravated rather than solved by the paperwork of politics and law. What is necessary is at once simpler and more difficult: only that financiers, bankers and stockholders must turn themselves into real people and ask themselves exactly what they want out of life—in the realization that this strictly practical and hard-nosed question might lead to far more delightful styles of living than those they now pursue. Quite simply and literally, they must come to their senses—for their own personal profit and pleasure.

The difficulty is that most of our very high-ranking business executives live in a closed world. They are wafted from their expensive but unimaginative homes and clubs to offices of dreary luxury, wherein they are protected and encapsulated by secretarial staffs. They read only what is filtered through by underlings and consort only with others in the same Bigelow-lined traps. It is almost impossible for people outside their caste to communicate with them directly, for they are victims of a system (also a ritual) so habitual, so complex and so geared in to the whole corporate operation that the idea of changing it seems as preposterous as rewiring the human brain. Actually, this life is a form of role playing with the reward of status; its material rewards are meager—for one reason, because it is tiring and time-consuming. But to suggest that one should change an established role is to be understood by the player as suggesting that he become someone else, and this affront to his imaginary ego is such that he will cling passionately to a role of high status, however much it may be frustrating his natural and material inclinations. This would, perhaps, be commendable if the role being played fulfilled important responsibilities to society, and many businessmen do, indeed, feel themselves to be doing just that. But their closed world prevents the realization that in the vast, long-range world of material events, they are highly irresponsible—both to their children and to themselves. This is precisely why so many of their own children drift off to the dubious adventures of Haight-Ashbury or the East Village. They find the high life of Scarsdale or Atherton, Lake Forest or Beverly Hills inconceivably dull.

Hopefully, there are signs that some of these very children are getting through to their parents, since it's tough to put a secretary between yourself and your son. Is there any historical precedent for the revolt of a younger generation against the older on the present scale? So widespread? So radical—in politics, morals, religion, dress, art and music? So vociferous—with such powerful techniques of communication as are now available? I do not believe that the elders will ultimately reject the children; it's against nature. But to make peace, the elders will have to move a long, long way from their present position.

Less hopeful are the prospects of a change of attitude in the ranks of successful blue-collar workers, who, as now organized in the once very necessary but now highly reactionary labor unions, constitute the real and dangerous potential for American fascism. For the unions operate under the same confusion of symbol and reality as the investors: The wage is more important than the work and, because all must conform to union hours and (mediocre) union standards, any real enthusiasm for a craft is effectively discouraged. But a work force so robotized is all the more inviting its replacement by machinery, since a contrivance that won't work must inevitably be replaced by one that will. The basic assumption of unionism was not the dignity but the drudgery of labor, and the strategy was, therefore, to do as little as possible for as much pay as possible. Thus, as automation eliminates drudgery, it eliminates the necessity for the unions, a truth that is already extending up to such "high-class" unions as the musicians'. The piper who hates to play is replaced by a tape, which does not object when the payer calls the tune. If, then, the unions are to have any further usefulness, they must use their political pressure, not for a greater share of profits (based on rising prices to pay for rising wages) but for total revision of the concept and function of money.

The fear that adequate production and affluence will take away all restraint on the growth of population is simply against the facts, for overpopulation is a symptom of poverty, not wealth. Japan, thus far the one fully industrialized nation of Asia, is also the one Asian country with an effective program of population control. The birth rate is also falling in Sweden,

West Germany, Switzerland and the United States. On the other hand, the poorer nations of Asia and Africa resent and resist the advice that their populations be pruned, in the feeling that this is just another of the white man's tricks for cutting down their political power. Thus, the one absolutely urgent and humane method of population control is to do everything possible to increase the world's food supply and to divert to this end the wealth and energy now being squandered on military technology.

For, from the most realistic, hardheaded, self-interested and tactically expert point of view, the United States has put its Armed Forces in the control of utterly incompetent strategists—a bunch of essential "bad shots" who do not know the difference between military skill and mere firepower, who shoot at mosquitoes with machine guns, who liberate countries by destroying their territories, whose principal weapon is no weapon at all but an instrument of mutual suicide and whose political motivations, based on the puerile division of the world into "good guys" and "bad guys," cannot allow that enemies are also people, as distinct from demonic henchmen of a satanic ideology. If we were fighting in Vietnam with the honest and materialistic intention of capturing the wealth and the women of the land, we would be very careful to leave it intact. But in fighting for abstract principles, as distinct from material gain, we become the ruthless and implacable instruments of the delusion that things can be all white, without the contrast of black.

Timothy Leary was not so wide of the mark when he said that we must go out of our minds (abstract values) to come to our senses (concrete values). For coming to our senses must, above all, be the experience of our own existence as living organisms rather than "personalities," like characters in a play or a novel—acting out some artificial plot in which the persons are simply masks for a conflict of abstract ideas or principles. Man as an organism is to the world outside like a whirlpool is to a river. Man and world are a single natural process, but we are behaving as if we were invaders and plunderers in foreign territory. For when the individual is defined and felt as the separate personality or ego, he remains unaware that his actual body is a dancing pattern of energy that simply does not happen by itself. It happens only in concert with myriads of other patterns—called animals, plants, insects, bacteria, minerals, liquids and gases. The definition of a person and the normal feeling of "I" do not effectively include these relationships. You say, "I came into this world." You didn't; you came *out* of it, as a branch from a tree.

So long as we do not effectively feel this to be so, there is no motivation for forms of politics that recognize the interdependence of all peoples, nor for forms of technology that realize man's inseparability from the entire network of natural patterns. How, then, is the sense of self to be changed? By scientific education? It convinces the intellect but not the emotions. By religion? The record is not hopeful. By psychotherapy? Much too slow. If anything is to be *done* about it, and done in time, I must agree with Aldous Huxley (and with the sober and scholarly Arthur Koestler in his *Ghost in the Machine*) that our only resort may be psychopharmacology—a chemical, a pill, that brings the mind to its senses.

Although I have experimented very sympathetically with such methods (LSD, etc.), I would be as reluctant to try to change the world by psychedelics as to dose everyone indiscriminately with antibiotics. We do not yet know what ecological damage the latter may have done, how profoundly they may have upset certain balances of nature. I have, therefore, another and perhaps equally unacceptable suggestion.

This is simply that nothing be *done* about it. Shortly before his death, Robert Oppenheimer is said to have remarked that the whole world is, quite obviously, going to hell—adding, however, that the one slim chance of its *not* going to hell is that we do absolutely nothing to stop it. For the greatest illusion of the abstract ego is that it can do anything to bring about radical improvement either in itself or in the world. This is as impossible, physically, as trying to lift yourself off the floor by your own bootstraps. Furthermore, the ego is (like money) a concept, a symbol, even a delusion—not a biological process or physical reality.

Practically, this means that we stop *crusading*—that is, acting for such abstract causes as the good, righteousness, peace, universal love, freedom and social justice, and stop fighting against such equally abstract bogeys as communism, fascism, racism and the imaginary powers of darkness and evil. For most of the hell now being raised in the world is well intentioned. We justify our wars and revolutions as unfortunate means for good ends, as a general recently explained that he had destroyed a village in Vietnam for its own safety. This is also why we can reach no genuine agreement—only the most transitory and unsatisfactory compromises—at the conference tables, for each side believes itself to be acting for the best motives and for the ultimate benefit of the world. To be human, one must recognize and accept a certain element of irreducible rascality both in oneself and in one's enemies. It is, therefore, an enormous relief to realize that these abstract ambitions are total nonsense and to see that we have been wasting untold psychic and physical energy in a fatuous enterprise. For when it is understood that trying to have good without evil is as absurd as trying to have white without black, all that energy is released for things that *can* be done. It can be diverted from abstract causes to specific, material undertakings—to farming and cooking, mining and engineering, making clothes and buildings, traveling and learning, art, music, dancing and making love. Surely, these are excellent things to do for their own sake and not, please *not*, for one's own or anyone else's improvement.

"I'm sorry, Senator, it's some more of those crackpot conservationists."

RAY BRADBURY

THE VACATION

"we're let out, darling," he'd said, "and we'll never come back to the silly damn dull routines"

It was a day as fresh as grass growing up and clouds going over and butterflies coming down could make it. It was a day compounded of silences of bee and flower and ocean and land, which were not silences at all, but motions, stirs, flutters, risings, fallings, each in their own time and matchless rhythm. The land did not move, but moved. The sea was not still, yet was still. Paradox flowed into paradox, stillness mixed with stillness, sound with sound. The flowers vibrated and the bees fell in separate and small showers of golden rain on the clover. The seas of hill and the seas of ocean were divided, each from the other's motion, by a railroad track, empty, compounded of rust and iron marrow, a track on which, quite obviously, no train had run in many years. Thirty miles north it swirled on away to farther mists of distance, thirty miles south it tunneled islands of cloud shadows that changed their continental positions on the sides of far mountains as you watched.

Now, suddenly, the railway track began to tremble.

A blackbird, standing on the rail, felt a rhythm grow faintly, miles away, like a heart beginning to beat.

The blackbird leaped up over the sea.

The rail continued to vibrate softly until at long last around a curve and along the shore came a small workman's handcar, its two-cylinder engine popping and spluttering in the great silence.

On top of this small four-wheeled car, on a double-sided bench facing in two directions and with a little surrey roof above for shade, sat a man, his wife and their small seven-year-old son.

As the handcar traveled through lonely stretch after lonely stretch, the wind whipped their eyes and blew their hair, but they did not look back but only ahead. Sometimes they looked eagerly, as a curve unwound itself, sometimes with great sadness, but always watchful, ready for the next scene.

As they hit a level straightaway, the machine's engine gasped and stopped abruptly. In the now-crushing silence, it seemed that the quiet of the earth, sky and sea itself, by its friction, brought the car to a wheeling halt.

"Out of gas."

The man, sighing, reached for the extra can in the small storage bin and began to pour it into the tank.

His wife and son sat quietly looking at the sea, listening to the muted thunder, the whisper, the drawing back of huge tapestries of sand, gravel, green weed and foam.

"Isn't the sea nice?" said the woman.

"I like it," said the boy.

"Shall we picnic here while we're at it?"

The man focused binoculars on the green peninsula ahead.

"Might as well. The rails have rusted badly. There's a break ahead. We may have to wait while I set a few back in place."

"As many as there are," said the boy, "we'll have picnics!"

The woman tried to smile at this, then turned her grave attention to the man. "How far have we come today?"

"Not ninety miles." The man still peered through the glasses, squinting. "I don't like to go farther than that any one day, anyway. If you rush, there's no time to see. We'll reach Monterey day after tomorrow, Palo Alto the next day, if you want."

The woman removed her great shadowing straw hat, which had been tied over her golden hair with a bright yellow ribbon, and stood perspiring faintly, away from the machine. They had ridden so steadily on the shuddering rail car that the motion was sewn in their bodies. Now, with the stopping, they felt odd, on the verge of unraveling.

"Let's eat!"

The boy ran with the wicker lunch basket down to the shore.

The boy and the woman were already seated by a spread tablecloth when the man came down to them, dressed in his business suit and vest and tie and hat as if he expected to meet someone along the way. As he dealt out the sandwiches and exhumed the pickles from their cool green Mason jars, he began to loosen his tie and unbutton his vest, always looking around as if he should be careful and ready to button up again.

"Are we all alone, Papa?" said the boy, eating.

"Yes."

"No one else, anywhere?"

"No one else."

"Were there people before?"

"Why do you keep asking that? It wasn't that long ago. Just a few months. You remember?"

"Almost. If I try hard, then I don't remember at all." The boy let a handful of sand fall through his fingers. "Were there as many people as there is sand here on the beach? What *happened* to them?"

"I don't know," the man said, and it was true.

They had wakened one morning and the world was empty. The neighbor's clothesline was still strung with blowing white wash, cars gleamed in front of other seven-A.M. cottages, but there were no farewells, the city did not hum with its mighty arterial traffics, phones did not alarm themselves, children did not wail in sunflower wildernesses.

Only the night before he and his wife had been sitting on the front porch when the evening paper was delivered and, not even daring to open to the headlines, he had said, "I wonder when He will get tired of us and just rub us all out?"

"It has gone pretty far," she said. "On and on. We're such fools, aren't we?"

"Wouldn't it be nice"—he lit his pipe and puffed it—"if we woke tomorrow and everyone in the world was gone and everything was starting over?" He sat smoking, the paper folded in his hand, his head resting back on the chair.

"If you could press a button right now and make it happen, would you?"

"I think I would," he said. "Nothing violent. Just have everyone vanish off the face of the earth. Just leave the land and the sea and the growing things like flowers and grass and fruit trees. And the animals, of course, let them stay. Everything except man, who hunts when he isn't hungry, eats when full, and is mean when no one's bothered him."

"Naturally," she smiled quietly, "we would be left."

"I'd like that," he mused. "All of time ahead. The longest summer vacation in history. And us out for the longest picnic-basket lunch in memory. Just you, me and Jim. No commuting. No keeping up with the Joneses. Not even a car. I'd like to find another way of traveling, an older way . . . Then, a hamper full of sandwiches, three bottles of pop, pick up supplies where you need them from empty grocery stores in empty towns, and summertime forever up ahead . . ."

They sat a long while on the porch in silence, the newspaper folded between them.

At last she spoke.

"Wouldn't we be *lonely*?" she said.

So that's how it was the morning of the first day of the new world. They had awakened to the soft sounds of an earth that was now no more than a meadow, and the cities of the earth sinking back into seas of saber grass, marigold, marguerite and morning-glory. They had taken it with remarkable calm at first, perhaps because they had not liked the city for so many years and had had so many friends who were not truly friends, and had lived a boxed and separate life of their own within a mechanical hive.

The husband arose and looked out the window and observed very calmly, as if it were a weather condition, "Everyone's gone . . ." knowing this just by the sounds the city had ceased to make.

They took their time over breakfast, for the boy was still asleep, and then the husband sat back and said, "Now I must plan what to do."

"Do? Why, why you'll go to work, of course."

"You still don't believe it, do you?" he laughed. "That I won't be rushing off each day at eight-ten, that Jim won't go to school again ever. School's out for all of us! No more pencils, no more books, no more boss's sassy looks! We're let out, darling, and we'll never come back to the silly damn dull routines. Come on!"

And he had walked her through the still and empty city streets.

"They didn't die," he said. "They just . . . went away."

"What about the other cities?"

He went to an outdoor phone booth and dialed Chicago, then New York, then San Francisco.

Silence. Silence. Silence.

"That's it," he said, replacing the receiver.

"I feel guilty," she said. "They gone and we here. And . . . I feel happy. Why? I *should* be unhappy."

"Should you? It's no tragedy. They weren't tortured or blasted or burned. It went easily and they didn't know. And now we owe nothing to anyone. Our only responsibility *is* being happy. Thirty more years of happiness, wouldn't that be good?"

"But then we must have more children!"

"To repopulate the world?" He shook his head slowly, calmly. "No. Let Jim be the last. After he's grown and gone let the horses and cows and ground squirrels and garden spiders have the world. They'll get on. And someday some other species that can combine a natural happiness with a natural curiosity will build cities that won't even look like cities to us and survive. Right now, let's go pack a basket, wake Jim and get going on that long thirty-year summer vacation. I'll beat you to the house!"

He took a sledge hammer from the small rail car, and while he worked alone for half an hour fixing the rusted rails into place, the woman and the boy ran along the shore. They came back with dripping shells, a dozen or more, and some beautiful pink pebbles, and sat and the boy took schooling from the mother, doing homework on a pad with a pencil for a time; and then at high noon the man came down, his coat off, his tie thrown aside, and they drank orange pop, watching the bubbles surge up, glutting, inside the bottles. It was quiet. They listened to the sun tune the old iron rails. The smell of hot tar on the ties moved about them in the salt wind as the husband tapped his atlas map lightly and gently.

"We'll go to Sacramento next month, May, then work up toward Seattle. Should make that by July first, July's a good month in Washington, then back down as the weather cools, to Yellowstone, a few miles a day, hunt here, fish there . . ."

The boy, bored, moved away to throw sticks in the sea and wade out like a dog to retrieve them.

The man went on, "Winter in Tucson, then, part of the winter, moving toward Florida, up the coast in the spring, and maybe New York by June. Two years from now, Chicago in the summer. Winter, three years from now, what about Mexico City? Anywhere the rails lead us, anywhere at all, and if we come to an old offshoot rail line we don't know anything about, what the hell, we'll just take it, go down it to see where it goes. And some year, by God, we'll boat down the Mississippi, always wanted to do that. Enough to last us a lifetime. And that's just how long I want to take to do it all . . ."

His voice faded. He started to fumble the map shut, but before he could move, a bright thing fell through the air and hit the paper. It rolled off into the sand and made a wet lump.

His wife glanced at the wet place in the sand and then swiftly searched his face. His solemn eyes were too bright. And down one cheek was a track of wetness.

She gasped. She took his hand and held it tight.

He clenched her hand very hard, his eyes shut now, and slowly he said, with difficulty:

"Wouldn't it be nice if we went to sleep tonight and in the night, somehow, it all came back. All the foolishness, all the noise, all the hate, all the terrible things, all the nightmares, all the wicked people and stupid children, all the mess, all the smallness, all the confusion, all the hope, all the need, all the love. Wouldn't it be nice?"

She waited and nodded her head once.

Then both of them started.

For standing between them, they knew not for how long, was their son, an empty pop bottle in one hand.

The boy's face was pale. With his free hand he reached out to touch his father's cheek where the single tear had made its track.

"You," he said. "Oh, Dad, you. You haven't anyone to play with, either . . ."

The wife started to speak.

The husband moved to take the boy's hand.

The boy jerked back. "Silly! Oh, silly! Silly fools! Oh, you dumb, dumb!" And, whirling, he rushed down to the ocean and stood there crying loudly.

The wife rose to follow, but the husband stopped her.

"No. Let him."

And then they both grew cold and quiet. For the boy, below on the shore, crying steadily, now was writing on a piece of paper and stuffing it into the pop bottle and ramming the tin cap back on and taking the bottle and giving it a great glittering heave up in the air and out into the tidal sea.

What, thought the wife, what did he write on the note? What's in the bottle?

The bottle moved out in the waves.

The boy stopped crying.

After a long while he walked up the shore to stand looking at his parents. His face was neither bright nor dark, alive nor dead, ready nor resigned; it seemed a curious mixture that simply made do with time, weather and these people. They looked at him and beyond to the bay where the bottle, containing the scribbled note, was almost out of sight now, shining in the waves.

Did he write what *we* wanted? thought the woman; did he write what he heard us just wish, just say?

Or did he write something for only himself? she wondered, that tomorrow he might wake and find himself alone in an empty world, no one around, no man, no woman, no father, no mother, no fool grownups with fool wishes, so he could trudge up to the railroad tracks and take the handcar motoring, a solitary boy, across the continental wilderness, on eternal voyages and picnics?

Is that what he wrote in the note?

Which?

She searched his colorless eyes, could not read the answer, dared not ask.

Gull shadows sailed over and kited their faces with sudden passing coolness.

"Time to go," someone said.

They loaded the wicker basket onto the rail car. The woman tied her large bonnet securely in place with its yellow ribbon, they set the boy's pail of shells on the floor boards, then the husband put on his tie, his vest, his coat, his hat, and they all sat on the bench of the car looking out at the sea where the bottled note was far out, blinking on the horizon.

"Is asking enough?" said the boy. "Does wishing work?"

"Sometimes . . . *too* well."

"It depends on what you ask for."

The boy nodded, his eyes faraway.

They looked back at where they had come from and then ahead to where they were going.

"Goodbye, place," said the boy and waved.

The car rolled down the rusty rails. The sound of it dwindled, faded. The man, the woman, the boy dwindled with it in the distance, among the hills.

After they were gone, the rail trembled faintly for two minutes and ceased. A flake of rust fell. A flower nodded.

The sea was very loud.

"Just one little thing. In the ideal city of the future, I don't think we want the main shopping center quite so close to the ghetto."

JOHN STEINBECK

fable

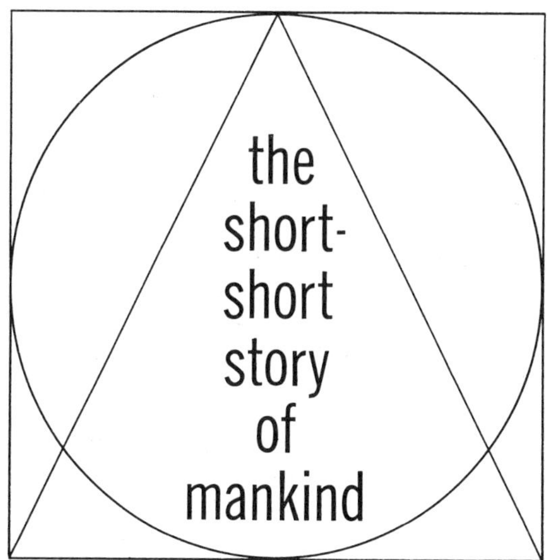

the short-short story of mankind

an improbable allegory of human history compressed for a very small time capsule

It was pretty drafty in the cave in the middle of the afternoon. There wasn't any fire—the last spark had gone out six months ago and the family wouldn't have any more fire until lightning struck another tree.

Joe came into the cave all scratched up and some hunks of hair torn out and he flopped down on the wet ground and bled—Old William was arguing away with Old Bert, who was his brother and also his son, if you look at it one way. They were quarreling mildly over a spoiled chunk of mammoth meat.

Old William said, "Why don't you give some to your mother?"

"Why?" asked Old Bert. "She's my wife, isn't she?"

And that finished that, so they both took after Joe.

"Where's Al?" one of them asked and the other said, "You forgot to roll the rock in front of the door."

Joe didn't even look up and the two old men agreed that kids were going to the devil. "I tell you it was different in my day," Old William said. "They had some respect for their elders or they got what for."

After a while Joe stopped bleeding and he caked some mud on his cuts. "Al's gone," he said.

Old Bert asked brightly, "Sabertooth?"

"No, it's that new bunch that moved into the copse down the draw. They ate Al."

"Savages," said Old William. "Still live in trees. They aren't civilized. We don't hardly ever eat people."

Joe said, "We got hardly anybody to eat except relatives and we're getting low on relatives."

"Those foreigners!" said Old Bert.

"Al and I dug a pit," said Joe. "We caught a horse and those tree people came along and ate our horse. When we complained, they ate Al."

"Well, you go right out and get us one of them and we'll eat him," Old William said.

"Me and who else?" said Joe. "Last time it was warm there was twelve of us here. Now there's only four. Why, I saw my own sister Sally sitting up in a tree with a savage. Had my heart set on Sally, too, Pa," Joe went on a little uncertainly, because Old William was not only his father, but his uncle and his first and third cousin, and his brother-in-law. "Pa, why don't we join up with those tree people? They've got a net kind of thing—catch all sorts of animals. They eat better than we do."

"Son," said Old William, "they're foreigners, that's why. They live in trees. We can't associate with savages. How'd you like your sister to marry a savage?"

"She did!" said Joe. "We could have them come and live in our cave. Maybe they'd show us how to use that net thing."

"Never," said Old Bert. "We couldn't trust 'em. They might eat us in our sleep."

"If we didn't eat them first," said Joe. "I sure would like to have me a nice juicy piece of savage right now. I'm hungry."

"Next thing you know, you'll be saying those tree people are as good as us," Old William said. "I never saw such a boy. Why, where'd authority be? Those foreigners would take over. We'd have to look up to 'em. They'd outnumber us."

"I hate to tell you this, Pa," said Joe, "I've got a busted arm. I can't dig pits anymore—neither can you. You're too old. Bert can't, either. We've got to merge up with those tree people or we aren't gonna eat anything or anybody."

"Over my dead body," said Old William, and then he saw Joe's eyes on his skinny flank and he said, "Now, Joe, don't you go getting ideas about your pa."

Well, a long time ago, before the tribe first moved out of the drippy cave, there was a man named Elmer. He piled up some rocks in a circle and laid brush on top and took to living there. The elders killed Elmer right off. If anybody could go off and live by himself, why, where would authority be? But pretty soon, those elders moved into Elmer's house and then the other families made houses just like it. It was pretty nice with no water dripping in your face.

So, they made Elmer a god—used to swear by him. Said he was the moon.

Everything was going along fine when another tribe moved into the valley. They didn't have Elmer houses, though. They shacked up in skin tents. But, you know, they had a funny kind of a gadget that shot little sticks . . . shot them a long way. They could just stand still and pick off a pig, oh . . . fifty yards away—wouldn't have to run it down and maybe get a tusk in the groin.

The skin tribe shot so much game that naturally the Elmer elders said those savages had to be got rid of. They didn't even know about Elmer—that's how ignorant *they* were. The old people sharpened a lot of sticks and fired the points and they said, "Now you young fellas go out and drive those skin people away. You can't fail because you've got Elmer on your side."

Now, it seems that a long time ago there was a skin man named Max. He thought up this stick shooter so they killed him, naturally, but afterwards they said he was the sun. So, it was a war between Elmer, the moon, and Max, the sun, but in the course of it a whole slew of young skin men and a whole slew of young Elmer men got killed. Then a forest fire broke out and drove the game away. Elmer people and skin people had to take for the hills all together. The elders of both tribes never would accept it. They complained until they died.

You can see from this that the world started going to pot right from the beginning. Things would be going along fine—law and order and all that and the elders in charge—and then some smart aleck would invent something and spoil the whole business—like the man Ralph who forgot to kill all the wild chickens he caught and had to build a henhouse, or like the real troublemaker, Jojo *au front du chien,* who patted some seeds into damp ground and invented farming. Of course, they tore Jojo's arms and legs off and rightly so because when people plant seeds, they can't go golly-wacking around the country enjoying themselves. When you've got a crop in, you stay with it and get the weeds out of it and harvest it. Furthermore, everything and everybody wants to take your crop away from you—weeds—bugs—birds—animals—men—— A farmer spends all his time fighting something off. The elders can call on Elmer all they want, but that won't keep the neighbors from over the hill out of your corncrib.

Well, there was a strong boy named Rudolph, but called Bugsy. Bugsy would break his back wrestling but he wouldn't bring in an armload of wood. Bugsy just naturally liked to fight and he hated to work, so he said, "You men just plant your crops and don't worry. I'll take care of you. If anybody bothers you, I'll clobber 'em. You can give me a few chickens and a couple of handfuls of grits for my trouble."

The elders blessed Bugsy and pretty soon they got him mixed up with Elmer. Bugsy went right along with them. He gathered a dozen strong boys and built a fort up on the hill to take care of those farmers and their crops. When you take care of something, pretty soon you own it.

Bugsy and his boys would stroll around picking over the crop of wheat and girls and when they'd worked over their own valley, they'd go rollicking over the hill to see what the neighbors had stored up or born. Then the strong boys from over the hill would come rollicking back and what they couldn't carry off they burned until pretty soon it was more dangerous to be protected than not to be. Bugsy took everything loose up to his fort to protect it and very little ever came back down. He figured his grandfather was Elmer now and that made him different from other people. How many people do you know that have the moon in their family?

By now the elders had confused protection with virtue because Bugsy passed out his surplus to the better people. The elders were pretty hard on anybody who complained. They said it was a sin. Well, the farmers built a wall around the hill to sit in when the going got rough. They hated to see their crops burn up, but they hated worse to see themselves burn up and their wife Agnes and their daughter Clarinda.

About that time the whole system turned over. Instead of Bugsy protecting them, it was their duty to protect him. He said he got the idea from Elmer one full-moon night.

People spent a lot of time sitting behind the wall waiting for the smoke to clear and they began to fool around with willows from the river, making baskets. And it's natural for people to make more things than they need.

Now, it happens often enough so that you can make a rule about it. There's always going to be a joker. This one was named Harry and he said, "Those ignorant pigs over the hill don't have any willows so they don't have any baskets, but you know what they do?—benighted though they are, they take mud and pat it out and put it in the fire and you can boil water in it. I'll bet if we took them some baskets they'd give us some of those baked mud pots." They had to hang Harry head down over a bonfire. Nobody can put a knife in the status quo and get away with it. But it wasn't long before the basket people got to sneaking over the hill and coming back with pots. Bugsy tried to stop it and the elders were right with him. It took people away from the fields, exposed them to dangerous ideas. Why, pots got to be like money and money is worse than an idea. Bugsy himself said, "Makes folks restless—why, it makes a man think he's as good as the ones that got it a couple of generations earlier," and how's that for being un-Elmer? The elders agreed with Bugsy, of course, but they couldn't stop it, so they all had to join it. Bugsy took half the pots they brought back and pretty soon he took over the willow concession so he got the whole thing.

About then some savages moved up on the hill and got to raiding the basket and pot trade. The only thing to do was for Bugsy, the basket, to marry the daughter of Willy, the pot, and when they all died off, Herman Pot-Basket pulled the whole business together and made a little state and that worked out fine.

Well, it went on from state to league and from league to nation. (A nation usually had some kind of natural boundary like an ocean or a mountain range or a river to keep it from spilling over.) It worked out fine until a bunch of jokers invented long-distance stuff like directed missiles and atom bombs. Then a river or an ocean didn't do a bit of good. It got too dangerous to have separate nations just as it had been to have separate families.

When people are finally faced with extinction, they have to do something about it. Now we've got the United Nations and the elders are right in there fighting it the way they fought coming out of caves. But we don't have much choice about it. It isn't any goodness of heart and we may not want to go ahead but right from the cave time we've had to choose and so far we've never chosen extinction. It'd be kind of silly if we killed ourselves off after all this time. If we do, we're stupider than the cave people and I don't think we are. I think we're just exactly as stupid and that's pretty bright in the long run.

interview

a candid conversation with MARSHALL McLUHAN *the high priest of popcult and metaphysician of media*

*In 1961, the name of Marshall McLuhan was unknown to everyone but his English students at the University of Toronto—and a coterie of academic admirers who followed his abstruse articles in small-circulation quarterlies. But then came two remarkable books—*The Gutenberg Galaxy *(1962) and* Understanding Media *(1964)—and the graying professor from Canada's western hinterlands soon found himself characterized by the* San Francisco Chronicle *as "the hottest academic property around." He has since won a world-wide following for his brilliant—and frequently baffling—theories about the impact of the media on man; and his name has entered the French language as* mucluhanisme, *a synonym for the world of pop culture.*

Though his books are written in a difficult style—at once enigmatic, epigrammatic and overgrown with arcane literary and historic allusions—the revolutionary ideas lurking in them have made McLuhan a best-selling author. Despite protests from a legion of outraged scholastics and old-guard humanists who *claim that McLuhan's ideas range from demented to dangerous, his free-for-all theorizing has attracted the attention of top executives at General Motors (who paid him a handsome fee to inform them that automobiles were a thing of the past), Bell Telephone (to whom he explained that they didn't really understand the function of the telephone) and a leading package-design house (which was told that packages will soon be obsolete). Anteing up $5000, another huge corporation asked him to predict—via closed-circuit television—what their own products will be used for in the future; and Canada's turned-on Prime Minister Pierre Trudeau engages him in monthly bull sessions designed to improve his television image.*

McLuhan's observations—"probes," he prefers to call them—are riddled with such flamboyantly undecipherable aphorisms as "The electric light is pure information" and "People don't actually read newspapers—they get into them every morning like a hot bath." Of his own work, McLuhan has remarked, "I don't pretend to understand it. After all, my stuff is very difficult." Despite his convoluted syntax, flashy metaphors and word-playful one-liners, however, McLuhan's basic thesis is relatively simple.

McLuhan contends that all media—in and of themselves and regardless of the messages they communicate—exert a compelling influence on man and society. Prehistoric, or tribal, man existed in a harmonious balance of the senses, perceiving the world equally through hearing, smell, touch, sight and taste. But technological innovations are extensions of human abilities and senses that alter this sensory balance—an alteration that, in turn, inexorably reshapes the society that created the technology. According to McLuhan, there have been three basic technological innovations: the invention of the phonetic alphabet, which jolted tribal man out of his sensory balance and gave dominance to the eye; the introduction of movable type in the sixteenth century, which accelerated this process; and the invention of the telegraph in 1844, which heralded an electronics revolution that will ultimately retribalize man by restoring his sensory balance. McLuhan has made it his business to explain and extrapolate the repercussions of this electronic revolution.

For his efforts, critics have dubbed him "the Dr. Spock of pop culture," "the guru of the boob tube," a "Canadian Nkrumah who has joined the assault on reason," a "metaphysical wizard possessed by a spatial sense of madness," and "the high priest of popthink who conducts a Black Mass of dilettantes before the altar of historical determinism." Amherst professor Benjamin DeMott observed, "He's swinging, switched on, with it and NOW. And wrong."

But as Tom Wolfe has aptly inquired, "What if he is right? *Suppose he* is *what he sounds like—the most important thinker* since Newton, Darwin, Freud, Einstein and Pavlov?" Social historian Richard Kostelanetz contends that "the most extraordinary quality of McLuhan's mind is that it discerns significance where others see only data, or nothing; he tells us how to measure phenomena previously unmeasurable."

The unperturbed subject of this controversy was born in Edmonton, Alberta, on July 21, 1911. The son of a former actress and a real-estate salesman, McLuhan entered the University of Manitoba intending to become an engineer, but matriculated in 1934 with an M. A. in English literature. Next came a stint as an oarsman and graduate student at Cambridge, followed by McLuhan's first teaching job—at the University of Wisconsin. It was a pivotal experience. "I was confronted with young Americans I was incapable of understanding," he has since remarked. "I felt an urgent need to study their popular culture in order to get through." With the seeds sown, McLuhan let them germinate while earning a Ph. D., then taught at Catholic universities. (He is a devout Roman Catholic convert.)

His publishing career began with a number of articles on standard academic fare, but by the mid-Forties, his interest in popular culture surfaced, and true McLuhan efforts such as "The Psychopathology of *Time* and *Life*" began to appear. They hit book length for the first time in 1951 with the publication of *The Mechanical Bride*—an analysis of the social and psychological pressures generated by the press, radio, movies and advertising—and McLuhan was on his way. Though the book attracted little public notice, it won him the chairmanship of a Ford Foundation seminar on culture and communications and a $40,000 grant, with part of which he started *Explorations*, a small periodical outlet for the seminar's findings. By the late Fifties, his reputation had trickled down to Washington; in 1959, he became director of the Media Project of the National Association of Educational Broadcasters and the United States Office of Education, and the report resulting from this post became the first draft of *Understanding Media*. Since 1963, McLuhan has headed the University of Toronto's Center for Culture and Technology, which until recently consisted entirely of McLuhan's office, but now includes a six-room campus building.

Apart from his teaching, lecturing and administrative duties, McLuhan has become a sort of minor communication industry unto himself. Each month he issues to subscribers a mixed-media report called "The McLuhan Dew-Line"; and, punning on that title, he has also originated a series of recordings called "The Marshall McLuhan Dew-Line Plattertudes." McLuhan contributed a characteristically mind-expanding essay about the media—"The Reversal of the Overheated Image"—to *Playboy's* December 1968 issue. Also a compulsive collaborator, his literary efforts in tandem with colleagues have included a high-school *textbook and an analysis of the function of space in poetry and painting.* Counterblast, *his next book, is a maniacally graphic trip through the land of his theories.*

In order to provide its readers with a map of this labyrinthine terra incognita, Playboy *assigned interviewer Eric Norden to visit McLuhan at his spacious new home in the wealthy Toronto suburb of Wychwood Park, where he lives with his wife, Corinne, and five of his six children. (His eldest son lives in New York, where he is completing a book on James Joyce, one of his father's heroes.) Norden reports, "Tall, gray and gangly, with a thin but mobile mouth and an otherwise eminently forgettable face, McLuhan was dressed in an ill-fitting brown tweed suit, black shoes and a clip-on necktie. As we talked on into the night before a crackling fire, McLuhan expressed his reservations about the interview—indeed, about the printed word itself—as a means of communication, suggesting that the question-and-answer format might impede the in-depth flow of his ideas. I assured him that he would have as much time—and space—as he wished to develop his thoughts."*

The result [which appeared in the March 1969 issue of Playboy*] has considerably more lucidity and clarity than McLuhan's readers are accustomed to—perhaps because the Q. and A. format serves to pin him down by counteracting his habit of mercurially changing the subject in mid-stream of consciousness. It is also, we think, a protean and provocative distillation not only of McLuhan's original theories about human progress and social institutions but of his almost immobilizingly intricate style—described by novelist George P. Elliott as "deliberately antilogical, circular, repetitious, unqualified, gnomic, outrageous" and, even less charitably, by critic Christopher Ricks as "a viscous fog through which loom stumbling metaphors." But other authorities contend that McLuhan's stylistic medium is part and parcel of his message—that the tightly structured "linear" modes of traditional thought and discourse are obsolescent in the new "postliterate" age of the electric media. Norden began the interview with an allusion to McLuhan's favorite electric medium: television.*

Playboy: To borrow Henry Gibson's oft-repeated one-line poem on Rowan and Martin's *Laugh-In*—"Marshall McLuhan, what are you doin'?"

McLuhan: Sometimes I wonder. I'm making explorations. I don't know where they're going to take me. My work is designed for the pragmatic purpose of trying to understand our technological environment and its psychic and social consequences. But my books constitute the *process* rather than the completed product of discovery; my purpose is to employ facts as tentative probes, as means of insight, of pattern recognition, rather than to use them in the traditional and sterile sense of classified data, cate-

"The young will continue turning on no matter how many of them are turned off into prisons. Such legal restrictions only reflect the cultural revenge of a dying culture against its successor."

"The Eskimo is a servomechanism of his kayak, the cowboy of his horse, the businessman of his clock, the cyberneticist—and soon the world—of his computer. In short, to the spoils belongs the victor."

"The hostility of my critics is the customary human reaction when confronted with innovation—a practice refined by the Chinese emperors, who used to execute messengers bringing bad news."

gories, containers. I want to map new terrain rather than chart old landmarks.

But I've never presented such explorations as revealed truth. As an investigator, I have no fixed point of view, no commitment to any theory—my own or anyone else's. As a matter of fact, I'm completely ready to junk any statement I've ever made about any subject if events don't bear me out, or if I discover it isn't contributing to an understanding of the problem. The better part of my work on media is actually somewhat like a safecracker's. I don't know what's inside; maybe it's nothing. I just sit down and start to work. I grope, I listen, I test, I accept and discard; I try out different sequences—until the tumblers fall and the doors spring open.

Playboy: Isn't such a methodology somewhat erratic and inconsistent—if not, as your critics would maintain, eccentric?

McLuhan: Any approach to environmental problems must be sufficiently flexible and adaptable to encompass the entire environmental matrix, which is in constant flux. I consider myself a generalist, not a specialist who has staked out a tiny plot of study as his intellectual turf and is oblivious to everything else. Actually, my work is a depth operation, the accepted practice in most modern disciplines from psychiatry to metallurgy and structural analysis. Effective study of the media deals not only with the content of the media but with the media themselves and the total cultural environment within which the media function. Only by standing aside from any phenomenon and taking an overview can you discover its operative principles and lines of force. There's really nothing inherently startling or radical about this study—except that for some reason few have had the vision to undertake it. For the past 3500 years of the Western world, the effects of media—whether it's speech, writing, printing, photography, radio or television—have been systematically overlooked by social observers. Even in today's revolutionary electronic age, scholars evidence few signs of modifying this traditional stance of ostrichlike disregard.

Playboy: Why?

McLuhan: Because all media, from the phonetic alphabet to the computer, are extensions of man that cause deep and lasting changes in him and transform his environment. Such an extension is an intensification, an amplification of an organ, sense or function, and whenever it takes place, the central nervous system appears to institute a self-protective *numbing* of the affected area, insulating and anesthetizing it from conscious awareness of what's happening to it. It's a process rather like that which occurs to the body under shock or stress conditions, or to the mind in line with the Freudian concept of repression.

I call this peculiar form of self-hypnosis Narcissus narcosis, a syndrome whereby man remains as unaware of the psychic and social effects of his new technology as a fish of the water it swims in. As a result, precisely at the point where a new media-induced environment becomes all pervasive and transmogrifies our sensory balance, it also becomes invisible.

This problem is doubly acute today because man must, as a simple survival strategy, become aware of what is happening to him, despite the attendant pain of such comprehension. The fact that he has not done so in this age of electronics is what has made this also the age of anxiety, which in turn has been transformed into its *Doppelgänger*—the therapeutically reactive age of *anomie* and apathy. But despite our self-protective escape mechanisms, the total-field awareness engendered by electronic media is enabling us—indeed, compelling us—to grope toward a consciousness of the unconscious, toward a realization that technology is an extension of our own bodies. We live in the first age when change occurs sufficiently rapidly to make such pattern recognition possible for society at large. Until the present era, this awareness has always been reflected first by the artist, who has had the power—and courage—of the seer to read the language of the outer world and relate it to the inner world.

Playboy: Why should it be the artist rather than the scientist who perceives these relationships and foresees these trends?

McLuhan: Because inherent in the artist's creative inspiration is the process of subliminally sniffing out environmental change. It's always been the artist who perceives the alterations in man caused by a new medium, who recognizes that the future is the present, and uses his work to prepare the ground for it. But most people, from truck drivers to the literary Brahmins, are still blissfully ignorant of what the media do to them, unaware that because of their pervasive effects on man, it is the medium itself that is the message, *not* the content, and unaware that the medium is also the *massage*—that, all puns aside, it literally works over and saturates and molds and transforms every sense ratio. The content or message of any particular medium has about as much importance as the stenciling on the casing of an atomic bomb. But the ability to perceive media-induced extensions of man, once the province of the artist, is now being expanded as the new environment of electric information makes possible a new degree of perception and critical awareness by nonartists.

Playboy: Is the public, then, at last beginning to perceive the "invisible" contours of these new technological environments?

McLuhan: People are beginning to understand the nature of their new technology, but not yet nearly enough of them—and not nearly well enough. Most people, as I indicated, still cling to what I call the rearview-mirror view of their world. By this I mean to say that because of the invisibility of any environment during the period of its innovation, man is only consciously aware of the environment that has *preceded* it; in other words, an environment becomes fully visible only when it has been superseded by a new environment; thus, we are always one step behind in our view of the world. Because we are benumbed by any new technology—which in turn creates a totally new environment—we tend to make the old environment more visible; we do so by turning it into an art form and by attaching ourselves to the objects and atmosphere that characterized it, just as we've done with jazz, and as we're now doing with the garbage of the mechanical environment via pop art.

The present is always invisible because it's environmental and saturates the whole field of attention so overwhelmingly; thus, everyone but the artist, the man of integral awareness, is alive in an earlier day. In the midst of the electronic age of software, of instant information movement, we still believe we're living in the mechanical age of hardware. At the height of the mechanical age, man turned back to earlier centuries in search of "pastoral" values. The Renaissance and the Middle Ages were completely oriented toward Rome, Rome was oriented toward Greece, and the Greeks were oriented toward the pre-Homeric primitives. We reverse the old educational dictum of learning by proceeding from the familiar to the unfamiliar by going from the unfamiliar to the familiar, which is nothing more or less than the numbing mechanism that takes place whenever new media drastically extend our senses.

Playboy: If this "numbing" effect performs a beneficial role by protecting man from the psychic pain caused by the extensions of his nervous system that you attribute to the media, why are you attempting to dispel it and alert man to the changes in his environment?

McLuhan: In the past, the effects of media were experienced more gradually, allowing the individual and society to absorb and cushion their impact to some degree. Today, in the electronic age of instantaneous communication, I believe that our survival, and at the very least our comfort and happiness, is predicated on understanding the nature of our new environment, because unlike previous environmental changes, the electric media constitute a total and near-instantaneous transformation of culture, values and attitudes. This upheaval generates great pain and identity loss, which can be ameliorated only through a conscious awareness of its dynamics. If we understand the revolutionary transformations caused by new media, we can anticipate and control them; but if we continue in our self-induced subliminal trance, we will be their slaves.

Because of today's terrific speed-up of information moving, we have a chance to apprehend, predict and influence the environmental forces shaping us—and thus win back control of our own destinies. The new extensions of man and the environment they generate are the central manifestations of the evolutionary process, and yet we still cannot free ourselves of the delusion that it is how a medium is used that counts, rather than what it does to us and with us. This is the zombie stance of the technological idiot. It's to escape this Narcissus trance that I've tried to trace and reveal the impact of media on man, from the beginning of recorded time to the present.

Playboy: Will you trace that impact for us—in condensed form?

McLuhan: It's difficult to condense into the format of an interview such as this, but I'll try to give you a brief rundown of the basic media breakthroughs. You've got to remember that my definition of media is broad; it includes any technology whatever that creates extensions of the human body and senses, from clothing to the computer. And a vital point I must stress again is that societies have always been shaped more by the nature of the media with which men communicate than by the content of the communication. All technology has the property of the Midas touch; whenever a society develops an extension of itself, all other functions of that society tend to be transmuted to accommodate that new form; once any new technology penetrates a society, it saturates every institution of that society. New technology is thus a revolutionizing agent. We see this today with the electric media and we saw it several thousand years ago with the invention of the phonetic alphabet, which was just as far-reaching an innovation—and had just as profound consequences for man.

Playboy: What were they?

McLuhan: Before the invention of the phonetic alphabet, man lived in a world where all the senses were balanced and simultaneous, a closed world of tribal depth and resonance, an oral culture structured by a dominant auditory sense of life. The ear, as opposed to the cool and neutral eye, is sensitive, hyperaesthetic and all-inclusive, and contributes to the seamless web of tribal kinship and interdependence in which all members of the group existed in harmony. The primary medium of communication was speech, and thus no man knew appreciably more or less than any other—which meant that there was little individualism and specialization, the hallmarks of "civilized" Western man. Tribal cultures even today simply cannot comprehend the concept of the individual or of the separate and independent citizen. Oral cultures act and react simultaneously, whereas the capacity to act without reacting, without involvement, is the special gift of "detached" literate man. Another basic characteristic distinguishing tribal man from his literate successors is that he lived in a world of *acoustic* space, which gave him a radically different concept of time-space relationships.

Playboy: What do you mean by "acoustic space"?

McLuhan: I mean space that has no center and no margin, unlike strictly visual space, which is an extension and intensification of the eye. Acoustic space is organic and integral, perceived through the simultaneous interplay of all the senses, whereas "rational" or pictorial space is uniform, sequential and continuous and creates a closed world with none of the rich resonance of the tribal echoland. Our own Western time-space concepts derive from the environment created by the discovery of phonetic writing, as does our entire concept of Western civilization. The man of the tribal world led a complex, kaleidoscopic life precisely because the ear, unlike the eye, cannot be focused and is synaesthetic rather than analytical and linear. Speech is an utterance, or more precisely, an *outering*, of all our senses at once; the auditory field is simultaneous, the visual successive. The modes of life of nonliterate people were implicit, simultaneous and discontinuous, and also far richer than those of literate man. By their dependence on the spoken word for information, people were drawn together into a tribal mesh; and since the spoken word is more emotionally laden than the written—conveying by intonation such rich emotions as anger, joy, sorrow, fear—tribal man was more spontaneous and passionately volatile. Audile-tactile tribal man partook of the collective unconscious, lived in a magical integral world patterned by myth and ritual, its values divine and unchallenged, whereas literate or visual man creates an environment that is strongly fragmented, individualistic, explicit, logical, specialized and detached.

Playboy: Was it phonetic literacy alone that precipitated this profound shift of values from tribal involvement to "civilized" detachment?.

McLuhan: Yes, it was. Any culture is an order of sensory preferences, and in the tribal world, the senses of touch, taste, hearing and smell were developed, for very practical reasons, to a much higher level than the strictly visual. Into this world, the phonetic alphabet fell like a bombshell, installing sight at the head of the hierarchy of senses. Literacy propelled man from the tribe, gave him an eye for an ear and replaced his integral in-depth communal interplay with visual linear values and fragmented consciousness. As an intensification and amplification of the visual function, the phonetic alphabet diminished the role of the senses of hearing and touch and taste and smell, permeating the discontinuous culture of tribal man and translating its organic harmony and complex synaesthesia into the uniform, connected and visual mode that we still consider the norm of "rational" existence. The whole man became fragmented man; the alphabet shattered the charmed circle and resonating magic of the tribal world, exploding man into an agglomeration of specialized and psychically impoverished "individuals," or units, functioning in a world of linear time and Euclidean space.

Playboy: But literate societies existed in the ancient world long before the phonetic alphabet. Why weren't *they* detribalized?

McLuhan: The phonetic alphabet did not change or extend man so drastically just because it enabled him to read; as you point out, tribal culture had already coexisted with other written languages for thousands of years. But the phonetic alphabet was radically different from the older and richer hieroglyphic or ideogrammic cultures. The writings of Egyptian, Babylonian, Mayan and Chinese cultures were an extension of the senses in that they gave pictorial expression to reality, and they demanded many signs to cover the wide range of data in their societies—unlike phonetic writing, which uses semantically meaningless letters to correspond to semantically meaningless sounds and is able, with only a handful of letters, to encompass all meanings and all languages. This achievement demanded the separation of both sights and sounds from their semantic and dramatic meanings in order to render visible the actual sound of speech, thus placing a barrier between men and objects and creating a dualism between sight and sound. It divorced the visual function from the interplay with the other senses and thus led to the rejection from consciousness of vital areas of our sensory experience and to the resultant atrophy of the unconscious. The balance of the sensorium—or *Gestalt* interplay of all the senses—and the psychic and social harmony it engendered was disrupted, and the visual function was overdeveloped. This was true of no other writing system.

Playboy: How can you be so sure that this all occurred solely because of phonetic literacy—or, in fact, if it occurred at all?

McLuhan: You don't have to go back three thousand or four thousand years to see this process at work; in Africa today, a single generation of alphabetic literacy is enough to wrench the individual from the tribal web. When tribal man becomes phonetically literate, he may have an improved abstract intellectual grasp of the world, but most of the deeply emotional corporate family feeling is excised from his relationship with his social milieu. This division of sight and sound and meaning causes deep psychological effects, and he suffers a corresponding separation and impoverishment of his imaginative, emotional and sensory life. He begins reasoning in a sequential linear fashion;

he begins categorizing and classifying data. As knowledge is extended in alphabetic form, it is localized and fragmented into specialties, creating divisions of function, of social classes, of nations and of knowledge—and in the process, the rich interplay of all the senses that characterized the tribal society is sacrificed.

Playboy: But aren't there corresponding gains in insight, understanding and cultural diversity to compensate detribalized man for the loss of his communal values?

McLuhan: Your question reflects all the institutionalized biases of literate man. Literacy, contrary to the popular view of the "civilizing" process you've just echoed, creates people who are much less complex and diverse than those who develop in the intricate web of oral-tribal societies. Tribal man, unlike homogenized Western man, was not differentiated by his specialist talents or his visible characteristics, but by his unique emotional blends. The internal world of the tribal man was a creative mix of complex emotions and feelings that literate men of the Western world have allowed to wither or have suppressed in the name of efficiency and practicality. The alphabet served to neutralize all these rich divergencies of tribal cultures by translating their complexities into simple visual forms; and the visual sense, remember, is the only one that allows us to *detach;* all other senses involve us, but the detachment bred by literacy disinvolves and detribalizes man. He separates from the tribe as a predominantly visual man who shares standardized attitudes, habits and rights with other civilized men. But he is also given a tremendous advantage over the nonliterate tribal man who, today as in ancient times, is hamstrung by cultural pluralism, uniqueness and discontinuity—values that make the African as easy prey for the European colonialist as the barbarian was for the Greeks and Romans. Only alphabetic cultures have ever succeeded in mastering connected linear sequences as a means of social and psychic organization; the separation of all kinds of experiences into uniform and continuous units in order to generate accelerated action and alteration of form—in other words, applied knowledge—has been the secret of Western man's ascendancy over other men as well as over his environment.

Playboy: Isn't the thrust of your argument, then, that the introduction of the phonetic alphabet was not progress, as has generally been assumed, but a psychic and social disaster?

McLuhan: It was both. I try to avoid value judgments in these areas, but there is much evidence to suggest that man may have paid too dear a price for his new environment of specialist technology and values. Schizophrenia and alienation may be the inevitable consequences of phonetic literacy. It's metaphorically significant, I suspect, that the old Greek myth has Cadmus, who brought the alphabet to man, sowing dragon's teeth that sprang up from the earth as armed men. Whenever the dragon's teeth of technological change are sown, we reap a whirlwind of violence. We saw this clearly in classical times, although it was somewhat moderated because phonetic literacy did not win an overnight victory over primitive values and institutions; rather, it permeated ancient society in a gradual, if inexorable, evolutionary process.

Playboy: How long did the old tribal culture endure?

McLuhan: In isolated pockets, it held on until the invention of printing in the sixteenth century, which was a vastly important qualitative extension of phonetic literacy. If the phonetic alphabet fell like a bombshell on tribal man, the printing press hit him like a 100-megaton H-bomb. The printing press was the ultimate extension of phonetic literacy: Books could be reproduced in infinite numbers; universal literacy was at last fully possible, if gradually realized; and books became portable individual possessions. Type, the prototype of all machines, ensured the primacy of the visual bias and finally sealed the doom of tribal man. The new medium of linear, uniform, repeatable type reproduced information in unlimited quantities and at hitherto-impossible speeds, thus assuring the eye a position of total predominance in man's sensorium. As a drastic extension of man, it shaped and transformed his entire environment, psychic and social, and was directly responsible for the rise of such disparate phenomena as nationalism, the Reformation, the assembly line and its offspring, the Industrial Revolution, the whole concept of causality, Cartesian and Newtonian concepts of the universe, perspective in art, narrative chronology in literature and a psychological mode of introspection or inner direction that greatly intensified the tendencies toward individualism and specialization engendered two thousand years before by phonetic literacy. The schism between thought and action was institutionalized, and fragmented man, first sundered by the alphabet, was at last diced into bite-sized tidbits. From that point on, Western man was Gutenberg man.

Playboy: Even accepting the principle that technological innovations generate far-reaching environmental changes, many of your readers find it difficult to understand how you can hold the development of printing responsible for such apparently unrelated phenomena as nationalism and industrialism.

McLuhan: The key word is "apparently." Look a bit closer at both nationalism and industrialism and you'll see that both derived directly from the explosion of print technology in the sixteenth century. Nationalism didn't exist in Europe until the Renaissance, when typography enabled every literate man to *see* his mother tongue analytically as a uniform entity. The printing press, by spreading mass-produced books and printed matter across Europe, turned the vernacular regional languages of the day into uniform closed systems of national languages—just another variant of what we call mass media—and gave birth to the entire concept of nationalism.

The individual newly homogenized by print saw the nation concept as an intense and beguiling image of group destiny and status. With print, the homogeneity of money, markets and transport also became possible for the first time, thus creating economic as well as political unity and triggering all the dynamic centralizing energies of contemporary nationalism. By creating a speed of information movement unthinkable before printing, the Gutenberg revolution thus produced a new type of visual centralized national entity that was gradually merged with commercial expansion until Europe was a network of states.

By fostering continuity and competition within homogeneous and contiguous territory, nationalism not only forged new nations but sealed the doom of the old corporate, noncompetitive and discontinuous medieval order of guilds and family-structured social organization; print demanded both personal fragmentation and social uniformity, the natural expression of which was the nation-state. Literate nationalism's tremendous speed-up of information movement accelerated the specialist function that was nurtured by phonetic literacy and nourished by Gutenberg, and rendered obsolete such generalist encyclopedic figures as Benvenuto Cellini, the goldsmith-*cum-condottiere-cum*-painter-*cum*-sculptor-*cum*-writer; it was the Renaissance that destroyed Renaissance Man.

Playboy: Why do you feel that Gutenberg also laid the groundwork for the Industrial Revolution?

McLuhan: The two go hand in hand. Printing, remember, was the first mechanization of a complex handicraft; by creating an analytic sequence of step-by-step processes, it became the blueprint of all mechanization to follow. The most important quality of print is its repeatability; it is a visual statement that can be reproduced indefinitely, and repeatability is the root of the mechanical principle that has transformed the world since Gutenberg. Typography, by producing the first uniformly repeatable commodity, also created Henry Ford, the first assembly line and the first mass production. Movable type was archetype and prototype for all subsequent industrial development. Without phonetic literacy and the printing press, modern industrialism would be impossible. It is necessary to recognize literacy as typographic technology, shaping not only production and marketing procedures but all other areas of life, from education to city planning.

Playboy: You seem to be contending that practically every aspect of modern life is a direct consequence of Gutenberg's invention of the printing press.

McLuhan: Every aspect of Western *mechanical* culture was shaped by print technology, but the modern age is the age of the *electric* media, which forge environments and cultures antithetical to the mechanical consumer society derived from print. Print tore man out of his traditional cultural matrix while showing him how to pile individual upon individual into a massive agglomeration of national and industrial power, and the typographic trance of the West has endured until today, when the electronic media are at last demesmerizing us. The Gutenberg Galaxy is being eclipsed by the constellation of Marconi.

Playboy: You've discussed that constellation in general terms, but what precisely are the electric media that you contend have supplanted the old mechanical technology?

McLuhan: The electric media are the telegraph, radio, films, telephone, computer and television, all of which have not only extended a single sense or function as the old mechanical media did—i.e., the wheel as an extension of the foot, clothing as an extension of the skin, the phonetic alphabet as an extension of the eye—but have enhanced and externalized our entire central nervous systems, thus transforming all aspects of our social and psychic existence. The use of the electronic media constitutes a break boundary between fragmented Gutenberg man and integral man, just as phonetic literacy was a break boundary between oral-tribal man and visual man.

In fact, today we can look back at three thousand years of differing degrees of visualization, atomization and mechanization and at last recognize the mechanical age as an interlude between two great organic eras of culture. The age of print, which held sway from approximately 1500 to 1900, had its obituary tapped out by the telegraph, the first of the new electric media, and further obsequies were registered by the perception of "curved space" and non-Euclidean mathematics in the early years of the century, which revived tribal man's discontinuous time-space concepts—and which even Spengler dimly perceived as the death knell of Western literate values. The development of telephone, radio, film, television and the computer have driven further nails into the coffin. Today, television is the most significant of the electric media because it permeates nearly every home in the country, extending the central nervous system of every viewer as it works over and molds the entire sensorium with the ultimate message. It is television that is primarily responsible for ending the visual supremacy that characterized all mechanical technology, although each of the other electric media have played contributing roles.

Playboy: But isn't television itself a primarily visual medium?

McLuhan: No, it's quite the opposite, although the idea that TV is a visual extension is an understandable mistake. Unlike film or photograph, television is primarily an extension of the sense of touch rather than of sight, and it is the tactile sense that demands the greatest interplay of all the senses. The secret of TV's tactile power is that the video image is one of low intensity or definition and thus, unlike either photograph or film, offers no detailed information about specific objects but instead involves the active participation of the viewer. The TV image is a mosaic mesh not only of horizontal lines but of millions of tiny dots, of which the viewer is physiologically able to pick up only fifty or sixty from which he shapes the image; thus he is constantly filling in vague and blurry images, bringing himself into in-depth involvement with the screen and acting out a constant creative dialog with the iconoscope. The contours of the resultant cartoonlike image are fleshed out within the imagination of the viewer, which necessitates great personal involvement and participation; the viewer, in fact, becomes the screen, whereas in film he becomes the camera. By requiring us to constantly fill in the spaces of the mosaic mesh, the iconoscope is tattooing its message directly on our skins. Each viewer is thus an unconscious pointillist painter like Seurat, limning new shapes and images as the iconoscope washes over his entire body. Since the point of focus for a TV set is the viewer, television is Orientalizing us by causing us all to begin to look within ourselves. The essence of TV viewing is, in short, intense participation and low definition—what I call a "cool" experience, as opposed to an essentially "hot," or high definition–low participation, medium like radio.

Playboy: A good deal of the perplexity surrounding your theories is related to this postulation of hot and cool media. Could you give us a brief definition of each?

McLuhan: Basically, a hot medium *ex*cludes and a cool medium *in*cludes; hot media are low in participation, or completion, by the audience and cool media are high in participation. A hot medium is one that extends a single sense with high definition. High definition means a complete filling in of data by the medium without intense audience participation. A photograph, for example, is high definition or hot, whereas a cartoon is low definition or cool, because the rough outline drawing provides very little visual data and requires the viewer to fill in or complete the image himself. The telephone, which gives the ear relatively little data, is thus cool, as is speech; both demand considerable filling in by the listener. On the other hand, radio is a hot medium because it sharply and intensely provides great amounts of high-definition auditory information that leaves little or nothing to be filled in by the audience. A lecture, by the same token, is hot, but a seminar is cool; a book is hot, but a conversation or bull session is cool.

In a cool medium, the audience is an active constituent of the viewing or listening experience. A girl wearing open-mesh silk stockings or glasses is inherently cool and sensual because the eye acts as a surrogate hand in filling in the low-definition image thus engendered. Which is why boys make passes at girls who wear glasses. In any case, the overwhelming majority of our technologies and entertainments since the introduction of print technology have been hot, fragmented and exclusive, but in the age of television we see a return to cool values and the inclusive in-depth involvement and participation they engender. This is, of course, just one more reason why the medium is the message, rather than the content; it is the participatory nature of the TV experience itself that is important, rather than the content of the particular TV image that is being invisibly and indelibly inscribed on our skins.

Playboy: Even if, as you contend, the medium is the ultimate message, how can you entirely discount the importance of content? Didn't the content of Hitler's radio speeches, for example, have some effect on the Germans?

McLuhan: By stressing that the medium is the message rather than the content, I'm not suggesting that content plays *no* role—merely that it plays a distinctly subordinate role. Even if Hitler had delivered botany lectures, some other demagog would have used the radio to retribalize the Germans and rekindle the dark atavistic side of the tribal nature that created European fascism in the Twenties and Thirties. By placing all the stress on content and practically none on the medium, we lose all chance of perceiving and influencing the impact of new technologies on man, and thus we are always dumfounded by—and unprepared for—the revolutionary environmental transformations induced by new media. Buffeted by environmental changes he cannot comprehend, man echoes the last plaintive cry of his tribal ancestor, Tarzan, as he plummeted to earth: "Who greased my vine?" The German Jew victimized by the Nazis because his old tribalism clashed with their new tribalism could no more understand why his world was turned upside down than the American today can understand the reconfiguration of social and political institutions caused by the electric media in general and television in particular.

Playboy: How is television reshaping our political institutions?

McLuhan: TV is revolutionizing every political system in the Western world. For one thing, it's creating a totally new type of national leader, a man who is much more of a tribal chieftain than a politician. Castro is a good example of the new tribal chieftain who rules his country by a mass-participational TV dialog and feedback; he governs his country on camera, by giving the Cuban people the experience of being directly and intimately involved in the process of collective decision making. Castro's adroit blend of political education, propaganda and avuncular guidance is the pattern for tribal chieftains in other countries. The new political showman has to literally as well as figuratively put on his audience as he would a suit of clothes and become a corporate tribal image—like Mussolini, Hitler and F. D. R. in the days of radio, and Jack Kennedy in the television era. All these men were tribal emperors on a scale theretofore unknown in the world, because they all mastered their media.

Playboy: How did Kennedy use TV in a manner different from his predecessors—or successors?

McLuhan: Kennedy was the first TV President because he was the first prominent American politician to ever understand the dynamics and lines of force of the television iconoscope. As I've explained, TV is an inherently cool medium, and Kennedy had a compatible coolness and indifference to power, bred of personal wealth, which allowed him to adapt fully to TV. Any political candidate who doesn't have such cool, low-definition qualities, which allow the viewer to fill in the gaps with his own personal identification, simply electrocutes himself on television—as Richard Nixon did in his disastrous debates with Kennedy in the 1960 campaign. Nixon was essentially hot; he presented a high-definition, sharply-defined image and action on the TV screen that contributed to his reputation as a phony—the "Tricky Dicky" syndrome that has dogged his footsteps for years. "Would you buy a used car from this man?" the political cartoon asked—and the answer was no, because he didn't project the cool aura of distinterest and objectivity that Kennedy emanated so effortlessly and engagingly.

Playboy: Did Nixon take any lessons from you the last time around?

McLuhan: He certainly took lessons from somebody, because in the recent election it was Nixon who was cool and Humphrey who was hot. I had noticed the change in Nixon as far back as 1963 when I saw him on *The Jack Paar Show*. No longer the slick, glib, aggressive Nixon of 1960, he had been toned down, polished, programmed and packaged into the new Nixon we saw in

1968: earnest, modest, quietly sincere—in a word, cool. I realized then that if Nixon maintained this mask, he could be elected President, and apparently the American electorate agreed last November.

Playboy: How did Lyndon Johnson make use of television?

McLuhan: He botched it the same way Nixon did in 1960. He was too intense, too obsessed with making his audience love and revere him as father and teacher, and too classifiable. Would people feel any safer buying a used car from L. B. J. than from the old Nixon? The answer is, obviously, no. Johnson became a stereotype—even a parody—of himself, and earned the same reputation as a phony that plagued Nixon for so long. The people wouldn't have cared if John Kennedy lied to them on TV, but they couldn't stomach L. B. J. even when he told the truth. The credibility gap was really a communications gap. The political candidate who understands TV—whatever his party, goals or beliefs—can gain power unknown in history. How he uses that power is, of course, quite another question. But the basic thing to remember about the electric media is that they inexorably transform every sense ratio and thus recondition and restructure all our values and institutions. The overhauling of our traditional political system is only one manifestation of the retribalizing process wrought by the electric media, which is turning the planet into a global village.

Playboy: Would you describe this retribalizing process in more detail?

McLuhan: The electronically induced technological extensions of our central nervous system, which I spoke of earlier, are immersing us in a world-pool of information movement and are thus enabling man to incorporate within himself the whole of mankind. The aloof and dissociated role of the literate man of the Western world is succumbing to the new, intense depth participation engendered by the electronic media and bringing us back in touch with ourselves as well as with one another. But the instant nature of electric-information movement is decentralizing—rather than enlarging—the family of man into a new state of multitudinous tribal existences. Particularly in countries where literate values are deeply institutionalized, this is a highly traumatic process, since the clash of the old segmented visual culture and the new integral electronic culture creates a crisis of identity, a vacuum of the self, which generates tremendous violence—violence that is simply an identity quest, private or corporate, social or commercial.

Playboy: Do you relate this identity crisis to the current social unrest and violence in the United States?

McLuhan: Yes, and to the booming business psychiatrists are doing. All our alienation and atomization are reflected in the crumbling of such time-honored social values as the right of privacy and the sanctity of the individual; as they yield to the intensities of the new technology's electric circus, it seems to the average citizen that the sky is falling in. As man is tribally metamorphosed by the electric media, we all become Chicken Littles, scurrying around frantically in search of our former identities, and in the process unleash tremendous violence. As the preliterate confronts the literate in the postliterate arena, as new information patterns inundate and uproot the old, mental breakdowns of varying degrees—including the collective nervous breakdowns of whole societies unable to resolve their crises of identity—will become very common.

It is not an easy period in which to live, especially for the television-conditioned young who, unlike their literate elders, cannot take refuge in the zombie trance of Narcissus narcosis that numbs the state of psychic shock induced by the impact of the new media. From Tokyo to Paris to Columbia, youth mindlessly acts out its identity quest in the theater of the streets, searching not for goals but for roles, striving for an identity that eludes them.

Playboy: Why do you think they aren't finding it within the educational system?

McLuhan: Because education, which should be helping youth to understand and adapt to their revolutionary new environments, is instead being used merely as an instrument of cultural aggression, imposing upon retribalized youth the obsolescent visual values of the dying literate age. Our entire educational system is reactionary, oriented to past values and past technologies, and will likely continue so until the old generation relinquishes power. The generation gap is actually a chasm, separating not two age groups but two vastly divergent cultures. I can understand the ferment in our schools, because our educational system is totally rearview mirror. It's a dying and outdated system founded on literate values and fragmented and classified data totally unsuited to the needs of the first television generation.

Playboy: How do you think the educational system can be adapted to accommodate the needs of this television generation?

McLuhan: Well, before we can start doing things the right way, we've got to recognize that we've been doing them the wrong way—which most pedagogs and administrators and even most parents still refuse to accept. Today's child is growing up absurd because he is suspended between two worlds and two value systems, neither of which inclines him to maturity because he belongs wholly to neither but exists in a hybrid limbo of constantly conflicting values. The challenge of the new era is simply the total creative process of *growing up*—and mere teaching and repetition of facts are as irrelevant to this process as a dowser to a nuclear power plant. To expect a "turned on" child of the electric age to respond to the old education modes is rather like expecting an eagle to swim. It's simply not within his environment, and therefore incomprehensible.

The TV child finds it difficult if not impossible to adjust to the fragmented, visual goals of our education after having had all his senses involved by the electric media; he craves in-depth involvement, not linear detachment and uniform sequential patterns. But suddenly and without preparation, he is snatched from the cool, inclusive womb of television and exposed—within a vast bureaucratic structure of courses and credits—to the hot medium of print. His natural instinct, conditioned by the electric media, is to bring all his senses to bear on the book he's instructed to read, and print resolutely rejects that approach, demanding an isolated visual attitude to learning rather than the *Gestalt* approach of the unified sensorium. The reading postures of children in elementary school are a pathetic testimonial to the effects of television; children of the TV generation separate book from eye by an average distance of four and a half inches, attempting psychomimetically to bring to the printed page the all-inclusive sensory experience of TV. They are becoming Cyclops, desperately seeking to wallow in the book as they do in the TV screen.

Playboy: Might it be possible for the "TV child" to make the adjustment to his educational environment by synthesizing traditional literate-visual forms with the insights of his own electric culture—or must the medium of print be totally unassimilable for him?

McLuhan: Such a synthesis is entirely possible and could create a creative blend of the two cultures—if the educational establishment was aware that there *is* an electric culture. In the absence of such elementary awareness, I'm afraid that the television child has no future in our schools. You must remember that the TV child has been relentlessly exposed to all the "adult" news of the modern world—war, racial discrimination, rioting, crime, inflation, sexual revolution. The war in Vietnam has written its bloody message on his skin; he has witnessed the assassinations and funerals of the nation's leaders; he's been orbited through the TV screen into the astronaut's dance in space, been inundated by information transmitted via radio, telephone, films, recordings and other people. His parents plopped him down in front of a TV set at the age of two to tranquilize him, and by the time he enters kindergarten, he's clocked as much as four thousand hours of television. As an IBM executive told me, "My children had lived several lifetimes compared to their grandparents when they began grade one."

Playboy: If you had children young enough to belong to the TV generation, how would you educate them?

McLuhan: Certainly not in our current schools, which are intellectual penal institutions. In today's world, to paraphrase Jefferson, the least education is the best education, since very few young minds can survive the intellectual tortures of our educational system. The mosaic image of the TV screen generates a depth-involving *nowness* and simultaneity in the lives of children that makes them scorn the distant visualized goals of traditional education as unreal, irrelevant and puerile. Another basic problem is that in our schools there is simply too much to learn by the traditional analytic methods; this is an age of information overload. The only way to make the schools other than prisons without bars is to start fresh with new techniques and values.

Playboy: A number of experimental projects are bringing both TV and computers directly into the classrooms. Do you consider this sort of electronic educational aid a step in the right direction?

McLuhan: It's not really too important if there is ever a TV set in each classroom across the country, since the sensory and attitudinal revolution has already taken place at home before the child ever reaches school, altering his sensory existence and his mental processes in profound ways. Book learning is no longer sufficient in any subject; the children all say now, "Let's *talk* Spanish," or "Let the Bard be *heard,*" reflecting their rejection of the old sterile system where education begins and ends in a book. What we need now is educational crash programming in depth to first understand and then meet the new challenges. Just putting the present classroom on TV, with its archaic values and methods, won't change anything; it would be just like running movies on television; the result would be a hybrid that is neither. We have to ask what TV can do, in the instruction of English or physics or any other subject, that the classroom cannot do as presently constituted. The answer is that TV can deeply involve youth in the process of learning, illustrating graphically the complex interplay of people and events, the development of forms, the multileveled interrelationships between and among such arbitrarily segregated subjects as biology, geography, mathematics, anthropology, history, literature and languages.

If education is to become relevant to the young of this electric age, we must also supplant the stifling, impersonal and dehumanizing multiversity with a multiplicity of autonomous colleges devoted to an in-depth approach to learning. This must be done immediately, for few adults really comprehend the intensity of youth's alienation from the fragmented mechanical world and its fossilized educational system, which is designed in their minds solely to fit them into classified slots in bureaucratic society. To them, both draft card and degree are passports to psychic, if not physical, oblivion, and they accept neither. A new generation is alienated from its own three-thousand-year heritage of literacy and visual culture, and the celebration of literate values in home and school only intensifies that alienation. If we don't adapt our educational system to their needs and values, we will see only more dropouts and more chaos.

Playboy: Do you think the surviving hippie subculture is a reflection of youth's rejection of the values of our mechanical society?

McLuhan: Of course. These kids are fed up with jobs and goals, and are determined to forge their own roles and involvement in society. They want nothing to do with our fragmented and specialist consumer society. Living in the transitional identity vacuum between two great antithetical cultures, they are desperately trying to discover themselves and fashion a mode of existence attuned to their new values, thus the stress on developing an "alternate life style." We can see the results of this retribalization process whenever we look at *any* of our youth—not just at hippies. Take the field of fashion, for example, which now finds boys and girls dressing alike and wearing their hair alike, reflecting the unisexuality deriving from the shift from visual to tactile. The younger generation's whole orientation is toward a return to the native, as reflected by their costumes, their music, their long hair and their sociosexual behavior. Our teenage generation is already becoming part of a jungle clan. As youth enters this clan world and all their senses are electrically extended and intensified, there is a corresponding amplification of their sexual sensibilities. Nudity and unabashed sexuality are growing in the electric age because as TV tattoos its message directly on our skins, it renders clothing obsolescent and a barrier, and the new tactility makes it natural for kids to constantly touch one another—as reflected by the button sold in the psychedelic shops: IF IT MOVES, FONDLE IT. The electric media, by stimulating all the senses simultaneously, also give a new and richer sensual dimension to everyday sexuality that makes Henry Miller's style of randy rutting old-fashioned and obsolete. Once a society enters the all-involving tribal mode, it is inevitable that our attitudes toward sexuality change. We see, for example, the ease with which young people live guiltlessly with one another or, as among the hippies, in communal ménages. This is completely tribal.

Playboy: But aren't most tribal societies sexually restrictive rather than permissive?

McLuhan: Actually, they're both. Virginity is not, with a few exceptions, the tribal style in most primitive societies; young people tend to have total sexual access to one another until marriage. But after marriage, the wife becomes a jealously guarded possession and adultery a paramount sin. It's paradoxical that in the transition to a retribalized society, there is inevitably a great explosion of sexual energy and freedom, but when that society is fully realized, moral values will be extremely tight. In an integrated tribal society, the young will have free rein to experiment, but marriage and the family will become inviolate institutions, and infidelity and divorce will constitute serious violations of the social bond, not a private deviation but a collective insult and loss of face to the entire tribe. Tribal societies, unlike detribalized, fragmented cultures with their stress on individualist values, are extremely austere morally and do not hesitate to destroy or banish those who offend the tribal values. This is rather harsh, of course, but at the same time, sexuality can take on new and richer dimensions of depth involvement in a tribalized society.

Today, meanwhile, as the old values collapse and we see an exhilarating release of pent-up sexual frustrations, we are all inundated by a tidal wave of emphasis on sex. Far from liberating the libido, however, such onslaughts seem to have induced jaded attitudes and a kind of psychosexual *Weltschmerz.* No sensitivity of sensual response can survive such an assault, which stimulates the mechanical view of the body as capable of experiencing specific thrills, but not total sexual-emotional involvement and transcendence. It contributes to the schism between sexual enjoyment and reproduction that is so prevalent, and also strengthens the case for homosexuality. Projecting current trends, the love machine would appear a natural development in the near future—not just the current computerized datefinder, but a machine whereby ultimate orgasm is achieved by direct mechanical stimulation of the pleasure circuits of the brain.

Playboy: Do we detect a note of disapproval in your analysis of the growing sexual freedom?

McLuhan: No, I neither approve nor disapprove. I merely try to understand. Sexual freedom is as natural to newly tribalized youth as drugs.

Playboy: What's natural about drugs?

McLuhan: They're natural means of smoothing cultural transitions, and also a short cut into the electric vortex. The upsurge in drug taking is intimately related to the impact of the electric media. Look at the metaphor for getting high: turning on. One turns on his consciousness through drugs just as he opens up all his senses to a total depth involvement by turning on the TV dial. Drug taking is stimulated by today's pervasive environment of instant information, with its feedback mechanism of the inner trip. The inner trip is not the sole prerogative of the LSD traveler; it's the universal experience of TV watchers. LSD is a way of miming the invisible electronic world; it releases a person from acquired verbal and visual habits and reactions, and gives the potential of instant and total involvement, both all-at-onceness and all-at-oneness, which are the basic needs of people translated by electric extensions of their central nervous systems out of the old rational, sequential value system. The attraction to hallucinogenic drugs is a means of achieving empathy with our penetrating electric environment, an environment that in itself is a drugless inner trip.

Drug taking is also a means of expressing rejection of the obsolescent mechanical world and values. And drugs often stimulate a fresh interest in artistic expression, which is primarily of the audile-tactile world. The hallucinogenic drugs, as chemical simulations of our electric environment, thus revive senses long atrophied by the overwhelmingly visual orientation of the mechanical culture. LSD and related hallucinogenic drugs, furthermore, breed a highly tribal and communally oriented subculture, so it's understandable why the retribalized young take to drugs like a duck to water.

Playboy: A Columbia coed was recently quoted in *Newsweek* as equating you and LSD. "LSD doesn't mean anything until you consume it," she said. "Likewise McLuhan." Do you see any similarities?

McLuhan: I'm flattered to hear my work described as hallucinogenic, but I suspect that some of my academic critics find me a bad trip.

Playboy: Have you ever taken LSD yourself?

McLuhan: No, I never have. I'm an observer in these matters, not a participant. I had an operation last year to remove a tumor that was expanding my brain in a less pleasant manner, and during my prolonged convalescence I'm not allowed any stimulant stronger than coffee. Alas! A few months ago, however, I was almost "busted" on a drug charge. On a plane returning from Vancouver, where a university had awarded me an honorary degree, I ran into a colleague who asked me where I'd been. "To Vancouver to pick up my LL. D.," I told him. I noticed a fellow passenger looking at me with a strange expression, and when I got off the plane at Toronto Airport, two customs guards pulled me into a little room and started going over my luggage. "Do you know Timothy Leary?" one asked. I replied I did and that seemed to wrap it up for him. "All right," he said. "Where's the stuff? We know you told somebody you'd gone to Vancouver to pick up some LL. D." After a laborious dialog, I persuaded him that an LL. D. has nothing to do with consciousness expansion—just the opposite, in fact—and I was released. Of course, in light of the present educational crisis, I'm not sure there isn't something to be said for making possession of an LL. D. a felony.

Playboy: Are you in favor of legalizing marijuana and hallucinogenic drugs?

McLuhan: My personal point of view is irrelevant, since all such legal restrictions are futile and will inevitably wither away. You could as easily ban drugs in a retribalized society as outlaw clocks in a mechanical culture. The young will continue turning on no matter how many of them are turned off into prisons, and such legal restrictions only reflect the cultural aggression and revenge of a dying culture against its successor.

Speaking of dying cultures, it's no accident that drugs first were widely used in America by the Indians and then by the Negroes, both of whom have the great cultural advantage in this transitional age of remaining close to their tribal roots. The cultural aggression of white America against Negroes and Indians is not based on skin color and belief in racial superiority, whatever ideological clothing may be used to rationalize it, but on the white man's inchoate awareness that the Negro and Indian—as men with deep roots in the resonating echo chamber of the discontinuous, interrelated tribal world—are actually psychically and socially superior to the fragmented, alienated and dissociated man of Western civilization. Such a recognition, which stabs at the heart of the white man's entire social value system, inevitably generates violence and genocide. It has been the sad fate of the Negro and the Indian to be tribal men in a fragmented culture—men born ahead of rather than behind their time.

Playboy: How do you mean?

McLuhan: I mean that at precisely the time when the white younger generation is retribalizing and generalizing, the Negro and the Indian are under tremendous social and economic pressure to go in the opposite direction: to detribalize and specialize, to tear out their tribal roots when the rest of society is rediscovering theirs. Long held in a totally subordinate socioeconomic position, they are now impelled to acquire literacy as a prerequisite to employment in the old mechanical service environment of hardware, rather than adapt themselves to the new tribal environment of software, or electric information, as the middle-class white young are doing. Needless to say, this generates great psychic pain, which in turn is translated into bitterness and violence. This can be seen in the microcosmic drug culture; psychological studies show that the Negro and the Indian who are turned on by marijuana, unlike the white, are frequently engulfed with rage; they have a low high. They are angry because they understand under the influence of the drug that the source of their psychic and social degradation lies in the mechanical technology that is now being repudiated by the very white overculture that developed it—a repudiation that the majority of Negroes and Indians cannot, literally, afford because of their inferior economic position.

This is both ironic and tragic, and lessens the chances for an across-the-board racial *détente* and reconciliation, because rather than diminishing and eventually closing the sociopsychic differences between the races, it widens them. The Negro and the Indian seem to always get a bad deal; they suffered first because they were tribal men in a mechanical world, and now as they try to detribalize and structure themselves within the values of the mechanical culture, they find the gulf between them and a suddenly retribalizing society widening rather than narrowing. The future, I fear, is not too bright for either—but particularly for the Negro.

Playboy: What, specifically, do you think will happen to him?

McLuhan: At best, he will have to make a painful adjustment to two conflicting cultures and technologies, the visual-mechanical and the electric world; at worst, he will be exterminated.

Playboy: Exterminated?

McLuhan: I seriously fear the possibility, though God knows I hope I'm proved wrong. As I've tried to point out, the one inexorable consequence of any identity quest generated by environmental upheaval is tremendous violence. This violence has traditionally been directed at the tribal man who challenged visual-mechanical culture, as with the genocide against the Indian and the institutionalized dehumanization of the Negro. Today, the process is reversed and the violence is being meted out, during this transitional period, to those who are nonassimilable into the new tribe. Not because of his skin color but because he is in a limbo between mechanical and electric cultures, the Negro is a threat, a rival tribe that cannot be digested by the new order. The fate of such tribes is often extermination.

Playboy: What can we do to prevent this from happening to America's Negro population?

McLuhan: I think a valuable first step would be to alert the Negro, as well as the rest of society, to the nature of the new electric technology and the reasons it is so inexorably transforming our social and psychic values. The Negro should understand that the aspects of himself he has been conditioned to think of as inferior or "backward" are actually *superior* attributes in the new environment. Western man is obsessed by the forward-motion folly of step-by-step "progress" and always views the discontinuous synaesthetic interrelationships of the tribe as primitive. If the Negro realizes the great advantages of his heritage, he will cease his lemming leap into the senescent mechanical world.

There are encouraging signs that the new black-power movement—with its emphasis on Negritude and a return to the tribal pride of African culture and social roots—is recognizing this, but unfortunately a majority of Negro Americans are still determined to join the mechanical culture. But if they can be persuaded to follow the lead of those who wish to rekindle their sparks of tribal awareness, they will be strategically placed to make an easy transition to the new technology, using their own enduring tribal values as environmental survival aids. They should take pride in these tribal values, for they are rainbow-hued in comparison with the pallid literate culture of their traditional masters.

But as I said, the Negro arouses hostility in whites precisely because they subliminally recognize that he is closest to that tribal depth involvement and simultaneity and harmony that is the richest and most highly developed expression of human consciousness. This is why the white political and economic institutions mobilize to exclude and oppress Negroes, from semiliterate unions to semiliterate politicians, whose slim visual culture makes them hang on with unremitting fanaticism to their antiquated hardware and the specialized skills and classifications and compartmentalized neighborhoods and life styles deriving from it. The lowest intellectual stratum of whites view literacy and its hardware environment as a novelty, still fresh and still status symbols of achievement, and thus will be the last to retribalize and the first to initiate what could easily become a full-blown racial civil war. The United States as a nation is doomed, in any case, to break up into a series of regional and racial ministates, and such a civil war would merely accelerate that process.

Playboy: On what do you base your prediction that the United States will disintegrate?

McLuhan: Actually, in this case as in most of my work, I'm "predicting" what has already happened and merely extrapolating a current process to its logical conclusion. The Balkanization of the United States as a continental political structure has been going on for some years now, and racial chaos is merely one of several catalysts for change. This isn't a peculiarly American phenomenon; as I pointed out earlier, the electric media always produce psychically integrating and socially decentralizing effects, and this affects not only political institutions within the existing state but the national entities themselves.

All over the world, we can see how the electric media are stimulating the rise of ministates: In Great Britain, Welsh and Scottish nationalism are recrudescing powerfully; in Spain, the Basques are demanding autonomy; in Belgium, the Flemings insist on separation from the Walloons; in my own country, the *Quebecois* are in the first stages of a war of independence; and in Africa, we've witnessed the germination of several ministates and the collapse of several ambitiously unrealistic schemes for regional confederation. These ministates are just the opposite of the traditional centralizing nationalisms of the past that forged mass states that homogenized disparate ethnic and linguistic groups within one national boundary. The new ministates are decentralized tribal agglomerates of those same ethnic and linguistic groups. Though their creation may be accompanied by violence, they will not remain hostile or competitive armed camps but will eventually discover that their tribal bonds transcend their differences and will thereafter live in harmony and cultural cross-fertilization with one another.

This pattern of decentralized ministates will be repeated in the United States, although I realize that most Americans still find the thought of the Union's dissolution inconceivable. The U. S., which was the first nation in history to begin its national existence as a centralized and literate political entity, will now play the historical film backward, reeling into a multiplicity of decentralized Negro states, Indian states, regional states, linguistic and ethnic states, etc. Decentralism is today the burning issue in the fifty states, from the school crisis in New York City to the demands of the retribalized young that the oppressive multiversities be reduced to a human scale and the mass state be debureaucratized. The tribes and the bureaucracy are antithetical means of social organization and can never coexist peacefully; one must destroy and supplant the other, or neither will survive.

Playboy: Accepting, for the moment, your contention that the United States will be "Balkanized" into an assortment of ethnic and linguistic ministates, isn't it likely that the results would be social chaos and internecine warfare?

McLuhan: Not necessarily. Violence can be avoided if we comprehend the process of decentralism and retribalization, and accept its outcome while moving to control and modify the dynamics of change. In any case, the day of the stupor state is over; as men not only in the U. S. but throughout the world are united into a single tribe, they will forge a diversity of viable decentralized political and social institutions.

Playboy: Along what lines?

McLuhan: It will be a totally retribalized world of depth involvements. Through radio, TV and the computer, we are already entering a global theater in which the entire world is a Happening. Our whole cultural habitat, which we once viewed as a mere container of people, is being transformed by these media and by space satellites into a living organism, itself contained within a new macrocosm or connubium of a supraterrestrial nature. The day of the individualist, of privacy, of fragmented or "applied" knowledge, of "points of view" and specialist goals is being replaced by the over-all awareness of a mosaic world in which space and time are overcome by television, jets and computers—a simultaneous, "all-at-once" world in which everything resonates with everything else as in a total electrical field, a world in which energy is generated and perceived not by the traditional connections that create linear, causative thought processes, but by the intervals, or gaps, which Linus Pauling grasps as the languages of cells, and which create synaesthetic discontinuous integral consciousness.

The open society, the visual offspring of phonetic literacy, is irrelevant to today's retribalized youth; and the closed society, the product of speech, drum and ear technologies, is thus being reborn. After centuries of dissociated sensibilities, modern awareness is once more becoming integral and inclusive, as the entire human family is sealed to a single universal membrane. The compressional, implosive nature of the new electric technology is retrogressing Western man back from the open plateaus of literate values and into the heart of tribal darkness, into what Joseph Conrad termed "the Africa within."

Playboy: Many critics feel that your own "Africa within" promises to be a rigidly conformist hive world in which the individual is totally subordinate to the group and personal freedom is unknown.

McLuhan: Individual talents and perspectives don't have to shrivel within a retribalized society; they merely interact within a group consciousness that has the potential for releasing far more creativity than the old atomized culture. Literate man is alienated, impoverished man; retribalized man can lead a far richer and more fulfilling life—not the life of a mindless drone but of the participant in a seamless web of interdependence and harmony. The implosion of electric technology is transmogrifying literate, fragmented man into a complex and depth-structured human being with a deep emotional awareness of his complete interdependence with all of humanity. The old "individualistic" print society was one where the individual was "free" only to be alienated and dissociated, a rootless outsider bereft of tribal dreams; our new electronic environment compels commitment and participation, and fulfills man's psychic and social needs at profound levels.

The tribe, you see, is not conformist just because it's inclusive; after all, there is far more diversity and less conformity within a family group than there is within an urban conglomerate housing thousands of families. It's in the village where eccentricity lingers, in the big city where uniformity and impersonality are the milieu. The global-village conditions being forged by the electric technology stimulate more discontinuity and diversity and division than the old mechanical, standardized society; in fact, the global village makes maximum disagreement and creative dialog inevitable. Uniformity and tranquillity are not hallmarks of the global village; far more likely are conflict and discord as well as love and harmony—the customary life mode of any tribal people.

Playboy: Despite what you've said, haven't literate cultures been the only ones to value the concepts of individual freedom, and haven't tribal societies traditionally imposed rigid social taboos—as you suggested earlier in regard to sexual behavior—and ruthlessly punished all who do not conform to tribal values?

McLuhan: We confront a basic paradox whenever we discuss personal freedom in literate and tribal cultures. Literate mechanical society separated the individual from the group in space, engendering privacy; in thought, engendering point of view; and in work, engendering specialism—thus forging all the values associated with individualism. But at the same time, print technology has homogenized man, creating mass militarism, mass mind and mass uniformity; print gave man private habits of individualism and a public role of absolute conformity. That is why the young today welcome their retribalization, however dimly they perceive it, as a release from the uniformity, alienation and dehumanization of literate society. Print centralizes socially and fragments psychically, whereas the electric media bring man together in a tribal village that is a rich and creative mix, where there is actually *more* room for creative diversity than within the homogenized mass urban society of Western man.

Playboy: Are you claiming, now, that there will be no taboos in the world tribal society you envision?

McLuhan: No, I'm not saying that, and I'm not claiming that freedom will be absolute—merely that it will be less restricted than your question implies. The world tribe will be essentially conservative, it's true, like all iconic and inclusive societies; a mythic environment lives beyond time and space and thus generates little radical social change. All technology becomes part of a shared ritual that the tribe desperately strives to keep stabilized and permanent; by its very nature, an oral-tribal society—such as Pharaonic Egypt—is far more stable and enduring than any fragmented visual society. The oral and auditory tribal society is patterned by acoustic space, a total and simultaneous field of relations alien to the visual world, in which points of view and goals make social change an inevitable and constant by-product. An electrically imploded tribal society discards the linear forward-motion of "progress." We can see in our own time how, as we begin to react in depth to the challenges of the global village, we all become reactionaries.

Playboy: That can hardly be said of the young, whom you claim are leading the process of retribalization, and according to most estimates are also the most radical generation in our history.

McLuhan: Ah, but you're talking about politics, about goals and issues, which are really quite irrelevant. I'm saying that the result, not the current process, of retribalization makes us reactionary in our basic attitudes and values. Once we are enmeshed in the magical resonance of the tribal echo chamber, the debunking of myths and legends is replaced by their religious study. Within the consensual framework of tribal values, there will be unending diversity—but there will be few if any rebels who challenge the tribe itself.

The instant involvement that accompanies instant technologies triggers a conservative, stabilizing, gyroscopic function in man, as reflected by the second-grader who, when requested by her teacher to compose a poem after the first Sputnik was launched into orbit, wrote, "The stars are so big / The earth is so small / Stay as you are." The little girl who wrote those lines is part of the new tribal society; she lives in a world infinitely more complex, vast and eternal than any scientist has instruments to measure or imagination to describe.

Playboy: If personal freedom will still exist—although restricted by certain consensual taboos—in this new tribal world, what about the political system most closely associated with individual freedom: democracy? Will it, too, survive the transition to your global village?

McLuhan: No, it will not. The day of political democracy as we know it today is finished. Let me stress again that individual freedom itself will not be submerged in the new tribal society, but it will certainly assume different and more complex dimensions. The ballot box, for example, is the product of literate Western culture—a hot box in a cool world—and thus obsolescent. The tribal will is consensually expressed through the simultaneous interplay of all members of a community that is deeply interrelated and involved, and would thus consider the casting of a "private" ballot in a shrouded polling booth a ludicrous anachronism. The TV networks' computers, by "projecting" a victor in a Presidential race while the polls are still open, have already rendered the traditional electoral process obsolescent.

In our software world of instant electric communications movement, politics is shifting from the old patterns of political representation by electoral delegation to a new form of spontaneous and instantaneous communal involvement in all areas of decision making. In a tribal all-at-once culture, the idea of the "public" as a differentiated agglomerate of fragmented individuals, all dissimilar but all capable of acting in basically the same way, like interchangeable mechanical cogs in a production line, is supplanted by a mass society in which personal diversity is encouraged while at the same time everybody reacts and interacts simultaneously to every stimulus. The election as we know it today will be meaningless in such a society.

Playboy: How will the popular will be registered in the new tribal society if elections are passé?

McLuhan: The electric media open up totally new means of registering popular opinion. The old concept of the plebiscite, for example, may take on new relevance; TV could conduct daily plebiscites by presenting facts to 200,000,000 people and providing a computerized feedback of the popular will. But voting, in the traditional sense, is through as we leave the age of political parties, political issues and political goals, and enter an age where the collective tribal image and the iconic image of the tribal chieftain is the overriding political reality. But that's only one of countless new realities we'll be confronted with in the tribal village. We must understand that a totally new society is coming into being, one that rejects *all* our old values, conditioned responses, attitudes and institutions. If you have difficulty envisioning something as trivial as the imminent end of elections, you'll be totally unprepared to cope with the prospect of the forthcoming demise of spoken language and its replacement by a global consciousness.

Playboy: You're right.

McLuhan: Let me help you. Tribal man is tightly sealed in an integral collective awareness that transcends conventional boundaries of time and space. As such, the new society will be one mythic integration, a resonating world akin to the old tribal echo chamber where magic will live again: a world of ESP. The current interest of youth in astrology, clairvoyance and the occult is no coincidence. Electric technology, you see, does not require words any more than a digital computer requires numbers. Electricity makes possible—and not in the distant future, either—an amplification of human consciousness on a world scale, without any verbalization at all.

Playboy: Are you talking about global telepathy?

McLuhan: Precisely. Already, computers offer the potential of instantaneous translation of any code or language into any other code or language. If a data feedback is possible through the computer, why not a feed-*forward* of thought whereby a world consciousness links into a world computer? Via the computer, we could logically proceed from translating languages to bypassing them entirely in favor of an integral cosmic unconsciousness somewhat similar to the collective unconscious envisioned by Bergson. The computer thus holds out the promise of a technologically engendered state of universal understanding and unity, a state of absorption in the logos that could knit mankind into one family and create a perpetuity of collective harmony and peace. This is the *real* use of the computer, not to expedite marketing or solve technical problems but to speed the process of discovery and orchestrate terrestrial—and eventually galactic—environments and energies. Psychic communal integration, made possible at last by the electronic media, could create the universality of consciousness foreseen by Dante when he predicted that men would continue as no more than broken fragments until they were unified into an inclusive consciousness. In a Christian sense, this is merely a new interpretation of the mystical body of Christ; and Christ, after all, is the ultimate extension of man.

Playboy: Isn't this projection of an electronically induced world consciousness more mystical than technological?

McLuhan: Yes—as mystical as the most advanced theories of modern nuclear physics. Mysticism is just tomorrow's science dreamed today.

Playboy: You said a few minutes ago that *all* of contemporary man's traditional values, attitudes and institutions are going to be destroyed and replaced in and by the new electric age. That's a pretty sweeping generalization. Apart from the complex psychosocial metamorphoses you've mentioned, would you explain in more detail some of the specific changes you foresee?

McLuhan: The transformations are taking place everywhere around us. As the old value systems crumble, so do all the institutional clothing and garb-age they fashioned. The cities, corporate extensions of our physical organs, are withering and being translated along with all other such extensions into information systems, as television and the jet—by compressing time and space—make all the world one village and destroy the old city-country dichotomy. New York, Chicago, Los Angeles—all will disappear like the dinosaur. The automobile, too, will soon be as obsolete as the cities it is currently strangling, replaced by new antigravitational technology. The marketing systems and the stock market as we know them today will soon be dead as the dodo, and automation will end the traditional concept of the job, replacing it with a *role,* and giving men the breath of leisure. The electric media will create a world of dropouts from the old fragmented society, with its neatly compartmentalized analytic functions, and cause people to drop *in* to the new integrated global-village community.

All these convulsive changes, as I've already noted, carry with them attendant pain, violence and war—the normal stigmata of the identity quest—but the new society is springing so quickly from the ashes of the old that I believe it will be possible to avoid the transitional anarchy many predict. Automation and cybernation can play an essential role in smoothing the transition to the new society.

Playboy: How?

McLuhan: The computer can be used to direct a network of global thermostats to pattern life in ways that will optimize human awareness. Already, it's technologically feasible to employ the computer to program societies in beneficial ways.

Playboy: How do you program an entire society—beneficially or otherwise?

McLuhan: There's nothing at all difficult about putting computers in the position where they will be able to conduct carefully orchestrated programming of the sensory life of whole populations. I know it sounds rather science-fictional, but if you understood cybernetics, you'd realize we could do it today. The computer could program the media to determine the given messages a people should hear in terms of their over-all needs, creating a total media experience absorbed and patterned by all the senses. We could program five hours less of TV in Italy to promote the reading of newspapers during an election, or lay on an additional twenty-five hours of TV in Venezuela to cool down the tribal temperature raised by radio the preceding month. By such orchestrated interplay of all media, whole cultures could now be programmed in order to improve and stabilize their emotional climate, just as we are beginning to learn how to maintain equilibrium among the world's competing economies.

Playboy: How does such environmental programming, however enlightened in intent, differ from Pavlovian brainwashing?

McLuhan: Your question reflects the usual panic of people confronted with unexplored technologies. I'm not saying such panic isn't justified, or that such environmental programming couldn't be brainwashing, or far worse—merely that such reactions are useless and distracting. Though I think the programming of societies could actually be conducted quite constructively and humanistically, I don't want to be in the position of a Hiroshima physicist extolling the potential of nuclear energy in the first days of August 1945. But an understanding of media's effects constitutes a civil defense against media fallout.

The alarm of so many people, however, at the prospect of corporate programming's creation of a complete service environment on this planet is rather like fearing that a municipal lighting system will deprive the individual of the right to adjust each light to his own favorite level of intensity. Computer technology can—and doubtless will—program entire environments to fulfill the social needs and sensory preferences of communities and nations. The *content* of that programming, however, depends on the nature of future societies—but that is in our own hands.

Playboy: Is it really in our hands—or, by seeming to advocate the use of computers to manipulate the future of entire cultures, aren't you actually encouraging man to abdicate control over his destiny?

McLuhan: First of all—and I'm sorry to have to repeat this disclaimer—I'm not advocating *anything;* I'm merely probing and predicting trends. Even if I opposed them or thought them disastrous, I couldn't stop them, so why waste my time lamenting? As Carlyle said of author Margaret Fuller after she remarked, "I accept the Universe": "She'd better." I see no possibility of a world-wide Luddite rebellion that will smash all machinery to bits, so we might as well sit back and see what is happening and what will happen to us in a cybernetic world. Resenting a new technology will not halt its progress.

The point to remember here is that whenever we use or perceive any technological extension of ourselves, we necessarily embrace it. Whenever we watch a TV screen or read a book, we are absorbing these extensions of ourselves into our individual system and experiencing an automatic "closure" or displacement of perception; we can't escape this perpetual embrace of our daily technology unless we escape the technology itself and flee to a hermit's cave. By consistently embracing all these technologies, we inevitably relate ourselves to them as servomechanisms. Thus, in order to make use of them at all, we must serve them as we do gods. The Eskimo is a servomechanism of his kayak, the cowboy of his horse, the businessman of his clock, the cyberneticist—and soon the entire world—of his computer. In other words, to the spoils belongs the victor.

This continuous modification of man by his own technology stimulates him to find continuous means of modifying it; man thus becomes the sex organs of the machine world just as the bee is of the plant world, permitting it to reproduce and constantly evolve to higher forms. The machine world reciprocates man's devotion by rewarding him with goods and services and bounty. Man's relationship with his machinery is thus inherently symbiotic. This has always been the case; it's only in the electric age that man has an opportunity to *recognize* this marriage to his own technology. Electric technology is a qualitative extension of this age-old man-machine relationship; twentieth-century man's relationship to the computer is not by nature very different from prehistoric man's relationship to his boat or to his wheel—with the important difference that all previous technologies or extensions of man were partial and fragmentary, whereas the elecric is total and inclusive. Now man is beginning to wear his brain outside his skull and his nerves outside his skin; new technology breeds new man. A recent cartoon portrayed a little boy telling his nonplused mother, "I'm going to be a computer when I grow up." Humor is often prophecy.

Playboy: If man can't prevent this transformation of himself by technology—or *into* technology—how can he control and direct the process of change?

McLuhan: The first and most vital step of all, as I said at the outset, is simply to understand media and its revolutionary effects on all psychic and social values and institutions. Understanding is half the battle. The central purpose of all my work is to convey this message, that by understanding media as they extend man, we gain a measure of control over them. And this is a vital task, because the immediate interface between audile-tactile and visual perception is taking place everywhere around us. No civilian can escape this environmental blitzkrieg, for there is, quite literally, no place to hide. But if we diagnose what is happening to us, we can reduce the ferocity of the winds of change and bring the best elements of the old visual culture, during this transitional period, into peaceful coexistence with the new retribalized society.

If we persist, however, in our conventional rearview-mirror approach to these cataclysmic developments, all of Western culture will be destroyed and swept into the dustbin of history. If literate Western man were really interested in preserving the most creative aspects of his civilization, he would not cower in his ivory tower bemoaning change but would plunge himself into the vortex of electric technology and, by understanding it, dictate his new environment—turn ivory tower into control-tower. But I can understand his hostile attitude, because I once shared his visual bias.

Playboy: What changed your mind?

McLuhan: Experience. For many years, until I wrote my first book, *The Mechanical Bride,* I adopted an extremely moralistic approach to all environmental technology. I loathed machinery, I abominated cities, I equated the Industrial Revolution with original sin and mass media with the Fall. In short, I rejected almost every element of modern life in favor of a Rousseauvian utopianism. But gradually I perceived how sterile and useless this attitude was, and I began to realize that the greatest artists of the twentieth century—Yeats, Pound, Joyce, Eliot—had discovered a totally different approach, based on the identity of the processes of cognition and creation. I realized that artistic creation is the playback of ordinary experience—from trash to treasures. I ceased being a moralist and became a student.

As someone committed to literature and the traditions of literacy, I began to study the new environment that imperiled literary values, and I soon realized that they could not be dismissed by moral outrage or pious indignation. Study showed that a totally new approach was required, both to save what deserved saving in our Western heritage and to help man adopt a new survival strategy. I adapted some of this new approach in *The Mechanical Bride* by attempting to immerse myself in the advertising media in order to apprehend its impact on man, but even there some of my old literate "point of view" bias crept in. The book, in any case, appeared just as television was making all its major points irrelevant.

I soon realized that recognizing the symptoms of change was not enough; one must understand the *cause* of change, for without comprehending causes, the social and psychic effects of new technology cannot be counteracted or modified. But I recognized also that one individual cannot accomplish these self-protective modifications; they must be the collective effort of society, because they affect all of society; the individual is helpless against the pervasiveness of environmental change: the new garbage—or mess-age—induced by new technologies. Only the social organism, united and recognizing the challenge, can move to meet it.

Unfortunately, no society in history has ever known enough about the forces that shape and transform it to take action to control and direct new technologies as they extend and transform man. But today, change proceeds so instantaneously through the new media that it may be possible to institute a global education program that will enable us to seize the reins of our destiny—but to do this we must first recognize the kind of therapy that's needed for the effects of the new media. In such an effort, indignation against those who perceive the nature of those effects is no substitute for awareness and insight.

Playboy: Are you referring to the critical attacks to which you've been subjected for some of your theories and predictions?

McLuhan: I am. But I don't want to sound uncharitable about my critics. Indeed, I appreciate their attention. After all, a man's detractors work for him tirelessly and for free. It's as good as being banned in Boston. But as I've said, I can understand their hostile attitude toward environmental change, having once shared it. Theirs is the customary human reaction when confronted with innovation: to flounder about attempting to adapt old responses to new situations or to simply condemn or ignore the harbingers of change—a practice refined by the Chinese emperors, who used to execute messengers bringing bad news. The new technological environments generate the most pain among those least prepared to alter their old value structures. The literati find the new electronic environment far more threatening than do those less committed to literacy as a way of life. When an individual or social group feels that its whole identity is jeopardized by social or psychic change, its natural reaction is to lash out in defensive fury. But for all their lamentations, the revolution has already taken place.

Playboy: You've explained why you avoid approving or disapproving of this revolution in your work, but you must have a private opinion. What is it?

McLuhan: I don't like to tell people what I think is good or bad about the social and psychic changes caused by new media, but if you insist on pinning me down about my own subjective reactions as I observe the reprimitivization of our culture, I would have to say that I view such upheavals with total personal dislike and dissatisfaction. I do see the prospect of a rich and creative retribalized society—free of the fragmentation and alienation of the mechanical age—emerging from this traumatic period of culture clash; but I have nothing but distaste for the *process* of change. As a man molded within the literate Western tradition, I do not personally cheer the dissolution of that tradition through the electric involvement of all the senses. I don't enjoy the destruction of neighborhoods by high-rises or revel in the pain of identity quest. No one could be less enthusiastic about these radical changes than myself. I am not, by temperament or conviction, a revolutionary; I would prefer a stable, changeless environment of modest services and human scale. TV and all the electric media are unraveling the entire fabric of our society, and as a man who is forced by circumstances to live within that society, I do not take delight in its disintegration.

You see, I am not a crusader; I imagine I would be most happy living in a secure preliterate environment; I would never attempt to change my world, for better or worse. Thus I derive no joy from observing the traumatic effects of media on man, although I do obtain satisfaction from grasping their modes of operation. Such comprehension is inherently cool, since it is simultaneously involvement and detachment. This posture is essential in studying media. One must begin by becoming extraenvironmental, putting oneself beyond the battle in order to study and understand the configuration of forces. It's vital to adopt a posture of arrogant superiority; instead of scurrying into a corner and wailing about what media are doing to us, one should charge straight ahead and kick them in the electrodes. They respond beautifully to such resolute treatment and soon become servants rather than masters. But without this detached involvement, I could never objectively observe media; it would be like an octopus grappling with the Empire State Building. So I employ the greatest boon of literate culture: the power of man to act without reaction—the sort of specialization by dissociation that has been the driving motive force behind Western civilization.

The Western world is being revolutionized by the electric media as rapidly as the East is being Westernized, and although the society that eventually emerges may be superior to our own, the process of change is agonizing. I must move through this pain-wracked transitional era as a scientist would move through a world of disease; once a surgeon becomes personally involved and disturbed about the condition of his patient, he loses the power to help that patient. Clinical detachment is not some kind of haughty pose I affect—nor does it reflect any lack of compassion on my part; it's simply a survival strategy. The world we are living in is not one I would have created on my own drawing board, but it's the one in which I must live, and in which the students I teach must live. If nothing else, I owe it to them to avoid the luxury of moral indignation or the troglodytic security of the ivory tower and to get down into the junk yard of environmental change and steam-shovel my way through to a comprehension of its contents and its lines of force—in order to understand how and why it is metamorphosing man.

Playboy: Despite your personal distaste for the upheavals induced by the new electric technology, you seem to feel that if we understand and influence its effects on us, a less alienated and fragmented society may emerge from it. Is is thus accurate to say that you are essentially optimistic about the future?

McLuhan: There are grounds for both optimism and pessimism. The extensions of man's consciousness induced by the electric media could conceivably usher in the millennium, but it also holds the potential for realizing the Anti-Christ—Yeats' rough beast, its hour come round at last, slouching toward Bethlehem to be born. Cataclysmic environmental changes such as these are, in and of themselves, morally neutral; it is how we perceive them and react to them that will determine their ultimate psychic and social consequences. If we refuse to see them at all, we will become their servants. It's inevitable that the world-pool of electronic information movement will toss us all about like corks on a stormy sea, but if we keep our cool during the descent into the maelstrom, studying the process as it happens to us and what we can do about it, we can come through.

Personally, I have a great faith in the resiliency and adaptability of man, and I tend to look to our tomorrows with a surge of excitement and hope. I feel that we're standing on the threshold of a liberating and exhilarating world in which the human tribe can become truly one family and man's consciousness can be freed from the shackles of mechanical culture and enabled to roam the cosmos. I have a deep and abiding belief in man's potential to grow and learn, to plumb the depths of his own being and to learn the secret songs that orchestrate the universe. We live in a transitional era of profound pain and tragic identity quest, but the agony of our age is the labor pain of rebirth.

I expect to see the coming decades transform the planet into an art form; the new man, linked in a cosmic harmony that transcends time and space, will sensuously caress and mold and pattern every facet of the terrestrial artifact as if it were a work of art, and man himself will become an organic art form. There is a long road ahead, and the stars are only way stations, but we have begun the journey. To be born in this age is a precious gift, and I regret the prospect of my own death only because I will leave so many pages of man's destiny—if you will excuse the Gutenbergian image—tantalizingly unread. But perhaps, as I've tried to demonstrate in my examination of the postliterate culture, the story begins only when the book closes.

"The only serious drawback I can see about bringing this weapon into production is that it might bring civilization, as we know it, to an end."

BIOGRAPHICAL NOTES

JAMES BALDWIN (b. 1924), American novelist and essayist, was born in New York City. His prize-winning drama *Blues for Mr. Charlie* was produced on Broadway in the 1963–64 season. He has published several novels, among them *Go Tell It on the Mountain* (1952), *Giovanni's Room* (1956), *Another Country* (1961), and *Tell Me How Long the Train's Been Gone* (1968). His collections of essays, notably *Notes of a Native Son* (1955), *Nobody Knows My Name* (1961), and *The Fire Next time* (1963), established him as a distinguished spokesman for black Americans and the civil rights movement. His most recent publication is a collection of children's stories (1970).

RAY BRADBURY (b. 1920) is America's master of the science fiction story. He has written more than a thousand stories and several novels of fantasy, many of which have appeared in such periodicals as *The New Yorker, Harper's,* and *The Saturday Evening Post* and have been collected into book editions. He was awarded the California Gold Medal for his book *Fahrenheit 451* (1953), which was later made into a film, and in 1963 was named Interior Design and Idea Consultant for the U.S. pavilion at the New York World's Fair.

ELDRIDGE CLEAVER (b. 1935), black militant and minister of information of the Black Panther party, went into what he calls political exile in 1968 when his parole from the California prison system was revoked. (Earlier in 1968 he campaigned as the Presidential candidate of the Peace and Freedom party.) He surfaced in Cuba, moved to Algeria, and has since visited North Korea and Moscow. *Soul on Ice* (1968) was hailed by *The New York Times* as one of the year's ten best books; in it Cleaver comments on the cultural alienation of the black American. Another book, *Post-Prison Writings and Speeches*, was published in 1969.

WILLIAM SLOANE COFFIN (b. 1924), American clergyman and chaplain at Yale University, describes himself as a Christian revolutionary. In 1968 he went on trial with Benjamin Spock and three others for advocating resistance to the draft as a measure indicating opposition to the Vietnam War; he was found guilty of conspiracy. He has worked with Operations Crossroads in Africa and is on the board of directors of the Peace Corps. Two of his sermons have been published in *Sermons to Intellectuals from Three Continents* (1963, edited by F. H. Littel).

FRANK DONNER (b. 1918) is a New York lawyer who specializes in constitutional law and civil liberties cases. He has been supervisory attorney for the National Labor Relations Board and general counsel for several labor unions. A frequent contributor to *The Nation*, Donner is the author of *The Un-Americans*.

WILLIAM O. DOUGLAS (b. 1898) has been an associate justice of the United States Supreme Court since 1939. He has taught law at Columbia and Yale universities and is a prolific writer. Douglas' books include *An Almanac of Liberty* (1954), *America Challenged* (1960), *Mr. Lincoln and the Negroes* (1963), and, most recently, *Points of Rebellion* (1970). His interest in the world's varied people and places and his long experience in mountain climbing have provided subjects for such books as *Of Men and Mountains* (1950), *Russian Journey* (1956), *Exploring the Himalaya* (1958), *Muir of the Mountain* (1961), and *Farewell to Texas* (1967).

LESLIE FIEDLER (b. 1917), American author and educator, is presently professor of English at the State University of New York at Buffalo. He has also been chairman of the English department at the University of Montana and Gauss lecturer at Princeton University. He is an associate editor of *Ramparts* and a contributing editor of *American Judaism*. Often a contributor to scholarly journals, Fiedler has published *An End to Innocence* (1955), *Love and Death in the American Novel* (1966), and the autobiographical *Being Busted* (1970).

ROMAIN GARY (b. 1914), French writer and diplomat, born in Russia, has been honored by the French government with the titles Officier de la Legion d'Honneur and Campagnon de la Liberation and also with the Crois de Guerre for service in the war from 1939 to 1945. From 1956 to 1960 he was French Consul General in Los Angeles. An adroit writer, Gary received the Prix de Critiques for his first novel, *Forest of Anger* (1944), and in 1956 he was awarded the Prix Concourt for *The Roots of Heaven*. Among his best-known novels are *Lady L* (1959), *The Ski Bum* (1965), and *The Dance of Genghis Cohn* (1967). In 1967 he wrote and directed a film, *The Birds of Peru*, and he has written a number of plays.

HERBERT GOLD (b. 1924), American essayist, novelist, and social critic, has been visiting professor of literature at Cornell, Berkeley, Harvard, and Stanford. In 1951 he launched his literary career with a novel, *Birth of a Hero.* Since then he has published a number of books, including *The Age of Happy Problems* (1962), a collection of his nonfiction, *Salt* (1963), *Fathers* (1967), and *The Great American Jackpot* (1969).

PAUL GOODMAN (b. 1911), American writer and literary critic, is sometimes regarded as the father of the New Left. His defense of youth in *Growing Up Absurd* (1960), together with his *Community of Scholars* (1962) and *Compulsory Mis-Education* (1964), attests to his position as America's utopian social critic. He is also poet, short-story writer, dramatist, and historian. Two of his well-known novels are *The Empire City* (1942–59) and *Making Do* (1963). He has been a lay psychotherapist with the New York Institute for Gestalt Therapy and has conducted seminars on education for the Institute for Policy Studies. His latest book is a collection called *Essays in American Colonial History* (1969).

GERALD GREEN (b. 1922), author of *The Last Angry Man* (1957), has written and produced such television shows as "Today," "Wide, Wide World," and "Chet Huntley Reporting." Two of his recent books are *To Brooklyn with Love* (1968) and *The Artists of Terezin* (1969).

NAT HENTOFF (b. 1925), jazz and movie critic, novelist, and protean social commentator, is a frequent interviewer for *Playboy.* In 1953 he became an associate editor for *Down Beat;* in 1958 he helped found *The Jazz Review;* in 1960 he became a staff writer for *The New Yorker;* and he has long had a popular column on jazz and the contemporary scene in *The Village Voice.* Among his several books are *The New Equality* (1964), *Our Children Are Dying* (1966), and *Journey into Jazz* (1968).

KARL HESS (b. 1923) lives in Washington, D.C., where he is an associate fellow at the Institute for Policy Studies. Formerly the articulate speechwriter and phrasemaker of Barry Goldwater's 1964 Presidential campaign, Hess has since changed camps and is currently involved in New Left activities. He co-edits a bimonthly paper, *Libertarian Forum,* contributes to such periodicals as *Ramparts,* and occasionaly ghostwrites a book.

ROLF HOCHHUTH (b. 1931), German playwright, shook the conscience of Europe with his controversial play *The Deputy* (produced in New York in 1964), for which he received the Gerhart Hauptmann and Younger Generation prizes of West Germany.

The play has been produced in many countries, though it was banned in Rome for its comment on Pope Pius XII. In 1967 Hochhuth published another historical but polemical drama, *The Soldiers*, on the wartime activity of Sir Winston Churchill.

ERIC HOFFER (b. 1902), longshoreman and social philosopher, achieved fame in 1951 with the publication of *The True Believer*. The self-educated Hoffer who prefers to live and work along the San Francisco waterfront, has served on the President's Commission on Civil Disorder and has written *The Passionate State of Mind* (1955), *The Ordeal of Change* (1963), and *The Temper of Our Time* (1965).

JULIAN HUXLEY (b. 1887), English biologist and writer, was knighted in 1958 for his services to science and the British government. He has been professor of zoology and an honorary lecturer at Oxford, the Rice Institute, the University of London, and the University of Chicago. From 1946 to 1948 he was director general of UNESCO. His views on evolution and ethics have been articulated in all media, including articles, reports, books, television programs, film commentaries, and lectures. Among his more recent books are *Essays of a Humanist* (1964), *The Human Crisis* (1963), and *The Wonderful World of Evolution* (1969).

ALFRED KAZIN (b. 1915), American writer, critic, and teacher, is Distinguished Professor of English at the State University of New York at Stony Brook. His books include *On Native Grounds* (1942), *A Walker in the City* (1951), *The Inmost Leaf* (1955), and *Contemporaries* (1962). He is a frequent contributor to periodicals such as *Fortune, Partisan Review, Harper's,* and *Commentary. Starting Out in the Thirties* (1965) is an autobiographical account of his literary career, which includes producing editions of such socially aware writers as Blake, Emerson, Dreiser, and Henry James.

MARSHALL MCLUHAN (b. 1911), professor of English at the University of Toronto, is also director of the Centre for Culture and Technology there. He is best known for his revolutionary theories on mass communications, especially for his startling book *The Medium Is the Message* (1967). His many publications include *The Mechanical Bride* (1951), *The Gutenberg Galaxy* (1962), and *Understanding Media* (1964). In 1968 he co-authored *Through the Vanishing Point: Space in Poetry and Painting,* and *Man and Peace in the Global Village*.

CAREY MCWILLIAMS (b. 1905), American author and longtime editor of *The Nation*, was educated in law, which he practiced in

California for many years. He has written many books, beginning in 1929 with a biography of Ambrose Bierce. Some of his other books are *Factories in the Field* (1939), *Brothers Under the Skin* (1943), and *North from Mexico: The Spanish-Speaking People of the United States* (1949). In 1968 he became the editor of *The California Revolution.*

KEN W. PURDY (b. 1913) is a prolific short-story writer and a regular *Playboy* contributor. He has been an editor with The Free Press, *Argosy,* and *Look.* He assisted Stirling Moss in writing Moss's autobiography, *All But My Life* (1963), and collaborated with Horst Baumann on *The New Matadors* (1965). His own books include *The Wonderful World of the Automobile* (1963) and *Young People and Driving* (1967).

KENNETH REXROTH (b. 1905) is a productive leader of the Bohemian spirit in America. A distinguished artist, Rexroth was one of America's first abstract painters. Also one of the country's most respected poets, he has received the California Literary Silver Medal award and has been a Guggenheim fellow in poetry. He is a columnist for *The San Francisco Examiner* and a correspondent for *The Nation,* and in 1966 he published *An Autobiographical Novel.*

IRWIN SHAW (b. 1913), American author, playwright, and storyteller, has lived as a self-willed expatriate in Switzerland since 1951. *The Young Lions* (1948) was the best-selling novel that brought him fame; he has also written *Lucy Crown* (1956), *Two Weeks in Another Town* (1960), and *Voices of a Summer Day* (1965). Since his war drama *Bury the Dead* (1936), he has continued to write stories and plays, and in 1963 he combined these skills with his extensive experience in the cinema by co-producing *In the French Style,* a film based on two of his own stories.

JOHN STEINBECK (1902–68), a Nobel Prize winner in literature in 1962, is internationally known for such books as *Of Mice and Men* (1937), which earned him the New York Drama Critics Award, *The Grapes of Wrath* (1939), for which he won the Pulitzer Prize, *East of Eden* (1952), *The Winter of Our Discontent* (1962), and *Travels with Charlie* (1962). While Steinbeck concentrated heavily on the California locales he knew well, his novels and stories vivify that which is genuinely American, good and bad.

NORMAN THOMAS (1884–1968), American author and lecturer, succeeded Eugene V. Debs as leader of the American Socialist party in 1926. Formerly a Presbyterian clergyman, Thomas was devoted to the cause of American pacifism; he was a six-time

Presidential candidate between 1928 and 1948 on the Socialist ticket. Among his many published works are *The Conscientious Objector in America* (1923), *The Prerequisites for Peace* (1959), and *Choices*, published posthumously in 1969.

NICHOLAS VON HOFFMAN (b. 1929), a syndicated columnist with *The Washington Post*, recently attracted national attention with his coverage of the Chicago conspiracy trial. He is the author of *Mississippi Notebook* (1964), *Multiversity* (1966), *We Are the People Our Parents Warned Us Against* (1968), and *Life at the Post* (1970).

JON R. WALTZ (b. 1929), lawyer, educator, and author, has been a book critic with the *Chicago Tribune* and an editor of the *Yale Law Journal*. He has been at Northwestern University since 1964 where he has taught law as full professor since 1965 and where he presently teaches medical jurisprudence. Waltz co-authored *The Trial of Jack Ruby* (1965), *Cases and Materials on Evidence* (1968), and *Principles of Evidence and Proof* (1968). Since 1968 he has been a panel member of the American Arbitration Association.

ALAN WATTS (b. 1915), philosopher, writer, and lecturer, was once a priest in the Episcopal church and chaplain at Northwestern University. He was on the teaching staff of the College of the Pacific in comparative philosophy and psychology from 1951 to 1957 and has since been guest lecturer at many colleges and universities in and out of the country. He is perhaps best known for his interpretations of Zen Buddhism and has written copiously on East Asian thought. Among his many publications are *The Spirit of Zen* (1936), *The Meaning of Happiness* (1940), *The Way of Zen* (1957), and *Psychotherapy East and West* (1961). Recently he was research consultant at the Maryland Psychiatric Research Center.

A 1
B 2
C 3
D 4
E 5
F 6
G 7
H 8
I 9
J 0